WORLD PHILOSOPHIES

World Philosophies presents in one volume a superb introduction to all the world's major philosophical and religious traditions. Covering all corners of the globe, Ninian Smart's work offers a comprehensive and global philosophical and religious picture.

In this revised and expanded second edition, a team of distinguished scholars assembled by the editor, Oliver Leaman, have brought Ninian Smart's masterpiece up to date for the twenty-first century. Chapters have been revised by experts in the field to include recent philosophical developments, and the book includes a new bibliographic guide to resources in world philosophies. A brand new introduction which celebrates the career and writings of Ninian Smart, and his contribution to the study of world religions, helps set the work in context.

Ninian Smart (1927–2000) was Emeritus Professor of Comparative Religion and of Religious Studies at the Universities of California and Lancaster and one of the world's most foremost scholars in religious studies. He was President of the American Academy of Religion for 2000, and authored many acclaimed books, including *The Religious Experience*, *Dimensions of the Sacred* and *The World's Religions*.

Oliver Leaman is Professor of Philosophy at the University of Kentucky, and is the author most recently of *Islam: The Key Concepts* (Routledge, 2008) (with Kecia Ali).

WORLD PHILOSOPHIES

REVISED SECOND EDITION

Ninian Smart

Edited by Oliver Leaman

Routledge
Taylor & Francis Group

LONDON AND NEW YORK

First published 1999 by Routledge

Second edition published in 2008
2 Park Square, Milton Park, Abingdon, Oxon. OX14 4RN

Simultaneously published in the USA and Canada
by Routledge
270 Madison Ave., New York, NY 10016

Routledge is an imprint of the Taylor & Francis Group, an informa business

© 2000 and 2008 the estate of the late Ninian Smart

Typeset in Sabon by
HWA Text and Data Management, London
Printed and bound in Great Britain by
The Cromwell Press, Trowbridge, Wilts

British Library Cataloguing in Publication Data
A catalogue record for this book is available from the British Library

Library of Congress Cataloging in Publication Data
A catalog record for this book has been requested

ISBN 10: 0-415-41188-2 (hbk)
ISBN 10: 0-415-41189-0 (pbk)

ISBN 13: 978-0-415-41188-2 (hbk)
ISBN 13: 978-0-415-41189-9 (pbk)

CONTENTS

List of revisers		vi
Preface		vii
Preface to the second edition		viii
Introduction to the second edition		ix
1	The history of the world and our philosophical inheritance	1
2	South Asian philosophies	13
3	Chinese philosophies	70
4	Korean philosophies	117
5	Japanese philosophies	126
6	Philosophies of Greece, Rome and the Near East	151
7	Islamic philosophies	191
8	Jewish philosophies	223
9	Europe	243
10	North America	330
11	Latin America	353
12	Modern Islam	370
13	Modern South and South-east Asia	384
14	China, Korea and Japan in modern times	406
15	African philosophies	433
16	Concluding reflections	453
Bibliography		467
Index		554

REVISERS

PREFACE

I wrote this work so that general readers could have a clear guide to the philosophies of the world. This is useful in helping to solidify a sense of global solidarity and diversity. I use 'philosophies' in the plural because a number of Western philosophers use the singular only to refer to a particular kind of Western philosophy.

Mine is a guide to intellectual thought from all parts of the world. I have limited its scope up to shortly after World War II, say the 1960s, and chiefly to the dead. This is partly because of limitations of my own knowledge and because of the desire for my descriptions to be confined to complete philosophers, namely dead ones. This has generally led to the underplaying of some recent movements, including feminism, environmentalism and postmodernism. It has led to the neglect of otherwise excellent philosophers, such as my brother.

I am indebted in launching and preparing the book to Laurence King of Calmann and King, Adrian Driscoll, Anna Gerber and Maria Stasiak of Routledge, and Ellen Posman and Marilyn Sarelas of the Department of Religious Studies of the University of California Santa Barbara. The latter helped to reconstruct the Bibliography. I should express my gratitude to numerous students who inspired my labours.

Ninian Smart
Santa Barbara, California
May 6, 1998

PREFACE
TO THE SECOND EDITION

It was not easy to tackle a revision of Ninian Smart's book since we as a group had such respect for it, and did not like the idea of changing it. On the other hand, he did end his survey in the 1960s and we felt that it would be helpful to tweak his material to bring it more up to date and in line with current research in the many areas that he discussed. The revisers should not be assumed to agree with everything that Smart asserts in his volume, of course, and we have certainly not altered his opinions or his arguments. The grandeur of the original conception remains, and we hope that readers will find what we have done useful rather than obtrusive.

Let me outline what our revisers have done. Chris Bartley has worked on Indian philosophy (Chapters 2 and 13); David Bradshaw on Greek and classical philosophy (Chapter 6); Cynthia Gayman, North American philosophy (Chapter 10); Aaron Hughes, Jewish philosophy (Chapter 8); Muhammad Kamal, modern Islamic philosophy (Chapter 12); Gereon Kopf, Japanese philosophy (parts of Chapters 5 and 14); Safro Kwame, African philosophy (Chapter 15); Susana Nuccetelli, Latin American philosophy (Chapter 11); Sor-hoon Tan, Chinese Philosophy (parts of Chapters 3 and 14); Patrick O'Donnell, the bibliography; and Donald Wiebe wrote the introduction to the second edition. I looked after the chapters and sections on Korean philosophy, classical Islamic philosophy, European philosophy, and am responsible for editing the whole volume. Errors that remain should, and no doubt will, be laid at my door. I also added to the Bibliography, which is sizeable and we hope will be useful in helping readers orientate themselves in the area and pursue topics and thinkers who interest them.

Many people have contributed to this second edition, not just the authors who have set about revising Ninian Smart's material, but also at Routledge Gemma Dunn who was with the project when it started and Lesley Riddle who supported it throughout. The Ninian Smart Trust gave permission for the project as a whole. We are grateful to them all.

Oliver Leaman
October 2007

INTRODUCTION
TO THE SECOND EDITION

When first published, *World Philosophies* was widely appreciated. Reviewers described it variously as 'a masterpiece of lucid description, analysis, and interpretation', an 'insightful, incisive, and reliable' reference work, and 'an encyclopedia of wonders, a treasure store complete with accounts of philosophy and religion from around the world'. It is all of these things and more.

Although intended as a guide to the philosophies of the world for the general reader, as Smart asserts in the Preface, he clearly intends to do more than simply provide readers with a reference work crammed with information. His primary aim is to bring them to a consciousness of the interconnectedness of the world and to show how 'the varying centers of civilization and culture ... have contributed divergent themes to the sum of human thought', as he puts it in the introductory chapter to the book. His project, consequently, involves 'something necessarily plural' even though it is focused on 'the philosophical thinking of the whole world'; it is this dual focus, he suggests, that may make possible the emergence of a global, corporate philosophy.

Smart's interest in comparative philosophy long antedated the publication of *World Philosophies*. His earliest book, *Reasons and Faiths: An Investigation of Religious Discourse, Christian and Non-Christian* (1958) put into question the widely held assumption of the autonomy of philosophy – the Western view of philosophy as a unitary enterprise – and provided evidence that philosophy had much to gain from a historical and comparative analysis of philosophical problems as conceived in different cultural contexts. In an academic paper on 'The Analogy of Meaning and the Tasks of Comparative Philosophy' which he published thirty years later, Smart urged philosophers to recognize that not all cultures even have a word that univocally corresponds to 'philosophy', let alone that they operate with the assumption 'that somehow there is a clearly and well-defined place in [the] intellectual firmament for what is called philosophy'. Nevertheless, he points out that this does not constitute grounds for believing that thinkers in other cultures lack analytical insight or are in any other way intellectually inadequate. What Western thinkers need to appreciate, he maintains, is the dual contextual nature of much non-Western philosophical thought: that is, both its horizontal context (in which key concepts are embedded in different types of systematic structures of thought) and its vertical context (in which key concepts are embedded in a different form of life, which is to say that they are tied to particular social and spiritual attitudes and behaviour). To acknowledge this, claims Smart, is to see that cross-cultural or comparative philosophy (and particularly so the philosophy of religion) is not easily distinguishable from what he calls worldview construction which encompasses a wide variety of styles of thought which he thinks deserve the label 'philosophy'. Consequently, readers will find that Smart's *World Philosophies* catches them up in a history of worldviews and in worldview analysis. And with much of the worldview construction in non-Western cultures being heavily influenced by the 'vertical context' as described by Smart, therefore, it should not surprise the reader that Smart takes seriously the role of religion in his consideration of the symbolic life of humanity as a whole.

The figure of the professional philosopher who holds a position in a modern university and who is primarily concerned with matters of science, logic, and analysis, does not, then, determine the framework of Smart's enterprise in *World Philosophies*. It is important, therefore, that the reader give special attention to Smart's delineation of the variety of possible 'philosophical styles of thought' to be found in other cultures. Indeed, it is part of his agenda to persuade the reader of a 'wider meaning of philosophy' exemplified in this account of the world's philosophies; to assist the reader to see elements of significance in the abstract and critical reflections on life by intellectuals in both Western and non-Western cultures. Though this may seem a daunting task given the ten different kinds of philosophers Smart describes in the introductory chapter, the complexity is tamed somewhat in that, according to him, only three motifs or themes can be seen to emerge from them which Smart describes as follows: 'First, there is the theme of wisdom, whether it be spiritual, political, or ethical. Second, there is the theme of worldview whether metaphysical, scientific, or religious. Third, there is the theme of critic and questioner.'

One element in Smart's motivation to write this book, then, is simply to recover intellectual traditions of thought that are in danger of being lost, or of being excluded from consideration because of the dominance of Western modes of discourse. But Smart's enterprise here is not simply that of a scholarly preservation project. Smart is of the conviction that humankind faces serious difficulties and is in need of a common worldview within which they can be discussed and debated. Moreover, he considered himself to be involved in just such a task of worldview construction. In his Gifford Lectures – *Beyond Ideology: Religion and the Future of Western Civilization* (1981) – he did more than merely review and analyse religions and ideologies; he attempted to contribute to the construction of a philosophical framework that would press 'differing cultures and political systems ... [into] continuing and intimate interplay' that could lead to the resolution of the problems of modern society. He was convinced then, as he is in the conclusions he draws in this book, that our multiple cultures must enter 'into the same global debate and dialogue'. And in his estimation, every culture, small-scale and large, has something to contribute to this dialogue, this 'reflective synthesis'; together they constitute 'a treasure house of resources'. As he puts it in his above-mentioned article on the tasks of comparative philosophy: 'If we look on the various philosophical heritages as resources, then we may hope that ideas drawn from them might help to resolve some of the major world-view problems of the new intellectual world taking shape through the meeting of cultures.' For him, it is a grounding principle that we assume every cultural tradition to embody some value or an aspect of truth that enables each culture to contribute something distinctive to world culture. Thus in his judgment, everyone can participate in what he calls 'a general diffusion of human values on the world scene'.

This book was meant to be a contribution to achieving such a world culture. And in that, it expresses an enthusiastic idealism that is more characteristic of the mid-twentieth century than today. Nevertheless, there is something refreshing and stimulating in that unabashed idealism that may well prompt a rethinking of global values in the twenty-first century.

Donald Wiebe
Trinity College, University of Toronto

1

THE HISTORY OF THE WORLD AND OUR PHILOSOPHICAL INHERITANCE

We are living through one of the most transformative times in world history. Indeed, ours is the age when histories have come together into a single process. This is because of a blend of world wars and singular inventions. By pitting colonial powers against each other, World War I raged over virtually the whole globe, from the Somme to East Africa and from Tientsin to the Atlantic. World War II even more dramatically and deeply enmeshed the globe, and burned from Glasgow to Hiroshima and from Papua New Guinea to Murmansk. Satellite communications, jet airliners and computers have helped to knit together the globe in meshes of more or less instantaneous exchanges and almost time-free travel. In older days it was arduous or impossible to travel from one of the main centers of civilization to another. It took years to travel from Europe to East Asia, and hardly less from India. Great swathes of the world were unknown to the rest – the interior of Africa, large parts of South and North America, large stretches of Siberia and many islands of the Pacific. Regions were relatively discrete from one another, and so we are wont to think of countries' histories separately: we think of Chinese, Japanese, Indian, Tibetan, Persian, German, Italian history. But in our day, all these histories have flowed together to form, from now on, a single stream – world history. By the same token we are all (or virtually all) included in the processes of global economics, geopolitics and planetary ecology. From now on we are forced to think globally. And yet often our traditions of education and culture, especially in the West, because the West has not endured the impact of the West as a colonial power-source, lead us to think in terms merely of our own tradition.

Thus philosophy for many scholars and interested lay persons means Western philosophy, literature means Western literature, music means Western music and so on. In this book, I shall attempt to give a picture of the philosophies of all the world. It may be that from now on humans will speculate together in a global manner: but now more than ever it is vital to remember the diversities of the past. The varying centers of civilization and culture, together with their outlying peripheral civilizations, have contributed divergent themes to the sum of human thought. We need to be conscious of our ancestors of all races, religions and intellectual climates, who have helped to shape human living and human ideas. They can be our critics and can remain sources of ideas and new slants on things. Especially because we all belong to a cross-cultural world, the plural past can be amazingly invigorating. We can exploit several kinds and sources of riches. But the shape of a project of thinking about the world's philosophies depends on what we mean by 'philosophy' and its plural. The word, after all, is a Western word, and there is no guarantee that it has a clear equivalent outside of the West.

Actually, even in its home territory, the word is controversial and confusing, in part because of the changing nature, through history, of how the enterprise of philosophy has been conceived. Or rather, we should say 'enterprises'. For Plato it was a kind of critical wisdom about both the ultimate realities and this world. For Plotinus it was a religious worldview. For Aristotle it was systematic knowledge and indistinguishable from science. For Aquinas it was greatly implicated with theology. For the later Wittgenstein it was a method of examining language in ways which would dissolve previous metaphysical problems. All this is without considering the differing slants provided by, say, Chinese and Indian philosophy. Indeed, the nature (and the worth) of philosophy is itself a philosophical problem. As Aristotle succinctly observed, 'Whether or not one should do philosophy is itself a philosophical issue: so you have to philosophize.' Even so, we need to think through the main varieties of speculative and critical thinking to which, in the West, the term 'philosophy' has been attached. And in order to arrive at something of a global consensus we need to add meanings which come from other great centers. Let me then, before delineating the chief patterns of philosophy, sketch briefly the chief powerhouses of thought among the varied civilizations of the human race.

It is not a cause of disrespect to other fertile intellectual and spiritual areas of human culture to point to a 'great three' which have proved to be especially rich in human civilization: namely, China, South Asia (India, roughly) and the West. They have helped to procreate other regions of dynamic philosophy: China has fertilized Japan and Korea; South Asia has fertilized Tibet and South-east Asia; Europe has generated offspring in the Americas and the Islamic world. There are of course other wonderful areas of human culture whose creativity will no doubt tell us more in the future than it has in the past, such as Black Africa and the Caribbean. But we can simplify human intellectual history by saying that three great regions have particularly vivified it. And about them, we can ask: do the conceptions which we find in Chinese and Indian civilizations give a separate slant on what 'philosophy' is? Do they add something to the Western tradition about the nature of the enterprise?

Much emphasis is given in China to the role of the reflective sage and adviser, who thinks deeply about ethical and political problems, problems of human nature, and how to act in conformity with nature and, above that, Heaven. This stress upon practical wisdom is of course also not unknown to the West. But it looms much larger in the Chinese and its related traditions. In India, speculations tend to be more theoretical, but often they are tied to release or salvation. The bond between religion and philosophy is closer than in China or in the West; but the varieties of religion are greater. Especially to be noted are the mutually critical relations between the Buddhist and Hindu schools. To complicate our sketch, Buddhism migrated to almost all of South-east and East Asia, and particularly to China. It helped to fertilize the dialectical relations between Taoism and Confucianism, while it added a more individualistic and cerebral dimension to Chinese thought, and the three formed the three traditions of China, living in partial harmony and interplay, together with varieties of folk religion.

The sage and the guru, and their traditional critics, are not at all absent from Western thought and religion. But I mention them so that we are not mesmerized by the narrower confines of modern English-speaking professionals' account of what philosophy is. It comprises not only the more critical and technical kinds of thinking which have come to dominate Western academic philosophy, but also those more sagely and spiritual aspects of human thought that have often been prominent in China and India and their surrounding regions. It is wise to add, because of sensitivity on this matter, that philosophy outside the West and above all in India has a rich vein of technical and epistemological writings which rival the intricacies of some modern Western writings in the field.

Because sometimes philosophy comes to be embedded thoroughly in a religious culture or civilization, it is useful to treat its manifestations in these ambiences. It is convenient therefore to speak of Jewish and Islamic thought (separate chapters indeed are devoted to these two). In addition, there are areas of human experience which have in classical times produced little that formally might be thought of as philosophy (as judged by the great trio of civilizations considered above), such as classical African cultures, which nevertheless contain important strands of the material of philosophy. There are traditional worldviews, including myths of origin and accounts of human nature in relation to the wider world, ethical values and proverbial lore. Such material may be called 'worldviews' for short. And the articulation of such worldviews, their critique and adaptation, may be fairly called philosophy.

People are of course sensitive about the achievements of their cultural regions and national identities. They can become upset to think that in singling out some areas and epochs of human history as being highly productive, other countries are being downgraded. But the dignity of the human being is not related to the putative glories of her or his ancestors. Moreover, if we look at human life in a broader sweep, we see that the future is as vital as the past. Black Africa, for instance, whose past has not been as scintillating as that of ancient Greece or the T'ang (Tang) dynasty of China will no doubt have a highly creative future with which to contribute to the glories of humanity. So while some cultures have not attained to richness in philosophical debate and articulation, there are future veins to be mined: and in any case, philosophy is not the only human activity by which to judge traditions. Spiritual power, musical achievement, painting, human welfare and a whole number of other yardsticks may be used.

SOME HUMAN TYPES REPRESENTING PHILOSOPHY

One way of approaching the question of what philosophy is by considering what the main human types are in diverse civilizations whose work is in some sense philosophical. For instance, the great historian of Chinese philosophy, Fung Yu-lan, prefers the phrase *che-hsüeh (zhexue)* as a translation of 'philosophy'. This derives from the term *che-ren (zheren)* or 'sageman', or more briefly 'sage'. So philosophy is the 'learning of sages' or 'sage-learning'. Indeed, classically the idea of the philosopher as sage is by no means absent in the Western tradition. In ancient Greece, Pythagoras and Plotinus can be cited as sages – people who have a charismatic or mystical wisdom. The very term 'philosophy' does after all mean the love of wisdom; and *sophia* might well be used for the kind of knowledge that a sage has attained. And so one type of philosopher might be thought of as the sage.

By contrast, a differing ideal is often set forth – the philosopher as dialectician, the person who is clever at arguments. This arises partly because reason is often recognized as a vital component of the philosophical approach, and so the person who can conduct reasoning well is admired. In ancient Greece we have the figure of the sophist. As the name's history indicates, there were ambivalent feelings about reasoning power: it could be used in opposite directions, or unscrupulously. In China, one of the six chief recognized schools in ancient times was that of the *pien-che (bianzhe)* or Dialectical school, much concerned with logic and the relation of names to reality.

Another type is that of the spiritual analyst – that is, the analytical thinker who uses his powers to lay out a religious position. I am thinking here of some of the great *ācāryas* of the Hindu tradition, such as Śaṅkara; of St Thomas Aquinas in the Roman Catholic tradition; and such acute thinkers as Nāgārjuna and Buddhaghoṣa in the Buddhist religion. In fact, perhaps the greatest spiritual analyst of all is the Buddha himself. He perhaps combined the role of sage and spiritual analyst. All these people produced analytical ideas of spiritual importance. Thus St Thomas argued for the five ways of reasoning to God, and the all-important distinction between knowledge based on natural reasoning and that which is based on revelation.

The spiritual analyst – as I have called this type – is not always different from the theologian. But I have not used the latter term for several reasons. First, it is not quite comprehensive enough: it implies someone who reasons about God; but not all religions have a serious God (for instance Buddhism does not), and there are philosophies or ideologies such as Marxism which reject theology, though their intellectual articulators play roles very similar to those of theologians in God-centered religions. Second, the word 'theologian' should really contain a prefix to mark the tradition which he claims to expound (for typically theologians are recognized, and so authoritative, persons within a faith tradition). Anyway, we may note that what I have called a spiritual analyst may be dubbed by others a theologian, though not – as I have spelled out – in all cases.

Another rather different ideal of the philosopher is as the super-scientist. In ancient times there were speculative cosmologists, such as the proponents of the yin-yang theory in China, or the Atomists in India and Greece, who claimed to possess a kind of key to all knowledge. Aristotle presented the ideal of a thinker whose immense scope sought to bring about a synthesis of all knowledge. So successful indeed was Aristotle that his articulated vision of science dominated Western thought to the Renaissance and beyond. In more recent times, history and social science have been drawn into the super-scientists' grasp, and we have such seminal figures as Marx and Popper who have sought to produce overarching theories to deal with human life as well as the natural sciences.

Not dissimilar is the ideal type of the metaphysician who claims to give a picture of ultimate realities which lie beyond the immediate scope of the natural or social sciences. In ancient China something of this flavor is caught in the idea of the *hsuan-hsüeh (xuanxue)* or 'learning of the mystery'. That which is mysteriously 'beyond' the world as it presents itself to us is what metaphysics is about (as is commonly thought). Not only the ancient Taoists but also such modern Western figures as Hegel and Heidegger might be seen as metaphysicians in this sense.

Because of the prizing of dialectics, and the fact that ideally reasons have to be given for philosophical positions, there is another type which has proven important in different cultures: that of the skeptic. He or she is the person who finds the usual reasons for positions to be wanting. Absolute skepticism issues in silence, and that was the stance adopted in India by certain *munis* or silent sages, and in ancient Greece by Cratylus. But a skeptic does not need to be so extreme, using language for ordinary purposes and out of habit, while remaining skeptical about the ultimate justifications of what we take to be knowledge. Perhaps, though, we should see the skeptic as just one variety of a more important type: the questioner.

For another way in which we see the philosopher is as the questioner of what we claim to be true. The great paradigm was Socrates: but in more modern times we can think of philosophers who have called into question the commonly held assumptions of society – great critics, such as revolutionary writers like Tolstoy and Lu-Hsun (Luxun), thinkers like Proudhon and Kropotkin, and poets like Lorca and Lucretius. The image of the questioner is akin to that of the critical reasoner, though more volcanic fires may burn beneath her or his challenges to social or intellectual convention. Of all modern Westerners perhaps the most important is Nietzsche, and who knows whence came the fierce flames of his bold challenge to Western tradition?

But in the last forty years a more conventional figure has come to prominence (in part because of the great expansion of universities in so many countries, and above all in the English-speaking world). That figure is the professional philosopher: usually conceived as technically very competent and therefore familiar with modern logic, and often too wedded to a particular ideology springing from the linguistic analysis and modern empiricist traditions; devoted mostly to a scientific worldview. She or he is a type derived from the Enlightenment, in so far as reason is claimed to be the chief determinant of opinion. As a professional, the philosopher is in danger of becoming tamed by the very institutions that have begotten him. The image of suit and briefcase flit through the mind, and hours completed at the knowledge-plant from nine till five.

As another type we can maybe nominate the modern, or mathematical, logician. Technical logic is used as a means of defining and elucidating philosophical problems. But with the separate development of the field, much of logic has taken off on its own or in close liaison with mathematics – much as psychology, once regarded as part of philosophy, has attained its separation and independence.

Finally, to revert to Confucius and Chinese philosophy, we may note that the sage is often perceived as the adviser: the person of sagacious intellect who surveys the scene and gives advice on values. In a party regime he may be the ideologist. The adviser is a public intellectual who can comment on affairs perceptively: and this is sometimes seen as the role of the philosopher – as with such figures as Confucius himself, Plato in Sicily, Aristotle as tutor of Alexander the Great, and various modern intellectuals prominent in public affairs and debate – Ortega y Gasset, Dewey, Bertrand Russell, Sartre, Croce, Radhakrishnan, Karl Popper, Lukaćs and so forth.

All these types are a mixed lot. They emerge as embodying, however, three main themes. First, there is the theme of wisdom, whether it be spiritual, political or ethical. Second, there is the theme of worldview, whether metaphysical, scientific or religious. Third, there is the theme of critic and questioner.

A SKETCH OF THE WIDER MEANING OF PHILOSOPHY

From the foregoing discussion of types of philosopher, we can begin to delineate roughly speaking what the scope of philosophy is, given a wider and cross-cultural view. It is useful to think, in this connection, who we would *not* count particularly as philosophers, and why.

Why, for instance, does it seems inappropriate to think of Jesus as a philosopher, though it is quite easy to consider the Buddha one? I believe it is because the Jesus of the Gospels is a poetic, mysterious figure, given to healing, to flashing images, to profound parables, to unexpected action: but he is not liable to produce analytic discourses or to dwell on eight thises or twelve thats, in the way of the Buddha. He does not deal in abstractions or metaphysical-sounding concepts, but rather with concrete metaphors and numinous similes. His task is not that of systematic instruction. He belongs to a different world. Maybe in some sense he has a philosophy of life: but he does not expound it in an articulated manner. It was for others to build upon his life and images – people such as Paul and Cyril and Augustine.

Nor do we think of Horace as a philosopher, though again he had a philosophy of life. But his chief task was to fashion lovely verses and to bend the Latin language to a sweet variety of meters. Nor is Li Po a philosopher; nor Charles Darwin; nor Turgenev; nor Murasaki Shikibu. These have all been ornaments of creative writing – but they did not primarily concern themselves with analysis, worldview-construction or political or ethical advice (even though no doubt from every great artist wise advice can be mined).

As we noted above, it is possible to extract a worldview from a person's thinking and living even when he or she is not mainly concerned with presenting a system. The same applies to societies and the world of traditional myth. For instance, Jesus looked upon God as his Daddy, Abba. We can if we wish elaborate on this whole image and construct a more abstract delineation of the divine Being as transcendent and personal (or having an analogy to a human person). Or we may take some tribal world and sketch out its worldview – as has been done by anthropologists and others in works on various groups such as the Dogon, the Kikuyu (by Jomo Kenyatta) and the Ndembu.

Such worldview-articulation is especially obvious in these latter days. For colonial impingement upon traditional small-scale societies, together with the impact of modern technology and bureaucratic arrangements, has challenged them to imitate the incoming forces by expressing an ideology or worldview which somehow plays in the same league. Sometimes the process works through a double development of a wider cultural merger and an overall set of values. For instance, both classical African culture and Native American societies are moving in this direction. It is not uncommon now to hear of African ideas and Native American beliefs, as though they form unitary units. Sixty years ago such wide-ranging notions would not have occurred. Now there are many courses in colleges on African religion and Native American ideas. So there is a variety of responses that have come about during these colonial and postcolonial days: the articulation of particular worldviews by anthropologists; and the modernizing of such worldviews through synthesis and greater abstraction. In these ways, relatively non-philosophical societies have grown philosophies. The whole process can be seen as one of worldview-articulation and worldview-adaptation.

I have used the word 'philosophies' in the plural just now. A philosophy can be said to be a product of philosophy. That is, philosophical thinking, whether it be in the service of articulating the old but inchoate, or critically replacing the old, serves to produce some system of ideas which broadly we have called a worldview, and which can also be called a philosophy. Philosophizing relates to method: philosophies are what comes out as a result of applying the method. As may be seen, to include the various kinds of philosophies in what we mean by philosophy we move far beyond what is technically and fairly narrowly deemed to be philosophy by modern professional philosophers. This more catholic purview helps to resolve some of the problems which are posed by the need to be cross-cultural, since my project involves something necessarily plural, namely a history of the philosophical thinking of the whole world. It resolves those problems because a wider collection of philosophies will more easily embrace the difference in concepts exhibited in non-Western civilizations.

For instance, we have noted that Chinese ideas of sage-learning, and of the learning of the mystery, are analogous to Western ideas of philosophy and metaphysics. We could point also to the Indian notion of *darśana* or viewpoint (or vision: the word is based on a root meaning 'to see'), to describe the philosophical positions which occur in Indian thought. It is sometimes used as a translation of 'philosophy'. It fits very well with our idea of worldview. If we define one main activity of philosophy as being that of worldview-articulation and worldview-construction, then I think it readily embraces the slants which belong to Chinese and Indian civilizations.

But in our review of the types of philosopher we meet those whose primary purpose is not so much worldview-construction as the questioning and criticism of received values. Even the adviser must be to some degree a questioner. Also it often happens that a deeper questioning leads to the framing of possible answers. In various ways the critical function of philosophy complements the constructive function. There is an interplay between worldviews and critical questions. The guru is undermined by the critic: but the sage perhaps is someone who has reflected enough to frame his or her own critiques of received values, and is then able to present a considered and revised worldview.

We may bring these differing points together to say that the process of philosophizing typically creates critical conclusions which articulate worldviews, usually of a relatively abstract kind. At one extreme lies the guru who reveals a worldview or set of values; at the other is the skeptic who falls into merited silence.

I use 'worldview' in a rather stretched way, for even where the aim of the critique of ordinary concepts is designed to present an 'empty' point of view, as may be encountered in certain forms of Buddhist philosophy, there is as it were the ghost of a worldview which is pointed to. The Buddhist dialectical thinker who believes that all our concepts fail to grasp pure experience would no doubt wish to deny that he is putting forward a positive worldview or philosophical position. He is positionless. Nevertheless there is a flavor to his account which distinguishes it from other ways of viewing and acting upon the world. So I shall ascribe to him, however tenuously, a worldview. But broadly the term will be used for religious systems of ideas and political ideologies as well as more purely 'rational' systems. I shall return to this point in a short while.

But before that it is worth saying that we can make a rough distinction between philosophy as an activity, or even a way of life, and philosophies or worldviews. As we have noted, the latter are products, for the most part, of the activity. The latter follows some method or recognized perception of valid utterance. In recent times in the English-speaking world the method of analyzing language with a view to clarifying or even dissolving philosophical problems has been prominent: there is also the use of logic and rigorous argument, as with such writers as Bertrand Russell. Hegel claimed to follow a dialectical method. Even being a reflective sage, like Confucius, involves some kind of method – observing human behavior, classifying types of virtues, practicing different means of education, gaining experience in statecraft and so on. But there is no single philosophical method, because any position on how to do philosophy is itself debatable. The plural world of intellectual diversity is always liable to hit back at rigid orthodoxies (and how much more so in a situation like the present, with its cross-cultural meetings). Because of this, the concept of philosophy in the singular which roughly speaking refers to method will always be open-ended and plural.

MYTH, METHOD AND CONTENT

If we can broadly distinguish between philosophy as method and the philosophies which it gives rise to, it is worth reflecting too on the question of style. Many of the world's cultures have well-developed myths or narratives and while these may contain, implicitly, sketches of the world and of the nature of living beings and humankind, they are not primarily thought of as philosophical creations. This is often because philosophy seems to belong to a reflective period in a society's evolution. But it is also because, relatively speaking, a culture's philosophy or set of philosophies typically has a relatively abstract form. It deals in the interplay of forces rather than the clashing of heroes, and in the delineation of ultimates rather than the depiction of old battles and amours.

This more abstract character is something often shared with religious doctrines. For instance, while the New Testament speaks of Jesus and God in highly personal ways, the doctrine of the Trinity as in due course evolved at the Council of Nicaea in 325 CE contained the formula of 'three persons in one substance' or (putting the Greek into a better translation) 'three beings in one entity'. A great deal of subsequent, including modern, theology has had this dark and abstract character. In rather recent times, Tillich wrote about 'man's ultimate concern' as being the focus of religion. There is a story about Jesus inquiring of his disciples as to who people say he is: on learning the deep abstractions of modern theologians he is profoundly puzzled: do we then classify philosophy and religious doctrine together? I think it will be useful to do this in this present narrative of the world's philosophies. Doctrines do have their reflective aspect. Admittedly they are often collective in character. The same applies often to political ideologies, especially as forced by modern governments or defining a political party. But group doctrines do have their place in the evolution of human thought, and so I shall include them.

But myth represents a very different style. It is useful to explore briefly here the function of myth in human societies before depicting its relation to philosophy and philosophies. Myths, first of all, are narratives, and typically they involve accounts of gods or other significant forces in human life and creation. Myths often sketch the interaction between significant humans, such as the first man and woman, and divine beings. They may depict the saving acts of heroes and others – such as the story of Jesus' life, death and resurrection, and the story of the Buddha's enlightenment. These stories (which may also of course be seen as historically true) give a vivid sense of powerful acts which mean something central to the human race. Some myths, because they are seen as taking place in a 'never-never' time at the beginning of history, are in modern times looked on as allegories or creative fictions – as with the story of the Garden of Eden, now looked on as no longer to be taken as literally true, though it may express something very vital in the relationship between God and human beings. The emphasis in modern times has shifted in two directions – towards the creation of fiction, which does not usually pretend to have taken place actually, though it may contain actualities of human nature and truths about the human condition; and towards the historical. The actual history of a nation's or an individual's past becomes important. Scientific history (but suitably selected) becomes the basis for establishing a people's claims to identity.

All this is part of a modernizing intellectual trend, in which a degree of abstraction has become the norm. For instance, in the last hundred years or so remarkable interest, and often enthusiasm, have been directed towards dialectical theories of history, notably that of Marx. Relative abstractions such as those of class, profit, exploitation, revolution, proletariat and so on are wielded in the context of unfolding events. Similar more 'scientific' abstractions are used in sociology and economics. It is all part of a turning away from more mythic formulations. Thus Christian theologians often write of human alienation from the divine Being, preferring such language rather than the more direct talk of Adam's sin. Unvarnished myth is a good deal less credible today than it was once, and so we have a relative doctrinalization of the mythic. The metaphysical is brought in to give depth to stories. So myth has a tendency to turn into history, and the historical reaches out behind itself to the darker mysteries of philosophy, ideology and doctrine.

Something of this owes itself to the spread of Western-style higher education, which has produced world-wide a new intelligentsia. The spread was brought about substantially by the colonial epoch. As nations were subdued by Western powers, they began to contemplate measures to assert their independence, which became an especially vivid goal with the spread of the ideal of modern nationalism from the time of the French Revolution onwards. National resurgence needed to borrow some or many of the tools of the colonial powers – the West's weapons with which of course to combat the West. Main among these weapons was ideology: some philosophy with which to rebuild a nation, and something too which could stand up to the process of higher education (itself the key to more mundane values, such as Western literacy for bureaucratic purposes, science for engineering and so on). The various major countries groped around for doctrines which would give them the direction and *élan* to combat rampaging colonialism. India devised its own form of democratic Neohinduism, under the inspiration of such figures as Swami Vivekananda and Mahatma Gandhi. Japan devised its own Westernized system, and grafted onto it the values of Shinto seen as an expression of national identity. China adapted its enemies' enemy, namely Marxism, in the guise of Mao Zedong thought, which was used successfully in overcoming both internal and external foes. (Whether such ideologies prove to be more effective in economic development is another matter.)

Small-scale societies have not been exempt from such exigencies of ideology. Thus we see the gradual confluence of ideas and forces in Native American thought to form a new, nature-related and ecologically sensitive ideology; and similar events are occurring among Australian Aborigines. Such notions have been formed as 'the Pacific Way' (among the inhabitants of the South Pacific) and 'Africanness' (among Black Africans).

In short, new identities and ideologies are being formed, which in some degree confer a certain abstractness on thinking about cultures. This is part of the trend towards moving away from pure myth or history towards a more philosophical and metaphysical stance. Even where myth is collected and prized, it is often seen under the rubrics of psychoanalysis (particularly Jung), as revealing deep patterns in human thinking and feeling.

We may see all this as part of a postcolonial globalization of thinking. Such a world perspective may in the long run reduce variety and tend towards the homogenization of cultures. Already we may note that most Western organizations (for instance, associations of philosophy and the like) are dominant. This is why the present book is urgently needed, to remind us all of the plural riches of the human race's reflective heritage.

SOME CONCLUSIONS ABOUT WORLD PHILOSOPHY

As has been noted, we are here treating philosophy in the widest possible way – to cover worldviews which are both collective and individual, traditional and critical, religious and ideological, affirmative and skeptical. Such a wide embrace is important so that we may preserve some sense of the plural character of human thinking.

In what follows I shall attempt to sketch the evolution of human thinking on a regional basis. I shall treat separately such areas as South Asia, China, Korea and Japan, even though they obviously have a great deal of interplay. In particular, because Buddhism (so important both religiously and philosophically throughout Asia) spread from India to China and from there further afield, it is important to begin our Asian sequence with South Asia first. This already dictates one main sequence of chapters and treatments.

Also I think it is salutary for Western readers in particular but really for all readers, to begin their reading of world thought outside of Europe. This will help them, and us, escape from being too confined in the strait-jacket of a conventional view of the history of the field. It will enable us to look with fresh eyes upon the patterns of the world.

Sometimes, because of the vitality of the religious ambience, it is useful to talk of developments not just by region but by spiritual culture. For this reason, after dealing with ancient and later Greek and Roman thought I shall move to Islamic and Jewish cultures, which had one of their main flowerings in the early medieval period. After dealing with Western thinking, particularly the postclassical and modern (even postmodern) ideas of the West, including both North and South America, I return to more traditional cultures and their way of expressing the modern condition – from modern Islamic to Japanese and South-east Asian philosophies. In this sequence I include African and other philosophies, as notions which have emerged seriously only in postcolonial times. For this reason, for instance, I do not have any earlier premodern African philosophy. It seemed best to treat African classical worldviews in immediate conjunction with the modern period and the evolution of postcolonial ideologies and worldviews.

Each chapter will contain a conclusion which will sketch in some of the major themes of the various traditions. I would hope that these, together with my final section of summation in the book, will provide a mosaic of important values and questions for the human race to reflect on and absorb.

For, after all, the whole story is a thrilling one. There are subtle skepticisms and affirmations of the Buddha, the fires of Upanishadic speculation, the mysterious profundities of the Vedānta Sutras, the elaborate Indian schools, new logic, Chinese Buddhism, the networks of Hua Yen (Yan), the elliptical speech of Ch'an (Chan/Zen), Neoconfucian profundities, the Taoist heritage, the continuing sagacity of Confucius, the Yin and the Yang, Korean extensions of Chinese thought, Japanese richnesses, the whole vast gamut of ancient Hellenistic philosophy, medieval Islamic and Jewish thought, the wonderful flowering of modern Judaism, Renaissance Italian thought, nineteenth-century German philosophy, African varieties, Latin American Arielism and the influence of Krause – and a whole lot of riches besides. Into that history, and into many more familiar episodes, we now plunge. We shall float on the many minds of the world, through many streams that in due course have become the single wide river of today.

2

SOUTH ASIAN PHILOSOPHIES

INTRODUCTION: THE CULTURAL AREA

The cultural area known as South Asia covers a number of countries which are now to be seen on the political map: India, Pakistan, Bangladesh, Nepal, Tibet, Bhutan and Sri Lanka. The major divisions in recent times have occurred because of the split between mainly Hindu India and chiefly Islamic Pakistan and Bangladesh. Others have been somewhat adventitious – for instance Ceylon or Sri Lanka was incorporated as a separate colony into the British Empire, separate from India itself (then chiefly under the control of the East India Company, basically a trading organization) after the conquest of the hill capital, Kandy, in 1815. Confusingly, the term 'India', which was used for the whole of the land from the Himalaya mountains down to Cape Kanyakumarin (Comorin) at the southern tip, is now used only for a part, namely that which belongs to the Republic of India with its capital in Delhi. For the most part, in the present chapter I shall use the word 'India' for the whole of the subcontinent. Thus by Indian philosophy I shall mean, as other writers indeed do, the philosophy of the great traditional region from the borders of Afghanistan to the Indian Ocean.

We take the story up to the verge of the modern period – effectively up to about 1800. From this time on colonial forces were making a real impact. Moreover, in the latter part of this period the Islamic culture of the Mughals was rather dominant. To some extent this Muslim phase will be taken care of through my account of Islamic thought, treated separately.

The two main streams of traditional Indian philosophy have been those of Buddhism and of the Hindu tradition. There have been others of marked, but lesser, importance – notably the Cārvākas or Materialists and the Jains. The Buddhist stream flowed on

13

elsewhere – into Sri Lanka first of all, and into parts of south-east Asia; even more importantly into China and much of the rest of East Asia; and finally into Tibet and Mongolia. In the Far East especially it saw new flowerings, with such schools as Huayen in China and Zen in Japan. It became part of the indissoluble fabric of East Asian civilization. But though it has greatly faded in India itself, Buddhism is one of the great religions (and philosophies) of India. It should not be overlooked (as some today might do because of the predominance of the Hindu tradition in the Republic) as one of the two great pillars of Indian civilization. Or one of three, if one wants to include a third pillar, Islam, which has played such a strong and creative role in the subcontinent in the last few hundred years. But in our treatment here we shall be confining ourselves to traditional formulations of philosophy, and so primarily to Buddhist and Hindu varieties.

We can point to some major periods in the unfolding of Indian thought. The first great flowering was from about the fifth century BCE onwards, particularly with the emergence of Buddhist, Jain and other schools as well as the speculations of the classical Upanishads. From about the second century BCE we have the creation of the Mahāyāna varieties of Buddhist thought, together with the emergence of the great sutras or aphoristic texts of the major Brahmin schools. This is the main period of the formation of the so-called Six Schools of Hindu thought. From about the eighth century CE onwards into the medieval time there evolved some of the great commentarial literature – above all the great formulations of Hindu Vedānta: the apogee, so it might be said, of Hindu theology. There were other developments too, such as the evolution of schools, such as Kaśmir Śaivism and Tamil-based devotional Śaiva Siddhānta. In addition, there is the formation of a great period of Indian logic. Very crudely, then, we can divide the periods into: the Early Period; the Classical Period; and the Medieval Period. After that (but for us the subject of another chapter) is the Modern Period.

The most common way of treating the history of Indian thought is to begin with the *Ṛg Veda*, the ancient hymns, maybe going back to 1000 BCE, often seen as very early deliverances of the Aryan culture which came into India in the period from about 1500 onwards. It is of course the Veda which serves as the beginning point of the holy tradition of the Brahmins, who in becoming the dominant priesthood of a whole civilization, have laid their stamp upon the Hindu world. In this context, the Buddhists are seen as breakaways, rebels, reformers, perhaps above all as protestants against a prevailing ethic. It may be that there is some truth in this picture. Yet there is a much clearer view of the nature of Indian society and thinking as seen through the Buddhist texts than can be afforded via the rather obscurer treatises, composed between the seventh and first centuries BCE, known as the Upanishads. Not only this, but some of the things which the Buddhists take for granted are only beginning to be felt in the late Vedic literature – the idea of rebirth or reincarnation, the operation of karma from life to life, the great and recurring character of the world's evolution and periodic subsidence and so on.

These ideas were already fairly common too among other schools of the period, such as the Jains, Ājīvikas and others who were after the same audience as the Buddha himself. Moreover, a new and flourishing civilization was taking shape along the Ganges river, in such new cities as Pataliputra (now Patna), Vaisali, Banaras and others. To the new mercantile classes the Buddhists and other followers of the so-called śramaṇic schools appealed. Though the Brahmins had their place in this new society, they were away from the ancient heartlands of Brahmanic culture, the Āryāvarta, to the West (near and north of what is now Delhi). It is common in many of the texts to use the significant combination *brāhmaṇśramaṇas*, in other words, the Brahmins and the *śramaṇas*. The latter were the wandering recluses and holy beggars who practiced the spiritual life. The Buddha himself and his followers were typical of such world-renouncers. In being coupled with Brahmins there is a suggestion that they had some equality of status: so the traditional priests of Aryan tradition were paired with those who had gone from home to homelessness.

For a long period of Indian history the forces of Buddhism (and other śramaṇic movements such as Jainism) lived side by side with the developing religiosity of the Hindu tradition, in all its variety.

It is thus a bit misleading to see the Buddhists as a kind of breakaway from an ancient Hindu tradition. As it happened, what we now know as Hinduism had not yet come into existence at the time of the Buddha, in the fifth century BCE. It was several centuries before anything like the complex caste system had arisen; nor were there temple complexes and elaborate worship of the gods (in the Vedic hymns, worship is conducted more on a nomadic basis); there was as yet no wide acceptance of reincarnation and the idea of merit; the ideal of *mokṣa* or ultimate spiritual release was not yet dominant; many of the major myths had not yet emerged; we look in vain for the notion of avatars or incarnations of the great God Viṣṇu. All this essentially belongs towards the end of this first period, not to its beginning.

And so it is for such reasons that I am going to begin our history of Indian philosophy unusually with the Buddha, and only from there move on to the other śramaṇic movements and to the later Hindu philosophical schools. This maybe a slightly unusual perspective; but I think it will prove to be rewarding.

One final point about periods and dates: a recurrent problem with much of the relatively earlier Indian material is that we are uncertain about dates. Good scholars can differ by a few hundred years on such matters as the dating of the *Bhagavadgītā*.

THE BUDDHA'S TIME: ITS CIRCUMSTANCES

Over a long period, perhaps a thousand years, elements of Brahmin lore had been handed down. By the sixth century BCE there were in existence at least three main collections of hymns (the Vedic hymns), of which the most important was the *Ṛg Veda*. Not yet assembled into final form was a fourth collection known as the *Atharva Veda*: it was this that ultimately constituted the fourth part of the Vedic canon. Other works were in process of composition and some of these had reached perhaps their present form, as handed down orally in rigid succession by trained Brahmins, these being the Brāhmaṇas or ritual texts, and some Upanishads.

The Brahmins were a hereditary priesthood, who for certain purposes had achieved ritual prominence and indeed great respect. Often they functioned as advisers and ministers to kings and princes. Later, as the predominant group, they came to control those practices which we identify with Hinduism: not only their traditional command of sacrificial techniques, but also the worship which went on in temples, festivals and pilgrimages, and rites of passage, such as marriage and funerals. But at the time of the Buddha there was considerable fluidity. By no means did the Brahmin ideology command the scene. Many rejected the idea of a supreme or ultimate sacred reality, sometimes identified with a personal God and sometimes with the holy power implicit in the acts and powers of Brahmins and implicit ultimately in the fabric of the whole universe, called Brahman. There were plenty of alternative religious teachers and specialists, usually thought of collectively as the śramaṇas. While these wandering recluses and holy beggars had a variety of worldviews, they did share some broad values. They did not tend to accept Brahmin claims. They did not think of the Veda as revealed. They believed in reincarnation or rebirth: humans, animals and other beings were in a perpetual round of rebirth, until they might gain ultimate release. They saw virtues in asceticism and in the life led outside of, though in interface with, normal human society.

The area which is described in the Buddhist passages is what is today Uttar Pradesh and Bihar: that is, the region along the mighty Ganges river, and ranging up to the distant foothills of the Himalayas. Here in effect a new civilization was in the making. Prosperous cities were being established along the river. Agricultural surpluses were being created. Villages and towns not only had enough to support themselves, but wandering religious teachers as well. The large kingdom of Magadha was growing in power. Some of the lesser ethnic groups were being absorbed into larger units. In such a period of growth and prosperity there were opportunities for the spread of new religions. Among those which were successful were the Buddhists and a group known as the Ājīvikas and a revived movement known as the Jainas (or Jains), under the leadership of a great contemporary rival of the Buddha, Mahāvīra. Woven into folk religion was no doubt great variety, and it was out of varying mixtures that in due course the full complexities of the Hindu tradition were created.

It was much at this time, we suppose, that the speculative treatises known as the Upanishads were being put together. These represent new directions in Brahminic thinking: for instance (as we shall see later) towards the idea of a unified divine Being pervading the whole universe, and towards belief in reincarnation. In this, philosophy and religion drifted away from the vibrant multiplicity of the hymn collections, dedicated to a number of gods, and as yet with little if anything to say about yoga and rebirth, two vital later themes. We are unclear as to the dates of the principal Upanishads: some are older than the time of the Buddha. There is evidence in the Pāli canon (the primary texts of the Theravāda or 'Elder Doctrine' written in the Indic language of Pāli, as distinct from the more formal and sacred language of Sanskrit) of the doctrines of the Upanishads. If we assume that the Buddha's teachings were handed on from the region of Magadha then it might have been that the Upanishads had their main locus to the north-west of there, in the older heartlands of the Aryan folk and of Brahmin influence. Where the Pāli canon criticizes Brahmins it is often for their adherence to three collections of hymns, with attendant sacred lore and expertise, and for their sacrificial and other ritual practices. Buddhism had a more ethical slant on religious practice, and was willing to praise the 'true Brahmin', that is the person who followed ethical precepts and had good self-control and so on.

Broadly, then, what we know about are two main streams of religious practice: one centered on Brahmin ritual and the other focused on reverence for wandering ascetics. There were some recognized groups who held distinctive philosophical views. The Ājīvikas believed in *niyati* or fate. Individuals were destined to experience all kinds of existence, ending up as recluses fated to be finally released at the end of this life. Good or bad actions did not affect the outcome. Then there were the Lokāyatas or people who believed in this world *(loka)* alone: in other words, they were materialists and rejected all sacrifices, rituals, prayers and so on. Third, there were Agnostics or Skeptics, who refused to assent to any of the speculative ideas then current. Finally, most important, were the Jains, already mentioned, who refused to take life and acted with great care so as to not harm living beings; and who believed that by the practice of extreme austerity, and ultimately self-starvation, one could attain release. They also affirmed a kind of relativism, holding that from one point of view such-and-such is the case, but from some other perspective it is not so. As mentioned, there were Brahmins who held that there is a supreme Lord (over and above all the other gods) or that there is an ultimate impersonal divine principle or Being, which may or may not be identical with the cosmos.

THE BASIC TEACHING OF THE BUDDHA

The Buddha was probably raised in the place known as Kapilavastu, close to the modern Nepalese border in the second half of the fifth century BCE. At the age of 29 he left home, and a wife and small son, with a view to discovering the ultimate truth which would explain and cure the suffering which he had observed, despite his sheltered youth. For six years his pursuit took him to various teachers from the range of schools cited above.

Finally at Bodh Gaya (now the greatest of the four major pilgrimage centers connected with the Buddha's life – the others being the place of his birth in Lumbini, of his first sermon in Sarnath near Banaras, and of his death) he achieved enlightenment or *bodhi,* and so became the Enlightened One or Buddha. Thereafter he preached his first sermon to some former associates, who like him had renounced normal social relationships, and thence more widely for the rest of his long life.

It is of course difficult to disentangle the original teaching of the Buddha from some of the later developments ascribed to him. In some ways it does not matter: the main thing to grasp is some of the basic teachings of Buddhism as they came to emerge from this early period. But there can be little doubt about the originality of the Buddha as an individual. He managed to leave his stamp upon the growing movement. In many ways, Buddhism in all its multifariousness became the most creative of all the strands of philosophy throughout Asia.

In one way the doctrines of the Buddha are deceptively simple. These were summed up in one way through the Four Noble Truths which he presented at his first sermon, in the deer park at Sarnath. First, life is permeated by frustration or – as it is sometimes translated – suffering (*dukkha* in Pāli and *duḥka* in Sanskrit). Second, the cause of frustration or dis-ease is craving or thirst. Third, there is a cure for this. Fourth, the cure consists in the Noble Eightfold Path. This latter culminates in three stages which signify differing kinds of meditation or contemplative practice. As a consequence the individual, successfully cured of suffering, will no longer be reborn at the end of this life. He will become an enlightened being or *arhant*; or to put it another way, he will have attained nibbāna (in Pali: nirvāṇa in Sanskrit).

In order to help one another with this spiritual task, the Buddha formed a Saṅgha or monastic order (later including nuns as well as monks). This Saṅgha would also be a vehicle for the transmission of the Teaching (Sanskrit: *dharma,* and Pali: *dhamma*). The Buddha, the Dharma and the Saṅgha were later deemed to be the three refuges of the Buddhist, and affirming them as such constitutes a profession of faith. Out of these arrangements there grew the decentralized world-wide manifestation of Buddhist monks, nuns and lay persons.

The task of self-training might be thought to be hard, but the general principle is fairly straightforward. But the Buddha's teaching had a much deeper substratum, which has given rise to many of the subtleties and controversies within Buddhism and between it and other schools. That substratum consists in the affirmation that nothing in the world is possessed either of self (*ātman* in Sanskrit and *attā* in Pali) or of permanence *(nitya/nicca).* So all things lack essential identities, permanence and are full of suffering. These are the three marks of existence. Eventually, they all boil down to the fact of impermanence, since it is basically because of that that no being can have a permanent identity, and it is because of it too that nothing (other than liberation or nirvāṇa) is ultimately satisfactory. The thesis that everything is impermanent led to the Buddha's basic repudiation of the notion of a substance or thing. The world is a complex of *events,* each having short duration.

This was an original vision. The solid world of objects dissolved into an ocean of events. Partly because of this the Buddha seems to have concluded that language is misleading. Thus that cunning little word 'I' seems to stand for something positive: but actually I am like everything else, a complex of events. There is nothing firm or substantial underlying the foam of change. It is frequently the case that language produces misconceptions, in part because it is built up of nouns and the like, which have a wrong appearance of solidity.

The denial of an eternal soul brought Buddhists into collision with a number of other schools as time went on. Most significant perhaps for the early period were early manifestations of later Sāṅkhya, one of the main orthodox schools of Hinduism. By 'orthodox' is here meant that it was a school which recognized the authenticity and validity of the authorless Vedic canon as an infallible source of knowledge about the supernatural. By contrast the Buddhists, the Jains, the Ājīvikas and the Materialists rejected Vedic authority. Anyway, the Sāṅkhya position was that there was an infinity of eternal *puruṣas* or individual souls wandering through the cosmos in the process of reincarnation and embedded within the complex structure of matter or nature (*prakṛti*). Each soul was numerically distinct. Buddhism repudiated such a metaphysics, which is also contrary to those positions of the Upanishads, which assumed the existence of an eternal *ātman* at the heart of each individual, sometimes thought of as essentially dependent upon God, or as non-individual and identical with the divine essence. This changeless something was thought to be that which lay beyond everyday awareness, a further fact over and above the stream of consciousness that presupposes it.

The reductive analysis of the world into a mass of impermanent events was itself a startling enough vision. The Buddha went further and had a more particular analysis for each human individual – as being composed of five 'groups' or 'bunches' (Sanskrit: *skandhas;* Pali: *khandhas*); that is, groups of events, or types of events. Each individual is composed of bodily events, perceptions, feelings, dispositions and conscious events. It is when this collection is put together harmoniously that you have what we call persons. Such a teaching was, however, more than a mere analysis: it was also designed to assist self-awareness (which is the seventh in the limbs of the eightfold path). One can realize how one is put together through analysis and introspection, and this in turn helps with self-control. Moreover, the thesis that each of us has no soul has experiential confirmation. Beyond the evanescent states of the various groups there is nothing left over and nothing is changeless.

This analysis of the individual has to bear the weight of rebirth, karma and liberation. That is, the Buddha argued that we do not need a persisting soul to bridge the distance from one life to the next, or for that matter from one instant to the next. It is sufficient that there is a causal or regular connection between events, whether the transitions are of a micro kind from one moment to the next or of a macro kind from one life to the next. How we are reborn is itself a question of largely psychological karma: if your thoughts are relatively virtuous and generous, pure and collected, then you are likely to be reborn in a good state, for instance in a heaven. Indeed, it became the prime concern of the generous lay person, who gave alms to the Order and may have donated land or other things to the growing body of monks and nuns, to be reborn if possible in a heaven. You could live like a god for ages, though eventually you would exhaust your karma and be reborn in a lower realm, say as a human being. Also, the Buddha did not think that it is necessary to postulate a soul to account for nirvāṇa. That blessed state would occur at death, for one who has understanding and perfect serenity. Nirvana is the extinction of the fires of greed, hatred and delusion. It is not necessary to specify further the nature of nirvana. It is a kind of metaphysical end point: an ultimate Event, we may say (not a Thing or Substance).

In this connection, the Buddha specified certain questions of a transcendental kind as being basically to be set aside, undetermined or unanswerable questions. He used the simile of a fire: where does a fire go when it goes out? The question is after all meaningless. Similarly, there are questions such as whether the Tathāgata (a title of the Buddha) exists after death or not, or whether he both does and does not, or whether he neither does nor does not, which cannot be answered. Since the Tathāgata has dissolved as an identifiable flow of events, there is, so to speak, nothing to talk about after death. Similar questions relate to the eternity and infinity of the universe, and whether the living spirit and body are identical. (The Buddha did not here use the term *ātman*, but rather the word *jīva*.) There has been much discussion of why these questions are unanswerable. Although the Buddha used, as well as the simile of the fire, the simile of the arrow (you do not ask who it was that discharged it before you have medical attention in getting it extracted), which might suggest a merely pragmatic account, as though you should not allow yourself to get distracted from the process of salvation, it seems likely that he had in mind the profounder reasons why these questions are beyond ordinary human categories. In the Mahayana they were extended, so that all theories of ultimate reality have to be set aside – at least according to Nāgārjuna and his school.

A final major idea may go back to the Buddha, and that is the conception of what is often translated as 'dependent origination'. According to this, there is a network of conditions which explains death and decay. The sequence stretches from there through existence *(bhava)*, attachment *(upādānd)*, craving (tṛṣṇa), feelings *(vedanā)*, sense-contact *(sparśa)*, sense-fields *(āyatana)*, psychophysical complex *(nāmarūpa)*, consciousness *(vijñāna)* and ignorance *(avidyā)*. Parts of this network are clear enough. What makes you grasp is your craving, but this in turn is dependent upon feelings, which arise out of contact with the outer world; but such contact itself is channeled through the sense-faculties which are dependent on the functioning psychophysical complex (the body–mind complex). But that in turn cannot survive without consciousness. Ultimately it is averred that the whole network depends on lack of insight, for true insight would spell release or nirvana which would, in some sense, do away with the whole network.

Later Buddhism was to swing between relatively realistic and relatively idealistic interpretations of these ideas. From one point of view dependent origination tells the ultimate story of the individual: the real world carries on once he has been eliminated through nirvana. But on a more cosmic interpretation the whole cosmos is itself determined by the force of ignorance of the truth that there are no permanent identities.

These may be held to be the primary teachings of the Buddha. But he was keen to show that they had a directly practical side. The path culminated in *samādhi* or contemplation. But it also stressed ethics, and the combination of moral attitudes and contemplative methods is well seen in his use of the so-called *brahmavihāras* or divine stations, or more naturally, the divine virtues. Through suffusing the different quarters of the universe and all their living beings with these four attitudes, one may free one's mind. The virtues are benevolence, compassion, sympathetic joy and equanimity. Of these the second is often singled out as the most characteristically Buddhist, namely *karuṇā,* compassion.

Because there is nothing permanent, the idea of a supreme Creator is rejected. But the Buddha does not seem to have denied the many gods and spirits pervading the cosmos. They are not important for liberation, but they have a certain limited power. Generally the cosmology does not seem to have been very different from that of some other śramaṇa groups. The universe exists over huge periods and then relapses into a kind of sleep, to be stimulated once again and to develop into its large and manifest form. This 'pulsating' cosmos came to be the normal picture in later Hindu beliefs – one of a number of motifs it has taken over from the śramaṇa groups.

The Buddha's rejection of things or *substances* went with his theory of causes and effects. One major Indian model of causation was to be that of transformation, as when milk turns into curds. This transformation theory was opposed by the Buddha, who saw the relation between causes and effects as external – one set of conditions simply gives rise to another set and so on. It may be that his resistance to ideas of substances transforming themselves was part of a deeper critique of the sacrificial and sacramental religion of the Brahmin tradition. The expertise of Brahmins was in bringing about mysterious changes which themselves reflected the way the divine Being transforms itself into the world.

We have briefly sketched some of the main ideas of the Buddha and of the early period of that religious and philosophical tradition. It was to develop in diverse directions. As far as philosophy went, perhaps the great conundrums turned out to be as follows. First, could a consistent ontology of events be held which did not implode inwards into an incoherent mist of instantaneous events? Second, does a reality exist 'out there' independently of our perceptions?

Meanwhile, let us turn to look at the beginnings of the great alternative tradition, which was in due course to gel into Hindu orthodoxy.

THE NATURE AND TEACHINGS OF THE UPANISHADS

The Vedic collections were essentially oral transmissions of hymns in verse which were used in the course of rituals. They yield knowledge to us of the varieties of gods. Some of these were later to become very important in the Hindu tradition, notably Rudra or Śiva and others were already vital, such as Agni the firegod, and Indra the great warrior and stormgod. Some of the late hymns of the collection known as the *Rg* contain speculative ideas. For instance R.V.x.121 ascribes the whole creation to a single Lord. And R.V.x.129 ends with a mysteriously agnostic note:

> The source from which the cosmos has come,
> And whether it was made or not made,
> He alone knows who rules from highest
> Heaven, the all-seeing Lord – or does he not know?

There is, however, little in the Vedic hymns to foreshadow the great teachings of the Upanishads, nor clear reference to the doctrine of reincarnation, which later was to be such a pervasive feature of Indian culture. In many ways the religion of the Veda reflected strands of Indo-European religion found elsewhere, for instance in Iran, though deeply pervaded by a sense of ritual complexity, no doubt arising from the dominance of the Brahmin class.

The shift we can see as we move from the ancient hymns, some of which may go back to 1000 BCE and beyond, through the compositions known as Brāhmaṇas, to the Upanishads or Secret Discourses (which like the rest of the corpus were handed down orally, and were not meant for diffusion beyond the upper three sacred classes of Indian society, and which were probably first of all handed on with even greater restrictions as to audience), is considerable. Structures of language remain similar, and more or less the same cast of gods appears, but deep down there has been a double shift. The emphasis has moved from the rituals in which the hymns were embedded to the meaning of ritual itself. The rituals came to be understood as sustaining the cosmos. Second, there is an increased interest in and awareness of yoga practices and the whole process of training the self. There is a voyage inwards into the soul, as well as a voyage outwards into the universe. It coincides with the revelation of a new doctrine – that of reincarnation. Vedic belief had thought of the spirits of the dead wandering off to the moon and sun: now there was a newer teaching about the possibility of death and redeath, over long cycles.

The quest to find the inner meaning of the sacrifice arose in part because of the increasing complexity of sacrificial acts and techniques – involving a whole succession of oblations in which portions (of ghee, meat or whatever) are poured or set in the sacrificial fire, presided over often by a number of specialized priests. But one may surmise also that a system originally designed for the life of the Indo-Aryan warrior no longer made much sense in the mercantile and agricultural communities of Uttar Pradesh and Bihar, and elsewhere in the settled regions of north India. In the Upanishads we observe an interiorization of ritual from two points of view. On the one hand, self-discipline and yoga came to stand for the inner reference of the outer ritual acts. On the other hand, what counted was not just sacred performance but *knowledge* of its meaning. This knowledge is what gave power to skilled practitioners. It was this that gave prominence to the whole idea of *vidyā* and its negation, ignorance or *avidyā*.

Meanwhile the concept of holy power or *brahman* had been expanding. It was not just the power implicit in the priest and in the sacrificial act – that power which animated the sacred class of Brahmins (*brāhmaṇas*, to use the correct term, in short, those endowed with *brahman*). It came to be thought of as that which sustains and vivifies the whole cosmos. Sacrifice as a key notion was applied to the understanding of the universe as a whole. So *brahman* came to be used of the Holy Power which (monistically) was identified with the whole of the world or which (non-monistically) was seen as the root of the world – the creative source from which the material cosmos emerged. Sometimes, the creative source of everything is described in the Upanishads as being personal, as Prajāpati, the father of creatures.

These doctrines came to be fully elaborated in later Hindu philosophy as Vedānta or the 'End of the Veda', varieties of theology or metaphysics which took seriously differing strands in the thought of the Upanishads, which are not of course homogeneous works, but varied in their doctrines and styles. That strand which drew out the monistic impulse provided the background for Advaita Vedānta, and those strands which issued in theism were the basis for varieties of theistic Vedānta, such as the thought of Rāmānuja and of Madhva. These more systematic developments were nearly a millennium and a half or more away.

From the various speculations which came to be collected together in the classical Upanishads, certain main themes emerged. The first is that of *Brahman* as the subtle power within everything that is (as we have sketched it above). The second is the idea of an eternal self or *ātman* within the individual, and also within the cosmos as a whole. Third, there is the motif of liberation, conjoined with the belief in reincarnation (for if we are continuously being reborn and dying again and again, how do we ever come to escape this fate?). The three sometimes come to be fused together. According to the great formulas such as in the *Chāndogya* and *Bṛhadāraṇyaka* Upanishads, the Self within is ultimately one with *Brahman*, the cosmic power. Knowledge of the timeless Self is something which is given in the inner quest: and if this direct existential knowledge is yoked to the secret truth that *Brahman* and *ātman* are identical, then this gnosis itself brings about release from ignorance and from the round of rebirth.

Another theme which is vital is the indescribability or inexpressibility of the higher knowledge. The self is thought of as something which we cannot know in the ordinary way. Up to a point this is a commonplace of the mystical path, finding many echoes round the world. But it rests too, in the Upanishads, on an epistemological point. For I cannot have the normal subject–object knowledge of the I since then there would need to be another I to know that I. If I say 'I know what I am', the first 'I' would have to lie deeper, so to speak, than the second 'I' which it knows. We have here the stage set between the Buddhist view that a changeless self is useless because all causation involves changes, and the thesis that nevertheless we have some need for the idea of a transcendental self, lying as it were behind all experience, which is beyond description and beyond change.

Already many key concepts of Indian theology and philosophy are foreshadowed in the early Upanishads: such notions as the self as inner controller of the individual – an idea which could be seen as meaning the capacity of God to guide the soul from within; the notion of the personal Lord who might become the focus of *bhakti* or loving adoration (basically a later development); and the conception of the cosmos as something illusory (though *māyā* did not yet quite mean 'illusion' it already had some sense of 'magic').

Already too there are some hints of Sāṅkhya ideas, later worked up into one of the main six systems of orthodox philosophy. Such ideas had a curious double existence during the major part of the Hindu tradition. On the one hand, they were integrated elements in a coherent system which we know as Sāṅkhya. This set of claims about the world was originally non-theistic. Second, though, the Sāṅkhya categories were taken over by Vaishnava and Shaiva theologians to explain the mechanisms of the processes of creation. In other words, they were commonly housed within a theistic framework. It is something of this second pattern which is evident in the Upanishadic material.

Before we leave the preliminary sketch of thought in the Upanishads, let us pause to see any discernible patterns at work. The fact that reincarnation comes into what in other ways is a highly Vedic milieu, and as a new and esoteric teaching, may indicate that certain notions drawn perhaps above all from *śramaṇa* circles were beginning to affect the Brahminical climate. Indeed, the central equation of *Brahman* and the self – the formulas *tat tvam asi* ('That art thou') and *aham brahmāsmi* ('I am the Divine'), to quote the best-known versions – can be perceived as a synthesis between certain inward-looking yogic motifs, set against the background of belief in asceticism, reincarnation and the hope of liberation, and new Brahminic speculation about a single Divine Being. Far from our seeing śramanic ideas, and especially those of the Buddha, as a revolt against a pre-existent Brahmanism, we may see the latter as a confluence between *śramaṇa* and Brahmin values. In short, non-orthodox notions are central to the Upanishadic synthesis.

24

This also chimes in with the prominence given in some of the Upanishadic dialogues to *kṣatriyas*, i.e. warriors who are not members of the priestly class. We may also note that the situation in north India in the sixth and fifth centuries and beyond was surely so much more complicated than we can know, that we can only have a small grasp of the development of religious and philosophical thought during this period. Meanwhile, it is useful to begin to move into the classical phase of Indian culture by considering Sāṅkhya as a system, and with it some other systems, notably the Materialists, Jainas and Ājīvikas.

THE SĀṄKHYA SYSTEM

Although the first extant work we have is the Sāṅkhyakārikā of Īśvarakṛṣṇa possibly of the fourth century CE, the structure of thought is undoubtedly much older. Moreover, there are some general analogies between it and Buddhist and Jain thought, which have led some scholars to see the system as belonging to that ancient non-Brahminical and śramaṇa complex of beliefs, although it counts as orthodox or *āstika* in that by the time classical Hinduism came into existence it recognized the canonical scriptures as being revelatory (that is to say, the Vedic hymns and what was attached to them, such as the Brāhmaṇas and the Upanishads). Yet, though orthodox, Sāṅkhya obviously diverges in its whole worldview from the Vedic hymns and likewise from the Upanishads. It is atheistic, and postulates a myriad of eternal souls or persons (*puruṣas*), transmigrating continuously, save when any of them may have gained liberation, through the world of material nature (*prakṛti*). Whereas each of the souls is distinct, nature is one enormous substance.

The name of the school means 'Count' or 'Enumeration' and supposedly derives from its delight in categorizing entities. It lists categories with verve. But its outlook is that of the world renouncer. It sees all life as suffering. The great hope is to acquire a certain kind of knowledge, which will bring about release from the world of nature, and ensure a quiescent, painless liberation.

Over huge ages the world evolves and periodically relapses into the quiet state, a phase in which material nature reassumes its unmanifest character. It is a kind of soup of three *guṇas* or constituents, namely *sattva* (which I shall translate as 'brightness'), *rajas* ('force') and *tamas* ('darkness'). The first is bright and subtle, and the material basis of intellects and other manifest entities. The second is energetic, and helps to constitute people and material forces such as fire and storms which are volatile, while the third is sluggish, weighing and slowing down processes. At the end of a quiet period the equilibrium between the three constituents of the cosmic soup is slightly disturbed, and the *guṇas* begin to distill out. An infinite pointillism of brightness-strands forms, as the *buddhis* or intellects. These are attached to the infinity of souls which through this connection become implicated in the round of rebirth (the quiet period has been a cosmic rest for them). The distillation out of brightness gives an extra force to *rajas,* which in its dynamism helps to form, for each intellect, a 'self-maker' or individuating factor. In addition there accrete the sense-faculties, etc. – not only the five senses but also, as is typical of the Indian way of thinking, the *manas* or mind-organ – in other words a kind of 'common sense' that synthesizes the reports of the other senses. As well as these there form the organs of activity (speech, handling, locomotion, waste-extrusion and generation).

These developments are on the mental side and as it were create the relevant attachments for each soul. The soul itself is pure inactive consciousness. On the more material side of evolution, the primeval soup gives rise to material counterparts of the more psychic side of the universe. (However, as elsewhere in Indian thought, both intellects, for example, and material entities all count ultimately as belonging to material nature or *prakṛti*: the Indian tradition does not draw the same line between the mental and the physical as has been typical in the West.) The beginning of the material side of evolution is the distillation out from the mass-stuff of an inert substratum, divisible in space, which therefore functions as an individuating factor in regard to material objects. Thence emerge minute subatomic entities, rather like quarks, which form into atoms. They possess the principles of sensible properties, such as taste, though they themselves are imperceptible. In short, though Sāṅkhya looks upon *prakṛti* or material nature as being a single substance, it has within it the turbulences which go to make up a plural, atomically constituted world. All this activity results, then, in the manifestation of the world as we experience it. The intellects and other living adjuncts as it were entangle *puruṣas* or individual souls, which are non-material, in the round of reincarnation. The intermingling of the light of consciousness and the activity of matter generates personal individuality.

The theory of Sāṅkhya supplies the scaffolding of knowledge which will bring ultimate release. The person needs to see intuitively and with understanding the essential difference between soul and nature. This knowledge is called *viveka* or discrimination. When at a later point Sāṅkhya got itself paired with, and allied with, the school known as Yoga, it was thought that the purification of consciousness which could bring about the realization of *viveka* itself had to be achieved by the practice of yogic methods.

Whereas the atoms are spatial, souls are not. They are treated by Sāṅkhya as being all-pervasive, though each soul, unless it has attained release, is hitched to a particular individual, with a particular place and cosmic history. At final 'isolation', as the state of liberation is called, the soul floats, as it were, in a non-localized sphere, and is free from suffering. It is not a state of positive bliss, but rather one of absence of pain and unhappiness. Some have thought that this is a state little different from annihilation: but evidently it is not the same for the depersonalized individual souls endure as self-aware monads.

It may be noted that the quiet and manifest periods of the cosmos, lasting over immense periods, and giving rise to an unending sequence of further expansions and collapses of the cosmos, occur automatically. It is the 'mere presence' of the *puruṣas* that gives that slight impulse which disturbs the equilibrium of the cosmic soup. Obviously this is insufficient to explain generation and retraction since the souls are ever present. Originally there is in Sāṅkhya no Lord or Creator. In the Yoga system there is a Lord (but not strictly a Creator) who is the one soul never implicated in material nature, serving as an inspiration, and according to some a help, in the practice of contemplation leading to liberation.

The enumeration of categories or underlying principles (*tattva*), from contentless consciousness and *buddhi* through the various faculties and subtle elements to the gross elements making up bodies, consists in twenty-five realities. These interact in various ways, and enable the Sāṅkhyan philosophers to enumerate further categories. Moreover, through the idea of the three *guṇas* a kind of psychology was built up, according as individuals exhibit differing mixtures of brightness, energy and mass.

The Sāṅkhya system is attractive in sketching a model of the development of the manifest cosmos. It gives a quasi-mechanical account of how things gel out and interact. It begins, however, with a stark dualism between the souls and material nature. In so far as there is a symbiosis between the two, it occurs not just negatively through the mysterious implication of the souls in reincarnation but more positively since the round of rebirth, through bringing suffering to individuals, provides the motive for trying to gain release.

In brief, the Sāṅkhya school has its eyes on liberation, but has strong protoscientific leanings, in trying to give a coherent picture of the evolution of the cosmos and of the nature of the individual. It is atheistic, and it is (in an important sense of the term) dualistic. That is, there is a strong ontological distinction between souls and nature. It is of course monistic as to nature and pluralistic as to souls. Despite its exiguous use of the Vedic inheritance, save in so far as the Upanishads already had incorporated some Sāṅkhyan motifs, it counts itself orthodox or *āstika*.

THE SCHOOLS OF INDIAN PHILOSOPHY

The affinities of Sāṅkhya may have been with the unorthodox śramaṇic schools, but because of its acceptance of *śruti* or 'what is heard', that is to say Vedic revelation, it is orthodox. Traditionally, Hindu thinkers came to categorize the main schools as six in number. They are often referred to as the Six Darśanas or Six Viewpoints. As a classification, this old way is not satisfactory, but let me first describe it briefly.

The Six come in three pairs. The first pair is Sāṅkhya-Yoga, since these two were increasingly coupled together. Like other schools their positions were initially handed down orally, and then reduced to aphoristic sentences, known as *sūtras*. These in turn attracted commentarial and other systematic literature. Because of the gnomic quality of *sūtras,* there was room for diversity of interpretation. The second pair lies at the heartland of Brahmanic study: it comprises Uttara-Mīmāṃsā or Vedānta proper, which is a set of systems of varying monistic and theistic metaphysics based on the *Brahma Sūtras,* perhaps of the fourth century CE, and on the Upanishads and *Gītā* (the last was not strictly a work of *śruti,* but had such prestige that later writers felt impelled to compose commentaries on it). There was another branch of Mīmāṃsā which is known as Pūrva- Mīmāṃsā, or Mīmāṃsā for short, which deals with the exegesis of sacred texts, notably the Vedic texts prescribing rituals. Oddly, this has an archaic worldview which owes very little to its twin viewpoint. It reduced all Vedic utterances to injunctions, denied gods except in so far as their names were mentioned in the course of the rituals and saw temporary heaven (*svarga*) as the goal.

The third pair is Nyāya, which is devoted to the study of reasoning and epistemology, and which may briefly be translated as Logic, and Vaiśeṣika, which sets forth a metaphysic based upon a form of atomism. Both these viewpoints have a less immediate relation to religious questions than the others.

The Six Darśanas have their unorthodox or *nāstika* rivals, of which the most important are the Buddhist schools, followed by Jain philosophy and Materialism.

But the general schematism is unsatisfactory, for various reasons. First, both Vedānta and Buddhism proliferate into many important and distinct schools. Thus just to start with, there are the three major varieties of Vedānta: Advaita (non-dualism), Viśiṣṭādvaita (organic unity of a complex reality) and Dvaita dualism, associated with Śaṅkara, Rāmānuja and Madhva, respectively. There are other important schools too. But second, even regarding Hindu theological treatises, the Vedāntin ones do not exhaust the range. There are, for instance, many vital works of dualistic and non-dualistic Kashmiri Śaivism as well as the Tamil devotional Śaiva Siddhānta (Śaiva doctrine). Third, as we have seen, there are vitally diverse Buddhist schools – ranging from the Theravāda to the important manifestations of Mahāyāna thought, the Mādhyamika and the Vijñānavāda. There are also new varieties of logic evolved both by Buddhists and Hindus in the early medieval period. Fourth, as indicated above, some of the so-called viewpoints are not primarily schools of philosophy, so much as methods: so Pūrva-Mīmāṃsā has to do with ritual and textual exegesis, and Yoga is primarily oriented towards techniques of self-control and meditation.

JAIN PHILOSOPHY

Both Buddhism and Sāṅkhya do without either a God or an Absolute. The same is true of Jainism, a rival to Buddhism in the early days, and showing signs of greater archaicness. Like Sāṅkhya it conceived of many souls involved in the round of rebirth, but these were conceived more materially, as entities which fill up the bodies to which they belong. The chief means of liberation is by the practice of severe austerity, which in the best circumstances would end with a saint's starving himself to death. The asceticism was hitched closely to the ideal of non-injury or *ahiṃsā*. Not taking animal life was central to Jain ethics, and killing was the gravest sin. Lay people should not be engaged in pursuits, such as farming, which mean that they have to take life. Ideally, disciples become monks or nuns.

This path to salvation was taught in the Buddha's time by Mahavira, also called Vardhamāna, who left home like the Buddha to become a wandering ascetic, and who attained liberation and omniscience. However, the Jain claim has consistently been that Mahāvīra, as he was entitled (the Great Hero), was restoring previous teachings, and in effect refounding an existent spiritual tradition. Some details of the cosmology appear very archaic. Thus the cosmos is likened to a giant human being. We exist at the level of the waist. Below are various purgatories, and above an ascending scale of gods. At the summit of the person's head is a region where motion is impossible. When a liberated person rises there he remains ever motionless, beyond communication with humans or other inhabitants of the cosmos, victorious and utterly serene. Symbolic of this condition of the supremely indifferent saint are the colossal Jain statues, such as the most famous at Sravana Belgola in south India, of a saint who stands upright, completely naked, and so without possessions – so oblivious of his environment that creepers have started to twist up his legs.

Together with such archaic symbols, the Jains had some philosophical attitudes which were both interesting and sophisticated. Thus they held to a theory of perspectives, according to which judgments about objects were categorized as varying under seven differing perspectives. One could see a thing under the generic perspective which applied: see something as a neem tree for instance; or without distinguishing its specific or generic properties; or as having specific properties (its branches being of a peculiar shape, say); or as being given now, without regard to its past or future (without for example considering that or how it got planted); or as being referred to by such words as 'neem tree'; or as being described by other terms; or as displaying characteristics relating to both 'neem tree' and alternative words. Such perspectivism already displays a sophistication about the relation between the world and language.

Another general Jain doctrine may be called relativism, or perhaps 'soft relativism'. For the formulas expressing the doctrine are of the following kind: (1) 'Could be it is'; (2) 'Could be it is not'; (3) 'Could be it is and is not'; (4) 'Could be it is inexpressible'; (5) 'Could be it is and is inexpressible'; (6) 'Could be it is not and is inexpressible'; and (7) 'Could be it is and is not and is inexpressible'. I may assert that a temple flower exists, but in making a distinction I am saying that a tiger does not exist at that spot. But there is no way of expressing how it both is a temple flower and not a tiger. And so on. Not only does this Jain scheme place judgments under seven forms but it prefaces each with a 'Maybe': *syād* or 'Could be', from which the doctrine is called *syādvāda* or 'Could-be-ism'. This sense of the perhaps reflects Jainism's thought that all viewpoints are partial. Perhaps it may be a form of intellectual non-violence. This is illustrated by the simile of blind men grasping different parts of an elephant and giving different reports – all true up to a point but all false too. This simile is often used to illustrate the relations between differing religious traditions. Its application, of course, depends on our having a privileged view of the elephant as a whole, which is not vouchsafed to the blind participants. But I think the Jains were perceptive in tacking on the 'Maybe': no worldview can conclusively establish itself over against others, even if one may have some reasons for believing one more than others. The softness of the *syād* is in my view entirely right and helps too to explain why some adherents of religions and ideologies are so strongly and abrasively assertive, for they recognize the uncomfortable truth of uncertainty behind every stance we take towards the cosmos.

It is perhaps therefore something of a paradox that a religion with a soft theory at its philosophical core should have such a hard and rigid view of the need to use the greatest austerity to annihilate bad karma, and so to rid souls of their weights and let them float free to the top of the world and a painless still peace. It shows that commitment is not proportionate to proof: it cannot be, nor maybe should it be.

MATERIALISM AND SKEPTICISM

At the time of the Buddha there were already followers of Cārvāka, who were materialists, denying the soul and the afterlife. In later accounts there is some confusion between this school and that of skeptics. The materialists rejected inference as a basis of knowledge on the grounds that our limited experiences cannot lead us to the true general propositions that are integral to valid deductive procedures, and relied solely on perception. These two, together with *śabda* or verbal testimony, usually meaning scriptural testimony as to matters transcendental, were the main sources of knowledge (*pramāṇa*) debated in Indian epistemology. But rejecting inference (naturally the materialists rejected *śabda*) would eventually lead to skepticism and agnosticism about anything except what was given immediately to perception. Probably we have two strands of the rejection of religious positions: one which boiled the whole of reality down to what was composed of matter and in particular earth, air, fire and water; and the other which in restricting itself to empirical evidence eschewed speculation about the possibility of transcendental realia. While the Materialist school lived a long time, it has left very little in the way of texts, so that we have a very exiguous view of it as a systematic philosophy. Its main problem was in accounting for consciousness. The main argument deployed here was to cite the analogy with fermented liquor. If you take two or three material substances and mix them in a certain way and proportion, fermentation will occur. The property of being alcoholic, which belonged to none of the individual ingredients, will now pertain to the cooked mixture. Similarly, it was argued, if you put together the right material ingredients you will get consciousness arising as a new property.

If there is nothing beyond this world, then of course the whole apparatus of Brahmin religion falls down, as well as the spiritual pursuits of the unorthodox. The Materialists rejected sacrifices, prayers, hope of heaven, reincarnation, God and gods. We are left with a mild ethical hedonism – 'enjoy yourself while you can'. Theirs was a powerful voice of criticism at this early period. But in some ways the spirit of protoscience was better represented by Śaṅkara and by the Vaiśeṣika school, both of which were bolder, because they were uninhibited in making inferences and so going beyond the perceptual.

THE TRANSITION TO THE CLASSICAL PERIOD

We have briefly reviewed some of the main ideas, both orthodox and unorthodox, which had emerged by the fifth century BCE and a little after. In the succeeding centuries, the transition occurred to the classical forms of the great Indian religions. The Brahmins had absorbed some aspects of śramanic philosophy, and in the meantime were spreading further south and beyond the confines of the Gangetic region. The growth of a new urban civilization began to see the building of Buddhist and Jain monasteries, and then of Hindu temples, housing the gods. This came to be the chief classical manifestation of Hindu religion. The worship of the many gods came to focus greatly upon certain supreme forms. Ultimately these were three in number – Śiva, Viṣṇu and the Goddess. Such devotionalism or *bhakti* religion came to be dominant in Hindu piety. It had some expression in the great Epics which were being evolved in the last two centuries before the Common Era, and in the famous religious poem the *Bhagavadgītā,* incorporated into the *Mahābhārata.* The cult of the gods came under the control chiefly of the Brahmins. The dominance of this class reinforced the importance of ritual purity in the framework of classical Hinduism, and so helped to solidify the caste system.

This latter had as its scaffolding the structure of the four 'colors' or classes (*varṇa*), namely the three twiceborn classes of the Brahmins, *kṣatriyas* (rulers and warriors) and *vaiśyas* (merchants and farmers), together with the lowborn *śūdras,* whose function is that of serving members of the three higher estates. Below these was an even lower category, the various untouchables – sweepers, leatherworkers, butchers and others belonging to unclean occupations. Inside this general structure came to arise the fragmentation of even more narrowly conceived *jātis,* castes proper. Bound by ties of endogamy and commensality, these are the actual units of social organization. They did not typically intermarry or eat together. All this maze of social relationships was sticky: it caught up other groups – early Christians, Jains, Buddhists – in its embrace. How could you be excluded from intermarriage without becoming an endogamous group of your own?

There were other motifs in the growing pattern of Hinduism – the practice of pilgrimage to such holy places as Banaras, teaching by wandering holy priests or gurus, the practice of austerity, the use of tantric and taboo means of realizing and expressing higher spiritual truth, great local variations in gods and rites, the formation of an all-India Sanskrit overlay, the theory that the various gods are all related to the great God, the virtually universal acceptance of the belief in reincarnation, and the cult of avatars or incarnations of Viṣṇu.

Side by side with this mixture were the non-orthodox religions and particularly Buddhism. During the reign of the great emperor Aśoka in the mid-third century BCE these groups had had powerful patronage. As Buddhism developed, its organization, through the Saṅgha, proliferated; its temples grew; pilgrimages were encouraged; eventually the elaborated canon was written down; Buddha statues became common; alternative Buddha figures came to be worshiped; the ideal of the Buddha-to-be or Bodhisattva, who puts off his own salvation to help others, flourished; the idea of merit became central to piety; forms of Buddhist *bhakti* grew. And during this period different recensions of the scriptures were composed. During Aśoka's reign Buddhism took root in Sri Lanka, and in the first century CE the canon was put into writing.

The elaboration of scriptures meant divergence of texts, and to some degree it meant differences of doctrine. From the mid-fourth century BCE we note the emergence of an Eastern school, centered on the imperial capital of Pataliputra, called the Mahāsaṅghikas (Great Saṅgha school), who took a less rigorous view of the attainment of arhant-ship (sainthood or the attaining of nirvāṇa). A piquant question was whether the *arhant* could be seduced by a female spirit (meaning, whether he could have a wet dream). The more relaxed view led to a higher standard, by contrast, for the Buddha himself. This was a factor in the evolution of the doctrine of a world-transcending Buddha, the *Lokottaravāda*. This coincided with greater emphasis on Buddha statues and the growth of devotion.

The *arhant* question was a more particular form of the issue as to whether a person who had attained *nibbāna* could fall away. Among other important questions debated in these early centuries were: (1) Is there a person (*pudgala* in Sanskrit; Pali, *puggala*) that transmigrates? Or is the term a merely conventional one of ordinary speech with no ontological significance? (2) Is progress in understanding the truth gradual or sudden? (3) Is the Buddha transcendental? (4) Are all events momentary? The first of these perhaps constituted the most angst-laden question. It called into question the denial of the doctrine of *anattā* or non-self. The second continues as a debate right through to Zen Buddhism, at the other end of the Buddhist world (the Zen school is divided into two main sections, one favoring sudden enlightenment and the other gradualism). The third question prepared the way for the whole religious expansion of Mahāyāna Buddhism, with celestial Buddhas and Bodhisattvas acting as foci of worship and dispensers of grace. The fourth question raised the profoundest issues of Buddhist philosophy. If events dissolve into a powder of momentariness, can causation still work? If it does not, then does not the whole edifice of our theories about the world collapse? And is this the true meaning of Buddhist philosophy? Powder into nihilism, so to say.

Meanwhile during the period before Aśoka there emerged the Sarvāstivāda school, who were one of eighteen recorded divisions to appear in the Saṅgha during this classical period. This school received the powerful patronage of the Kushana emperor Kaniśka (mid-second century CE). But like the other major schools it largely vanished, and the major representative of Lesser Vehicle Buddhism came to be the Pāli Buddhism of Sri Lanka and south-east Asia. Nevertheless it was an important influence and itself may be symptomatic of a certain syncretic mode in which early Buddhism lived.

For the name of the school means 'Everything-exists-ism'. Its proponents held that the basic ingredients or atomic factors (*dharma*) which make up complexes really exist in past, present and future. So a dharma manifests itself momentarily but nevertheless pre-existed in unmanifest form. Now though these Realists, as I shall call them, held to a generally orthodox position, denying a permanent soul for instance, nevertheless their position on causation came close to that of Sāṅkhya. They posited atoms as the substratum of matter, such atoms flashing into manifestation to form complex states of affairs. Thus seven microatoms join to form a perceptible atom. This is not dissimilar to Sāṅkhya doctrine. So we may see Realism as a Buddhist version of Sāṅkhya-type thinking. But it is something of a paradox that the school should have made permanence so pervasive.

Indicative of some conceptual troubles liable to remain with Buddhism is the fact that the school nominated three uncompound entities, namely the two forms of nirvāṇa (up to, and beyond, death) together with space. How to categorize space was a constant difficulty, since it is not a compound or changing thing or event.

The Theravādins, while remaining realist about the external world, rejected the notion that the past and future exist. It seemed cleaner and more economical, as well as more in the spirit of the Buddha's own teaching, to suppose that past events no longer exist. It is the more original teaching and preserves the freshness of the Buddha's version. The Sarvāstivāda seems to make too many compromises with more substantialist ways of looking at the world.

Probably the most striking heretical movement of this period was the so-called *pudgalavāda* (Sanskrit) or *puggalavāda* (Pali). It postulated a 'person' or *pudgala* as the bearer of the *skandhas,* i.e. of the various groups or types of events that go to make up the individual. To what do states of consciousness, dispositions, perceptions and so on belong? Evidently many Buddhists felt uneasy about the non-self doctrine, especially in relation to the question of a person's making the transition from one life to the next. Thus it was argued that moral responsibility implies the existence of a 'bearer' of responsibility; likewise, compassion would be pointless if there were no one 'there' to be compassionate for. Moreover, knowledge implies an active subject. Now though the Personalists (as I shall call them) claimed that the person was impermanent, merely manifesting itself in various actions, nevertheless there was a sense that the underlying substratum was indeed permanent. It thus was just a sophisticated version of the self. Their opponents accused them of rejecting the *anattā* doctrine. It is interesting, incidentally, that the term used, *pudgala,* explicitly avoided the use of *ātman*: this is a tribute to the strength of the tradition that the Buddha rejected the idea of a permanent self. Eventually Personalism died out: and in any case the only branch of the so-called 'Lesser Vehicle' to survive into medieval and modern times was the Theravāda, found in Sri Lanka, Burma, Thailand and Cambodia.

The other developments in Buddhism of the period helped to sow the seeds of the Mahāyāna or Great Vehicle. Meanwhile, both the Buddhist and Hindu traditions were making the transition towards their classical manifestations. In the case of the Theravāda the formation of the canon in Sri Lanka in the first century BCE paved the way for a monastic Buddhism with great emphasis on learning and the patronage of the monarchy. In the great city of Anuradhapura there came to be established flourishing monasteries, great temples and a center of pilgrimage. The shape of the Theravāda remained loyal to a scholasticism in which the Abhidhamma portion of the canon involved an elaborate analysis of the various factors comprising both the cosmos and the psychology of the individual. The distinction between the transcendent state of nirvana and the round of worldly existence, namely *saṃsāra*, remained clearly defined. This was one of the Theravādin distinctions that came to be challenged by the Great Vehicle.

THE RISE OF THE MAHĀYĀNA

We have noted that Buddhism as a religion had grown in richness and devotion. But as well as the development of piety there were philosophical changes which were of profound importance. These emerged in the first century CE; a class of writing known as the Perfection of Wisdom or Prajñāpāramitā represented a new genre of Mahayana *sūtra*. There is for instance the Perfection of Wisdom of Eight Thousand Verses, which purports to recount instructions of the Buddha to the disciple Subhūti. Various other varieties of scripture emerged, including such famous texts as the *Vajracchedika* and the *Lotus Sutra,* together with the biographical text about the life of the Buddha, the *Lalitavistara,* and the text of the Pure Land school, the *Sukhāvatīvyūha.*

Part of the Mahāyāna development was philosophical, and involved some exciting ways of interpreting the doctrine. Part of it was ethical, and part was religious. The ethical side of it had to do with the ideal of the Buddha-to-be or Bodhisattva. The Lesser

Vehicle was criticized for not resolving the tension between liberation and compassion. It could well seem that the monk or nun who spent his or her life striving for perfection and the attainment of nirvana was in the highest sense selfish. Self-abnegation and self-control were ultimately in the service of one's own disappearance from the suffering world. How could such a selfish aim square with the Buddha's insistence on the great virtues, and above all that of compassion for other living beings? The ideal of the Bodhisattva, already present in the *Jātaka* or birth-stories, recounting the Buddha-to-be's heroic deeds in previous lives, was extended. The compassionate Bodhisattva would help others towards liberation, and would indeed not be happy until all living beings were liberated. This ideal was extended to all beings: everyone could be a Bodhisattva, and so everyone was in principle a Buddha.

This ethical notion had religious significance. The Bodhisattva had already gained enough merit to attain liberation, but sacrificed himself for others. He thus acquired a vast amount of surplus merit. This could be transferred to the otherwise unworthy faithful, and functioned in the Mahāyāna as a rough equivalent to the idea of grace in the Christian tradition. Celestial Buddhas and Bodhisattvas, such as Amitābha, the creator of the paradise of the Pure Land, and Avalokiteśvara, the Bodhisattva who looks down on living beings with compassion, were worshiped – the focus of *bhakti*.

Such florid growths of piety and ethics were attractive. But the most exciting new trends were philosophical. Particularly important were the notions contained in Perfection of Wisdom literature and in the writings of Nāgārjuna. Both stressed the emptiness of phenomena. This *śūnyavāda* or 'Doctrine of Emptiness', takes up a theme which is there, but only mildly, in the Theravāda literature. Everything is empty, in the sense that it has no self-existence or own-nature, *svabhāva*. In short, there are no essences. This is a critique of the Sarvāstivāda tenet that the ultimately real types of atoms underlying all mental and material phenomena are distinguished from macroscopic composites in virtue of their possession of immutable intrinsic natures. As such they would be uncaused or self-created, otherwise they would be 'borrowing' their natures from external causal factors. Nāgārjuna not implausibly thinks that auto-generation is impossible. Moreover if essences are immutable, the universe, qua manifestation of atoms with essential natures, would be static and intellectual and moral progress towards nirvāṇa would be out of the question.

Nāgārjuna, probably originally a Brahmin of south India, who did most of his work at the famous Buddhist university of Nālandā in North India, lived at about the end of the first century CE. He was the principal figure in the Middle school called Madhyamaka. His most famous work is the *Mūlamadhyamakakārikā* or *Verses on the Middle Way*. His originality consists in a number of things – his extension of the idea of 'undetermined questions' to cover all philosophical issues, his claim not to have a position at all, his distinction between higher and empirical truth, and his dialectical method of revealing contradictions in all positions. He pointed out the flaws in many of the philosophical theories current at his time, deploying the technique of *reductio ad absurdum* (*prasanga*). Of course, some of these ideas were foreshadowed in the canon and in earlier Buddhist teaching – he does after all claim to be the true interpreter of the Buddha's message. But the flavor of his work is original and exciting. It happens that in recent decades a great deal of interest has been shown in the West, among those in touch with the Buddhist tradition, in Nāgārjuna's 'position' (or non-position!).

He considered that the fourfold negation which earlier texts had applied to a range of undetermined questions, such as whether the Tathāgata or Buddha exists after death, should be applied to all fundamental positions, for instance regarding the nature of causation and change. He criticized the idea of time as self-contradictory. So that which is past cannot relate to what is present or future without itself overlapping with the present or future, i.e. by itself being present or future (which destroys its pastness). Regarding causation, he contended that nothing has arisen from itself, from others, from both itself and others, or from no cause. The first point rejects the Sāṅkhya view, which will be adopted by Vedānta, that effects pre-exist in their material causes. The second rejects the Nyāya-Vaiśeṣika view that a totally new effect is produced by the rearrangement of causes. The third rejects the Buddhist realist view. The fourth repudiates a materialist view that things just occur naturally without any causal explanation. The arguments are that self-generation is pointless. If something already exists it does not need to re-invent itself. If something were to arise from others, anything could arise from anything and causality would be unregulated. If something were to arise from itself and others, the previous two problems would still obtain. If something were to arise from no cause, it would follow that everything would arise from everything all the time. So Nāgārjuna tries to show that no coherent account of causation can be formulated.

If all theories of time and causation are self-contradictory, all theories about the world are defective. Nothing has its 'own existence' or 'own nature', and can thus be described as empty. In saying that causes do not exist, Nāgārjuna also wants to claim that it is equally absurd to say that it is not the case that they do not exist, nor that they both do and do not, nor that they neither do nor do not.

All this makes sense of the Buddha's claim not to have a viewpoint (*diṭṭhi* in Pali; Sanskrit: *dṛṣṭi*). It is true that one of the links of the Eightfold Path is right view, but at a profounder level the Buddha, it is held by Nāgārjuna, did not adhere to any position. His view appears to have been that all philosophical theories or any 'grand narrative' pretending to offer an account and explanation of reality as a whole are doomed to failure since we cannot detach ourselves from the limitations of our particular and parochial categories of thought and language and achieve the Olympian standpoint requisite for formulating the Grand Unified Theory.

If there are no essences, the Sarvāstivāda distinction between ultimate and conventional reality, between nirvāṇa and saṃsāra, collapses. If the Buddha taught that there is a way to nirvana this was part of his skill in adapting his message to the condition of hearers (this is why he propounded the Lesser Vehicle first, according to Mahāyānists). The only genuine difference between the person who is liberated is epistemological – such a person understands the Middle School account (or non-account) and grasps the true meaning of emptiness.

Does this mean that Nāgārjuna did not hold to the doctrine of dependent origination? He did and he did not. He evolved an explicit idea of two levels of truth: the higher level is unstatable but is pointed to by the philosophical arguments which he used dialectically to undermine all positions. The lower or empirical truth is what we use for ordinary traffic in the world, and at this level the doctrine of dependent origination holds. Indeed, dependent origination articulates emptiness, the essencelessness and interdependence of phenomena. This two-level notion was something which was taken up several centuries later by Śaṅkara and the Advaita school of Hindu theology.

The emptiness of phenomena fitted in with the traditional Buddhist stress upon the importance of the contemplative way. If philosophy, by showing that our concepts do not describe objective reality but are conceptual constructs convenient for human purposes, empties the head of concepts of causation and the like, contemplation empties the consciousness of discursive thought and images. Moreover, the pure consciousness at which the Buddhist aims has no distinction *(ex hypothesi)* between subject and object (it is like the Sāṅkhya notion of consciousness in this respect). This means that there is no gap between the contemplator and the 'ultimate truth' of emptiness, and no gap between him or her and Buddhahood itself. All saints thus are Buddhas, and all living beings potentially Buddhas. So the whole scheme of Mahāyāna religion dovetails together neatly – the Bodhisattva ideal, the ethics of compassion, the idea of emptiness, the nature of contemplation, the worship of Bodhisattvas and Buddhas, the idea of grace for the faithful.

THE SCHOOL OF REPRESENTATION-ONLY

A somewhat different slant to Mahāyāna philosophy is found in the school of Vijñānavāda or Representation-only. This derived from the work of Maitreya in the late third and early fourth century CE. Its chief exponents were the brothers (if they were so – there are scholarly debates about who Vasubandhu was and whether there were more than one Vasubandhu) of the fourth century. Because the school emphasized the practice of yoga it is sometimes called Yogācāra (school of yoga practitioners). It is often interpreted as a kind of idealism although in one main respect, as we shall see, this may be rather misleading.

The system of thought derives in part from the observation that ordinary consciousness is subject–object in character. The 'grasper' grasps that which is grasped; and as such it is projective in character. In other words, all perception and other forms of grasping the outside world involve subjectivity – so for instance if I look at a daffodil I am projecting certain concepts such as 'daffodil' and 'flower' which are human creations, and certain colors and other properties, which also are creations of the mind.

The early Yogācāra theorists saw all phenomena as displaying three characters – as being fictive creations of consciousness, or projections; as being the product of dependent origination; and as being perfected or having the indescribable nature of suchness *(tathatā)*. Sometimes the dependent origination is described in a special way, namely that phenomena arise out of seeds contained in the subconscious 'store-consciousness' or *ālayavijñāna*. This doctrine is elaborated by Vasubandhu in his famous treatise *Triṃśika* or Thirty Verses, widely used later as a textbook of the school. Unenlightened experience is structured by the subject–object dichotomy. Thinkers of this school try to show the incoherence of the notion of a mind-independent objective sphere. Once it is accepted that objectivity is impossible, the other pole of the dichotomy, subjectivity or individual selfhood and its attachments is dissolved.

In so far as the school held that phenomena result from dependent origination, one may see it as holding to an admittedly minimal doctrine of a noumenal process that underlies manifestations of consciousness. Process or processes in themselves are 'out there', except that of course all the concepts including 'out there' are projected by consciousness. But the doctrine of *ālayavijñāna* gives the school a more overtly idealistic flavor. There is some 'universal mind' from which the phenomena of the world flow. And so in reality the world of phenomena is a mind-created mirage.

HINDU DEVELOPMENTS: THE GĪTĀ AND THE BRAHMA SŪTRA

While Buddhist trends were, as we have seen, highly analytical, the Hindu viewpoints unfolded in a heavier, more mythic fashion. Perhaps in the third century BCE (but dating here is highly conjectural) the poem known as the 'Song of the Lord' or *Bhagavadgītā*, or *Gītā* for short, was incorporated into the Great Epic, the *Mahābhārata*. It was to acquire a phenomenal fame, and although it was not strictly part of the mainstream revelation or *śruti*, its weight turned out to be greater than many revealed books. It became one of the three pillars on which the Vedānta stood, and attracted important commentaries from most of the great figures of the Hindu tradition.

Its tale, of the hero Arjuna hesitating before a great battle in the major civil war of legendary India, for fear of the harm done by killing his relatives, is the prelude to teachings and a numinous manifestation of the God Kṛṣṇa as an avatar of Viṣṇu. It is striking, dramatic, awe-inspiring: and this is no doubt why it has retained such a strong grip on the Indian imagination. It has powerful ambiguities – suggesting to some that our duties as soldiers are paramount, to others that we should practice non-violence. The mysterious many-sidedness of the poem could look like incoherence: but it is a strength in rounding its appeal. Its main message is religious, rather than philosophical, and it preaches the importance of throwing oneself on divine grace and love. In this it foreshadows the theology of Rāmānuja. There are also philosophical aspects to the poem, within the framework of a work of strong devotional drive.

First, the *Gītā* depicts how each person has within herself or himself a spiritual nature, which is eternal. Though in some ways the poem reveals Buddhist influence, here is a distinctly non-Buddhist motif to start with. The assurance of immortality should, second, give the hero and anyone else assurance about following his *dharma* – the ethical and ritual norm which defines his place in society. Thus the job of a warrior, like Arjuna, is to fight. But third, one truly does one's *dharma* when acting unselfishly, not doing it with an eye to the fruits one gains oneself. This is the secret of recognizing the law of karma which in its infinitely long webs of action casts its net over the whole of human life, without being bound or entangled by it. As with the Buddhists, the poem makes the operation of karma intentional. If you do not wish for the fruits but act out of a pure sense of duty, then they will not cling to you.

The way the picture of the individual is depicted in the *Gītā* owes much to the vocabulary of Sāṅkhya. Here we seem to meet another stream of Sāṅkhya but coalescing in its own way (different, that is, to the examples of 'pure Sāṅkhya' and Sāṅkhya-influenced *pudgalavādin* Buddhism or Personalism). Nature is seen as *prakṛti*, and in it like an infinity of plums in an enormous pudding are embedded the souls – these being the eternal or spiritual part of humanity and of living beings. Individuals represent mixtures of the *guṇas* and the *Gītā* links the *guṇa* to the way karma operates. But beyond the more conventional language there is another idea which was to be immensely fruitful in later Indian thinking about the Divine. It is the idea that God too is the self within. God controls persons from the interior.

It is of course a most notable feature of the poem that the initial expositions of nature and of the individual are only the prelude to the numinous unfolding of the doctrine that the whole universe is the scene and focus of God's creative activity. The theophany of God in the poem is one of the great passages of the world's religious literature, and can make the reader's (as well as Arjuna's) hair stand on end. It was a decisive passage for Rudolf Otto's famous exposition of the numinous in his *The Idea of the Holy*. The fact that God creates and guides the cosmos itself gives another perspective on all that has been said hitherto about doing one's dharmic duty. If one does it not merely indifferently but for the sake of the Divine, that is a higher message too. In all of this, the *Gītā* attempts to combine differing paths. There is the path of knowledge or *jñāna,* in which the individual practices a kind of yoga of contemplation and attempts to discriminate between the eternal and the non-eternal. There is then the path of duty or *dharma*. Here the individual sees herself or himself within the web of social relationships. Then there is the path of devotion or *bhakti,* in which both knowledge and duty are subsumed under the head of devotion to God (and of course ultimately the Lord's devotion to his creatures).

These then are some of the highlights of the *Gītā*. It is probably reasonable to say that it was Rāmānuja among the classical Hindu commentators whose view of God actually came closest to the viewpoint expressed in the poem. But there are such diversities of interpretation in the Indian tradition that my judgment here is not going to settle the issue.

The fact is there are two very different strands going back to the Upanishads and displaying themselves most prominently in the Hindu tradition. One could say three strands if you wanted to include the slant which typifies early Buddhism and some of the śramanic schools. The first strand has its most vivid presentation in the *Gītā*. It is that which highlights a personalistic Creator and Divine Being. This has been powerful right through the Hindu tradition, and there are times when it is important in Buddhism, as with the Pure Land school, where the focus of a personal celestial, somewhat creative, Buddha is at the fore. The second strand is that of a more impersonal Absolute – the Divine Being thought of as going beyond the more personal characteristics of the Creator and object of worship: the impersonal *Brahman,* in other words (and it has a brother in the emptier absolutes of the Mahāyāna). The third strand is that pluralistic and non-absolutistic picture of the world, with no personal or impersonal single Being as the backdrop to human striving.

The *Gītā* has the more personal flavor: the *Brahma Sūtras* have the more impersonalistic taste. Since the composition is in typical Hindu *sutra* style, of such mind-bending brevity that it needs a commentary to make sense of it, it is open to debate as to what precise doctrine it does espouse. Maybe it belongs to a trend known as the *bhedābheda* or the philosophy of identity in difference. For Śaṅkara and the *advaita* a non-dualistic teaching can be safely quarried from it. For Rāmānuja you can get a personalist theism out of it. It is the master work, composed by the sage Bādarāyaṇa and finished perhaps in the early centuries of the Common Era. What is clear is that the aphorisms of the *sutra* do attempt to express the deeper position of the Upanishads, that is the major early texts of the Vedānta. In short, the *Brahma Sūtra* is an attempt to put into systematic, though admittedly cryptic, form the main teachings of Hindu sacred theology, as it was understood typically in Brahmin circles.

Any view of the Upanishads has to make sense of the great sayings, the mysterious identity-statements which somehow affirm the unity of the soul within and of God who lies 'outside', within and beyond the visible cosmos. Moreover, there is a like question of the relation between the manifest world and the *Brahman* who lies within it or behind it. Since the Upanishads see *Brahman* as source of all, the clear conclusion is that the cosmos is the result of *Brahman's* manifesting itself. *Brahman* transforms its divine substance into a new form, both unmanifest and manifest. And within the living individual the soul appears as somehow divine: possibly as the inner controller. Whether the Upanishads wish to affirm that the soul or self and the Divine are literally identical is of course one of the great points of discussion within the wider tradition.

Bādarāyaṇa's work not only includes positive delineations of how the absolute appears, but counterarguments against other schools, notably against the Sāṅkhya, the Nyāya and the Buddhists. It is notable that the work is already heir to a vigorous period of mutual debate between schools.

It may be useful to pause a moment here to consider the differences between the Mahāyāna doctrines and the 'high' Hindu doctrines represented in differing ways by the *Gītā* and the *Brahma Sūtra*. It is clear that in parallel both Hindu-style and Buddhist religion involved a sense of devotion, and came to worship not altogether different gods (indeed, at a later stage the Buddha was himself incorporated into the Vaiṣṇava pantheon as a tricky avatar). Superficially it seems that the great Mahāyāna 'absolutes' such as *Śūnyatā* or *Tathatā* (Emptiness or Suchness) had a force similar to divine *Brahman*. Out of the womb of the absolute celestial being Buddhas emerged just as the personal God appeared from out of an undifferentiated sacred background. Yet the subtle divergences remain. The Hindu concept of the Absolute remains both heavily sacred and substantial: it is as if *Brahman* retains a kind of sticky and raw darkness which hints so much of the numinous, whereas there remains something playful and illusory about the great foci of Buddhist worship – as though in the end they are all going to be unmasked as the Buddha's skill in means. Yet Buddhism was in the later Mahāyāna on the verge of that whole movement which has come to be known as Tantra, and which has an aura of sacramental magic. Tantric Buddhism became effectively close to Tantric Hinduism in mood and method. Still, in the Great Vehicle there remains that divergence of spirit. At the root of the world lies not power but emptiness (even if emptiness can display its own power); at the basis of analysis lies not substance but event; at the heart of authority lies not revelation but the guiding and replaceable words of the Buddha.

And so, to return to the *Brahma Sūtras,* they are part of that major debate running through Vedānta, as to how that closeness between the visible world and the one great divine Substance is to be conceived. Are they identical, or different, or both? Are they fused in unity without possessing strict identity?

ŚAṄKARA AND ADVAITA VEDĀNTA

There is no doubt that the most brilliant of the early medieval commentators on the major texts – Upanishads, *Gītā* and *Brahma Sūtra* – was Śaṅkarācārya *or* Śaṅkara the Teacher (*ācārya*). A renouncer, he was heir to the unitive tradition of the Upanishads. He is traditionally credited not only with great organizational and intellectual achievements (the foundation of a powerful monastic order, composing philosophical and theological major texts, Upanishads, *Gītā* and *Brahma Sūtra* pilgrimages and writing devotional hymns) but also he was at the forefront of a great Hindu revival, beginning in the Kerala area in the south-west where he was born. He achieved all this, it is said, during a very brief life. Born in 788 CE, he is supposed to have died in 820. It is more likely that he flourished during the first half of the seventh century CE.

He was influenced by a famous thinker, Gauḍapāda who died somewhere around 500. He had been influenced by some Buddhist works but his primary focus of commentary was the Upanshiad Māṇḍūkya. Evidently, he influenced Śaṅkara, who was in his time accused by more old-fashioned adherents of orthodoxy of being a crypto-Buddhist, largely owing to his denial of individual agency. Gauḍapāda's verses on the Māṇḍūkya were commented upon by him, and this formed one of Śaṅkara's principal writings, together with commentaries on the three major pillars of Vedānta.

Śaṅkara's non-dualistic or Advaita Vedānta is important for two main reasons. First, it was influential in its day and gave impetus to a whole school of interpretation of the tradition. Second, in recent times, especially since the life of Swami Vivekananda, the Hindu reformer and revivalist, and eloquent exponent of Indian nationalism, most famous for his dramatic intervention at the Parliament of Religions held in 1893 at Chicago, an adapted version of Śaṅkara's philosophy has been the underpinning of much Hindu philosophizing and apologetic. Modern Hinduism, especially among the English-educated elite, often expresses itself though a version of Advaita Vedānta. So in relatively recent times Hindus have found inspiration in the thought of Śaṅkara.

From Buddhism, Śaṅkara borrowed the distinction between 'higher truth' and 'ordinary' or 'pragmatic truth' – between *pāramārthika* and *vyāvahārika*. The former is something which cannot be stated discursively, but can be experienced directly in the act of liberation. It is also pointed to in certain great utterances in the Upanishads. Ordinary truth concerns everyday existence and religion at its pragmatic levels. Most of what is found in *śruti* belongs to this lower level: and indeed most of human knowledge is of this lower and secondary kind. This distinction between levels is an important device for Śaṅkara in providing a consistent interpretation of revelation. Thus there are diverse pictures of the Divine in the Upanishads. Sometimes the Divine Being is treated as Lord and personal Creator; and sometimes *Brahman* is non-personal and indescribable. Similarly, texts sometimes relate to the ordinary religion of worship and sacrifice and sometimes they relate to the deepest meaning of the spiritual quest. Śaṅkara's two-level theory helps to reconcile apparent tensions and contradictions in the Upanishads and elsewhere. (Actually, it is really a three-level theory, since in ordinary experience we have to distinguish between provisionally correct deliverances of perception and – in the ordinary sense – illusions, such as mirages in the desert. The higher truth stands to ordinary knowledge as the latter does to illusions.)

The distinction enables Śaṅkara to deal with a number of problems implicit in the Upanishads and evident too in the attempt to impose a monistic framework on Vedānta. One problem has been mentioned: whether God is non-personal or a personal Lord. The answer is (in a sort of way – what sort we shall shortly see) both. Another problem is related to the possibility of monism. If there is but one Substance, it is still necessary to account for the appearance of multiplicity. Somehow, beginningless ignorance leads us to understand reality as differentiated into individual objects, persons and actions. It generates the illusion of individual agency and subjection to ritual duties and rebirth.

From the conventional point of view, there are many beings and a kaleidoscopic world to experience; the truth is that there is only One without a second. The distinction could also more particularly deal with two levels of religion and piety. The higher level represents the interiorized unitive experience of the contemplator. At a lower level, the Divine is seen as other, to be the recipient of *bhakti* or devotion. Similarly, the elaborate ritual life of the Brahmins could be subsumed under this lower level. It was perhaps at this point that Śaṅkara attracted the most opposition – for the truth seemed to be that his doctrine was ultimately subversive. As an orthodox Hindu he could hold that Vedic knowledge and the Vedic path are the norm, yet of course his notion of a higher truth ultimately falsified the lower respect that he inculcated for the sacred tradition. It would not be unnatural if many Brahmins found his teachings a threat. His distinction also helped with the problem of how to make consistent the equation of self and *brahman*. The self which is identical with the Divine is not the empirical or everyday self, or even some individual spark lying as it were at the bottom of the psyche. It was something which transcended ordinary speech, and it was, so to speak, a unitary self shared by all sentient beings. Human beings are usually at the lower level and so in a state of *avidyā* or ignorance, and so they identify the permanent self with their empirical egos. The higher knowledge involves ridding oneself of this illusion. (Incidentally, this move brought Śaṅkara close to Buddhism since he denied all individual souls or selves as being permanent.)

The chief difference between Śaṅkara's system and that of the Śūnyavāda before him comes from the fact that Śaṅkara conceives of his ultimate as being a unitary Substance – a Being. It is true that nothing can properly be predicated of it, beyond such facts as that its essential nature is consciousness (later Advaitins were to adopt the formula of saying that *brahman* essentially consists in being, consciousness and bliss). Despite its indescribability, Brahman is still a substantial reality, and this contrasts with the intent of the doctrine of emptiness in the Mahāyāna, where the ultimate is a no-thing. But we are at rarefied levels here, and some commentators have seen an essential convergence between the two systems of ideas.

Śaṅkara's worldview has a brilliant simplicity about it: one without a second, that is the authentic reality. It presents us with a mysterious One: glowing, so to speak, in the darkness of our ignorance, and lying silently beneath and within everything that we see and hear and worship. It lights up our inwardness, being beneath every state of our shifting consciousness. The picture is vivid, compelling, decisive. It has a certain starkness, and yet warmly leaves room for popular religion, for back down on the lower level there is a God or Goddess to worship. There are hymns to be composed, temples to be frequented, merit to be gained, pollution to be avoided, social hierarchy to be respected. Yet the transitions between levels cause uneasiness and paradox. According to one story, probably apocryphal, an untouchable upbraided Śaṅkara who had paused on a street in Banaras, fearing too close contact with this human polluter – upbraided him for not being true to his higher doctrine, for did not the laborer and the sage share the one eternal Self?

The doctrine of the two or three levels was not in any case enough to deal with all the puzzles and problems left behind by the magisterial claim that there is only One without a second. Some of these questions are epistemological. How do we know that reality is as Śaṅkara says it is? And some of these relate to a search for suitable analogies to illuminate the picture presented. As to the first kind of problem, Śaṅkara is conventional in relying on, among other things, scriptural testimony and inference. Testimony relates to things transcendental: for him the 'great sayings' in the Upanishads testify or point to the higher truth. But their operation must be different from ordinary texts, which in some way describe what is. Because of the simple, monolithic character of the higher truth, the great sayings must stir the relevant knowledge in the person who hears them. So there is at the end of the day an existential, experiential basis for the system, but it is not a question of ordinary experience (which in any case belongs to the realm of ignorance).

We might think of this higher experience as a kind of transcendental intuition. It itself serves as the basis for recognizing differing levels of truth, since it has the effect of falsifying ordinary knowledge. It is like waking up from a dream: it shows the falsity of the dream, even if within the dream everything is both vivid and consistent. So there is an analogy at work: as waking is to dreaming, so is transcendental intuition to ordinary experience.

Yet within the sphere of ordinary experience we can use inference and other modes of reasoning. Thus we can be intuitively aware of our ignorance and at the same time know that there is a self behind our ignorance. Śaṅkara is happy to argue for the necessity of a Self to lie behind the various states of the individual. He is also happy to use inferential argument to show that behind the cosmos there must be a perpetual Creator. But when we go more deeply into the concepts of the Self and Lord we see that their ordinary associations, like individuality and personhood, dissolve away.

The world which presents itself to unenlightened consciousness is itself a projection. Our modes of cognition and perception are what give rise to the sense of multiplicity before us. This projection or *adhyāsa* applies equally to our sense of being an individual. We wrongly attribute individuality to selves. In this we mistake the empirical self as being the Self. It is as when we think of the separate spaces contained in various jars, for instance, as being separate (but there is really only one space). Objectively the world is *māyā* or illusion; and subjectively it is the result of ignorance or *avidyā*. In both capacities it hovers so to speak between existence and non-existence. The illusion is not nothing, but it is nothing fully real. In this, Śaṅkara uses as his criterion of full reality the notion of being permanent. The things in the world, including our empirical selves, are not permanent. Whether this is a good criterion is open to question, and indeed this was questioned by Rāmānuja.

There seems to be the puzzle as to why the cosmos as presented to us in illusion exists. Can Śaṅkara give an explanation of why the grand illusion is there, before us, as it were? Not strictly: he can of course give an analysis, which he does by considering it a projection. But in a deep sense no explanation can be possible. Anything which could serve as a Cause of the world is itself an illusion: this is why God after all shares the magical semi-reality of the creation. Anything which lies beyond the impermanent cannot serve strictly as explanation, and anything which could explain the world would itself require explanation. So the nature of the world is ultimately indefinable.

Looked at from another angle, the one Self is refracted through various limiting conditions into an apparent multiplicity of selves. But it is self-luminous in itself, and so when the individual sheds 'his' or 'her' sense of refraction, liberation is achieved. In the last resort therefore, *vidyā* or knowledge is powerful, for it brings about salvation, in which the individual, no longer trammeled by limiting conditions, does not go on being reborn. By understanding existentially the true meaning of the scripture the individual rises above individuality and attains that self-luminous bliss which is one of the three marks of Brahman.

Sometimes writers describe the liberating event as if a person becomes Brahman. This is not so. According to Śaṅkara's view each life-monad really is the Divine but does not realize it, because of the powers of projection and self-limitation. The achievement of liberation is an act of knowledge, but what is known existentially is that you were Brahman all along. It is not a change of ontological status but a change in the state of knowledge.

The individual who achieves release has to have knowledge, according to Advaita, of the Vedic texts and of the linguistic tools for dealing with them, and also has to have certain virtues and existential insights – insight into the difference between what is permanent and transient; disinclination to worldly pleasures; distaste for enjoyments and a desire for knowledge; and self-control. With these accomplishments and dispositions in place the wise person is ready for liberation. If he achieves it, he will go on living, using up the surviving fruits of karma, like the potter's wheel continuing to spin after the potting is finished, using up its inertia. In other words, Śaṅkara advocates a version of the doctrine of *jīvanmukti* or living liberation, when the sage goes on existing, apparently normally, though with the luminous Self blazing within and informing all his feelings and actions.

Śaṅkara's system had a brilliant simplicity about it. But by its two-level theory of truth it was able to accommodate the complexities of scriptural interpretation. At the ordinary or this-worldly level he was able to make use of some of the commonplaces of traditional cosmology. So a Sāṅkhya account of the creation and evolution of the cosmos, a regard for the empirical otherness of the Lord, and a conservative regard for tradition could combine with his most radical view of the monistic character of reality. He grasped with unerring dedication the principle that if Brahman and the Self *(ātman)* are truly identical, then there can only be one Self and so the apparent multiplicity of selves is a delusion. He grasped the point, too, that if monism is true then there can be no question of our becoming Brahman because that is our true nature already. His radical monism prepared the way for other developments – in particular dialectical and subjectivist versions of Vedānta, which we shall come back to.

Why do we need the apparatus of Brahmanical religion? It may help us on the way to intuitive insight into the identity of the soul and the Absolute, by providing moral guidance and mental purification. But this is something not fully explained by Śaṅkara and it represents an Achilles' heel in his system. Nevertheless, it is overall an impressive edifice, and it had a great influence on the Indian intellectual scene. Perhaps it had too much, in the sense that its power masked the fact that over so much of Indian religious life it was the light of worship and devotion which shone, and it was forms of theism that proved to be the most influential religiously (theism which itself was diffused and refracted through the many gods of local practice).

CLASSICAL YOGA AND ATOMISM

During the main period of formation of what may be called classical Hinduism, during, that is to say, the early centuries of the Common Era, the major 'orthodox' schools took shape – those that accepted the Veda with its ancillaries as canonical. Among these schools was Yoga, which virtually took over Sāṅkhyan ideas as its metaphysical base, but which came to develop a form of theism; and the Nyāya-Vaiśeṣika combination, which welded together a school of logic and epistemology with an elaborate atomistic worldview. We may also mention the emergence of a formal school of exegetical method, known as *Mīmāṃsā* which had some characteristic views about reality, dictated by its special doctrines about how to deal with sacred formulas. As the formalization of Indian philosophy emerged, three pairs of schools came to be recognized – Yoga-Sāṅkhya Nyāya-Vaiśeṣika and Mīmāṃsā-Vedānta. Despite their incompatibility in many matters and manifest divergences about epistemology and method, they all could count themselves as orthodox. From this time on *pandits* or skilled practitioners of intellectual sciences could specialize in one or other of these traditions. Those who dealt with potent, sacred texts could be adept at Mīmāṃsā. Those who knew about the theory of knowledge and modes of reasoning, including logic, could immerse themselves in Nyāya. Those who theorized about material processes could follow Vaiśeṣika or Sāṅkhya. Those who had deeper metaphysical or theological ambitions could work in one form or another of Vedānta. So far we have looked at Sāṅkhya and Vedānta of the Advaitin or Non-dualistic variety.

The chief teachings of Yoga as a system are to be found in the *Yoga-Sūtras* ascribed to Patañjali (sometimes identified with the famous Indian grammarian of that name, but probably wrongly). Some put his date as the second century BCE. Certainly since early times there are references to yoga, including in Buddhist texts and in the *Gītā*; but these relate to general uses of self-control and meditation of one form or another rather than to the formal school of this name. I am inclined to use Yoga with a capital Y to refer to the school, and yoga with a small y to relate to various broad practices of meditation. The school of Yoga was further reinforced by the Yogabhāsya or Yoga-commentary attributed to Vyāsa who flourished perhaps in the fourth century CE, or later.

The chief divergence between Sāṅkhya and Yoga has to do with belief in God or *Īśvara*. It is evident that there was some pressure towards theism among canonical practitioners of Yoga, possibly because of the atheistic character of the chief rivals of orthodoxy (among the Buddhists and Jains, who also underwent their own kinds of meditational discipline). As Yoga developed right through to almost modern times, its theism became more pronounced. But in its initial phase, its God was not such a dynamic Being. Rather, the Lord was a kind of shining ideal: he was the one soul which had not been entangled in the round of rebirth. Splendid in his permanent isolation he could serve as a beacon for the inward voyager – the person who was adept at the skills and armed with the virtues that the true Yogin had to have if he or she were to escape into the Beyond – the state of release. The path of Yoga, as described practically, has, like the Buddha's path, eight stages, involving restraint or moral training; ascetic discipline; the practice of postures or *āsanas*; the control of breathing; withdrawal from sense-objects; concentration, which is like the early stages of Buddhist *dhyāna*; formless meditation; and higher modes of trance. The effect of this path is to bring the adept to an awareness of the essential difference between the soul or self and the psychophysical organism. The utter purification of the *buddhi* or intellect means that it shines like a mirror in which the soul is as it were visible. The Yogin in this way achieves liberation in this life and at death the final detachment of his soul from the migrating *buddhi* and the rest of his organism. In this state the permanent self is beyond sorrow. But this does not mean that it exists in a kind of positive bliss. Feelings, such as joy and sorrow, belong all on this side of the divide between the self and the organism. Feelings are, in a word, material, and thus they belong in the realm of *prakṛti*.

This says something too about the performance of religious duties. These are often thought to bring about heavenly joys. This is the promise of doing wealthy sacrifices and employing virtuous and chanting Brahmins. But such rewards are essentially of this world and do not pertain to ultimate release. So in a sense Yoga reflects a perspective not so very different from that of Advaita Vedānta. This ties in too with a social fact: the religious wanderer or holy recluse leaves the whole of society behind him: even the gods are part of that social fabric. He transcends the world of caste, of the Veda, of Brahmins. The ancient Indian distinction between Brahmins and *śramaṇas* lives on in the notion that in Yoga one goes beyond the realm of the sacrifice and the sacred. Yet the Yoga system has made a concession to orthodoxy. It recognizes the Veda as *śruti* or revelation, and as far as doctrine goes it acknowledges a God who has never been implicated in the moil of the world.

The fact that Yoga in accord with its name puts its emphasis upon very practical ways of controlling the body and breathing, and in the medieval period succeeded in evolving the meditational gymnastics called Haṭha Yoga (which in the last quarter-century has been enthusiastically taken up in the West as a means of physical fitness, though not so much spiritual elevation), implies that it has a different view of release from that outlined in its sister system the Sāṅkhya. The latter places its stress upon knowledge. One has to have metaphysical knowledge of the difference between the self or soul and the world of nature or *prakṛti*. It aims at a kind of gnosis, while the Yoga system tends towards the higher flights of meditation. In the one the consciousness has intellectual content, in the other transcendental purification. But despite this theoretical difference it is doubtful whether in practice there is so much divergence. For gnosis is not book knowledge or just something one can learn by heart listening to the wise words of a *pandit*: while Yogic knowledge or purification, for all its self-emptying nature, has to occur within a certain framework of theory, to be accepted as defining the path which has to be trod if one is to gain ultimate success in ridding oneself of the trammels which bind one to the otherwise endless and suffering round of rebirth.

As we have noted before, Sāṅkhya categories also came to be absorbed or taken up in the theologies of Vedānta, particularly those with a strong Vaiṣṇava coloring. The whole idea of the *guṇas* and of the evolution of *prakṛti* or nature come in to delineate the ways God spins out the formation of the cosmos from its inert state into its formed state (as we know it today). Though Sāṅkhya exists in theory as a separate school within the orthodox frame, it in fact is usually well integrated into more mainstream religious formulations. It represents in part a kind of protoscience, and with its theory of miniscule 'potentials' or (to use a modern word a little wildly) 'quarks' and of atoms, as microwaves so to speak within the wider soup of nature, it has some analogy to the more overtly atomistic Vaiśeṣika school. But it is worth noting briefly at this point that Sāṅkhya Yoga espouses the transformation theory of causation, which is one of the two great options in Indian debate, in which cause and effect are compared to two different states of the same substance – for instance milk and curds (a favorite example). By contrast Buddhism and Vaiśeṣika espouse the non-identity theory in which cause and effect are not identical to one another but bear an external relationship. There is a third theory, namely Śaṅkara's view that the effect is an appearance of the (real) cause. But this is not a genuine theory of this-worldly causation, since it is employed to label the relationship between Brahman and the *māyā* or illusion which is the product of the projection of ignorance upon the one Real. Within the world of illusion he makes use (in this theistic context, for, as we have noted, God shares in the illusory form of the world he supposedly has made and is continuously making) of the Sāṅkhyan model, in accord with orthodox practice. Anyway, the two main theories are the identity (or transformation) and the non-identity views. The latter is more in accord with modern thinking, especially from the time of David Hume onwards.

The Vaiśeṣika school allied itself with Nyāya, which is a summing up of some of the main results of thinking about thinking in the early tradition. There is plenty of evidence, in the Upanishads and in Buddhist works, of sophisticated reasonings about how we come to know things, including the use of inference and of forms of inference or syllogisms. The *Nyāya-Sūtras* which deal aphoristically with these matters were perhaps put together in their present form in the second century of the Common Era. They already show signs of the merger between Nyāya thinking and the worldview of Atomism or Vaiśeṣika. The aphorisms summing up this school are attributed to the legendary and ancient Kaṇāda, but may in fact belong to about 100 CE. It was not until the eleventh century that the full merger between the two traditions occurred. They may be considered two sides of protoscientific inquiry in ancient India – the one dealing with method, the other with content. The chief feature of the Vaiśeṣika school is its elaboration of the theory of atoms, though other subtraditions in fact had such theories, notably Buddhism realist schools and in its own way, as we have seen, the Sāṅkhya.

The general theory of atoms was that they were four in kind when combined – namely the elements of earth, air, fire and water, which combined to create macroscopic entities. In addition there was space, conceived as all-pervasive. Each atom is infinitesimally small. When one combined with another, a dyad was formed, which had a minute magnitude. Three such dyads combine to form a molecule, and this involves another quantum jump. Atomists had trouble with the continuum and the transition from the infinitesimal to the unit possessing magnitude. Apart from the question of quantum jumps, there was a problem with number: only the number one is possessed intrinsically by atoms. All other numbers are, as it were, superimposed on reality, through a faculty known as the connective understanding. In other words, all numbers beyond one were mind-dependent.

It may be noted too that according to Atomist theory these claims about atomic and molecular behavior rest upon inference, since they are not observable. Partly for this reason there was a disinclination to suppose that the particularity of objects in the seen world owed all their kinkiness or idiosyncrasy to the possession of differing numbers or combinations of atoms. So the idea of particularities (*vaiśeṣas*) was introduced. It is from this notion that the school takes its name (*vaiśeṣika* is an adjective based on the noun *vaiśeṣa*). In addition, the school wished to ally itself with common sense, and drew up a list of categories to which observables related: such as substance, property – such as sense-properties – number, magnitude, separateness, disjunction and conjunction, long or short duration, weight, etc.; also, selves (which are not treated as atomic, but as all-pervasive) have properties, such as sorrow, knowledge, willing, etc. As well as all the above there exists the unseen force or *adṛṣṭa*, which governs destinies and guides what we more popularly know as karma. Other categories, beyond substances and properties, are motion, directionally defined as upwards, downwards and so on, universality, particularity (as described above) and inherence. This last category shows how there is a very special relationship between a property and the substance in which it inheres. Such then are the various categories which Atomism makes use of.

Living beings too are made up of atoms in combination, and it may be noted that while the rest of the organism is complex, the *manas* or mind-organ, which is a kind of synthesizer which puts together the reports of the various senses, is itself atomic. As usual in the Indian scene the main constituents of the mind, such as the *manas* and the senses, are material. But the self or soul is an immaterial principle of identity and, as we have seen, the soul is all-pervasive. This may be held to make it easier to see how the unseen force or karma can cause a self which dies in one place to be reborn in another place. Generally, action at a distance is ruled out, though whether this counts as an exception is a moot point.

The system as a whole has a certain messiness, since three kinds of ingredients are built in to it: the atoms, the categories and the Nyāya epistemology. Its spirit is, however, empirical, despite its having to concede that its chief postulates, namely atoms, have to be inferred. Though it is orthodox and recognizes the Vedic revelation, it does not rest its deliverances upon a revealed basis as such. It holds that we can infer the existence of God. Thus revelation has validity because it is the work of an omniscient author whose existence can be established on the basis of perception of the universe and inference as to its cause. Indeed, a famous eleventh-century CE book called the *Kusumāñjali* (or 'Handful of Flowers') by Udayana is devoted to the arguments for the existence of God. Among the arguments is a version of the teleological: together with the system-particular one that you need a cosmic connective understanding to project number onto things. It could be countered of course that it is not a very strong argument to claim the existence of God on the basis of what after all is a weakness in the system, namely that it cannot properly account for the numberedness of substances.

There is also, by the way, a problem with the Atomist defense of revelation as being the product of an omniscient author. Is it? What about alternative books of revelation? And what about the thesis that all books have human authorship so that at best a book of putative divine authorship is inspired by God (and then does not the omniscience get filtered and muddied by the human intellects through whom God necessarily has to work?). It is interesting that fearful of such objections the Mīmāṃsā school preferred to hold that śruti or revelation is without authorship, even of the divine variety. Its authority thus for them became intrinsic. This notion of authorless testimony became an important and controversial bone of contention in the Indian philosophical scene. It may be noted that the term for 'authorless' was *apauruṣeya*, an adjective derived from the negative prefix *a-* and the stem *puruṣa* which is a normal word for a person and is naturally applied also to God as a person. (It is also the word used in Sāṅkhya for the soul or self.)

We see then that the rather naturalistic schools which have something of a scientific air about them, namely Sāṅkhya and Vaiśeṣika, become theistic after a fashion once they are drawn into alliance with their twins, and once they come regularly to accept the authority in some fashion of the Vedic revelation. This is perhaps testimony to the fact that the pressurers towards belief in a Lord or God of some kind were, in the period of the formation of the classical Hindu tradition, rather strong. Indian metaphysics had begun to bifurcate into a theistic or absolutistic form in the shape of Hinduism and an atheistic form in the shape of Buddhism, Jainism, Ājīvikism and Materialism. Or to put it another way, the orthodox schools tended to theism, and the unorthodox ones to atheism. Yet of course Buddhism's flowering into the Mahāyāna did create something of a devotional faith, and personal Buddhas and Bodhisattvas became phenomenologically hard to distinguish from gods. They were lighter in texture, less heavy with sacrament and mystery, but nonetheless celestial saviors and dispensers of heavenly merit.

But by a strange paradox it was the school at the heartland of the Brahmanical enterprise and the sacred twin of Vedānta which turned out to be most uncompromisingly atheistic among the orthodox traditions. It was Mīmāṃsā, dispensing the rules of exegesis to be wielded by those who mediated by their memories and chants the vibrant sounds of the Vedic revelation – that which for the pious Hindu is 'to be heard', which so stressed the sacrality of revelational sound that it denied God to make sure that the Veda did not have an author.

MĪMĀṂSĀ: A PARADOXICAL WORLDVIEW FOR AN ACTIVE PRIESTHOOD

It is common enough to have people deny God in order to knock religion, but rarer to have it happen in order to defend absolute orthodoxy. Nor did the Mīmāṃsā go along with usual views of *mokṣa* or liberation. For Buddhists, Jains and Hindu schools such as Sāṅkhya-Yoga and Vedānta, liberation was of a distinctly transcendental kind. The eternal soul at the decease of a saint disappears from the entangling round of rebirth, and typically occupies a state which shuts out sorrow and which is generally characterless. It is a state beyond heaven. In a Pure Land such as that of the devotional Buddhists the individual persists and enjoys herself or himself. Those who do good deeds and attain high levels of meditation may live millions of years in a heaven. But liberation is something so much more radical. The person who goes to heaven in due course works off her or his karma and comes back down again to a human level. But the individual who makes it to *mokṣa*, beyond heaven, is thoroughly depersonalized. (If you find such a loss of personality to be distasteful, then this only shows how far you are from the attitudes and serenity which bring about ultimate release.) All this view, which essentially belongs to the śramanic heritage of India, is rejected in the Mīmāṃsā system. (At least in most forms, though there was a later version of Mīmāṃsā which incorporated it.)

The main point of concern for Mīmāṃsā was Vedic ritual. This had its fruits in this world, and ultimately in rebirth in heaven. It held, consistently enough, that sacrifices and the like had their effects quite independently of the gods. Indeed, the gods of the Vedic tradition, together with any transcendent God, had no potency: they were merely names that occurred in Vedic texts! It was the texts and the mantras which possessed power. This they had intrinsically. They were not, moreover, descriptive utterances but rather injunctions. The whole corpus of scripture was to be interpreted as a bundle of imperatives. Their meaning was to be found in the ritual acts performed by the Brahmins. And as we have already seen, the potency of the words did not derive from their authorship by God. It was not to be thought that there was some external sacred power, *Brahman,* which breathed through the words of the canon, so to speak. *Brahman* as sacred power inhered only in the words of the holy tradition. So in order to defend the self-authenticating character of the Veda, Mīmāṃsā denied God and an external *Brahman.* This affected their cosmology too: for it led them to reject the usual picture, in the Indian tradition both Hindu and Buddhist, of the cosmos as 'pulsating' – alternately resting in a quiet phase (sleeping, so to speak) and evolving dynamically (waking, so to speak). This pattern which seems to have stemmed from the early Buddhist tradition and to have been absorbed into the orthodox Hindu framework was unacceptable, because it would imply that the scriptures would disappear every so often into the formless rest state and so would need to be recreated every so often. Better, then, to reject the pulsating cosmos, and to preserve the unique and intrinsic power of the Veda.

All this implied something about the Sanskrit language which is interesting. Obviously its meanings had to be intrinsic to it. It was the primordial language, the sacred tongue *par excellence,* whose sounds were coupled by inner power to their meanings. It was not a human invention, nor was it true by convention. Whereas the Buddhists claimed that language is a mere customary formulation, and is dependent on human convention, the Brahmins of the Mīmāṃsā tradition held that Sanskrit was uniquely the system of sounds that reflects the true nature of the cosmos. That humming and vibrating Om, that wondrous chanting of *mantras,* that reverberating memory of primordial sound – all this was an echo of the heart of things. It was the essence of the universe in sound. It was to be heard, and it was to be acted upon, as sacrifice and holy rite. Being authorless, revelation is everlasting, actualized from time to time in the sacred utterances of those who possess the Brahmin power, who are of course the Brahmin priesthood.

It is a strange system. There is no God: the gods are mere names used in the rites. There is no ultimate release beyond sorrow, but rather the reward of heaven for those who cause the sacrifices to be properly conducted and who otherwise perform the *dharma*. It is sacramental atheism.

A SUMMATION OF THE SITUATION IN THE EARLY MIDDLE AGES OR LATE CLASSICAL PERIOD

We have brought the story of Indian philosophy up to the time of Śaṅkara and early Advaita. Already in existence were the six schools of orthodox Hinduism: Sāṅkhya-Yoga; Nyāya-Vaiśeṣika; Mīmāṃsā and Vedānta. Buddhism had proliferated beyond the Lesser Vehicle (as its critics called it) into the Mahāyāna, and here we may note the following varieties – the Theravāda, the Sarvāstivāda, the Śūnyavāda and the Yogācāra or Vijñānavāda. In addition there were the Jainas, the Ājīvikas and Materialists. The last two, however, were destined to fade: while in south and south-east Asia the Theravāda was due to become the dominant school. The Mahāyāna's chief contribution was going to be (and already by this time was) delivered in China and the rest of East Asia. In India itself the balance of power was about to shift in a number of ways.

First, as the instance of Śaṅkara showed, much of the vigorous Vedānta speculation was going to take place in south India. This was largely under religious stimulation. For example, the great contributions of Rāmānuja and Madhva, the foremost exponents respectively of the Qualified Non-dualist and Dualist Vedānta, were spurred by the vigor of south Indian Vaiṣṇavism. For Rāmānuja the eloquent spiritual hymns of the Tamil saints, the Alvars, were immensely important. Second, Buddhism was beginning to fade. In North India it suffered greatly because of the Muslim incursions – into Sind during the eighth century, this being an area where Buddhism had a certain strength, in Ghazni (in modern Afghanistan), and in Uttar Pradesh and Bihar in the eleventh century CE, where key monasteries and centers of learning were sacked. Muslim Turks considered, conveniently but no doubt sincerely, that Buddhist statues were idolatrous. Third, as is evident from this beginning of Islamic influence, a new civilization was about to be shaped in the subcontinent, dominated by the Sultanate of Delhi and the Mughal Empire. This suppressed some of the vigor of traditional Hinduism. As it happened, the south was less susceptible to Muslim influence. The effects of Islam were somewhat to reinforce certain kinds of *bhakti* religion, since it was itself a form of this; while conversely mystical Islam, or Sufism, drew power from the yogic and meditative traditions of the Hindu–Buddhist environment. Fourth, because of the decline of Buddhism we have to look at the frontiers of India itself to see its active continuance. It remained a strong force in Sri Lanka, beyond the Hindu south; and it became deeply entrenched in Tibet, where a form known as the Diamond Vehicle (Vajrayāna) was to be dominant. In Bengal also forms of Tantric Buddhism survived. The more magical sides of Buddhism were evident in the Vajrayāna, and are sometimes labeled the

Mantrayāna (the Vehicle of the Mantra or Sacred Formula) and the Tantrayāna (the Tantra Vehicle). Although in Sri Lanka Mahāyāna motifs were woven into Buddhism in the Middle Ages, it was Theravada which dominated, and this underwent relatively little philosophical development, though the commentaries made systematic efforts to list and characterize all the various *dharmas* or events which go to make up the empirical work. Also, Buddaghoṣa (fifth century CE) composed among other things a magisterial *Visuddhimagga* (Path of Purification), intended as a summation of the whole religion of the Buddha – what he himself might have composed if he had had the leisure to sit down and write out the essence of his teachings. The Theravāda came to be dominant too in south-east Asia.

But meanwhile in India proper the most powerful motifs were those spun forth by theistic Vedānta, together with schools such as those of Śaivism in Kashmir and the devotional Śaiva Siddhānta in the Tamil country of the south. The aim of these schools was to replicate something like Vedānta philosophy and theology, though from the standpoint of religious movements less perfectly assimilated into the Brahmanical and Vedāntin tradition. We can select as examples of these positions the doctrines of Rāmānuja and Madhva, of Abhinavagupta and Meykaṇḍa, and of the late Vedāntins Vallabha and Caitanya. Some of these endeavored to combine theism with a sort of monist ontology, wishing to affirm somehow the unity of God and the cosmos while at the same time allowing for the differences between souls and God which make the practice *of bhakti* meaningful.

THE VIŚIṢṬĀDVAITA OF RĀMĀNUJA – INDIA'S MOST POWERFUL THEISM

Śaṅkara's system had a profound effect on Indian culture, for it led to a revival of Hindu values and offered a way of undercutting and subsuming Buddhist teachings. By his establishment of monasteries Śaṅkara also gave new life to the spiritual vocation of those who wished to 'leave the world' but within a definitely Brahmin and Hindu context. Yet there were two features of his thought which were obnoxious to those like Rāmānuja who were powerfully moved by devotion and by the tradition of poet-saints in the Tamil language who had given such vivid and fervent expression to the southern religion of devotion. He lived in the twelfth century CE, and died in the holy center of Śrīrngam. His chief works were commentaries on the *Gītā* and *Brahma Sūtra* and expositions of the Vedānta such as the *Vedārthasaṅgraha* or 'Compendium of the Meaning of the Vedas'. His chief concern was to expound a version of the sacred tradition which could do justice to the passionate Vaiṣṇavism which he espoused. The two features of Advaita thought which he wished to combat were the doctrine of illusion or *māyā* and the absolute monism of this system. It was clear to Rāmānuja that a real relationship to God implied some difference between the individual and the Divine Being. How could there be worship of that which is identical with one's self? It also by the same token implied the reality of the individual and therefore of his or her world. The God, moreover, whom Rāmānuja worshiped was a highly personal Creator and Sustainer of the world, and could not be seen simply as the nirguṇa *Brahman* or qualityless Divine Being whom Śaṅkara put at the forefront of his picture.

It was then on this double front that Rāmānuja sought to attack the ideas of Śaṅkara. At the same time he wished to be faithful to the three pillars of Vedānta, the Upanishads, *Gītā* and the sacred aphorisms. In some respects his task was not so difficult, since the predominant trend of the *Brahma Sūtras* was perhaps some theory of 'identity in non-identity' *(Bhedābhedavāda)*, while the Song of the Lord was undoubtedly theistic. The Upanishads do not have any single completely consistent point of view, I would say, even though the natural assumption of writers like Sāṅkhya and Rāmānuja was undoubtedly that coherent teachings were to be found there.

Rāmānuja had of course to make sense of the Great Sayings of the Upanishads: such as the great *tat tvam asi* or 'That art thou'. He had to affirm a strong solidarity between the soul or self and God. The great analogy which he used to underline the unity between God and the world (while asserting their difference) was that of soul and its essentially dependent body. This simile relates the Lord to the cosmos. The cosmos is his body, and so there is an intimate union, one indeed of essential dependence according to Rāmānuja, between God and the universe. A body is defined as that which is subservient to a soul, and each soul needs a bodily vehicle or instrument. But in the case of human beings the body is imperfectly subservient to the soul – for instance there are all sorts of inner events, let us say, of the liver or the heart, over which we have little or no control; in the case of God he is perfectly in control of the cosmos. This analogy preserves a sense of solidarity between the material and spiritual aspects of reality. It makes sense of those texts which seem to refer to the material universe as part of God (just as if we injure a person we do not just say that we harm his body but rather that we harm him, thus identifying him in part with his body).

There is of course the question of where the myriads of human and animal souls fit in all this. If each of us has a body and that body is part of the *prakṛti* or natural world which makes up God's body, then what about the individual soul? Here Rāmānuja claims that the soul of an individual is also in a sense part of God's body. He is the soul of the soul – or to use another term is the *antaryāmin* or inner controller. This notion not only makes the situation symmetrical, but it is also handy in expressing the way in which God's grace works in guiding us towards salvation, if we only have faith. This is part of the logic of *bhakti* religion, for the worshiper ascribes all holiness and loving care to the Lord, out from whom flows goodness on to the worshiper.

As for the question of the reality of the world, Rāmānuja directs various arguments against illusionism or *māyāvāda* as expressed by Advaita. He affirms that to say something is an illusion is to draw on a contrast. The contrast is with veridical or right perception.

To try and say that every perception is illusory is to rob the contrast of meaning and with that the very idea of perception. Moreover, all perception has some basis in reality. If I see a piece of rope as a snake, there is still something I am looking at and seeing – a twisty something or other. Even a mistake then involves the real apprehension of something. Rāmānuja, then, wished to affirm the reality of the world in which we are immersed. As individuals we have a real existence: but it is an existence which occurs in total dependence upon the Lord.

The visible world is the result of a transformation of the subtle body of God. In this and other ways Rāmānuja follows the cosmology of Sāṅkhya. Everything below God is depicted in terms more or less closely derived from this system. But there was a major difference of some interest. The Sāṅkhyan scheme had *puruṣas* or souls as being all-pervasive. But Rāmānuja, following the tāntric Pāñcarātra system of ritual and theology, saw the *ātman* or self of the individual as being atomic. In certain respects, however, it is Godlike. It is permanent and blissful and it may be active – that is, none of its desires is frustrated when it is liberated and provided with supernatural spheres of experience.

Rāmānuja saw release or salvation as consisting in life in proximity to the Lord, in his heaven. The self exists in happy dependence on the Lord. Because of God's acting as inner controller it is he who brings the individual to such a state. It follows from this that somehow God is in charge of the unseen force of karma. This is something which flows from theism. For such systems as Buddhist and Jain thought, the operation of karma is, so to speak, automatic. The consequences of acts or intentions come about without a chief administrator. But theism implies that God brings about salvation, and so must have charge of karma. Rāmānuja's doctrine of the inner controller is one way of taking care of this. For him, good and bad karma are expressions of divine pleasure or displeasure.

Incidentally, Rāmānuja does not deny that those who see release as consisting in unification with Brahman gain their objective – he is thinking of the non-dualist *yogin*. But it is an inferior kind of release since it does not have room for that joyous basking in dependence upon the Lord. (He does not think that such dependence implies any inferiority, because the highest happiness of a living being lies in accordance with its true nature: and for creatures that involves a sense of dependence on the Creator.) In effect he here reverses Śaṅkara's priorities. For Śaṅkara the higher truth and the higher religion are that of realizing one's identity with Brahman. The religion of devotion is inferior to this, though Śaṅkara himself did write hymns of a *bhakti* character. For Rāmānuja devotional faith culminating in heavenly dependence on God is the higher religion, and the religion of realization of unity with Brahman is inferior. In this he sees the non-personal Brahman as a lower aspect of the Lord. Probably he is much nearer in this view to the intentions of *Gītā*.

Rāmānuja's realism is reinforced by his appeal to common sense and ordinary language. Such locutions as 'I know P' and 'I remember Q' presuppose the existence of a self, which remains unchanging through the differing memory-states. And just as the individual can have a changeless aspect as well as a changing aspect (her or his body), so there is no contradiction between holding that the Lord too is both changeless in himself and changeable, in his creative activities.

Rāmānuja derived his picture of the world from revelation. But he did not think that the truth about God could be derived from reasoning, though of course he used reasoning in presenting his picture. He therefore devoted great energy and acuteness to assaulting the usual Indian arguments for the existence of God (as we noted, these were systematized in the famous *Kusumāñjali* of Udayana, not very long before Rāmānuja's time). Thus he attacked the influential teleological argument, and there is an intriguing overlap with the famous points made by the eighteenth-century Scottish philosopher, David Hume. Among his strictures on the claim that the universe resembles an artifact and so we should infer an intelligent author are the following.

First, though experience shows that pots and so on are the product of intelligent authors, we neither know the material composition of oceans, mountains and so on, nor have perceived their being produced, and have no right to infer an intelligent agent. Second, even if the argument were valid, we have no right to say that the world is produced by a single author. Third, was the cosmos made at one time or at different times? If the former, then that weakens the idea of an agent, since we see things being made over a period of time: but if the cosmos were made over time then the thought that it was caused by a series of agents becomes more plausible. Fourth, we only have the right to infer a finite agent or agents, since this is what we have experience of. Fifth, agents act through their bodies: do we then have to suppose a body for God? Here we are liable to get into an infinite regress. Sixth, the stronger the argument, the greater the likeness between the Lord and finite agents: the more exalted the Lord, the weaker the argument. There is a tension between the feeling of the worshiper who wishes to exalt the Lord and sees his or her own inferiority and the desire of the philosopher to strengthen the argument.

As to the subsidiary argument that the universe bears a resemblance to an organic body and so demands a soul to 'hold it together', Rāmānuja replies that the resemblance is at best weak – animated bodies typically breathe but we do not see the mountains or the oceans breathing. Second, the maintenance of a living body only requires the right combination of parts and so we do not need to postulate a soul as keeping it together. Third, intelligence is not the only condition of maintaining a body in life. And so on. Rāmānuja also attacked some more particular arguments of the Nyāya-Vaiśeṣika school, such as the need for a cosmic mind to account for numbers above one, necessary to explain the quantum jump from the infinitesimal to the finite, etc.

It may be repeated that Rāmānuja used his counterarguments on the side of faith, and not against it, since knowledge of the Lord flows through revelation to the faithful. But the Nyāya-Vaiśeṣika school had a much stronger stake in the inference to God, since they relied on the *pramāṇas* or sources of knowledge constituted by perception and inference. It was dependent on these that scriptures, seen as the work of an independently established Lord, gained their veridicality.

In general Rāmānuja's *Viśiṣṭādvaita* (the compound word means, 'unity of a differentiated organic reality') works well as an interpretation of the *Gītā,* and it chimes in with the more personalist passages in the Upanishads. It reflects at least part of the main thinking of the *Brahma Sūtras.* In taking up passionate themes from the Alvars and the sacred poetry of the south, it well expresses the fact that the majority of Hindu practice, especially from the medieval period onwards, has been theistic. But virtually throughout the Indian tradition there has been a polarity between those who turn in worship and *bhakti* to a God and those who tread a mystical or interior path, accompanied by asceticism, towards a non-personal goal, whether it be one described minimally as nirvāṇa or through the Śūnyavāda, or more floridly expressed through the ontology of Brahman-Ātman.

Meanwhile, theism could be expressed not through a body–soul analogy, or using the model of attribute and substance (as though the world and souls were attributes of a divine substance – another picture which Rāmānuja drew), but through a frank theism. This is found above all in the Dvaita or dualism of Madhva, another famous southerner, from Udipi near the West coast, in Karnataka, to whom we can now turn.

THAT ART NOT THOU: MADHVA'S DUALISTIC VEDĀNTA

Traditionally Madhva's dates have been held to be 1197 CE to 1276 CE. His chief works were commentaries on the Upanishads, on the *Gītā* and on the *Brahma Sūtra.* He also wrote a book called 'Light on Principles' or *Tattvoddyota.* To him are ascribed certain miraculous acts, including walking on water, which have led some to think that there might have been Christian influences on him (the Thomas Christians were active in that and other parts of south India near the coast from early times). But there are other easy explanations of his views, which stem from the perception, both on religious and philosophical grounds, of a duality between God and souls and God and the world. Other influences, such as Jain, may have come into play. Of course early Christian influences must have become woven into the very fabric of south Indian religiosity: they were like another Hindu sect or movement, from the standpoint of the general population, one imagines.

Madhva dealt with the problem of the great sayings in the Upanishads by simply supposing that there was a submerged negative prefix *a-* there. The Sanskrit *sa ātmā tat tvam asi,* which was written all together as *sātmātattvamasi* could in theory have been *sa ātmā atat tvam asi* or 'That self not-that art thou'. He was committed to a highly pluralistic worldview in which distinctions were vitally important – not only the distinction between the Lord and other souls, but also between each soul and every other, and between souls and non-intelligent substances; and indeed between each such substance and every other. The cosmos was like a huge shoal of myriad fish, each swimming independently, yet under the overall guidance of the Lord. Madhva thought of each substance as made up of a whole lot of 'relative particulars' or particular features. He retained the schematism of the Sāṅkhya in so far as he thought of these substances as being evolved through God's activity out of a unitary *prakṛti* or nature (thought of as female and represented mythically as Lakṣmi, who is Viṣṇu's consort).

This doctrine of the individuality of particular souls enables Madhva to see the operation of karma as a kind of predestinationism. The Lord recreates the cosmos, which in its quiet phase dissolves into a fine powdery chaos, and sets the souls going once more on their paths, in accord with the inner characteristics which each possesses. He, as it were, draws from them the implications of their inner natures. Thus we discover through the unfolding of events in the universe, which must occur in some kind of harmony under God's influence and guidance, how each soul will fare. That which binds a soul to the world is its ignorance, but each instance of ignorance is different from any other. Because Madhva thought of individuals as particular he postulated differing fates for them. Alone among major Indian thinkers he thought that some souls would be destined to everlasting punishment: others always conceived of purgatories as finite, however long and grisly the torments in them might be. There were different grades of salvation, moreover. Some have seen in his work a kind of resemblance to Calvinism, and because Madhva sees eternal torment as a possibility for souls there have been suppositions, again, of Christian influence. But of course his idea of multiple kinds of fate fits directly with his ontological pluralism. It is much more likely that he was influenced by Jainism, which held to a view very similar to relative particularism.

The metaphysical scheme put forth by Madhva seems to limit the power of God, since he has to work out the fates of creatures in accordance with their inner natures. By a paradox the dualistic Vedānta he proposes, while stressing the difference between the Lord and his or her creatures, and so the gap between the majestic Creator and the ignorant worshipers who ascribe to him all praise, nevertheless limits him or her. The total system has its own inner logic. The difference between God and creatures is this – that the Lord is self-dependent or *aparatantra,* while all the rest of the cosmos is dependent or *paratantra.* While God activates herself, others are activated under her influence, as chief among the network of causes which draws out each substance's destiny.

Madhva wished, like Rāmānuja, to combat Śaṅkara's Non-dualism. But he, like Śaṅkara and so many others in the Hindu tradition, thought that meditation is an essential spiritual practice: through it one gains direct apprehension of the Lord. But it was meditation surrounded, so to speak, by *bhakti,* and was similar in flavor to other forms of theistic mysticism. All in all, his was an interesting and powerful attempt to stress certain things which have vital echoes in European philosophy. He was on the edge of a theory of the pre-established harmony of all things, so that his cosmology was not distant from that of Leibniz. His relative particularism as applied to souls is close to latter-day views about the individuality of persons, themselves based on some elements in the Christian heritage.

ŚAIVA VARIANTS ON THE MOTIFS OF MAINSTREAM VEDĀNTA

One of the main early sects of Śaiva worshipers is known as the Pāśupatas, who go back to the beginning of the Common Era and beyond. They elaborated some doctrines which compared souls to animals *(paśus)* who were benignly controlled by the Lord or *Pati*. Much later, some of these notions were taken up in Tamil Nadu by Śaiva poets corresponding to the Alvar tradition which lay behind Rāmānuja, as we have seen. The Tamil works combined with Sanskrit texts or *āgamas* to form a corpus of sacred literature which was an alternative canon to the Vedas, and is sometimes seen as a Fifth Veda. The ideas of this tradition were most systematically expounded in what is known as the Śaiva Siddhānta or Śaiva Doctrine, and most philosophically in the writings of the thirteenth-century Meykaṇḍa.

In formal structure the system is not unlike that of Madhva. Indeed, the Mādhva tradition emerged out of south Indian Śaivism. There are three separate entities or sorts of entities: the Lord, who is Creator; the world which is nature – sometimes represented by God's female creative energy and consort *(śakti)*; and innumerable souls. These souls are immersed in matter and afflicted by a substance (called '*mala*') which obscures knowledge and inhibits agency. This obscuring substance combines with impurities with which the soul is drenched to act as the deep predicament from which the self has to gain ultimate release. For this it needs the help of God, though acquaintance with the material world and its sufferings helps. In particular we need the guidance of a guru of the Siddhānta tradition: such a guru is seen as an incarnation of Śiva. He can guide the individual in the meditative life to effect a union with Śiva, sometimes likened to the sexual union of male and female on earth. There is an interesting thought at this point: even in the state of living liberation, when the saint has attained union here on earth, and in the state beyond death when the soul lives with God it still keeps a shadow of its former ignorance and impurity. This touch of darkness is a reminder that the soul can after all fall again: and so depends still on Śiva's grace even when it has reached the summit of spiritual attainment.

Sexual themes are more explicit in the Śaiva traditions of the North, where in the early Middle Ages Tantric practices began to flourish. Some of these involved the use of normally prohibited activities to achieve a disinhibited expansion of consciousness transgressing the confines of one's sense of identity sanctioned by orthodoxy, such as eating forbidden meat and drinking wine, as well as sexual intercourse outside (but also inside) marriage. From the early part of the tenth century CE a form of this, known as Trika or Triad Śaivism, flourished in North India, principally in Kashmir. It gets its name from a triad of goddesses who are worshiped, one benign and the other two wild – having between them the characteristics of Kālī, with whom they were associated. Abhinavagupta (about 975 to about 1025) formulated a comprehensive metaphysics which drew on Trika Śaivism and which gave the moment a sophisticated ideology. The system is often referred to in Indian texts as *Pratyabhijñā* or Recognition.

The meaning of this term will soon become apparent, when we see the picture which is presented: Śiva is Consciousness alone, which exists in absolute freedom, and which projects forth the universe. It is like a silver screen projecting a movie onto itself. This movie is not, however, an illusion, because it is argued that being produced by Consciousness it must be in the last resort made of the same sort of stuff. It is fleeting and without its own substance but it is real.

As part of the 'movie', Śiva as absolute Consciousness pours out a cloud of unknowing, and it is because of this obscuration that individuals do not realize that their essential inner nature is simply that light of transindividual Consciousness which is Śiva. The individuals, however, in part through God's act, are turned back towards himself, their divine Source, and in them is gradually reawakened a memory of their origin. This is the remembrance or recognition of their Source. In order to attain liberation it is necessary, drawing on God's grace or *anugraha,* to practice intense meditation and so to gain *samādhi* or rapt concentration in which the individual experiences directly the non-dual state of merging with the divine Consciousness. He is the light and all his ignorance is dispersed in this glorious realization. Naturally, the figure of the two-in-one or sexual union is apt in conveying the sense of spiritual rapture obtained (this could also justify the use of Tantric techniques in pursuit of the highest bliss).

SOME VAISṆAVA THEISMS: VALLABHA AND CAITANYA

It may be noted that Abhinavagupta and the Śaivite tradition keep to a kind of absolutism in which the Absolute projects forth the cosmos and then draws the souls immersed in the world back to himself (or herself). Its absolutism is not as stark as that of Śaṅkara, because it affirms the reality of the world. We might call it a kind of panentheism – everything being enveloped in God. Anyway, it maintains the feasibility of piety and a provisional duality by affirming the real nature of the world as a projection of the Divine. A similar move can be seen in the work of Vallabha.

His parents came from Andhra Pradesh, but he was raised in Banaras, in the late fifteenth and early sixteenth centuries (1479–1531). He founded a sect of Vaiṣṇavism. His philosophy came to be known as Śuddhādvaita or Pure Non-dualism. Actually it does not differ too markedly from Rāmānuja's system, but its resemblances to the

Pratyabhijñā are quite striking. The supreme Being is Kṛṣṇa who sends forth the cosmos, which is a projection out of himself: so too are individual souls. Each one of us is a scintilla or fragment of the Divine: but we forget, through egoism. In order to draw us back to realization of the blissful unity of the Divine he appears as Kṛṣṇa to teach us *bhakti*. Vallabha tries to resolve the reason for the creation in an attractive way: God makes the world out of himself in an act of playfulness. The cosmos is God's sport, and mythologically this is told in the stories of Kṛṣṇa's delicious naughtiness both as a child and as a young man in Brindaban.

Caitanya (1486–1533) was a contemporary of Vallabha, and came from Bengal. He, like Vallabha, stressed piety towards Kṛṣṇa and challenged Islam by leading chanting parties devoted to the ecstatic utterance of his name. Philosophically he claimed to express *Acintyabhedābheda* or the Unthinkable *(Acintya)* Theory of Identity in Difference. The various kinds of absolutistic theism which we have been considering in some sense claim that God is both the same as the cosmos and different. It is probable that some form of *Bhedābhedavāda* lay behind the thinking of the *Brahma Sūtras,* as we have seen. Caitanya took the bull by the horns and simply affirmed that logical reasoning could not cope with the idea. That both difference and non-difference coexisted was to Caitanya evident enough, not just because of the scriptures, but because of the polar nature of religious experience. But maybe it was best not to try to pretend that their coexistence was logically thinkable. Regarding the personal side of the Lord, figured by Caitanya as Hari (Kṛṣṇa), he ascribed to him superiority over the non-personal (Śaṅkara's Brahman) which turns out to be merely an aspect of the Lord. This echoes a view we have noted in Rāmānuja.

It may be noted that theists in India did not make use of the idea of the creation of the world out of nothing. Rather, in order to emphasize the absolute control of God over the cosmos it was often affirmed that God was not only the efficient or creative cause of the world but its material cause as well. So the cosmos is, for instance, God's subtle body transformed. This view has often been labeled pantheism, but its motivation is theistic, since belief in a personal God always seems to intensify into the belief in the absolute and unqualified sovereignty of God over the material processes and spiritual destinies of his or her creatures. Also, the imagery of self-transformation fits in with a main strand in Upanishadic thinking, and chimes in with the Sāṅkhya account of causation.

LATE BUDDHIST DEVELOPMENTS IN INDIA AND TIBET

From about the beginning of the seventh century onwards there were trends in the Buddhist tradition which drew it increasingly towards the Hindu spirit. There was the emergence of incantatory methods – of the use of ritual formulas to inculcate Buddhist progress on the path. Such a form of Buddhism is sometimes referred to as the Mantrayāna or the Vajrayāna (Diamond Vehicle). It may have been a factor in the ultimate demise of Buddhism in India that it came to be too Hindu. Another related development was the proliferation of sexual imagery and sometimes practice, as part of an antinomian movement both in Hindu and Buddhist circles, attempting to go beyond the *dharma* by sacramentally flouting its rules. Third, there were ways in which the *bhakti* forms of Buddhism progressively led to a more theistic explication of doctrine. Thus there came to be theories of an original or Adi-Buddha who is self-existent and who transforms himself into the cosmos. As Buddhism spread into Tibet, the Vajrayāna flourished there: but Tibetans also absorbed more orthodox and earlier forms of the Mahāyāna, as well as Lesser Vehicle movements. A complex religious civilization came to be established in Tibet. Among important Tantric teachers we may mention Padmasambhava of the eighth century CE, who introduced the Vajrayāna into the country and Tsong-ka-pa (1357–1419), founder of the Gelugpa order. As elsewhere, Buddhism forged an acceptable interface with pre-existent forms of religion, and in the ever-proliferating Buddhist iconography goddesses known as Tārās were absorbed, and Tantric motifs were used to express the coalescence of male and female both in creation and in the mystical quest.

Some of the later schools preserved in Tibet also came to be vital in China and in East Asia generally: we shall deal with them when we move into that region. Meanwhile, it is useful to sum up some main strands of Tibetan thought on practice by considering the fourfold division of methods or *tantras* which is found in the Tibetan Tripiṭaka. Thus some texts are primarily concerned with outer rituals, or *kriya*; others stress the inner and esoteric meaning of rituals in meditation; then there are texts which delineate ways of ultimate yoga or *anuttarayoga* – these often include the visualization of celestial Buddhas, notably Vairocana (in general, Tibetan Buddhism lays a lot of store on the use of visual symbols, including *maṇḍalas*); and in between the ritual texts and the *anuttarayoga* are yoga texts which combine ritual and yogic methods. The series is a gradual progression to the highest forms of sacramental symbolism.

SOME THEMES OF THE CLASSICAL INDIAN TRADITION: PROTOSCIENCE

We have noted that some of the *āstika* schools were heavily engaged in trying to understand the world from a naturalistic point of view. Both Sāṅkhya and Vaiśeṣika had their own forms of atomism. But in both cases the simplicity of the underlying model was overlaid with concerns for listing categories, and the two levels of description did not fit well together. The most sophisticated version of atomism was Buddhist in looking to infinitesimal events in a constant flow. But the Buddhists also showed greater interest in classifying the different *dharmas* or elements which go to make up the world. The works known as *Abhidharma* contained very complex lists, based on observation and introspection. They were chiefly interested in listing those elements operative in human life (including material components of the individual). Differing schools held divergent views about their status: for instance sense-fields, which are the objects of the sense-organs, are considered to be only secondarily real by the Lokottaravādins (a transitional movement on the way to the Mahāyāna) because their existence depends upon the *skandhas* or groups of events which go to make up the individual. In other words, outer phenomena from this point of view are mind-dependent. But the Theravāda and some other schools look upon outer phenomena as real, though necessarily the form in which they present themselves depends upon the nature of the receptor senses.

The great interest which has existed in yogic practices of one sort or another gives Indian introspection and classifications of inner events a remarkable density. There is a whole body of psychological classifications waiting to be explored in a modern systematic manner. Some of the ways in which Indian schemes differentiate such inner faculties such as intellect or *buddhi,* the *ahaṃkāra* or individuating factor, and the *manas* or 'common sense', synthesizing the reports of the diverse outer senses, are worth taking seriously, especially if we are concerned with creating a transcultural psychology.

Another important area of Indian concern is traditional medicine, which had some effect on philosophy, partly because of issues debated about the transmission of karma and its relation to the relative contributions of the male and female parents. The four noble truths of the Buddha were framed like a medical diagnosis and prescription, and this sets the scene for the naturalistic way in which Buddhism came to approach most topics, often substituting a moral message for a magical rite or mythic story. It is also worth noting the vast, almost limitless scale of the Buddhist and hence the Indian universe. This contrasts very vividly with other cultures' universes, especially the Western.

INDIAN EPISTEMOLOGY AND LOGIC

From early times there was a great interest in epistemology, partly because differing schools evaluated sacred traditions differently. Thus one of the hot concerns was whether verbal testimony should count as a source of knowledge or *pramāṇa*. The secret of this discussion was that it was necessary to count *śabda* (testimony) as such if successful appeal were to be made to transcendental revelation. Supposedly the words of the sacred canon would tell you about things beyond the realm of human perception and inference. Most critics of treating testimony as a separate source of knowledge argued that it itself depends upon perception and inference. Thus if I am told that it has rained in Cornwall, I presume that those who tell me so have either seen the rain itself or derived their knowledge somewhere along the line from someone who has seen it.

There are issues about perception itself which are of interest. For instance, many Indian thinkers took it in an extended sense, that is, to include yogic perception. This is analogous to debates in the West as to whether religious experience should be treated as a valid source of knowledge. Also, perception is typically drenched in concepts, in the sense that you have to learn a concept in order to see an object as a typewriter (for example). Without knowing what a typewriter is, you would not properly speaking see one (of course you could see a complex lump of metal which later you discover to be a typewriter). Indian writers therefore came to distinguish between *savikalpa* perception, that is, concept-laden perception, or perception making use of imagination or memory plus conceptual knowledge, from primary experience of undifferentiated wholes *(nirvikalpa)*.

One of the most eminent of Buddhist logicians, Dignāga (*fl.* sixth century CE) held that there are just two methods, perception and inference, by which knowledge may be acquired. Perception is pre-linguistic sensation, free from judgment or conceptual construction (*kalpanā*). It refers to the flux of instantaneous particulars (*svalakṣaṇa*) that constitute objective reality. Inference involves generalities, mental constructs, and is the imposition of words for universals, qualities, actions, individual substances and proper names upon the data supplied by perception. Thought and language are inseparable; conceptual thought is born out of language and language is born out of conceptual construction.

In the area of logic, Dignāga also formulated rules of correct formal reasoning, that would exercise considerable influence within and outside the Buddhist camp. A correct inference uses an observed feature as a sign of something unobserved. One property can be the sign of another (the signified) just in case three conditions are satisfied: the sign must be seen to be a property of the subject of the inference; the sign must be observed to co-occur with the signified property in objects other than the subject of the inference; the sign must not occur in objects where the signified property is absent. The procedure was reinforced by Dignaga's successor Dharmakīrti (600–60) who realized that the limited range of our observations could not guarantee the link between sign and signified, between *liṅga* (or *hetu*) and the *sādhya*, the signified that is to be established by inference. A connection based purely upon empirical evidence could always be falsified by a future counter-example. So he introduced the notion of essential connection (*svabhāva-pratibandha*) between the two terms. The essential connection consists in either a causal relation (e.g. between fire and smoke) or shared identity of essence (if something is an oak, it is a tree). The latter applies in cases where one item falls under a subset of the other.

Dignāga was also concerned with the problem that if there are no objective general features and no truly shared properties, how do general terms apply to individuals? The answer is that while there is no positive property that is common to all cows, what cows have in common is their being different from whatever is not a cow. This is called, 'exclusion of what is other'. 'Difference from non-cows' is not a positive feature or even a resemblance. The word 'cow' does not stand for a property, essence or real natural kind. Objective reality is the flux of momentary particulars. It serves human purposes to organize its fluctuations into what we call categories and kinds. The boundaries posited by thought and language are purely human conventions. This realization about the fragility of our experience helps us on the path towards detachment and selflessness.

There are also issues about negation in relation to perception. Can I be said to perceive the absence of something? Śaṅkara, for instance, held that I can know that I am ignorant of such-and-such. It is as if there is a penumbra of nescience surrounding our positive perceptions. Some schools also wanted to postulate analogy as another valid source of knowledge. If you are told that there is a yeti in the jungle and that a yeti is a bit like a gorilla, then when I see a suitable strange beast in the jungle then I can know that it is a yeti. This was, however, criticized as being superfluous: the example could be dealt with by combining perception and inference.

Indian forms of inference are different in style from Aristotelian ones, and typically they are concerned with inductive inference. This is in line with the belief in India that sources of knowledge should be regarded as sources of *new* knowledge. Usually we have the following pattern: (1) the hill possesses fire; (2) because of its possessing smoke; (3) where there is smoke there is fire – as in a kitchen; (4) this hill possesses smoke; (5) therefore it possesses fire. In this sequence the first fire (on the hill, its locus) is the inferendum. Obviously much weight falls on (3), so that quite a lot of Indian concern about inference dealt with criteria for testing the reliability of this proposition – which was formally thought to need support from a typical example.

Later logicians developed the *Navyanyāya* or New Logic school, which was paralleled by like developments among Buddhist thinkers – an increased concern with the formalization of arguments. But the main thrust of Indian logical research related to ways of conducting induction effectively, in the quest for new knowledge.

Not unconnected with this was the problem of which theory of causation should be adopted. As we have seen, two main models offered themselves: the transformation or identity theory and the non-identity theory *(asatkāryavāda)*. There were problems in both directions, and these were the subject of a powerful critique by Nāgārjuna, who wished to destroy all positions or viewpoints. Therefore, to undermine all theories of causation had obvious attractions. The fact that Buddhism denied the concept of substance or thing meant that it could scarcely adopt the transformation theory. But the problem with the non-identity view is that it seems to dissolve reality into a disappearing powder of instantaneous events. There were problems with the continuum also in Vaiśeṣika, in that it made the atoms infinitesimal and so had trouble arriving at finite quanta – into making the transition from the atomic to the visible.

THEMES IN CLASSICAL INDIA: REALISM AND IDEALISM

It was above all Buddhism, with support from some other schools, that turned the gaze inwards in order introspectively to discover the patterns of feeling and perception in human beings. It was not surprising that this should lead to a keen analysis of the processes of perception. It was seen that typically perception has a subject–object character. It is split, as it were, into two components – the grasper and what is grasped. It was not difficult to make the move which came to characterize the Vijñānavāda school of Buddhism: to see all 'reality' as being infected, so to speak, with qualities which were supplied by the perceiver. It was possible to suppose either that perceptions were ordered internally, or to suppose that they are all in the mind, and this led to the postulation of the *ālayavijñāna* or storeconsciousness containing the seeds of subsequent perceptions. One could also suppose that behind the perceptions lay an unknown process which nevertheless gave rise to the perceptions. It is just that *ex hypothesi* one can never get to the process in itself. There was a theory, however, that the Buddha, in cleansing his senses through meditation and in clarifying his insight to a high degree, was able to see processes as they really are, behind the more confused sense-data which present themselves.

There were those too in the Advaitin tradition who took a subjectivist position. Śaṅkara had thought of the world as being projected but not in a strictly subjectivist manner; but following him there was a school of *dṛṣṭisṛṣṭivādins* or perception-creationists, that is, those who saw the world as being created by perceivers. But on the whole a more commonsense realism prevailed, especially among theists like Rāmānuja. The reality of the world as revealed in perception helped to establish the reality of the distinction between humans and God, which was of course a necessary ingredient in the phenomenology of *bhakti*. On the whole, Buddhism adopted a middle path – seeing the world as being subjectively shaped, but seeing subjects as being shaped by the world.

THEMES IN CLASSICAL INDIA: THE CONCEPT OF THE SELF

A constant preoccupation is as to the nature of the self and of consciousness. Mostly in India the *cit* or consciousness, or permanent self, is distinguished from the mental faculties of various kinds, such as intelligence, for these require consciousness to light them up, so to speak, if they are to function. They are made of a subtle kind of matter. The materialists of course denied the sharp distinction, for they abolished consciousness as some soul-like entity. They argued that it was a supervening characteristic which arose from the mingling of certain elements to form an organic body. The Buddhists also in a sense denied the distinction between consciousness and the rest of the organism. The *vijñāna* or consciousness was itself just one of the groups of events which went to make up the individual human being.

The status of *cit* had another dimension. It could be argued that it was an offshoot of the one divine consciousness, or that it was actually identical with the Divine. It was the attempt to interpret this rigorously which led Śaṅkara into the thickets of māyā – for the fundamental aspect of the latter was the ego's conviction that it was separate, as if the space in a jar were to become conscious and think that it was separate from the rest of space. Our psychophysical organisms are our jars, creating the illusion of individuality.

The Mahāyāna perspective was different, and yet in practice it came close to the viewpoint of Śaṅkara. The non-dual experience of the Void or Emptiness was the basis for thinking oneself to be a Buddha, for in the non-dual there are no distinctions. In Buddhism the place of the soul was in effect taken by the notion of *nirvāṇa*. In the Theravada this of course is a sort of deathless or permanent state, beyond the states or events which swarm to make up the world. In the Mahāyāna *nirvāṇa* is equal to *saṃsāra* and the empirical round of existence, for the hidden nature of events is that they are empty. Instead then of a soul which exists behind the world there is emptiness and nirvana.

Notions of the freedom of the self usually revolve around the idea of absolute freedom or liberation in the Indian tradition. But there is also a strong sense of free will in certain systems, notably in Buddhism. But freedom is merely inner determination in Madhva, yet that is something built in by the system of idiosyncratic particulars which leads to a kind of predestination.

Naturally, with the concept of karma being so pervasive and with the notion of rebirth being taken largely for granted, freedom had to be seen in the context of a succession of lives. It made free choice less dramatic, but perhaps ultimately more effective.

As for arguments about rebirth: there were the commonplace empirical ones – memories of previous lives, recognitions of people and places hitherto save in a former life unseen, the manifestation of exceptional genius, and so on. Of more metaphysical ones, there was the observation that a permanent soul ought to imply pre-existence as well as post-existence: and if it is 'natural' for a soul to have a body, then reincarnation would seem to follow. Also, the Buddhists argued that if some mental states are not totally physically caused then there must exist some prior mental state before the first one experienced in this lifetime. This is because every event has a cause. But the Materialists growled in the background, ascribing all supposed mental states to physical causes, and complaining that no one 'came back' to tell us anything of prior lives.

THEMES IN CLASSICAL INDIA: THE NATURE OF ULTIMATE REALITY

Though there is much in Indian thought of a technical philosophical kind – the theory of inference, the problem of the sources of knowledge, the question of the continuum, the nature of human psychology, and so on – there is little doubt that the most important discussion has usually seemed to turn on the nature of the ultimate – Brahman or God – and with it the character of and way to liberation. There are those who think that Westerners in particular overemphasize the religious or spiritual nature of the Indian tradition. Maybe they do, if we take this as a general proposition: the landscape of India bustles with merchants, hedonists, generals, armies, prostitutes, family councils, castes, occupations – with all the tumult of the world and seemingly more. But it is one of the most interesting things about what we call Indian philosophy that so much of it points to what is ultimate. This is not a defect but in its own way a great glory. As we have seen, the picture is dominated by a small number of images: the image of Brahman as the Lord and Creator (if so, how are we to picture the cosmos? As his or her body? Or as the manifestation of the Lord in material form?); the image of Brahman as impersonal and as unthinkably consisting of being, bliss and consciousness; the image in between, of God as being mysteriously the same as and different from the cosmos; the image of no God but rather the possibility of final release or *nirvāṇa* from the undulating events which interactively make up this world; the image of Emptiness within all, with nothing having its own nature, but creating a vast interaction in which all are mutually dependent, and of a universe in which realizing existentially one's own Emptiness means to live in both *nirvāṇa* and *saṃsāra* together; or the image of this world alone as existing, with no Beyond, whether state or being. These and other choices (Jaina, for instance, or Yoga) make up the picture of the ultimate which we are invited to look at and search through.

CONCLUSION AND ONWARD

There will be time later to see what happened in India in the modern period, when after the Hindu desolations of the Muslim period and the birth of new syntheses, such as Sikhism, India was challenged by quite a new civilization, that of the marauding British and the proud Westerner. And we shall see how out of that challenge arose a renaissance both of the Hindu and the Buddhist traditions. And we shall also be able to see, in China and elsewhere, the transformation of Buddhism and its fruitful forms, melding into East Asian civilization; and to note how the Theravāda helped to vivify south-east Asian culture, already fructified by Indian influences as well as its own genius. In looking to classical India we have experienced a glimpse of a very rich vein of philosophizing, by no means all yet explored and rediscovered, but whose main schools and themes present distinctive worldviews.

3

CHINESE PHILOSOPHIES

SOME KEY DIVISIONS OF HISTORY AND THOUGHT

The sweep of Chinese philosophy was enriched by the coming to China of the Buddhist tradition. This added foreign, but subtle, concepts to the insights of the major indigenous traditions, namely Confucianism and Taoism/Daoism. Though in some sense we may call Confucius' teachings and the varied explorations of early thinkers including the Taoists philosophical (while Buddhism was always a highly philosophical religion among its elite), complications arise in our survey because Taoism became a religion, or perhaps one should say that Westerners use the name to label a religion, which took up into its fabric, among many other strands, a reverence for the teachings of Lao-Tzu (Laozi) the legendary author of the famous *Tao-te Ching (Daodejing) (The Classic of Tao and its Power),* so that Taoist philosophy was absorbed into a complex, ritual-rich, magical and contemplative religion. (In this chapter I give *pinyin* renditions of traditional Western versions of Chinese words and names.) Then the corpus of writings which Confucius (K'ung) (Kong) edited and transmitted were used as part of an imperial ideology, and a State cult of Kong projected Confucianism as part of a State religion. More than this, it has become quite common in the West to link on to this idea of Confucianism a whole mass of popular religion at village and local level. Finally, China in effect welded these different phenomena and ideas together into a functioning system incorporating the three religions, as they were called – Confucianism, Taoism and Buddhism. People would participate in the rites of all three for different social purposes and spiritual quests. Some modern scholars would prefer to list the religions of China not as the *San chiao (Sanjiao)* or Three Teachings, but as four: Confucianism, folk religion, Taoism and Buddhism – but this is a bit artificial as it would mean slicing each at the waist, so to speak, since folk religion is entwined with the 'great traditions'.

It is as if the more metaphysical and philosophical thoughts of men like Kong, Laozi and Chuang-tzu (Zhuangzi) had been hijacked by more ritually oriented religious movements many centuries after they lived. Thus the main founder of religious Taoism, Chang Tao-ling (Zhang Daoling), lived in the second century CE, some seven centuries after the supposed dates of Laozi. It was in the seventh century when the T'ang (Tang) dynasty decreed temples to Confucius throughout the Empire. This hitched on to the prevailing reverence for ancestors – a practice which is often thought of as part of Confucianism, though of course it is also part of popular religion. It is probably wise therefore to sort out some of the terminology.

Generally speaking, I shall use the phrases 'religious Taoism', 'religious Confucianism' and 'religious Buddhism' to refer to the three as religions. I shall use the Chinese expressions Tao-chiao (Daojiao), Ju-chiao (Rujiao) and Fo-chiao (Fojiao) to refer to the more intellectual presentations of the traditions, and the English terms Taoism, Confucianism and Buddhism to refer to the same, together with such other expressions, now well entrenched to indicate philosophical developments, as Neo-Taoism and Neo-Confucianism. We may note, by the way, that certain less important (in a Chinese context) faiths such as Nestorian Christianity, Manichaeanism and Islam have been present significantly in Chinese history, but their worldviews will be dealt with elsewhere than in this chapter.

It is usual to think of Chinese philosophy in four periods. The first lasts down to the establishment of the Ch'in (Qin) dynasty of 221 BCE when a dictatorial regime was established which suppressed the competing schools and burnt many of the traditional books. This Early Period is followed by what I shall call the Classical Period, to 960 (the date of the establishment of the Sung (Song) Dynasty). The third period lasts until the fall of the Empire and the creation of the Republic (1911–12); but I shall take it up to 1840 (the Opium War). This I shall call the Postclassical Period. I truncate it there so as to be able to deal separately with modern, that is in effect postcolonial, developments separately in the chapter on Modern China and Korea. This I shall call the Modern Period. In brief, then, I shall be fairly conventional in dividing China's intellectual history into the Early, Classical, Postclassical and Modern Periods.

THE EARLY PERIOD: THE MYTHIC AND COSMOLOGICAL BACKGROUND

When Kong started to teach, in the sixth century BCE, he could look back upon some ancient collective memories – of the three kings who at the outset of history gave humans their various crafts and skills, of old dynasties, beginning with the first legendary emperor (really the first emperor should be dated from the third century

BCE), misty dynasties such as the Hsia (Xia), the Shang (Shang) and above all the Chou (Zhou), beliefs in *Shang-ti (Shangdi)* the High God under the Shang, in oracle bones, in varied methods of divination, in virtuous rulers and the growth of dissolution, of the passing of rule from the Shang to the Zhou, at first based in the West near Sian and then further East near Loyang, of the imaginative and meritorious life of Wen Wang, near the end of the Shang era, of the coming to power of the Zhou under the leadership of Wen Wang's son, and of the model life of Chou-kung (Zhougong), the Duke of Zhou, hero of Kong. From 771 onwards, under the eastern Zhou, the dimmer shadows of prehistory lighten somewhat, during the Spring and Autumn Annals period, so-called after one of the classics which Kong came to edit, and which lasted until the period of the Warring States from 453 BCE onwards.

Emerging in this partly mythic history is the concept of the Mandate of Heaven *(t'ienming) (tianming),* that is, the sanction of Heaven or God possessed by the virtuous ruler which he forfeits if he engages in misconduct. Dissolute and cruel emperors have the Mandate of Heaven withdrawn from them. So we have emerging the theory of divine power being channeled downwards through the emperor: it was he who engaged in sacrifices on the altar of Heaven.

It is against this background that we should see Kong's life, in a period of much feudal struggle and disorder, harking back to the supposed 'good old days' of the times of Zhou. Actually, Kong was an innovator and had a highly creative mind, but he preferred to present his teachings under the guise of the restoration of tradition. The themes which we have outlined supplied some of the vocabulary of his philosophy.

THE PHILOSOPHY OF MASTER KONG

Kong's originality lay in his critical yet positive view of institutions. He took traditional concepts and social norms and transformed them, in the service of education, humane life and good political rule. He was not, however, terribly successful in worldly terms. There were three attempts on his life from apprehensive rulers; he had to leave his native Lu for a long period; he never gained the unquestioned status of political adviser to a prince; and though he later became a minister in Lu and a magistrate, he never reached the heights that his unquestioned abilities might have suggested. His chief accomplishments were as an educationist, and his disciples (probably seventy in number, though the figure of 3,000 is also quoted) carried on a tradition which helped to shape Chinese civilization. He had a vision which was realized, but long after his death.

This vision turned on various key ideas. One was that of *li* or ceremonious behavior. He saw education as training the young in formal patterns of acting, and he laid great store by traditional rites and music. One of the books which he is supposed to have edited is the *Li chi (Liji) (Record of Rites)* and another is the lost *Classic of Music (Yüeh ching) (Yuejing)*. It is through the cultivation of correct performance that one learns to deal with other human beings in the proper manner: it is the basis of respect.

In the post-World War II period much attention was paid in the English-speaking world of philosophy to the concept of the performative utterance, mainly through the classes and publications of the Oxford philosopher J.L. Austin: that is to say, an utterance that does something, as when in saying 'I promise' I make a promise. It is as if the Western world has rediscovered something vital in Kong's perception – that learned behavior or etiquette is a major ingredient in communication. To put Kong's point in another way, a person is a being towards whom one acts in a certain way. The concept of a person is a performative concept, or if you prefer the Chinese, a *li* concept. For Kong, persons were embedded in society and that is to say that they were embedded in relationships. He took the most important of these (ruler – subject, father – son, husband – wife, sibling – sibling and friend – friend) and analyzed them as the bases of differing patterns of behavior. If these mutual relationships are healthy and decorous then society is productive and calm.

Now in taking *li* as a central phenomenon, Kong was building on something traditional which could easily be meaningless and arid. He saw in religious and other rituals more than repetitious behaviors: he transformed them into acts which had a deep inner meaning, in expressing the fabric of the ceremonial in a virtuous society. As we shall see, there were plenty of critics who thought that Kong overemphasized formality. But he saw with clarity the vital role which formal and educated behavior plays in the ongoing patterns of civilized society. Kong does not stress rights: but the emphasis on *li* towards others is a counterpart to the notion. One person's rights are how others should perform towards her or him.

The danger, though, with a stress on *li* is that behavior might become insincere and mechanical. So Kong also talked a lot about human-heartedness or *jen (ren)*. The person of *ren* masters himself and returns to propriety or *li*. He is earnest, loyal to friends, truthful and generous. In fact *ren* sums up all the virtues. It is on the basis of Kong's praise of it that many scholars see in him a humanist. In the general sense that his ethic is one of concern for human welfare this is true. But together with humaneness there goes respect or awe in the face of Heaven. In his brief summation of his life he wrote:

> At fifteen my mind was fixed on learning; by thirty my character had been formed; at forty I had no more confusions; at fifty I understood the Mandate of Heaven; at sixty it was easy for me to hear the truth; at seventy I could follow my desires without transgressing what was right.
>
> *(Analects 2.4)*

In one important respect the idea of Heaven had to do with politics, in so far as the ruler stood in a special relationship to God. But for Kong the concept of heaven was much broader and more existential. It stood for the divine moral presence. It seems to have been something always there in his consciousness, and he hoped that his disciples would stand in respect of it and its ethical pressures. While it does not seem to have represented a vivid personal God, but has a rather impersonal air in Kong's words, it is given a strong ethical meaning. This was no doubt a transformation in traditional ideas which Kong had wrought. So it was that rituals directed towards Heaven were not mere rituals, but helped to cement intentions to perform the good. As he remarked, 'He who offends against Heaven has no place left where he may pray' (*Analects* 3.13). On the other hand, he was not much interested in the lower forms of religion. He did not wish to discuss ghosts and spirits and the like, though he was committed to veneration of ancestors. He believed that he derived his virtue from Heaven, and there is therefore little doubt that he thought of ethics as grounded in a Transcendent Being, even if he did not talk much about such matters as the afterlife. When he was ill and thought to be close to death, his disciples wished to attire themselves grandly, like stewards of some high dignitary, no doubt to give him a suitably grand send-off, but he asked them whether he would deceive Heaven. In brief, the ethics which he espoused were humane and humanist, but they were grounded in respect for Heaven and the heavenly law.

Though the idea of *ren* is so important (it occurs in nearly 10 per cent of the *Analects* passages, an anthology of Kong's sayings and conversations), other concepts were brought in to fill out the moral picture, notably the idea of *shu*. Kong once said that a single thread ran through all his teachings, and this was understood to refer to reciprocity or *shu,* together with loyalty to one's own moral nature. Unless one had personal integrity, one might despise oneself and in that case reciprocity would not have the desired quality. But given self-respect, then reciprocity (not treating others in ways in which you would not like them to treat you) becomes foundational of moral attitudes. Moreover, the humane person exhibiting *ren* would want to raise the moral insight and stature of others as he would wish to raise his own.

In all this, Kong's teachings were often a critique of the behavior of rulers and of the nobility. This is no doubt why he was not a great success in merely worldly terms. He sought by ethical teachings to put trammels on power. Not only this: his very passion for education, to which in a sense he devoted the whole of his life, involved a new conception of aristocracy. He lived in a feudal and hierarchically organized society, and there are elements of hierarchy in his thought (he emphasized the higher status of the ruler and of the male and so can be considered to agree with a kind of patriarchy). But he did not think of aristocracy in a simply hereditary way. On the contrary, his ideal was of the superior man or *chün-tzu (junzi)* as one who exhibits gentlemanly behavior. The *junzi* stands in awe of Heaven; is wise, benevolent and courageous; knows what the basic issues of life are; understands the Mandate of Heaven; follows what is right and does not concentrate on a high standard of living; helps to elevate his friends; is careful in speech and deed; and is not a mere 'utensil', being good for one sort of specialism and nothing else (he is thus in the broadest sense truly educated). There are echoes of Kant in the last: you should never treat another human being merely as a means – so you should not yourself be merely an instrument to others or to the State. We can see in all this that the gentleman or *junzi* is defined, as has happened too in English, in a moral and behavioral way. So Kong did not see the aristocrat as someone just born into a certain position. We can draw a parallel with the Buddha's treatment of the true Brahmin not as someone born a Brahmin but as someone who practices self-restraint.

We may note that in his own life Kong rose to eminence largely by his own efforts in educating himself. He was the son of the third wife of a poor official. He married at 19, by which time he had already given himself a wide range of knowledge, so that in his early twenties his reputation for education was such that he began to take pupils. He was concerned with teaching in line with his own upward mobility: it was through learning that a person elevated himself in spirit and in expertise and so gained gentlemanly or aristocratic status in the true sense. Whether or not he edited the Classics as traditionally has been held (he probably, however, himself wrote the *Spring and Autumn Annals*), he nevertheless upheld the idea that immersion in the values of the tradition was at the heart of learning; and through this ideal he stamped China with the most important idea of recruiting its chief officials through a Confucian examination system. Meritocracy was to be the pattern of imperial administration. Education became the central mode of Chinese commitment over more than two thousand years (it was Mao Zedong who turned this on its head by saying that you only need to read a very few books: his own library, however, was extensive).

Later the Classics were nominated as the collection known as the *I ching (Yijing)* or *Classic of Changes,* dealing with matters of divination (which had been a most important feature of rulers' methods since the Shang period); the *Shih ching (Shijing)* or *Classic of Poetry;* the *Shu ching (Shujing)* or *Classic of History;* the *Li chi (Liji)* or *Record of Rites;* together with the *Ch'un ch'iu (Chunqiu)* or *Spring and Autumn Annals.* To these were added the Four Books or *Ssu shu (Sishu)* – the *Analects,* the *Great Learning* and the *Doctrine of the Mean* (the *Lun-yü,* the *Ta-hsüeh* and the *Chung-yung*), all of which contain traditions of Kong's own teaching, and the *Mencius Book (Meng-tzu) (Mengzi),* expressing the outlook of his illustrious successor. Together with commentarial and other works amounting to thirteen in all, including the Five Classics and the Four Books, the collection became in later times the basis for the official examination system. We can speak about an imperial education system from 124 BCE when the Emperor Wu ti (Wudi) founded the imperial academy or T'ai hsüeh (Taixue).

But before all this formalization it can be said that Kong came to be the main inspirer of Chinese culture with the vital flame of education. And this was in part because he held to a critical view of tradition and society, which was summed up in his idea of the true gentleman or *junzi.*

The foregoing ideals of *li, ren, shu* and *junzi* had direct application to politics. On the whole Kong bent his gaze on the role of the ruler. He was eager that rulers should conform their behavior to ethical norms and this was the best protection for the people. The ruler should act in accord with *li* – indeed it was the mark of the good ruler that he would get others to obey not by the use of force but by the authority of his performative utterances. He should exercise *ren* because he was concerned with the happiness and welfare of his subjects, who were like an extended family to him. Reciprocity would take a special form, defined by what Kong saw as the rectification of names or *cheng-ming (zhengming)*. A person, such as a government minister, should act in accordance with his function as defined by his title, as a father should or a son. This idea could easily, unless informed by the proper inner spirit, become too formalistic – but the meaning of Kong's idea is plain: that a person should act impartially and unselfishly in conformity with the office and title which he had been given in life. When a person becomes a father, then he has to rule his actions in relation to his son or daughter in accordance with the best interests of the latter. The doctrine of the rectification of names has some analogy to the ideal of altruism.

Moreover, the ruler should serve as an example to his subjects. His own capacity to rectify his own conduct is relevant to getting his people to rectify theirs. A man who displays *ren,* he claimed, in wishing to realize his own moral character, helps to establish the character of others. This ideal of a moral spirit running through social harmony accords with the rigid application of law. The proper reason for punishment is education, not the terrorization of people into behavioral conformity.

To sum up: Kong had a vision of the gentleman who displays benevolence or humaneness and has at heart the welfare of others, and of a society which is harmonious because it is morally ordered. A key value at the center of all this is *li* or appropriate performative behavior, under the moral pressures, however, of Heaven seen as the presiding moral presence in the universe. All this was a vision which, of course, has had a profound effect on Chinese society down the ages. The figure of the *ru* or scholar – more like learned sage, perhaps – came to be a key one in Chinese civilization and that of its surrounding areas such as Korea, Japan and Vietnam, which came so heavily under the centripetal forces of the great culture of the Central Kingdom.

THE TAOIST ALTERNATIVE: THE MYSTERY OF THE WAY

Traditionally it is held that Laozi was a contemporary of Kong. The two are supposed to have met. But it is more probable that Laozi is a label for a group of sages, some of whose poetical and mysterious utterances came to be put into an anthology known as the *Laozi* or *Laozi Book,* better known as the *Daodejing,* or the *Classic of the Tao and its Power.* Some scholars think that this work dates from a century or more later than

Laozi. Possibly it is a working out of some of his basic teachings, handed down over the years. So we are in doubt as to whether he existed as a specific individual. If he did not, then that of course is highly proper for one who claimed that we should act by not acting. He founded a wonderful tradition perhaps by not founding it and not even existing! Yet of course through Chinese history he is the focus of much piety, and phenomenologically is an important figure in the imagination of the Chinese people – as a contrast to the more formal Kong.

The *Daodejing* is a beautiful and mysterious work which has attracted a myriad of translators and many differing interpretations. It has a mystical quality, but it also in its own way has a political message. It affirms the quietude and contemplative life of the inner voyager and the anarchic vision of the revolutionary. It has inspired deep religiosity and many thoughts of freedom from the oppressions of Confucian formality. It revolves around the concept of the Tao or Way which underlines or governs the life of the universe; and it is from this that the doctrines of the movement it expressed and stimulated are called Daojiao. Yet the notion of the Way was natural too to Kong's thought: it is just that Kong and Laozi had different views of the nature of the Way, whether it be the Way that governs the cosmos or the Way that should govern the life of the human being and of society.

The opening lines of the anthology set the mysterious scene:

The way that can be followed is not the eternal way;
The name that can be named is not the eternal name;
That which is without name is of heaven and earth the beginning;
That which is nameable is of the ten thousand things the mother;
He who is eternally without desire perceives the spiritual side of it;
He who is permanently with desire perceives the limit of it;
These two things are the same in origin but different in name;
Calling them a name is a mystery;
Indeed it is the mystery of mysteries; of all spirituality it is the gate.

Another passage reads:

There was something containing all, before heaven and earth it exists;
Tranquil, oh! Incorporeal, oh! Alone it stands and does not change;
It goes everywhere and is not hindered; it can thereby become the universe's
    mother;
I know not its name; I characterize it by calling it the Way;
Forced to make a name for it I call it the Great;
Great I call the elusive; the elusive I call the far;
The far I call the returning.

Both these passages pose great difficulties as to their purport. But there seem to be two or three things which are clear. In line with much mystical writing, the ultimate (that which is fundamental to the life of the cosmos and of human beings) cannot be described. It is the nameless, the ineffable. When Daojiao came to merge with certain aspects of Buddhist thought, in Ch'an (Chan), this idea of the ineffability of things came to be a vital teaching. The ineffability of the Tao matched the Mahayana Buddhist thesis that all language is a thorough distortion and covers up the Emptiness of the events of the cosmos. The marriage between Daojiao and Fojiao bore great fruit; and fertilized both Korean and Japanese civilization through Sŏn and Zen, respectively.

At the same time the *Daodejing* affirms something which does possibly have a name, the Mother of all things, a kind of matrix of the cosmos, existing before the advent of heaven and earth ('heaven and earth' often functions as a short description of the cosmos, as also does the expression the 'ten thousand things'). This creative power reminds one of Brahman as described in the *Iśa* Upanishad, which is both far and near, and pervades this world. So too the Way is not just a nameless X which somehow is source of reality: but it is also a dynamic Being.

Yet as the book goes on to relate, the Way acts with perfect spontaneity and without effort. For this reason the phrase 'dynamic Being' could be misleading if we are too used to dominant Western ideas of dynamism and Being. Perhaps it would be better to call it Non-being. Again there are echoes of Greater Vehicle ideas. At any rate, the Way acts by not acting. It is like the hole inside the pot, which is its whole point; or like the valley, the emptiness which holds mountains apart and defines them; it is like the way water flows or the sea surges.

The human being ought to live in harmony with the cosmos, and to do this he too needs to act spontaneously, in a sense to act through not acting. It seems that the early Taoist sages practiced a quietude in which they could ultimately attain a contemplative plenitude in which they could feel united to nature and in harmony with the Way governing all things (or flowing within all things: again 'governing' is no doubt too positive a notion).

There is also mention of those two forces which were so prominent in Chinese accounts of the cosmos, the Yin and the Yang. The former is female, dark, passive, centrifugal; the latter is male, active, light, centripetal. There was a school of early Chinese thought which is called the Yin–Yang school, which combined this bipolar theory with the doctrine of the five dynamic elements – the *wu-hsing* (*wuxing*), namely water, fire, wood, metal and earth. One main effect of the Yin–Yang theory was to reinforce the trend in Chinese thought to merge the microcosm and the macrocosm – to see the same forces at work both in human life and in the universe at large.

There is also a stress in the *Laozi* Book on oneness, from which derived later criticisms of the social hierarchy and distinctions which were built into *the Ju-chiao (Rujiao)*. The spirit of the Tao is democratic, while the Taoist theory of knowledge, implying sweeping from the mind concepts which had been handed down by tradition, was in its own way empiricist.

OTHER SCHOOLS OF THE EARLY PERIOD: MOISTS, LOGICIANS AND LEGALISTS

So far we have glanced at the early roots of the Rujiao and the Daojiao, as well as at the early Yin–Yang school. Two other streams of thought are of interest in this Early Period. One is Moism, following the teaching of Mo-tzu (Mozi). At one time it was the major rival to the Kong tradition. Like the Taoists, Mo was critical of the hierarchical and formal aspects of Kong's vision of society. He held a much more fervid and personal view of Heaven, and saw in universal love the central value favored by Heaven. He lived in a turbulent period of Chinese history, at the beginning of the phase known as that of the Warring States (403–221 BCE): his dates are possibly 370–290. His concern with peace and mitigating conflict took a practical mode, in that he acted as mediator in certain conflicts. He criticized the Confucians for watering down *ren* by placing it in the context of differing social relations. His stress on universal love was one which saw all humanity as equal. His religion was direct: he thought of elaborate rituals and sacrifices as a waste of time and resources, and instead he relied on a direct relation to Heaven. On his death, his followers formed an order which carried on his teachings.

He also interestingly set out standards with which to test policies or teachings. They should be in line with the best ideas already recognized, should harmonize with experience and should tend towards desirable ends. These in turn could be judged by a fourfold set of criteria: do they conduce to the enrichment of the poor; the increase of population; the removal of danger; and the regulation of disorder? There are analogies with Western utilitarianism. His diagnosis of the chaotic condition of society was that it was primarily due to selfishness, and the cure therefore for the chaos of the Warring States should be the application of the ideal of universal love, as commanded by Heaven.

The school known as Dialecticians or School of Names, *Ming-chia* (*Mingjia*), also advocated universal love; but its prime concern was with matters of logic and the question of whether there are universals. The most interesting figure in this school was Kung-sun Lung (Gongsun Long) (early fourth century BCE), who composed a number of paradoxical dialogues including the famous one on the white horse, establishing that a white horse is not a horse. This was designed to show that the universal which a horse participates in is his horseness. Another paradox of the same purport declares that all quadrupeds have five legs (because their four legs participate in the universal leg). The logicians of this kind were somewhat hampered by the structure of the Chinese language which made the formation of abstract words less easy. Gongsun Long's contemporary Huishi (380–305) was more concerned to emphasize the fluidity of universal change, so that names or words, in giving relatively hard edges to things, are misleading. Among his paradoxes are these: 'Going to the state of Yue today, one arrives there yesterday' (on the relativity of time); 'An egg has feathers' (it changes into a chicken); 'Eyes do not see' (you need the mind together with the eyes in order to be able to see). The Dialecticians' work had a somewhat sophistical air, but encouraged a critical attitude to language, in the middle between the blanket skepticism of the Taoists and the conventional traditionalism and realism of the Confucians.

The Legalists emphasized *fa* or positive law. They saw that the most vital thing in the State was obedience; law should be clearly enunciated and defined in advance, and then rigorously enforced. They were not concerned with the moral content of law: they were rather more committed to order. They rejected a number of activities and attitudes which weakened the State – such as caring for the old, living unemployed off others, the pursuit of beauty and love, ambition and in general virtuous conduct. They were thus fiercely against both the Confucian and the Taoist, as well as Moism, and by implication the School of Names. Their severe concern for law and order made them the ideology of the Qin dynasty between 221 and 206 BCE, which saw the establishment of a virtually totalitarian regime, and the burning of books. There was one sphere where their rigid doctrine were successful – they were keen on the standardization of measures and of language, etc., and this was achieved by the Qin to a remarkable degree – a major factor in the continued unity of the vast Chinese empire in later times. But there was a backlash against Legalism which led to the dominance of Confucian thought during much of the subsequent period. In a way it was a compromise between the egalitarianism of the Tao-chia (Daojia) and the Moists and the authoritarianism of the Legalists.

The most eminent of the Legalists was Han Fei (Hanfei), who died in 233 BCE. His *Hanfeizi* or *Book of Master Hanfei* gives a systematic defense of the position. The attack on morality is based on the fact that the moral appeal could at best sway a small minority of the population, and yet the State has to deal with the majority. The publication and enforcement of this law at least squared with people's natural egotism. It is by force that the law is properly to be applied. Force is essential to the State, indeed, which is above all a war-making machine. It was the consistent focus on this view of matters that led the Qin ruler to conquer most of China and impose universal rule.

As well as these schools, two others may be mentioned as having some influence during this Early Period. One is the thought of Yang chu (Yangzhu) that appears in a mid-third-century encyclopedia, the *Lü-shi Ch'un Ch'iu (Lushi Chunqiu)* and in some interpolated chapters of the *Mengzi*. It is the doctrine that health and longevity are what count. Better to lose an empire than a hair of your head. It is wiser to pursue your own life than to take public office with all its attendant risks. The theme of health and old age is worth noting because it became such a strong feature of Chinese ambition, especially as expressed in the religious Taoist tradition and its attendant alchemy in search of the secret elixir which would bring immortality.

Another movement was that of the agriculturalists or Tillers *(Nung-chia) (Nongjia)* as they are sometimes called, who advocated living in small communities and making their living by working the land. They wished to emphasize equality and self-sufficiency: the ruler should be making his living with his own hands instead of taxing his subjects. The Tillers were clearly a protest against the growing centralization and bureaucratization of power.

THE BOOK OF MENCIUS: ANOTHER PHASE IN CONFUCIAN THOUGHT

Mengzi (Mencius), after Kong, is the most important Confucian. He lived probably from 372 to 289 BCE, and his teachings are contained in the book the *Mengzi*. This, as we have seen, became one of the Four Books of the *Rujiao* canon and part of the subject-matter of the imperial examinations.

Mencius' chief contribution was to see moral cultivation, in which innate goodness is cultivated, growing outwards from the heart or *hsin (xin)*. That human beings are innately good can be seen from the reaction of people to a small child approaching a well – they instinctively move forward to protect her or him from disaster. In the heart are the sprouts or *tuan (duan)* of the primary virtues, which he sees as *ren, li* (propriety or right behavior), dutifulness *(i) (yi)* and *chih (zhi)* or knowledge – that is primarily of right and wrong. These virtues, especially that of *zhi*, are to be carefully cultivated. It follows from Mencius' idea of the innate goodness of human beings that vicious dispositions themselves are the consequences of unfortunate experiences. It is evil society and bad company which bury the developing sprouts. It is the duty of the State to foster good conditions which will allow the virtues to grow and flourish.

Mencius not unnaturally sees the government as being in the hands of morally developed *junzi* or gentlemen, who in turn are able to ensure the ethical training and welfare of the people. He thought that the superior person who has to serve under a bad ruler should remonstrate with him, but if this were without effect then it would be his duty to withdraw to another State. He was also by conviction a pacifist: the ruler should gather an empire only because people were eager to join it – expansion should not be by military force. At the turbulent time when he lived it was becoming apparent that a new unifier of empire might arise, and Mencius traveled from state to state in search of such a paragon: both the theory of the Mandate of Heaven and his own idea of the innate goodness of human nature pointed to a voluntary drawing together of peoples into the one empire. In fact, as we have seen, it was the brutalities of harshly applied Legalism which brought this unity.

Mencius much prized the formalism of proper behavior, but nevertheless saw it as something in the service of humanity: it was not to be inhumanely imposed. All in all, Mencius was a radical dreamer and at the same time fond of tradition, which he saw as helping to nurture human nature and therefore feed the sprouts of goodness residing in the *xin*.

CHUANG-TZU (ZHUANGZI): A DELIGHTFUL SAGE IN THE TRADITION OF THE TAO

Zhuangzi is second only to Laozi in the esteem in which he is held as a carefree exponent of philosophical Taoism. He lived from about 369 to about 286 BCE but not too much is known about his life. The book which is ascribed to him, the *Zhuangzi,* contains three main layers of material, the so-called 'inner chapters' being the most original, and possibly stemming from Zhuangzi himself. He developed the idea of spiritual freedom which is implicit in the *Laozi*. This comes out in his style, which incorporates a great deal of whimsy, of sometimes scandalous stories about Confucians and rulers, of tales of strange birds and animals and of pointed anecdotes. The most famous of these is the story of how Zhuangzi dreamt he was a butterfly

> flitting and fluttering about, happy and doing as he wanted. He didn't know he was Chuang Chou. Suddenly he woke up and there he was … But he didn't know if he was Chuang Chou who had dreamt he was a butterfly or a butterfly dreaming he was Chuang Chou.

In his world everything is in flux: by living in harmony with this flux the Taoist sage gains complete freedom. This harmony implies *wu-wei (wuwei)* or acting through not acting – flowing with the flux of things. The *Zhuangzi* offers a joyful vision of Taoist mysticism.

But it is a vision which goes beyond opposites, beyond joy and sorrow therefore. Zhuangzi holds to the doctrine of the equality of all things – that an underlying unity is there beneath the usual oppositions that meet us on the surface: beyond life and death, right and wrong and beauty and ugliness. It is not just that such oppositions are relative: things have the knack of creating their opposites. One needs to adapt to this universal process of transformation and to live in line with underlying unity, the Tao. The sage person forgets everything, and travels in the realm of infinity. He achieves the greater knowledge and the greater concord, and throws away small knowledge. He should be sagely within and kingly without, and thus combine his perception of both the transcendent sphere and the mundane, which are united in the Tao. A person should have a grasp of his own individuality, which should not be ignored: it too is part of the natural order of things.

This rather anarchic vision cuts against the formalisms of the *Rujiao*. It reacts against the ideal of a worldly education. It seeks to take people into a fresh vision of the world in which they can be truly free. One might say that Zhuangzi and Mengzi represent differing poles of early Chinese philosophical consciousness – the one with optimism about the malleability of human beings and the need for *li*, the other expressing a joy which runs beyond any *li* and reacts against the hierarchy of society. The one distances himself from nature and learns from it at a distance; the other seeks to enter the swirl of being and non-being, and finds insight in merging with nature. The one is conservative about government and about training the aristocracy; the other minimizes government and affirms a fresh equality of human beings. The one is destined to be the ideal of empire, the other the ideal of rebellion against authority.

HSUN-TZU (XUNZI) AND THE CORRECTION OF HUMAN EVIL

During the final years of the Early Period and through the era known as that of the Hundred Philosophers (so complex and turbulent were the debates about the nature of the cosmos and of society), the most important Confucian was Xunzi. There is some wide variation in the calculation of his dates, but he may have lived from 306 to 212 BCE, or 298–238, and in any case until the time of the unification of the Empire. Two of his main disciples, Hanfei and Li Ssu (Li Si) played a leading role in the new regime. Li Ssu became premier and Hanfei, as we have seen, was a leading theoretician of Legalist totalitarianism. Because of this, Xunzi's reputation suffered in the Confucian tradition. In fact he occupied an important place in Confucian debates, and can be said to have occupied a mid-point between *Rujiao* and Legalism.

The reason for this is that he held an opposite view to that of Mencius on human nature. He saw the latter as evil, being characterized by greed and envy. His key chapter on this matter begins with the clear statement: 'The nature of the human being is bad; goodness is acquired.' His educational theory therefore concentrated on ways of making human nature good. It was like the operation of a craftsman. He must mold and shape the characters of the young, as a woodworker carves wood. And absolutely crucial in this is the practice of *li*. Xunzi stood squarely in the Kong tradition in stressing the vital role of *li* and formalized behavior acquired by education. If anything, education was more important to Xunzi than to any other of the *ru* school because of his perception of the underlying badness of humans in the raw state. But the fact that he had a somewhat pessimistic view of the human starting point did not dampen his hopes for the educational process. Any person could become like a sage-king, he averred. His views had an egalitarian or perhaps it should be said meritocratic emphasis.

It was because of the need to restrain human turbulence that Xunzi emphasized the role of law in the State. The polity, by its laws, helps to shape subjects. It was not a long step from Xunzi's view of the law to the rigorism of the Legalist school. But of course, as one in the tradition of Kong, Xunzi did see the law under the presence of Heaven.

Heaven is constant, and is not swayed by either the virtuous or the evil ruler. However, Xunzi saw in Heaven a positivist character: it is nature and the logic of concepts which dictate what the law is to be.

Whereas Mengzi had seen *li* as an expression of inner sincerity and benevolence, Xunzi saw it as a means of external control, part of the teaching process which molds the individual towards proper behavior and orderly functioning in society. It is as if one can shape feelings from the outside in, while Mengzi thought of shaping behavior from the inside out.

As the Confucian tradition developed over the centuries, it retrospectively adopted Kong and Meng as its supreme sages: Xun was relatively neglected. But he shared with Kong and Meng the same ideal – of human welfare arising from a well-ordered society which is governed by well-ordered individuals shaped by moral education into a benevolent and decorous set of attitudes towards their fellow human beings. His pessimistic realism is a counterpoint to the perhaps too hopeful optimistic idealism of Meng and of those who, like modern liberals, tend to think of human nature as being essentially good.

THE FOUNDATION OF THE HAN DYNASTY AND THE INCREASING DOMINANCE OF *RUJIAO*

The burning of the books in 213 marked a terrible setback for the tradition of Kong: but it was not so long afterwards that Liu Fang overthrew the Qin, in 206 BCE and founded the Han dynasty. The new emperor was somewhat impatient of Confucian advice that he received, and is supposed to have declared, 'I conquered the empire on horseback and I'm going to rule it on horseback,' to which a scholar replied, 'You may conquer an empire on horseback but you can never rule it from horseback.' In short, the new empire for its stability required an administrative class. The emperor subsequently is reported to have sacrificed an ox to the memory of Kong. But though Confucians steadily gained ground in the first hundred years, Taoism in fact was the more dominant religious and philosophical outlook – there being a concentration on relative simplicity and so cheapness of government. Yet the empire more and more needed an educated elite, and this was where the strength of the *ru* showed. In the second century BCE the emperor Wudi was sufficiently impressed by the advice of a prominent *ru*, namely Tung Chung-shu (Dong Zhongshu) (176–104) to establish a State academy, based on the Confucian classics, and to favor *Rujiao* as the official ideology. The academy lasted right down the ages until the early part of the twentieth century, and though from time to time other ideologies were adopted by the empire, the Confucian heritage has certainly been the most influential and important. It always acted as a counterpoint to the more anarchic tendencies of the Daojiao and to the private pieties of the Buddhist tradition. Its chief notion, that there is a harmony or correspondence between Heaven's will and human society, has been a vital ingredient in official ideologies of the role of the emperor as mediating between Heaven and earth. Both virtue and prosperity are ensured by the proper behavior of the Emperor as cosmic lynchpin.

Dong Zhongshu was chiefly responsible for the official use of the Confucian outlook: yet it was a worldview which was syncretic. It incorporated the ideas of yin and yang and the doctrine of the Five Elements or agents. There was a complex view of the correspondences between different phenomena according to their classification under the Two Great Forces and the Five Elements. This could generate a new interest in varying kinds of divination. The *Yijing* could become a central text for imperial prognosis of the future and as a guide to action.

On the question of the elements, it should be noted that they were perceived as activities or processes. The translation 'element' is too static. For one thing the Chinese classical language makes no sharp divides between a noun and a verb. The grass greens as much as it is green. So the elements of earth, water, fire, etc. are perceived as dynamic goings-on: something considered as a mixture of earth and water could be better thought of as earthing and watering.

Dong's overall philosophy, though predominantly Confucian in spirit, had woven into it elements from other worldviews. He thus had a rather personalistic view of Heaven as deity, in line with Moism. He thought that bad rule would bring about prodigies as signs of heavenly anger, and in the worst instance, with the expiry of the Mandate of Heaven, God would terminate a dynasty. He connected the *ju-chiao (Rujiao)* relational theory of ethics to the yin–yang. The yang or male he saw as the superior force, and identified it with the ruler, the father and the husband, and the yin with the subject, the son and the wife.

At any rate, his synthesis proved to be attractive as an ideology of the State. He is chiefly responsible for the success of Confucianism as a political ideology. But other forces were gathering in the first centuries of the Classical Period. These were religious Taoism and the metaphysical religion of Buddhism, which came into China via the Silk Route from the first century CE onwards. The former had various strands – the veneration and indeed worship accorded to the figure of Laozi as Lao-chün (Laojun) or Lord Lao who was seen as a great God who comes down to earth in order to reveal various truths and scriptures. There was some confusion with incoming Buddhism: the legend that Laozi had traveled to the far West became part of the basis of the belief that the Buddha was Laozi. Indeed, many Taoist terms were used to translate key Buddhist ideas. Second, there was a Utopian strand connected with the book known as the *T'ai-ping ching (Taipingjing)* or *Classic of Great Peace* – looking forward to the establishment of an ideal polity on earth. Third, there was the movement started by Zhang Daoling in the second century CE which became an organized religion of mysterious and sacramental power, based on supposed revelations from the celestial Laozi. These and other forces merged together to form a general movement which rivaled Buddhism and played a powerful role not merely in folk religion but also in the political life of the masses, often generating messianic revolts.

And so we see the beginnings of that synthesis which wove together, in a somewhat chaotic way, the three religions of China together with the myths and rituals of folk religion and the pervasive veneration of ancestors, into that complex which came to be known as the *sanjiao,* the 'three teachings' or 'three religions'. The interaction between Buddhism, as a foreign faith, and Taoism was especially fruitful both philosophically and religiously. Meanwhile, though, there were metaphysical ideas fermenting which were built on the earlier *Daojiao*. These were not unimportant in relation to the syntheses between Taoist and Buddhist ideas later on in China.

THE CLASSICAL PERIOD: TWO NEO-TAOIST THINKERS

In the early part of the third century CE there was a great revival of Taoist thought, which sometimes was referred to as 'mysterious learning' or *hsüan-hsüeh (xuanxue)*. It looked back to the two main classics of the early Tao, namely the *Laozi* and the *Zhuangzi* together with the *Yijing*. One of the profoundest of commentators on these works was Wang Pi (Wang Bi) (226–49), who left major commentaries, the second unfinished, on the first and last of these. The movement was a conscious attempt to return to the simplicity and depth of the earliest *Daojiao*, which had been overlaid by excessive scholasticism. The three texts represented for it the three mysteries, laying forth darkly the metaphysical doctrines of the early sages.

Wang Bi, despite his early death, produced some fundamental ideas which were destined to have a big influence in the future. Above all, he brought about a new appreciation of the meaning of the negative *wu,* as in *wuwei* (the Taoist idea of acting by not acting). For him the central claim of Laozi is found in the paradox that the 'ten thousand things come into existence from being; and being comes into existence from non-being'. What could this mean? For Wang Bi the crucial aspect of the idea of non-being is that it is not this or that – it has no finite determination or characteristics. It is unspeakable, a kind of ineffable no-thing. We can recall too in this connection that as we have noted already the Chinese classical language does not demarcate between noun or verb: there is, as it were, a dynamic quality to nothing (to take a leaf out of a book of the twentieth century, nothing *noths,* as we might translate Heidegger). There are, in Wang Bi's interpretation of the *Laozi,* two sides to the universe – one side, the deeper, dark, mysterious side, has to do with *wu*; and there is the side of phenomena, the myriad or ten thousand things, as the *Laozi* sometimes puts it. The world of phenomena is changing, full of flux, restless; it is multiple, impermanent. The mystery of nothing is dark, silent, indefinable, not plural, inactive, peaceful. It is a stillness that mysteriously moves the many, and so it is that everything in the world has its dark, silent side; but it also has its overt, definable side. The world of phenomena is that defined by space and time, and the things contained in it are given names.

There was an anarchic element in Wang Bi's account: for whereas the Confucian scholars and the *ming-chiao (mingjiao)* or School of Names were concerned with the rectification of names, that is, making words correspond to realities and in particular making the titles of offices correspond to the expected behavior of those who bore those titles, there lurked always in Wang Bi's interpretation of the Tao the thought that the mysterious and metaphysical side of things was at least as important as the definable side. Indeed, later interpretations of Neo-Taoism often verged towards an otherworldliness where the silent side of things was more important. But Wang Bi's view was a balanced one. Moreover, he recognized the worth of Kong, but saw his teachings as being limited to the side of the myriad things and to the realm of useful function *(yung) (yong)*.

Although Buddhism was already coming into China in his day, it is doubtful whether it could have had any influence on his thought: yet his philosophy has a remarkable similarity to some Indian ideas and to some Buddhist philosophy in particular. His notion of the ultimate *wu* as being unspeakable is like the *neti neti,* 'not this, not that', formula in the Upanishads, pointing to the ultimate Brahman. More particularly his idea of the negative *wu* prepared the way in a most striking fashion for the reception in China of the doctrine of the void, emptiness – the *śūnyavāda*.

In treating the *wu* as being the root of the cosmos or *pen (ben)*, Wang Bi gave it a rather positive role. But he was throughout insistent on its indefinability. The whole point of the writings of Laozi and Zhuangzi was to move out of language towards the silent ultimate. Wang Bi saw Kong's words rather differently: he saw him as a sage whose directions were entirely directed towards the sphere of existence and of the 'ten thousand things'. In this he exhibited a synthetic trend at the heart of Taoism, which tried to embrace all people and varying values in a wider embrace. This notion became important for imperial ideology, since the Han Chinese empire itself took in many who were not Han: they were tribal and peripheral groups of all kinds – and Taoism could function as an egalitarian philosophy relevant to the absorption of these other peoples better than did Confucianism with its overt Chinese and traditionalist values.

In brief, Wang Bi came up with the mysterious view of the *wu* as having a positive as well as a negative significance. Nothing is not just nothing. The other great figure from the Neo-Taoist movement that we are about to look at, Kuo Hsiang (Guo Xiang), who died in 312 CE, was at odds with Wang Bi over this. Every pendulum must swing, it seems and Guo was much more rationalistic than Wang. His cosmos was not without its contemplative beauty. He still held that there was supreme peace in uniting with the underlying principle of the real world. But his picture of the universe was much more naturalistic. The cosmos does not have a cause outside of itself. It is everlasting and self-generating. Likewise, phenomena come into being out of their own nature. In this he was to be at odds with the Buddhist metaphysics, where phenomena lack self-existence or own-nature. Anyway, though the Great One governs the universe, it does so subject to the fact of the limitation of individual beings. The limitations assign to beings their places in the cosmos and in society and create their natures. So a person should accept his limits and his destiny. Yet the names the individual has, her or his place in society, are merely superficial and need to be forgotten if she or he is to be in union with the Great One – the universe in its pulsation and flux.

Guo Xiang was propounding a kind of monism, and this in turn prepared the way for the emphases of the Hua-yen (Huayan), one of the great schools of Chinese Buddhism.

THE SUCCESS OF BUDDHISM IN PERMEATING CHINESE CULTURE

There were some distinct clashes between Chinese traditional values, and especially those of the Confucian tradition, and the new religion which was coming into China along the Silk Route (and to a lesser degree by sea from the second century CE). There was a strong otherworldly streak in Buddhism which contrasted with the Confucian concern for the administration and good order of this world, where earth and Heaven were a single fabric. Then Buddhism tended to individualism – it was the individual that gained nirvana, and it was the individual who left the world and joined the Saṅgha. The celibacy of the monks and nuns tugged against the strong family emphasis in China. Then there was the belief in *karma,* somewhat bizarre and foreign from a Middle Kingdom point of view. It was also an odd thing to take over a religion which was barbarian. What good could come from outside of China, which is after all the center of the world?

But there were some favorable factors too. The consonances between the *Daojiao* and the *Fojiao* became evident. The nothingness of the Tao echoed, as we have seen, with the emptiness of the Buddha-nature. The Mahāyāna idea of the salvation of all beings could jibe with the ancestor-veneration of traditional China. The various meditation techniques had some counterparts in Taoism. Moreover, the *Rujiao* was after all an elitist doctrine absorbed primarily by a very small upper class; while Buddhism in varying ways appealed to the masses. The promise of heaven, the idea of merit, the frequenting of temples, Buddhist pilgrimages, congregational affiliation and a whole lot of other features of popular Buddhism could appeal well to the masses. Not for nothing was the theory put about that the Buddha's teachings were really those of Laozi who had supposedly traveled to the Far West in order to reveal the truth to the heathen, who now brought it back into China. Moreover, northern China between the third and fifth centuries, before the reunification of the empire, was often ruled over by non-Chinese, who were more favorable to Buddhism.

The Buddhism that came to China was of various sorts. Moreover, there were lots of opportunities to diversify once in China: and there is the phenomenon of the sinification or Chinese-ification of Buddhism in the Middle Kingdom. This was assisted by varying factors. One was the complexity of the task of translating the great weight of texts, despite the efforts of such great scholars as Kumārajīva (344–413 CE) and his colleagues. Second, there were important impulses to see Buddhism in Chinese terms, particularly Taoist. The pervasive grip of language was here vital, because it was difficult to use terms like *tao* (widely used in connection with Buddhist concepts) without bringing with it the flavor and meanings of its religious and philosophical heritage. Third, South China in particular was rather far from the main overland conduit of Buddhism; and the number of pilgrims who could penetrate to Buddhism's homeland of India was rather small. So the Chinese monks were often left very much to their own cultural devices. Out of such a situation and over the centuries there emerged new emphases in China, as well as the more traditionally expressed Indian Buddhist schools.

Some of these sinifications were largely religious without implying much in the way of philosophical theses. For instance, the great Buddha-to-be Avalokiteśvara was transformed into the female Kuan-yin (Guanyin), a lovely Madonna-like figure. Again the Chinese came to stress the theory of different ages of Buddhism which led to the view that strenuous Buddhism was hard or impossible to perform successfully in 'these latter days' – and so we have a fervid fideism leading to rebirth in the paradise of the Pure Land. But three main schools emerged out of the creative interplay between China and India which were of some great significance. One, the T'ien-t'ai (Tiantai), is less philosophical, but still betrays a certain overall tendency important in Chinese thought. The other two, Hua-yen (Huayan) and Ch'an (Chan) are of great interest from an intellectual point of view.

It was primarily during the era of the reunification of China during the Sui and Tang dynasties (from 589 to 907 – though there was persecution of Buddhism in the late Tang, especially in 845), that Buddhism flourished and consolidated its position in China. This was a creative period not just for what was no longer a new religion, but for other schools in so far as they had to respond to the subtle ideas of the Buddhist *sūtras* and commentaries. Let us then see the shape of the three systems, the Tiantai, the Huayan and the Chan.

BEYOND THE LOTUS SŪTRA TO THE HEAVENLY TERRACE MOUNTAIN OF CHIH-K'AI (ZHI KAI)

Zhi Kai (or Zhi) lived at the time of the reunification and preached before the architect of this great event, Sui Wen-ti (Sui Wendi), first emperor of the new Sui dynasty. From 575 he moved to Tiantai (Heavenly Terrace Mountain), and it is after this that the school which effectively he founded (though two previous masters are acknowledged) is called. His massive system was designed to follow the political example and to unify Buddhism. He found a system of interpretation that not only made sense of the diversity of Buddhism but also welded together doctrine and practice, which could so easily split apart. He was active himself not only in intellectual work but practical religious accomplishments as well: he is supposed to have seen to the building of thirty-five monasteries, and to have trained over thirty advanced students; he wrote voluminously, forty-six works being attributed to him, though some are forgeries. His close relations with the dynasty were the cause of considerable patronage. Altogether he was a marvelous organizer and teacher. Some of his ideas had profound influence. He is maybe chiefly responsible for the later sense of unity in Chinese Buddhism, allowing different strands to carry on their ways. but sensing in their differing styles a united loyalty to the teaching of the Buddha himself.

The most important *sūtra* for Zhi Kai was the Lotus or Saddharmapuṇḍarīka. Here the most important concept was that of *upāya,* or the skill in means of the Buddha in adapting his teaching to the various conditions of his hearers. Zhi's chief use of this was to demarcate differing periods in the Buddha's life when he produced differing discourses with various teachings. Zhi was thus able to match the main schools based on differing *sūtras* to the various times of the Buddha's career. Just before his death he – according to Zhi – preached the Lotus, immediately before the *Mahaparinirvāṇasūtra (The Great Vehicle Sūtra of the Great Decease).* This led to the doctrine of the Five Periods.

Immediately after his enlightenment he presented the Huayan or Avataṃsaka teaching: as it were, a fresh and sudden account of his experience – but too much for most people to accept. Then he went on to the Deer Park near Banaras where he preached the Lesser Vehicle doctrines. Then later in his life he taught the Great Vehicle's glories, then the *Prajñāparamitā* doctrines. Finally he taught the last two great teachings mentioned above: because they were more or less simultaneous, they jointly count as one period. The Lotus constitutes the true Perfect Teaching and indeed contains all the others. All this was an ingenious way of subsuming all the disparate schools under one more or less coherent scheme.

In synthesizing doctrine and practice, Zhi used a new method of exegesis, which he described in a work known as the *Words and Phrases of the Lotus Sūtra.* There are four kinds of explanation of a text: one outlines the benefits of the Buddha's teaching; another deals with the place of a teaching in the total life of the Buddha, in other words, contextualizes the text in the scheme outlined above; the third deals with the question of whether a text is basic or peripheral; and the fourth deals with the kind of meditation taught in a text, either directly or by implication. In this way, Zhi is able to keep theory and practice together. The meaning of any theory in Buddhism must relate to some form of meditation.

Probably the most profound of Zhi's ideas was his improvement on the traditional Indian differentiation of truths into 'higher' and 'conventional', according to whether the ultimate emptiness is being indicated or the conventional world of plural experience. Zhi described three sorts of truths: the first is empty, that is, it deals with emptiness; the second sort is provisional; the third is middle *(chung) (zhong)*. So we have everyday truths, the second of the above; there is the ineffable truth of the empty, the first of the above; and the affirmation of everyday truths *sub specie aeternitatis* – the affirmation of both provisional and higher truth simultaneously. The universe as it stands is already identical with the absolute (emptiness). For this reason all entities already possess the Buddha-nature. This idea of the middle truth is highly characteristic of Chinese culture and of Chinese Buddhism. And from the time of Zhi Kai onwards there is scarcely anyone in Far Eastern Buddhism who does not affirm in one way or another the middle position and the universal possession of the Buddha-nature.

The Tiantai came to be influential in various ways in Chinese culture: it also, in the form of the Tendai, played a vital role in the evolution of Japanese Buddhism. Various important figures came after Zhi Kai, such as Chih-li (Zhi Li) (*b.* 960), who took part in one of the great debates of the Tiantai tradition, as to whether the focus of meditation should be the actual empirical mind of the individual, stained as it was with ignorance and defilements; or whether it should focus on the 'true mind' – the purified mind of Buddhahood. Zhi Li argued for the former, which was the orthodox position (and it is more in accord with the idea of 'middle truth': we have to seek emptiness within the flow of plural experience).

The Tiantai's ambition was to unite the differing paths, whether of the *arhat* or of the *bodhisattva* or of the lay person, whether of the Great or Lesser Vehicle, into a single path. It did not really do this, for it became in effect another denomination, but its embracing tolerance and eclecticism had their effects throughout Far Eastern Buddhism.

THE HUAYAN – A CHARACTERISTICALLY CHINESE WAY OF LOOKING AT DEPENDENCE

In the early part of the fifth century CE an important Indian text was rendered into Chinese, reflection upon which was one of the main sources of the school known as the Huayan. This phrase is the Chinese for the short version of the Sanskrit name of this text, the Avataṃsaka or 'Flower Garland'. It is a long work filled with radiant beings, *bodhisattvas,* world-systems, dancing attendance on the Buddha. It is a work of poetic myth, but it is supposed to be anchored in an actual event, namely the period immediately following his enlightenment under the Bodhi tree. In the glorious light of his absorption, with the nature of the world glorified under his knowing scrutiny, the Buddha preaches this supernatural message. This is before he repairs to the Deer Park (where he does not think it fit to preach the Huayan message because even ascetics are not ready for it as yet). It is the philosophy contained in this great discourse by the Buddha that is explicated in the Huayan system.

Its beginnings go back to the Sui dynasty, to a group of monks centered on the Chung-nan (Zhongnan) mountains south of the then capital of Sian. The third patriarch of the lineage of the Huayan school was Fa-tsang (Fa Zang) (643–712), probably the most important thinker of the school.

The chief feature of the Huayan is the positive interpretation it places on the classic Buddhist doctrine of dependent origination or *pratītyasamutpāda:* the trend among Indian Buddhist thinkers was to underline the negative – to emphasize that because of dependent origination each event or *dharma* is empty. For Huayan the universe is a universally interconnected set of *dharmas*. As the famous Huayan simile has it, it is like the jewel-net of Indra (the leading Rigvedic god). We must image a net connecting myriad jewels. Each jewel has many facets, so many indeed that it can reflect not only the rest of the net as an interconnected whole but also every other jewel in its particularity. So each *dharma* is particular, but in its particularity contains a representation of every other particular. All this was a positive picture of the meaning of dependent origination. Nothing has its 'own being' in the sense that it depends on all the others for its particular placement in the system. This grand picture completes the various insights of the other main schools which are each of them partially correct.

The Huayan in this connection evolved a fivefold scheme for looking at the other Buddhist teachings. The Lesser Vehicle taught rightly the emptiness of things, as being compound, and the selfless nature of living beings; but did not adequately represent the emptiness of the constituent *dharmas*. The root Mahāyāna taught the emptiness idea and the notion that the mind ignorantly projects reality on to the world; but it did not see the other side of the same truth, that the mind contains a deeper wisdom and insight and a deeper purity. The teaching associated with the notion of the *Tathāgatagarbha* (Womb of the Thus-come or Buddha) was right in seeing the Buddha-nature in all sentient beings, but it undervalued the events of the world which merely became signs or symbols of the underlying Buddhist truth. Those who stressed the suddenness of enlightenment and the non-conceptual nature of insight (the forerunners of classical Chan Buddhism) were right to see that language is essentially misleading and can foul up our worldview; but in their emphasis on suddenness and spontaneity tended to underplay the need for solid practice guided by teachings which are of necessity to be expressed in language. It could be an easy shortcut to a liberation which stayed at the superficial level. By contrast, the Flower Garland school had a realistic middle course with respect to the other schools. The particular is as vital as the universal; emptiness is there, but so also is reality; spontaneity is important, but so also is practice; words mislead, but we must use them; the world as it presents itself is a projection, but it is not unreal.

The image of Indra's net is meant among other things to promote the thesis that there is no obstruction between phenomena and the principles or *li* underlying them.

The interpenetration of emptiness and manifestation renders the empty manifest and the manifest empty. When one has realization of this in one's experience, and not just at the theoretical level, then one has attained *bodhi* and has entered on nirvana. Fa Zang preached before the empress in the Imperial Palace in 699, and we have a work based on this sermon, called 'The Golden Lion' – he used the gold lion in the palace as an illustration of his philosophy, comparing the gold to the *li* and the lion aspect to the phenomena *(shi)*. At the end he said:

> When one sees this lion and this gold, the two characters are annihilated, the passions do not arise, and although beauty and ugliness are manifested before the eye, the mind stays calm … This is called 'entering nirvana'.

This indicates how the philosophical position has a practical effect when taken the right way, in existential or experiential terms, and not just abstractly. In this it follows the mainstream Buddhist way.

It is clear that the more positive interpretation of dependent origination is in line with the values of Neotaoism. It also searched for a kind of monism which was compatible with a pluralism of the manifest. There is a transcendental aspect to Fa Zang's thinking which is reminiscent more of Wang Bi than of Guo Xiang. What is interesting is that the Huayan creates its organicity internally – that is, it tries to show how the universe is an organic whole by starting with the microcosm. Thus each *dharma* shares six metaphysical characteristics – universality, particularity; similarity, difference; integration and disintegration. It is argued that each of these polarities implies the other. This is the structure surrounding the idea of mutual reflection as pictured by the image of the jewel-net of Indra. This makes Huayan in some ways a subtler view than anything which the Neotaoists had hitherto produced. It also foreshadowed some of the developments within Neoconfucianism.

Taoist influence, especially at the esthetic level, can also be seen in the rise of the other great indigenous Chinese school, that of Chan. The *Daojiao* emphasized spontaneity, minimum means and a love of emptiness, and these features appeared in the formation of Chan Buddhism. This is traditionally associated with the arrival in China of Bodhidharma, supposedly in 520 CE.

CHAN BUDDHISM – BETWEEN TAOIST HARMONY AND BUDDHIST IDEALISM

Some doubt whether Bodhidharma, a wonderful figure who had great potency in later art, really existed: but his legend helps to hitch Chinese Meditation Buddhism to an Indian root – in fact it is supposed to have been conveyed by direct transmission, from person to person, from the Buddha himself. But in its more shaped form it can be said to go back to the patriarch Hui-Neng (Hui Neng) (638–713) – though naturally it has roots before that, both in the Taoist tradition, in Chinese thought and in Indian *sutras*. Among Chinese antecedents of the movement was Seng-chao (Seng Zhao) (317–420 CE), who was much attracted to and influenced by both the *Daodejing* and the *Zhuangzi,* but became a Buddhist and used Taoist ideas to fill out understanding of the *Prajñāpāramitā* tradition (the perfection of wisdom, known in China as the Three Treatises or San Lun tradition). Four of his essays were gathered together in the *Chao lun (Zhaolun)* or Treatises of Chao (Zhao), and were influential. Another vital forerunner was Tao-sheng (Dao Sheng) (360–434 CE). According to him, the seventh stage of the Bodhisattva path, usually considered crucial (since then, after gaining non-dual insight the Bodhisattva can no longer 'fall away', though he postpones enlightenment of course until all other beings are saved), must involve sudden enlightenment. The underlying Absolute is permanent, indivisible and without any qualification at all: non-dual insight into it must be of exactly the same nature – unqualified, all-embracing, radical; and sudden in its onset, not a gradual construction built upon previous experience; but rather a radical turning.

We may note that from here on in the Buddhist tradition there is a division between what are sometimes called 'subitists' (advocates of the idea of sudden enlightenment, from a word meaning sudden, familiar in Italy: *subito*) and 'gradualists'. This division found its way into Chan itself; but it also divides the other philosophies of China. The Confucian path is usually seen as gradualist: it has to do with a gradual build-up of education and moral refinement whereby the superior person becomes a *junzi*. But Taoism favors the subitist theory. Thus Tao-sheng (Dao Sheng) drew on Taoist sources in interpreting the central Buddhist notions. The belief in the suddenness and ineffability of the experience of the Tao or of the higher truth is typically Taoist and could well be given a Buddhist dressing. So we see forerunners of the teaching which Bodhidharma is supposed to have brought from India. He was, according to the art, a fierce-looking character, an eccentric, highly forthright. He is reputed to have told the Chinese emperor Wudi, founder of the Liang dynasty, that there is nothing holy or meritorious in pious deeds such as the erecting of temples or the recitation of *sūtras*. At one level Chan is against importance being attached to ritual. Bodhidharma, however, amazed the faithful by sitting for nine years gazing at a wall, a form of meditation which led, legend has it, to his legs falling off.

At any rate the message which developed, whether it was brought by Bodhidharma or not, was summed up in a famous poem of four lines, as follows:

A special tradition outside of the scriptures;
No depending on words or letters;
Direct pointing to the human heart;
Seeing into one's own nature and gaining Buddhahood.

In other words, what was being thought through was a purely experiential form of Buddhism, which did away with the elaborations of doctrine, rituals, merit-working, and other paraphernalia of the religion. But if the Truth was something which could only be experienced and could not be described, how could it be conveyed? Was not experience something which was individual and in some sense private? What of loyalty to the Buddha and to the tradition? Part of the answer to these questions lay in Chan's emphasizing the role of the master or 'teacher' who passed on the experience to the pupil, who alone could stimulate it and recognize it. Since it was supposedly sudden and spontaneous, the only tests could consist in the judgment of persons: and it was in the master–pupil relationship that Chan sought its continuity.

Despite the apparent repudiation of scripture, some texts were important to the budding movement. The traditional Indian *sūtras* of greatest importance were the *Lankāvatāra Sūtra* and the Diamond Sutra of the *Prajñāparamitā* literature. The former is a long and complex work which takes its name ('Descent on Lanka') from the idea that the Buddha preached the discourse there, having been invited by Ravana the king of the demons (who is an important figure in the Indian epic the *Ramāyana,* by the way). Its basic metaphysical idea is that nothing but thought exists in the cosmos. There are eight kinds of consciousness, the Store Consciousness or absolute mind (as the Westerner might say), the six senses and *manas* or 'common sense', the imaginative and synthetic function. But basically these last seven amount to waves in the ocean of absolute consciousness. This idealism was mainstream Mahāyāna, but it had a feature of crucial importance to the Chinese tradition. The absolute mind was identified with the *Tathāgatagarbha* and with the Buddha-nature.

Together with the idea of the projective character of the plural world of phenomena, the Chan movement fostered a radically critical view of language. Here elements of the Mādhyamaka dialectic were important. But the attack on language carried on through language took a poetic form in Chan. There was the attempt somehow to express by oblique and esthetic modes a sense of the immediacy of experience and of sudden enlightenment. Crucial to these developments was the life of Hui Neng, the sixth patriarch, who is a seminal figure in what became the Southern school. For in 732 the Chan movement divided: the Southern school was subitist, the Northern gradualist. Before Hui Neng, the fifth patriarch or leader of the movement (which had become monastic, though it had originated in wandering monks), had groomed his disciple to become patriarch. There was a contest between him and the relatively illiterate Hui Neng, who worked in the granary at the monastery. Shen Xiu's verse was a fine four-liner:

The body is the bodhi tree;
The mind is a clear mirror;
Take care to keep it always clean:
Allow not a speck of dust on it.

But Hui Neng's spontaneous rejoinder seemed to the other monks even better:

> Originally there is no bodhi tree;
> Nor is there a stand with a clear mirror;
> From the beginning not a single thing exists:
> What then is a speck of dust to cling to?

The book which is attributed to Hui Neng is called the *Sūtra of the Sixth Patriarch* – the only work of Chinese provenance given the exalted title of *sūtra,* which is normally given to a discourse which is attributed to the Buddha himself (but if all distinctions are in the long run projective then so is the difference between the Buddha and Hui Neng!). The book is a compilation, and we do not know with any precision what Hui Neng's own teachings really were. But the wisdom is expressed in negative terms, such as 'no mind'. The non-dual insight is in being non-dual a kind of merging (to put it in our, earthly, terms) with the ultimate, which is the same as the Buddha-nature: but neither the insight nor the absolute are to be described and so are better treated by a sort of *via negativa*. It is because of this that the Southern school came to adopt the technique of the *kung-an* (*kongan*) or 'public document'. A vital figure in the formulation of this method was Lin-chi (Linji) (who died in 867 CE), after whom the Southern school is named (actually there were five lineages at one time, but effectively that of Linji came to be the norm in the Southern school).

He was formative in that many of his interactions with his students in which he explored techniques of spontaneity are recorded. Among other methods he used a sudden shout with which to interrupt trains of thought, to shake a student up, and so on. His view was that special means of training are needed because the non-attachment which brings freedom is something applying as much to intellectual and spiritual commitments as it does to material and emotional ones. Greed can be found in ideas and teachings as well as in food and drink. The shout and the *kongan,* a kind of riddle, are designed to flummox the intellect, so that we are rid of conceptual overlays on our original experience. So such famous riddles as 'What is the sound of one hand clapping?' are a kind of conceptual torment through which the student learns to go beyond concepts.

The trouble with both shout and riddle is that they get to be standard ways of teaching, and the result is stereotyped behavior. It is necessary to be continuously vigilant if the true spontaneity of Chan is to be retained. The most important collection of riddles was put together in the eleventh century CE by Yuan-wu K'o-ch'in (1063–1135), but his disciple and successor had the copies of the work burned. Some copies did, however, survive, on which a later edition was based. But the story reveals how dangerous from a Chan point of view it was to have records of *kongan*.

The Chan school had immense influence in both Korea and Japan, and had effects on the Neo-Confucian tradition in later Chinese thought. Its blending of esthetic themes from the *Daojiao* tradition with those of Buddhism gives it a central place in thinking about Chinese painting. Thus in the middle of the thirteenth century we have the work of the famous Muchi (Muji) and Ying Yü-chien (Ying Yujian), which was dramatic: the spontaneous use of ink was an exciting exhibition of the meaning of spontaneity.

There is of course a question of how far the paradoxes of Chan can be sustained. If we wish to transcend all concepts, how can we really communicate such teachings as that of the Buddha-nature? The Chan thinkers were happy to be iconoclastic even about the Buddha's own teaching. But ultimately there is the question: if there is nothing ultimately to be said, why attach this silence to one tradition rather than to another? Why attach this silence to one practice rather than another? The practice of being a Chan monk is pretty severe, after all. Chan therefore had to give positive meaning to the transcending of all concepts. Part of that meaning was to be found in absolutely fresh harmony with nature: experiencing the environment directly and then seeing it as ripples on the surface of the Buddha-nature. The experiencing of nature was a Taoist theme: and the whole flavor of Chan is partly Taoist and partly Buddhist, and is therefore a Chinese creation.

TANG DYNASTY BUDDHISM AND THE PERSECUTION OF 845

The Tang Dynasty was for the first part a period of great patronage for Buddhism which flourished in various forms already mentioned. As we have seen, the Tiantai, the Huayan and Chan were indigenously constructed forms of Buddhism and correspondingly attractive and influential. Also of high popularity was Pure Land Buddhism with its strong devotionalism. Even in the types of Buddhism whose metaphysics were rather impersonalist there was room for a personal representation of the ultimate, since the higher truth was mediated by some Buddha or other, and so that Buddha could stand for the Absolute or the Nothing. So Buddhism was suffused by devotionalism as well as with a strict thinking and austere methods of contemplation. The Pure Land in effect substituted the hope of heaven (the Pure Land) for that of Nirvana: but even here, in theory heaven was merely a propitious place for human beings to graduate to final liberation. Nirvana lay, as it were, at the other end of heaven. To a greater or lesser degree it was possible for this very rich religion to blend in with religious Taoism and with the Confucian and folk heritages. But there were jealousies. Confucian practice and theory revived in the ninth century, and Taoist functionaries were gaining influence at court. The inevitable backlash occurred. Buddhism's golden period came to an abrupt end, for the time being, with the persecution of 845. Over 40,000 temples were closed or destroyed; and over a quarter of a million monks and nuns were compelled to disrobe and go back to lay life. These events had a profound effect on Buddhism's wealth, and though it later recovered somewhat from these events, it tended to have a simpler form.

As it happened, Chan, with its emphasis on the lay life and austere esthetics, was best able to adapt to the new less luxuriant conditions. Pure Land could also flourish, with its wide roots among the masses.

CONFUCIAN REVIVAL: GOVERNMENT, PRINTING, CITIES, ACADEMIES, THOUGHT

Though the traditions of Kong carried on through the early Sui-Tang period, it was towards the end and during the subsequent Five Dynasties time (tenth century) that its strength began to reappear. The effects of Buddhism and to some degree Taoist thought had been debilitating. Although the achievements of the early philosophers had been impressive, it would not be hard to see how Buddhism, though foreign, had a depth of metaphysical subtlety that made it the leading intellectual force for a time in China. The *Rujiao* achievements of the Sui-Tang period were rather feeble, until towards the end, when there was some revival through the thought of Han-Yü (Han Yu) (768–829) and Li Ao (flourished about 800 CE). The former refined Mengzi's theory of the goodness of human nature through a compromise in which he described three grades of human nature, according to whether a person possesses all five virtues or not (namely the virtues *ren, li, yi, zhi* and *xin* – humaneness, propriety in behavior, righteousness, wisdom and faithfulness). Li Ao had been influenced by Chan thought, and argued for spontaneity. But Han Yu was fiercely anti-Buddhist and anti-Taoist. In a famous essay he attacked Laozi, arguing that he did not pay attention to humaneness and justice, and so helped to diminish natural principles of human relations. In other words, the *Daojiao* was antisocial, as indeed was Buddhism, both because of its otherworldliness and because its attempt to go beyond concepts involved it in going beyond moral behavior (and so undermining morality as well as humanity).

But Confucian scholarship was solidifying. The use of the classics in the imperial examinations and the reduction in patronage of the other two religions helped to restore Confucianism to its role as official ideology of the State. The wider use of printing gave new impetus to traditional scholarship. The increased urbanization may have helped too in the restoration of Confucian fortunes. Scholars could more easily meet, and out of this there arose the various academies which fostered scholarship and matched some of the monastic schools which anchored Buddhist (and in some degree Taoist) learning. All these were a factor in restimulating Confucian thinking. When the great revival came it was in the form of what is generally known as Neoconfucianism, especially in the Song Dynasty (tenth to twelfth centuries).

There was a weakness in traditional Confucianism, and that was its great concentration on matters of ethics and politics. This meant that its metaphysical side was rather rudimentary. On the other hand, the new Taoist philosophers paid a lot of attention to the mysterious side of the universe and in probing the cosmic secrets evolved doctrines which seemed impressive. The Configurations of the Indian schools were highly metaphysical, and must have seemed especially so to Chinese scholars. At the same time the ethos of Buddhism did not appeal. It was necessary, to combat it effectively, to adopt intellectual weapons on a par with its complexity. But there were other motivations too of the great revival of Confucianism which is known as Neoconfucianism.

NEOCONFUCIANISM OR THE LEARNING OF PRINCIPLE

The very name 'Neoconfucianism' is of course a Western invention. The movement is known differently in Chinese. It is sometimes spoken of as the *hsing-li-hsüeh (xinglixue)* or learning of nature and principle. Sometimes it is called the *Sung-Ming-li-hsüeh (Song-minglixue)* or learning of principle in the Song and Ming dynasties (that is, from the tenth to the seventeenth centuries). Most simply it is called the 'learning of principle'. All this implies that the key notion in the various systems of thought gathered together under this rubric is that of *li* or principle. This is a different character from *li* meaning proper behavior, etiquette, etc. The one *li* dominated early *rujiao*; the other later *rujiao*.

Probably the most important early figure in the revival was Chou Tun-i (Zhou Dunyi) (1017–73). He was thought by Chu Hsi (Zhu Xi) (1130–1200) who was chief formulator of mainstream Neoconfucian philosophy to be the founder of the new lineage of thinkers in the tradition of the Learning of Principle. Zhou elaborated an impressive cosmology which was based on a traditional diagram which he probably got from a Taoist priest and which had been used in a quasi-magical way by adherents of Taoism to pursue immortality. But Zhou Dunyi took it and used it as a sketch of a metaphysical theory which delineated the relationships in the universe.

The diagram has at its apex the Great Ultimate or *t'ai-chi (taiji)*. Yet the very first sentence of Zhou's famous book *T'ai-chi t'u-shuo (Taijitushuo)* or *Explanation of the Great Ultimate* starts: 'The Non-Ultimate! And also the Great Ultimate.' The phrase here translated as 'Non-Ultimate' is *wu-chi (wuji)*. This is the same negative, the *wu* or Nothing, which figured so much in Neotaoism. Some have seen a strong Taoist influence here in Zhou's thought. Some influence cannot be denied, as the provenance of the diagram indicates: but we may note that Zhou wants to affirm both sides – the being and non-being of the Ultimate. He captures for the Confucian tradition both the positive ground of the cosmos and that negative ground which figures so largely in Buddhism and Taoism. This positive and negative possesses both dynamism and passivity. From the one proceeds the yang principle and from the other the yin. It is also the source of the five phases or elements, the processes known as fire, water, wood, metal and earth. These processes in turn give rise to the 'ten thousand' things, that is the myriad particulars in the universe. Zhou also makes use of ideas drawn from the

Yijing relating to the *ch'ien (qian)* or heavenly principle and the *k'un (kun)* or earthly principle, themselves reflecting the male–female polarity. But though Zhou describes modes of evolution out of the Great Ultimate and wields various distinctions, he also sees the whole as an organic unity. Humanity is important in the scheme of things because it possesses the five processes in their most refined form and can exhibit the five virtues. There is a potential harmony between humans and nature of a profound kind, which the sage ought to cultivate by desirelessness and peaceful behavior. There is obviously much in all this that harmonizes well with the Taoist cosmology and ethos. It is Zhou's achievement to have produced a schema which could incorporate so much of the Buddhist and Taoist key concepts: in this way he bids to make the *rujiao* the fundamental and all-embracing philosophy (though Zhu Xi thought that in his ethics he went too far in a Taoist direction).

Shao Yung (Shao Yong) (1011–77) also used the *Yijing* to advantage, and struck on the notion that number is the key to cosmology. The *Yijing* says that the Great Ultimate gives rise to four forms of yin and yang (each seen in a major and minor phase), and these four in turn serve to bring about the eight hexagrams which are used in *Yijing* divination. So it was from this that he took the number four as crucial, and so classified everything into four kinds (for instance, four kinds of living forms, namely animals, birds, grasses and other plants). He was, despite this bias in favor of four, relatively empirical and thought that processes in the world were well organized and predictable. They should be examined on their own terms. Unlike many Confucians he was not much interested in history and where he does discuss it, he is overeager to see repetition and pattern. He was, connectedly, little concerned with politics, but fascinated by trying to reach an orderly view of how the cosmos actually works. Other scholars of the Learning of Principle tendency were highly critical of his pure naturalism.

A third important figure in the early Neoconfucian movement was Chang Tsai (Zhang Zai) (1020–77) who clearly expressed an important polarity, that between substance and function, which was later a vital ingredient in the Learning of Principle. He also emphasized the centrality of the idea of material force or *ch'i (qi)*. This is operative through the polar forms of yin and yang, which are not really separate. Indeed, they are one with the Great Ultimate. In its original form it is of the nature of substance *(t'i) (ti)*: as it manifests itself by a process of condensation (*qi* or material force means 'steam' and has the suggestion of a kind of ether), it takes on the role of function *(yung) (yong)*. Through the pulsations of the material force through the yin and yang and the five processes or elements, the universe proceeds in overall rhythmic harmony. Like Zhou Dunyi he has also a negative description of the Great Ultimate as the Great Empty *(t'ai-hsü) (taixu)*.

All this might at first sight seem to be a form of materialism, and sometimes Zhang has been seen in this way. But rather he was striving for a qualitative monism – that is, a theory which would unite the cosmos as to its composition, so that everything could be explained ultimately by one sort of thing. In this case it is *qi* or material force (perhaps 'vital force' might be a better way of putting it). So Zhang could say that the spirits (gods and demons, that is, positive and negative spirits) are also made of *qi*. But his view is not that of a reductive or rationalist materialist in the ordinary sense. Thus he sees Heaven as emanating from the Great Empty, and the Tao in the mode in which *qi* changes itself, and so the nature or *hsing (xing)* of things and living beings. A highly refined form of vital force is consciousness, which forms, when united with nature, the mind.

Zhang Zai was critical of both Buddhists and Taoists. The former he accused of subjectivism, based on a lack of understanding that the Great Empty is manifested by nature which operates according to certain necessities according to the laws of yin and yang. They operate according to the principle that existence comes from non-existence, and this cannot be. Moreover, in seeking a return to the ultimate they seek non-existence; while the Taoists in their alchemical frenzies seek individual eternity. But the nature of things is to consolidate and then disintegrate, returning to the *Taixu*. The sage knows this and hits the mean between the extremes represented by the other schools.

There is a strong spiritual and ethical sense permeating Zhang Zai's thought which is well brought out in a text which he had inscribed on the Western window of his study, the so-called 'Western Inscription' or *Hsi-ming (Ximing)*. It is an excerpt from a larger work. It is a moving passage, and shows Zhang's humaneness and lofty spirit in a poetic way. It begins:

Heaven is my father and earth my mother, and even such a small being as I finds an intimate place in their midst. So that which extends through the cosmos I look on as my body and that which directs the universe I look on as my nature. All people are my brothers and sisters, and all things are my companions.

Later on he writes, in the same text:

Wealth, honor, blessing and benefit are meant for the enrichment of my life, while poverty, humble station, care and sorrow will be my helpmates to fulfillment. In life I follow and serve. In death I shall be at peace.

Zhang Zai derived from his monism this ethic of universalism. We all, as it were, flow into one another, and all humans are the object of my *ren*. In substance, we are all one: but we have differing functions and stations in life. Zhang was able to combine a Moist universalism with the traditional more hierarchical view of society associated with the Kong tradition.

Also important in his thought was the figure of the sage *(sheng)*. Because he has knowledge of the way things are, he is able to 'form one body with the universe'. It is this which inspires his noble vision of peaceful death quoted above. In harmonizing with the rhythms of the world as it presents itself, he acts differently from the Buddhist saint or the Taoist. Either metaphysically or socially they flee the world as it is. This does not of course mean that Zhang adopts an uncritical posture: he is a powerful critic of those who do not see all people as their sisters and brothers, and is a critic of the bad ruler and the careless administration. But he is at one with the social as well as the natural world and flees from neither. The ideal of the sage comes increasingly to occupy the attention of Neoconfucian thinkers.

Another major contribution made by Zhang Zai was that he was the teacher of the two Cheng brothers, who were crucial to the development of the concept of principle which was to give the whole movement its flavor and name.

THE CHENG BROTHERS AND THE IDEA OF *LI* OR PRINCIPLE

The two brothers, Ch'eng Hao (Cheng Hao) (1032–85) and Ch'eng I (Cheng Yi) (1033–1107) were in fact nephews of Zhang Zai, and also studied with Zhou Dunyi. They conceived of principle in a new way. It is not just that each thing has its principle, i.e. its constitutive essence, or something like a Platonic Form; but all principle is one and is all-pervasive. All particular principles manifest the one principle which is the principle of Heaven *(t'ien-li) (tianli)*. They went a step further and saw principle as the same as the human mind or nature *(xing)*. This slogan that nature is principle became important in the later unfolding of the Learning of Principle. The identification of inner and outer affected the way they saw the investigation of things, which became the primary methodological quest of the Neoconfucians. Thus Cheng Hao could write that the ways to investigate things include discussing and reading about truth and principles; talking about people and events of the past and distinguishing which are good and which are bad; and through handling affairs. (So there was not a strong empirical strand in Cheng Hao's thinking.)

Cheng Yi began the process of making a relatively sharp distinction between principle and material force, between *li* and *qi*. Some thought that this made him a dualist. But at any rate the general theory of the universe held that each thing has two sides to it – *li* as form and *qi* as matter.

The brothers, in identifying the mind somehow with *li*, were much on the side of Mengzi. The original goodness and clarity of human nature get overlaid with selfishness and other forces which Cheng Hao identifies with turbid material or *qi*. In principle everyone can be changed: and the sage is himself an example to other people. Cheng Yi sought to unify ethics by seeing *ren* as the basic seed of other virtues. There was thus a strong egalitarian motif underlying his moral teachings, for it was not merely that every person's nature is good but humane and benevolent behavior towards all human beings was the essence of virtue. In dealing with self-cultivation, both brothers placed a lot of emphasis on the virtues of seriousness *(ching) (jing)* and sincerity *(ch'eng) (cheng)*. The latter was a highly important ingredient in Confucian morals to counterbalance the possible formalism of *li* or proper behavior and the outer adherence to rituals.

In all the foregoing developments key ideas were coming together waiting to be synthesized – and the major task here was performed by perhaps the greatest of Chinese philosophers, namely Zhu Xi (1130–1200). The elements that were assembling were as follows: the theory of the Great Ultimate; the dialectical interplay between negative and positive; the contrast between *li* as principle and *qi* as material or vital force; the task of *ko-wu (gewu),* namely the investigation of things; the role of the sage or *sheng*; the ideal of 'forming one body with the universe'; the underlying centrality of *ren*; the importance of *cheng* or sincerity; and the rhythms of the universe as represented by such traditional notions as *yin* and *yang*. Most of these were fertile ideas. They in some measure also embraced values or posed countervalues meaningful to the Buddhist and Taoist rivals to the new *li-hsüeh (lixue)* or Learning of Principle.

For instance, there is considerable emphasis among some of the foregoing thinkers on the negative side of the Great Ultimate. This corresponded to the *śūnya* or Empty of the Mahāyāna Buddhists. The match between the mind of the human being and the ultimate had many echoes too in Buddhism, and took a suitable midpoint as its stance, between absolute idealism and realist materialism. The idea that the sage conforms to the flow of manifest things had its *Daojiao* affinities. But it did not imply either revolt from or withdrawal from the world, including the social world. The new emphasis in the Neoconfucian perspective of the *sheng* or sage is interesting. Cheng Hao, for instance, thought that the sage exhibits a sort of transcendental quality of *shen*. *Shen* means god or spirit. The naturalist streak in the new thinking saw in gods and demons special manifestations of *qi,* and not a special transmundane sort of entity. There were no essential breaks in the unity of the cosmos. But *shen* exudes, so to speak, a special quality, something like holiness. Indeed, the idea of the *sheng* does already include a quality of the awe-inspiring or saintly, a kind of mysterious power and goodness. This is emphasized in Cheng Hao's thought. So the sage in his own way becomes a religious figure, and so can serve as a counter to the other ideals of holiness found in Buddhist and Taoist monasticism. Though there are obvious rationalist elements in Neoconfucianism, there is also a strong spiritual or religious side to it, and this is best summed up in the ideal of the *sheng*.

But the *sheng* is rather different from the saintly or charismatic figures of other religions. He plays his part in the world, and is involved in administrative or political affairs. At the same time he is a cultivated person who has a deep knowledge of history and literature and the *Rujiao*. It is an attractive ideal, for it depicts a holiness which is engaged with both the affairs and the values of the civilization which helped to create the ideal. (In modern times there is such a tendency to specialization of function that we tolerate politicians who are ignorant and conscienceless, often enough.)

CHU HSI (ZHU XI), THE GREAT SYNTHESIZER OF THE LEARNING OF PRINCIPLE

Zhu Xi passed the imperial civil service examination at the age of 18, and served for seven years in Fukien province; after a break of fourteen years he became a regional prefect in Nan-k'ang in Kiangsi province. For a brief period he was at the imperial court. His activities included the creation of granaries to protect against famine and reviving education through the re-establishment of Confucian academies. These practical points are worth mentioning because like other Neoconfucians Zhu Xi sought to unite theory and practice in public affairs. He was ever disturbed by the state of the empire in his time: the northern area was partly under the control of a foreign power (the Chin).

His philosophy became normative. His commentary on the Four Books (the *Ta-hsüeh (Daxue)* or *Great Learning*; the *Chung-yung (Zhongyong)* or *Doctrine of the Mean*; the *Lun-yü* or *Analects*; and the *Mencius (Mengzi)*) was to be part of the curriculum of the imperial examinations down to the time they were abolished in 1905. But during his lifetime he was in disfavor, partly because of his constant desire that the imperial court should be reminded of the need for moral reform.

Zhu Xi identified the realm of *li* with the Great Ultimate, which is both the sum of all the principles and the one principle lying within all principles. The Ultimate is the root creative force, but it is not in itself changeable: it lies beyond the dynamic interchange of the yin and the yang. It is not itself subject to activity or tranquility, but it contains within itself the principles which give rise to these manifestations. Since the creative process is forever throwing up new phenomena, there have to be new principles emerging from the infinite store of principles in the Great Ultimate. The Ultimate itself is not restricted as to space and time, and is in itself eternal and changeless. But it exists not as something absolute by itself, but is always in co-ordination with its manifestation through *qi*. Without that the principles would have nothing to be embedded in. In theory, principle would carry on even after the dissolution of the cosmos: but in fact the existence of a cosmos seems a necessary adjunct to the Great Ultimate in Zhu Xi's scheme. There is, though, a sense in which in his treatment the Great Ultimate is transcendent. But at the same time it works within everything, especially within the human mind. It is there working in every instance of a principle in the apparent flux of vital force or *qi*. The mind of humans is composed of very refined *qi* which makes it luminous to principles. In all this Zhu Xi emphasizes the difference between *li* and *qi* as well as their mutual necessity.

While *li* is unchanging and good, material force is corporeal, shifting, individual, destructible, and can be both good and evil. It needs principle for its forms; while principle needs material force for its embodiment. There was a danger in this kind of distinction, since Zhu Xi could be criticized as over-idealizing principle and by contrast denigrating material force. Was he after all so far from the Buddhists?

Because the Great Ultimate considered in itself is not to be defined as either active or tranquil (and by implication does not carry any other predicates), Zhu Xi defends Zhou Dunyi's reference to it as the Non-Ultimate; but the tenor of his discourse is overwhelmingly positive and so has a very different flavor from Taoist speculation about the Tao. There is a naturalist aspect of his thinking which suggests certain features of physical cosmology: so he thinks that at the outset of the cosmic process the circular movement of the yin and the yang caused the sedimentary part of the material force to coalesce in the center, so forming the earth; while the lighter parts swirled round to form the sky, which continues in perpetual circular motion. This indicates that his system is in broad terms naturalistic.

But the fact that the Great Ultimate has its transcendent aspect combines with his view of the natural affinity of the *xin* or mind to the Ultimate to drive a wedge into his universe. Thus he thinks of the human being's original mind as being the *Tao-hsin (Daoxin)* or 'mind of the Tao', being imprinted with pure principle and with *ren* or humanheartedness as the seed of all the virtues. This original nature of the human is distinguished from the 'human mind' *(renxin),* which is embodied in material force and contains turbid elements causing a person to be selfish. So Zhu Xi argues for the development of the mind of Heaven and the correction of the human mind. It is as if the transcendental mind shines through once the turbid mind has been clarified.

Strenuous effort is needed to cultivate the human mind, and Zhu Xi advised both study and 'quiet sitting' (meditation), seriousness in self-training combined with the effort to investigate things. Such investigation could deal with moral concepts as well as material things and should proceed systematically. Since a principle would be present in each instance of a species it was not necessary to do a wide range of inductive investigations: it was enough to deal thoroughly with an instance of a *li*. Thus it was that Zhu Xi's methods involved both introspective exploration and outer investigations.

Apart from his philosophical work, Zhu Xi was much concerned with re-establishing Confucian orthodoxy: his account of the lineage of teachers, coming in more recent times through Zhou Dunyi and the brothers Cheng, became officially recognized. He was very loyal to Kong himself, starting every day with an offering of incense before his portrait. He was punctilious and sincere in the performance of rituals, and was conventionally most pious.

His chief rival was Lu Hsiang-shan (Lu Xiangshan) (1139–93) who took a more idealist position. His views have come to be called the *hsin-hsüeh (xinxue)*, the Learning of Mind. The two scholars met in two famous debates at Goose Lake Monastery in Jiangxi province. Lu did not accept the distinction made between the transcendental mind or mind of Heaven and the human mind. He held to an extreme application of Mengzi's doctrine of the goodness of human nature and therefore of the human mind. Lu was critical of the conservative aspects of Zhu's educational philosophy, complaining that he paid too much attention to texts, commentaries and rituals, and too little attention to the cultivation of one's own moral nature. Zhu thought that Lu's position was optimistic in thinking that one could rely on one's own insights in order to gain an objective moral position. Lu's firm commitment to the thesis that 'the universe is my mind and my mind is the universe' led him to see the classics in effect as footnotes to the process of true self-discovery. His position has some analogy to the idea of pointing directly at the original mind, in Chan Buddhism. It is doubtful whether his viewpoint is correctly described as subjective idealism, a claim sometimes advanced by Western commentators. The point he wished to underline is that the principle or mind underlying the cosmos cannot be dualistically separated from the mind found in each one of us. In some ways his views are reminiscent of the *bhedābhedvāda* tradition in India. At any rate, while he was traditional in favoring Confucian learning, his standpoint was a good deal less conservative than that of the great synthesizer Zhu Xi. Zhu Xi had of course distinguished between the transcendental, moral mind and the human mind in order to explain evil in the universe. Lu's explanation was that it was merely because humans did not think that they conceal from themselves the truth: again, this has something of an Indian ring to it – the cause of our problems is ignorance, the root of all evil.

It will be seen from the foregoing that the Neoconfucian scholars were much concerned with cosmology and an analysis of the nature of the universe. Its emphases on the sage and moral self-cultivation flowed from the relevant worldviews they cultivated. Their more metaphysical interests, as we have seen, owed a lot to the need to take on the more elaborate Buddhist schools. And to some extent they were influenced in their practical ideas by Buddhist methods of meditation.

TAOISM AS A RELIGION: MEDITATION, MONASTICISM, CELESTIAL HIERARCHY, ALCHEMY, ANARCHISM

It was in the period of the Tang dynasty and later that Taoism's various strands came together in a form recognizable as being like modern Taoist religion. The increased emphasis on meditation itself helped to encourage the formation of Buddhist monasticism, more or less on the model of Buddhism. Many techniques of inner visualization were used by Taoist adepts. Important in these developments was Wang-che (Wangche) (1112–70), whose methods were not dissimilar to those of Chan. Taoist monasticism ran in parallel to the dispersal through the rural communities of China of Taoist priests, concerned with rituals directed at a celestial hierarchy of gods, presided over by the Jade Emperor, and including heavenly immortals such as a deified Laozi. Meanwhile, another strand of Taoist thinking and practice was the whole enterprise of alchemy, including the use of complex formulas which would, if ingested, help to promote immortality. At the same time Taoist techniques and popular myths incorporated many messianic elements, and this gave the religion a rebellious dynamic. The canon of Taoist scriptures was not, however, assembled in final form until 1445, when it was printed under imperial auspices. It includes a huge variety of material, ranging from the *Daodejing* to alchemical works, and such messianic books as the *T'ai-p'ing ching (Taipingjing)* or *Classic of the Great Peace*. This preoccupation with a visionary and utopian future was a vital lever of emotions in times of economic crisis and peasant uprisings.

THE PENDULUM SWINGS AGAIN: WANG YANG-MING (WANG YANGMING) IN OPPOSITION TO THE ZHU XI TRADITION

The Mongol or Yūan (Yuan) dynasty from 1280 to 1368 was relatively tolerant, first favoring Taoism and then Buddhism, and using Neoconfucian ideology. But it was in the succeeding dynasty, the Ming, that the last great flowering of the *rujiao* took place – a flowering associated with the name of Wang Yangming (1472–1529).

Wang was raised on the Yangtze River delta, where he had much pressure put on him to excel at learning and in the examinations, as his father before him had done. But he was somewhat rebellious and only passed the examination at the third go. He is supposed to have told a teacher that there was something more vital than book learning and that is learning how to become a sage. He dabbled in Buddhist philosophy, Taoist prescriptions on how to attain long life, military history, etc. But his main drive was towards understanding the *rujiao*. Impressed by Zhu Xi's prescription to investigate things, he spent seven days sitting in front of a grove of bamboo trying to see the principle inherent in it and in this way to acquire personal knowledge through the inquiry into outer things. But his attempt proved to be sterile: and this led him into skepticism about Zhu's system. Something much more direct was called for and he turned to a fresh and introspective inquiry into his own true self.

During his official duties he was critical once of a powerful eunuch. The Emperor, incensed, had him flogged and banished to a small and remote post in the mountains of Kweichow (Guizhou) province. This turned out to be a blessing in disguise for while he was there he experienced enlightenment and a breakthrough in his thinking.

There were some affinities between Wang's thought and those of Cheng Hao and Xiangshan. Thus he argued for the solidarity between the individual and the universe. He saw the unity between Heaven, earth and the myriad things, on the one hand, and the sage on the other. But a small-minded person shrinks into himself and cuts himself off from the cosmos of which he or she is part. So we 'form one body with Heaven'. In this he was in line with the thought of Cheng Hao. From Lu he derived the thought that the human mind and principle are the same. All principles are contained in the mind of the human being which is also the mind of Heaven. It follows that through the knowledge – the good or ethical knowledge – which is innate in us, it is possible to understand the inner nature of the universe. Through exploring inwards, partly through study but more intensely through quiet sitting (here Wang echoes the meditative methods of the Buddhism and Taoism which had attracted him when he was young), one can gain insight into the principles governing life. The innate knowledge which could be found within had a profound role in his thinking. It was not just a clear consciousness of the mind, but it was also its original substance. It was the equilibrium or balance before the passions are aroused, and it was the principle of Heaven and the very spirit of creation. Like Buddhist thinkers, Wang had a notion of the non-dual relation between pure consciousness and the Absolute. And because this original principle is present in each one of us, we can all become sages (there are echoes of the notion of the Buddha-nature here).

But knowledge goes with action. The contemplative introspection which reveals the interior principles also throws light on the virtues. It is from it that we have an insight into them. But it is not enough to have a merely experiential intuition. We must practice a given virtue to understand it (just as we have to experience pain to know what pain is). So in order to understand filial piety one needs to behave in a certain way towards one's parents, etc.

There are various consequences of this point of view. One is to give an account which, while rejecting Zhu Xi's emphasis on the outer investigation of things, nevertheless makes sense of how it is that Zhu came to be mistaken in his understanding. The knowledge of filial piety has to proceed from inside: but it does have two outer characteristics. One is that it is of its nature directed towards other people in society. Our innate knowledge proceeds with the recognition that we exist in the wider society including the whole cosmos. Second, in order to have practical understanding, the individual has to act outwardly. But the direction is inward to outward, and not a dualistic mishmash of outer knowledge and inner insights.

An interesting sidelight on Wang's notion of forming one body with the cosmos is that he posits a sense of fellow feeling with the non-animal world. Thus in his *Inquiry into the Great Learning* of 1527 he writes:

> [W]hen he sees a child about to fall into a well he cannot help having a feeling of alarm and compassion. This shows that his humaneness *(ren)* forms one body with the child. It may be objected that the child belongs to the same species as he does. Yet when he observes the pitiful cries and frightened behavior of birds and animals he cannot help feeling an 'inability to bear' their suffering. This shows that his humaneness forms one body with birds and animals. It may be objected that birds and animals are sentient beings. But when he sees plants broken and destroyed he cannot help a feeling of pity … Even when he sees tiles and stones shattered and crushed he cannot help a feeling of regret.

Another important aspect of Wang's philosophy was his espousal of 'the extension of the innate knowledge of the good'. He gave a dynamic interpretation to the notion of learning from the innate heavenly *li*. This in part followed from his practical development of knowledge cited above: but it came too from his vision that in sharing a primordial consciousness all humans are alike capable of attaining sagehood. The eliciting of the meaning of our nature results in our being pointed onwards to the summit of human excellence. We extend our instincts to become a sage. Sageliness is, as it were, built in to us: it is quite a natural thing.

AFTER WANG YANGMING: A SWING TOWARDS THE PRACTICAL AND EMPIRICAL

Wang Yangming's philosophy gave Confucianism something of the religious and psychological power of Buddhism. But perhaps inevitably there came to be some reaction against the metaphysical sides both of Zhu and Wang. Thus Ku Yen-wu (Gu Yanwu) (1613–82) and Tai Chen (Dai Zhen) (1723–77) moved away from the speculative mode to arguing that knowledge has to be gained by the pursuit of empirical and practical learning. Ku was a remarkable textual critic who brought in new and realistic methods of hermeneutics, to get at the original meanings of the Classics. He also used empirical methods with regard to water management, geography, etc. Dai Zhen argued for a materialist view of the universe in which everything can be explained in terms of orderly patterns in material force or *qi*.

Such criticisms of the grander modes of speculation did prepare the way for a positive appreciation of the achievements of Western science during the modern, colonial period. But we shall move to consideration of that in a later chapter. Meanwhile it is worth glancing back at some of the main themes of Chinese philosophy in the Early, Classical and Postclassical Periods.

TURNING AGAINST NEOCONFUCIAN METAPHYSICS

Evidential research (*kaozhengxue*), consisting in empirical investigation of texts with comparative and inductive methods gained center-stage in Qing Classical studies (*jingxue*). Development of philological tools such as etymology, phonology, paleography, and collation during the Qing dynasty contributed significantly to our understanding of the Confucian Canon. While some praise it for developing and applying 'scientific method', critics consider evidential research a complete turn away from philosophy, concerned only with textual authenticity, the relationship between texts, and philological details. However, the movement had its roots in Neoconfucian philosophical debates. Since all parties to Neoconfucian debates claimed to be propagating the teachings of Confucius and other ancient sages, it is important to determine what the sages actually said or wrote by establishing the authenticity of the Classics, which had been revered as containing their words of wisdom. Moreover, linguistic differences between ancient and contemporary times render painstaking philological study necessary to recover the ancient meanings of the Classics.

Song–Ming scholars might recognize textual criticism as a means of resolving philosophical disputes; but Qing scholars went much further in considering textual criticism indispensable, and capable of eliminating all such disputes. Gu Yanwu, often considered the founder of evidential research, recognized that the purpose of Classical studies is 'to illuminate the way'; but for him, there is no Learning of Principle outside Classical studies. Even though he was critical of the methodological inadequacy of all Neoconfucian interpretations, Gu continued the philosophical legacy of Zhu Xi, who in Gu's view advocated grounding Confucian moral cultivation in an understanding of the Classics.

Gu blamed Wang Yangming's subjectivistic interpretation of Confucian doctrines such as the 'investigation of things' and the 'innate knowledge of the good' for late Ming scholars' tendency to justify whatever conclusions they favored with claims of unverifiable personal 'intuitions', thereby distorting the sages' teachings. While the Cheng–Zhu school gained more popularity, the Lu–Wang school did not disappear completely. Huang Zongxi (1605–95) consciously supported the latter philosophical tradition as interpreted by Huang's teacher Liu Zongzhou, even though Huang also criticized late Ming neglect of textual studies. Huang's fellow student, Chen Que (1604–77), wrote an essay on the *Great Learning*'s date of authorship, with the aim of depriving Zhu Xi's view on the relation between conduct and knowledge of its textual basis.

The best *kaozheng* scholars presented a philosophical vision radically different from that of Song–Ming scholarship. Neoconfucians had debated the relative importance of honoring moral nature (*zundexing*) and study-inquiry (*daowenxue*), and their relationship in the quest for sageliness; study-inquiry in the form of evidential research reigned supreme in Qing philosophy. While Neoconfucians understood *li* as the metaphysical moral principle that gives shape and meaning to things, Dai Zhen, in whose scholarship evidential research reached its zenith, employed etymological evidence to argue that *li* refers to the 'internal patterns of things'. Rather than being grasped through meditations or intuitions, *li* is discovered through empirical and textual investigation. Dai went much further than Zhu Xi in emphasizing the priority of study-inquiry. Moral nature has only a subordinate role, beginning with unenlightened ignorance, it could become sagely intelligence only through study-inquiry. For Dai, evidential research enables us to retrieve the 'original meaning' of the sages' teachings regarding the pattern of things and the way. Dai's *Commentaries and Annotations on Word-Meanings in the Mencius* employed *kaozheng* results to explicate Confucian cosmology and philosophy of human nature. It is an indication of the spirit of the times that, despite Dai's influence, his contemporaries and followers did not value this work highly.

The orthodoxy of evidential research was not without its challengers. Zhang Xuecheng (1739–1801) objected to its narrow focus on the six Classics. Zhang saw himself continuing the intellectual lineage of the Lu–Wang school, through Huang Zongxi, who may be considered the founder of Qing historiography. Huang emphasized both the Classics and historical texts as embodying Confucianism, and was highly respected for his *Record of Ming Scholars*. Zhang argued that historical scholarship is of paramount importance because principles and the way are understood by grasping how they operate in concrete situations, not through metaphysical speculation. To Zhang, 'the six Classics are all history' since they show the historical operation of *dao* as it had evolved up to the sages' times. While he shared Dai's rejection of metaphysical interpretations, Zhang differed philosophically from Classical studies masters. For Zhang, the way constantly evolves and recovering the 'original meaning' of the sages' teachings will not give contemporary Classics readers the *dao* that applies to themselves. The sages' *dao* in the Classics must be understood within a larger historical context combined with a grasp of contemporary reality for a full grasp of *dao*. Besides including a larger corpus for textual study, Zhang also adopted different hermeneutical methods that belie his adherence to the Learning of Mind. In studying texts, one must 'grasp the large whole' and 'leap into the minds of the ancients' instead of getting lost in philological details and other piecemeal narrow investigations as Classical studies proponents tended to do.

Internal fragmentation played a part in the eventual decline of evidential research. This took the form of a revival of the Han controversy over the Old and New Texts. The New Texts were transmitted orally, and written down in the script of that time by Confucian Masters and formed the Confucian Canon of the early Han dynasty. The Old Texts were written in ancient script, but purportedly discovered towards the end of the Western Han. Scholars disagreed over which was more authoritative. The Old Texts became accepted as canonical during the Tang dynasty. Yan Ruoju's (1636–1704) *Inquiry into the Authenticity of Old Text Book of Documents* proved that the text was not fourth-century as believed but a later forgery. This revived interest in the New Text Classics, beginning with Zhuang Cunyu (1719–88), whose work on the *Gongyang* tradition represented by Dong Zhongshu did not gain recognition for half a century.

The *Gongyang* tradition, based on the *Gongyang* commentary on the *Chun Qiu* (*Spring and Autumn Annals*) instead of the *Zuo* commentary of the Old Text Classics, believed that Confucius wrote the *Chun Qiu*, which was not history, but a depository of enduring principles on how to unify China with ideal institutions. Confucius' 'great meanings conveyed in subtle words' had to be interpreted in the light of actual contemporary politics in order to fulfill his vision. Evidential research methods are not adequate to this task which requires a broader, more liberal interpretive stance and greater attention to contemporary realities. The rise of the New Text or *Gongyang* school in the nineteenth century accompanied a turn towards the practical. The resulting combination of New Text interpretation of Classics and practical philosophy is best exemplified by the works of Kang Youwei (see Chapter 14). New Text hermeneutics was more amenable to developing radical and creative understanding of and for a Chinese society tumbling into the modern age, tripped by one crisis after another.

MATERIALISM AND AFFIRMATION OF DESIRES

Despite its eventual triumph, evidential research was only one among plural reactions against Neoconfucian metaphysical tendencies. Against the Cheng–Zhu school's emphasis on *li* over *qi*, and the Lu–Wang school's emphasis on *xin*, there was a trend towards *qi* cosmologies, which have been compared with materialism in contrast to idealism, although vital force or *qi* is not matter and operates quite differently. Neoconfucians took the doctrine of 'preserving heaven's principle, eliminating human desires' to such extremes that reaction against it was inevitable. Many Qing scholars affirm the legitimate place of desires in moral life. Wang Fuzhi's (1619–92) philosophy exemplifies these trends. Wang was among those who fought the Manchu invaders. He chose to live in seclusion for the last four decades of his life after all hopes of restoring the Ming was lost. Although his surviving works were printed only in 1842, various aspects of his philosophical views were shared (but less systematically expressed) by other Qing thinkers. Some consider Wang the most important and innovative Qing philosopher, with significant influence in the nineteenth and twentieth century.

In Wang's cosmology, *qi* constitutes everything. He rejected Zhu Xi's view that *li* is ontologically prior to *qi* even though the two coexist and are inseparable. According to Wang, *li* is the order within *qi*, 'how *qi* ought to be'. Wang also criticized the Learning of Mind for mistakenly thinking that there can be heart-mind without *qi*, and that the heart-mind can be conscious or know without the aid of physical organs, and that the object of consciousness and knowledge is other than physical objects existing independently of the knower. Although influenced by Zhang Zai, who also claimed ontological-cosmological priority of *qi*, Wang did not posit *qi* as metaphysical substance or great vacuity (*taixu*), with material objects manifesting its functioning. Like *li* and *qi*, substance and function are inseparable and both are immanent in material objects. Wang's metaphysics is materialist in the sense that he does not posit any separate metaphysical entity prior to or above material or physical entities. Contrary to Neoconfucian division of *dao* as metaphysical or 'above physical forms' (*xingershang*) and phenomenal existents (*qi*, literally 'vessels' or 'implements') as 'below physical forms' (*xingerxia*), Wang understood *dao* as evolving within phenomenal or physical existence. '*Dao* comprises of ways of material existence; physical entities cannot be called implements of the way. … There is no way of the father before there is a son; there is no way of the elder brother before there is a younger brother. Many ways could exist that do not yet exist.'

Wang's monistic *qi* cosmology understands heaven as the totality of natural phenomena. Neoconfucian ideas maintained that morality is grounded in heaven-endowed human nature. From Wang's perspective, the cosmos or heaven is constantly changing, and the good is that which continues the process. Human nature is not the origin but the continuation of that good in human individuals, it is the evolved order of human life. In Wang's understanding, human nature is not fixed at birth, but rather develops over time, as knowledge and abilities constantly change with experience. One values that which is developed in human nature, while in nurturing that development, one 'selects the excellent and grasps the enduring'. At birth, human nature is *li*, the order within the *qi* we received from heaven. This provides the basis for human virtues; but this *li* has to be renewed daily and perfected through practice. Moral cultivation, especially rites, is 'the nurturing of the order of life and pattern of nature, and then refining them to fulfill their functions'. Wang's view resembles but is better explicated than Huang Zongxi's late-in-life claim, that 'the heart-mind has no substance, that which is attained by skilful effort (*gongfu*) is its substance'.

Given the continuity between nature and morality in his conception of human nature, Wang rejected the Neoconfucian opposition between heaven's principle and human desires. Desires are unavoidable as long as human beings interact with things, and are therefore ineliminable. The Neoconfucian recommendation 'to eliminate desires' is not only impossible to follow, following it would undermine the effort 'to preserve heaven's principle'. Wang shared Zhang Zai's belief that since desires are natural, heaven's principle is found within them. Insofar as desires motivate actions, they are the means of realizing principle. Wang is however not a hedonist. He advocated moderation as indulgence in any one desire blinds oneself to all other possible objects of desire. There should be fairness (*gong*) in satisfying desires because all desires are equal in being natural. Heaven's principle prevails only when everyone's desires are satisfied. Wang viewed indulgence of any desire as a matter of ignorance; its cure lies in knowledge of heaven's principle and human nature.

Among the early Qing Confucians, Chen Que also gave desires a legitimate place in his ritual ethics. Chen insisted that Confucians only advocate reducing desires, not eliminating them. 'Human heart-mind originally does not have what is called heavenly principle; heavenly principle is revealed in human desires … Without human desires, there can be no heavenly principle.' People act immorally not because they have desires but because they have failed to develop good habits through ritual practice. Chen understood the claim that 'human nature is good' as involving a process of developing potential goodness into actual goodness. This process, rather than eliminating desires, fulfills them, thereby also fulfilling heavenly principle.

Chen Que and Wang Fuzhi anticipated Dai Zhen's ethics which argues for a unity of desire, emotion, and reason. For Dai, the absence of desires does not guarantee that a view or action is right, comprehensive understanding of principle and practical ability to

113

apply it are also required. Moreover, Neoconfucian moral absolutism opened the way for the powerful to ignore the demands and welfare of the people as 'human desires'. Reaffirming the moral legitimacy of human desires is part of the critique of despotism. The trends towards materialist cosmologies and towards rejecting moral absolutism and affirmation of human desires signified and contributed to the 'practical turn' of Qing scholarship.

THE PRACTICAL TURN: ORDERING THE WORLD (*JINGSHI*)

Most early Qing scholars criticized Neoconfucianism for turning away from practical, especially socio-political, concerns in their metaphysical preoccupations and their predilection for meditational practices. Although the most prominent Neoconfucians such as Zhu Xi and Wang Yangming were not guilty of this, many late Ming scholars probably fit Yan Yuan's famous description: 'At leisure they spoke of heart-mind and human nature with folded sleeves; without even half a plan to meet difficult times, they could only repay the emperor by committing suicide.' In contrast, Gu Yanwu, Huang Zongxi and Wang Fuzhi all fought the Manchu invaders, and remained keenly interested in politics even though they refused to serve the Qing court. Their philosophical reflections included critiques of the despotism that they believed brought down the Ming dynasty.

Huang Zongxi's *Waiting for the Dawn: A Plan for the Prince*, written in 1662, was an attempt to order the world according to Confucian principles. For Huang, to order the world is to ensure the people's welfare, distinct from the rise and fall of dynasties. He analyzed and drew on the Classics and historical texts to construct his ideal 'great system', and proposed, *inter alia*, rectifying understanding of rulership, government re-organization, restoring independence of schools and their ancient function, land, tax and currency reforms. He argued that ancient sages served the people and did not see rulership as a prize; later kings thought differently because they treated the world as their personal property, illegitimately supplanting the common good with their private interests. Ministers should serve not the ruler alone but everyone under heaven. Contrary to other Confucians, Huang argued that 'only when we have governance by law or *fa* can we have governance by men'. Since the Three Dynasties, there has been no law because instead of establishing institutions for the people's welfare, rulers used coercive regulations or 'unlawful laws' to safeguard themselves and their interests. Huang objected to over-centralization of power and advocated that officials, led by a prime minister, should share in government instead of merely taking orders from the ruler. Governmental power should also have external checks. One such check is schools, which should not be subjected to political interference; their purpose is not merely to train officials but to independently 'determine right and wrong'. *Waiting for the Dawn* became influential at the end of the Qing dynasty as an early Confucian argument for democracy. Although it still awaits a prince, its insistence that rulers should not be obsessed with passing on the throne to their descendents and its recommendation of decentralization of power and checks on government, and its focus on institutions are aspects that approach government by the people.

Yan Yuan (1635–1704) and Li Yong (1627–1705) took the most extreme position on the idea of *jingshi*, agreeing wholeheartedly that 'the central purpose of Confucian learning consists in ordering the world'. Initially a devoted follower of Zhu Xi's ritual teachings, Yan's subsequent revolt against Neoconfucianism was more thorough than other early Qing scholars. Contrary to evidential research scholars, Yan considered Han Classical studies as disastrous a mistake as metaphysical Neoconfucianism: one produced impractical pedants, the other bred idle talkers. *Dao* is not a metaphysical entity or linguistic construct; it is the way of action, embodied in the deeds of the sages, distilled in the plain words of Confucius and Mencius. Neoconfucians differ from Confucius not in their words but in their deeds; instead of making a real journey, a Neoconfucian would study a map and thinks that he knows all about journeys. In Yan's understanding, Confucianism is about the ideal economic-socio-political order that resulted from intelligent design and dynamic action. Instead of abstract discourses, the sage taught people practical things ranging from household management to government. Such tasks require technical skills acquired through practice (*xi*). Yan's philosophy emphasizes the values of activeness, practicality, use, and technical competence, with little room for book-learning.

The turn to evidential research in the seventeenth century was encouraged by the Qing state's suspicion of Confucian 'practical' philosophy which was often mixed up with anti-Manchu political tendencies. Nearly two centuries later, there was a strong revival of *jingshi* thinking. While Yan Yuan's generation still looked solely towards the Confucian tradition for practical guidance, in the nineteenth century, *jingshi* scholars such as Wei Yuan (1794–1856) had to consider learning from the West, especially after the Opium War (1839–42). The crises of state and civilization turned scholars' attention once more to finding practical solutions, as they became aware that Qing evidential research had replaced useless metaphysics with equally useless textual investigation.

SOME THEMES IN THE HISTORY OF CHINESE PHILOSOPHY

There can be little doubt that Chinese philosophy always retained a practical orientation, especially if we look to the *rujiao* with its continuous concern, even in its most metaphysical, that is to say Neoconfucian phase, with the sources of morality and the debate about the goodness or otherwise of human nature. If Kong set one agenda in his passion for moral education, Mengzi set another in his bold doctrine of innate human goodness. Buddhist philosophy in its Chinese phase was ultimately concerned of course with liberation and enlightenment – having a more spiritual than directly ethical orientation. Here the three schools with the most Chinese flavor have a positive feeling, especially Huayan and Chan, and in this import Chinese feeling into Indian otherworldliness. The Neo-Taoists are perhaps more darkly metaphysical: but their doctrines bear on the question of engagement in the social world and harmony with nature. This question of whether spontaneity and ultimate harmony mean getting out of normal social obligations and interest in politics remains a theme down the ages.

Another concept which is vital in the tradition is that of the ultimate principle governing the cosmos. This debate about Heaven, the Tao and the Great Ultimate has a very different flavor from Indian debates about Brahman and God. Though Chinese thinking is in its own way religious, the Ultimate is usually seen in relatively non-personal terms.

The nature of the self or human nature recurs in debates, but it is typically placed within a social context. It is an important observation in Chinese philosophy that the individual is importantly defined by his or her embedment in the social order.

The concept of *li* as ceremonial stays central to Confucian thinking about human interactions; the virtue of *ren* or human-heartedness remains pivotal in ethics; the contrast of *ti* and *yong* – substance and function – and of *li* and *qi* – all these remain crucial to Confucian debates. In the background the old cosmology of yin and yang and of the five processes dance before the backdrop of the Tao and Tian. There is in most systems a predilection for the concepts of cosmic harmony and organic interconnectedness. These are very prominent in the Neotaoist schools and in the wonderful system of Huayan.

These are some of the primary themes in the Chinese debates about the universe and the nature of human society. The atmosphere is very much other than that of India, and yet the two interacted most fruitfully in the Chinese voyage of Buddhist values.

4

KOREAN PHILOSOPHIES

A SKETCH OF RELEVANT KOREAN HISTORY

Korea was for much of its history under the spell, and sometimes the rule, of China, and suffered from invasions both from the north and from Japan. Its primary philosophies have been variants on Chinese Confucianism and Buddhism, often fresh and vigorous, but tracing out partly Chinese trajectories. After the early period of tribal leagues there emerged the Three Kingdoms – first the northern state of Koguryo, then the Paekche and Silla kingdoms. The last of these became dominant on the peninsula, during the time from 668 CE to 935. During the Three Kingdoms period, Buddhism became well established, and Paekche, which was an advanced seafaring state, was able to send Buddhist missionaries successfully to Japan: in this way Korea was a vitally important bridge (as geography dictated) between China and Japan. The Silla dynasty not only saw the introduction of the important Chinese schools such as Tiantai and Huayan, but also used Confucian learning and philosophy as an ideology of centralized administrative rule. The coming of Sŏn or Chan Buddhism to Korea was also momentous, as it was to be the single most influential form of Buddhism in the peninsula. The succeeding Koryo dynasty was a time of great prosperity for Buddhism; but the Yi dynasty, which lasted from 1392 to 1910, turned increasingly to Confucianism, and it was during this period that there came to be a distinctly Korean school of Neoconfucianism, with such notable thinkers as Yi Hwang, better known as T'oegye (1501–70), and Yi Yulgok (1536–84). The Hideyoshi invasion from Japan (1592) and the Mongol invasion (1636) did not staunch the flow of Confucian debate, and various noted scholars emerged in this late period, including Yun Hyu (1617–80) and Chong Yagyong (1762–1836). In the 1870s and 1880s ports were successively opened to Japan and Western powers, preparing the way for Japanese annexation in 1910. After World War II, Korea was divided into North and South (1948), the former being ruled under the iron principles of the dictator Kim Il-sung, and the South having a more open culture. We shall deal with modern developments, from the late nineteenth century, in a subsequent chapter.

Religiously, Korea was dominated until recent times by the systems of Buddhism and Confucianism, with indigenous shamanism and folk religion playing an ongoing part. More recently, Christianity has made a very strong impact, especially forms of Protestantism.

KOREAN HUAYAN: UISANG AND WŎNHYO

As has been mentioned above, the Chinese schools of Buddhism had a strong influence in Korea. Tiantai, with its syncretic and embracing nature, had appeal: but the Huayan, with its positive organicism, also proved important, and later effected a synthesis with Sŏn or Chan Buddhism. During the Silla period the stability of the regime, together with possibilities of travel to China, cemented relations with Chinese Buddhism. One noted traveler was Uisang (625–702), who studied with the famous scholar of the Huayan tradition, Chihyen (Zhiyan) (602–68), together with a later most distinguished fellow student, Fazang (643–712), much his junior. On his return to Korea, Uisang warned the then king of Silla, Mummu, unifier of Korea and founder of the Silla dynasty, of an impending Chinese attack: forewarned, the Koreans fought off the incursion, and in gratitude Mummu helped with the building of Pusok monastery. This became the intellectual headquarters of Korean Huayan under Uisang's headship. Uisang combined Pure Land piety with his espousal of Hwaom (Huayan) philosophy. While not a great theoretician, he played a central part in making the Huayan presence felt in Korea.

His colleague Wŏnhyo was much more prolific in literary output. He was also tireless in proselytizing for the Buddhist faith, hoping that it would get firmly established as the national faith under the unified Silla dynasty. Two of his commentaries, one on the *Avataṃsaka Sūtra* or *Huayan ching* had a strong influence on Fazang, and for this reason he is often counted as one of the founders of the Chinese Huayan tradition, though not himself, of course, Chinese. But his interest was a wider one than promoting Huayen philosophy. He sought to reconcile the various important denominations and texts (for instance the Mādhyamika and Yogācāra traditions, and Indian and Chinese slants on Buddhist philosophy). He did this in the main by differentiating between those texts which were primarily aimed at expounding the idea of dependent origination and those which were concerned more with the idea of 'return to the source', abandoning the pluralism of the phenomenal world. The former texts were often negative: exploding things and persons through the relentless analysis of the complexes of causes going to make up apparent entities. The latter texts were positive: talking of higher consciousness and the original mind lying within or behind events. In this and other ways, Wŏnhyo looked for ways to bring together the varied forms of Buddhism. For this reason he has been seen in Korea as being the founder of the Popsong (Dharma Nature) school of Buddhism.

Though the scholastic schools could find it easy to schematize the varied texts, they were not at all at ease with Sŏn or Chan Buddhism, which was introduced during the unified Silla period. The most prominent wing of this new movement was predominantly of the lineage which came to form Linzhi Chan, and was known – because of the sites of principal monasteries founded by various monastic leaders after returning from China – as the Nine Mountains school. Resistance to the rather alarming anti-intellectual doctrines of Sŏn and the idea of sudden enlightenment led to confrontation between the scholastics and the Sŏn movement. But during the Koryo period, the attempt was made, for instance by Uich'on (1055–1101) to unify the two sides. He traveled to China to receive the imprimatur of the Tiantai lineage, and on his return to Korea formally set up the Ch'ont'ae. The Tiantai ideas were familiar already, but in setting up a formal organization of the school, Uich'on hoped to use it as an umbrella under which both the Meditation school and the others could shelter. But his death at an early age frustrated his aim. He, incidentally, compiled an amazing catalogue of Buddhist texts, for which he sent out to all of Asia. Though the woodblocks from which the texts were printed were burned during the Mongol invasion, his catalog survives as a monument to his imaginative scholarship.

His ambitions were better fulfilled a century later by the Sŏn master Chinul (1158–1210) who reconciled meditation and scriptural teaching and study (kyo). He is thought of as the founder of the Chogye school of Sŏn, which is a genuinely Korean form of Chan. He accepted the idea of sudden awakening, but then sketched a procedure of gradual cultivation of insight as leading the searcher onwards. At both stages scriptural understanding is important, but it is so because it points towards the experiences which take the adept onwards. He was much interested in method and pioneered, in Korea, the use of the *hwadu* or *kungan* (Japanese *koan*) – the spiritual riddle. Its use destroys conceptual understanding and so stimulates awakening. By going beyond the concepts and concentrating on the mere sound of the words one attains a kind of mindlessness which gives way to the sudden awakening. This sets the adept on the path. In all this, Chinul gave reassurance to those concerned about the textual heritage of Buddhism that its directions would in broad outline be followed; but at the same time he was very insistent on the experiential side of the Path. Between the paradoxes of many of the scriptures and the riddles used in meditation there was no wide gap.

THE YI STATE AND THE TRANSFORMATION OF KOREAN SOCIETY

The foundation of the Yi dynasty led to what might be called a slow revolution in Korean society, towards a polity which was based on Neoconfucian principles and which set great store by education and by the propagation of Confucian ethics. The culmination of this movement was the philosophy of high Korean Neoconfucianism in the sixteenth century. This was represented above all by the two thinkers, Yi T'oegye and Yi Yulgok. During the previous century Confucian pressures had led to severe restrictions on Buddhism. Temple lands were confiscated. The various schools were merged into two – one which put together the Sŏn, the Ch'ont'ae and the Vinaya schools, and the other fusing the scholastics into the Kyo or Doctrinal school. Temples were forbidden in the capital and in the larger cities. So while the influence of Confucianism was in the ascendant, the Buddhist tradition suffered. The effects are still evident in modern Korea.

Yi T'oegye served as an administrator under three kings, who all treated him with respect; and he succeeded in defining his position as an independent scholar, not merely serving the immediate political needs of the times. But he did lay out a form of orthodoxy which resisted the attractions of Wang Yangming's subjectivist philosophy, then making its influence felt in Korea. He followed Zhuxi, but he helped to clarify a major point left muddy in Zhu's writings. The latter had frequently enough affirmed the superiority of *li* or principle over *qi* or material force. But what was the nature of this superiority? Was it somehow that *li* was ontologically prior, and if so, in what sense? Did it mean that the *li* really existed before the material cosmos? But then what could 'exist' mean here, since *li* could not manifest or define itself except in terms of material force? Yi T'oegye took the line that *li* and *qi* were locked together ontologically. Rather, it was that *li* was superior as a kind of ethical force. So if *li* manifests itself, it will create good, while if material force obscures *li*, ignorance and evil will come to the fore. So *li* is not just morally prior in the sense of having greater value: it is an actual force in the production of good.

Since individual existence is determined ultimately by material force, this explains the relative worth of individuals as they actually are: but of course nature can be improved. This is the whole point of Confucian education. What is needed is for people to be recalled to their inner goodness. The mind itself contains innate knowledge of *li*, of principle and principles of good conduct. But its ability to recall this goodness and make it into a force in life is often prevented by the forces of selfish desires. There is a clash between the ethical mind and the human mind (a distinction often debated, as we have seen, in the Chinese tradition). The rectification of the human mind gives rein to the ethical mind.

In all this Yi T'oegye made a distinction between two states: one where *li* is the leader, and one where *qi* is the leader. In other words, though *li* and *qi* are everywhere interwoven, and are, so to speak, inseparable mates, in some cases *li* has the predominant role and in others *qi* does.

Considering rational thought to be important, T'oegye rejected Wang Yangming's skepticism about outer investigative inquiry. His exclusive concentration on the introspective method was dangerous, for it was important to work at moral cultivation day by day, and this could involve not just learning from past sages and scriptures but also testing out morality in the light of practical affairs.

T'oegye's doctrines of the actual generative or creative power of *li* and of its ethical (rather than ontological) priority became vital loci of debate in later Korean Neoconfucianism. As an independent thinker he gained respect because of his critical mind, and he also stressed the importance of sincerity and seriousness (old Confucian values) in the daily pursuit of knowledge. He helped to establish the Yongnam school of Confucianism which took a distinctive position on the question of the relation between the so-called Four Beginnings (or seeds) and the Seven Feelings. These traditional classifications of the origins of moral attitudes and of the basic emotions were to be found originally in the *Mencius* and the *Lizhi* (Book of Ritual), respectively. The former were the senses of compassion, shame, respect and right and wrong; the latter were pleasure, anger, sorrow, fear, love, hate and desire.

In a debate between T'oegye and another Korean philosopher, Ki Taisŭng (1527–72), T'oegye's position came under fire. He traced the Four to emergence from *li* and the Seven to *qi*. Ki held that the Four are actually included in the Seven. Besides, T'oegye would have difficulty in illuminating human psychology if the Four and the Seven are separated; and his account looks dualistic, separating *li* and *qi* unnaturally. If there were such a dualism, then it would be hard to say how it is that the individual human mind has a natural sense of right and wrong. T'oegye was not altogether swayed by these arguments, though he modified his position by using the analogy of a man riding a horse: the man, representing *li* and the Four Beginnings is dependent on the horse, representing *qi* and the Seven Feelings. All this prepared the way for a non-dualistic view as expressed by the other towering figure of Korean Neoconfucianism, Yi Yulgok (1536–84).

YI YULGOK AND SOME CRUCIAL DEBATES IN THE NEOCONFUCIAN TRADITION

Yi Yulgok (the latter is a *nom de plume* in the Korean tradition drawn from the name of his native village) studied until he was 16 with his mother, known as a poet and painter. In grief at her death, he retired to a Buddhist monastery for a while, but later performed brilliantly in the civil service examinations and rose quickly in the bureaucracy to hold various ministerial posts and to be royal tutor. He was in the activist tradition of Confucian scholarship. His followers kept to this mode and were at the center of power for the remainder of the Yi dynasty.

Yulgok was disturbed by the dualism inherent in T'oegye's position. For the latter this came out in various ways and not just in the question of the Four and the Seven: for instance, it came out in a kind of split between the *taoxin* and the *renxin,* that is, between the universal mind and the individual mind (literally the 'way mind' and the 'human mind'). The universal or good mind issues from *li* or principle and the individual mind from material force. Yulgok resisted this split. To understand why, we have to go back to his general cosmology.

For Yulgok, the universe is a dialectical unity. The Great Ultimate or *taizhi* is nothing other than the interplay of yin and yang. Its substance is change, and this change occurs in the *qi* or material force according to certain patterns, that is, in accord with *li*. So he does not look on the Great Ultimate as a kind of basis for the universe, but rather as another name for it. In its primordial or quiescent state, when yin predominates, it is the Great Emptiness. But there is no time when *qi* is not present. Indeed, Yulgok has usually been considered as taking *qi* to be predominant, and in this way he becomes a sort of materialist. Yet if it is materialism, it is materialism of a special kind. For one thing he finds a harmony between human and cosmic events, so that the sage can affect the universe just as the universe affects humanity. Basically, he holds that the cosmos is a changing organic complex, according to certain laws. These laws are invisible to us, rather like dynamic 'things-in-themselves' (to take an analogy from Kant) lying behind phenomena. It is the job of the wise person to investigate things with a view to understanding how the cosmos works.

There is another dialectical contrast in the traditional literature: between the heavenly mind and the individual mind. The former somehow enters into human life and inspires moral feelings, but how? Here Yulgok, in accord with his cosmology, resists the dualism of supposing that ethics spring from the *taoxin* and evil from the *renxin*, as though particularity and individuality were inherently bad, and indeed as though material force itself were evil. Both the heavenly mind and the individual mind are joint products, so to speak, of *li* and *qi*. For him the image of the human on horseback can be highly misleading, if we were to take the two entities as being separable – as though *li* (the human) could exist separately from the horse. At best the image has to be taken as a symbol of interdependence – the horse carries the human and the human guides (and feeds) the horse. It is best not to make *li* into a substance or thing: it is, rather, the collection of individual patterns which lie behind the richness of cosmic and human manifestation. This is why Yulgok does not want to split *li* from *qi* in the debate of the Four and the Seven. He therefore has to say that the Four are inherent in the Seven: the moral impulses are indeed natural, but not by invoking a cosmic Nature: but we can see them embedded in the ordinary functioning of human nature.

In criticizing T'oegye he first points out that Zhuxi's dictum that the Four and the Seven are due to the issuance of *li* and *qi* does not imply 'respectively'. It can just be taken as a general observation – both being jointly the product of *li* and *qi*. But it was T'oegye who established the theory of alternate issuance or production in saying 'the four beginnings are the *li*-issuance and *qi* follows thereafter; the seven feelings are the *qi*-issuance and *li* rides thereon'. For Yulgok, however, just as one should not make a dualism of substance out of the aspectual distinction between *li* and *qi*, so one should not make some ontological distinction out of the Four and the Seven. The Four are simply the good side of the Seven. So we should be able to set forth how it is that the Four relate to the Seven.

The Four are humanity or compassion *(ren)*, righteousness *(i/yi)*, proper behavior *(li)* and knowledge of right and wrong *(zhi)*. They have their roots in the feelings, since *ren* springs from love, shame springs from hate, proper behavior and respect for persons spring from fear, and right and wrong spring from knowledge of the rightness and wrongness of different manifestations of the Seven Feelings. The beginnings are the seeds or nuclei from which fully-fledged feelings and behaviors will develop, and Yulgok considers that he has given an adequate account of how they are rooted in the basic feelings. The *tuan* or beginnings are nothing other than the good side of the feelings – their potentiality for good conduct and good attitudes.

This debate on the origins of the beginnings is interesting since it shows the preoccupation among Confucianists with making morality intelligible in terms of the actualities of human nature. But here there is an extra factor which we have not yet mentioned and which is not just vital to Yulgok's thought but also has a significant place in the *rujiao* – the idea of will or *yi*. The notion goes back to Kong when he wrote, 'At fifteen years my mind was set on learning.' The *yi* itself influences *qi* and can make it into a tool of moral behavior. As we shall see, there is also a question of the relation of the establishment of the will to the cultivation of sincerity. But for the moment let us note that there is for Yulgok an inspirational side to the will, since its power can be sapped by not heeding the glowing example of the sage: the sage serves as a beacon to attract ordinary people. Sometimes, however, ordinary people recognize in themselves a lack of wisdom which causes them despair. How can such a person seriously hope to become a sage? And yet study and application can improve a person's wisdom immensely. One needs ambition. In short, faith, hope and courage are needed to aspire to the condition of the sage. We may note how once again we see, in the Confucian tradition, the ideal of the sage. He is a person who serves, as it were, as a conduit between Heaven and earth. He is charismatic: he is beyond ordinary notions of wisdom and learning (and yet it is striking how book learning is itself a component of this elitist vision: can it be democratized?).

It is through the exercise of will, then, that material force is bent towards good action. It is through lack of will that it becomes dark and evil. If it becomes good, then this is how the Four are developed out of the Seven, and how it is that the Universal Mind becomes incarnate, so to speak, in the individual mind.

SINCERITY AND THE THEORY OF KNOWLEDGE IN T'OEGYE AND YULGOK

Cheng or sincerity has always held a vital place in the *rujiao*. There was in Korean Neoconfucianism some interesting debate about the degree of its priority. This relates to the voluntarism of Yulgok. T'oegye held that reverence or *jing* is the crucial attitude with regard to learning. Respectful attention is needed in the investigation of things, and if the latter is successful, then sincerity will follow. But Yulgok considered *cheng* to be absolutely basic. And the reason for this was partly that he sought a heavenly counterpart for the Four Beginnings. These he found through the interpretation of a significant hexagram (called the Creative) in the *Yi jing*. According to this interpretation, heaven has four good forms of behavior: sublimity or *yuan*, *heng* or order, *li* or harmony and *chen (zhen)* or perseverance. Sublime behavior correlates with *ren*, orderliness with *li*, harmony with *i* and perseverance with *zhi*. They are the Four Beginnings of Heaven. So the wise person, acting in accordance with the Four, participates in the heavenly Four. The operation of the heavenly Four is the *cheng* or sincerity of Heaven. So we may think of *cheng* as acting in accord with one's true nature – so it is the true nature of the sun and moon to be bright, of seasons to alternate, of yin and yang to be in interplay, for mountains to be high and oceans to be deep. Consequently *cheng* has a cosmic as well as a human significance. We can see from this that Yulgok's rejection of T'oegye's treatment of sincerity as a side effect of reverent attention, etc., is deeply rooted: for him the *li* or pattern of the universe requires sincerity since it is through this that the sage takes part in the rhythms of the cosmos itself. When he achieves this ('he' because in the Confucian context the sage was usually conceived as being male), he achieves a harmony with the Tao, with the cosmos. So the sage has to use no effort in investigating things and aligning his mind with the cosmos. Here is an echo of the Taoist ideal. Of course he has had to labor mightily to become a sage, starting as a student and rising through the status of the superior man or *junzi*. But he comes to the *cheng* of non-action.

T'oegye and Yulgok represent differing streams of the Cheng–Zhuxi tradition, known respectively as the schools of Principle and Material Force. But both professed loyalty to their sources. Generally speaking, Zhuxi's ideas remained the official orthodoxy in Korea. However, there was an interesting variant in the position taken up by Yun Hyu (1617–80), rival of the highly orthodox Song Siyol (1607–89). Yun was deeply disturbed by events next door – the overthrow of the Ming dynasty by the Ch'ing (Qing) or Manchu dynasty. This he saw as challenging the Korean orthodoxy. He perceived Korea itself as a bastion of Confucian civilization, and in expressing loyalty to the values of this civilization he challenged Zhuxi's position somewhat. He thought of Confucianism as a constantly changing and evolving culture, stretching into the distant past, and adapting itself to varying conditions of the world. Thus now in these latter days Korean Confucianism needed to change, but in a spirit of loyalty to the wide and ancient achievements of the past. He himself wrote commentaries on the *Chung-yung (Zhongyong) (Doctrine of the Mean)* and the *Ta-hsüeh (Daxue) (Great Learning);* and this was perceived by his contemporaries as almost a blasphemous act and a challenge to established orthodoxy. In identifying Confucianism with a civilization, Yun was in many ways modern in his thinking.

SOME REFLECTIONS ON KOREAN THOUGHT IN THE PREMODERN PERIOD

Some of the most significant debates in the Confucian tradition took place, as we have seen, in Korea. The issue of the nature of the mind in relation to Mencian doctrine was taken up in the debates on the Four and the Seven, to which we have paid some attention here. The polarity between the schools of *li* and *qi* drew out some of the tensions inherent in Zhuxi and the brothers Cheng. Yulgok's dialectical non-dualism was a consistent treatment of Neoconfucianist cosmology, while Zhuxi exploited the transcendental aspects of the *rujiao* (transcendental traits which of course militated against a non-dualist position). In short, the Korean development of Neoconfucianism was fruitful. Its transformations of Buddhism were less striking, but its syncretic tendency was important, while Korea itself served as a vital road from China to Japan in the transmission of religions and philosophies. All this foreshadowed great changes due to take place in the late nineteenth century, with the onset of the colonial period. As it happened, Korea was to be heavily influenced by Protestantism, and is after the Philippines now the most Christian country in Asia. But that is a story which we shall come to later.

One final comment on the Confucian thread through China and Korea. The strong interest in the question of the goodness of human nature and the ways through which it enters into life is unmistakable. What does it suggest today? There are issues in all this of both a conceptual or theoretical and of an empirical nature. It is an interesting fact that differing cultures regard different emotions as basic and differing moral virtues as fundamental. How do we determine, in an emerging world civilization, who is right? And to what extent can questions about Mencius be settled empirically?

5

JAPANESE PHILOSOPHIES

AN OVERVIEW

The Meiji restoration of 1868 caused a profound change, as is well known, in Japanese society. The modern period has seen a rich interaction between Japanese thought and Western ideas. We shall be dealing with that interplay in a later chapter. In this chapter we are chiefly concerned with patterns of Japanese philosophy and religious ideas during earlier centuries. Japanese civilization was formed not just of native ingredients, such as the religious tradition that has gelled into Shinto; but also of imported elements, especially from Korea and China. Japan was in the orbit of Chinese culture, yet always independent. It therefore absorbed much from its 'central' neighbor, but also developed some new patterns of value, extending some of the lines in the traditions of Buddhism and Confucianism in particular.

The official introduction of Buddhism into Japan from Korea in the sixth century CE prepared the way for the system during the Nara period onwards (from 710) of the mutual dependence of the State and the saṅgha (Japanese: *sō*) and of imperial law and Buddhist *dharma* (Japanese: *hō*). During the following Heian period (794–1185) some vital Japanese variants on Chinese movements were established, such as the Tendai (Chinese: *Tiantai*) and Japanese esoteric Buddhism, Shingon (Sanskrit: *mantra*). But it was probably in the Kamakura period (1185–1333) that the full flowering of typical Japanese Buddhism took place. It was during these times that we see founded the Pure Land schools, including the True Pure Land school of Buddhism founded by Shinran (1173–1262), Nichiren Buddhism (founded by Nichiren – 1222–83), Rinzai Zen and Sōtō Zen. There was also during this period a revival of Confucianism, which in one form or another had been present in Japan since early times, though it was largely during the Tokugawa shogunate (or military government) that Neoconfucianism really flourished, known as the Shushi-gakuha or School of Zhuxi. As a backlash the Kogakuha or School of Ancient Learning sought to go back past the commentaries of Zhuxi to the original Confucian texts. It was also during these times that syncretic Confucian Shinto thought was consolidated (there had also been syncretism between Shinto and Buddhism, such as Shingon Shinto). In the seventeenth century there was the Kokugaku or School of National Learning, which sought to disentangle Shinto from the other traditions and to establish an independent Shinto thought. This so-called restoration Shinto (*fukkō shintō*) emphasized an intellectual tradition unique to Japan and was thus easily co-opted by nationalist theories that prepared the way for the post-Meiji ideology and underpinned Japan's expansionist ventures before World War II.

There were also imported Taoist/Daoist ingredients in Japanese culture. Their chief impact ultimately was upon the so-called Zen arts, especially in painting and the medical traditions of the Japan of the Edo period. If one is to make a comparison between the three religious systems in China and the Japanese scene it would be to see Buddhism, Confucianism and Shinto as the three ingredients in the complex structures of Japanese observance, piety and philosophy. Because Shinto is the name for the way of the gods or *kami* there was no great difficulty in its being integrated with Buddhist practice, as indeed happened up to the Meiji time, when a forcible separation of Buddhist temples and Shinto shrines was decreed; for Buddhism has never attacked the gods, but has allowed them to live somewhat peripherally beside the great icons of the true faith. Often the gods became manifestations of Bodhisattvas or Buddhas-to-be. Though tensions existed between Confucian teaching and Buddhist otherworldliness, the two traditions often enough functioned side by side. So if one is to ask what the Japanese worldview was, say during the Kamakura period, the answer would be necessarily a complex one.

In the present treatment of Japanese philosophies I want to focus upon those movements that are unique to Japan or underwent a significant transformation in Japan. After all, Japanese Buddhists and Confucianists used old and foreign texts, and to this degree there was nothing very original about their mainstream interpretations of the two traditions. But in certain ways they developed the lines of these traditions in a most original way. For example, the Buddhist schools of the Nara period were deeply steeped in the commentary tradition of Indian and Chinese Buddhism. But in the Heian period, we see attempts to break free from this tradition in method and rhetoric in order to create new forms of Buddhism. It is to these developments that we shall turn, then. And here we begin with brief accounts of Tendai and Shingon.

TENDAI: SYNCRETIC BUDDHISM AND ORIGINAL ENLIGHTENMENT

It was Saichō (764–822 CE), also known posthumously as Dengyō Daishi, who came back from China with a set of Tiantai texts and set up the Japanese version of the school. He thought that the Japanese had reached a stage when they would benefit from the perfect teachings of the One Vehicle or *Ekayāna,* which was promoted by the *Lotus Sutra.* He desired to employ Buddhism in the service of the emperor and the country and thought that it was above all in Japan that true Buddhism would reach its peak. He held too that salvation was readily attainable, and he rejected the more traditional Buddhist view that it could only be obtained by a few after eons of struggle. In this he prepared the way for later Japanese views about easy liberation through faith. Ironically, however, the Buddhism he proclaimed as an alternative to what he saw as the lax practices of Nara Buddhism was rigorous and owed a lot to the mountain practice known as Shugendō. He was also very interested in and adept at esoteric ritual practices, which attracted court attention and favor, and caused Tendai to overlap with and also quarrel with the Shingon movement, which was being introduced at much the same time.

As Tendai Buddhism developed, it paid increasing attention to the theory of original enlightenment (Japanese: *hongaku*). This idea had been present in Chinese thinking, but had a stronger expression in Japan, both in Tendai and in Shingon. Three forms of learning or enlightenment were postulated: original enlightenment as a kind of pure non-dual consciousness lying behind the flux of phenomena; *shikaku* or actualized enlightenment, as experienced by individuals; and *fukaku* or ignorance in which conditioned existence appears, but which ultimately stems from *hongaku*. This model reflects in some way Zhiyi's threefold theory of truth. As mentioned earlier, the first truth, the truth of emptiness suggests that all phenomena are empty of self-nature and that emptiness itself constitutes the real; the provisional truth implies that all phenomena are not non-existent but constitute temporary entities and that linguistic expressions, including that of the truth of emptiness, cannot claim absolute truth value. The middle truth combines the insight of the previous two and suggests that both are provisional yet empty. In one sense, this idea is analogous to the belief that the kingdom of god is present on earth – seeing the divine in the mundane, as if the Light can be seen in the manifestations of the visible. In another sense, it suggests a thorough co-dependence if not interfusion of emptiness and provisionality, the absolute and the everyday, to the degree that the mere juxtaposition of these terms is construed as provisional itself. Tendai Buddhism uses the term 'three thousand worlds in one thought' (*ichinensanzen*) to describe this rather non-dual relationship of the divine and the mundane. So it is that even in ignorance original enlightenment shows itself.

The introduction of *hongaku* theory is substantially due to the work of Enchin (814/15–891/2), who studied in China, and used the theory as part of the underpinning of his combination of Tendai with esoteric practice derived from the Shingon school. The implication of *hongaku* is that all conscious beings are already endowed with enlightenment. He was chief founder of the Taimitsu or Tendai esotericism, as distinguished from the Tōmitsu or Shingon esotericism. The syncretic tendencies of Tendai were also increasingly reflected by a unification of Shinto and Buddhism (Japanese: *shinbutsu shūgō*), whose philosophical grounding can be found in the *honji-suijaku* doctrine, which identified the gods or *kami* of Shintoism as the manifestations of the Buddha. The Tendai influenced Sannō Ichijitsu Shinto and the Shingon sect called Ryōbu Shinto were both the result of this syncretism. Later there was proposed a reverse doctrine in which the Buddha was seen as a manifestation of the *kami*.

The work of Ennin (794–864) is also worth noting. After falling ill and retiring to Mount Hiei awaiting death he was miraculously healed after having had a vision of the Buddha in a dream. He set off the following year to China with great energy and eventually returned to Japan with a large number of texts and other materials, together with a detailed account of his travels in China. His work was vital for various strands of Japanese thinking, since the texts he brought back vitalized later Pure Land, Zen and Lotus Sūtra schools. He was thus a most significant figure in the rich Tendai synthesis which stood at the heart of the transmission of Buddhism in Japanese history.

SHINGON BUDDHISM: ESOTERICISM IN THE JAPANESE MODE

The monk Kūkai (774–835), posthumously titled Kōbō Daishi, whose friendship with Saichō deteriorated into a bitter rivalry in their later years, was the one who brought Shingon teachings back from China – secret teachings or *Mikkyō*. They derived from Chinese and, ultimately, from Indian *tantra,* focusing on the figure of the Buddha Mahāvairocana (Japanese: *Dainichi nyorai*). According to Kūkai, the overt teachings of Buddhism were disseminated by Śākyamuni, but these were supposed merely to prepare the way for the higher secret doctrines coming from Mahāvairocana, who was identified with the *dharmakāya* (Japanese: *hosshin*) or Truth Body of the Buddha, and so with ultimate reality. He is a cosmic being pantheistically conceived as embracing the universe. In accord with the teaching of Three Bodies, two other forms of Buddhahood were to be discerned: the Transformation Body (Sanskrit: *nirmāṇakāya*; Japanese: *ōjin*), that is, the Buddha as earthly being or Śākyamuni; and the Enjoyment Body (Sanskrit: *sambhogakāya*, Japanese: *hōjin*), in which a Buddha appears in celestial form, virtually as an enlightened being. Mahāvairocana is inherent in all human beings and in this the position of Shingon was similar to that of Tendai. However, Shingon differed from it in two significant ways: first, to Kūkai, the cosmic principle was thoroughly personal; second, the practitioners are believed to become the manifestation of Mahāvairocana in the esoteric ritual. To express the philosophical significance of this embodiment of the transcendent, Kūkai coined the phrase 'becoming Buddha in the present body' (*sokushin jōbutsu*). Philosophically, this conception collapses the dichotomies between the human body and Buddhahood, the individual and the universal, and between body and spirit.

Thus, the aim of Shingon practice is to realize the integration of the individual with the Ultimate, that is, with Mahāvairocana. Various forms of practice were laid down, including the repetition of cosmically powerful syllabi or formulas (Sanskrit: *dhāraṇī;* Japanese: *ju*). Part of the philosophy behind this is that the Ultimate manifests both internally as enlightened consciousness lying behind all phenomena, and externally as phenomena. It follows that for individuals to follow the true path they need to engage both in meditational or inner practice and in ritual or external practice. From an inner point of view the experience of enlightenment is non-dual, so that one becomes the ultimate. From the outer point of view there needs to be integration between meditation and bodily activity; or more particularly, making use of the so-called 'three mysteries' (Japanese: *sanmitsu*), i.e. body, speech and mind, so there needs to be a fusion of bodily, vocal and mental acts. As far as the first two go, this involves the use of *mudras* (Japanese: *inzō*) or formalized sitting positions and positions of the arms and hands, and of *mantras* or sacred prayers. In all of this, Buddhist *tantra* (Japanese: *tantora*) in India had drawn very close to Hindu *tantra*: it was a convergence of practice, in which Buddhists found the justification for ritual activities very like those which originally had been dismissed by the Buddha as irrelevant. In Japanese Buddhism the moves helped the synthesis between the cults of the *kami* and Buddhist orthodoxy, though as time went on it was probably esoteric Tendai that was the more influential.

Both Tendai and Shingon contained elements which were to be formative for some of the most Japanese of Buddhist forms – notably the schools of Pure Land and Zen Buddhism. It may be noted that in their differing ways Tendai and Shingon tended to stress the solidarity between the Ultimate and the empirical. In human terms this prepared the path for the fusion of religious and lay life. Since each person, for instance, contained within herself or himself the original enlightenment or the mind of Mahāvairocana, in the final analysis there could be no sharp distinction between the nun or monk on the one hand and the lay person on the other. The ideal of the Bodhisattva, moreover, was a Great Vehicle notion, which gave much more meaning to lay practice. So it was that Pure Land and Zen in their different modes integrated faith and ordinary life. It was no surprise if Zen ideas were utilized in and conflated with the practice of archery or of flower arrangement. A further idea which helped to contribute to the distinctive working out of Japanese forms of practice was the Buddhist theory that history is running downhill the farther we get from the time of the Buddha. By the eleventh century wide currency had been given to the concept of the 'latter end of the *dharma*' – of the *mappō*. This was the third great period of Buddhist history. In the first, the Buddha's teachings were fresh and powerful and people were ready to receive them, so many became enlightened. In the second age confusion was rife and few were able to meet the demands of the *dharma* or hear its music. Then there is the final age, when practice has thoroughly decayed and even the idea of enlightenment is neglected; the Order is in disorder and the sound of the Buddha's message is little but a distant echo. However, the Buddha in his wisdom has prepared through his skill in means a message of hope and faith. Saichō had written a treatise on the subject called *The Lamp to Light Up the Age of Final Dharma (Mappō Tōmyoki)*. The notion had been worked out in China, but it had more impact in Japan. Part of the idea was that after 2,000 years the *dharma* would have fallen into this great decay. The Chinese thought that the decease of the Buddha had happened in 849 BCE and the onset of the final age was due therefore in 552 CE, but the Japanese used other calculations and the year 1052 came to have a vivid meaning as ushering in the new age.

The concept had a double effect. On the one hand, it called for an easy way to be saved (for instance, by calling on the Buddha Amida in faith). On the other hand, it rendered obsolete the precepts and moral austerities of the Buddhist past. So even if monks did not live up to their calling they were still to be treated with grave respect, and older Buddhist shunnings of people who made their living in an evil and violent way were no longer to be applied (so warriors, prostitutes, hunters, and so on should not be ruled out from the fold in the community's quest for salvation).

It may be remarked in all this that the Japanese inherited both from their own experience and from the Chinese values through which they had absorbed a lively sense of history. The *mappō* idea also corresponded with a period of hardship and anarchy in Japanese life in the eleventh century. The Tendai school was influential in bringing the *mappō* idea to the fore, even if it was not until some time after Saichō that it bore its full fruit.

HŌNEN AND THE PURE LAND SCHOOL

The idea that there is a Pure Land or *sukhāvati* (Japanese: *jōdo*) goes back to Mahāyāna Buddhism in India; and the school of *Qingtu* was important in China. But it was in Japan that the Pure Land idea met its apogee. Among the vital founders and teachers in the tradition, the most vital no doubt was Hōnen (1113–1212). He trained at the Tendai headquarters on Mount Hiei. He was rather disillusioned by the decadent state of monasticism and the rise of militarism among monks. In 1175 he became convinced that salvation must lie in the invocation of the name of Amida Butsu (the Buddha Amitābha). This invocation was known for short as the *nembutsu*; and in 1197 Honen wrote, at the request of the then First Minister, his most vital book on the idea of this invocation *(Collection of Passages on the Original Vow of Amida in which the Nembutsu is Chosen above all*; Japanese: *Senchaku hongan nembutsushū)*.

In this he distinguished between the more difficult Buddhist path, that of the sages, from the easier, the gate of the Pure Land. The former path is one in which the individual is self-reliant, i.e. relying on his or her own exertions. This was known as *jiriki*. The Pure Land relies on the work of another, or *tariki*: namely, one relies on the work of the Buddha Amida. Perhaps somewhat inconsistently, Hōnen held that repeated invocation of Amida's name was important in ensuring that body and mind stay purified. On this issue his followers divided, after his death, in that continued repetition of the name could be construed as a ritual practice with its own significance and power, preparing the way to embody aspects of Tendai and Shingon techniques in the movement. Nevertheless, these debates raise a question central to every form of *tariki* faith. Does the vow of Amida relieve the practitioner from religious practice and moral behavior and thus invite laziness and immorality? If not, does it not introduce the notion of self-power through the backdoor?

To look at the Pure Land movement in Indian terms: it was a school of *bhakti*. In Christian terms, it was close to the sentiments of early Protestantism. It is said that Francis Xavier, the gifted Jesuit missionary, declared on his arrival in Japan that Luther had got there before him. The emphasis on ideas akin to grace is unmistakable, and was to become even more pronounced, as we shall see, with Shinran and the Jōdo Shinshū. It may also be noted that there were elements in Buddhist doctrine which made these movements in effect a form of theism.

For one thing, Amida was identified with the underlying Absolute (as had happened with Mahāvairocana in Japanese Tendai) and source of phenomena. And although the divine might be held to reside in each one of us, the phenomenology of Pure Land Buddhism was to have a sense of the otherness of Amida – the object of worship, the source of salvation, the pure one over against the defiled creation and the decayed human race, incapable of virtue through its own efforts, but always relying upon the Other. The reasons for espousing such a theism were not primarily philosophical, though the concepts of Tendai, itself synthesizing so many philosophical and other texts, entered into it; the worldview found its justification more in the visions of its saints and in the sense of loving presence which was shared by the faithful. In short, the main motivations were religious, and reflected a sense of the numinous combined with a prizing of personal relationship with the Transcendent. Here was a very different phenomenological basis from that which inspired the Theravāda and other forms of the self-help wing of Buddhism (here the mystical, inner experience was prominent, rather than numinous visions). The Tendai–Shingon encouragement of the practice of visualization (of celestial forms of the Buddhas and of abstract *mandalas*) was a halfway house to the pietistic love of Amida displayed in the Pure Land movements. We now turn to Shinran's radical extension of Honen's teachings about faith.

SHINRAN: THE JŌDO SHINSHŪ AND AMIDA'S POWER OF ELECTION

Shinran (1173–1262) was led by a vision to become a disciple of Hōnen. As a result of criticism from other monks, Hōnen and some of his disciples were exiled from Mt Hiei for a few years. During this time Shinran, as a result of a dream he had of Kannon or the Bodhisattva Avalokiteśvara – who, in China, is revered as the goddess Guanyin and, in Japan, as the rather androgynous Kannon – got married and raised a family. This was to show among other things that the good works of becoming a monk did not bring salvation: celibacy did not produce the requisite merit. Instead merit flowed down to humanity from Amida. Eons ago he had as a Bodhisattva made a vow to save human beings through translating them on death to the paradise of the Pure Land, and it was the power of his virtually limitless store of merit that made the Pure Land; it was his surplus merit too that broke through the ordinary modes of working of karma. The round of rebirth was short-circuited. Grace could take the faithful straight to a new nirvāṇa, namely the Pure Land paradise.

Shinran's comments, especially those collected by his disciples in the famous *Tannishō*, are rather provocative. For example, he famously claimed that an evil person could be more easily saved than a good one. This phrase has to be understood in the context of the *tariki* rhetoric characteristic of Pure Land Buddhism. Only a person who is aware of his or her limitations and, even more fundamentally, fallibility will rely on Amida and practice the *nembutsu* to begin with. Ultimately, however, Shinran believed that all living beings are equal to the Buddha, for all reflect the original divine consciousness. He took the idea of the power of the Other (the *tariki*) to its logical conclusion. If a person is not saved because she or he does good works, but solely through faith as manifested in her or his uttering of the *nembutsu*, calling in devotion on the name of Amida, then that person is not saved because she or he dredges up the willpower to do such homage. Rather, the faith of the individual and her calling on Amida are themselves the work of Amida. The uttering of the *nembutsu* is a sincere and spontaneous expression of faith, not a calculated means of gaining rebirth in paradise. It is an expression, then, of a faith which itself is created by Amida.

Shinran took this reasoning one step further and argued, not unlike Blaise Pascal in his famous wager, that he did not even know whether or not the *nembutsu* constitutes a valid method for the attainment of Buddhahood. He rather suggests that faith in Amida logically follows from the basic human limitation, cognitive and otherwise. More concretely, Shinran admits that his ignorance and inability are so thorough that incapable of knowing the truth and of practicing the *jiriki* way he does not have a choice except for entrusting himself in the original vow of Amida. If the Pure Land teaching is not true he is condemned to hell anyway since he is unable to engage in the practices offered by other Buddhist schools and to attain Buddhahood by himself. In other words, Shinran's practice of the *nembutsu* is not a result of or reflects his conviction and strength but rather his awareness of his own limitations.

One great advantage of these doctrines is that the faithful follower of the True Pure Land school need not leave his or her worldly life. Shinran himself set up meetings in people's houses. If his movement took off as a separate denomination, this was hardly his intention. However, his daughter Kakushinni set up a mausoleum for her father east of Kyoto which became the nucleus of the Hongani temple, and this came to be the center of a variant on the Jōdoshū, namely the Jōdo Shinshū, or True Pure Land school.

The Pure Land movements, then, are an important strand in Japanese piety and take further the pietistic type of Buddhism found in China and before that in India. They draw out one strand of the Tendai synthesis, and exploit the theory of *mappō*. Somewhat associated with them but bearing a more aggressive stamp is the movement which has come to be known as Nichiren Buddhism, after its founder. This has been especially vital in recent times since a modernized form of it is the Soka Gakkai, one of the most powerful of the so-called new religions of Japan. It is also one of the main sources of three other new religions.

NICHIREN BUDDHISM: THE PRIMACY OF THE LOTUS SŪTRA AND THE IMPORTANCE OF JAPAN

Nichiren (1222–82) had a stormy life, for he came into conflict not only with other Buddhists but also with the government. It was a rough time of political strife, inundations, famines and threatened invasions by the Mongols. Such evils he said were to be traced to the lax views of the regime, which he claimed patronized false forms of religion and failed to bow to the primacy of the *Lotus Sūtra*. When Korean envoys came to Japan in 1268 bearing demands for the payment of tribute to the great Khubilai Khan, by then ruler of China and the great Mongol potentate whose power stretched over much of Asia, Nichiren reminded the Hōjō regents of the time that he had foretold this in a book he had presented to the court some eight years before. His position regarding other forms of Buddhism was uncompromising, and he denounced them with an evangelical fervor that was not typical of Buddhist attitudes.

For him the supreme text was the *Lotus Sūtra*. Salvation could be gained only by the recitation of the formula *Namu Myōhōrengekyō* or 'Adoration to the Lotus of the True Law'. The Lotus was regarded by most exegetes of the time to consist of two parts, the first fourteen chapters, which dealt with the teachings of the manifest Śākyamuni (the historical Buddha), and the second fourteen dealing with the eternal Śākyamuni, a transcendental figure. It was this latter Śākyamuni that was the sole real object of worship. Nichiren Buddhists also pay homage to a sacred diagram depicting the eternal

Śākyamuni and other beings surrounding the sacred title of the Lotus. The logic of Nichiren's idea that homage to the Lotus could bring liberation is this: the true meaning of the Lotus is what it points to, and this is the Ultimate. So in paying homage to the Lotus we are paying homage to the ultimate, eternal Śākyamuni. With these doctrines Nichiren adapted some of the principles of Tendai in a new way. By simplifying the ritual demands to repetition of the name of the Lotus he democratized esoteric Buddhism; and by being fiercely critical of other schools he gave his own movement a sharp edge. At the same time he appealed strongly to national sentiment, which was helped to form through the threat posed from outside by the Mongol fleet.

We see then various movements which promised easy salvation and which owed part of their power to ideas mediated by the Tendai school. With the advent of Pure Land Buddhism we find a typical form of Japanese worldview, making creative use of the eschatology of the *mappō*. Though it has its roots in earlier Buddhism, it has its full flowering in Japanese culture, and remains vigorous today.

ANOTHER TYPICAL JAPANESE MOTIF: ZEN BUDDHISM

At the end of the spectrum of Buddhism from the Pure Land was Meditation Buddhism. Its concentration upon meditation practice gives it some of the straightforward traditionalism of the Theravada, but its incorporation of new techniques, including the use of 'secular' arts such as calligraphy, gives it both originality and a special place in Japanese culture and society. Like other movements it was derived from China and brought into Japan: it was then absorbed and digested, to take a characteristic Japanese form.

It was at about the same time as the labors of Hōnen and Shinran that Zen gained its foothold in Japan and was a part of efforts to reform and revive the Buddhist tradition during a period of degeneration. Tendai was dominant, with its embracing doctrines, but it was also decadent. Monks were often taken up with political intrigues, while militarism had developed in the monasteries. Eisai (1141–1215), who was born of a priestly family, is credited with the first main introduction of Zen – and in particular Rinzai Zen – practices and ideas into Japan (though he himself credited Saichō, four centuries earlier, with a knowledge and appreciation of Zen). He made two trips to China. The first of these only lasted six months and was chiefly aimed at the gathering of Tendai texts. This was at the age of 28. It was in his late forties that a more momentous journey to China occurred, for during it he came in touch with a Chan master, who granted a certificate of enlightenment. Eisai on his return began to set up centers for the practice of Zen, but met a lot of opposition from the official Tendai. In defending himself Eisai wrote a significant book which argued on behalf of Zen: that it was Buddhism in a nutshell; that it had been known to Saichō and so was not some great innovation; that it involved the proper observance of Buddhist precepts and discipline; and that it could lead to new life in Buddhism in Japan which in turn would assure the well-being and security of the nation. A side interest of his was tea drinking, and the introduction of the herb to Japan had a large effect both on secular culture and the life of the monks (it was useful for keeping awake). Though his defense of Zen did not cut much ice with the Tendai establishment, he did get backing from the shogunate. This meant that Zen could at least take root in Japan, and later gained great influence.

Zen Buddhism was a contrast to the Pure Land in that it was a form of 'self-reliance' rather than 'reliance on the other'. Based on Yogācāra notions, it nevertheless and especially in its Rinzai form came to be anti-metaphysical. Its primary emphasis, as in China, was on experience or *satori* – that is, realization or enlightenment. In the Rinzai school it taught that such enlightenment was sudden: it came out of the blue. The rival Sōtō school believed in gradualism and stressed the deepened significance of the method used to achieve the goal, namely sitting meditation or *zazen*.

DŌGEN AND THE ESTABLISHMENT OF SŌTŌ ZEN

The chief exponent of this second form of Zen was Dōgen (1200–53). As with many other leading figures in Japanese Buddhism he studied Tendai at Mount Hiei. Hagiographies suggest that the source of his spiritual quest was twofold. Having lost both parents at an early age, Dōgen was driven by his insight into the impermanence of all of reality. Furthermore, while on Mount Hiei, he was puzzled by the seeming contradiction between the notions of *hongaku* and *shikaku*, original enlightenment and acquired enlightenment. If human beings are bestowed with original enlightenment, why is practice necessary? To solve this conundrum, so the later hagiographical accounts of his life go, he turned to Zen Buddhism and went to China where he studied under the Caodong master Rujing (Japanese: *Nyojō*). On his return he promoted the practice and theory of *zazen*, described the confirmatory experience as 'casting off body and mind' *(shinjin datsuraku)*, and wrote a number of works, the most famous of which is *Shōbōgenzō (The Treasury of the True Dharma Eye)*.

His main teachings were in part practical and in part theoretical. On the side of practice he was utterly devoted to sitting meditation and established detailed monastic rules. It is in this meditation that the Buddha-nature becomes most evident. For Dōgen did not think of the Buddha-nature as a special ingredient within each one of us, like a soul. He radically combined the Mahāyāna insights about the Buddha-nature with the ancient Buddhist concern with the idea of the transiency of all things. So he thought of the Buddha-nature as itself a changing, not a fixed or eternal, entity which is present in every event, both conscious and non-conscious. The very impermanence that characterizes everything *is* the Buddha-nature. In this way Dōgen takes most seriously the equation that nirvāṇa is saṃsāra.

In his *Shōbōgenzō, Dōgen* develops a rather radical non-dual philosophy in which Buddhas and sentient beings, practice and attainment, individual and the cosmos are neither one nor two. Rather Buddhahood is 'made present' (*genjō*) by the practice of the individual. In other words, the practice of *zazen* reveals that the self does not constitute an independent system or substance, but rather equally discloses all Buddha ancestors, the 'ten thousand things' (*manbō*), and all of nature. As long as the practitioner assumes an egocentric perspective, the self mistakenly believes itself to possess a substance and to be separate from the world. If, however, the practitioner assumes the standpoint of the ten thousand things, the fallacy of substantialism and dualism is revealed. Dōgen underscores this non-substantialism by conceiving of reality as radically dynamic – he uses the phrase 'total working' (*zenki*). Analogously, practice has to be understood as the continuous activity (*gyōji*) that participates in and makes present the creativity of the Buddhas.

In addition, Dōgen's position implied that time is inherent in all beings: time and being are not separate entities, but neither are beings located in time, yet they express time. To illustrate his position, Dōgen coins the term 'being-time' (*uji*). This means, that every single event, Dōgen calls them 'dharma positions' (*hōi*), fully manifests Buddhahood and is self-contained. While Dōgen focuses his conception of time on the 'absolute now' (*nikon*) rather than the progression from a past to the future, he does not abrogate the sense of continuity but emphasizes that the present has the character of a 'passage' (*kyōraku*); he also observes wryly in his *Shōbōgenzō Genjōkōan* that 'once firewood has become ashes, it does not return to be firewood'.

All this led Dōgen to reject the theory of *mappō*. He thought not only that the Buddhanature and so the essential teachings of the Buddha were present here and now: but also that through the practice of *zazen* liberation was open to all. Nevertheless, the tendency of Dōgen's thought and so that of Sōtō Zen was elitist, even if in the later evolution of the movement it came to fashion rituals of death for funerals and memorials to the dead. In the Edo period, Sōtō temples increasingly took to administering medicine and related health care services, especially to the rural population. Such a popular interface no doubt helped Sōtō to gain a popular following but also encouraged a two-tier religion.

ZEN AND THE MARTIAL AND OTHER ARTS

Some of the philosophy of Zen accounts for the way in which it influenced the martial and other arts. A strong element in it was the idea of harmony with nature, partly derived from Taoism and partly from the nature-oriented character of Japanese Shinto. This harmony was grounded in two features of Zen and more broadly in Buddhist thought. One was the notion that the conceptual distinctions we necessarily use in language are themselves projections upon the world around us – they introduce a cultural and artificial mode of thinking about and reacting to nature. It is necessary to scrape away our concepts. For this purpose Rinzai Zen introduced the mind-boggling riddles the *kōans* (Chinese: *gongan*) that are based on encounter dialogues. The other is the perception that time is of the essence of things, and so we strive to live in the now, not trying to stop the movie, but taking part in its flow. Such attitudes generated an appreciation of harmony, spontaneity and the vitality of non-verbal communication (or at least not straightforward verbal communication). It became the fashion for monks and others to try to convey their enlightenment in a brief, and oblique, poem, to practice highly expressive calligraphy and painting, and to adopt various arts where practice could eliminate self-conscious thought and enhance a full spontaneity. Some of these arts were the martial ones – such as swordsmanship, spearmanship, archery, wrestling and even (later on) riflery. There was, moreover some synthesis in medieval Japan between Zen attitudes and the values of the warrior or *Bushidō*. Indifference to death went with living for the moment. Buddhist discipline combined with the requirements of feudal loyalty and Confucian filial piety. Skill at war could be greatly enhanced by training in naturalness. Moreover, the abolition of the distinction between nirvāṇa and saṃsāra opened up faith to the lay person, for he already had the Buddha-nature present to the very temporal fiber of his being (or one should say becoming).

The master–pupil relationship is vital to Zen, because of its emphasis on non-verbal communication. Only someone who has gained enlightenment can see it in others; and only he can teach others to tread upon the paradoxical path. This means that though Zen in other respects is in principle egalitarian, it has its own hierarchical structure. But the ideal of non-verbal communication is present in another way in the arts: they have their own rules and each is in its different mode a self-contained system. It is like a language but it is not a language. So in exercising an art to perfection one is conveying something, but it is not through language. There can also be (so to speak) poetical or metaphorical asides. Thus the shooting of an arrow at a target is itself a metaphor for aiming at the center, or aiming at enlightenment or happiness. And yet you cannot achieve happiness by aiming directly at it, nor indeed spontaneous enlightenment. You must strive for these things by not striving, and the path turns out to be an oblique one.

One of the most famous manuals that combine Zen insights and martial art training is Takuan Sōhō's (1573–1645) *The Mysterious Record of the Immovable Wisdom* (*Fudō chishin myōroku*). In this text, he distinguishes between two states of mind, the 'delusional mind' (*mōshin*) that 'abides in a place' (*jūchi*) and the 'no-mind' (*mushin*) that flows freely through the body of the practitioner as well as the body of the opponent. The no-mind, Takuan explains, flows like water and is illustrated by the thousand arms of Kannon Bodhisattva. Kannon can move her arms simultaneously since she is not attached to any individual one of them. In other words, the ideal mental state, to Takuan, is that of complete detachment. The practices of both Zen meditation and sword fighting are designed to transform the delusion of the every mind that is attached to thoughts, emotions, and to the objects of the senses into no-mind. No-mind is the state, Takuan continues, where 'all Buddhas and sentient beings are one'. Such an attitude of detachment is not only beneficial to combat but constitutes the attainment of Buddhahood. Interestingly enough Takuan adds the suggestion that such mind also realizes that the three teachings, Buddhism, Shintoism, and Confucianism, are originally one. He thus applies the Chinese notion of the 'three teachings' (*sanjiao*) to the Japanese context.

HAKUIN AND THE REVIVAL OF RINZAI ZEN

The intellectual side of Zen looked fresh and innovatory, but in practice it could be seen as importantly rooted in the old monastic ideal. It was not surprising, especially in view of the rivalry of the Pure Land schools, which were highly popular and well suited to mass appeal, that as time went on Zen practice became diluted. Moreover, the Zen practitioners wished to maintain their interface with the rest of Buddhism. As with most other movements, practice began to degenerate. By the eighteenth century Rinzai was in need of reform, and this revival was supplied by the many-faceted work of Hakuin (1685/6–1768/9) during the Tokugawa shogunate. Buddhism during this period was under strict central control through something like a parish system. This State supervision could induce a deadness, and it was true that Zen practice had become too formalized. After years of study under various masters he set about restoring the *kōan* system and reviving the practices of early Zen teachers in Japan. He was particularly keen to underline the necessity of meditating in the midst of ordinary life, and he was against making meditation a special and secluded practice. He brought in a highly rigorous training schedule. He also himself continued the artistic tradition – quite a number of his sketches and calligraphic exercises are preserved. His reform was successful, so that all the Rinzai masters of today trace their lineage back to Hakuin.

Hakuin suggests that *satori* is necessarily preceded by 'great doubt' (*daigi*) and 'great death' (*daishi*). The practitioner has to be able and willing to let go of all securities and beliefs and throw himself or herself into the abyss of emptiness. Hakuin urges the practitioner to abandon all discriminating thought, to form the 'ball of doubt' (*gidan*), and to penetrate the One Mind. This, Hakuin says, is the experience of 'great death'. Only then is the practitioner able to solve the 'great matter' (*daiji*) and to attain 'great awakening' (*daigo*). Hakuin's own experience of *satori* was so violent that he suffered what he referred to as 'Zen sickness' (*zenbyō*). He overcame this sickness with the help of a Daoist mendicant who taught him medical practices and the therapeutic effects of recitation. Nevertheless, in his letters, he praised sickness as a pedagogical tool that teaches the practitioner the urgency and necessity of meditation since it focuses one's undivided attention on the suffering characteristic of the world of birth and death (*shōji*).

In brief, Zen has taken on a Japanese form in its austerity, economy, artistic tendencies, capacity to integrate with warrior and other modes of secular existence and its peculiar harmony with nature, often expressed in its characteristic art and poetry. Its anti-intellectualism has an intellectual basis in the Mādhyamika dialectic, though its spirit has also been influenced by Kegon or Huayan. In its single-minded concern for meditation it has strong analogies to the Theravāda, as though in the turning of the wheel from Sri Lanka to Japan that wheel had come full circle. Its love of paradox and its love of action have made it popular in the West (in part because it resolves intellectual difficulties by destroying concepts from within and thus destroying the intellect that caused the problems in the first place). I will treat the modern period separately in a later chapter.

Meanwhile, there is another aspect of Japanese Buddhism which it is important to look at, as it had some relevance to developments in the modern period. This is the relationship between Shinto and Buddhism, which we have already touched upon. Here we step back to consider the primordial patterns of Shinto thought, rooted in the myths of early Japan.

SOME MAIN SHINTO IDEAS: *KAMI*, PURITY, HUMANITY

Shinto or 'the way of the gods' is the name given to the collection of myths and rites which are rooted in early Japanese conceptions of the *kami*. These spirits are anything which may inspire awe, but predominantly have been associated with natural phenomena, although many are also deified heroes. Originally the rites were performed in beautiful or awe-inspiring spots, but later were held in shrines. (It is customary to refer to Buddhist *temples* and Shinto *shrines*; the latter are in fact temples.) Worship was designed to please the gods. A vital place came to be held by the idea of purity.

This notion, which had a ritual meaning (in that one could for instance purify oneself before worship by water), also had a metaphysical meaning in relation to the human heart. The *magokoro* or 'true heart' is pure and sincere. This links with the belief that the divine light which illuminates the *kami* is also found in the human heart. It is like a mirror which needs polishing and cleaning, to clear away the dust and dirt which obscure it. These conceptions could easily be linked with the Confucian belief in the heavenly nature of the mind and with the Buddhist concept of the Buddha-nature. Over much of its history therefore Shinto existed in subordination to Confucian and particular Buddhist institutions and ideas. The *kami* were seen as manifestations of Buddhas and Bodhisattvas. For instance, Shingon Shinto identified Mahāvairocana (who was symbolized by the sun) with the foundational goddess Amaterasu, from whom the royal family were supposedly descended.

This situation itself suggested a backlash. While in the Edo period most Shinto shrines were controlled by Buddhist monks, a rival form had grown up called Yoshida Shinto, founded by Urabe Kanetomo (1435–1511), who was a priest from the Yoshida shrine in Kyoto. This worked out its own theology, which included the idea of a supreme god, Taigen Sonjin (Great Exalted One) who was creator of the universe and all beings. This form of Shinto took over certain ideas from Shingon and incorporated some of its rituals. This was a reverse application of Shinto–Buddhist synthesis.

ATTEMPTS AT A SYNTHESIS BETWEEN SHINTO AND CONFUCIANISM

In the seventeenth century the revival of Confucian scholarship also led to ways of combining Shinto and Confucian values. The *kami* nature in the human being is identified with *li* (Japanese: *ri*; principle), according to one version of this philosophy, which is obscured by egotism or *qi* (Japanese: *ki*; the material force). It is necessary to purify the *li*. The ethic of the school centers on the three treasures of benevolence, loyalty and service (a trio useful in an ideology designed to commend itself to the State). Another important school was known as Suiga Shinto, which had influence later when the shogunate was overthrown, preparing the way for the Meiji restoration of 1868. It was started by Yamazaki Ansai (1618–82), who was given the name Suika as his Shinto religious name. He had originally trained to be a Zen priest, but had gained some knowledge of Zhuxi in the course of his studies. With this he came to see an important alternative to Buddhism and left the monastery. He began to teach the thought of Zhuxi. Many of his students were members of the samurai class, and this gave him some political influence. He was as it happens a good popularizer. He also was opposed to pure scholarship and was much more interested in the moral side of the Neoconfucian philosophy. It is not surprising therefore that he prized reverential seriousness over the investigation of things through external inquiry and book learning (thus changing Zhuxi's priorities). He saw Confucianism and Shinto as distinct systems in so far as they had different national origins, but as being parallel. His 'Japaneseness' gave his school a nationalist edge and prepared the path for other developments, such as the Kokugaku or National Learning school.

THE NATIONAL LEARNING SCHOOL AND THE THOUGHT OF MOTOORI NORINAGA

Motoori Norinaga (1730–1801) was sent by his family, which was of the lowest, merchant class to Kyoto to study, and learned, among other things, the art of medicine. But he became more interested in literary research, especially because his imagination was fired by reading a book on Japanese poetry written by a Shingon monk. This inspired his delving into the great works of Japanese literature. Through this he sought to have a restored appreciation of the essence of Japanese traditional thinking, going back to the earliest Shinto scriptures. For instance, he wrote a commentary on one of the two fundamental collections, the *Kojiki*. It was in the course of writing about the famous *Tales of Genji* that he formulated his well-known concept of *mono no aware* or 'feelings after experience'. That is, he looked to the feelings arising immediately after you experience something as being vital and serving as the key to understanding the *Tales of Genji*. It was a way of coming to terms with the essence of Japanese estheticism. By adopting this naturalistic approach to literature he freed his mind of the moralizing which often typified traditional criticism. In removing this crust of moralism he restored a sense of the freshness and vigor of the ancient texts of Japan. This involved a kind of national revival of pride in what was distinctively Japanese in the Japanese heritage.

It is interesting that in his criticism of the synthesis between Shinto and Confucianism that had been so fashionable in the previous generation, despite his reservation towards the Chinese tradition, Norinaga received inspiration from the thought of Zhuangzi: one needed to achieve harmony with nature, itself controlled by the *kami*. An earlier thinker, Kamo no Mabuchi (1697–1769) had appropriated Laozi for similar reasons. He had seen Confucian and Buddhist ways of interpreting Shinto as basically artificial and unnatural. They were the products of human imagination. Mabuchi advocated rather the spontaneity and acting-through-not-acting of the Taoist tradition, as a key to perceiving the true naturalness of the old Japanese tradition of the *kami*.

Ultimately Norinaga's thought was radically anti-rationalistic. He argued on the basis of the *Kojiki* and nativistic ideas against what he perceived to be foreign, that is Chinese, rationalism. The goal of scholarship is to recognize the purity of the text, the text of the *Kojiki*, and to return to the original sound and meaning of its words (*kotodama*). Words have spiritual power and evoke the 'spirit of ancient Japan' (*yamato damashii*). Rationality, on the contrary, Norinaga argues, lacks two basic aspects. First, it ignores the importance of emotions; second, rationality fails to account for even the most obvious facts of life such as the obvious existence of evil and negative emotions; yet they do exist. A philosophy based on scripture, that is, the *Kojiki*, and emotions rather than reason is more realistic and holistic; it recognizes the *mono no aware*. The more realistic and natural attitude towards life than rationality is, according to Norinaga, awe.

An important successor to Norinaga was Hirata Atsutane (1776–1843), who was interestingly enough influenced by what he had read of Christian writers, notably of Matteo Ricci, the famous Jesuit. Actually his philosophy, referred to as Hiratagaku, was somewhat influenced by Christian ideas. Contrary to Norinaga, who insisted on a literal reading of *Kojiki* and believed that the world was created by the divine couple Izanagi and Izanami and is now ruled by the sun goddess Amaterasu, Atsutane aspired towards what he perceived to be a more contemporary interpretation of the Shinto mythology and thought. He suggested a main deity, Amenominakanushinomikoto, who was the head of the trinity of three *kami* that did create and are in charge of the triple world of heaven, earth, and the netherworld. He also fashioned his vision of the afterlife on the Christian model. Where Norinaga accepted the existence and inevitability of the netherland (*yomi*) as described in the *Kojiki*, Atsutane assigned a great *kami*, *Ōkuninushinomikoto*, to judge over the dead in the next world and to assign punishments and rewards. The cosmos is thus conceived of as an impermanent home in which humanity is tested – a vale of soul-making, so to speak. In the end, Atsutane tried to reconcile traditional Shinto cosmology, which postulated a three-tiered cosmos, with the Newtonian astronomy he had learned of through Western books. His researches into ancient Japan led him to believe that the imperial system prevailed then: this became an implicit critique of the shogunate and the system of non-imperial military dictatorship. This and other factors brought him into conflict with the government and he was ordered to stop writing in 1841.

The Kokugaku was also able to give new meaning to the goddess Amaterasu in her creative role. She was also the imperial ancestress. So it was that religious sanction was given to the restiveness which led in due course to the overthrow of the Tokugawa shogunate. The ideology therefore of the Kokugaku is crucial in understanding the forces that gave rise to modern Japan. In some degree we can see the attacks on Confucian and Buddhist values as a backlash against the foreign influences that had fertilized Japanese culture.

Shinto, then, was a vital component in Japanese self-understanding. It was not a philosophically inclined system, unlike Buddhism which from the beginning had a vital doctrinal component and Confucianism which from the start had an educational and literary side to it. But if Shinto as an independent force were to be re-established – and this was an obvious move among Japanese nationalists – then it had to be given some philosophical clothing to stand up to the other systems. This was why Motoori Norinaga could reach out to Taoism and Atsutane could make use of Christian sources. To some degree the new movement towards a new sense of national pride was a literary one and not bound up exclusively with Shinto. But Shinto gave the movement power. The story of how Shinto later fared after the Meiji restoration we leave until another chapter: but it is interesting and ironic that the Japanese constitution ruled it not to be a religion, so that adherence to its values, required of all Japanese, would not conflict with the constitutional provision of freedom of religion to all citizens. This was another twist in the history of Shinto.

Meanwhile we have to turn the clock back from the Edo period in order to contemplate the way in which Confucianism developed in Japan.

CONFUCIANISM IN JAPAN BEFORE THE TOKUGAWA REGIME

It was chiefly during the Tokugawa shogunate that Confucian scholarship really flourished in Japan. Hitherto it had been overshadowed by Buddhism, although Confucian principles had a very ancient foothold in Japan, as early as Prince Shotoku. During the fourteenth century the Ashinaga shogunate had set up a Confucian academy, where Buddhist books were banned; but much of the study of Neoconfucianism had taken place in the Zen monasteries, where the practice of maintaining reverence and quiet sitting appealed as an adjunct to *zazen*. To some extent Confucian ideology had been used politically, especially before the installation of the system of shoguns. But most patronage had gone to the Buddhists, and it was only during the Tokugawa era that a restlessness had brought about not merely the revival of Shinto described above but also a new interest in the Confucian worldview.

Generally speaking, Japanese culture underplayed the tensions between Buddhism and the Confucian ethos. This was partly because so much of Japanese Buddhism was world-affirming. The fact that there could be married monks reduced the conflict between family-oriented Confucian values and those of the Buddha's path. Metaphysically there was no great gap between some forms of Neoconfucianism and Huayan (Kegon) and Tendai. Still, the fact remains that Confucianism often looked upon itself, in the Chinese context and so ultimately in the derivative Japanese context, as a rational alternative to 'superstitious' Buddhism. The rift was sooner or later going to show itself. In the fourteenth century the Ashigaka's Confucian academy banned the use of Buddhist works. But it was during the Tokugawa regime, from 1603 to 1868 that the 'teaching of the literati' (*rujiao*) really came into its own in Japan.

THE TOKUGAWAS AND THE SHUSHI SCHOOL

Even before he became the shogun, the powerful Tokugawa Ieyasu had consulted with the foremost follower of Zhuxi, Fujiwara Seika (1561–1619) with some view of making Shushi (Zhuxi) Confucianism his ruling ideology. Seika deputized his student Hayashi Razan (1583–1657) to the Tokugawa. Hayashi's son and grandson followed him as head of the Confucian academy in Edo (Tokyo), and formulated the educational policy of the regime. Hayashi himself took a hard line against other worldviews, though he himself had started out as a Zen Buddhist. Much of his work was taken up with polemics against Laozi and Taoism and various forms of Buddhism, together with Christianity (which was suppressed in Japan, only to emerge once again during the Meiji restoration). But in fact Buddhist influences remained strong in early Tokugawa times, and especially the Buddhist–Shinto synthesis: the shogun Ieyasu was elevated to the status of a *kami*. Hayashi accepted a position at court analogous to that of a priest, wearing a special

144

robe and having his head shaved: this conflicted with the usual ideal of the Confucian entering ordinary administrative work. But he did succeed in gaining a recognized place in the ruling structure for a sort of official Confucianism. He propagated Zhuxi's theory of *li* and *qi*, the importance of rites to bridge the gap between heaven and earth, and the five virtues – human-heartedness, righteousness, observance of rites, wisdom, and loyalty – a list compiled in the Han dynasty that added loyalty to Mencius' four virtues. He engaged in sectarian politics and was critical of deviant forms, such as the Wang Yangming school (called in Japanese *Oyōmeigakuha*); he rather allied himself with such populist Confucianism as that expressed by Kaibara Ekken (1630–1714), who wrote among other things an ethical handbook for women called *The Great Learning for Women (Onna daigaku)*. Ekken believed that doubt constituted the means of clarification and intellectual progress. He further recommended a dual method of knowledge and practice. Even though he identified himself as a member of the Shushi school, he criticized Zhuxi's metaphysics for what he perceived to be its inherent dualism and suggested as an alternative a monism of the all-pervading *ki* (Chinese *qi*), that is, the ultimate life-force. Ekken argued that if *li* is conceived of as the *li* of *qi*, the two are necessarily inseparable. This re-interpretation of Zhuxi's metaphysics under the influence of Buddhism and Taoism could be reconciled with the Chinese medical system. Contrary to Buddhism and Taoism, however, Ekken suggested that the primary principle of the 'Great Ultimate' (Chinese: *taiji*; Japanese: *taikyoku*) has to be grasped in terms of 'being' rather than 'non-being'.

THE IDEALIST ALTERNATIVE TO THE SHUSHI SCHOOL

As a counterbalance to the formalism of the Shushi school, Ōyōmei's idealism had attractions. It was probably Nakae Tōju (1608–48) who was the most important figure in establishing this form of Neoconfucianism in Japan. The teaching of the Ōyōmei school in Japan, which was also dubbed the 'study of the mind', focused on the unity of the principle (Chinese: *li*; Japanese: *ri*) and the mind (Chinese: *xin*; Japanese: *shin*) as well as the unity of knowledge and practice. Metaphysically, this conception resulted in a mentalism that denied the existence of external objects. In a similar vein, this school attempted to balance the intellectualism of the Shushi school especially with regards to ethics, and rather recommended the cultivation of the mind, the purpose of which was the re(dis)covery one's inborn conscience. This was in line with Tōju's personalistic ethics, in which he concentrated on filial piety as the central virtue. There could be an attitude, in line with this, to the universe as a whole, through allegiance to the Great Lord. He did not put forward filial piety or loyalty as a means precisely of reinforcing hierarchical modes in Japanese society, since it applied equally to all. But it provided the moral and emotional glue holding society together and reinforced a sense of patriotism

145

through the figure of the emperor. But these latter implications of his thought owe much to followers, who drew out from his teachings some of the values fermenting during the late Edo period which prepared the path for the Meiji restoration and for modern Japanese nationalism. His own appeal to filial loyalty was universal, and his general stance had some analogies to the Christianity of the period. His most vital follower was Kumazawa Banzan (1619–91), who rose high in the service of the provincial lord of Okayama, where he effected striking reforms and at the same time attracted enemies. His teachings were under suspicion because the Shushi variety were the officially approved form. The stress on innate knowledge and introspective cultivation was a license for an individualism which Kumazawa displayed in his own life, and might be thought to encourage it in others. The Ōyōmei school certainly underlined the intuitive side of Japanese culture: the attraction of the contrasting Shushi school was its formal adherence to Chinese ways and an outer discipline of ritual and correct behavior.

But the most vital of all the forms of Confucianism in Tokugawa Japan was undoubtedly the movement known as Kogaku or Ancient Learning, which was opposed both to the Shushi and the Oyomei varieties of thought.

THE ANCIENT LEARNING SCHOOL: CUTTING THROUGH COMMENTARIES AND ACCRETIONS

The chief idea of Ancient Learning was to go back to the original Confucian canon. This was to look behind the screen of commentaries put up by Zhuxi and Wang Yangming. An important figure in its formation was the scholar Yamaga Sokō (1622–85), who wrote a sharp criticism of Zhuxi in his book of 1666 on *The Essence of Confucianism (Seikyō yōroku)*. He was able to show that the idea of the Great Ultimate was an importation into original Confucian thinking. All that cosmology needed were the principles of yin and yang. In fact, the notion of the Great Ultimate was something dragged into Confucianism from Buddhism. Though he could not deny that the doctrines of Mencius were part of the ancient heritage, he took an intermediate position about human nature, as being both good and evil. One of the reasons for his being drawn to the ancient Confucian ethic, before it was overlaid by a preoccupation with scholarship, the investigation of things and intuitive introspection, was its relevance to the ethos of the warrior. He had written extensively on military matters (and underlined, among other things, the importance of firearms). He wished to outline a comprehensive ethic for the fighting man, who would hold to loyalty to his lord, with sincerity, serenity and self-restraint. But his attack on the Shushi orthodoxy led to his being exiled and during that time he developed a very strong patriotism, arguing for Shinto, and extolling Japanese achievement as being much greater than those of a decadent China. Indeed, he saw Japan as being the true central kingdom.

His military writings on ethics are probably his most lasting achievement for they helped to shape and express that system of values known as *bushidō* or the way *(do)* of the warrior *(bushi)*. This self-sufficient, courageous, impassive, loyal, self-restrained, self-sacrificing ethic became widely spread among the samurai class of the Tokugawa era.

Because of his military interests and his later rather extreme patriotism, Yamaga was, though an early proponent of the Ancient Learning, not a mainstream example. Perhaps such a position should be assigned to Itō Jinsai (1627–1705) who founded a highly influential academy in Kyoto. His metaphysics were drawn above all from the *Yijing*, the *Analects*, and the *Mencius*, and he put aside what he considered to be accretions which had been laid upon the original foundations of early (pre-Han) Confucianism. He suggested a monism of *qi*, which manifests itself in the mutual progression (*sōgo igyō*) and dependence (*sōgo ison*) of yin and yang, earth and heaven. Heaven and earth are eternal and self-caused; they constitute one life. Within heaven and earth, movement, goodness, and life are included, but rest, evil, and death are excluded. Later terms comprise transformations, that is, corruptions or even the lack of the former. This view not only reflects the optimism of Mengzi (Mencius) expressed in his belief that the original nature of human is good but also evokes the four hearts of compassion, shame, modesty, and the ability to distinguish between right and wrong which constitute the basis of the 'four virtues'. Especially with regards to ethics, Jinsai called for a return to Kongfuzi (Confucius) and his 'way of heaven' as the source of morality focusing on the importance of human-heartedness (Chinese: *ren*; Japanese: *jin*) as the highest virtue and ethical ideal. Human-heartedness is characterized by righteousness, observance of rites, and truthfulness. However, Jinsai went one step further and defined human-heartedness as 'love of human beings'. His influence was very great, largely through his many pupils, but also because in his own life he embodied to a high degree the virtues, which he taught. His interpretation of Ancient Learning was not, moreover, very polemical, though he was critical of alternative ways of life; and he was reverential towards spirits and the rituals of Japanese society. Also personalistic in his view of heaven was Ito's follower Ogyū Sorai (1666–1728), who was a strong Sinophile. He was concerned on the political front to apply ancient Chinese ways to modern statecraft, and though he was a sort of fundamentalist (his slogan was 'Back to antiquity') who considered his own interpretations of the old canon to be helped by Heaven, he had many innovatory ideas, including a scheme for making the samurai economically self-sufficient. Sorai followed the example of Kongfuzi and Mengzi and evoked the sage kings of Chinese antiquity as the model for all government; they had created a set of ideas and institutions which could be applied universally. In this way, he put the notion of human-heartedness in particular and Confucianism in general in the service of politics. Chinese cultural values could through correct education be inculcated in society and so become natural to Japan.

147

A SUMMATION ON JAPANESE PHILOSOPHIES AND THOSE OF EAST ASIA

When we look back on the various trends in Japanese philosophy in the premodern period we may note certain tensions, some of them no doubt creative. It will be noted that Japan in a very striking way received many of her values from outside. Buddhism came to her in Chinese and to a lesser extent Korean clothing. Confucianism also came, not merely fully clothed, but in a particular uniform for the most part – that of the Neoconfucian tradition. And so one of the tasks of Japanese religious leaders and philosophical thinkers was to adapt these extraneous ideas to Japanese forms of life. At the same time, Japanese indigenous culture, in so far as it was expressed in what came to be called the Way of the Gods or Shinto, was doctrinally very weak in the face of the intricacies of Buddhist metaphysics and the sonorities of Confucian values and sagacities. It was only at a rather late stage that there was the boldness to elevate Shinto to a predominant system. It could ride on the back of Confucianism or fuse with Buddhism. It was probably in the syncretic form of Shinto, in which it combined with Confucian values, that it had the strongest position. The question of the place of Shinto in Japanese culture came to be vitally important during the Meiji era.

It may be noted too that the tension between Confucianism and Buddhism took quite a different form in Japan from that which it manifested in China. The reason was to do with the sequence of events. China already had a well-established Confucian tradition well before the advent of Buddhism. The flowering of the two systems was a thousand years apart. So Buddhism could be resisted by Confucians, and indeed appeared at first for obvious reasons as being 'un-Chinese'. It is a commonplace observation that foreign systems have to work hard and long to become established in another culture where there is a long-standing literary tradition. Considering the circumstances, it is remarkable how well Buddhism adapted to Chinese conditions and how it came to pervade Chinese culture. But in Japan Buddhism itself came together with Confucianism as part of a package of Chinese culture. It was only very late indeed that the tension between Kong and the Buddha really manifested itself. Also, as Buddhism came in varying ways into Japan, through the efforts in the main of Japanese monks traveling to China and coming back with armfuls of texts and particular enthusiasms, it was sometimes the most sinified varieties that appealed: in particular, forms of Pure Land and Zen. These Chinese-oriented types of Buddhist worldview appealed because they were world-affirming and socially fitting to Japanese forms. In regard to these forms, the Japanese, as we have seen, took them further and gave them added sharpness.

When the Confucian revival did occur in Japan, its chief contribution was the school of Ancient Learning. This was a kind of fundamentalism, disguising its essential modernity with a return to origins. As for ethics, it provided a new ethos in that of the *bushidō*. Japanese Confucianism, however, was less innovative than Korean, where in any case the Confucian tradition had a much more direct role to play in the functioning of the State.

148

The dialectical relations in China between Confucian and Buddhist traditions help to explain the emergence of Neoconfucianism as a synthesis. The synthesis did not really occur in the opposite direction – that is, with Buddhism taking up themes explored by the other tradition. Buddhism was so diverse that syncretic energies were exhausted in the theories, such as that of Tendai, which brought together the various schools and movements.

But we may note the positive effects of Taoism on Buddhism. The more positive interpretation of the concept of dependent origination which led to the 'Indra's net' metaphysics of the Huayan was in line with Taoist feeling. Though Japan did not harbor Taoism except as a secondary Chinese import, it had the shamanistic and nature-spirit background to make Taoist ideas in principle congenial. So a positive Buddhism blending the Buddha and the Tao was destined to have strong appeal – hence the success of Zen in Japan.

I have referred to the dialectic character of Chinese thought, in that we have three major strands in tension and interplay; in particular there is the contrast between Buddhism with its outsider origins and Indian nature as contrasted with the indigenous Chinese philosophies, notably the *ru* and Tao traditions. It can often be that such a dynamic is fruitful: the tensions and contradictions stimulate debate. This is especially important because Chinese culture was in many ways remarkably conservative and backward-looking (if this be taken in not too pejorative a sense), for it held that the key to wisdom lay in the high past – either that represented by the early Confucian texts or that represented by the various texts flowing along the Silk Route out of India. Schools and movements tended to be classified by the texts which they relied upon. Even the relatively innovative Huayan took its title from a text (the *Avatṃasaka*). One of the engines of change was the tension between schools, therefore. But the tensions were less in Japan, where for so long Buddhism was the dominant worldview. Yet there remained the bigger question, which came to the fore during the Tokugawa period, of the relationship between Japanese values and foreign culture. The forging of a new nationalism, stimulated by intimations of a foreign threat, began the shaping of ideologies and philosophies which could help towards the remarkable political synthesis achieved by Japan in the modern period. The dialectic between foreign and indigenous values helped to bring about a very fertile period of philosophizing in Japan after the Meiji restoration. By comparison the Chinese response was rather impoverished.

I have pointed to the relatively less important role played by Confucianism in Japan because of its importation from China, together with a more dominant Buddhism. But even when it came to flourish somewhat during the Tokugawa period, it did so under an important handicap. Much of Confucian writing about politics relates to the behavior of the emperor and of his ministers. Ethics are an important ingredient of political theory, as is education. But in the Japan of the Edo period (and Japan previously) the emperor had been relegated to a position of ritual significance but no real political power. One could of course argue – on Confucian lines, as some scholars did – for the restoration of the imperial system. But the fact was that the Tokugawa regime was one with a military dictatorship and a sort of constitutional monarch (a role which could be dovetailed into a modern constitution after the Meiji restoration). The Confucian assumption about the place of the emperor simply did not hold in pre-modern Japan. This modified the role which Confucianism could play.

We shall later return to the Eastern scene: to see how the varying philosophies of China in the twentieth century crumbled in the face of Marxism, and how this in turn was given a Chinese face in Mao Zedong's Thought; to perceive the modern changes in Korea; to look at the rich development of Japanese philosophy in the last hundred and twenty years or more. During this modern period there has come to be some migration of values from East to West, although because of power and economic dominances and for other reasons it has been the exuberant West that has had the greater impact on the East.

6

PHILOSOPHIES OF GREECE, ROME AND THE NEAR EAST

THE SIGNIFICANCE OF THE GREEK EXPERIENCE, AND OF SURROUNDING CULTURES

Ionian and mainland Greece, which were to be the parents of Greek thought, were richly placed in that they had living contacts with some of the high cultures of the period, in the sixth and fifth centuries BCE, when the first major stirrings of philosophy took place. The Persian empire to the east had, under Cyrus the Great, conquered most of Asia Minor, together with Babylonia and Media, by the year 630, when he was killed. It remained for his heir to bring Egypt into subjection. So most of the Middle East was unified, with cultural heritages tracing back to ancient Sumer and Babylon, Egyptian civilization and the traditions of the Persians themselves. Only certain elements of these cultures turned out to be important in the later history of ideas. First, Babylonian astronomy and Egyptian geometry were to some degree absorbed by the Greeks, who notably developed mathematics and especially geometry. Second, Zoroastrian ideas (which we shall describe later) not only influenced Judaism and through that Christianity, especially in regard to the figure of the Devil and in the belief in the resurrection of the dead, but they also had a strong presence in Manichaeanism, a once important faith which stretched from the Roman empire (and there had its effects upon Augustine) to China. Third, and most importantly, Jewish ideas made a strong impact on the world of the Roman empire, especially through the wide-ranging success of the new religious movement which came to be known as Christianity. Christian beliefs coalesced with those of Neoplatonism to constitute classical Christian doctrine. We shall deal with these influences upon later philosophies in the course of recounting the narrative of the development of Greek and Roman philosophy. The roots of Zoroastrian and Jewish ideas stretch back before the period of the rise of the first Greek speculations: but we shall nevertheless deal with them in the order of their impact upon the wider world, rather than strictly chronologically.

It was, then, on the Ionian mainland of Asia Minor that the first seeds of free-ranging thought sprouted. Eventually, as we know, the main center for philosophy came to be Athens, partly because of the free spirit of that city, partly because Socrates performed his probing work there, and partly because of the high level of its literary culture, of which Plato's works were a fine and perhaps the most impressive body.

The Ionian school began the quest to find the underlying basis of the world: for Thales it was water and for Anaximander it was *apeiron* or the limitless. Thales was much interested in and a practitioner of navigation and is supposed to have predicted an eclipse – making use no doubt of Babylonian and Egyptian data and techniques. So his postulation of water as the stuff from which things are made can be seen in the context of a wider pursuit of scientific knowledge – or at least that is how it might look from our point of view, since we have at least a rough distinction between philosophy and science. But the speculation that there might be a single material source of the universe corresponds to one of the traditional forms of philosophy. In this sense the Ionians stand at the beginning of a powerful process which led through the Presocratics to Socrates and beyond to Plato and Aristotle, Stoicism and a whole number of other schools. These provided something of an intellectual religion for the Greeks and Romans. For myth had already conceived of some primeval substance out of which the world had been formed. But the new speculations had a different spirit, one in which reliance on tradition was unimportant and something of a free and new look at the world was taking place.

THE IONIAN SCHOOL AND THE SEARCH FOR A FIRST *ARCHÉ*

Thales, who lived in Miletus, flourished at about 580 BCE. We do not have his original writings and the fragmentary evidence we have about him we owe principally to Aristotle. We know that he thought that everything was composed of water and that the earth itself floated on water (in its pure form). No doubt the observation of phenomena such as steam and ice were suggestive in showing how water could easily change its properties. He also more mysteriously held that everything is full of gods. Perhaps he meant that everything contained a sort of animation or capacity for self-motion. Later writers were to ascribe to him a whole range of achievements – including some proofs in geometry, the inclination of the zodiac, the explanation of the light of the moon, and so on. They no doubt exaggerated his achievements, but it is fair to say that these supposed discoveries lay within the range of his interests.

Anaximander was a younger contemporary of Thales, and held a more dialectical view, seeing the four substances of hot, cold, dry and wet as being in polar interplay. But if so, the basic material or stuff of the cosmos must be something which is not bounded or defined in the way in which these forces are. The very possession of particular properties seemed to rule out a substance as the primordial source-material. And so he posited the limitless or unbounded. This lies beyond perception. In a vital way, Anaximander is the father of theory in the West, for his postulation of the imperceptible *apeiron* takes him beyond the manifest surface of things.

It was also a bold conception because he seems to have held that there are many *kosmoi* – many cosmoses. In the case of our world, he conceived of the earth as like a spherical column suspended in the middle of the space between the sphere of the heavens. Because it has no reason to go one way rather than another, it remains motionless. It and the rest are the result of something triggering off the polar forces of hot and cold (respectively dry and damp) and Anaximander explains the particular features of the cosmos in terms of these forces. The ocean, for instance, is the moisture left after the congealing of the earth under the influence of the hot. As for men, they have come from animals, which first formed in the ocean before coming onto dry land. This is a primitive anticipation of evolutionary theory. We can see from all this that the bent of Anaximander is naturalistic. He stands at the dawn of human science.

If for Anaximander the *arché* or primordial substance was the *apeiron*, for Anaximenes (flourished 545 BCE), the third of the great Milesians, it was *aer* or air, which can rarefy into fire or condense into wind, water, earth and rock in successive stages. He did not like the idea of 'separating off' which had been brought in by Anaximander to explain the transition from the *apeiron* to the polarity of hot and cold. He wanted to see all manifestations as due to the varying states of the one substance *aer*. Quantitative change of this one mode of things led to qualitative differences. But in some other ways Anaximenes' account of the world was more simplistic than that of Anaximander.

THE PYTHAGOREAN SCHOOL AND THE FASCINATION OF NUMBERS

Another Greek, for he came from the island of Samos, Pythagoras (c.570–490 BCE) migrated to Croton in South Italy where he became leader of a community there. It is possible that it was he who invented the word *philosophia*. At any rate the notion of the love of wisdom was vital, for his community and its sisters in other cities in South Italy were religious in character and aimed at cultivating the soul, partly through intellectual inquiry and partly through ascetic practices, like abstaining from the eating of meat and beans. The cosmos was seen as a harmony in which limit or *peras* was imposed on the *apeiron*. Human beings and animals were thought of as being in the process of transmigration or rebirth from one life to the next. The cosmos was a vast system of things whose inner nature was numerical. The discovery that musical harmonies could be represented mathematically was considered to be of profound importance. The universe itself was seen therefore as a huge mathematical and musical harmony.

This model of numbers as forming the basis of things in part reflected the fact that already mathematics was beginning to develop in Greece and could be seen as the paradigm of knowledge, being certain and precise. This idea of the priority of numbers had a grip on Plato and was to have momentous consequences in the evolution of science in the West.

Pythagoreanism was a religious movement and had strong affinities with the contemporary movement known as Orphism, focusing on the enchanter and musician Orpheus, master of animals, traveler down to the underworld, and savior of souls. According to one source, Pythagoras himself wrote books under the name of Orpheus. The soul of humans was, according to the *Orphics*, a fragment of the Divine destined to return to its origin, but so long as it remained contaminated by the world it was fated to follow the round of reincarnation. The Orphic slogan was *soma sema* – the body is a tomb. But the shining and incantatory figure of Orpheus, mysterious from Thrace, and offspring of that great master of animals Apollo, could lead humans who joined in his sacramental ceremonies and observed his prohibitions to ultimate escape.

Pythagoras' genius seems to have been to have changed the rules of Orphism. The asceticism and the sense of the Divine remained, and belief in reincarnation – but salvation was not by sacrament as such but by following the way of a community devoted to sacred knowledge: in brief to philosophy. That knowledge was mathematical in a vital aspect as we have seen. The discovery that the scale could be represented by the proportions 1:2 (octave), 3:2 (fifth) and 4:3 (fourth), and that these numbers, 1 to 4, made up the teractys, a triangle of dots arranged in four lines (1 at the top, 2 in the next row down, 3 in the third row, and 4 in the bottom row) and a sacred symbol for the Pythagoreans, was astounding. The later discovery of irrational numbers, that is, those numbers which cannot be represented as a ratio of integers or whole numbers, was profoundly disturbing. The Pythagoreans speculated that all things were made up of points (represented by 1); straight lines (represented by 2); minimal triangles (represented by 3); and tetrahedrons, the minimum solid (represented by 4). It was the planting of numerical limit into the limitless which was the beginning of the evolution of the cosmos. The initial unit in the formation of the universe was thought to be fire and as the universe grew outwards from its core, the heavenly bodies were formed. These, being in motion, gave off a sound, the 'music of the spheres', in harmony. Indeed, the cosmos was a perfectly orderly and harmonious entity. It was a noble vision, and it remained a vital ingredient in Greek thinking down the centuries until late antiquity (the third and fourth centuries CE).

Apart from the famous claim that the universe is basically mathematical, the other key idea in Pythagoreanism was the notion of the orderly and beautifully harmonious universe: the cosmos. There has perhaps ever since in Western thinking been a supposition that the universe has this orderly nature, so that science is the attempt to delineate the principles of this order. But for Heraclitus of Ephesus (in Asia Minor, again) the Pythagorean view was too bland. In fact the key to the universe is strife.

HERACLITUS, FIRE, FLUX AND STRIFE

Heraclitus, who flourished about 501 BCE, was a mysterious and poetic writer, castigated by Aristotle for his obscurantism. We do not have more than fragments of his major work, and there is some dispute as to what precisely his reasonings and conclusions may have been. But some things stand out. He considered, according to some dubious ancient accounts, the stuff of the cosmos to be fire in varying forms. But in order to explain change it is necessary to postulate strife, a force opposite to love, which stirs things up in the world. It tears things apart, as love brings them together. This dialectical interplay explains change. Change itself is continuous: as Heraclitus's famous dictum has it, *panta rhei*, all things flow. You cannot step into the same river twice. (Cratylus later went further and said that you cannot step into the same river once – such extreme flux in the world led him to the conclusion that nothing could be properly said, and he gave up speech.) In all this Heraclitus, for all his darkness of utterance, clearly saw something – that you could combine the notions of change and stability by postulating a law or formula according to which things regularly change. This principle he called Logos – a word of wide-ranging meaning in Greek, meaning reason, or formula, or definition or – most commonly – word. It is of course the term which was later in the New Testament used for the Word, or underlying principle of Creation. Heraclitus thus had a dialectical and formulaic notion of the way things operate in the world, which was more important than his identification of fire as the fundamental element underlying the cosmos.

The problem of change and permanence had already of course been posed in principle by the Pythagoreans. Numbers seem unchanging, but the cosmos appears to change. It was the members of the Eleatic school, and in particular its chief figure, Parmenides, who posed the question in the starkest form. If it is the case that there is something unchanging, and yet *panta rhei*, then what are we to make of this?

PARMENIDES AND HIS THREE WAYS: WITH SOME INDIAN COMPARISONS

Parmenides (b. c.515 BCE) of Elea in southern Italy (hence the name 'Eleatic' to pinpoint his school) produced a very striking and influential poem, possibly called 'On Nature'. In this he is in dialogue with a goddess (quite who is obscure), who delineates three ways of thought. The first is the way of Truth, and asserts that 'It is': in other words,

Being, or the object of thought, is. The second way is absurd – it is the way of non-being. But what does not exist is unthinkable. It absolutely is not. The third way, about which the goddess warns the reader, is that of seeming. It is the way of mortals, for they confusedly suppose that there are things which exist at one time and not at another. Oddly enough, however, there is a description of the content of mortal beliefs, with a fairly detailed cosmology in which the polar pair of Fire and Night play a vital role in the creation of the sun, stars, etc. It is probably Parmenides' own cosmology, though there are some reminiscences of Heraclitus's schema. It is, however, a puzzle: if the way of seeming is as the goddess says it is, why is a cosmology included at all?

It looks as if Parmenides accorded some provisional reality to the way of seeming. It is after all the philosopher's mind which emerges under the rubric of the way of seeming, in the shifting world of sense-perception, which grasps the way of Truth. There may be here some analogy to Indian ideas of provisional truth, as distinguished from 'higher' truth. The latter is found through higher experience, which invalidates all that has gone before. The second way, which is that of non-being, corresponds to the path of emptiness in the Buddhist tradition (but there the fact that it is unthinkable is not regarded as a disadvantage, since it is possible to have non-dual experience of it). There are also incidentally those variations evident in Chinese and Japanese philosophy which take the 'third way' as being a simultaneous affirmation of the changeable and the empty. And there is the identity-in-difference school of Hindu Vedanta which tries to combine the way of seeming and the way of Truth.

Parmenides' most influential follower was Zeno (b. c.490 BCE), who proposed various paradoxes, of teasing and theoretical interest, to show the contradictory character of pluralism and motion, etc. We can here cite two of these. Against pluralism there is this argument: if there were many things, then each would have to have unity and self-identity. But nothing can have unity if it has size, for whatever has size can be divided into parts. So if there were many things, each would be sizeless. But on the other hand, if a thing did not increase another when added to it (or decrease it when subtracted), it would be nothing. So a thing must have size. As to the most famous paradox against motion, this is known as Achilles and the Tortoise. The tortoise starts ahead of Achilles but the latter, though so swift of foot, never catches up. For during the period that he proceeds from his starting point A to B, where the tortoise starts, the tortoise has moved forward a bit, to C. The same argument can be repeated in regard to B and C, and so on to infinity. The tortoise is always a tiny fraction ahead.

Another follower of Parmenides was Melissus, also of the fifth century. It is not quite clear whether he produced anything original: he was in the main extending the arguments for Parmenides' position. He held that the one being is infinite, both as to space and time. Parmenides had compared it to a sphere, which has led a number of commentators to suppose that he held that it is spatially finite, though infinite in time. This is open to some question. It was the homogeneity of a solid sphere which he sought to stress, rather than its finitude. Melissus (more explicitly than the Parmenides of the fragments) insists that the world of sense-experience, in reporting change, registers contradictions and so is an illusion.

The importance of Parmenides is that he posed a severe question to those philosophers who wished to affirm something eternal or unchanging. The very idea of a thing suggested something unchanging beneath changing appearances. It was partly because of him that Aristotle opted for a theory of substances which dictated the norm for Western philosophy, which only rarely broke out into an ontology of events. The solidities of Michelangelo and Titian were preferred to the *pointillisme* of Seurat.

But there were moves towards atomism. One of those came through the religio-philosophical thought of Empedocles of Acragas in Sicily.

EMPEDOCLES, THE FOUR ELEMENTS AND REINCARNATION

Empedocles, dating from the first part of the fifth century BCE, was a political leader in his own city before being exiled; he practiced healing, had wide scientific interests, wrote two major poems, and claimed to be divine: he was an all-round sage! Probably his chief contribution to the later development of ideas was his notion of the four elements. He agreed with the principle which had been laid down by Parmenides, namely that nothing can come out of nothing. But he felt that anything which would explain the cosmos would have to be multiple. You could not get differentiation out of a single substance like fire or water. So he postulated a theory of four elements, the everlasting particles bodies of which combined or uncombined under the influence of the two cosmic forces of love and hate. The four 'roots of all things' are earth, air, fire and water. This theory of elements was taken up by, among others, Plato and Aristotle. The mingling and unmingling of the 'roots' proceeded according to a certain rhythm and periodicity, so that the cosmos is first in a state of fusion, when the elements are evenly intermingled, and then evolves into a formed state and then reverts to the fused state. But Empedocles, as well as believing in the material roots of things, also postulated a soul. Thus individuals also obey the law that nothing can come from nothing. Rather, they are continually being reborn. He thought of himself as an immortal spirit or *daimon* who had by some fault been forced from the company of the blessed gods and condemned to rebirth again: but he was ready for his release back into the blessed sphere. His book on Purifications describes some of the means to purity, including abstaining from eating meat, beans and various other substances (here are echoes of Pythagoras).

Governing the whole was a divine being, who was incorporeal and was seen as 'holy mind, darting through the whole cosmos with rapid thoughts'. It is hard, in view of the incomplete nature of our sources, to say how Empedocles' theology fitted together. Perhaps love was the nature of God and fragments of love became human souls, helping thus to keep organic creatures together as unified wholes. The early stages of creation seem to have been idyllic, as closest to the state of elemental fusion and the dominance of love in the material sphere. Then, with degeneration, souls enter bodies and embark on their long round of reincarnation. In some ways Empedocles' system resembles that of the period of the late Upanishads.

ANAXAGORAS AND THE IDEA OF MIND OR NOUS: AND BEYOND TO ATOMISM

Anaxagoras (?500–428 BCE) was from Clazomenae in Asia Minor, but settled in Athens and started the famous Athenian tradition of philosophy (though he was voted into exile on a charge of impiety, probably because in his actual cosmology his position appeared materialistic, although his appeal to a universal Mind made him a sort of theist). He postulated Nous as causing the initial mixture of elements of the cosmos to rotate, out of which the present differentiated world emerges. He had an interesting theoretical distinction between homogeneous and differentiated substances – cut a bar of gold in half and you have two pieces of gold; cut a baby in half and you do not have two babies (in fact none). It is not quite clear what part the distinction played in the details of his cosmology. His guess that the heavenly bodies are very hot rocks did not commend itself to Athenian traditionalists and may have brought on his prosecution and exile.

On the side of cosmology, the various schools of thought we have looked at point towards the atomic theory which was to be put forward primarily by Leucippus and Democritus. About the former we know little, but he probably lived in the second part of the fifth century, while Democritus' life may have been from 460 to 370, in Abdera. He is supposed to have starved himself to death during a plague: but generally was known for his cheerfulness, being nicknamed 'the laughing philosopher'. His writings were extensive and it was he who worked out the details of the atomistic worldview.

The fact is that the attempt to work out a cosmology by postulating one or more substances, such as fire or water, raised the issue of particles of such substances. Moreover, the Parmenidean principle that nothing comes from nothing, so what is must be everlasting, was highly persuasive. The Pythagorean notion of a cosmos suggested a self-sufficient entity. If you put these thoughts together you may come to think that the universe is composed of a void with scattered in that void an infinite number of atomic, that is indivisible or uncuttable, entities. These, swirling about, form larger combinations and out of this we have the formation of the world as we know it. Since there is no reason why atoms should be one shape rather than another, they have an infinity of different shapes.

The Atomists, consistently, had a materialist view of the soul, which was composed, according to Democritus, of round atoms, good for smooth penetration; and an account was given of the engagement of the senses with images coming from outside. In general the Atomists rejected all notions of design in the cosmos. Everything was to be explained in terms of the necessities arising from the constitution and combination of atoms. As for the theory of knowledge, Democritus held a kind of modified empiricism. The data which we have about the world come through the senses, but sense-experience can be very misleading. We have to go beyond it in order to understand the world, for by and large the atoms themselves are invisible. And as the world is to be explained by atomic theory, so ethics does not have a supernatural sanction. Moral behavior should be moderate, and the pleasures of the soul are better than those of the body. Nevertheless Democritus did not deny the existence of gods, who seem to be refined denizens of the cosmos. There are, consistently with his theory, a large number of worlds, many without sun or moon or water.

THE VARIOUS THEORIES AND THEIR EASTERN COUNTERPARTS

The various Presocratic philosophies have some general resemblance to the world of the Buddha and of the early Upanishads. The Greeks seem to have been more inclined towards physical science; in India medicine was best developed. There was of course speculation in ancient India about the ultimate material or substantive cause of the universe or of the one divine reality. The *śramaṇic* movements tended to believe, with Anaximander and others, that there are many *kosmoi*. Similarly, in both cultural spheres there is a marked predilection for the theory of reincarnation. But the detailed account of the relationship between mathematics and music pioneered by Pythagoras is not evident in the early Indian world. It is a pity we do not know more about Heraclitus, since his view that everything flows or changes brings him close to Buddhism. Of all the parallels perhaps the greatest is between the doctrines of Parmenides and the kind of monism found in the Upanishads, with its suggestion of an ordinary world which has a magical (and later this was seen as illusory) world given to perception behind which lay the changeless Divine Reality.

But the worlds of religion in the two cultures, while not without analogies, are dissimilar. There is not the same emphasis in the Greek case on the role of severe asceticism. There is no strict analogy to the idea of *mokṣa* as a state of radical break with the round of rebirth, even though there are echoes of the idea, notably in Empedocles' readiness to rejoin the blessed gods with whom his soul was in the beginning in communion. There is little, in the early period in Greece, refined practice of yoga. Moreover, already in India the brahmins have a vital role, even if it is not yet as dominant as later. They and the *śramaṇas* were the chief mediators of religion and philosophy in northern India. But the rising intellectuals of Greece had a more miscellaneous character. Some, like Pythagoras, seem to have been charismatic spiritual leaders, but others were not śramanic in type. Moreover, though the Greeks were beginning to feel a sense of ethnic unity as belonging to a common civilization, there was not, as in India, a more homogeneous class system developing, with, in particular, the brahmins on top. The sense of cultural unity is, however, probably earlier in Greece than in India in one particular at least. In the period in question the dominance of the Homeric epics and in some degree of Hesiod too was recognized. The relevant dominance of the Indian epics was doubtless a few centuries later, with the formation of classical Hinduism, and the synthesis between popular Indo-European religion and the ritual and intellectual edifice of Brahmanism. One factor in all this was the more advanced state of literacy in the Greece of the period. Because of the importance of ritual for brahmins, the very accurate transmission of memories was an imperative, while the Buddhists, Jains and others had socially institutionalized ways of ensuring the orthodoxy of transmission. So though ancient India produces great variety in thought and doctrine, it was subject to a less individualistic regimen than ancient Greece.

It is also noticeable that at an early date the Indian schools began to work out a complex psychology, with entities such as the *ahamkara* and the *buddhi*, which diverge somewhat from Western ideas. This is no doubt in part because the yogic interest flowed over into introspective methods which were the foundation for later manuals of contemplation.

The fact is also that in the one case the Indo-Europeans mingled with one culture and in the other with a different culture. The civilizations of the period were therefore divergent syntheses. Moreover, geography played its part. The Greeks turned themselves into a great seaborne civilization, while the Indians became an essentially land-based culture. The former favored greater looseness and fragmentation. The latter, while containing an astonishing variety due to the assimilation of so many peoples, customs and myths, nevertheless had a greater opportunity to impose a more homogeneous set of hierarchies, including the monastic arrangements of the śramaṇic religions. The one found its apogee in the city-state; and the other in kingdoms and empires.

THE SOPHISTS: TOWARDS SOCRATES

The Sophists, who might be described as a new class of critical educators, one of whose main interests was rhetoric, have been given a bad name by both Plato and Aristotle, who accused them of producing sham knowledge or wisdom in order to make money, and of using rhetoric in a cynical way. They could be thought to be destructive of received or traditional ideas (but so were Plato and Aristotle).

In some ways their nearest analogy elsewhere are ancient Chinese philosophers, especially in the tradition of Kong. Their interest too was educational. They thought that virtue could be enhanced or taught, and while they were less given to ritual, they nevertheless had a strong concern with the performative. For it was above all by the 'magical' use of words that we persuade one another. Moreover, some Sophists appealed to innate or natural tendencies as the basis of law and ethics: thus Protagoras (500–430 BCE) held that *aidōs* or shame is imparted to all humans, who will find it to be in their interests to conform to the particular laws of the State (which are relative to each State's situation and concerns). With his interest in rhetoric he made a pioneering study of grammar.

Gorgias of Leontini in Sicily (c.483–c.375 BCE), reacting in part to the Eleatic school, propounding varied paradoxes to show that notions such as motion or change are contradictory, argued that nothing exists, for if there were anything it would either be eternal or non-eternal. Both positions he holds to involve contradictions. Second, there is no knowledge, for there cannot be knowledge of non-being. Even if there were knowledge, it could not be communicated, since each sign is different from that it is supposed to signify. Modern Western commentators have been puzzled by this doctrine: surely Gorgias could not have meant it seriously? But he may have been offering what may be called a substantial nihilism, as if the underlying 'reality' of the world were a void or nothingness. From the viewpoint of the emergence of Mahāyāna about four centuries later, Gorgias is not unintelligible (leaving aside the problem of the coherence of such a position).

At one time during his early days Socrates (c.470–399 BCE) was involved with the cosmological and other interests of his predecessors, notably Archelaus. But he turned from speculative interests to chiefly ethical ones, pursued by the dialectical or conversational method. Metaphorically, therefore, Socrates referred to himself as, like his mother, a midwife – of ideas. His quest was for universal definitions of such attributes as courage or piety. It is because of his method, no doubt, that Plato regarded it as justifiable to show Socrates in his dialogues as uttering or coming to Platonic doctrines. The universals in Plato were now labeled the Ideas, which transitory substances or things resemble, if imperfectly. Since Socrates held a version of the thesis that virtue is knowledge, Plato allowed himself to fill out what 'knowledge' meant. It meant knowledge of the universals as arrived at dialectically, by cross-questioning people. Mathematics was also like this – susceptible to midwifery, as Plato tried to demonstrate in the *Meno*, by having Socrates draw out previously unrecognized geometrical truths from a slave-boy, simply by cross-questioning him. And so in a general sense the Socrates of the dialogues is faithful to the spirit of Socrates, even if the substance of the worldview presented is Plato's.

The predecessors of Plato, including Socrates, all contributed to his philosophical thought. Despite his criticism of the Sophists, he too built a cosmological theory, and was in his own way an encyclopedist. Parmenides taught him that the real is to be apprehended by the mind and cannot be grasped by the senses, though he gave belief based on empirical observation an intermediate status. One could multiply such influences. Plato's genius was to create a highly complex and wide-ranging worldview incorporating mathematical and other scientific elements, which yet had at its summit the idea of the Good, which possessed both ethical and religious meaning.

PLATO'S SCHEME OF THINGS

During the middle part at least of his writing career, between his early Socratic dialogues devoted chiefly to the probing of the essence of various virtues, such as courage, and his later works of a more technical character, Plato formulated his famous Theory of Forms, which was intended to indicate the presuppositions of thinking of what is permanent within or beyond the world of change. It related a bit untidily to mathematical knowledge and cosmology, on the one hand, and to the highest focus of his spiritual belief, namely the Idea of the Good, on the other. It also formed a key link in the chain of reasoning which led him to belief in the eternity of the soul and to the doctrine of reincarnation.

If we look to the *Timaeus*, a fairly late work, we see a full picture of the universe as conceived by Plato. God, or the Craftsperson (*Demiourgos*), has his attention focused on the unchanging Forms of things as he makes the universe. But he does not make it out of nothing. There is already there what is known as the Receptacle or Space, together with the primary qualities, which the Demiurge fashions into images of the Forms. God gives these qualities geometrical shapes, themselves formed out of types of triangles, and they become elementary powers, formed of pyramids (fire), cubes (earth), octahedrons (air) and icosahedrons (water). Thus Plato sketches a synthesis between the Pythagorean mathematization of reality and the more commonsense notion of the four elements. Out of these elements are built up the various substances of the world. And so we have a picture of the creator God who is given a necessary 'material' to work with, namely the chaotic flux of the Receptacle: he is also constrained by the theory of Forms, and by that Form in particular which is called the ideal Living Creature, comprising within itself the Forms of the gods, the birds, fish and animals. In bestowing order upon the cosmos God also 'gives' it life, that is to say a World Soul. In resembling the Forms, the various contents of the world have a shadow of the timeless, but in changing they necessarily have time: this time is a 'certain living likeness of eternity'.

The particulars in this world imitate their Forms and in some degree participate in them. But likewise somehow Forms partake in one another. By the process of arriving at definitions and aligning genera with their subordinate species a whole hierarchy can be mapped. But ultimately all forms partake in the One or the Good. This supreme Good is the apex of the whole system (and there are questions, naturally enough, about the relation of God to the One: are they the same?).

Lower than the Forms proper are the mathematical entities, which have an ideal and timeless existence – for instance, the true triangle is ideal when compared with the however accurately drawn triangle on paper. In the diagram of the Line in Plato's *Republic* there is such a thing as mathematical knowledge, but it is inferior to the still more elevated conceptual knowledge (*noesis*) of the Forms. It is discursive understanding or *dianoia*. But of course knowledge of the shifting things of this world is not true knowledge at all – it is mere *doxa* or opinion, and divides into belief or *pistis*, which concerns shifting 'realities', while apprehension of images, without realizing that they are mere images, is what is known as imagination or *eikasia*. The line represents the ascent from imagination to true knowledge. And within that highest realm of *noesis* one may ascend finally to the knowledge of the Good, which is ultimate and ineffable.

This One lies at the summit because of its perfection. It is in this perfection that each Form shares, for each is an ideal and changeless schema of the shifting and imperfect things which we see in this world. It is because we have intellectual access to the Good that we can grasp fully the life of virtue. It was in this way that Plato extended the view of Socrates that virtue is knowledge. This in turn had a profound influence on Platonic political theory.

In his own manner Plato had political ambitions. These were to be fulfilled by proxy, a little in the mode of Kong, through his influence upon Dion and through him his nephew Dionysius II, ruler of Syracuse (in all, the philosopher made three trips to that city: the bulk of his later book *Laws* seems to have been composed as a blueprint for a constitution for the ruler to adopt – it is in effect a much softened version of the vision set forth in the *Republic*). The major point which informed Plato's thinking was that since virtue, to be deep, involved the higher knowledge, including geometry and the dialectical inquiry into the arrangement and hierarchy of the Forms, not excluding the ultimate and unspeakable vision of the Good, there is need of a ruling class of wise people. Philosophers thus shall be kings. There is in this way a solidarity between ethics and politics.

This is also brought out by Plato's thinking of human psychology as a kind of microcosm of the polis. The human soul according to him has three aspects. Highest is the *logistikon* or rational aspect. Next there is that aspect which is full of spirit: we might call it the courageous aspect. Then there is the lowest aspect which is the appetitive. Roughly these correspond to the three main classes which Plato envisages. Going in converse order: there are the producers of various kinds, such as farmers, carpenters, merchants, and so on. In accord with their predominantly appetitive nature, they will be rewarded by consumption. The next class, living communally and provided for by the producer class, are the auxiliaries, who are trained soldiers guarding the State and subject to rigorous physical and intellectual education. From among these are selected the guardians, who at a relatively advanced age, especially for those days (50 years and more), will be selected to rule the city–state. Arranged marriages and the community of children looked after collectively would ensure that the best in the guardian genes would be propagated. Unfortunate specimens could be relegated to the producer class. Education in poetry and music would, like other aspects of life, be monitored, and Plato was highly critical of tradition, especially in the works of Homer and Hesiod, for representing the gods as acting immorally. God is author of the good alone. Here we may note in passing that in an important sense Plato was a dualist in relation to the two ultimate 'forces' in the cosmos. God, as we saw in the description of the *Timaeus*, is limited by the existence of the chaotic in the shape of space and the primary qualities waiting as it were to be assembled by the Creator into an organized cosmos.

Naturally we, with totalitarian regimes fresh in our memories and here and there still active in the world, shiver at the implications of Plato's ideal State. From a modern point of view it has justly attracted the criticism so powerfully expressed in Karl Popper's *The Open Society and Its Enemies*. It is in its own way a product of Pythagorean communitarian ideals together with disillusionment with democracy as understood in Athens, which had been responsible for the trial and execution of Plato's saintly master Socrates.

If the rich dialogues remained a monument to Plato's thought, there was another that for many centuries was perhaps even more vital: the Academy. This community of inquirers lasted until 529 CE, when Justinian forbade the teaching of Platonism as such, though of course Plato had, through Neoplatonism, an immense influence upon Christianity. The Academy was not a kind of university, but was devoted to knowledge and to mutual teaching through the joint practice of dialectic. There is a nice passage in Plato's *VIIth Letter* (344b) where he writes:

> Eventually, after names, definitions, visual and other sense-impressions have been rubbed together and sifted amicably by persons using the method of question and answer with no malicious rivalry, suddenly there shines forth enlightenment about each one, and intellectual grasp (nous) stretching human powers to their uttermost.

Perhaps too the ascent to the One had a genuinely mystical side to it. Plato's language is often religious, and he was also through his beautiful myths, in which invisible things are obliquely presented, such as the voyage of the soul beyond this life, aware of the ineffable and analogical character of much spiritual discourse and experience. It is certainly true that through Neoplatonism Plato's religious side was expressed and extended (some might say it was rather exaggerated). Since the Christianity that came to dominate both the Greek East and the Latin West is essentially a blend of Judaism, Pauline motifs and Neoplatonism, Plato can be represented as one of the founders of the faith. It is at any rate convenient here to trace some of the later history of Platonism leading up to the point of merger. Later we shall return to Aristotle, the Stoics and others in the line of Greek philosophy.

EARLY AND MIDDLE PLATONISM

Speusippus, a nephew of Plato, succeeded him as head of the Academy from 348/7 to 339/8. His position involved in part some regression to the Pythagorean schema, since he seemed to have abandoned ideal numbers in favor of the intermediate mathematical entities as the patterns out of which the cosmos as built. However, he saw God as emanating from the One, and may have identified it with the World Soul. There are hints here of Neoplatonism. But Aristotle and others left the school, complaining that metaphysics was being displaced by mathematics. Among later leaders of the Academy there were some significant advances in astronomy – thus Heraclides Ponticus held that some of the planets and maybe all revolve around the sun: he also evolved an atomic theory. There were also growing impulses to blend Platonism, Aristotelianism (especially the Aristotle of the dialogues, now lost to us) and Stoicism. Also interesting was the Jewish maverick Philo (c.25 BCE–c.50 CE), who helped to fashion the way towards a fusion of Christian and Platonic values.

For a period under Arcesilaus (315/14–241) the main teaching of the Academy was skeptical: the appeal was to Socrates' questioning of received truths. In later developments a more dogmatic temper prevailed. One of the key thinkers in the transition to Neoplatonism was Alcinoubinus (second century BCE). For him there was a First God, unmoved, who operates through Nous or Intellect and the World Soul. The Forms are ideas in the mind of God. Albcinous drew on the Symposium for the picture of the ascent of the soul to God through various levels of beauty. He also freely incorporated ideas from Aristotle (God as unmoved mover), Stoicism and other sources. Another notable synthesizer was Cicero (106 to 43 BCE), a sign too of the penetration of Greek philosophy into Roman culture. But ironically the greatest Roman or rather Latin-writing philosopher was the Christian convert, Augustine. The old Roman–Hellenistic civilization by then was beginning to fade.

NEOPLATONISM, AND THE CREATION OF A FULLY SPIRITUAL PLATONISM

The sun in the firmament of later Platonism is undoubtedly Plotinus (205–70 CE), who was influenced not only by the earlier trends and by other systems, but also by his teacher Ammonius Saccas, who in turn may have had some knowledge of the Indian philosophy of the period. It was to learn more about such Eastern systems that Plotinus joined the military expedition of the Emperor Gordianus III to Persia and further East. There are some resemblances between Neoplatonism and proto-*Bhedābhedavāda* (the identity-in-difference school of Vedānta). But the major part of his inspiration was without a doubt Plato. But it was Plato systematized and given an overtly mystical interpretation, since Plotinus saw as the culmination of the philosophical life the ascent of the soul to the Divine Being.

Plato had referred to the One (or the Good) as *epekeina tēs ousias*, 'on the other side of being'. This transcendence is stressed likewise by Plotinus, even if the contemplative life can bring one a direct 'vision' of the One – a flight of the alone to the Alone. As first God, the One stands there indescribable and unmoved. It is indeed a full unity, so much so that it does not even have within itself the distinction between known and knower: it is in this sense without self-consciousness. But from it there flows forth or emanates the next figure in the Hierarchy, namely Nous or Intellect. Inside of Nous there is a plurality, for this aspect of the Divine contains within itself the Forms. It is them and it knows them, but it knows them in a unified manner. Below the Nous is the World Soul, which has an upper aspect, more akin to Nous. In its lower aspect it is the Soul of the Cosmos. So for Plotinus the universe is a beautiful living thing, constrained by its material nature admittedly but colored and breathing with living harmony. In it the souls of living creatures wander, in a process of reincarnation: others leave upwards to become united in the one Soul.

Though there is an otherworldly element in Plotinus, it is a moderate one. He was strongly critical of the dark side of Gnosticism, which saw the human soul as trapped in the darkness of the material world. It is true that the soul descends into its incarnate state. But this is not so much a cause for a feeling of gloom and entrapment as a recognition that this world is rather distant, by emanation, from the full beauty and goodness of its Source. The world is a wonderful place, created as it is by the Demiurge, Nous. Suffering and evil exist, but are to be seen in the widest, cosmic context, where they become in effect, necessities.

This beautiful picture of reality is coordinated to a view of praxis, of the practical implications of this worldview. The spiritual person wishes to ascend to the indescribable and luminous One. He must first, under the impulse of a noble Eros, strive to become like God; and in the early stage should practice the virtues – wisdom, self-control, justice and courage. They purify the soul, which by its descent has had its true nature covered over, as it were, by mud. Then the soul should turn away from sense-perception and rise towards the Nous, through the practice of philosophy. Beyond that the soul is carried upwards to a communion with Nous, still keeping its self-awareness. Finally, the soul gains union with the One, and is 'grown one with the light in its purity, without burden or weight, transformed into Godhead, indeed being in essence the Divine' (*Enneads* 6.9.10).

OTHER NEOPLATONISTS, AND SOME REFLECTIONS

Probably the two most important successors to Plotinus were his disciple Porphyry (b. ?232 CE) who arranged the Enneads and was a disciple of Plotinus during the latter's last years. Porphyry was concerned to paint philosophy as a way of salvation, and to defend 'paganism' (that is, the old Greek religion with its attendant philosophies) against encroaching Christianity. Myths could be allegorized to provide popular vehicles of higher, philosophical religion. Christian appeals to the Bible met with Porphyry's critique of the scriptures. Thus, he denied that Moses could have been author of the

Pentateuch and showed up contradictions and tension between the four Gospels. In all this he anticipated modern scholarship. Proclus (410–85), a man of wide-ranging knowledge, tended to multiply the stages of emanation, in part following Iamblichus (d. c.330). If the latter laid a stress on the life of ritual and of priesthood, Proclus was more concerned with the life of contemplation. He saw the practice of virtue and the spiritual life as a kind of turning back, which is the mirror image of the whole process of emanation. The soul turns back to its Source, through self-control, asceticism, higher knowledge and finally the unitive vision of the One. He also held that everything in the world reflects every other, somewhat like Huayan.

There are those, of course, who see a large gap between Plotinus and Neoplatonism on the one hand and Plato on the other. There are two or three points of some divergence. Thus the later Platonists were less Pythagorean than Plato himself. Their interests were less in science than in religion or salvation. Second, whereas the Forms were depicted by Plato as if they hung loose from God, they are firmly anchored in the Nous in Neoplatonism. Third, Plato may or may not have thought of his vision of the Good in mystical terms, that is, as a 'vision' yielded by contemplative or yogic practice; but this is the main thrust of Neoplatonism. It thus converged with the growing interest in mysticism exhibited in Christianity. The ascetic life was a way of affirming values which were likely to wither once Christianity became the official faith of the Empire. Meanwhile let us retrace our steps and see something of the alternatives to the Platonic tradition which became important from the fourth century BCE onwards.

THE ARISTOTELIAN DIVERGENCE: THE HIGHER COMMON SENSE

When Aristotle (384–322 BCE) was sent to Athens to study by his guardian Proxenus, he remained at the Academy about twenty years, until the death of Plato in 367. He seems during this time to have been an enthusiastic supporter of Plato's doctrine of Forms. But during his middle period, when among other things he studied biology on the island of Lesbos, he broke away from many of Plato's detailed ideas. After three years tutoring the young Alexander the Great he came to Athens to found his own school at the gymnasium called the Lyceum. Because of his width of knowledge, intelligence and conformity to commonsense observations he came to be the predominant figure in European scientific thought for centuries. It was largely by breaking away from Aristotle that modern science was born. His was a marvelously well-wrought worldview, but because of its amazingly long influence it was – and perhaps still is – a disaster for the West. By turning away from Plato's transcendentalism (despite his espousal of an unmoved moving God) he also turned away from that skepticism about ordinary language and perception which is a condition of fresh thinking about the world. It is perhaps ironic that modern science should have arisen in the West, when the Indians, especially through the Buddhists, were earlier expressing a much more modern approach to language and to perception. One factor could have been the contradictions which appeared so sharply in the West's thinking because of the Renaissance and its aftermath. Also the emergent and highly rationalist account of God, especially from Aquinas onward, prepared the way for a questioning of the universe as perhaps displaying the mind of God and hence conforming to rational patterns. But despite the rather damaging effect of Aristotelianism's very success, the edifice of Aristotle's own thought is wonderfully articulate and in its own way beautiful.

The main thing he did, of course, was to bring Forms from heaven to earth. He also cleaned out Plato's receptacle or space as depicted in the *Timaeus*: instead he put in a substrate or primary matter. Change occurs when the substrate acquires a form it did not previously have. This analysis requires three notions, that of matter and those of privation and form. Another distinction, not always tidily coordinated to the above analysis, is that between potentiality and actuality. What brings a thing from potential to actual existence is a cause or causes. These are characterized as formal, material, final and efficient. So a statue is made out of, say, stone, its material cause; it has a certain shape, its formal cause; the purpose of the sculptor (the plan of the sculpture in her mind) is the final cause; the action of the sculptor is the efficient cause. Though he allows that some things can be explained by material and efficient causes alone, he does in general bring final causes into play, and sees them as pervasive in nature which he says (*De caelo* A.4, 271a33) 'does nothing in vain'. Such teleology played a decisive part in his advanced biological investigations, and even today the language of purpose has a heuristic role in such inquiries.

Aristotle considered – and such a thought is natural enough for human actors, for we note the effort required for many movements and activities which we undertake – that motion or more generally change requires explanation: things are naturally at rest until they are moved by something else. Since you cannot in his view have an actual infinite in the chain of causes there must, for the universe, be a First Cause, itself unmoved. This Being – God – has to be unmoved: if he had to be efficient cause he would be involved in a kind of shoving. He acts by not acting, but by being there as First Final Cause.

It is because of the later adaptation of Aristotle by Aquinas that we have a fuller picture of the Aristotelian God than Aristotle had. For one thing he was not the only unmoved mover. Such intelligence moved the layers of heavenly spheres that accounted for astral motions: they were, being intelligences, capable of responding to the Final Cause which was God. God was transcendent in the sense of being beyond the world of ordinary substances, but he was not conceived as being either creator in the normal sense or as providence. In fact, he was not an object of worship or prayer, for he could not have any intercourse with human beings. There could not be *bhakti*, since he would have no way of returning our love, and in what sense could we be said to love God (*Magna moralia* 1208b26–32)? Though elsewhere Aristotle may occasionally use the language of popular religion, it is mistaken to think of his God as God in our sense. His situation is more like that of the *Tirthankaras* in Jainism, though they are not given a teleological role: essentially they do not communicate any more with us. Or perhaps God has analogies to the supreme Buddha of some Greater Vehicle schools. Yet even here we may be misled: it is natural to think of Buddhas at least as having personhood. It is doubtful whether Aristotle's God is personal, though he does involve himself changelessly in *noesis* or thought. However, the object of thought is not the universe but what is changeless, namely himself (and maybe also all necessary truths – though he cannot have knowledge of the changeable universe).

Aristotle's whole metaphysics depends on his substitution of the notions of the causes and of actuality and potentiality for the work of the Forms. The idea that Forms could be separate from, rather than embedded so to speak in the particulars and the species and genera which exist as secondary substances (the particulars being primary substances), is absurd. Because of his biological work and for other reasons he was less interested in the mathematical model of the material world than was the Pythagorean Plato. His world was one of classification and final causes. It was a non-evolving hierarchy of unchanging genera and species. Both in his acceptance of thing-words and the rough adequacy of ordinary language and in his relatively unmathematical approach to reality he missed out on the main ingredients of science as it ultimately developed.

In certain ways he remained a Platonist. Though his primary view of the soul is the actualization of the body and its form (to which the body is the matter), a view ingeniously and perceptively expounded in the *De anima*, he yet postulated an immortal part – the nous. This nous as active imprints forms upon the passive nous. It is alone immortal. It is imperishable; but the passive intellect gets wiped out at death, so that a person may survive death as an individual but without memory. Is not then his individuality gone? And if so, is there but one Active Intellect for all humans? These questions were left unanswered by Aristotle.

It is perhaps in his treatment of ethics and politics that Aristotle's teleological language appears to best advantage. Moral and political cultivation aims at happiness or *eudaimonia*. This is defined as activity in accordance with virtue, pursued not on a short-term basis, but over a whole (or the greater part) of a life. The virtues include both intellectual and moral ones. The former have their summit in the activity of contemplation, of the highest and most sublime objects in the universe – the heavens and God. The moral virtues are in the middle between excesses and deficiencies (there are resemblances to the Chinese doctrine of the mean). In politics Aristotle is much more moderate, as one might expect, than Plato, favoring aristocracy as the best form of government, or at least a democratic constitution with property limitations, so that the State is ruled by the middle class, who are likely, he thinks, to be trusted both by the upper and lower classes.

In sketching the above we have of course only touched on the wonderful extent of Aristotle's writings, which include long-lived masterpieces such as his Categories, his

169

logical writings, his Poetics and so on. The picture he presents is even more complete than that of Plato. Its very vigor and universal range were bound to make it influential. It was especially in the medieval period that, adapted, it came into its own. His thought in the ancient world remained long unpublished – not until the first century BCE, though there were holdings of manuscripts both at the Lyceum and in the great library at Alexandria. But he did leave a major stamp upon Western civilization until and beyond the Renaissance, when his physical and biological thought was gradually dismantled. His treatment of substances stayed hypnotic, so that even in the twentieth century books are still being written on things and individuals which owe something to the rich Aristotelian tradition. The massive character of Aristotle's achievement explains why the West remained so long satisfied with the general shape of ordinary language and ordinary perception (forgetting that the simplification of outer reality by the senses is necessary for practical survival and activity, and that it is a hard and counterintuitive business to wrestle for a theoretical understanding of what in nature lies beyond the senses). But for all that, Aristotle's complex vision of a grand hierarchy of the universe crowned by the self-thinking and impassive Prime Changer is both attractive and inspiring.

OTHER SYSTEMS OF GREEK THOUGHT IN THE HELLENISTIC PERIOD

While Aristotelianism did not develop into a way of life in the manner that Platonism did, with its strong religious and contemplative overtones, some other schools presented such a face. The most forceful of these was Stoicism, founded by Zeno of Citium (c.336–c.264 BCE) at the Stoa in Athens. Stoicism had its own interest in logic and rhetoric, but as a worldview it was keen to remove dualisms between forms and individual entities and between souls and bodies. For the Stoics there were only particulars, apprehended by sense perception, and then classified through memory and through general ideas formed by nous or reason. There are active and passive forces in the cosmos, but essentially the universe is a single entity, moved by fire, which is also identified with God, who is the dynamic soul of the cosmos. He sows in the world the seed principles or *logoi spermatikoi*, which unfold as individuals. Every so often the world goes up in a universal conflagration and then is renewed in a new cycle of existence, when everything is repeated exactly as in the prior world-period. There is no radical human freedom, therefore: freedom is doing consciously and with agreement what would happen in any event. Fate rules all, or to put it more mildly, the Providence of God. All is ordered for the best, even if viewed by itself an act or happening may seem bad and/or painful. In the wider scheme of things there is perfection.

Life should be lived in accord with nature, that is, the necessities of the universe. Virtue means being in consonance with reason, the ruling pattern of nature and identical with Zeus or Fire. Moral evil in essence consists in the attitudes brought to bear by human beings, while virtue is its own reward. The Stoics sought above all to cultivate equanimity in the pursuit of the four chief virtues of Wisdom or *Phronesis*, Courage, Self-Control and Justice. Pleasure, sorrow, desire and fear are the feelings we possess and should be eliminated, for they are irrational. Humans therefore should aim at a heroic self-sufficiency.

An important side to Stoicism was its cosmopolitanism. All humans equally share in Reason, drawn from God, and so we should see ourselves above all as citizens of the cosmos as a whole. The attractions of this ethical outlook, especially its courageous self-control and equanimity, to late Republican Romans, wishing to restore the virtues of the older Roman State, gave Stoicism a certain influence in the Roman world. Some noble Romans followed its example of suicide as an honored way to go in the face of dishonor.

Epicurus, who opened his school at Athens in 306 BCE, created a worldview at variance with Stoic values. For one thing Stoicism still stuck to the language of religion despite its materialistic monism; Cleanthes' famous hymn to Zeus is colored with the sensations of loving devotion. Epicurus sought rather to get away from fear of the gods. This desire was forcibly expressed by Lucretius (91–51 BCE) in his famous poem *De Rerum Natura*. Epicurus saw the cosmos as composed of innumerable atoms of various weights, forms and sizes, existing in a vast empty void. Teeming downwards in oblique paths, they collide and form larger entities as they get stuck to one another. Vortices are formed out of which emerge various worlds separated from one another by huge empty spaces. Human souls are composed of atoms too, and dissolve at death. The Epicureans did not deny the gods, who (also material) live a luxurious life in the interstices between worlds. They can be honored, but fear of them is ridiculous. They have neither interest in nor access to human worlds. Pleasure is the highest goal for humans, but to get the best out of it, it needs to be pursued in moderation.

Over against the positive schools which propounded relatively dogmatic worldviews were two important movements of questioning. One was that of the Skeptics, founded by Pyrrho of Elis (c.360–c.270 BCE) and formulated systematically by Aenesidemus (first century BCE). He employed skeptical argumentation to question all theories, and he criticized the skeptical strand in the Academy (which drew upon the idea of doxa or opinion, holding that at best hypotheses about the sense-world are probable) for making the distinction between the probable and the improbable. Formally, he is similar to Nāgārjuna in his dialectical approach to claims presented by other philosophers. A fuller account of skepticism is to be found in the writings of Sextus Empiricus (maybe third century CE). He was, as his sobriquet indicates, an empiricist, but used dialectical arguments against all transphenomenal claims. This led to suspension of judgment or *epoché*, which in turn produced *ataraxia* or equanimity. Naturally, there was a strong overlap between Stoicism and Skepticism.

The Cynic movement, harking back to the 'Dog', as he called himself, Diogenes (b. c.324 BCE), questioned human conventions and laws, and cultivated fairly extreme asceticism in the cause of attaining natural self-sufficiency – for which reason the life of animals was commended. The Cynics liked to shock, and some got a bad name for their offensive behavior. But there were others such as Dion Chrysostom (b. about 40 CE) who became a saintly critic of contemporary materialism and preacher of cosmopolitanism. In his commendation of the natural life he echoes early Taoism, and the Cynics had a similar anarchic disposition to that of the Taoists.

The more challenging schools, as well as the Stoics and Epicureans, died out effectively with the success of Christianity. Platonism and Aristotelianism lived on as part of that faith.

Marcus Aurelius, who was Emperor from 161 to 180 CE, was maybe the last great Stoic. He followed in the footsteps of the former slave Epictetus (c.50–138 CE) whose noble and moderate Stoicism was highly attractive. He stressed the innate morality of human beings, though they do need education in the good. He was the Mencius of the Western world.

But much of ancient philosophy came, as we have just noted, to be displaced by Christianity. This, over a longish period, carried with it a penumbra of Gnosticisms, which were latter day Orphisms, born out of a Jewish–Christian background. Though Judaism itself never had the startling success of its daughter Christianity, it was nevertheless a vital force in the Hellenistic and Roman imperial world. Both these religions betrayed some Zoroastrian influence, while the same was true of the complex faith known to us as Manichaeism (or Manichaeanism). Let us then retrace our steps to the days of the Persian empire when it was rival to Greece, though succumbing to the military conquest of Alexander in the latter half of the fourth century BCE.

ZOROASTRIANISM AND ITS EFFECTS ON JUDAISM AND CHRISTIANITY

In an important way Zoroastrianism, with its emphasis on monotheism and its strong ethical content, can be called a prophetic faith. During the period of the Persian empire under the Achaemenids, it grew into a cosmology and theory of history, which saw it in three phases: the period of the primeval Human; the period of Zarathustra, the religion's focal founder; and the period of the Savior, Saoshyans. At the end of history, it came to be thought, there will be a universal conflagration when the faithful, resurrected now with purified and immortal bodies, will exist in a blessed state, praising the great God, Ahura Mazda. Angra Mainyu will have been defeated and evil banished. This system of ideas has been called dualistic, since both these great spirits, the one good and the other evil, existed together at the start of time. On the other hand, during the latter part of the Achaemenid period there arose a religious movement known as Zurvanism, called after the spirit Zurvan, which was postulated as the original Being out of which Ahura Mazda and Angra Mainyu emerged. This gave the religion a more rigorously monotheistic structure, but it allowed that evil had been created by or emanated out of God.

172

Judaism proper did not fully come into being until the third century CE – at least not in the form which was to persist until modern times. But its earlier currents felt the effects of Zoroastrianism. The Pharisees, for instance, adopted the notion of the resurrection of the body. This passed, chiefly through the writings of Paul, into orthodox Christianity. But Judaism of course existed in the Hellenistic world as well as within the orbit of Persia. It consequently, as did Christianity, absorbed the idea of the soul, which could survive the body. The two ideas were not so easily reconciled.

Philosophical influences on Judaism were most apparent in the writings of Philo of Alexandria (b. c.25 BCE). He anticipated some later Neoplatonist motifs, and pioneered the allegorical method. He was thus able to show that the teachings of the Hebrew Bible were consonant with philosophy as he understood it. But in pointing to the allegorical he did not sacrifice the literal, at least as far as injunctions went. Faithfulness to the Law could accompany an exalted sense of the transcendent. Also somewhat in the spirit of Platonism was his postulation of a Logos to serve as the agent of God and to substitute for the more Platonic term Nous. The Logos is where the Forms are, first in their eternal manner as thoughts of God and second as existing objectively in the created order. For Philo rejected the notion that the world is eternal on scriptural grounds. There are quite a number of original ideas in Philo. Probably the two most important are as follows. First, he held that we can know God directly by mystical intuition as well as by reasoning from the world. But in knowing God directly we do not know his essence but only his existence. This distinction was later vital in Christian writings: he held, moreover, that God in his own nature is unnamable, ineffable and ungraspable. In this he differed from the Aristotelian and Platonic traditions. Second, he modified Aristotle's cosmological argument to establish a Prime Changer or Mover, so that it started from the existence of the cosmos rather than its containing motion or change.

Philo was a key figure, since his pioneering synthesis between biblical religion and Greek philosophy cleared the way for later syntheses in which the three faiths of Judaism, Christianity and Islam expressed their theologies. His worldview was a liberal one, but he appealed also, deeply, to religious experience (and gave an interesting account of prophetic knowledge as a variety over and above other forms of knowledge in the Greek tradition). And above all he wished to be faithful to the injunctions of the Torah. He was thus a traditionalist in practice and an adventurer in philosophical ideas, as well as having a mystical side to him.

Christianity, as it made its way into the fabric of the Roman empire, became increasingly dependent on Greek philosophy. This was in part because of the growth of concern with the interior, contemplative life alongside the sacramental worship involved in the Eucharist and other rites.

Meanwhile, various rival religious movements had begun to grow on the edges of Judaism and therefore, too, on the edges of the young Christian faith. These involved chiefly three themes: first, the need for gnosis or knowledge for salvation; second, the idea that the world is evil; and third, varying myths in which there emerges out of the original and good God an evil being, often identified with the Creator as described in the Hebrew Bible, who creates the evil world. In this bad matter souls become trapped because of the primordial disaster, and they need to make their way back to the first Being. In Christian versions, Christ figures as the one who conveys the divine knowledge to humans here on earth. Mostly the Gnostic groups seem to have emphasized asceticism, in order that the elite souls destined for salvation should contaminate themselves as little as possible with the material world; and additionally, by sexual abstinence they did not populate this world further. Some versions, however, took the way of antinomianism and excess, as a different form of protest against the mainstream Jewish and Christian teachings.

The notion of gnosis is interesting. It sometimes means direct experience, this either in the form of exterior visions or, more often, with the apprehension of the inner light, as in so much other mysticism. But it can also mean the secrets which have to be revealed to initiates, so that salvation has a magical and sacramental side. Many of the documents of Gnosticism which we possess are supposed revelations, modeled after the sacred books of Judaism, particularly since at the period in question the Jewish myth was the most powerful of those exhibited in revealed writings. Of all the movements which may in a general sense be termed Gnostic, the most successful and powerful was that known as Manichaeism, after its founder Mani.

MANI AND THE MANICHAEAN TRADITION

Mani (216–77) felt his call to prophecy at the age of 24. The religion he founded had basic Zoroastrian elements, in particular the eternal contrast between good and evil principles (even if in the final consummation of history the evil power will be bottled up in a vast sphere and imprisoned beneath a huge stone). But it has also Buddhist, Christian and Gnostic elements; and was conceived by Mani and by the Persian emperor Shapur, who patronized him, as a universalistic religion with multiple appeal. It had its own scriptures, including a book of pictures, which were revealed through Mani, as well as using expurgated editions of other works, notably the New Testament. Salvation is, through knowledge, mediated through a savior figure (represented in the West as Jesus, though identified elsewhere with other salvific figures such as Laozi). Partly modeled on Christian and partly on Buddhist patterns, the Manichaean church was divided into two classes, the elect and the mass of followers, who might find an elect status through rebirth in a subsequent life. The ethics were rigorous, commanding the elect to abstain from eating meat or harming animals, to abstain from wrongful occupations, such as agriculture, and to abstain from sexual intercourse and marriage.

The tradition was a strong one, for its missionaries took it to Gaul at one end of the world and to Chinese Turkestan at the other. It was regarded as subversive by the

Roman emperors and attempts were made to suppress it. Later, the Christian church also wished to smother it, seeing it as a heresy – particularly because it was docetic, seeing Jesus' death as unreal, since he was a transcendent being who only seemed to come into the world (though as a form of the divine savior he was supposed to suffer with the evils of the world until the final victory). There were persecutions of the faith also in Persia; then with the advent of Islam it also underwent persecutions in the territories conquered by the Muslims. Despite that it occasionally has made its reappearance – as with the Bogomils in Eastern Europe and as the Albigensians. It also captivated Augustine, before his conversion to Christianity, and there are some of the rather gloomy strains of Manichaeism in his attitudes to original sin and the like. It remains as one of the strands woven into the rope of European and Western culture.

It was partly because of the Gnosticism of Marcion and others that Christian teaching came to define itself. And it was partly in response to such self-definition that the Judaism of the Talmudic period came to define itself. And so it is that somewhat indirectly these movements which eventually died away from the scene have contributed to the shapes that two of the great religions have taken. There is more than a little resemblance, moreover, between the ambition of Mani to be the Seal of the Prophets and the self-understanding of Muhammad.

THE DEVELOPMENT OF CHRISTIAN THOUGHT: THE ALIGNMENT OF THEOLOGY AND PHILOSOPHY

Repeated attempts to suppress Christianity, Judaism and Manichaeism were not successful. But what explains the imperial desire to persecute these religions, which were permeating the fabric of the Roman empire? And why was it that Christianity eventually became the official ideology, through Constantine's reversal?

The empire as such did not, until Christianity, have an official ideology. It is true that there were fragments of imperial myth which could be important, such as the story of the Aeneid. In a rather modest way the emperor was deified. This was an extension of the practice of elevating heroes and a kind of officially sponsored Euhemerism. The fact is though, that even if there was not much in the way of an imperial ideology, there was an imperial praxeology. There were due rites to be observed, both by the emperor in accordance with tradition and towards the emperor. Such rites fitted into that loose and general framework of the cult of the gods in the Roman empire. Within that framework there was a lot of latitude of belief. Even those who denied power to the gods, such as the Epicureans, did not greatly or even at all object to the custom of paying due homage. Such rites could help to maintain tradition and were good for civic solidarity. Varieties of both belief and more intense faith existed. The former were expressed through various philosophies or worldviews. Some of these as we have seen had a highly spiritual flavor, such as Neoplatonism; others were highly moralistic, such as Stoicism; others again were more scientific, such as Aristotelianism. Some were very challenging, such as Cynicism. But even the more disgusting acts of the Cynics were more shocking than objects of fear, still less of imperial fear. It is true that there were tendencies, as there were in contemporary Hinduism, to draw together the miscellany of Greco-Roman religion into a systematic whole, but this was in each case in part because of the impact of systematic religious movements (Christianity, for instance, in the West and Buddhism in South Asia). Later, for instance, Julian the so-called Apostate could attempt to reinstate a systematically conceived paganism. What, then, were the menacing characteristics of Christianity and Judaism? It was chiefly that in their desire to retain a purity both of life and of belief they repudiated the gods, including the political god. We shall return to this point.

In noting that there was a variety of philosophical beliefs open to the individual under the aegis of the Roman empire we left on one side the variety of more intense faith: this was represented above all by the various mystery religions, such as the cult of Isis and the initiations of Eleusis, the sacraments of Mithras, and so on. These, though they attracted prejudice in some cases, especially during their first introduction into Rome, could coexist alongside the more staid and unemotional sacrifices and rites. But the world religions, especially Christianity, combined faith as in the mysteries, with an uncompromising attitude to the official praxeology. It also had in its Catholic version a unified organization, even if there were plenty of heresies embodied in various movements moving like a flotilla alongside the main fleet.

A further factor was at work. While Judaism could define itself as the religion of a chosen people, even if it was open to converts, Christianity, making converts so widely among gentiles as well as Jews, had no single, albeit loosely conceived, identity as representing a people. It was not in any way an ethnic religion, even if it transported some of the values of the Jewish tradition into a wider world. So it came about that Christianity defined the boundaries of the New Israel not by descent or ethnicity, which, in their relative indelibility, give people a sense of security, however harsh the outside world may be from time to time, but rather by belief. Orthodoxy came to supplant orthopraxy.

Moreover, reinforcing this tendency towards a kind of intellectualism was the undoubted challenge represented by Hellenism and the Roman way, both including noble and astute philosophies. In rising to the challenge of alternative philosophies Christianity itself had to become philosophical even in refuting or rejecting philosophy. As Aristotle said, there is no avoiding philosophy, since the question of whether one should philosophize or not is itself a philosophical question. So Christianity had a double incentive to create an intellectual worldview, in which biblical revelation was seen in the light of Hellenistic philosophy. Thus, Tertullian (b. 160 CE), a convert to a rather puritanical kind of faith, could ask what Athens had to do with Jerusalem, and yet he already was fashioning a philosophical vocabulary in order to explain points of Christian doctrine: he spoke of the Trinity as having three personae without, however, having three *substantiae*, and he also in some degree drew upon Stoic ideas.

CHRISTIAN PHILOSOPHIES UP TO AND BEYOND CONSTANTINE

The Catechetical School of Alexandria was very important in the evolution of Christian thinking. Among its influential leaders were Clement (c.150–c.219) and Origen (185/6–254/5), who, however, left in his mid-fifties to found a school in Caesarea in Palestine.

Clement held to the growing view that the Greek philosophers prepared the way for the Christian message. The divine Logos enlightened people of diverse cultural traditions. Consequently the Greek philosophers saw some truths independently of the Jewish prophets – even if they also, as many Christians alleged, borrowed from the latter and passed off such truths as their own. And so in a sense Greek culture could be regarded as a parallel Old Testament, and Christians could be heirs to both the ancient Hebrew and the Greek traditions. Clement was influenced widely, but mostly by the Platonic movement, and held to a negative theology of the nature of the Divine Being. We can know what he is not, not what he is.

Origen's worldview was more imaginative, and got him into trouble, since he was led to deny certain tenets which were being defined as orthodox during this period. He saw the Divine Being as the Neoplatonic One. But though he is ever active and is Creator of the world, the world was, according to Origen, everlasting, since if it came into being at a particular time this would imply that God changes, which he held to be impossible. God creates matter as well as everything else, so Origen was orthodox in seeing everything in complete dependence upon the Creator. But it was usual to take Genesis at its face value and suppose that there is a creation in time. The world, in short, is finite: however, Origen's idea contradicted this orthodoxy. He also held that finally all souls will be purged of their sin, and so saved. This ran against the starkness of the pictures of hell in the scriptures. The Last Judgment was taken to be final and hell was not empty. Origen also believed in the pre-existence of the soul, while mainstream Christianity came to reject this idea as well as that variant of it known as reincarnation or rebirth. This element of Platonism was regarded as unscriptural. In these and some other matters Origen was thought of as heretical.

Compared with the Hellenistic universe, the Christian cosmos was highly dramatic. Its major myth centered on Christ, of course, but the very importance of Christ's mission on earth dictated that Christians heavily emphasized the fall of humankind through the transgression of the proto-humans Adam and Eve. But also, though hope of a more immediate coming of Christ had faded by the second century CE, there was vividly in the Christian imagination the picture of the end of history, with the Second Coming of

Christ and the judgment of the human race. Though of course both Greek and Roman civilization had a lively appreciation of history, there was no such dramatic sweep to their understanding of human life.

The chief stream of history stressed by Christians was, moreover, that alien one of the Jews and their Exodus, prophets and other elements. The cosmos as revealed in the Bible seemed to be a small one. The drama was heightened by the relative narrowness of the stage, and also by the denial of reincarnation, for each person had but one life and one destiny. The contrast between heaven and hell, softened later through the emergence of the doctrine of purgatory, dramatized human choice. The uniqueness of the Divine Being and more particularly the uniqueness of the Savior, Christ, made the choice of faith absolutely important. The skirmishing of the Devil, ready to devour individuals who did not cleave to the vine which could nourish humans with his life-giving blood, added to the menace and possible turbulence of the pilgrimage. Such a dramatic universe was moreover peopled by cruel persecutors and noble martyrs and holy persons, who in the glory of their lives added a Third Testament, so to speak, to the Old and the New. And even when the tumult subsided and the faith became imperial and respectable, the challenges were transposed to other fields – to the call to be a hermit or a monk or nun, there to wrestle with inner demons on the path upwards to the vision of the inner Light and communion with Christ and indeed the Trinity.

How could this rather narrow but yet dramatic universe be held together with the wider, lazier and less stringent cosmologies of Greek philosophy? Some synthesis seemed unavoidable. Rome itself might be an intermediary. For the Christian faith had two centers: Jerusalem, site of the Savior's death and glorification; and Rome, both as power-center of the world, and as the recipient of the martyred relics of the twin great apostolic pillars of the Church: Peter and Paul.

Because Christianity claimed to be a universal faith, which was in part expressed through a kind of philosophical ideology – a set of doctrines and a potent myth, it posed in a sharp form the question of imperial ideology. It was no longer sufficient to make do with a praxeology. In many cultures we see the same dilemma: the indigenous customs are challenged by an ideologically-framed outside force. The indigenous tradition needs either to reformulate itself and grow a countervailing ideology, or to succumb in the hope later of bending the incomer to its own social and spiritual needs. But Christianity was especially menacing to the older more chaotic and competing values of the empire, for in its strong and even violent rejection of the gods (Jewish purity gone universal and aggressive) it did not hold out promise of some tolerant synthesis – equating Christ with Apollo, the Virgin with Isis, the Father with the Demiurge, the Spirit with the World Soul, the saints with heroes, and so on. There would be such syntheses beneath the surface perhaps, and there were blends-to-be of a Platonism suitably purged and the biblical revelation, following in the steps of Philo.

It was therefore not surprising if Christianity became the official ideology of the empire, for a consistent and systematic opponent was scarcely available. This became a third factor in rigidifying doctrine. Not only was the new Israel defined by beliefs, and intelligent folk drawn into Christianity by synthesizing philosophy and the biblical tradition, but it also became a matter of imperial and civic concern to make sure that the faith was defined properly. This was the first task set the Church by Constantine when the Council of Nicaea was convened in 325.

The way of synthesis was expressed by various thinkers beyond Clement and Origen, both before and after Nicaea. I shall here mention two, one because he evolved a clear theory of the *praeparatio evangelica* or Gospel preparation implicit in Greek philosophy, and the other because he adumbrated, partly in terms borrowed from Plotinus and Philo, a mystical theology which was influential upon the major mystical writings of the late Roman empire, or early medieval period, namely these of Pseudo-Dionysius.

Eusebius of Caesarea (c.265–c.339), while critical of various forms of pagan religion, on which he tended to blame the great persecutions, saw in Greek philosophy and in Plato in particular a voyage towards the truth which is found consummately in Christian faith. It may be that Plato borrowed from the Old Testament, but nevertheless his ability to formulate the truth is commendable, and he stands parallel to Moses. In a sense Christianity is the 'crown of Platonism' (as later J.N. Farquhar saw Christ as the 'crown of Hinduism'). Moreover, Eusebius perceived in the Neoplatonic triad of the One, Nous and the World Soul an anticipation of the Trinity.

Gregory of Nyssa (c.335–c.95) followed Origen in holding to an idea of the return of all things to God and so the universal salvation of all, after a necessary purgation of evil through suffering. All this happens, of course, through God's grace. While Gregory laid great importance on treading the interior path to the higher levels where the soul comes into contact with the divine transcendence in a divine darkness, he sees all this as due to the guidance of the indwelling Christ. Naturally, the human being is oriented towards the visible world, through the senses: this is whence human knowledge is by and large drawn. But he recognizes that this world of the senses is not fully real. His despair at his limitations is a factor in God's drawing him back towards himself, so that he begins to tread the path towards the transcendent. Gregory's emphasis upon the divine darkness into and through which the soul progresses anticipates Pseudo-Dionysius' negative theology. (We may note in passing that while there are intellectual reasons for supposing that God is in himself indescribable, a typical major factor in leading thinkers both East and West to stress negative theology is an interest in mysticism, that is, in the contemplative or yogic inward path.)

THE TRINITY DOCTRINE AS DEFINED AT NICAEA

From the time of Constantine onwards the distinction between religion and philosophy, if it could ever be made clearly, eroded, for the universal Church dictated much of what was allowable in philosophy. Moreover, divine revelation as found primarily in the scriptures was in the Christian empire regarded as a respectable and indeed overarching source of knowledge. In Indian terms, the *sábda-pramāṇa* was pre-eminent. Though paganism, so-called, did not go down without a struggle, most philosophy after about the fifth century CE was religious philosophy, until the coming of the Renaissance. It is therefore useful for us to sketch briefly the heart of orthodox belief as it came to be formulated: this was the doctrine of the Trinity, pivotal in the scheme of Christian faith. This was, interestingly, formulated through the use, primarily, of Greek philosophical terminology, followed by Latin rough equivalents.

Christianity had a problem to solve and a value to express, both religious. The problem arose from Christ's saving work and the practice of Christians in worshiping him. Because of the Jewish heritage, with its strict emphasis upon monotheism, it was inconsistent for Christians to worship Christ without recognizing him as God. Indeed it would have been idolatrous. Similar remarks apply also to the Holy Spirit who played a developing role in Christian worship. In brief, Christ and the Holy Spirit had to be seen as fully divine (though Arians, against whom the Council of Nicaea was principally directed, did give Christ a lower status, since there was a time when he was not, they held). But if the three, Father, Son and Holy Spirit are each divine, does this not mean that Christianity is a tritheism, that is to say, a form of polytheism? The solution advanced by Athanasius and his allies at the Council was to see the Divine Being as consisting in three *hypostaseis* united in one substance or *ousia*. In Latin, this became the notion that God is three *personae* united in one *substantia* (*personae* suggested actors or three 'masks' – *prosopa* in Greek). Whether the 'solution' works or not is of course a matter of discussion between orthodox Christians and others, such as Unitarians, who continued to find the Trinity doctrine contradictory and/or unnecessary. But clearly the intention of the formula was to remove the sense of contradiction, so that Christians could affirm with a clear conscience that God is both three and one. This way the suggestion of idolatry and polytheism is removed.

The other side of the religious importance of the Trinity is that the notion of three loving Beings embracing one another in the most intimate and mutually pervasive fashion came to be the central symbol of Christian love. The Trinity was the highest expression of divine love, to be imitated by the Christian.

The attempt, however, to define the Trinity, and in parallel with this, to distinguish the divine and human aspects of Christ, led to a concatenation of disputes, to be settled, or not settled, by successive Councils of the Church. But gradually, though not in the most edifying way, the two halves of the Church which became the spiritual inheritor of the rifting empire settled down, though in dispute with one another, to generally agreed patterns of orthodoxy.

It will be convenient here to sketch the ongoing history of Byzantine philosophy until the fall of Byzantium. This had a considerable continuity with the world of Hellenism, even if often the atmosphere of the Eastern court and administration was far removed from the pluralism and fluidity of earlier days. I shall then revert to the West and say something about Augustine and Pseudo-Dionysius (not of course strictly a Western writer but one whose works in Latin translation had considerable impact later). These two writers can be said, from a Latin point of view, to mark the boundaries of the ancient world. Medieval philosophy in the West can conveniently be treated after we have contemplated the development of Islamic philosophy, which had a considerable part in the transmission and transformation of the classics, and concurrent Jewish philosophy. In all these three cases – Islamic, Jewish and medieval Christian philosophy – we are in a rather different world from that of Hellenism and the Roman empire. The great reverence in all three cases for books or writings regarded as divinely inspired altered the whole epistemology of these civilizations. Already of course we see this happening in the transition, say, from Plato to Philo, or Plotinus to Augustine, or Aristotle to Origen.

A BRIEF LOOK AT BYZANTINE PHILOSOPHY AND THEOLOGY

The Emperor Justinian (reigned 527–65) was strict and overwhelming in his decision to stamp out heathen thought. An edict caused the closure of the philosophical schools of Athens, which thus lost its pride of intellectual place in the Hellenic world. Theology and philosophy were concentrated by consequence upon the imperial capital of Constantinople. The Aristotelian center in Alexandria was at the same time taken over by Christians.

Nevertheless, Platonism, Neoplatonism and Aristotelianism, together with much of Greek science and literature, remained living forces in the Eastern world, and Byzantium produced over the centuries a whole host of commentarial writings, all important in the transmission of the ancient world to the modern. Naturally the major preoccupations of Byzantine speculation concerned God and the Trinity. There was much preoccupation with schemes, such as the complex one put forward by Maximus the Confessor (b. c.580), for understanding the triadic nature of God. Taking up a pattern of thought found in Porphyry, he elucidated a scheme in which God's nature is analyzed in terms of the triad of Being, Power, Act. Human life itself is moved by God to its 'Act' or perfection in a return to the divine source and an ultimate mystical vision of the Divine. A much later, but important, writer on Christian mysticism was Gregory Palamas (1296–1359), the chief theoretician of the mystical movement known as Hesychasm (from the Greek word *hesyche* meaning 'peace' or 'quiet'), which involved use of the Jesus Prayer and breathing techniques. The path of the Hesychast was deemed to culminate in the vision of the uncreated Light. This emanated from God but was not itself the divine essence, which is unknowable. Critics of the movement considered that Palamas brought a division into the Godhead, and had therefore fallen into something like polytheism.

Among the encyclopedists of Byzantine were John of Damascus (c.679–749), whose three-part compendium contained in its third part a systematic exposition of his understanding of Christian theology, and Photius (patriarch of Constantinople from 858 to 886 with a ten-year gap in the middle), whose *Bibliotheke* contained a modest section on philosophy as such. Another was Michael Psellus (1018–78), who wrote commentaries on Plato's *Timaeus* and on Aristotle, as well as producing a 'universal encyclopedia' (*Didaskalia pantodape*) heavily influenced by Neoplatonism.

Perhaps the most interesting figure was the humanistic Pletho (c.1355–1452). He attributed the decline of Byzantium to Christian influences and sought to evolve a restored Platonism which would express the spirit of ancient Greece. Thus renewed, Hellenism would conquer both Christianity and Islam. He became an important figure in the transmission of ancient classicism to the Western world, since he attended the Council of Florence in 1438 as an adviser, perhaps because of his learning and his Hellenic nationalism, rather than for his orthodoxy. At any rate, he came into contact with Western humanists, and was able to tell them much from his wide learning of the Pythagorean and Platonic heritages.

As it turned out it was the classical tradition of Byzantine scholarship which had the greatest impact on the European scene. The fall of Constantinople in 1453 was followed by a migration of scholars and texts to the West. The rediscovery of the ancient world during the Renaissance was an important part of the dialectical process whereby the contradictions in Western culture stimulated an onward movement of thought.

AUGUSTINE: THE GREATEST OF LATIN CHRISTIAN WRITERS OF THE EMPIRE

Augustine would have had a firm place in history if only for his pioneering autobiographical work, *The Confessions*. He lived at a time (354–430) of increasing chaos besetting the Empire – its division between East and West after Theodosius, the irruption into various provinces of different peoples, and the sack of Rome by the Visigoths in 410. It was a time of division between the old world and the emerging Christian civilization which would survive the collapse of the imperial system. He played, of course, a notable role in systematizing the thought of Christendom, since he wrote on psychology, the Trinity, ethics, the philosophy of history, and so on. The volume and system of his writings gave him immense later prestige and influence.

Augustine for a while was a Manichaean. His own somewhat depressed inner struggles maybe found the Manichaean dualism attractive. But when he converted to

Christianity it led him to repudiate and indeed argue against his older faith. In its own way, of course, Manichaeaism presented itself as a kind of Christian movement, since Mani was an apostle of Jesus Christ, but orthodox Christianity was clearly demarcated, and Augustine, moreover, had the benefit of the counsel of notable Milanese Christians (after he moved there to teach in the university), notably Ambrose (c.339–97). His position was that of a moderate otherworldliness. He saw the human being as created out of a fusion of soul and body. Though he was attracted for a time to the notion that the soul preceded the body, he was insistent on its created character. It differed from God, despite its immortality and immateriality, in being changeable. It was thus affected by sin and repentance, and was in general affected by the body, in being stimulated by bodily perceptions into sensual knowledge. The union of soul and body is a model of the hypostatic union of Christ's own divine and human natures. Moreover, though the soul is contaminated by the fall, it still bears, distorted, the image of the divine. Essentially, moreover, it strives for the highest good, namely beatitude – the *summum bonum*, which involves the contemplative life in communion with the Divine Being. In all this Augustine was able to make use, adapted, of the Neoplatonic heritage which he came to find to be so congenial.

His own experience seems to have helped dictate Augustine's views on sin and grace. He had after all wrestled with problems, both intellectual and ethical, before he became a Christian. It was his experience of conversion which clarified his life and led him away from subordination to fleshly desires and to wrong views. So it is not surprising that he reacted so strongly to the Celtic thinker Pelagius (c.360–c.431). The latter was a moral reformer, and wished to stress human freedom and moral obligation. Perfection is possible and so mandatory. Humans are not infected with original sin; it is rather that Adam set a bad example. So it is through his moral teachings and exemplary life that Christ saves. Such a 'commonsensical' attitude was anathema to Augustine. It destroyed the very logic of salvation: this involved the need to reconcile humanity to God through the saving acts and consequent sacraments of Christ. The Church was the continuing embodiment of the saving work of Christ. Worse, Pelagius' view did not give a central role to grace. It is through divine assistance that we can do good, as Augustine's own experience testified. Our freedom consists in the way in which God through his grace may draw us to the good. Humans, moreover, inherit the propensity to sin from Adam. We are incapable of goodness except through God's overcoming of this original sin. It follows that whether we are saved or not depends not at all upon us but simply on the grace of the Divine Being. In turn it is inexplicable why God saves one person but not another. Moreover, God knows in advance whom he will and whom he will not save. Thus Augustine was a prime pioneer of the doctrine of predestination.

But Augustine was eager to escape the conclusion that God brings about evil. And he certainly did not want to propound a separate source of evil. His Manichaean episode trod too hard upon the heels of his final faith. He resolved these matters chiefly by a theory, borrowed from Neoplatonism, that evil is mere absence of good. Naturally, the further you are from the central Light the more imperfection: this is not to be avoided. So God as creator naturally has to bring into being that which is less perfect than himself. Also, humans, in choosing evil, are free, though they are not under the direct influence in so acting of the grace of God.

Individual good and evil, though, need to be seen in the wider context of society, and Augustine made a major contribution to thinking about Church and State in his *The City of God*. In contrasting the heavenly city with the earthly one he was using ideal and indeed eschatological ideas; until we see the final judgment of God it is not possible to identify the two cities, except of course for the guidance of the Bible itself. Babylon or the earthly city, ruled by self-love rather than Christian agape, could thus be associated with Assyria during the Old Testament period. But in looking at the roughly contemporary scene which had produced the harsh, and by many overrated spectacle of the sack of Rome, it was easy to identify the earthly city with the Roman State. Augustine did not mean to do precisely that. But he did wish to hold aloof either from the theory that Rome was providentially the vehicle, despite the earlier persecutions, for the onward transmission of the faith, or from the view that it was because of the adoption of Christianity that the State had collapsed. But he did accede to the notion that the State should be subservient to the Church, in so far as the latter was an admittedly imperfect embodiment of the heavenly city. It could thus be used as an instrument to suppress Donatism. Augustine's somewhat reluctant acquiescence in this maneuver had fateful consequences in the later history of the Christian Church.

In his account of the relation between God and the created world, Augustine follows a generally Neoplatonic path. But he begins to adumbrate something of the distinction between primary and secondary causation which was later to emerge. He postulates *rationes seminales* or seminal reasons which bring things into being in due time, so that they follow natural laws or processes. This conception of a relatively independent nature in no way inhibits God from acting from time to time through miraculous means, though the greater miracle is the world itself, with all its signs of beauty. These beauties point to the invisible handiwork of the Divine Being. In a memorable passage (*Confessions* X.6.9–10), he pictures created things saying to him: we are not your God, so seek higher up. The idea is that a person should honor that which is higher and seek it – in other words should seek God. He is more interested in this practical message than in offering some kind of proof of God's existence. Indeed, though God leaves in the world pointers to himself, he is utterly transcendent, and according to Augustine is best known through ignorance.

The edifice that Augustine built was to be a landmark throughout the Middle Ages and beyond. The reason was in part his wide-ranging abilities and insights, but also a certain moderation which made him congenial to the ongoing Church. This comes out in his response to the Donatist heresy (heresy that is in retrospect from the standpoint of the victorious party). The Donatists were purists. They did not want to let back into the Church those who had shown themselves to be unworthy during the days of persecution. In particular there were priests who were unworthy to administer the sacraments. Sinners would need rebaptism to join the Church again. Augustine wrote strenuously against this. The Church is not a perfect organism: it is not indeed to be identified with the heavenly city. It contains sinners and people who are more or less penitent. But it is the extended body of the sacramental Christ. Augustine declared that for a priest like himself his root is Christ, whose blood, so to speak, flows through the veins of the Church. The rigorism of the Donatists was ultimately damaging to the Church. Later they were suppressed by imperial edict. In this, by a strange irony, the tables were turned. Those who had before been persecuted now turned themselves into forcible suppressors of what they took to be errant opinion. Perhaps Augustine, who used various arguments, including something close to Descartes' later *cogito ergo sum* to combat the skepticism which had become somewhat fashionable in the Academy, could have done with a bit more uncertainty.

Though he projected himself through his writings to the medieval period and had an immense influence there, he yet belongs unmistakably to late imperial civilization. He could see the attractions and achievements of the classical world at first hand. If his quest had taken him for a time into the arms of Mani it was as a result, no doubt, of a similar yearning for the authority of divine revelation which in the end drove him into the arms of Christ. But he was, though always ready to argue from scripture, well aware of the force of 'pagan' philosophy. The synthesis which he created between the revelatory and the philosophical ideas was as successful as any in the history of the Church. Yet of course he left many loose ends and pungent questions, above all those concerning free will and predestination. One feels sorry for Pelagius that his well-meaning position should have been declared heretical. But of course his subtraction of the doctrine of an inherited original sin left large questions about the saving work of Christ, though conversely Augustine's idea of the sexual transmission of sin left a dark blot upon sexuality.

ONE OTHER FIGURE: PSEUDO-DIONYSIUS

By 533 CE the works of the supposed Dionysius the Areopagite, the convert of Paul, were being cited as authoritative. They contain clear indications, however, of being influenced by Proclus (418–85). So they must have been composed somewhere a little before or after 500, no doubt in Syria. Their authoritativeness during the Middle Ages came, however, from their ascription to the Areopagite, and were often cited as very close to scripture. Had it been a Hindu context they would have no doubt had the status of *smṛti*.

Pseudo-Dionysius is the locus classicus, in the Christian tradition, for the distinction between the positive or cataphatic and negative or apophatic ways. The affirmative path leads us up a hierarchy, for Pseudo-Dionysius' picture of the world is of a vast chain of beings coming down from God, through Seraphim and Cherubim and various powers down to angels, all in the upper world, and Jesus and then the hierarchs of the Church down to catechumens on earth. God in himself, viewed positively, has such attributes as Wise and Good, but pre-eminently, so that he is super-essentially wise: human wisdom is but an imperfect reflection of this. It is caused or created by God, but at a lower level. But God is better thought of (or rather not thought of) apophatically. This path begins by denying of God the things which are farthest away from his nature – so fury, for instance, has no place in God. He is not furious. Pseudo-Dionysius gives the example of the way a sculptor strips away pieces of stone in order to reveal the true shape at which he aims. We use negatives to ascend higher, so that God is not even wise. Indeed he (or it) is invisible, intangible, unknowable. It is a kind of higher and supreme darkness into which the soul ascends, in which it is blinded as it were by light. It is a darkness of light.

This negative way reflects of course the practice of mysticism. Many of Pseudo-Dionysius' negative formulations remind us of the notion (or non-notion) of the *śūnya* or void in Mahāyāna Buddhism, and the contrast which Pseudo-Dionysius draws between negative and positive theologies has its Vedāntin echoes in the distinction between *nirguṇam* and *saguṇam Brahman*, Brahman with and without attributes. Sometimes his cataphatic theology leads him towards formulations which infringe upon the classical Trinity doctrine – that is, he sometimes writes as if there is one ineffable Godhead behind the manifestations of the Three Persons of the Trinity. Maybe such a tension between orthodoxy and the apophatic or negative mode is inevitable. It was, however, Pseudo-Dionysius' intent, in part at least, to struggle against the tendency to be anthropomorphic about God, which often arises from taking the Bible at face value.

A CONCLUSION

It is worth pausing here to draw a temporary conclusion, before proceeding onwards to contemplate the worlds of Islamic and Jewish philosophy. We have surveyed many of the major philosophical and other trends of the Hellenistic world and its aftermath, and before that the world of earlier Greece. We have touched on Zoroastrianism and Rome. We have glanced at certain aspects of Greek, Christian and other religions. It is of course obvious that while philosophy took into its purview the findings of science and logic, not to mention literary theory, psychology and so on, it also very importantly during the whole period had a moral and spiritual side to it. As such, the schools on the whole came to be different traditions of living, with divergent ultimate values. So in a way there is not such a great gap between Western philosophy of this major early period and the ruling conceptions of ultimate welfare in Eastern systems. Virtually every Hellenistic system had its notion of what is the ultimate good, and therefore a conception of what the highest human welfare or happiness consisted in. The tradition that knowledge is important for discerning all this is not so far removed from what became the classical Indian assumption – that every system of philosophy, even such a one as *Vaiśeṣika* which had much to do with protoscience, had as its ultimate goal the attainment of release.

But differing fates awaited the pluralisms of the two cultural spheres. The Buddhist Sangha had something of the cohesiveness of the Christian Church, and maintained differing segments of relative doctrinal unity. But it never had the motivation to try to suppress, however much it might have wished to replace, the alternatives. So the varying systems of thought of roughly a Hindu background, as well as some of the non-orthodox or *nāstika* systems were able, mostly, to survive. Moreover, the existence of the class and later the caste system gave a dominant cultural role to the priesthood or Brahmins. This resulted in a growing loose unity of the Hindu tradition. It cemented the revelatory aspect of Hindu culture. By contrast the Greco-Roman constellation never acquired a unified sense of authoritative tradition. It is true that the Homeric epics were revered, and in the later days of paganism their importance increased as a counterweight to the biblical books of the Christians. But Homer had not had the *Gītā* and the *Mokṣadharma* interpolated, and the Homeric writings never achieved that high and mysterious spirituality of the Indian epics.

Nor was the situation in China parallel to that in the West. Though there were periodic repressions of non-Confucian values (and even of Confucian values), the general position was that the Confucian tradition and its literary heritage served as the ideology of the imperial bureaucracy. This largely successful attempt to sustain a bureaucratically focused intellectual elite gave China greater stability than Rome. At the same time it opened the way to the evolution in the last thousand years of an organic symbiosis between different ideologies and spiritual paths, together with localized elements of an extensive peasant religiosity and the customary adherence to ancestral reverence.

But though Christianity simply replaced alternative systems and gradually extended its doctrinal homogeneity, save for the schism between East and West (which turned more on questions of Church governance than much in the way of real theological divergence), ancient philosophy had its future shaped in a new way. Essentially, Christian orthodoxy came to be a novel synthesis between biblical and Neoplatonic doctrines. In due course also Aristotelianism came to extend profound influence, adding a third element to the synthesis. But Greek and Roman philosophy did lose their independence, and became instrumental to the formulation of a Christian worldview. A similar thing happened, as we shall now see, in the Islamic world.

THE CONTINUITY OF GREEK PHILOSOPHY: THE CONCEPT OF LOVE

One of Plato's most famous dialogues, the *Symposium*, is an extended discussion of the particular kind of love known as *eros*. Each speaker, in offering his own view of *eros*, seems to hit upon something true while at the same time leaving much room for correction. Phaedrus begins by pointing out the moral benefits of *eros*, in that it can lead a lover to many fine acts of courage and self-sacrifice. Pausanias agrees in part, but insists that there is a distinction between the vulgar *eros* which aims only at bodily pleasure and the heavenly *eros* which seeks to cultivate virtue in the beloved. Erixymachus grants this distinction, but adds that both forms of *eros* must be seen as operative in the cosmos at large, the heavenly *eros* harmonizing divergent natural forces so as to produce peace and beauty, the vulgar *eros* setting them at odds so as to produce strife and destruction. Aristophanes counters these rather moralistic views with an unforgettable parable in which *eros* is the drive each of us feels to find wholeness by reuniting with his sundered other half. Finally Socrates describes how the desire to bring forth beauty in the beloved (the heavenly *eros* praised by Pausanias) can lead the lover upward, through successive fixations upon progressively higher and more abstract forms of beauty, to the vision of Beauty itself. This speech represents a marked turn from what are often regarded as the more typically 'Platonic' views of the *Phaedo* and *Republic*, for it describes a way in which bodily and emotional urges can contribute to the philosopher's quest for wisdom. (Indeed, Socrates playfully presents Eros himself as a philosopher.) Yet it is just as one-sided as the others, for it overlooks that *eros* is a fascination with and desire for, not just beauty in general, but a particular beloved human being. Perhaps the sequel to Socrates' speech, in which a drunken Alcibiades describes his own failed love for Socrates, is meant to highlight this important lacuna.

Plato's other dialogue dealing with *eros*, the *Phaedrus*, presents a more balanced and integrated view. Here there is no ladder in which the lover leaves behind his particular attachment to the beloved. Instead it is by working in and through a particular attachment, learning to love one particular person in the right way, that the lover's soul re-grows its 'wings' and recovers the vision of the Forms. Somewhat as in the speech of Aristophanes, love in the *Phaedrus* is thus a means to recovering a lost state of wholeness and integrity. The *Phaedrus* also explains, more explicitly than had the *Symposium*, why of all human drives only *eros* has this unique transformative power. The reason is that, of all the Forms which the soul beheld in its prior existence, the one which shines forth most clearly within the sensible world is Beauty.

Despite their differences, both dialogues present *eros* as an innate drive which, when pursued correctly, can re-connect us to the highest reality. It is a short step from such a view to seeing *eros* as the appropriate response to God, and God as the highest object of *eros*. Surprisingly enough this step was taken by that most unromantic of philosophers, Aristotle. Aristotle has little to say about the personal aspects of love so brilliantly explored by Plato. Instead he follows Erixymachus in seeing *eros* as a cosmic force which binds the disparate elements of the universe into a harmonious whole. The Prime Mover, since it is pure actuality, is both supremely intelligible and supremely desirable. This explains how it is able to move others without itself being moved: it moves them in being loved (*eromenon*). Such love need not be conscious. Plants and animals reproduce for the sake of partaking of the divine, and even processes of change among inanimate bodies, since they are a passage from potentiality to actuality, are a way of approximating to the perfect actuality of God.

In identifying the Prime Mover as that which is supremely desirable, Aristotle effectively assigns to it the role that Plato in the *Symposium* and *Phaedrus* had assigned to Beauty. When the views of the two authors were synthesized, as they were in Middle Platonism, the natural conclusion is intrinsically desirable and the highest object of love, and all other forms of love are in a sense directed toward this ultimate end. Christian authors embraced these ideas warmly. To cite only two examples, Gregory of Nyssa freely adapts the Ladder of Love passage from the *Symposium*, substituting God where Plato had spoken of Beauty; and Boethius in *De consolatione philosophiae* reworks the Aristotelian cosmic teleology into a hymn of praise to *amor quo caelum regitur*, the love by which heaven is ruled (a passage which would later influence Dante). Yet Christian authors could not simply adopt the classical view without change, for they saw God as not only an object of love but as one who actively loves others, and whose love is itself the perfect model of love. There was also an important terminological difference, for in the New Testament the love which God exhibits is identified not with eros but with agape, the self-sacrificing desire to help the beloved achieve his own proper good. The first epistle of John goes so far as to state that God is agape (4:8).

These Biblical ideas were synthesized with the classical heritage by Pseudo-Dionysius. Dionysius insists that God is both, on the one hand, the Beautiful and the Good, and on the other Love itself, in the sense both of eros and agape. Indeed in his case eros and agape are identical, since in seeking to draw others to himself God also seeks their proper good, which is none other than himself. This divine love Dionysius defines as 'a power to effect a unity and alliance and particular commingling in the Good and the Beautiful, because of the Good and the Beautiful'. Even more strikingly, Dionysius holds that the eros of God for creatures places him in a kind of ecstasy; God is 'carried outside himself in the loving care he has for all things', and 'is as it were enticed away from his transcendent dwelling place, and comes to abide within all'. This is a particularly vivid way of restating one of the fundamental themes of Dionysius's philosophy, that God is both transcendently beyond every name and all forms of knowledge, and immanent within creatures as their being, life, and other perfections. Dionysius refers to these perfections as the divine 'processions'. Considered in the first way, God is much like the Plotinian One; considered in the second way, he is much like Plotinian Intellect. The difference is that for Dionysius these are not two distinct hypostases, but two different ways of understanding – or better, of praising – the one God.

The later Byzantines carried these ideas even further. Maximus the Confessor holds that through agape God and man become 'paradigms' of one another, God being 'humanized' through love for man, and man deified through love for God: 'as much as God is humanized to man through love for mankind, so much is man able to be deified to God through love; and as much as man is caught up by God intelligibly to the one known [that is, to God], so much does man manifest God, who is invisible by nature, through the virtues'. Here each person's particular moral goodness is almost a second incarnation, a way in which God becomes sensibly manifest. Similar ideas are to be found in the last great Byzantine theologian, Gregory Palamas. Palamas understands deification in light of the Dionysian distinction between God as he exists in himself and as he is manifest within creation; the former he calls the divine essence, the latter the divine energies. Whereas the divine essence remains transcendently unknowable, the divine energies can be shared through acts of worship, obedience, and charity, as well as through the sacramental life of the Church. In doing so one comes to share in the active expression of God himself, and thereby to be deified.

Eros and agape provide, then, one thread in the long and complex skein which leads from ancient Greece to Byzantium. It is worth noting that the ideas of Dionysius, Maximus, and Palamas remain today part of the foundational theology of the Eastern Orthodox church. They constitute one of the many ways in which the philosophical legacy of ancient Greece continues to live within the modern world.

7

ISLAMIC PHILOSOPHIES

DIFFERENT STRANDS IN THE INTELLECTUAL LIFE OF ISLAM

Compared with the Jewish and Christian faiths, Islam's formation as an organic body of beliefs and practices was swift in its essentials. It arose basically within and shortly after the lifetime of the Prophet (*c.*570–632 CE). Naturally in the fuller delineation of its rituals, its law, its theology and political organization, the faith took a while to settle into its principal early forms. Still, it was a revealed faith, and the main essence of the revelation was to be found in the Qur'an. As standing in succession to both Judaism and Christianity, though at variance with them in a number of important ways, it drew on some elements of the myths and values of these religions.

The gist of the Qur'anic revelation can be summed up in five basic beliefs – in God, in angels, in revealed books, in God's messengers (above all in Muhammad as the last and the greatest of the prophets) and in the Last Day, when human beings will be judged. Practical action was summed up in the so-called Five Pillars of Islam: in the profession of faith: 'There is no god but God and Muhammad is his messenger'; in praying five times daily; in paying the alms tax; in fasting during the holy month of Ramadan; and, if financially feasible, in going on the great pilgrimage to Mecca. But Islam had, around these simplicities, a growing body of law or *Sharī'ah*. Apart from the evolution of schools of jurisprudence, there were other strands of intellectual and religious development which broadly speaking affected or comprised what may be broadly thought of as Islamic philosophy. There were the varied debates about Islamic theology and apologetics, which were known as *kalām*. This term, used as a translation, incidentally, of the Greek word *logos*, meant either the word of God, that is to say the Qur'anic revelation, or more pregnantly, the discipline of theology based upon

191

the word of God. Then there were the writings of that stream of spirituality known as Sufism: one may call this the mystical thought of Islam. There was also what Islamic culture dubbed *falsafah* – a borrowing of the Greek word *philosophia* – which referred to philosophy as based upon reason rather than upon revealed tradition. Though these differing strands of development can be distinguished well enough, it is somewhat artificial to treat them in isolation. Thus Islamic proponents of *falsafah* considered that reason pointed to God's existence, so in some ways the difference between *kalām* and *falsafah* was like that between revealed and natural theology in medieval Europe. On the other hand, many of the issues treated by *kalām* could be thought to be eminently philosophical – for instance the relation between God's activity and human free will. The Sufic constructions often incorporated materials which could otherwise be classified as falling under *kalām and falsafah*.

But philosophy in the sense of *falsafah* took quite a while to start up, for it was itself the result of the meeting of Islamic culture and Hellenistic culture, or rather its aftermath. Before Arabic thinkers could make much use of the Greek texts it was necessary for them to be translated, sometimes from Syriac and other translations, and sometimes directly from the Greek. A great impetus in this work was given by Abbasid caliph al-Ma'mūn, who reigned from 813 to 833, and who founded a scientific and philosophical academy in Baghdad.

The three major Greek philosophers known to the Arab world were Plato, Plotinus and Aristotle. Of these, the last was the most authoritative, particularly with regard to scientific inquiries. But often Islamic understanding of Greek philosophy contained sources of confusion – a text containing a substantial portion of the *Enneads* (books 4, 5 and 6) was found in paraphrase in a work called *The Theology of Aristotle*. A large sweep of commentaries on Aristotle were translated. The impact of all such works on Islamic intellectual culture was great. Through conquest Islam became in effect the inheritor of Greek, Persian and other resources, but of all of these the Greek influence was the most telling.

THE EMERGENCE AND THE CHALLENGE OF THE MU'TAZILAH AND THE ASH'ARITE SYNTHESIS

Although debates within the general definition of *kalām* had philosophical consequences, the initial impulses were practical. With the success of Islam and its evident status as a universal or world religion it became urgent to deal with the question of the Muslim who was a sinner. What if someone professes the faith through the requisite formula but commits a serious sin, such as adultery or murder? The first main school of interpretation of theology was the Kharijites, arising as a series of puritanical movements who took a rigorist line. A more systematic and somewhat less rigorist line was taken by the movement known as Mu'tazilah, founded by Wāṣil ibn Aṭa (699–748) and authoritatively formulated by Abu al-Hudhayl 'Allāf (748–820). In their own way they were rationalists. On the question of the sinning Muslim, they did not go so far as the Kharijites in holding him to be a non-believer, but they did not regard him as a Muslim either. He could belong to the community, and judgment was eventually up to God, depending upon the person's repentance. Human moral acts are free ones. God's role is in rewarding and punishing good and bad acts. Moreover, what is good and bad can be known by human reason without the benefit of revelation; indeed the fact that God nominates some things as good and bad is because they are good and bad: it is not the other way round, namely that they are good and bad because they are commended and condemned by God.

The Mu'tazilah were also very much concerned with the unity of the Divine Being, and so with the question of the status of his attributes. They were most strongly opposed to anthropomorphism and were therefore opposed to the *ḥadīth,* which they considered to be traditions not only unreliable in themselves but frequently given to anthropomorphic styles of expression. In order to safeguard both God's unity and his transcendence they held that the attributes of God are indissolubly part of his essence: on the other hand they resisted hypostasizing such things as 'knowledge' or 'life', in case it might be thought that these existed as more or less separate entities in God. In this case we would be involved in a form of polytheism. They also rejected the idea that the Qur'an is somehow eternal, and held with great vigor that it is created. All this creed was imposed by al-Ma'mūn. But this in turn created resistance, and eventually in the mid-ninth century traditionalism or the Sunni views became ascendant. The school known as Murji'ah, who were lax in their criteria of the true Muslim, were by reaction popular. The chief formulator of the orthodox Sunni position was al-Ash'arī (?874–?935). He founded a school, which became the single most important expression of orthodox Islamic theology. He had had some predecessors, such as ibn Kullāb (*d.* 855), but the clarity and system of his thinking gave him magisterial status.

He had been a member of the rationalist *kalām,* but had broken with it: his conversion was one of content of belief. If his conversion put him on the wrong side of his previous rationalist allies, his use of the *kalām* methods put him on the wrong side of radical literalists, who flourished by way of reaction to the Mu'tazilah. The literalism could be extreme, and the rejection of innovation stifling. As one writer put it (M.M. Sharif i.221), 'God's settling himself firmly upon his throne is known, the how of it is unknown: belief in it is obligatory; and questioning about it is an innovation'. So it was that al-Ash'ari sought a middle position, which he presented in a number of seminal writings, such as *The Clear Statement on the Fundamental Elements of the Faith.*

The Ash'arites argued that we cannot identify the attributes of God with his essence for that in effect washes them away and abolishes them. But they are inherent in God, and they are to be understood in a non-literal way. They are fundamentally different from the 'same' attributes which pertain to created beings. So they apply to God in an absolutely different manner. All this meant, by the way, that no attribute should be ascribed to God on the basis of our reasoning: only those cited in the Qur'an are legitimately ascribed to him.

As to the question of free will, the Ash'arite position was in theory a middle one, between free will and fatalism. For the conservative orthodox God has absolute power over everything, and so they adopted a position of fatalism about human acts. Now God, according to al-Ash'arī, creates everything, and therefore does indeed create human actions. But he also creates in human beings the power to make a free choice between two acts, and between right and wrong. God habitually creates what a person chooses. So the human being is free only in intending to do one thing rather than another, and in so intending he acquires the merit or demerit of his choice. This notion of acquisition was supposed to supply a modicum of freedom in human deeds. In other words, the human intention is part of the cause of an act, though it is in turn derived from the power placed there by God. Thus God creates, in the human being, the ability, choice and will to perform an act, and the human being, endowed with this derived power, chooses freely one of the alternatives, and wills to do the act. In accord with this intention, God completes the act.

Another bone of contention of the period was whether there was to be a beatific vision of God in the next life. The Mu'tazilah argued there was not, since God is not a physical object and so subject to being seen. Yet the claim that the saved will see God in the next life is contained in revelation. It is surely within God's capacity to create in humans a power to see him without the use of sense-organs.

The extreme literalists held that the Qur'an is eternal: some even argued that its cover and binding are external. But the Mu'tazilites argued that it is made up of parts and so must be created. The al-Ash'arī solution is to consider the inner and real meaning of it as being uncreated. It constitutes, so to speak, part of the mind of God. But in its outward expression in language, as in the written or recited Qur'an, it is of course created.

The Ash'arite metaphysics as it developed was highly interesting. It amounted to an atomistic occasionalism. They rejected other Aristotelian categories than substance and quality. Now qualities are mind-dependent, and as such are fleeting and transitory. But a substance cannot exist apart from its qualities, so it too is transitory. The eventual conclusion of such an analysis was that the world consists in a host of momentary atoms, coming into existence from nothing and dropping back into nothingness again. None of these atoms has any creative power of its own, and so we can only say that they are brought into and out of being by God (who *ex hypothesi* is not a thing or substance). Further, if nothing has creative power, then there are no patterns of secondary causality. There are no laws of nature: it is only that God has the habit of creating things in regular sequence. Regularity is a tribute to the relative consistency of God, not to the power of one thing to bring about another on some regular basis. All this, by the way, made the explanation of miracles easier. Thus the miracle of someone's receiving a prophetic message is simply an irregular activity on the part of God, compared with his usual, and as we might look upon the matter regular, habits.

This Ash'arite occasionalism was something startlingly new compared with the prior ideas of Greek thought. It also represented a rational way to look upon the predestinarian hints and messages of the Qur'an itself. As to the objection that the Ash'arite system, though based on revelation, is not contained therein, the answer is that there were quite a number of things undiscussed by the Prophet (though he and his companions did debate a number of theological and legal problems). The relevant questions had not come up, so the Prophet could not be said on these matters to have any opinion one way or another. Since the questions had arisen later, it is for us to make up our mind about them, but on the basis of course of revelation.

ANOTHER RELIGIOUS SOURCE OF WORLDVIEWS: THE GROWTH OF SUFISM

We saw in the case of al-Ash'arī and the evolution of an occasionalist metaphysics that certain religious impulses push thought in a certain direction. It is obvious that atomistic occasionalism in this case has primarily a theological function and arises in part at least from the Qur'anic emphasis on divine omnipotence and supremacy. In the days of the success of Islam, a movement which, analogously to monasticism in the case of Christianity, helped to combat the laxities born out of political success, also created new slants on the cosmos and the Divine Being. This movement was known as Sufism. It had an ascetic side to it (though this did not include celibacy, which was by and large anathema in the world of Islam), and it developed techniques of inner contemplation which assimilated it to both Christian mysticism and Indian forms of yoga. It often put on the appearance of heterodoxy, hence the bad fate of al-Ḥallaj (which we shall come to).

Eventually Sufism was to play a vital part in the conversion of populaces to Islam, particularly in Persia (Iran), India and South-east Asia. The cult of the holy man was a bridge between popular piety and elite spirituality, and Sufism itself as already indicated was a bridge between indigenous forms of piety and the incoming religion – between Christianity and Islam in India, between Hinduism and Islam in India, and between Buddhism and other religious manifestations and Islam in South-east Asia. Because of its mystical side it had some philosophical importance in reinforcing solidarity between Islamic revelation and Neoplatonic and other classical strands of thought.

Perhaps the first major mystic, properly speaking, was a woman (leaving aside such a noted ascetic as Ḥasan al-Baṣri (642–728), from Iraq, a notable area for the pursuit of other worldliness, in contrast with the luxury of its cities like Baghdad and Basra). She was Rābi'ah al-'Adawiyah (*d.* 801). There were stories of the rivalry between Ḥasan and Rābi'ah, no doubt apocryphal: but they included the chauvinist claim by the Ḥaṣan party that no woman could rival a man in piety. Ḥaṣan was a rather solemn, maybe morose, person. He thought that God should really not have created the world at all, and he was forever thinking of hell and of his own sins. But Rābi'ah took the view of the lover: the hope of paradise and the fear of hell are not the reasons for trying to come close to God. In a famous poem she expresses her love of God as being twofold: there is the selfish joy of God's presence, and there is the disinterested outward-going love.

A vital figure in the onward development of Sufism was Dhū al-Nūn (806–59), who introduced the notion of gnosis or *ma'rifah*. This is direct knowledge of God. It is brought about by God's direct communication of his light to the mystic; it is not a question of (literal) seeing, and it is indescribable, for the mystic gets lost in the light. Here there is a strong echo of much other mystical literature in the world's religions: the distinction between subject and object seems to vanish.

The sense of merger was dangerous from the angle of orthodox Islam. The mystics tended to minimize or even abolish the gulf fixed between Creator and creature. Thus we have tendencies to monism, as in the teachings of Abū Yazīd al-Bisṭāmi (*d.* 874), who had through his teacher, from Sind, some contact, direct or indirect, with Indian methods of yoga. He spent a long period as a wandering ascetic in the Syrian desert. Some of his writings have come down to us. One of them (maybe spurious, but still a testimony to the kind of thinking of this developing period) describes Abū Yazīd's re-enactment of the Prophet's night journey. There was a sense of being annihilated in God: this annihilation was known as *fanā'*. In other words, the empirical and self-conscious self disappears, to be replaced by the divine light (sometimes figured too as darkness). Abū Yazīd also described various inner experiences: the sense of the expansion and contraction of the soul, sometimes filling up the whole room, sometimes tiny like a flittering sparrow. His dramatic descriptions led some Muslims to describe his kind of mysticism as 'drunken' and the difference between drunken and sober forms of mysticism became a commonplace of later Sufism. It will be noted that the idea of gnosis or *ma'rifah* was put alongside discursive knowledge, i.e. the kind of knowledge that comes from scholarship, reasoning and the like. It of course was troublesome from an orthodox point of view that this gave Sufis an extra source of knowledge apart from those available to the theologian. Sufis tended too to back up points they made not just from the chief fonts of Islamic orthodoxy, namely the Qur'an and the Ḥadīth, but also from incidents and sayings in the lives of famous Sufis. The holy person became, as in the later Roman empire with Christianity, an extra scripture, as it were.

The night journey of Muhammad, by the way, corresponds to a well-known theme in the history of religions and has something in common with shamanistic experiences. The image of the ladder ascending to heaven, up which the Prophet ascends, having made a miraculous journey from Mecca to Jerusalem, is highly significant for Sufi mysticism, as it signifies the mode by which the soul ascends to the light of the Divine Being. At

Jerusalem Muhammad leads prayers together with Abraham, Moses and Jesus, thus indicating his supremacy over these earlier prophetic figures.

The collisions between Sufism and orthodoxy inherent in the tensions between the superiority of the Divine and the mergery motif in mysticism came to a head with al-Ḥallāj (857–922). He became an itinerant preacher, who emphasized moral regeneration and the life of union in love with God. He was not himself of any particularly philosophical bent, though he prepared the way for later Sufi systems of thought which stressed the unity of the creation with the Divine Being. But he did make use of the perilous sentence *Anā al-Ḥaqq* or 'I am the Real' (or 'I am the Truth'). The expression *al-Ḥaqq* was one of the attributes of Allah in traditional Islam. This, however, was not the sole cause of his later execution. Part of his problems lay in the fact that he had become a popular preacher, having discarded his Sufi gown in order to have freer access to the public. He was therefore repudiated by his teacher, al-Junayd (*d.* 910), who was an exponent of 'sober' mysticism. His conduct was a model of propriety and fulfillment of the Law. But al-Ḥallāj openly proclaimed his beliefs: generally hitherto, and indeed for much of the history of Sufism, the doctrines espoused by the masters were to be expounded to the inner circle of the mystical associations only. But al-Ḥallāj gave free vent to his own experience, and was imprisoned for eight years as a rabble-rouser before he was executed (he was flogged, mutilated, crucified and then decapitated, and his body was burned). But his shining love of God spread his reputation after his death.

He was especially rash because he loved paradoxes. Thus he counted the Devil or Iblis as one of his role models. He was the most committed of monotheists who yet was disobedient because God commanded him to bow down to Adam, which he refused to do. Al-Ḥallāj was also a great admirer of Jesus, so that crucifixion was thought to be highly appropriate.

He had in a rather informal way prepared the ground for the doctrine of the coincidence of opposites, a theme in much Sufi literature. One of the first to systematize thought in this matter, and to argue for the identity of God and his creation, was 'Ayn al-Quḍāt (1098–?1131), also executed for his unorthodoxy. There was a serious need to try to bring Sufism into some kind of synthesis with orthodox Islam, and this goal was achieved above all in the writings of al-Ghazālī (1058–1111). Since he drew upon philosophical ideas, and had studied philosophy, Ash'arite theology, Sufi writings and other sources, it now seems appropriate to turn back to the development of *falsafah* in the Islamic world.

FALSAFAH: CONVERGENCES WITH AND DIVERGENCES FROM REVELATION

The first major philosopher within the world of Islam was al-Kindi (*c.*801–73). He was a person of encyclopedic knowledge, and wrote on scientific matters (he was among other things a competent physician) as well as on philosophy. He believed quite strongly in the compatibility, indeed solidarity, between philosophy and revelation. Though his acceptance of a version of negative theology is derived from Greek examples, his account of God's relation to creation strikes a rather different tack. He argues that no body can be infinite. If it were, then you could subtract a finite body from it and be left with two infinites of differing size, which involves a contradiction. The same applies to an infinite chain of causes. So we can argue to the existence of a First Cause, namely God. Moreover, if you cannot have an actual infinite, then the creation of the world must have happened a finite time ago. So al-Kindī argued in accord with orthodoxy for the creation of the world in time. The only being who could be eternal is God.

Further, al-Kindī argued, we cannot think of the creation of the world a finite time ago after the model of the setting in motion of a static something, which becomes this world after it has got into motion. He considered the idea of a static body as being a contradiction in terms, because bodies are characterized by existence in space and time. The only eternal entity is God, who is not bodily. Now it follows from this that creation is by God out of nothing. Similarly the world will eventually dissolve. Moreover, things will perish automatically, al-Kindī holds, if they are not sustained by God. So he held a doctrine similar to Augustine's notion that the preservation of the world is a continuous creation.

A somewhat different view of creation was taken by al-Rāzī (865–925) who was a highly active physician. He was influenced by Plato's *Timaeus,* and thus held that God imposed order in the activity of creation. He thus did not espouse the doctrine of creation out of nothing, like al-Kindī. The latter, incidentally, had thought that the orderliness of the cosmos and its hierarchical arrangement pointed to a supremely Perfect Being. However, for al-Rāzī, the orderliness of the cosmos is constrained by the existence of various eternal principles – atoms, space, time and the world soul. These four together with the fifth, the Creator, make up the five eternal principles in his system. But though al-Rāzī was a theist, he was also against religion. Thus he rejects prophecy for two reasons – first, all humans are born equal in intelligence (he thinks) and differences arise from divergences of dispositions – some like to learn and others do not. So what sort of sense does it make to have some humans, namely prophets, guiding all the rest of humanity? Second, prophets in different religions contradict one another, so how do you choose? Al-Rāzī devoted part of his writings to an attempted exposure of the contradictions in various books of revelation. Reason was quite sufficient to tell you that God exists and give you the basis for knowing the difference between right and wrong.

Al-Rāzī also considered that wars tend to be caused by religion. It fosters the idea that the Creator favors one nation or group over against others. Naturally, his rationalism scarcely commended him to the orthodox. A common Islamic theme of the times was the fear of death, but al-Rāzī declared that there was nothing to fear. For either the soul is immortal and what lies in store for us is some kind of beatific vision or paradisal state; or alternatively we shall be unconscious, and this will mean the cessation of pain.

THE EXPONENT OF A UNIFIED PHILOSOPHY: AL-FĀRĀBĪ (870–950)

While both of the two above-described philosophers wrote in a fairly systematic fashion, the first main exponent of a holistic view of philosophy in the Islamic world was the Turkish writer al-Fārābī, who came from a village called Farab in Transoxiana. While learned enough in his earlier career, at the age of 50 he decided to study more fully at one of the major intellectual centers of the time. The last few years of his life were spent at the court of Saif al-Daulah in Aleppo.

Al-Fārābī held that there is a unity of philosophy. It really is all one school or discipline. He ascribed the differing schools, such as Peripatetics, Stoics and so on, to the fanaticism of followers of great philosophers who stressed points of divergence instead of trying to bring about harmonization. Moreover, philosophical method involves the use of logic, in which al-Fārābī became a master, and logic deals with structures of the human mind which is everywhere the same (for this reason, logic is pre-eminent over grammar, which deals with the variabilities of languages).

Al-Fārābī considered that philosophy and religion were also in harmony, if each is properly understood. They exist in parallel. It is true that he held to the everlasting character of the cosmos, which was scarcely strictly orthodox, since he took over important aspects of Aristotle's cosmology. But he had theories reconciling the two traditions, including a theory of prophecy, which we shall come to shortly. His universe was hierarchical. From the Necessary Being or God at the top emanates a first intelligence, which is the beginning of unity-in-multiplicity, since though it is in itself one, by its knowledge it knows another. Out of it in successive emanations come the intelligences, each associated with one of the nine heavens, down to the moon. In the sublunary world, ruled by the tenth and last intelligence, exist the four elements (earth, air, water, fire) and human souls. The source of the idea of the spheres revolving in circles above the earth lies of course in the geocentric cosmology of Aristotle. The causation of effects up the hierarchy arises from attraction or, in other words, final causation.

The last intelligence al-Fārābī identifies with Aristotle's active intellect. By the process of contemplation and philosophical reasoning, in a somewhat Platonic manner, it is possible for the philosopher (that is, any person who devotes his life to this enterprise) to rise to the level, virtually, of the active intellect, for his rational faculty at this level becomes the matter to which the active intellect is the form. This attainment of bliss is quite possible, though those who do not achieve it simply perish at death without attaining immortality. All this prepares the way for al-Fārābī's rather ingenious theory of prophecy.

He held a view, partially that of Aristotle, about the function of images, both in waking states and dreams. When we are asleep the imagination, relatively free from the distraction of the senses, creates new forms. It is possible, moreover, for it to compose images which reflect the nature of the spiritual world. If a person has a powerful imagination, it can get into communion with the active intellect which will supply it with images of the highest sublimity and beauty. So the prophet is a person of the most vivid imagination which gets inspired by the active intellect and so is filled with spiritual truths. Thus the active intellect has the same function as, and is effectively identified with, the Angel Gabriel.

The general principles of this explanation of prophecy were later taken over by a number of philosophers – by ibn Sīnā and ibn Rushd and by Maimonides. A similar position was expressed by Spinoza. There are hints in al-Fārābī that the divergences between religions arise out of differences in symbolism, rather than in genuine contradictions.

As the cosmos is hierarchical so ought society to be. Al-Fārābī's political philosophy owed much to the *Republic*. But in his case the philosopher–king is also the prophet–king. This general view tended to be accepted too by the philosophers who succeeded him. In brief, al-Fārābī proved himself to be not just a master of logic, but a highly influential moderate rationalist who more or less reconciled *falsafah*, considered by him to be a school or discipline, and religion, mainly that expressed in Islam.

IBN SĪNĀ: A DOMINANT ISLAMIC PHILOSOPHER

The philosopher ibn Sīnā (980–1037), or Avicenna as he came to be known by the Latin writers of the West, built upon al-Fārābī's emanationist structure, but he also had some special and interesting doctrines of his own. First, he noted that God is the only absolutely simple entity in the universe. In all other cases you can ask about the essence or definition of a thing and then about whether it exists or not. But in God essence and existence are one and the same. Moreover, ibn Sīnā was critical of the Aristotelian theory that a substance consists of form united to matter. For form in itself, being a universal, does not exist. On the other hand, matter, being pure potentiality, does not exist either. The union of two non-existents can hardly produce something which exists. So a third notion is needed, namely the thing's existence. But in itself a thing is merely contingent: to explain it you need something which necessarily exists, namely God. But it would be wrong to look on existence as so to speak, a third ingredient in a thing. It is a relation to the necessary existence, namely God.

All this allows ibn Sīnā to give a triadic rather than a dyadic scheme of emanation, thus supplementing al-Fārābī's picture. God, through an eternal act of self-intuition gives rise to an active intelligence which is necessitated by another, namely God himself, but is potential in itself. This in turn gives rise to another intelligence, a soul, and a body – this last being the outer shell of the cosmos. And so on down the chain of intelligences. Since this is an emanationist scheme and God is eternal, ibn Sīnā saw the world too as being eternal, that is everlasting 'backwards', without a beginning (or end).

Ibn Sīnā developed an interesting psychology and epistemology, which gave shape also to his theory of prophecy. With regard to the individual person, he has five outer sense-faculties. But ibn Sīnā postulated five inner ones, too. One was the *sensus communis,* much in the style of Aristotle. Second, there is the imagination (that is, memory) in so far as it conserves sensible images. Third, there is imagination which fuses and recombines sensible images. Fourth – and this is an original notion – there is *wahm,* which the West translated as *vis estimiva,* which judges things to be useful or harmful, loveable or hateful and so on. This becomes the basis of our character, for our cumulative experience and so estimation of things is what pulls us in one direction or another. Fifth, there is that which conserves intentions in one's memory.

Also original is ibn Sīnā's idea that universals come into our minds from outside, that is, from the active intellect. He rejects the view that somehow the emergence of universals in the mind is the mechanical result of the perception of so many particulars. This is not how it happens. It may of course be that reflection on the particulars may prepare the mind for the reception of the universal. But very often we note how somehow ideas come in, as it were, from outside, as when we say, 'It occurs to me that so and so.' We need to make an effort, but then ideas come into our minds. There is then in ibn Sīnā an important sense of the dynamic character of ideas in ordering our world (he sees the senses as passive by contrast, registering what lies in the outside world). So the mind is like a mirror which reflects ideas from the active intellect lying outside, and having something of the function of a God of our immediate world. At first our mirror is rusty and clouded over, but repetition of an item of knowledge polishes it up, so to speak.

All this prepares the way for his notion of prophecy. He notes that people differ very widely in their intuitive and imaginative powers. A person with a most vivid imaginative faculty can intuit truths given to them by the active intellect. The supreme example of this is the prophet. In one sense his mind becomes one with the active intellect, and so the divine speaks from within him. In another way, as a human being, he is non-identical with the revelatory active intellect. By his imagination he transforms the abstract truths about reality, and about God and his creation, into powerful images. Moreover, the true prophet has a charismatic power which enables him to lead human beings, stirring them up both by his images and by his character. He is strong enough too to be able to launch a new sociopolitical system, which can transform civilization.

The vivid nature of the prophetic imagination helps too to explain his experiences. So he actually comes to see and hear the very images which he conjures up in representing the universal truths contained in the active intellect. Pure intellect cannot be the basis of any religion. To impel human beings to action strong imaginative powers are needed.

201

So philosophy and religion are complementary activities. And because what revelation contains are figurative images, it needs to be interpreted to get out of it the higher spiritual truths.

It is worth adding that for ibn Sīnā the potential intellect in the human being, because it can come to hold within it ideas, which are non-spatial, is indivisible and immaterial. It comes into existence with the individual, but it is imperishable.

This relates to the notion that ibn Sīnā held that the creation, like God, is eternal. First of all, the nature of God is absolutely simple: in 'him' necessary existence and essence are one and the same. But God has a kind of mystical self-knowledge in which subject and object are identical, and so he knows what proceeds from his necessary existence. But because God is immaterial, he does not know particular events and persons by perception; however, he knows everything about them in a universal way. So though he might not know what happens at this instant, since he can have no perception of it, he knows everything about the qualities and their combination which go to make up the event. He therefore actually has no need of perception. But just as God does not need and cannot have perception, so the notion of God's will seems to be superfluous. The creation emanates necessarily from God. Of course he is aware of what is proceeding, and assents to it, so in this sense he wills it. But there is no time bound act of will.

Ibn Sīnā has religious as well as philosophical reasons for taking up his general view of the world. On the one hand, he disagrees with the atheists who consider that the world exists eternally, but without the benefit of a creator. Against them he hold that the world is contingent and therefore always needs the necessary existence of God lying beyond it to confer existence upon it. On the other hand, he wants to make a sharp differentiation between the world and God, since without it his doctrine might seem to be a kind of pantheism, which was abhorrent to the orthodox. By stressing the point that the cosmos is time-bound while God is non-temporal, he makes a powerful gap open up between the world and God, even though there is a price to pay, namely the fact that God cannot relate in perception to the creation. It might seem to some that there can thus be no real personal relationship between God and his worshipers, and so ibn Sīnā's religion might seem to be too philosophical and too cold.

While ibn Sīnā is generally thought of as the most famous and powerful intellect of the Islamic philosophical tradition, who had a strong influence, moreover, on the young Aquinas and a number of other medieval Christian philosophers and theologians, his orthodoxy was always somewhat in doubt. His doctrine of the eternity of the creation set him at odds with many orthodox teachers. His conception of prophethood did not always commend itself. Though in public he considered the notion of the bodily resurrection should be believed, in private he strongly rejected it, at least in its literal form. It was not surprising if he were one of the targets of al-Ghazālī's critique of philosophy, in his defense of a middle path in regard to Sufism.

AL-GHAZĀLĪ: THE MOST IMPORTANT INTELLECTUAL FIGURE OF THE ISLAMIC EAST

Al-Ghazālī (1058–1111) had a negative and a positive side. On the negative side, his critique of philosophy seems to have been a vital factor in the virtual demise of live philosophy in the then eastern parts of the Islamic world. It was to continue with some vigor in the West: Spain itself became a great intellectual and artistic center in which the values of Islamic, Jewish and Christian civilization were in interplay.

Al-Ghazālī came from north-eastern Iran, but most of his studies were conducted elsewhere. In due course he was appointed to a professorship of the Nizamiyah university in Baghdad, but after two years he underwent a spiritual crisis, which led him at the age of 36 to resign, and to devote himself to the wandering life of the ascetic and Sufi. He was influenced in part by the al-Ash'ari system, skeptical ideas and Sufism. He also studied the Isma'ilis or esoteric Shi'is, against whom the Caliph commanded him to write a critique.

On the positive side, al-Ghazālī created an important synthesis which helped to bring together both mystical and orthodox notions, entitled the *Revivification of the Religious Sciences*. This together with his *The Incoherence of the Philosophers* stand as the two greatest among his voluminous writings.

In due course al-Ghazālī returned to his native region, and lived his last days quietly, supervising pupils who ran his school. He died in 1111.

In a somewhat autobiographical work which was written to explain why it was that he had given up his university post, while at the height of his fame, his powers and his worldly success, al-Ghazālī divides the intellectual world into four groups – the theologians or al-Ash'arīya school; the mystics, that is to say the Sufis; the authoritarians who appealed to an imam or spiritual leader for authority; and the philosophers. He was himself raised in orthodox theological jurisprudence, and while he did have a short period of skepticism, it is doubtful whether he ever or at all doubted the root beliefs of Sunni Islam. It is true that he did say that it is necessary to question everything; he quoted the saying of the Prophet that every child born has the right attitude, but it is his parents who make him a Jew or a Christian or a 'follower of the Magi' – this of course already presupposes the truth of Islam. He was certainly most critical of taking anything on the authority of another, and this was why of the above-mentioned four groups he was most strongly critical of the imamites (and he had the Isma'īliyah most of all in mind). Indeed, underpinning his approach to the various schools was his method of doubt, which was also a method of openness. He wanted to probe what philosophers, theologians and Sufis had to say, and why they said it. He wanted to try to get at the foundations of each school or thinker. In all this the width of his experience should be underlined. He was probably the first theologian of the Sunni tradition who had a thorough grasp of philosophy. Hitherto most theologians had thought of philosophy with apprehension and distrust. Moreover, by giving up his professorship and devoting himself to the spiritual life, after experiencing a crisis of skepticism, unbelief and severe psychosomatic symptoms, he could claim to have a real inward knowledge of mysticism and of the experiences to which it appealed.

His knowledge of philosophy included a good grasp of logic, which he thought to be important methodologically and which he introduced into theological training. He wrote a masterly compendium of Aristotelianism which, when put into Latin, impressed Western thinkers as being the work of an Aristotelian, though in fact al-Ghazālī was highly critical of that tradition. In criticizing philosophers, he divided them into three groups: materialists; naturalists (who believed in a benevolent God, but not in the spiritual nature of the soul, etc.); and theists. He reserved his deeper scrutiny for the latter. Here he held that the work of al-Fārābī and ibn Sīnā was most important. Yet he considered that these had departed from Qur'anic claims for no very good metaphysical reasons, and he noted the gulf fixed between Qur'anic and Hellenic values.

He criticized the philosophers on various counts: regarding the eternity or everlasting nature of the cosmos; the inconsistency of their claim that this idea fits with the doctrine of creation by God; their notions about God's knowledge of either universals or particulars; their doctrine of souls of the heavenly spheres and of their knowledge; their theory of causation; their failure to prove or recognize the spirituality and immortality of the soul; their denial of the resurrection of the body. While some of their confusions are the result of indifference and the like, three are in basic conflict with Islam: their views on the eternity of the world; their views on God's knowledge of particulars; and their denial of the resurrection of the body.

Al-Ghazālī spends proportionately a great deal of space in dealing with the question of the eternity of the world and the related concept of the emanation of the world, in various stages, down from God. He is very fierce on these matters, since it offended strongly against his belief in, and feel for, the contingency of God's act of will in creating the world out of absolutely nothing. According to al-Ghazālī the philosophers assumed things about causation which there is no need to assume – that every effect has a cause, that a cause lies outside of the effect and that a cause will lead immediately to an effect. So they argued that if the world came into being at a particular time, there must be a cause of God's change of mind; but this is impossible since at the time in question *ex hypothesi* nothing else existed. So the world must have been in existence from all eternity. But al-Ghazālī counters this by showing that we could equally believe that the cause of God's willing lies within his mind. Moreover, God can will from all eternity that Socrates and Plato should come into being, but at differing times: there is no need for the effect to follow directly upon his willing. God's will is not in any case bound by anything, so why should his choice of a particular time not be entirely undetermined? But actually, of course, time comes into being with the creation of the spatial cosmos, since space and time are conceptually connected. Al-Ghazālī is especially critical of the philosophers because they are happy to think of God's knowledge as being of quite a different character than ours, but they continue to make close comparison between our will and his. Both are equally remote from our own experience.

The emanationist theory which involved the First Being and then the descent of various intelligences related to various heavenly spheres down to the sublunary world of the earth is criticized as mere fantasy. The very idea that something complex can emerge from what is simple seems to undermine an underlying belief that somehow by multiplying downward stages the philosopher resolves the paradox of the one and the many. Take the first intelligence which supposedly has emanated from the Divine Being. Is its self-knowledge something identical with its essence or is it not? It seems arbitrary to think of the first intelligence as having three aspects only, as the emanationists claim; it would be equally logical to think of it as having five aspects – its essence, its self-knowledge, its knowledge of the First Principle, its being a possible existent by itself and its being a necessary being having its necessity derived from outside of itself, namely from the First Principle. All such speculation can in any case be applied to the First Principle itself, giving it a multiplicity rather than simplicity of nature. In any event, the emanationists cannot avoid the idea that what is plural comes from something simple, and such multiplicity is necessarily inexplicable, even given their own assumptions.

And how indeed could they expect otherwise? The First Principle does what he wills. You cannot show either on the basis of inference or of self-evidence that such an idea is impossible. However, it is obvious that speculative attempts to penetrate the mystery of creation are vain, because in order to establish some understanding of the matter you would have to establish some link with experience, but creation itself involves bringing into being both that which is experienced and that which does the experiencing. To make this act intelligible would abolish its very creativity. So inquiring into the manner in which the world has proceeded from God's will is an idle and pointless venture, says al-Ghazālī.

Actually the philosophers really reduce God. He is supposed to have only knowledge of himself. But the first intelligence has knowledge, it is held, not only of the First Principle (God) but also of what proceeds from itself. What kind of a theory is it that gives God a lesser knowledge than that of his supposed creatures? Aristotle's idea of the Divine Being thinking himself blankly makes him like the dead, in an empty sort of dream. For all these reasons, then, al-Ghazālī excoriates emanationism. In effect it represents another worldview from that of orthodoxy, and one which is shot through with contradictions. Moreover, the philosophers relied on a view of causation which is itself entangled in problems. To al-Ghazālī's arguments on this front I now turn.

AL-GHAZĀLĪ'S CRITIQUE OF THE CONCEPT OF CAUSATION

His initial skepticism has to do with the very idea that the relation between cause and effect is a necessary one, as the philosophers seem to suppose. For there is nothing self-contradictory in supposing a given cause is followed by a different sort of effect. You can conceive that fire is not followed by burning, or that sunrise is not followed by light. Whether a given law holds or not is not discovered by reasoning, but is based, very simply, on observation. Necessity only applies within the order of thought, and has a use in logic. But it has no purchase on the world of nature. When we see that an effect follows a cause repeatedly, there is set up in us an association of ideas. The norm gets fixed indelibly in our minds. There is a bit of likeness here with logical necessity, because two things are associated in our minds, though their relation to one another is actually extrinsic. This psychological necessity is of course not absolute. We can deny the consequences which are usually experienced after a given event or set of events without being involved in a contradiction. (Hence, the denial of miracles without establishing their logical impossibility is a sign of mere obduracy or confusion.)

All this is relevant too to the question of God's knowledge of particulars, about which al-Ghazālī felt strongly. For ibn Sīnā and others, God does not have direct knowledge of particulars. But he knows himself, and as he is the First Cause of the universe, so he knows the universe. But this argument is unwarranted. For knowing himself as cause of the cosmos is something over and above knowing his essence. Of course, the philosophers get themselves into the morass of difficulties by wishing to preserve the unity of God's knowledge. But it is not sensible for them to make a sharp distinction between the knowledge of universals, on the one hand, and knowledge of particulars, on the other. Both involve a degree of multiplicity and should affect the alleged unity of divine knowledge. Further, given al-Ghazālī's analysis of causation, God's knowledge of himself as cause will not give a guide to the actual effects, which are not, as we have seen, necessitated.

Moreover, the contrast drawn by the philosophers between the eternality of God's knowledge and the temporality of our knowledge makes God irrelevant to my actual experience. I am forever living through the fleeting nows which make up my experience of life. The shifting continuum of nows is a vital ingredient in my religious experience, and yet it seems to be locked away for ever from the comprehension of the Divine Being. So in all sorts of ways the metaphysical theory of the unity of God and the emanations through which he creates (or is alleged to create) the world are seen, by al-Ghazālī, to involve a mass of contradictions. And far from preserving God's inviolate grandeur, it cuts him off from the world. The bridge which it supposedly builds between the one and the many is an illusion. They have produced more of a gulf between ontologically diverse levels of existence than a real bridge between them. Yet their God is 'smaller' than that of the pious al-Ghazālī.

AL-GHAZĀLĪ'S MAKING SUFISM ORTHODOX AND ORTHODOXY SUFI

In his *Revivification of the Religious Sciences* and other writings, al-Ghazālī sought to give a unified picture of the moral, spiritual and intellectual life which would show how mysticism has a rightful and indeed central place in Islam. His critique of the philosophers prepared the way for a warmer approach to the contemplative life and a more realistic (from an orthodox point of view) picture of religion. In ethics he stressed a number of Islamic virtues which were somewhat foreign to Greek civilization, such as repentance, reliance and fear of God. He held up the Prophet as the great exemplar of virtue. He connects fulfillment of the Law with the practice of asceticism, necessary if one is not to be too beguiled by the created world, and desirable as a means of training one's attention upon the Divine Being. At the end of the road there lies the supreme love of God, and in this relationship a person may have a *gnosis* or direct apprehension of the Divine. It is because the Sufi is plunged into the Light and loses self-consciousness that he is liable to utter those mad sentences which brought Sufis under suspicion among many of the orthodox, such as al-Ḥallāj's 'I am the Real' or 'Glory be to me!' These utterances are like those of a drunken person. When he gets over his state he will come to recognize that they are crazy, though they did rest upon genuine experience. Al-Ghazālī preaches a 'sober' Sufism. In this he had great success in establishing Sufism as respectable within Islam, until relatively recent times, when it has often come under criticism from the neo-orthodox.

In his moral psychology he also took a middle path. He tried to resolve the problem of God's determinism and its relationship to free will by conceiving the total universe as consisting of three levels. At the top is the level where God exists in his perfect self-subsistence. This is an area of perfect freedom. At the bottom level is the region of material entities, whose patterns are wholly determined by God. The world of human selves lies in between, since the self or soul is characterized above all by being a will, and so is like God in this. And as God transcends the world, so the soul transcends the body. On the other hand, only God is self-subsistent. There is, then, in al-Ghazālī a strong emphasis on the will. Yet the material side of life is controlled by God, and also the occurrence of those inner ideas and inclinations which precede actions. But the individual can either exercise his will in relation to these or not. And so within a world of determinism, the individual has his freedom.

The rich learning and many-sidedness of al-Ghazālī's experience and writings have given him a very central place in Islamic philosophy and religion. In a way, he could be regarded as a kind of apologist against another religion, that being the religion of Greek philosophy as interpreted in Arab or Islamic clothing. He was right in seeing that some of the assumptions of the philosophers were open to challenge and question, and belonged to a stock of ideas taken over a bit uncritically from the Hellenistic civilization which formed their milieu. Philosophy as understood among the Greeks and Romans was very imperfectly assimilated into the world of the Qur'an.

PHILOSOPHY IN SPAIN

Meanwhile at the other end of the Islamic world, in Spain, developments were taking place which culminated in the work of perhaps the greatest of the medieval Muslim philosophers, namely ibn Rushd (known as Averroes in Latin). The first notable thinker in the Spanish context was probably ibn Bājjah (*d.* 1139), who may have been Jewish, but a convert to Islam. He had wide-ranging interests, but two points are important in his development of ideas relating to the mystical life, in which he was interested, though outwardly he seems to have lived a worldly life. He thought of the active intellect as being a kind of intermediary between God and the soul. Moreover, he interpreted the mystical vision as involving a communion or contact of the soul with the active intellect, rather than as an actual union or merging. In this way he attempted to reconcile philosophical speculation and the apparent realities of the inner quest. He also foreshadowed something in ibn Rushd's thinking in arguing that the beatified souls who without cessation praise God are not countable because they lack material embodiment. So arithmetic does not apply to them.

Probably the most influential of ibn Bājjah's works was *The Rule of the Solitary Person*. He argues that the way upwards in reflecting philosophically on the world and God is by being solitary. His epistemology is rather *a priori*, so that a person can in principle by himself ascend to the level of the active intellect and so have a kind of rational union with the divine. His doctrine helped to stimulate one of the most famous works composed in Western Islam, by ibn Tufail (*d.* 1185), *Hayy bin Yaqzān*.

This romance concerns one Ḥayy, who is born spontaneously on a desert island, though legend had it that he had been abandoned there by his mother, secretly married to one Yaqzān. Anyway the lonely Ḥayy is raised by a doe. In due course he comes to realize his nakedness and covers his genitals with leaves. He also realizes that he is defenseless, and arms himself with a stick. From this he comes to see the superiority of the hand over the limbs of other animals. He also gets the concept of the stick as instrument. When the doe dies he realizes that there is a sort of animal soul for which the body serves as an instrument. The soul brings warmth and so shares a likeness with the sun. He then proceeds to analyze nature around him and comes to classify the differing kinds of animals, plants, minerals and so on. Each of the objects has a body, but each type has a different soul or form, which is, however, not strictly visible. He begins thinking of the unseen world, and comes to the conclusion that there is a first and necessary, bodiless, being which is the cause of all the others. This conception of God leads him to recognize his own immaterial essence or soul.

At this point, amid his amazing inductive and intellectual progress, Asāl, a mystic from a neighboring island appears. He had been looking for a solitary place to conduct his meditations. He now tells Ḥayy about the contents of the Qur'anic revelation: about the Prophets; about angels; about the Day of Judgment; and so on. Ḥayy intuitively recognizes the truth of these notions. But he does not especially like the strongly poetical and figurative language used in the Qur'an: it often seems to be couched in such a worldly way that people hearing it might not be impelled to pursue the upward course of the purely contemplative mystic, who should rise above earthly things. He returns with Asāl to the other island, with a view to converting them from their convention-ridden ways and to preach them the pure concepts which he had learned on his own. But the people do not understand him and find his utterances altogether too hard to apprehend. At this point Ḥayy realizes that the Prophet was eminently wise in expressing revelation in strongly sensuous and imaginative terms. And so he returns to his solitude in his own island, there devoted to the pursuit of the contemplative part which will bring him into communion with the Divine Being.

Ibn Tufail was stimulated, as we have noted, to write this famous piece by the theory of the solitary person developed by ibn Bājjah. But he considered that the latter was too intellectualist. If he was a mystic it was a highly rationalistic kind. Ibn Tufail therefore stressed rather more the need for reason to be supplemented by the pursuit of ecstatic experience in the life of Ḥayy. His treatise also served as a sketch of the origin of human life, and showed how the inductive intellect could be developed independently of any social milieu. It also aims at showing how the conclusions of philosophy and revealed theology coincide. But while the truths of religion are accessible to the philosopher, it is absolutely necessary for the masses to be presented with both law and imaginative revelation. All this in some degree corresponded to the ideology of the rather puritanical regime which ruled Morocco, at whose court ibn Tufail served. It provided a rationale for dividing people into an elite class, capable of wielding philosophical concepts, and the masses, who need to be fed a diet of imaginative revelation. The latter need to be obedient. The philosopher–mystic can gain the heavenly bliss of the divine light. The masses have to rest content with a second-rate kind of salvation.

Consequently ibn Tufail postulates union with God as being the ultimate good at which ethical behavior should aim. The human being is a mixture of three things, namely a body, the animal soul and the pure immaterial soul. On the first front he needs food, shelter and protection. On the second front, he should be clean and dignified, kind to animals and other humans, etc. At the last level, equipped with wisdom and the knowledge inherent in both negative and affirmative theology he should gain union with the divine essence.

It should be noted that ibn Tufail's romance of *Ḥayy bin Yaqẓān* had a strong influence far beyond its original cultural milieu. It was translated into a variety of languages – Hebrew, Latin, Russian, German, French and English among others. It influenced the Quaker movement, but was found alarming by the orthodox, since it called in question the doctrine of original sin and the fallen nature of human beings, including their reasoning faculties.

IBN RUSHD AND THE INFLUENCE OF AVERROISM

Some time after ibn Tufail (who died when ibn Rushd was 11 years old), an even greater and more influential figure appeared on the Western Islamic scene. Born in Cordova of a legal family, ibn Rushd, usually Latinized into Averroes, lived from 1126 to 1198. Towards the end of his life he was persecuted, having served as chief magistrate in Cordova and was patronized by some of the Almohad rulers, who had established themselves in Marrakesh in 1147; one of them indeed ordered him to write his famous commentary series on Aristotle (or what he took to be Aristotle). Conflict with the more narrowly religious *'ulama'* led to his books being burned. Many were translated, however, into Latin, and in the thirteenth century, therefore, he came to have more influence in the Christian West than in the Islamic world.

Apart from his commentaries and précis of the writings of Aristotle, ibn Rushd's two most important works related to philosophy were his *Faṣl al-Maqāl (The Decisive Treatise)* of 1177 and his celebrated attempted refutation of al-Ghazālī's *Incoherence of the Philosophers* aimed at al-Fārābī and ibn Sīnā. This refutation was called *Tahāfut Al-tahāfut* or *The Incoherence of 'The Incoherence'*, published in 1184.

The first of these works turns on the question of whether the *Sharī'ah* or Islamic law prohibits, permits, requires or recommends philosophical inquiry. The answer is that at least it is recommended, since the Qur'an enjoins rational consideration of the nature of the universe. This implies that people should use logic in the furtherance of processes of deduction, which can lead from the known to the unknown. Indeed, the objective of religion is to find the truth and right practice, and this is in one sense a philosophical task.

Ibn Rushd considers the relationship between philosophers, theologians and the mass of people. The philosophers, aiming at scientifically demonstrated truth, are highest of the three categories; the theologians are next, though their arguments depend on dialectical reasoning; the people, whose assent comes from the power of rhetoric, are the lowest. Sometimes there seems to be a conflict if a rational conclusion out of philosophy about God's nature conflicts with an orthodox interpretation of a text. Often Muslim scholars have drawn back from interpreting texts out of fear of confusing the minds of the common people. But strictly it is necessary to do something about conflicts such as these. The solution is to use *ta'wīl* or allegorical interpretation. But since the philosopher is best equipped to do this, and since what he said might be confusing to the masses, such allegorical ways of understanding texts should be kept as esoteric claims among philosophers and not widely broadcast.

Moreover, says ibn Rushd, the sources of law are the Qur'an, the *Ḥadīth*, *ijmā'* or consensus, and legal syllogism. But it is obvious that there are occasions when the Qur'an has to be rationally interpreted, and on matters of doctrine there is virtually no consensus among qualified jurists. It was thus wrong of al-Ghazālī to imply that philosophers are irreligious on the basis of any kind of supposed consensus. He condemned certain ideas, notably the three chief ones – the doctrine of the eternity of the world, philosophers' denial of God's knowledge of particulars and the denial of bodily resurrection. Certainly the first two of these cannot be regarded as contrary to articles of faith. And the notion of bodily resurrection is stated in that way primarily for the benefit of the masses. The notion of spiritual resurrection is compatible with philosophical speculation. It will be noted that in all this ibn Rushd essentially subordinates theology and religion to philosophy.

Moreover, he held to a close relationship between science and philosophy. In Aristotle the way 'being' is used in the *Physics* is not the same as, though it is analogous to, its use in the *De Anima*. Averroes did not accept these divergences between the sciences and the uses of being. The universe, including God, is a single, complex hierarchy of being. He therefore relied on some of al-Ghazālī's strictures on philosophy to restrict the pursuit of science (in favor of the mystical path). Conversely, ibn Rushd was influenced by what he saw as scientific considerations in arguing for the eternity of the world. The circular motion of the heavens is a perfect and infinite motion. This in turn requires above it the existence of an unmoved mover. This Being, which also is the supreme intelligence, is the cause of and animator of all the lesser intelligences in the cosmos. In all this, ibn Rushd was impressed with the correctness of Aristotle's general analysis of causation, and was thus critical of what stood at the heart of al-Ghazālī's criticism of the philosophers. Ibn Rushd accepted the doctrine of the four causes. This also held the clue to his dealing with the problem of God's knowledge of the particulars. For as creator God knows them through his acts of causation. Ibn Rushd criticized al-Ghazālī's idea that causation is a mere habit of mind, so that by association of the ideas of supposed cause and effect we come merely to expect one thing to follow from another. He likewise rejected Ash'arite occasionalism. Thus it was that ibn Rushd's attempted rebuttal of al-Ghazālī rested on two Aristotelian assumptions. One was the permanence of things. This, so to speak, ensured the stability of the world and tied up with his connection between belief in essences and relative permanence in substances. The other was the necessity of causation. He thought that the real reason why al-Ghazālī wanted to affirm the mere contingency of causal relations was so as to give an intelligible account of miracles. For ibn Rushd the supreme miracle of Islam was the Qur'an itself, but this does not run contrary to the laws of causation. In any event, he thought that the denial of efficient causes in what is evidently observed is mere sophistry. In attacking al-Ghazālī on this front he thought to destroy the very nerve of al-Ghazālī's complaint against the philosophers.

In many ways al-Ghazālī's conception of the contingency of causation was more forward-looking. But Averroes' impressive commentarial status could draw sustenance from the magnified reputation of Aristotle in the medieval world – where he was famous far beyond the bounds of Islam, and drew, for instance, much commentarial and critical treatment from Thomas Aquinas. It was also from Aristotle that he drew his idea of immortality (such as it was). He held to a mild emanationism, in the sense that he accepted the various levels of intelligence below God controlling the heaven, down as far as the active intellect, which because its nature was formal rather than material was a unified entity. It infused the passive intellect in human beings with forms which helped humans actively to understand what was given to them through the senses. The fusion of the active intellect and the passive intellect brought about the so-called acquired intellect. But all this created problems about the future life. The soul involved being the form of a body, and could not exist as an individual once the body had perished. What survived was the upward-yearning intellect, but it could not, being formal, exist as an individual entity. So immortality was possible, but was impersonal. This could be regarded as little different from annihilation. If my intellect survives but has no special memories attached or other connections to me, then is it any better than the survival of my bones (say)? My bones at least would be Ninian-Smart-shaped. Not that that would be much consolation to me. So there were reasons to criticize ibn Rushd as not being perfectly orthodox.

FROM PHILOSOPHY TO SUFISM ONCE AGAIN: IBN 'ARABI

Throughout this period there is a constant interplay between jurists or theologians, philosophers and Sufis. This was because all were, more or less, engaged in studies and life-activities which bore upon the nature of God. As we have noted, the treatment of philosophy as, so to speak, a single profession with some kind of ideology (if, however, also pursued in a professional manner, implying training in logic and the like), may give a misleading impression. Each party was given to the expression of a worldview, sometimes on the basis of the Greek tradition, sometimes on the basis of revealed scripture, sometimes on the basis of religious experience, and usually to some extent on the basis of all three, but with varying emphases.

Ibn 'Arabī (or ibn al-'Arabī) was born in Murcia in Spain in 1165. Much of his early education was in Seville, and he traveled widely, seeking out Sufis and others. After a very long apprenticeship he left the West during his thirties and went to Egypt and Mecca, and in due course settled in Damascus. He was probably impelled to leave the region of Spain and Morocco because of the intolerant attitudes of the schoolmen of the area, suspicious even of al-Ghazālī, and hardly likely to take kindly to ibn 'Arabī's startling philosophy, still less to the erotic imagery he often employed. He wrote, as a result of an encounter in Mecca, a wonderful and widely celebrated love poem *Tarjumān al-ashwāq* or *The Interpreter of Ardent Longings*. This has an inner meaning. The beautiful girl Niẓām, daughter of a Sufi *shaykh,* is the transfigured embodiment of the eternal woman, the Eternal Wisdom of the Divine. This poem may have influenced Dante in his depiction of Beatrice.

The mainspring of ibn 'Arabī's metaphysics lies in the thought of the unity of the universe when it is seen in its inner nature, beyond the multiplicity of phenomena which present themselves to the ordinary person. The problem in trying to perceive this inner truth lies in the subject–object dualism of ordinary consciousness. This comes about because the individual is conscious of his own ego. So in order to see the world as it really is, the person has to undergo rigorous training which removes his or her sense of ego. This discipline leads to the disappearance or *fanā* of the self. In this line of teaching, of course, ibn 'Arabī is in consonance with so much yogic and mystical thinking and practice. The final vanishing of the subject–object distinction may be held to be a commonplace of much of mystical thought. According to ibn 'Arabī, the culmination of the Sufi path is the realization of *Aḥad* or the absolute One. In its oneness it negates all plurality and therefore all things (indeed there is doubt about calling it One in case this be thought of as a number).

The Sufi who has attained egolessness and this sense of unity will see the world of multiplicity in quite a new light. He will see all things as one. Ibn 'Arabī says that the mystic must see with two eyes, seeing both the unity and the multiplicity of the world, as he survives beyond the extraordinary experience of absolute unity. It is as if in the unity we perceive the contraction of the world and in the many we see its expansion.

So far we may note that for ibn 'Arabī the experiential dimension of religion or life is central. Thus for him the path to the higher experience may be regarded in a sense as his philosophical method. It surely is reasonable for someone who thinks that ordinary experience needs to be transcended if we are to see things as they truly are to cultivate the kind of experience that will produce insight into the 'invisible'. Naturally, however, the appeal to Sufi gnosis was something regarded with suspicion by the orthodox: it set another revelation alongside of revelation.

The absolute unity of the Divine Being, who or which is beyond speech and differentiation, contains within itself the impulse to expand. To put the matter anthropomorphically, God wishes to have an object of love – something for him to love and to love him. The One therefore expands into the multiplicity of the world. This Absolute as manifested retains an essential unity, and the cosmos becomes as it were the mirror through which the One knows itself. The human being plays a crucial role here: he is made in the image of God and can, as a Sufi, progress along a path which begins in ignorance and illusion, in so far as he or she will imagine him- or herself to be an agent independent of the Divine, to the realization that we are but manifestations of the one God, who dwells in each of us. Everything in fact is ultimately dependent on God.

Though ibn 'Arabī's system has been thought of as pantheism, it in fact follows the logic of Ash'arī orthodoxy. There the Divine Being is entirely responsible for the patterns of behavior traced by the atoms. Secondary causation has no meaning. So in ibn 'Arabī's thought the world is everywhere directly dependent on God.

The original unity of the Absolute means that it is a complete mystery, being indescribable and unutterable. It is the *Ahad* or bare One. But at some point (so to speak) it starts to turn towards manifestation, and becomes articulated and ready to create. Thus the One becomes something more like the Allah of religion. It contains within itself articulated forms which it projects into the phenomenal world, which is the self-transformation of the One. In this way, as with other mystical thinkers within the theistic traditions, ibn 'Arabī's thought involves levels of the Divine.

We have already noted that God is desirous of love and the process of the universe is designed to find in self-manifestation a mirror. It is above all through human beings that God mirrors himself. He lies at the heart of each person, so that human beings are essentially fusions of the divine and the human. This is the truth lying within the Christian conception of Christ as Son of God. But it is above all in certain prophets and saints that God meets his perfect self-mirroring. It is above all in the perfect human being that the whole creative self-manifestation culminates, for in such a being there is a refusion of the manifested creature and the divine essence.

The picture which ibn 'Arabī drew was a deterministic one. With his rigorous doctrine of the unity of the One with the manifested cosmos there was no room for independence. The imperfections of the world are only apparent. Truly God acts through every single item in the phenomenal world. If the emancipated person is at all free, it is because in sharing the divine nature she or he shares in the ultimate freedom of the Divine Being itself.

Like a number of mystics, ibn 'Arabī was remarkably generous towards other religious traditions. Thus he wrote:

> My heart has become the receptacle of every 'form',
> It is a pasture for gazelles and a convent for Christian monks,
> And a temple for idols and pilgrims' Kabah,
> And the tablets of the Torah and the Book of the Qur'an.
> I follow the religion of love whichever way its camels take,
> For this is my religion and faith.

SOME OTHER TRENDS IN SUFISM

There are many other aspects of Sufism than the attempts to frame various mystically inspired worldviews. There were such poets as Farid ad-Dīn 'Attar (*d. c.*1230) and the famous Jalāl ad-Dīn Rūmī (1207–73), and there were founders of various Sufi orders. Rūmī started the Mevlevi order, using rotatory dances to help induce higher states of consciousness. Among other important ones are the Qadiriyah, founded by the famous saint al-Qaīdir (1088–1166), the Suhrawardīyah, founded by Abū Najīb al-Suhrawardī (*d.* 1162), and the Naqshbandiyah, founded by Baha' al-Dīn Naqshband (*d.* 1388), important in Mughal India.

Among mystical writers, it is important to mention Shīhab al-Dīn Suhrawardī Maqtūl (1153–91), who tried to revive what is often regarded as a kind of Zoroastrian-influenced theosophy, known as *ishrāqi* wisdom, which was to play an important role in the Shi'ah tradition. There is an appeal to a very different picture of the history of philosophy from that standard in the Islamic world at that time. Suhrawardī was highly critical of Aristotle, and appealed less to reasoning than to inner intuitions, following, as he considered it, the traditions going back to Hermes and Plato on the one hand and to Persian sages on the other. The language of his worldview was bathed in the imagery of light. *Ishrāq* means illumination, and Suhrawardī saw a connection between such light imagery and the importance of the East, that is Persia, compared with the more rationalistic West of the Islamic world. This tradition, which had influence both in Iran and in Mughal India, had comparatively little impact upon European philosophy, but some treatises were translated into Sanskrit and entered into the stream of Indian mystical writings.

IBN KHALDŪN: A NEW SCIENCE OF CIVILIZATIONS

Ibn Khaldūn (1332–1406) was born in Tunis, and his remarkable reputation for scholarship led to his being given positions in various courts across the Maghreb, from Morocco to Egypt; he suffered the vicissitudes of such a life. He devoted himself, even during prison and exile, to the systematic study of political power and human civilization. He can be said to be the first of modern historians, and he sought to give his researches and writings a scientific basis which could be said to be a philosophy of history. Here we do not quite leave the world of Islamic philosophy, with its tendency to debate old themes, such as the relation between revealed theology and the speculations of Greek philosophers. But we do meet with a fresh approach to history, seen as a natural science. If ibn Khaldūn wished to work in general with Aristotelian categories and schemas of the relation of the various sciences, the reason was that what we would now count as scientific investigation was part of philosophy in the wider sense. The work of such great figures as ibn Sīnā and ibn Rushd incorporated a lot of science, and owed much to Aristotle. What is surprising about ibn Khaldūn is his modern approach to history and his radical defense of his inquiry into the nature and operation of human culture. For he had to disentangle what he was doing from the work of jurists and political philosophers. He thought that his inquiries into the how of human events had lessons for the ought of law and politics, but was very different from these other thinkers. He was a descriptive and analytical figure, and he thought analysis and description to be important. Much of all this he wrote in his *Prolegomena* or *Muqaddimah* to his *History*.

Because he was an inheritor of the categories of Greek science and philosophy, it was less easy for him to make in a relatively simple and decisively clear way the distinction between the natural sciences, on the one hand, and the positive sciences based on divine law, on the other hand. In fact, the natural sciences were typically held to include metaphysics and theology, which were in a peculiar situation, being as it were free-floating ideas which might or might not have once related to a religious community, such as the followers of Plotinus. But they seemed to play roughly in the same league as the theological parts of Islamic studies as then understood.

But at any rate ibn Khaldūn was quite clear that his new science of culture was a natural science. It dealt with human beings in so far as they gathered by association into more or less stable groups. This was seen by him as a necessary attribute of humanity, which goes beyond questions of individual psychology. Humans recognize their individual weakness in relation to quite a number of other animals. It is association that gives them advantages in self-defense, etc. Ibn Khaldūn considered that the study of human sociability, its rise and corruption, its various basic manifestations, its giving rise to this or that political structure, etc., were all fit subjects of natural inquiry. It was an important science, and it was new, having virtually been invented by ibn Khaldūn. He thus set out some topics for approaching the study, which are of considerable interest.

First, there is the necessity for association. Human beings do not live in societies by accident, but because of the need to band together for defense (as just noted), for the fulfillment of agricultural and other such goals, and the wider life which becomes possible in an organized political community. Second, there is the descriptive question of the distribution of cultures on earth, and here ibn Khaldūn offers an inventory. Third, there are the effects of atmosphere on various cultures. Ibn Khaldūn indicates that even complex elements of a culture such as the importance given to philosophy and the rising in a culture of prophets, etc., depend in part on the temperacy or otherwise of the climate. Fourth there is the influence of climate on character. Fifth, there are the consequences of the abundance or otherwise of food in a particular region. Sixth, there is the issue of the presence of prophecy in a society. Here ibn Khaldūn begins to sketch a social psychology of religion (while by way of contrast, philosophers and theologians tend to treat the question in relation to the intervention or otherwise of God). A crucial factor running through ibn Khaldūn's analysis of the rise and fall of cultures is population density. And underpinning his whole analysis is the appeal to group feeling or 'aṣabīyah as being constitutive of human nature.

He was correct in supposing that he had created a new science. His naturalistic approach is the forerunner of so much in modern social science, history and religious studies as understood in the last twenty or thirty years.

REFLECTIONS ON ISLAMIC PHILOSOPHY BEFORE THE MODERN PERIOD

I have in this chapter sampled many of the great figures of Muslim philosophy, theology and mystical speculation. Certain obvious problems existed in the way intellectual life developed, despite the extraordinary richness and vigor of Islamic societies up to the time of Western colonial dominance, from about the sixteenth century onwards. One problem was the ambiguous position of philosophy itself. Since initially it was a foreign import, out of Hellenistic culture, into a largely Arabic-speaking world, it came as a kind of package, as we have more than once noted. That package was irrationally put together, in that philosophy was tradition-bound and constituted an amalgam of Aristotelian, Neoplatonist and other ingredients. In fact to a great extent it was the expression of a religious worldview, itself an alternative to both Christianity and Islam. In the case of Christianity we can say that a new faith emerged in effect, which was an ingenious and potent synthesis between Neoplatonist motifs, suitably transmuted, and Christianity as derived from Jewish sources, modified by cultural values found in the Roman empire of the time of the new faith's spread. In the case of Islam, there was at least a three-way tug of war – between orthodox, and mostly Ash'ari, Islam, philosophy and Sufism. The tension between theology and philosophy was heightened and distorted by the character of philosophy.

There was an extra problem. Philosophy as applied to the analysis of the nature of the Divine Being had much to offer – for instance a restraint upon anthropomorphism. But it was also linked on the other side of metaphysics, so to speak, with the natural sciences – physics, mathematics, astronomy, medicine, and so on. The separation of the scientific study of cultures (history, politics, and so on) from value-prone and revealed subjects like religious law was a remarkable one. It was also to the credit of the Persian thinker Mullā Ṣadrā (c.1571–1641) that he separated the natural sciences, with the exception of psychology, from metaphysics. This was later to be of some importance when Islam had to adjust to the new worldview presented by the sciences as they had been developed in the West. But through much of Islamic history the sciences were at least theoretically connected up with philosophy, and this might make anyone who rejected philosophy seem unnecessarily obscurantist, even if philosophy as expressing a religion divergent from classical Islam might quite reasonably be repudiated by those who wished to remain orthodox. On the other hand, the question of Sufism looked different. Since Neoplatonism itself had a strong mystical bent (the 'flight of the alone to the Alone'), a synthesis between Sufism and philosophy was always natural enough.

In fact, the *ishraqi* or illuminationist school of philosopher that was developed especially enthusiastically by Persian thinkers became one of the three main types of philosophical thought in Islam along with Peripatetic thought and Sufism. One of the major principles of *ishraqi* or illuminationist thought is that there is a type of knowledge which is so self-evident that it cannot be doubted. Of course, many philosophers have used the idea of such knowledge to serve as a foundation for other ideas. Descartes tries to start his system by pointing to a proposition which cannot be doubted, and the search for an incorrigible or perfect level of knowledge is a traditional philosophical concept. Self-evident knowledge for the *ishraqi* thinkers is that level of knowledge which is so much part of our idea of ourselves that in doubting it we would doubt ourselves, which is to imply doubting that which makes the activity of doubting possible in the first place. The conclusion is taken to be that such doubt is impossible. The truth which is presupposed by any perception is that the subject of perception exists, since otherwise it would have nothing to be about. Suhrawardī develops this notion of immediate knowledge in some detail, and he argues that it is so immediate and incontrovertible that it is known in more than an intellectual sense. They go beyond rational truths. There are propositions which we know through reason and which we know perfectly, in the sense that we grasp all aspects of them and can hold them in our minds all at once perfectly. We cannot doubt these propositions, but they rest only on reason. The sorts of knowledge which are called *'ilm al-ḥuḍūrī* are not only indubitable, but we can actually experience their indubitability. The light of knowledge which shines on them makes evident to us in more than merely an intellectual sense how true and genuine they are. Apprehension of the self has the advantage over discursive knowledge that the assumption is made that the self is basically a simple thing, so the use of our intelligence implies the activity of a simple self, a self which is characterizable in terms of its pure agency and can be experienced as simple also.

This might seem to be just wrong, since we often think of ourselves as highly complex. However, the key to the self is merely its capacity to represent our existence, and as such it is simple. Mullā Ṣadrā argues that in knowing anything we know ourselves, and that self-knowledge is basic epistemologically. He goes on to argue that we cannot even express that basic form of knowledge in propositional form, since it is so direct that we cannot construct a proposition around it. We cannot do this because the knowledge is so firmly an aspect of thought itself that expressing it propositionally would be to make complex that which is paradigmatically simple, and introduce issues of truth and falsity, and perhaps even doubt, where they have no place.

This theory fits in nicely with Suhrawardī's suspicion concerning propositions which are complex, the basis of his critique of the notion of definition and the basis of what is very distinctive about the illuminationist school, their opposition to Peripatetic Greek philosophy and its followers in the Islamic world. Aristotelian techniques of basing the syllogism on a definition, which is supposed to be a sound basis for such an argument, is misguided, they claim, since the aspects of the definition which are supposed to make up the logical properties which characterize the notion themselves require a proof before they are accepted as parts of the meaning, and so on ad infinitum. How can one be sure that in one grasp of apprehension, as it were, all the characteristics of a thing have been identified and properly described? It is worth pointing out here that the notion of the definition as lying at the basis of logical thought is fundamental to the Peripatetic tradition of philosophy At this point we need to distinguish between two kinds of knowledge in Mullā Ṣadrā, knowledge which is *ḥuḍūrī* and directly present to us, and knowledge which is *ḥuṣūlī* and which is acquired from without. There is nothing wrong with the latter kind of knowledge; on the contrary, it represents our role in the world of constant movement in which we seek to perfect our understanding by aligning our consciousness so that it represents better the plurality of ever-changing existence which both describes and constitutes reality.

What is perception for Mullā Ṣadrā? We have to recall here his antipathy to essences, as evidenced by his adherence to an ontology in which existence is more basic than essence. We also need to acknowledge the significance of change in his view of reality, so that we should not regard the perceiver as someone who seeks to come into contact with stable and pre-existing essences, which themselves in some way reflect divine reality. It is certainly true that when we know we come into contact with the divine creation, and we do this by moving from being able to know to knowing in actuality. Mullā Ṣadrā is suspicious of the traditional *mashshāʾī* understanding of knowledge as grasping the abstract forms which lie within things, since this is to reify essences in objectionable ways. He does adhere to the traditional idea of there being a variety of realms of understanding, ranging from the ordinary perceptual level to the higher intelligible, separated by the *barzakh* of the imaginative realm, but we certainly should not see this as a progress towards ever-increasing levels of abstraction. On the contrary, as we perfect ourselves we come closer to ever more basic forms of existence, and in this way come closer to the deity, as the supreme representative and cause of what really exists.

Light becomes significant in the illuminationist system in characterizing our knowledge, because it reveals that which exists, much of which remains hidden until it is affected by light. And light itself, of course, is also invisible, so that which is itself invisible brings to our attention what would otherwise be invisible. Light plays a large part in a large number of philosophies from different cultural traditions, and is certainly not limited to Islamic philosophy. For example, within Buddhism there is a traditional way of conceptualizing the mind as like a mirror reflecting the light of (potential) enlightenment which is ever-present in the universe. All we need to do is to blow the dust off the mirror, and then the pure light will be accessible to us.

Some Buddhists like Huineng go ever further and claim that the light is always present within us, and the idea that anything could really impede it is mistaken. It is this idea that when something is illuminated then one cannot be mistaken about it, which is such a crucial aspect of Mullā Ṣadrā's notion of perception. For at the root of our perception of everything outside us is our perception of what is within us, and the nature of the subject which is doing the perceiving must be known to us if anything is, since it is ever-present in the action of perceiving. There are many things which we can doubt, but as Descartes argued, the fact that we can doubt itself relies on certain facts which we cannot doubt, and those facts present themselves to us (they are *ḥuḍūrī*) in ways in which more dubious forms of experience do not.

Many objections have been made to the attempt at identifying such incorrigible experiences, and these objections are soundly based. They basically suggest that even if there are such incorrigible experiences, they do not actually provide us with anything which is really information. For example, the knowledge that my experiences are the experiences of a subject does not reveal anything about the nature of that subject, apart from the fact that it is a subject. So the idea, which is quite evidently there in Suhrawardī, of a series of fixed and final objects of knowledge, facts which we cannot doubt and which ground further claims to knowledge, are far from philosophically safe from doubt themselves.

Mullā Ṣadrā constructs an unusual ontology, based around the notion of the ambiguity of existence or *tashkīk al-wujūd*. Although there is no doubt that Mullā Ṣadrā also adheres to a doctrine of *waḥdāt al-wujūd*, of the unity of existence, it is what he does with this idea of unity which is so original. The concept of light, which brings everything together by lighting it up also serves as its grounds for differentiation, since it is the degree of light which determines the level of reality of each individual thing in existence, its level of radiance. As we increase our knowledge, we reach ever higher levels of perfection, we come into contact with more abstract and significant existences which are brighter and closer to the source of being itself, ultimately the deity itself.

Is this knowledge part and parcel of mysticism? It is difficult to know what to say about such a claim. Much of the technical language which Mullā Ṣadrā uses comes from ibn al-'Arabī and we know that he was interested in exploring a range of mystical approaches to knowledge. There is certainly a good deal in Mullā Ṣadrā which acknowledges the significance of *ḥikmah*, by contrast with other forms of rational thought, and which prioritizes the sorts of understanding of reality which come about through the personal contact between the individual and the creator. Mullā Ṣadrā's notion of the priority of existence over essence does not import any particular notion of mysticism, and that is true also of his use of the idea of the imaginal realm (*al-'alam al-khayālī*). All these concepts have profound mystical implications, yet there is no need to draw these implications in order to understand them. This is hardly surprising, since most ideas in Islamic philosophy have two sides, the *ẓāhir* (open) and the *bāṭin* (hidden), and we can understand them on each level without necessarily having to explore both levels. It is very much in the spirit of the School of Isfahan that we should accept that the mystical and the rational levels of discourse are capable of operating independently of each other, and it is within that spirit that the concept of knowledge was developed to operate both rationally and also as a gateway to deeper levels of understanding.

One of the most interesting analyses of the notion of *'ilm al-ḥuḍūrī* in modern times is that provided by Mehdi Ha'iri Yazdi, and he concentrates on the description of this kind of knowledge as specified by al-Suhrawardī, but it is essentially the same as that used by Mullā Ṣadrā. The basic argument is that at some level knowledge of ourselves is not to be classified as propositional knowledge, consisting of statements which could be true or false. If this knowledge was capable of being true or false then it would have to be assessable, yet any such assessment already presupposes the self which is doing the assessing. To take an example, there is much about which I could be mistaken, but I could not be mistaken that there is a self writing these pages. I could even get the name of the self wrong, but that there is a self acting here is incontrovertible. There are a variety of ways of expressing this idea. One is to say, as Wittgenstein does, that nothing could be evidence for the absence of such a self, since nothing could give us more grounds for disbelieving in such a self than in believing in it. That is, a world which turned out to justify the denial of such a self would be such a different world from that with which we are familiar that we would not know how to go on. In that case there is no more reason to deny the self than to assert it.

Another way of expressing this supposedly incontrovertible truth is to say that experience of the self is so perfect that it is undeniable. This is to take up a Cartesian strategy of taking some beliefs to be so clear and distinct that we can see everything that there is to see about them all at once, and are unable to deny them. The metaphor of light here is useful, since once something is lit up, it is there in front of us and we are immediately aware of it. But could we not be mistaken about its nature? We could be, we might for example imagine that we see something, that something is lit up, but really do not. We may be dreaming or merely having a powerful image before us to which nothing objective corresponds. Actually, this sort of objection will not work when brought up against *ishraqi* thought, since imagination and dreaming are within that tradition regarded as just as capable of yielding objective and significant experience as our everyday experience. In fact one might go further and suggest that dreaming and imagination is more capable of expressing reality than our ordinary experience, since it is while we are using our imagination that we are better able to represent to ourselves what is really important, as compared with what seems to be important as parts of our everyday existence.

The main problem with describing a particular type of experience which cannot be challenged is that to be persuasive the example has to yield very little detail. For example, it may be that as I am writing this I am having an experience of an 'I' doing the writing which I cannot challenge. I then say that this is an example of *'ilm al-ḥuḍūrī* because the experience of the self is so direct that it cannot be separated from the experience itself except as yet another example of the same experience. That is, if I consider the status of my experience of the self, then I am doing it through yet another experience of the self. But what does this actually show? It shows very little if anything about the nature of the self in question, merely that someone is having experience. It does not even show that it is the same subject which is having the experience of writing this paragraph that wrote the earlier paragraph, or is going to write the next one. Perhaps we need the mysticism after all to establish this sort of knowledge, and through such knowledge we can establish links between the different manifestations of the 'I'. If that is the case then it would be disappointing, since it is very much the direction of the argument that it will lead us to incorrigible propositions through the use of reason alone, and without making any specific religious commitments. After all, if to paper over the gaps in the argument we can use principles from mysticism then there seems little point to trying to establish the argument in the first place. For the School of Isfahan the level of *'irfan* is the most superior form of knowledge, but it does not follow that there are no other concepts of knowledge.

The influence of such philosophers as ibn Sīnā and ibn Rushd, known as Avicenna and Averroes, was of course great upon medieval Western thought. The interplay of ideas, Christian, Islamic and Jewish, in Spain was a notable episode in human history. But it could be argued that the less influential parts of Islamic philosophy (that is, less influential on the outside) were the most exciting and original – the occasionalism of Ashʿarism is attractive and intrinsically interesting; the monism of ibn ʿArabi is visionary and religiously engaging; al-Ghazālī's critique of the Aristotelian theory of causation is incisive and Humean before its time; and ibn Khaldūn's contribution to the human sciences was like fresh air (and only discovered rather late in the West).

Although some might think that the conjunction of terms 'Islamic philosophy' is a bit strange, it is quite obviously well justified. Here was a whole civilization which was built on firm and revealed principles. Though it had absorbed so much of what it had overrun, in the way of Greek philosophy, Persian art and so on, nevertheless it is quite clear that the religious question is always to the forefront. The main issues revolve round the nature of God, predestination, the theory of prophecy, the last things. Tensions tended to surround these topics, and institutionally there were struggles between universities and religious training schools, and between jurists and philosophers, not to mention Sufis. And so philosophy was conducted largely within the ambience, not of an Academy or a Stoa, but of a mosque: just as in medieval Christianity philosophy too was much the handmaid of theology. And so more or less throughout Islamic civilization, philosophy and speculation about the right worldview were indeed Islamic.

Within that constraint, Islamic civilization was indeed a glittering one – in many ways much more brilliant than the contemporary cultures of Latin Christendom and Byzantine Orthodoxy. It was thus a shock to Islam that it should have entered upon such a dead period from the seventeenth to nineteenth centuries. This was followed by something of a revival, but by no means a complete one. In a later chapter I shall revert to this sort of renaissance, when philosophers and others sought to adjust Islamic worldviews to the new realities uncovered by modern science and changes in political and social forces.

8

JEWISH PHILOSOPHIES

JEWISH PHILOSOPHY: WHY TREAT IT SEPARATELY?

In this chapter we shall discuss Jewish philosophy within the milieus of the prevailing Islamic and Christian civilizations up to about the eighteenth century. The reason is primarily that practicing Jews during these times found themselves partly or wholly segregated, and classified as belonging to their religious tradition. It is true that they were often able to play a leading role in the professional and mercantile life of these wider civilizations (a fact which gave them the wealth to patronize such activities as philosophy). Nevertheless, there was a sufficient degree of segregation and separate interest for it to make sense to treat Jewish philosophy separately. In the modern period, after the re-entry of Jews into the main stream of Western life it makes much less sense to talk of Jewish philosophy, though I shall be noting ways in which a specifically Jewish worldview is defended and articulated in modern circumstances (for instance, through work of Moses Mendelssohn and Franz Rosenzweig).

It may be as well here to recapitulate some salient and elementary facts about the Jewish tradition after the first century CE. The destruction of the Temple in Jerusalem in 70 CE and the crushing of the Jewish rebellion effectively meant that Judaism as a religion then developing was faced with a severe crisis. No longer could it focus on the great cult center in Jerusalem. Nor could it so effectively claim to represent a territorial nation. Instead, its chief thrust went into creating a religion that could well exist in dispersion. On the one hand, the synagogue provided a meeting point for Jews. On the other hand, the tradition of the oral Torah alongside of the written Torah encouraged the institution of rabbis or religious teachers, learned in the oral Law. Moreover, that Torah could be (paradoxically) written down, and so we have the formation of the Palestinian and

223

Babylonian Talmuds. This emphasis on the Torah meant that behaviorally Jews became well defined. It was two or three centuries after the thorough formation of Judaism that Islam swept through many lands with important Jewish populations. Meanwhile, from the fourth century Christianity became the official religion of the Roman empire. So it was that Judaism became constricted between two official religions. It was not until the ninth century that serious Jewish philosophy emerged, in the context of current Islamic philosophy (Jewish thinkers tended to write in Arabic, since it was the *lingua franca* of that civilization). In the eleventh and twelfth centuries in Spain, particularly, Jewish philosophy flourished. It culminated in the work, both philosophical and theological, of Moses Maimonides (1138–1204). To complicate matters, the mystical movement known as Kabbalah demanded attention from Jewish thinkers – some of the same tensions which had existed between the orthodox and Sufis became apparent. The story of Jewish thought continues through medieval Europe, and the Renaissance into modern times. As we noted above, we shall from the late eighteenth century onwards treat Jewish philosophy as woven into the fabric of Western philosophy in general.

The above-mentioned behavioral self-definition of Judaism, through the rules laid down in the Torah, means that Judaism is much less wedded to a doctrinal scheme than either Christianity or Islam. On the other hand, Judaism was almost inevitably drawn into the prevalent forms of the civilizations with which it found itself. Moreover, though it may be that Judaism is characterized more by orthopraxy than by orthodoxy, there are doctrinal questions to be faced, about the nature of God and creation, for instance. In what may be broadly called the medieval period, from late antiquity through to the Renaissance, Judaism came to have a similar question of interface between traditional faith and the rationalism of philosophy, and between traditional faith and the alternative tradition of Neoplatonist and Aristotelian philosophy, as faced both Islam and Christianity.

SA'ADYAH BEN YOSEF AND JEWISH *KALĀM*

Baghdad was a vital center of Jewish thought in the ninth and tenth centuries, where it was influenced heavily by the methods of Muslim theological reasoning or *kalām*. The Mu'tazilite movement in particular could have a universal appeal, since it claimed to be based on reason. Sa'adyah, originally from Egypt, became head of the rabbinic academy in Baghdad, and in his *Kitab al-Amānāt wa' l I' Tiqādāt* or *Book of Beliefs and Opinions* gave a wide-ranging defense and elucidation of the Jewish position.

He begins with an account of the sources of knowledge (we are reminded in this of Indian philosophical ways), which he identifies as the senses, the intellect, inference and testimony, that is, of reliable people. Generally speaking, skeptics exaggerated the fallibility of the senses which on the whole, he argued, are fairly reliable. The intellect has intuitive knowledge of ethical and mathematical truths. The inclusion by Sa'adyah of testimony suggests direct Indian influence, and the function of this source is the same as it is in the Indian tradition; that is, to verify transcendental truths and give a place for revelation. In attempting to defend revelatory tradition, Sa'adyah in effect wishes to show the compatibility between the fourth source and the preceding three.

Sa'adyah was hostile to the Aristotelian view that the cosmos is eternal, and he begins his general argument with an attempted refutation of that view. He avers that Aristotle's cosmology is in conflict with his physics. For if the universe is finite in space, as Aristotle thinks, then it contains only a finite amount of energy, and therefore must in due course run down. But that which is corruptible is generated. So the cosmos must have been generated, and a finite time ago. He also has difficulty with the idea of an infinite sequence of events to be gone through before we reach the present. Surely we would never reach a given moment. Consequently we have to postulate a finite universe in time. As a consequence of these arguments, Sa'adyah tries to show that the cosmos must have been brought into being out of nothing, by a Creator: were there some eternal matter out of which the cosmos was created, such matter would have been coeternal with God and so would be independent of God and thus possibly intractable. Moreover, arguments against an eternal cosmos would apply to matter too.

Sa'adyah holds that God's very nature is to be creative, and the other attributes ascribed to him such as power, wisdom and love, flow from that. He also derives from all this the notion that God is absolutely bodiless, and this leads him to purge interpretations of the Bible of anthropomorphic aspects. Anthropomorphic language has to be understood as pointing to pure and bodiless activities on the part of the Divine Being. It is our obligation to worship such a Maker, as we have an obligation to honor our parents. However, God needs to give us the right means to worship. Now worship should be accompanied, rationally, by good works. So it is that God gives us the Law. Naturally, in the cultural milieu of his time, Sa'adyah was faced with challenges to Mosaic Law. Christians followed Paul in thinking of Jewish Law as a kind of means towards the necessity of sin, and Muslims had their alternative Law or *Sharī'ah*. Sa'adyah was keen to put Mosaic Law on a rational basis, because he considered that God's grace is a reward for virtue; otherwise God would be merely capricious.

Now many of the rules laid down in the Torah are readily accessible to the human intellect which, as we saw, has the capacity among other things to apprehend ethical injunctions. The Torah strengthens these by giving commandments clear and more detailed definition. Some injunctions of the Law, however, are not directly intellectual or rational in this sense, but have an air of the arbitrary. They are revealed rather than rational Law. But they too have an indirectly rational basis. Given that we have a duty to worship God, then it is better that a period is set aside for it. Hence the Sabbath regulations. The period need not be from Friday to Saturday evening, but some decision is needed, which God provides.

Sa'adyah also involved himself in an apologetic polemic against Christians and Muslims. If the Law is superseded by a more perfect Law as found in the New Testament, then why did God not reveal the second Law first? He cannot be said to change his mind. Moreover, if Christians really do accept the Old Testament, they should attend to its own claims to its own validity. It would be much more consistent if Christians simply dropped their connection with the Hebrew Bible and claimed to be a thoroughly new religion. Again, even if the New Testament were held to be more perfect than the Hebrew Bible, what about the Qur'an, which is claimed to be superior to, and to supersede, the New Testament? If we carry on thinking in this direction there is no reason why there should not be some later revelation which supersedes the Qur'an. There would be no end to such a series. Since to stop at any one point is arbitrary we might as well stop at the first putative revelation, which is the Hebrew Bible.

Sa'adyah's view of the importance of good works, as an adjunct to the call to worship, introduces the topic of human free will. Here he does not follow what became the dominant trend in Islam, towards predestination and divine occasionalism. He held that human beings must be perfectly free, and should take responsibility for their action in the face of God's omnipotence.

There were ample precedents for this view in Judaism. But in Islam the doctrine of free will was viewed with some suspicion. The Mu'tazilite position proved to be too rationalist to remain the dominant one. On the other hand, Sa'adyah could be without strain a kind of Jewish Mu'tazilite. He argued that human freedom does not diminish divine omnipotence: it is just that God chooses to create agents, and agents are by definition beings capable of acting, and so possessing free will. It is true that God, being omniscient, will foresee my actions. But that does not mean that he causes them. You can foresee something because you know the patterns of causation involved, but such knowledge is not itself a causal factor in what comes to be.

Sa'adyah, in relying on testimony, that is, revealed texts, did not wish thereby to open up a gap between them and what is reasonable. So even the belief in the resurrection of the body in which new bodies are created to go with human souls (persisting because of their more spiritual substance) must be seen to be in consonance with reason. This is so because the notion of an ultimate judgment at the end of history is one version of the necessary reward and punishment exercised by God, to accompany the responsible free will with which every human being is endowed. A last judgment is not entailed by reason but it is perfectly compatible with it.

In conducting his rational polemic against Muslims and Christians, Sa'adyah was not unmindful of a threat from within Judaism, represented by the Karaites, who combined radical and traditional motifs. They were very old-fashioned in one way in rejecting the whole concept of the oral Torah, which was so central to rabbinical Judaism. On the other hand, they could represent themselves as radical in so far as they accepted much more fully the Mu'tazilah position. This involved that instantaneous atomism which we have sketched in the chapter on Islamic philosophy. With this went both occasionalism and the rejection of Aristotelian ideas of causation. Sa'adyah was as keen to combat this Jewish *kalām* as he was to defend Jewish revelation against its great rivals.

JEWISH PHILOSOPHY IN THE WESTERN (SPANISH) CONTEXT

Sa'adyah's contribution to Jewish rationality was impressive; but the next and in many ways the most fruitful area of Jewish philosophy was in the West – in the rich interplay of ideas in Muslim and Christian Spain, especially in the eleventh and twelfth centuries CE. Here the influences were generally Neoplatonic, through the work of al-Fārābī and ibn Sīnā. It was a civilization in which Jews were given the opportunity to play important professional roles. Arabic provided a common language.

The first major figure in the sequence of Jewish thinkers in the West was Solomon ibn Gabirol (*c.*1021–58), who composed liturgical and ethical works, as well as a more famous treatise, called *The Fountain of Life*. This was severely criticized by the contemporary writer Avraham ibn Daud (1110–80), and so came to have little influence upon subsequent Jewish thinking. But a Latin translation had some impact in medieval Christendom, since it made no use of proof texts or appeal to rabbinical authority. It was therefore taken as possibly a Christian document. It argued for the presence of matter as well as form throughout the hierarchy of the cosmos. But conversely the essence of the soul is intellectual, and it is by the practice of philosophy that the soul will ascend to its divine Source and gain immortality.

If ibn Gabirol was partial to philosophy, this cannot be said about Judaism's greatest medieval poet, Yehudah ha-Levi (1085–1141). He studied philosophy when a young man, and was entranced by it, but later turned against it. His only discursive book in which such matters are discussed is his famous dialogue, *Kuzari* or *Book of the Khazars*. The Khazars (a people of Southern Russia) did in fact convert, through their king, to Judaism, and the book is based upon this incident. The king has been visited by an angel, who tells him that though his conduct is good, his mode of worship is not. But what is the true religion? Ultimately in the dialogue four are on display, through their representatives – Christianity, Islam and Judaism, together with a philosopher. Halevi then presents the philosopher's case, based chiefly on the thought of ibn Bājjah and ibn Sīnā. He describes the nature of God as perfect and changeless, and tells how one can ascend to union with the active intellect, through self-purification (one may use the methods of the religions here, but it does not matter which). When the king hears from the Christian and the Muslim that both recognize the revelation of God to Israel, the king turns to a rabbi. He is somewhat dissatisfied with the philosopher, though finding him persuasive, because of the lack of importance in philosophy of the prophetic mode. The rabbi holds that there are many prophets in Israel because of the excellence of the spiritual soil through which it is cultivated. Prophets can communicate divine truths to all and sundry: philosophers can only speak and that too rather tentatively, to an elite. Besides, the faith of Israel embraces what the philosopher offers and much more. The First Cause, impersonal and indeed indifferent to the lives of human beings, is represented in the Bible as Elohim. But there is the personal Adonai, who intervenes in the world, and is revealed through the prophets. It is by being united to him that human beings can experience their greatest bliss. Being cut off from him is the greatest unhappiness.

The rabbi does not stop there. He delivers a sharp critique of philosophy. He admits that there are demonstrations in logic and mathematics, but much else is either contradictory or speculative. The physics of the philosophers, based upon the four elements, has scarcely been proved empirically. Their psychology contains the whole doctrine of the active intellect, which is riddled with absurdities. It may be that in this critique Halevi draws on al-Ghazālī's *The Incoherence of the Philosophers*. The rabbi in the dialogue recommends drawing upon the great ancestral tradition of the Jews. He sets forth for the Holy Land, as did Halevi, who died on the way there, probably in Egypt.

One element in all this dialogue seems highly uncritical from a modern standpoint. The rabbi persuades the king of the revelation at Mount Sinai on the ground that this was a public event, attested to by over six hundred thousand Israelites, which was clearly handed down. There is no proper discussion of the role of testimony and the canons of historiography.

Still, this was an interesting venture into dialogue. It showed how the multi-religious milieu of Spain could stimulate inter-religious debate. We may note here once again a motif which is found also in Islamic writings: that in effect philosophy comes to stand for a separate religion. It may also be noted that Halevi anticipates the later contrast between the God of the philosophers and the God of religion. Also, in setting so much store by the prophetic tradition, he in effect stresses the appeal to experience in the philosophy of religion, an important twentieth-century motif. But Halevi is also narrow. He confines prophets to Israel and so does not draw a vital conclusion from the appeal to religious experience, namely the thought that since religious experience of one sort or another is to be found in all major religions, they ought all to contain at least a modicum of truth.

IBN DAUD AND THE JEWISH USE OF ARISTOTELIANISM: MAIMONIDES

Avraham ibn Daud wrote both a highly influential history, *The Book of Tradition,* which takes the story of rabbinic Judaism from Sinai to his own times, with a valuable treatment of Judaism in Andalusia; and a noted work on philosophy, *al-'aqadiya al-rafiyah* or *The*

Exalted Faith. This was a notable attempt to synthesize Aristotelian theory with Jewish orthodoxy, and depended a lot on ibn Sīnā, with the procession of ten bodiless intellects down from God. He was critical of ibn Gabirol's idea of the material component being present at all levels of being in part because he wished to argue that the human soul is immaterial, as was witnessed by its pure or immediate self-awareness. His work, however, was primarily devoted to trying to reconcile God's foreknowledge and human free will. He thought that we could make a vital distinction between necessary events, which are events in this world determined by God and known by him as necessary because of his creative activity, and contingent ones which are the result of human decisions. Since they are so brought about, God does not know what will happen in advance. So in the woven fabric of God's knowledge of the necessary there are innumerable holes of human freedom.

But the fusion of Aristotle and the Torah had its apogee in the work of the greatest and most influential of Jewish philosophers, Moshe ben Maimon or Maimonides (1138–1204). He was born in Cordoba in Spain, but he and his family fled when it was taken over by the repressive Almohads in 1148. After a few years he settled in Fez, and thereafter made his way to the Holy Land. It was a hard time, for it was in the midst of Crusader warfare. He made his way to Cairo, where he practiced medicine and became leader of the Jewish community. His two most important writings were his *Mishneh Torah,* which was revolutionary in its systematic scope, and his philosophical *Guide of the Perplexed.*

From Maimonides' perspective, Moses was a philosopher as well as a prophet. His aim in the *Guide* is to elucidate the Bible from a philosophical point of view, while supplementing metaphysics from the Bible, since there are necessary limits to metaphysical thinking. In book 1 of the *Guide* he makes use of the *via negativa.* Human language is of necessity inadequate in trying to express the nature of God. Nevertheless, some truths can be established on the basis of reasoning – that God exists, is bodiless, is one and is simple.

On the other hand, Maimonides wished to resist the Aristotelian claim that the cosmos is eternal. There are good arguments either way. Nevertheless, in so far as the position of Aristotle rested on the assumption that the laws of physics apply without restriction, so that creation a finite time ago becomes an anomaly, the eternity claim is defective. For if indeed the creation did occur a finite time ago, it does not follow that there was some time before this, since time came into existence with the creation. Since both the eternity of the universe and creation can be argued for, ultimately which we believe is a matter of choice. It is not unreasonable, then, to believe in the biblical doctrine.

Maimonides was faced with defending the priority of Moses over Muhammad in the matter of prophecy. Accepting the rough framework of theory sketched by Islamic philosophers, namely that a suitably perfected individual is acted on by the active intellect, Maimonides argued that God could still withhold the unfolding of revealed messages to the suitably qualified. So ultimately it is a question of whether God actually intervenes or not. Then again, in the case of Moses, he had spoken to God face to face, as the Bible states. This could be interpreted to mean that God emanated his message to Moses directly without the mediation of the active intellect.

Since we cannot know the inner nature of God we do not need to follow those philosophers, unduly worried about the changeability of God, who deny that he can know particular events and people. In order to do this, would he not somehow have to enter into time? But we can accept that God is different and cannot just know the particular but protect the particular human being providentially. Moreover, God can know what a person will in fact do without himself thereby necessitating the action, so freedom of the individual can still be maintained.

The last section of his work deals with the rationality of the Torah. Naturally Maimonides wished to establish this. He goes through the legal system in some detail, trying to show in each case the rational basis of the law. He held that in promulgating the Torah Moses had to take account of existing traditions. The Law was meant in part to separate the people of Israel from their pagan neighbors among whom they lived. So legislation about sacrifice could not have represented too sharp a break with what had gone before. So in a sense Moses had to be a 'realist'.

It may be noted in this medieval period that differing exponents of the rival religions argued for the superiority of their own revelations and prophets, but did not express skepticism about the historical records. And so they did not conclude that arguments in favor of one tradition rather than another were necessarily soft.

While Maimonides' book *Mishneh Torah* is primarily concerned with a systematic ordering and interpretation of the Torah, and is very fresh and articulate as an expression of Jewish traditional practice, it has too its philosophical side, not just because Maimonides has to systematize ethical questions, but also because he regarded the study of philosophy as part of one's general obligation towards God. Philosophy was part of the Jewish heritage as well as belonging to Islamic and Christian civilizations. One reason for this view was his perception that in integrating the philosophical tradition into Jewish behavior and life he gave Judaism a proper universality, which might otherwise be missed among its critics. This is one reason for the continued influence of Maimonides over the following centuries.

Moreover, as the Islamic culture of Spain crumbled, under the remorseless impact of the Reconquista, culminating in the final conquest of Granada in 1492 and the expulsion of the Jews from Spain, the emphasis on Arabic writings faded. Jewish thought tended to express itself more in Hebrew than in Latin. This helped to consolidate internal dialogue in European Jewish culture, and helped to give Maimonides' major works a stronger influence during the next few centuries.

JEWISH AVERROISM AND ITS CRITICISM

While Maimonides left Cordoba, his rough contemporary ibn Rushd stayed on there. Had the two philosophers met, it might have made quite a change in Maimonides' expositions, since he did not have access to the more Aristotelian flavor of ibn Rushd's thinking. At any rate ibn Rushd's expositions of Aristotle had a marked effect on Jewish thought, as they did upon Christian natural theology. There were even attempts to read Averroistic interpretations into Maimonides, to the point of trying to reintroduce the notion of the eternal creation of the universe, a point which Maimonides had explicitly set aside. Such thinkers as Yitsḥak Albalag (flourished 1265), Yosef Kaspi (1270–1340) and Mosheh of Narbonne (d. ?1360), all of Southern France, belonged to this tendency. They were attracted too to the idea in ibn Rushd of impersonal immortality – for they share survival as departicularized expressions of the one active intellect.

The chief critic of the Averroistic tendency was Levi ben Gershom, known in Greek form as Gersonides (1288–1344), from Provence. He had a good knowledge of commentaries on Aristotle; but he did not hesitate to criticize aspects of the tradition with which he disagreed. Thus he was not impressed with the above-described theory of impersonal immortality. He considers that each human intellect is separately immortal, and in any case cannot become identified with the active intellect. Each intellect retains after death the intellectual knowledge which it has acquired during life.

This intellectualist strand in Gersonides' thought is attested too in his account of God's knowledge. He considers it useless to appeal to the *via negativa* to explain how God's knowledge differs from ours. Though his knowledge may be greatly superior, there yet must remain a link by analogy. However, what he said about God's knowledge turned out to be highly controversial, since he accepted the argument (rejected by Maimonides, but unclearly, thought Gersonides) that since God does not have sense-organs he cannot have knowledge of particulars. This hole in God's knowledge is useful for Gersonides in helping to explain why God does not have knowledge of future contingencies, thus allowing space for the exercise of human reason. God's omniscience therefore is in one sense restricted. God knows everything that can be known, but not future contingents, since if they were knowable in advance they would not be contingent.

Gersonides has an interesting view of creation. He believes, at least on the surface, in creation out of nothing. Nevertheless, and though this creation did occur a finite time ago, there is a way in which the cosmos is everlasting, since the 'nothing' out of which God created the world is not utterly nothing. It lies between absolute nothingness and the formless matter of Aristotle. It is impossible that there should be a vacuum, so his nothing is a kind of non-vacuum. Gersonides also thinks that the cosmos is infinitely long in a forward direction, since God could have no motive for destroying it. He surely could not think that he had made a mistake in making it, or a mess. So while he considers an infinite amount of time in a past direction to be impossible, he does not think the same about future time. Incidentally, he rejected Aristotle's notion of the present instant – the *now* which marks the boundary between the future and the past. Because it does so, there can be no beginning in time. But Gersonides held that a now may mark the beginning of a sequence (or the end): consequently the beginning of the world a finite time ago is conceivable.

Gersonides was a noted astronomer and retained concerns which nowadays might be called astrological. In his worldview the influence of celestial events on the terrestrial plane could help explain the superior knowledge of the Prophet, whose intellect could have been endowed with special knowledge given to him by one of the angelic intelligences. In general his was a rationalistic position, deviating from classical Aristotelianism. His God is not providential in relation to particular individuals, and even the seeds of the miraculous are planted in the world by the Creator, so that we do not need to appeal to particular interventions by God.

CRESCAS, THE AL-GHAZĀLĪ OF JUDAISM

The Spanish philosopher Ḥasdai Crescas (1340–1410) was much more radical than either Maimonides or Gersonides, since he undertook a sweeping critique of Aristotle, both as regards natural philosophy and in relation to metaphysics. He did not think it appropriate to base Judaism upon a weak foundation. He admitted the possibility, for instance, of two alleged impossibilities – the vacuum and the actual infinite. Both of these denials cut at the basis of Aristotle's arguments for a First Mover. Crescas envisaged the idea that our particular cosmos is surrounded by a vacuum and that there are various other universes. Nor did he rule out the idea that God created a succession of universes. He did not, incidentally, think that the belief in creation in time was necessary for Jewish belief. Even if the Bible had just started with the claim that God and a universe had existed from all eternity, there could still have been the Torah and the rest of the Jewish religion. Belief in a succession of universes and in other worlds in space were what Crescas thought of as optional beliefs, which Jews should be free to believe if they so chose.

For Crescas the physically based 'proofs' of God's existence do not work. But the fact is that the cosmos is composed of a series of contingent events. Whether the cosmos is eternal or not, its contingency demands the existence of a Necessary Being to confer existence upon it. This version of the cosmological argument may be regarded as a metaphysical proof.

He was also highly critical of the intellectualist character of the Aristotelians' view of the highest activity for humans and for God. The most important characteristic of God is his love, and humans should love him as he loves us. The gap between God and humans lies in his infinity, but given that gap there is the possibility of a mutual loving relationship. In a similar vein Crescas is critical of the idea that the human intellect is separable from the soul. The soul is a substance which can exist outside of the body, and continues to exist after death.

Since Crescas is free from the idea that God does not know particulars, for indeed he can know all that he causes, eternally, since he creates just this world and no other (events could take a different course in a different world), human acts are, as it were, fixed in advance by God's foreknowledge. Moreover, it can be observed that there are actual dispositions, influences and so on which account for why a person does this rather than that. However, though some kind of determinism is true, this does not actually restrict human freedom. For a person who is not compelled by an external cause to do something will do it, if he is self-aware, freely. (This view is similar to a modern one which argues that freedom and predictability-in-principle are compatible.) As for praise and blame, reward and punishment, these are natural divinely administered consequences of good and bad deeds.

Crescas' contribution may have been influenced in part by parallel anti-Aristotelian movements in Christian Europe, notably the work of Duns Scotus and of William of Ockham, not to mention the new physics being explored at the University of Paris. But at any rate it was a refreshing and critical look at the major issues exercising Jewish and Islamic philosophy.

THE FINAL CHAPTER BEYOND SPAIN: THE END OF MEDIEVAL JEWISH PHILOSOPHY

Spain and the Western Maghreb had been fruitful areas for the dialogue between philosophies and religions. The final expulsion of the Jews from Spain marked the end of an era. Not only did many Jewish intellectuals have to migrate, but in Italy and elsewhere the effects of the fall of Constantinople were already being felt. A fresher and clearer perception of the classical world was emerging, and a rather different Plato and Aristotle presented themselves to the new wave of scholars and thinkers. A symbol of the new philosophical world was Judah Abravanel (c.1460–1521). He wrote a book with an altogether new flavor to it – the *Dialoghi d'amore* or *Dialogues on Love*. Here he discusses the role of *eros* in the cosmos, inspired by the *Symposium* and the *Phaedrus*. Though Abravanel sees human intellectual love of God and God's reciprocal love of the whole of his creation as central, the spirit of inquiry is far removed from the older ways of commentary and exegesis.

Looking back on the philosophical discussions of medieval Judaism we can see them as bearing very similar marks to much Islamic discussion, and later Christian debate, itself indebted to both Muslim and Jewish sources. It was a creative time, and yet it was also restricted. The pressures of the community and the challenges particularly of Islam led to a certain defensiveness. For all that, certain thinkers, most notably Crescas, were open and free-ranging in their thought. Maimonides was, of course, extraordinarily influential, though his and others' reliance on Aristotle was going to prove, in the long run, a weakness. Anyway, the Renaissance was to herald new opportunities for Jewish thought, both as part of the main stream of Western philosophy and as preoccupied with the question of how to maintain the tradition while opening it up to the new breezes of modern knowledge. To these developments we shall turn later. Meanwhile we need to cast our eyes backwards a few centuries, to contemplate that trend in Jewish mystical thought which is known as the Kabbalah.

THE EMERGENCE OF A KABBALISTIC WORLDVIEW

Various strains of religion and mystical speculation went into the formation of the Kabbalah as it emerged in the thirteenth century. While the doctrines of this tradition (which is what Kabbalah means literally) had some interplay with the philosophical and commentarial literature we have been considering, the Kabbalah does represent a parallel and different development in worldview-construction. For our purposes we can begin with it in its fullness, namely in the expression of this ideology in a book called for short the *Zohar* (*Splendor* or *Glory*, viz. of God), which was mainly composed by Mosheh de Leon (1240–1305), of Castile. However, it was taken for the work of a second-century CE figure, namely Shimon bar Yoḥai. Its supposed antiquity gave it special status, and the respect the book was accorded is reminiscent of the way Christians treated the works of Pseudo-Dionysius. It attracted a considerable commentarial literature, therefore.

As Kabbalistic cosmology came to be worked out, it involved a distinction between the *Ayn Sof* or infinite Absolute, and various qualities or forces which emanate from it. The *Ayn Sof* has strong affinities to the One of Plotinus and other expressions of the indescribable ultimate in various religious traditions. It is a conception (or non-conception) typical of the mystical path, both in the East and West. It indicates, together with other evidence we have of practices such as stillness and breathing techniques, that here we have a genuine Jewish yoga. There are those who think it goes back unbrokenly to forms of mysticism prevalent at the turn of the millennium – the first centuries BCE and CE. It has affinities perhaps with so-called 'Chariot mysticism' (which I shall return to shortly) and to practices such as those of the Therapeutae in Alexandria, referred to by Philo (who was himself undoubtedly influenced by early mystical tendencies). It is doubtful whether medieval mysticism such as that of the adherents of the *Zohar* have anything like a direct connection. But generally speaking Judaism was not a religion much given to the practice of the mystical life. It was much more oriented towards the meticulous observance of the life of worship, and so more inclined to emphasize the Otherness of the Divine Being, but it was even more bound to the practice of the

Law, with its strongly ethical flavor, and its emphasis upon holiness of ritual and daily behavior. There were therefore tensions, as there also were in Islam, between official theology and interpretation of the Law, on the one hand, and those elements in Greek philosophy derived from Neoplatonism which emphasized oneness with God. Yet Maimonides among others had made use of the *via negativa*. However, most religions see the rise of mystical, interiorly contemplative religion, and Judaism proved to be no exception. What is interesting is that in medieval Kabbalah its speculative doctrines took such a distinctive form.

The usual Kabbalistic picture of the manifestation of the *Ayn Sof* or Infinite is of ten attributes, potencies or degrees, most usually simply called 'numbers'. That name itself goes back to older esoteric methods of interpreting letters in the Hebrew texts as numbers, in order to get at their secret meanings. In certain circles a deep and complex hermeneutics was developed. At any rate the ten *sefirot* or numbers were arranged in diagrammatic form to represent a giant human being or tree, which in turn stands for God as creative. And so at the highest stage of emanation the Infinite condenses itself, so to speak, into a complex set of properties. In arrangement there are four depicted in a central upright disposition, flanked by three on either side in the upper reaches of this pillar. At the top is an aspect known as the 'crown' or 'thought'. This emanates into the first two flanking properties, namely understanding and wisdom. Below understanding lies power or *din*, 'stern judgment'; and below wisdom is greatness or mercy. Incidentally, this pair is drawn from an old Talmudic tradition of mercy and stern judgment as being crucial to the Creator: they are kept in balance in the providential ruling, and before that the creation, of the cosmos. In the middle just below these two powers lies grandeur. Below stern judgment and mercy are splendor and eternity. These emanate downwards to a centrally placed attribute, foundation, and below that again lies kingdom.

In the main stream of Kabbalah these powers were regarded as making up the essence of the Divine Being. There was also the view that they are the vessels which contain the outflowing divine energy, or that they are the instruments through which God creates and governs the cosmos. For Kabbalists, the total universe is a hierarchy. At the uppermost level is the emanated world of the *sefirot*. Below that is the realm of the divine chariot and the higher angels. Then there is the world of angels, and below that again the world of action, both celestial and terrestrial.

We shall later see how this theory of emanations came to be bound up with new interpretations not merely of the significance of mystical ascent but with the keeping of the commandments. But let us first look at some of the techniques in use. Here a highly influential figure was Avraham Abulafia (1240–*c*.91). He was probably somewhat influenced by Sufism, and through him some Kabbalists used formulas reminiscent of al-Ḥallāj and others, such as 'I I', suggesting identification between the mystic's inner self and the Divine Being. He also made use of breathing techniques, and repetition of the divine names. Moreover, in aiming at a union with the active intellect, as seen within the framework of Maimonides' philosophy, Abulafia conceived of himself as aiming at the same state of consciousness as that of the prophets. As a consequence he claimed to be the Messiah, a pretension which caused a backlash among soberer interpreters of the Torah. Still, his technical ideas had wide circulation and proved to be influential. His methods, as we have indicated, look very similar to those in use among a wide spectrum of mystics, including Christian contemplatives, Sufis, Hesychasts and yogis.

If this caused problems about the respectability of Kabbalah, this had been partly offset by the work of Mosheh ben Naḥman (c.1194–1270), commonly known as Nahmanides, who won great prestige as an exegete and apologist. He had acquitted himself well in a public debate with a Christian convert from Judaism before the king in Barcelona. He considered that even beneath the usual layers of rabbinical commentary there lay a realm of meaning in the Hebrew texts which referred to the various secret names of God. Such a theory of interpretation was congenial to Kabbalists. Moreover, Nahmanides himself supported the Kabbalah. If such an orthodox and upright person could adhere to it, there was less to fear in it than might have otherwise been imagined.

It is clear how easy it might be to combine the main motifs of Kabbalistic cosmology and metaphysics with the Neoplatonic and Aristotelian traditions. So there were distinct possibilities here of a creative synthesis between the three elements of rabbinic tradition, philosophical inquiry and Kabbalistic thinking. External events also played a further part in the evolution of Kabbalah. The expulsion of the Jews from Spain in 1492 and other persecutions were especially depressing. The Jews were often pressed back into a private world in which they could only witness to their faith and their loyalty to the community through the meticulous practice of the commandments of the Torah. Later Kabbalah gave all this cosmic meaning.

By far the most important figure in the development of the new understanding of the mystical tradition was Isaac Luria (1534–72). Born in Jerusalem, he studied the Talmud. Thereafter he plunged into the study of the *Zohar*. In due course he settled in Safad in Galilee, where he gained a reputation for extraordinary saintliness, having mystical and other powerful experiences. He imparted to a circle of some thirty-five disciples a theology or theosophy which gained very wide acceptance across the Jewish world. He deepened the Kabbalistic practice of concentrating on the deeper meanings of the texts of prayers. Luria gave his disciples exercises, different for each, in which they concentrated on differing letter-combinations in the divine names.

According to Luria the processes of evolution out of the *Ayn Sof* are much more dramatic than had been portrayed in previous Kabbalah. First of all he explained what perhaps had been something of a puzzlement in the tradition. What room was there for creation when the Infinite, presumably, occupied everywhere? Luria adopted the idea of *tzimtzum* or contraction. The Absolute contracted itself to make room for the creation. This already hinted at problems for that which was to come. But as a doctrine it of course made clear that the system could not be described as pantheistic, a charge sometimes brought against traditional Kabbalah. Anyway, as the divine light emanated to begin the process of filling the space evacuated by the Absolute and to form a created cosmos, some of the channels containing the light fractured. Some of the light, imprisoned in its containers, fell into the void, bringing matter into being. The cosmic catastrophe meant that even the orderly universe has powerful elements of disruption. So the whole universe itself is in need of reparation or restitution, *tikkun*. Though disrupted, however, the universe is organic. What happens in the microcosm can affect the macrocosm. What happens on earth can help to restore heaven (this interconnectedness of things is in a way reminiscent of Chinese Huayan). So the Jew, by his attention to the pursuit of mysticism and adherence to the Torah, can help in this restoration of the cosmos. In other words, the people of Israel have a central place in the salvation of the whole cosmos and even the ruptured state of God himself. For the vessels' break-up also meant a division within the configuration of the *sefirot*. And so it turns out that God needs human beings for his salvation as they need him. The whole schema is interesting for various reasons. The fall of the sparks of light is reminiscent of the Gnostic and Manichaean heritages. But instead of this catastrophe being viewed in a pessimistic light, Lurianic Kabbalism is much more optimistic. Second, the idea that you can restore God gives the system a theurgic flavor. Yet instead of some sacramental magic, typical of theurgy, here we see that the following of the commandments with pure (though mystically suffused) intentions is the essential means of divine and cosmic restoration. It was also, obviously, a schema which, as I have noted, could give central meaning to the faithful continuance of the faith in dark times. This helps to explain why over three centuries or so Lurianic Kabbalah attracted such a wide following in post-medieval Judaism.

The emergence of European Jewry from the ghettoes, chiefly in the first part of the nineteenth century, and the surge of emigration to the United States, diminished the impact of the Kabbalah because other concerns came to the forefront, notably how Judaism was to cope with the values of the Enlightenment, the upsurge of nationalism and integration into American life.

SOME CONCLUSIONS ABOUT JEWISH PHILOSOPHY AND MYSTICISM

We can observe a general pattern which dominated the civilizations both of the Islamic world and of Christendom, in which Judaism was embedded. Both of the big religions came to identify, though in differing ways, the interests of religion and the State. Both were heirs, to some extent, of the Hellenistic and classical past. That heritage, however, was imperfectly understood. Both saw philosophy largely in the context of theology. But on the whole philosophy was understood as a tradition rather than a method, and that tradition was a kind of merger between Neoplatonic and Aristotelian motifs, in which scientific inquiry was appended as a large adjunct. We shall be noting how the relation between the traditions was worked out in the medieval Christian context, and how it was in Europe that the theological–philosophical synthesis there came to break down. But in its heyday the synthesis had a strong grip on the imagination of many thinkers, and so Judaism itself, existing within the broader fabric of the two civilizations, was in effect compelled into following the same pattern. So it was that Jewish philosophers could take up Islamic theories of prophecy and apply them to the Jewish tradition. But the net effect was to make all three attempts at synthesis between a required religion and a certain philosophical tradition relatively less challenging than things might have been if the Roman empire had lasted, say, another few hundred years, without being subjected either to Christian dominance in the North or Islamic conquest in the South and South-east. But these are speculations. Given the relative restrictions of intellectual life, both Jewish philosophy and mysticism flourished. It should also be borne in mind that throughout the long period from the formation of rabbinic Judaism to the coming of the Renaissance much greater energy was spent by Jewish thinkers and commentators on elucidating and understanding the Torah than in philosophical speculations. At the heart of Judaism lay orthopraxy. Part of that orthopraxy was study of the Torah. When eventually Judaism did burst the bounds of the ghetto, this devotion to study, and the Jewish predilection for argumentative debate, made a quantum leap into the brilliant contributions of the Jewish people to Western civilizations, including philosophy.

RECENT DEVELOPMENTS IN THE STUDY OF JEWISH PHILOSOPHY

The study of Jewish philosophy, at least in the medieval period, has recently shifted attention away from the great thinkers (e.g. Maimonides, Gersonides) to lesser-known ones in order to understand the various ways in which philosophical ideas were received and disseminated. The emphasis is now on the role that philosophical ideas played in shaping various Jewish cultures (e.g. Islamicate, Provençal, Renaissance). Second, it is important to remember that Jewish philosophy is a modern term, and none of the thinkers discussed in the pre-modern period would have employed it, or considered themselves to have been 'Jewish philosophers', or engaged in an activity we today recognize as 'Jewish philosophy'. Rather, they would have regarded themselves as Jews engaged in a larger project of explicating the thought of Plato and Aristotle. Finally, because philosophy is not autochthonous to Judaism, Jewish philosophy is essentially a response, whether positive or negative, to larger non-Jewish intellectual forces. As such, those engaged in the production of Jewish philosophy over the years and into the present, served and continue to serve as important conduits between Jewish and non-Jewish cultures.

Maimonidean controversies

The center of Jewish philosophical production until the early thirteenth century was located in al-Andalus (Spain and North Africa). It was here, for instance, that the great Jewish Neoplatonists (e.g. Shlomo (Solomon) ibn Gabirol, Abraham ibn Ezra, Abraham bar Ḥiyya) lived and wrote. These individuals, however, were not simply philosophers, but also important rabbinical figures, sacred and secular poets, grammarians, and mystics. Recent studies have begun to examine the role of mysticism and literature in such thinkers' thought and writings, with an eye to understanding topics traditionally ignored, such as aesthetics and poetics.

The zenith of philosophical speculation in al-Andalus is Moses Maimonides (1138–1204), who many consider to be the greatest Jewish philosopher. Although Maimonides represents a shift from Neoplatonism to Aristotelianism, many Neoplatonic ideas nonetheless remain in his writings. His works were to prove very controversial in the Jewish world. The Maimonidean Controversies revolved around the reception, role, and function of Maimonides' writings in a number of Jewish cultures. Although the Maimonidean Controversies reached Jewish communities in many countries, the epicenter was northern Spain and Provence. The initial impetus for the Controversies seems to have been the intersection of two distinct Jewish cultures, the rationalism associated with Judeo-Arabic synthesis and the more conservative Talmudism or rabbinism of Franco-German Jewry.

With the transmission of Judeo-Arabic philosophical terms and categories into regions that had been primarily versed in Talmudic and rabbinic study, we essentially see, depending upon the viewpoint, either the collision of or the synergy between two different worldviews, two different understandings of what Judaism was or should be. Almost immediately after the introduction of philosophy by, *inter alia*, the Ibn Tibbon family, philosophical principles and methods caught on rapidly and became popular. Provence subsequently became the locus of the Hebrew translation movement and thus the new center of Jewish philosophical activity. The Ibn Tibbons played such an important role in this because they translated many of those works of Jewish philosophy written in Arabic into Hebrew (including Maimonides' *Guide of the Perplexed*). It is also worth noting that the primary way that philosophy was disseminated in this period was not through technical treatises of philosophy, but through so-called 'secondary forms' (e.g. encyclopedias, philosophical Bible commentaries, philosophical sermons preached in the synagogue, dialogues).

The Maimonidean Controversies were not simply academic discussions, but vitriolic debates about what constituted Jewish culture. For example, what role if any should philosophical texts play in the Jewish educational curriculum? In 1232, critics of philosophy denounced the writings of Maimonides to the Church, which saw fit to burn parts of his *Mishneh Torah* and *Guide*. And in 1305 Rabbi Solomon Adret banned the study of philosophy for those under the age of twenty-five. Shem Tov ibn Falaquera (c.1225–c.1295), wrote, among other things, a commentary on the *Guide*, entitled *Guide to the Guide*, that was used by virtually all subsequent commentators. Although ibn Falaquera did not claim to be an original thinker, his many translations (from Arabic to Hebrew) and commentaries were responsible for ordering and disseminating philosophical principles to those not trained in the technical study of philosophy. Moreover, despite the conservative nature of the commentary genre, ibn Falaquera did not hesitate to disagree with those whose writings he was commenting upon or to innovate in the names of their authors.

Scholasticism and Kabbalah

The role and influence of Christian Scholasticism on subsequent Jewish philosophers is the matter of some debate. In the fourteenth century, Jewish thinkers such as ibn Kaspi (1279–c.1332) and Nissim of Gerona (1320–80) seem to have engaged certain ideas that were popular among Latin Scholastics (e.g. the problem of God's knowledge of future contingents, logic). It is also a matter of debate whether or not these Jewish thinkers would have obtained these ideas from reading Scholastic texts or from personal conversations with Christian philosophers. It is worth pointing out that no Jewish philosopher in the fourteenth century employed the *quaestio disputata*, the most important Scholastic method of discussion.

One possible exception is Abner of Burgos (c.1270–1344) who converted to Christianity and took the name Alphonso de Valladolid. This thinker was very interested in the metaphysics of action, especially the problems associated with the freedom of will. For Abner, human actions are voluntary in so far as they are the product of will, yet they are strictly determined because the will is part of a causal chain going back to the movement of the celestial spheres. It seems that Abner used this theory not only to protect divine omnipotence and omniscience, but also to justify his conversion to Christianity. Those Jewish philosophers opposed to his determinism, e.g. Isaac Pollegar (d. c.1330) and Moshe Narboni (d. c.1362), however tended to frame the debate with Abner by appealing to astrology: both experience and reason show that choice plays an important role in the production of actions. The debate between the two sides, however, is less one of Jew versus apostate than that between the older Islamic paradigm of Jewish philosophy and the newer Scholastic-influenced one. It also seems likely that the thought of Abner influenced later Jewish critics of Aristotelianism, such as Ḥasdai Crescas. The fifteenth century witnessed an increased presence of Scholasticism in the writings of Jewish philosophers, undoubtedly occasioned by the increased Hebrew translation of Latin texts. The writings of thinkers such as Joseph Albo (d. 1444), Abraham Bibago

(d. c.1489), Abraham Shalom (d. 1492), Isaac Arama (d. 1494), and Isaac Abravanel (d. 1509) all evince the use of Scholastic methods.

There was a trend in the fifteenth and sixteenth centuries that saw Jewish thinkers in Italy attempt to read Kabbalistic texts philosophically. An important figure in this was David ben Judah Messer Leon (c.1470–c.1535). For instance, he interprets the *sefirot* (divine hypostases/emanations) in light of the philosophical discussion of divine attributes. This synthesis was instrumental in the spread of Kabbala in Italy and the Ottoman Empire.

Modern Jewish philosophy

Moses Mendelssohn (1729–86) is generally regarded as the first modern Jewish philosopher. He argued that Judaism is not a revealed legislation that demands that Jews passively accept a set of dogmas, but a 'revealed legislation' requiring the performance of actions. As such, the eternal truths residing at the heart of Judaism are comprehensible to and verified by human reason (something that he argues is lacking in Christianity and its concept of faith). This notion that the Bible was a rational text chock full of intellectual truths would come under severe attack (in both Judaism and Christianity) by Baruch Spinoza.

One of Spinoza's biggest critics was Hermann Cohen (1842–1918), the founder of the Marburg school, which was responsible for reviving Kant's ethical principles. Cohen subsequently applied Kant's understanding of ethics, duty, and autonomy to Judaism. For Cohen, the laws of ancient Israel are not confined to one people, Israel, but are applicable to all of humanity, and it is the duty of all to fulfill its moral laws. It is the ceremonial laws, however, that provide Jews with the necessary prerequisites for obeying God *qua* rational will.

The notion that Judaism was a rational religion, nothing more than a particular manifestation of universal truths, did not go uncontested. One of the greatest and ablest critics of this reading of Judaism was Franz Rosenzweig (1886–1929), a student of Cohen's and perhaps the most profound thinker in modern Judaism. Influenced by the particularism of Judah Halevi, Rosenzweig argued that Judaism was not a historical religion (here it is important to juxtapose his thought with contemporaneous attempts to apply historical methods to Judaism), but a supra-historical one. It is the liturgical and ritual cycles of Judaism, according to Rosenzweig, that permits Jews to live outside of history, to achieve an authentic existence in which God, Jews, and the world exist in a unified and unifying relationship through the concepts of creation, revelation, and redemption.

The Shoah

The majority of Jewish philosophy in the modern period took place in Germany. All of this would of course come to an end with the Shoah, or Holocaust, in the 1930s and 1940s. Before examining some trends in post-Shoah Jewish philosophy, it is worth mentioning some response to this event. The extermination of much of European Jewry led many to question traditional assumptions (e.g. God, chosenness, freedom of will, history). Some (e.g. R. Rubenstein) argue that the Shoah is proof that God cannot exist and that the key to Jewish renewal resides not in history but in nature. Others (e.g. I. Maybaum) contend that all was part of God's plan and that God used Hitler in the modern period in the same way that God used Pharaoh or Nebuchadnezzar in biblical times. Still others (e.g. Y. Leibowitz) contend that the Shoah is neither more nor less unique than other national tragedies (e.g. destruction of the second temple, exile from Spain in 1492).

Contemporary Jewish philosophy

Contemporary Jewish philosophy puts primary focus on ethics. Emmanuel Levinas (1906–95), for example, argues that we become whole only through encounters with others. The 'Other', then, is responsible for putting demands on the self to such an extent that the very being of the 'Self' is called into question. (This differs from Martin Buber's concept of a reciprocal 'I and Thou' encounter.) For it is ultimately through encounters with others that the self encounters and experiences transcendence.

Another trend in contemporary Jewish philosophy is the proper way to understand traditional Jewish law (halakhah). Joseph Soloveitchik (1903–93), for example, argues that this law is not a rigid set of rules that hampers the Jew's ability to function in the modern world, but provides the means to true human perfection on both the physical and spiritual levels. In like manner, Yeshayahu Leibowitz, writing in Israel as opposed to the diaspora, argues that Jewish law is what provides Jews with autonomy and authenticity in this world. Any attempt to reform this law (as certain strands of Judaism do) is tantamount to accommodating Judaism and Jewish life to non-Jewish society.

9

EUROPE

THE EMERGENCE OF PHILOSOPHY IN MEDIEVAL CHRISTENDOM

Probably the single most significant event in the emergence of philosophical debate was the foundation of universities such as those of Paris and Oxford. Of them all, Paris was the most international and vital. The principal centers of learning were founded by papal or imperial charter and date from the thirteenth century CE. Being independent corporations with licenses to grant degrees they could be relatively free arenas for intellectual debate. So the great age of medieval philosophy was from the thirteenth century onwards. It may also be noted that times were propitious for the revival of learning. Intercourse between Muslims, Jews and Christians in Spain helped to promote the translation of works of such notable figures as ibn Rushd and ibn Sīnā (Averroes and Avicenna), and also classical works. This could permit, for instance, the resuscitation of Aristotelian ways of thinking, especially under the stimulus of the new synthesis produced by Thomas Aquinas. Prior to this great period, there was, too, in the twelfth century what might be described as the 'pre-university' of Paris, in that the Parisian schools were already attracting attention and scholars.

In the period before the thirteenth century we can note some important figures and centers – notably John Scotus Erigena or Eriugena (b. c.810), and Irish scholar, Anselm of Canterbury and the School of St Victor. The first of these was testimony to the continued vigor of the Celtic Church, seemingly on the very fringe of the Christian world, yet going on with an important tradition of learning.

The whole atmosphere of philosophy, of course, was suffused with orthodox Christianity as understood in the Latin West (but with some more direct access to Eastern Christian sources, such as the works of Pseudo-Dionysius). Apart from the Jewish tradition, and in Spain also Islam, there were no serious challenges to the Christian worldview, other than the Albigensian heresy in the South of France and Italy, during the second half of the twelfth century and the first half of the thirteenth. These Cathari derived in part from the Bogomil movement in Eastern Europe. Their picture of the universe was dualistic, and their general value-system was Manichaean, but with some Christian attributes. The Albigensian movement involved a division between the small elite or *perfecti,* who lived a life of great simplicity, eschewing sex, meat and the things of this world, and ordinary worshipers. But their worldview was perceived as a grave threat by the Church, which launched first a preaching crusade and then a military one against them. For the rest, though, there was a rough homogeneity of belief throughout Western Christendom which was only finally shattered, of course, at the Reformation, though there were challenges during the Renaissance, itself stimulated by the rediscovery of the wider values of the classical heritage. And so for the most part the atmosphere of medieval philosophy is not at all dissimilar to that of Islamic and Jewish philosophy of the preceding period. In short, a most vital concern was the proper relationship of theology and philosophy.

JOHN SCOTUS ERIUGENA: A CELTIC NEOPLATONIST

One of the features of Celtic monasticism was the continuance of the knowledge of Greek there. By contrast, elsewhere in Britain and on the continent of Europe there was little knowledge of the language and what there was owed itself to the influence of Irish monks. John Scotus Eriugena was commissioned by Charles the Bald and others to translate various works, including Pseudo-Dionysius. But his great achievement was a book composed between 862 and 866, called *De divisione naturae*. In this he produces a highly original synthesis between Neoplatonist and Christian ideas.

For him nature or *natura* means everything – the total universe including God, and not just nature as we might conceive of it. There is a fourfold division of nature into (1) nature which creates and is not created; (2) nature which both creates and is created; (3) nature which does not create but is created; and (4) nature which neither creates nor is created. The first of these, obviously enough, is God. From God emanates the rest of the universe, or the rest of nature, to use Eriugena's terminology. In the end the whole of the created realm returns to God. There is in Eriugena's vision a nice rhythm of symmetry. With regard to God, John Scotus adopts both the negative and the affirmative way. On the one hand, the nature of the Godhead is ineffable, but, on the other hand, we can predicate things of God in so far as we can see them through the effects. The fact that we have to say both that God is wise and not wise does not, however, involve a contradiction. As cause of wisdom in human beings, and in virtue of the applicability of the term to God, we can say that God is wise, but metaphorically

– *metaphorice* or *translative*. God is of course not literally wise the way a human being might be wise. We deny that God is wise in order to deny the literal application of the term to him. So there is no contradiction between the negative and affirmative ways. We should use a term like 'super-wise' to refer to God – here John Scotus echoes Pseudo-Dionysius. But of course we have no clear notion at all of what the prefix 'super' contains. Even to say that God is a substance is not right, so that we must affirm that God transcends our categories. Again, if we have to use the term it must be given the negative prefix of 'super'.

All this helps Scotus to satisfy himself that there is a real division between God and creatures. Nevertheless his account of creation is emanationist. It is as if God creates outside of time. He does not make use of the analogy of God's body, however, to describe that realm of nature which is created but does not create. In other ways his system is remarkably similar to that of Rāmānuja. But in one respect there is a gulf, because Scotus is still under the spell of Plato in postulating his second division of nature, namely that aspect which both is created and creates, which is the realm of ideas or archetypes. Out of the Godhead comes the Word, who somehow contains the archetypal ideas which have the patterns of all created things in them.

Since God is necessary to the existence of creatures, they are nothing apart from him. But though this is an intimate relation, it is the human being that provides an extra-special link between the natural world and the creator, since he is made in God's image. Human beings can attain, through God's grace, deification. Others will be suitably purged before the whole of nature returns to God in the end. John Scotus is then a universalist of a sort, though the elite will have in the end greater glory than the rest.

Altogether John Scotus built a highly integrated intellectual system. It could look, however, as though he were a pantheist and that he does not maintain a wide enough gulf between God and creatures. For such reasons his major work was condemned three and a half centuries after his death, by Pope Honorius III, who ordered the book to be burned. Though it was without a lasting influence in the Christian tradition, it was powerful.

ANSELM OF CANTERBURY AND THE ONTOLOGICAL ARGUMENT

Anselm, who came from Aosta, lived from 1033 to 1109 and at the age of 60 became Archbishop of Canterbury. In theology he was chiefly known for his explication of the doctrine of Christ's atonement for the sin of human beings, in his *Cur Deus Homo*. He also developed two arguments for God's existence which have attracted a lot of attention. One, in his work the *Monologium,* is from degrees of perfection observed in things, and reappears as Aquinas' fourth way (of arguing to God's existence). The other, much more renowned, is the famous ontological argument, in which he affirms that God necessarily exists, given his essence or definition. Thus, he defines God as 'that than which no greater can be thought'. But a God who exists is greater than a God who is merely conceived to exist. An extramental entity will be greater than that same entity (that is as described) which does not exist. For technical and philosophical reasons, due to the trickiness of concepts such as necessity, this argument has attracted an enormous amount of debate in later, and especially fairly recent, Western philosophy. Of course, in proffering the argument Anselm did not mean to imply that you should not have faith until you have gone through some such reasoning. Indeed, the work in which the argument appears was the *Proslogium* or Address (to God). But the argument could reassure faith.

Others who dealt in supposed proofs of God's existence were those attached to the Abbey of St Victor outside of Paris. Hugh of St Victor (1096–1141) devised or adapted proofs from self-consciousness, external change and teleology. In the first he argued that since we have not always been self-conscious, the soul must have a beginning. As a rational entity it must have a rational cause. Such a being must also be necessary, and is God. The other proofs prefigure ways of Thomas Aquinas. One of the proofs of Richard of St Victor (d. 1173) comes from the idea of possibility. None of the entities in the cosmos receives its possibility from itself. Such entities need to get their possibility of existing from another, which will be self-dependent and necessary.

All these arguments are preliminaries in the exercise of constructing a natural theology, which was most successfully accomplished by Thomas Aquinas.

AFTER AUGUSTINE: BONAVENTURE

Bonaventure (c.1217–74) was skeptical of the growing influence of Aristotle in Paris, and took more of a theological than a philosophical stance in expounding his ideas on the emanation of the world from God, Christ as exemplar, and on the consummation of the cosmos through a return to the Divine Being. A great deal of his thinking is in sympathy with Augustine. In affirming a more Platonic than Aristotelian position, Bonaventure also provided some original notions. For instance he had an interesting theory of knowledge, in which he combined the view of Aristotle that the mind is at birth a *tabula rasa,* and needs for knowledge the stimulus of the senses, with a Platonic view that calls on the notion of ideas in the mind of God which help to illuminate the process of acquiring knowledge. So in so far as we appreciate beauty or goodness in natural objects given to us through the senses, we draw upon divine ideas. This theory of the double source of knowledge, from outside through the senses, and from inside through the ideas, foreshadowed more modern theories.

Bonaventure can be considered the major Platonist before the coming of the Aristotelian revolution put in place by Aquinas. The new knowledge of Aristotle, transmitted via

Islamic civilization, and the perceived possibilities of a new structure of Christian ideas, combined to create this synthesis. Moreover, the growth of the universities and the new awareness of philosophical traditions favored the distinction, made by among others Albertus Magnus (1208–80), who was Aquinas' mentor, between philosophy and theology. This gave theologians some leeway in dealing with the Church, and provided an arena, namely philosophy, for some freedom of thought.

THOMAS AQUINAS AND THE NEW SYNTHESIS

Thomas of Aquino was born in 1224 or 1225, and died, by no means old, while on his way from Naples, where he had presided over a Dominican college (or *studium generale*) founded by him, to a Council at Lyons. The very wide range of his writings, from large works such as the *Summa theologica* and the *Summa contra gentiles,* through a large corpus of commentarial works, mainly on Aristotle, to smaller writings such as *De ente et essentia* (On Being and Essence) and *De veritate* (On Truth), testifies to his wide and systematic thought. The power of his argumentation and synthesis is highly impressive, and it is no surprise that his works, even if viewed with early suspicions, would come to enter into mainstream Catholic theology and intellectual life. Though his use of Aristotle was thought of in his day as being both innovative and controversial, it must also be recognized that what he came to create was not a baptized Aristotle, but a new and original crossing between Christian dogma and tradition on the one hand and Greek philosophy, chiefly Aristotelian, though not exclusively so, on the other. Hence Thomism itself came to be the new Christian philosophy.

Thomas' whole scheme is an ingenious interlocking system, and we may begin by considering his view of the material reality. Following Aristotle he analyzes the world as consisting of substances in which forms are embedded in matter. This hylomorphic view is important when taken together with other distinctions which Thomas wields – notably that between act and potentiality and that between essence and existence. These are overlapping polarities. This is because, important though the hylomorphic world is, it is not the only realm of existence. For Aquinas saw the universe as a hierarchy. There are inorganic substances, vegetables, non-rational animals, up to the rational animal, viz. human beings. At the summit of the hierarchy is the Divine Being – which is pure act or activity, is infinite, and whose existence and essence coincide. In this range of kinds of entities there is a place missing, which is one for entities which are finite, yet are without body. Such beings are angels. It was for Thomas logical that there should be such beings, each a separate species, by the way, since normal individuation requires the presence of matter.

Knowledge of all this hierarchy of beings can be derived from reason, from doing philosophy. Obviously on the other hand, there are truths which are relevant to the highest human well-being and which cannot be proved simply on the basis of rational argument, such as the doctrine of the Trinity. Such truths have to be derived from revelation. So there are two kinds of discourse about God. There is that body of knowledge based on natural reasons, which is called 'natural theology'; and there is that body which depends on revelation, and is known as 'revealed theology'. The scheme of natural theology in fact modifies revelation, in the sense that certain highly central ideas, notably the concept of analogy, influence the way in which theology is interpreted; or rather, more particularly, influence the way in which the *texts* are interpreted.

The most obvious thing about our hylomorphic world is the way in which it is subject to change. Explanation of such change forms the chief basis of the ways or arguments to the existence of God. In turn there is the possibility of arguing from what we know of the relation of the Necessary Being to the created order to various conclusions about the nature of the former. Here Aquinas both elaborates and uses his famous theory of analogy and its types. So in all this the supposed proofs of God's existence as used by Thomas are crucial. We have an elaborate edifice. On the basis of the analysis and observation of things in our cosmic environment we argue to the existence of God. From there, using analogy, we develop outwards our knowledge of the nature of God. All this, of course, gives the five proofs or ways which he recognizes and lays out a crucial role in his whole system.

We may note first, before going on to those proofs which Thomas thinks do work, that he is skeptical about our use of the ontological argument propounded by Anselm and others. Because God's essence and existence coincide, the argument should be valid for God, but not for us, since we do not have inner knowledge of his essence. We cannot then get to God from the end of essence, but have to begin from the world of existent things available to our senses.

The first of the ways to the existence of God has to do with motion or change. Change, according to the Aristotelian analysis, involves the reduction of a thing from potency to act. But this requires an agent already in act. Since an infinite series is impossible, it follows that there must be a first unmoved mover, and, as Aquinas says, 'All understand this to be God.' This argument was used for, among others, Maimonides and Albertus.

The second way was used by Avicenna and Albertus, again among others. It begins from the notion of the efficient cause. A thing cannot be the cause of itself, since to be a cause it would have to exist, and so it would have to exist before it did. Again, by excluding the chain of infinite length, we come to a first efficient Cause. Again Aquinas claims that by this all men would understand God.

The third way, which many consider the most essential of all the proofs, begins with the idea of contingency. Some things come into being and perish, and in this way they show that they are contingent – that is, they can either exist or not. But we need to explain why it is that contingent beings do exist. Ultimately they must owe their being to the existence of a Necessary Being – some being which cannot not be.

These three arguments are usually categorized by modern commentators as being three versions of the cosmological argument. The fourth argument is from degrees of perfection and has a Platonic origin. Despite this, it seems to contain the same principle as the foregoing arguments. It begins with the thought that where there are degrees of goodness, beauty or truth there must be a supreme exemplar. But further, contingent beings do not contain their goodness or truth in and from themselves. They must derive their perfections from the supreme example of perfection. And this is taken by all human beings to refer to God.

The fifth way, usually referred to as a version of the teleological argument or argument from design, notes that inorganic objects operate always or very often for an end. But they cannot do so on their own account, for they do not possess knowledge or intentions. There must be an intelligent being by whom all natural things are directed to an end. And this people speak of as God.

These somewhat abstract conclusions are used by Thomas to add to our metaphysical knowledge of God. For instance, God must be bodiless, for every embodied substance is in potentiality. But God as necessary being is pure act. God must be simple, for which reason his essence and existence are identical. For if you could separate out his existence then he would owe his existence to another. But this is impossible, because he is First Cause. Likewise he can be shown to be infinite, immutable, eternal, and so on.

All this generates a problem about language. It can be easily shown that when we ascribe attributes to God they are not used univocally. That is, we do not ascribe wisdom to God in the same sense as we ascribe this to human beings. On the other hand, we cannot be using the terms completely equivocally. If that were so it would be impossible to say or know anything about God. There must be some sort of middle path. This Aquinas found in his doctrine of analogy. And analogy can be of two kinds, originally called the analogy of proportion and the analogy of proportionality. By an unfortunate sequence of developments, these names have changed in more recent times, so that the analogy of proportion is now more usually called the analogy of attribution and the analogy of proportionality is called the analogy of proportion. All this is unnecessarily confusing, and I shall stick to the original usage of Thomas.

According to the analogy of proportion, being may be predicated both of God and creatures, in a way similar to, but also different from, the way in which being can be predicated both of a substance and an accident (that is, a property belonging to the substance but not essentially or by its very definition). A substance is defined as something which can bear different accidents, while an accident is defined in terms of substance. Now regarding God and creatures, the relations differ. Creatures have a real relation to God. They would not have being without God. But on the other hand, God does not have a real relation to creatures, for he would exist even if creatures did not. But because of God's real relation to creatures we can hold that there are some actual likenesses of creatures to God. These likenesses are controlled by the nature of God and of creatures. Because God brings all trees into being it does not at all follow that he is wooden or leafy. Woodenness and leafiness imply a material side. But God is immaterial by definition. On the other hand, there are some properties which a creature may have which neither imply materiality nor imperfection. Thus we can say that God is good or wise.

There is of course a complication in all this. It arises from the fact that if the doctrine is true, God is primarily wise and humans secondarily. The real wisdom lies in God; human wisdom is but a reflection of that, existing in a mode which is appropriate to embodied creatures. But we come to learn our language here below. We learn the concept of wisdom from human and not divine examples. And so the order of knowing is different from the order of reality. This complication has a big consequence relating to the proofs, to which I shall come.

The analogy of proportionality is like this: as seeing stands to the eye so does intellectual seeing stand to the intellect. When I say I see the solution to a problem or the point of a joke, the word 'see' is appropriate because of the analogy with sight. It might be argued that ultimately all analogical predication is of this kind, because of the restrictions we had to apply in relation to such cases as wisdom. There we had to note that wisdom applies to God in so far as no defect is implied and no materiality – such is the concept of wisdom. But is it not the case then that what we are saying is that God's wisdom stands to God's essence as human wisdom stands to the human being's essence? Anyway, whether this is so or not, Aquinas held to both kinds of analogy, even if in some of his later works he held more to the analogy of proportion.

Now all this implies that our capacity to take a middle way depends upon our accepting a real resemblance of creatures to God. Even then of course we are groping a bit in the dark. We can only have a very partial view of the nature of God. But that (it would be argued) is as it should be: it follows from our nature as creatures. But even this rather dim knowledge is fragile, in that it places a huge weight upon the Five Ways. The point is that the doctrine of analogy is a crucial part of the whole edifice of philosophical knowledge of the Divine Being, but it itself depends upon the acceptance of real resemblance. This itself flows in major part from the persuasiveness of Aquinas' proofs. It also depends on the notion, by no means self-evident, that effects resemble causes in some crucial respect. But what is the resemblance between my act in striking a match and the bursting forth of flames?

Aquinas was also very keen to preserve the notion of the simplicity of God. We ascribe various virtues or perfections to God – such as intelligence, unity, will, etc. But these cannot ultimately be different attributes of God. But we as finite beings come to them separately. Moreover, our language is typically subject–predicate in form. Hence we have space for many different predicates which can be applied to God. But in God they all fuse into a unified essence. The same prevails when we consider ideas in the mind of God. We want to say, and indeed we rightly say, that God has knowledge of many things, which in differing ways as creatures reflect the divine perfection, even if imperfectly. There is a sense in which ideas exist in the mind of God. To this extent Thomas is in the Platonic tradition. But whether this is strictly compatible with the simplicity of the divine intellect is hard to say: for Thomas it was evidently possible.

Metaphysically of course the primary distinction between the Divine Being and all creatures is that in God essence and existence are fused. All creatures have borrowed existence: you can always ask whether anything of a given specification, say, a cow or unicorn, exists. But God's existence is his essence. He is the 'I am' or He who is, *Qui est*.

Thomas' doctrine of creation goes a good deal beyond Aristotle. It is already apparent that, though built upon such abstract foundations, his concept of God is much richer. God is not just an unmoved mover (or better: unchanged changer), moving other beings magnetically as final cause. He actually creates out of nothing. Though Aquinas holds philosophically that God might have created an everlasting world – the world being like a violin melody which God has always been playing – and so we have to go to revealed doctrine for the belief in the temporal finitude of the cosmos, he does believe in creation out of nothing. The reasoning is powerful. God cannot have had to use some material. That would either be part of himself, which is impossible (since God is a spiritual not a material being), nor could anything exist independently of the First Cause. So God creates out of nothing, and that nothing is not some sort of miasmic material. Next, we have to ask why God creates. It cannot be because he needs anything, being a perfect being. And being perfect he must have acted freely, without necessity. He created because of his goodness and goodness is diffusive of itself. It spills over, so to speak. The world, then, is intrinsically good, though it is limited by its unavoidable finitude. Whether this is the best of all possible universes we can hardly say, though since God is omnipotent he could always produce something better. Now all this generates too the problem of evil, for does not creating a cosmos in which actually there are real evils create (and indeed will) those evils?

Strictly according to Aquinas, evil is not a being, but a *privatio* – an absence of what ought to be there. God could not be said to have created such absences, for absences are not things which you can or cannot create. Of course in willing a physical universe God does will that decay should occur: a universe with only incorruptible entities is less good than one which also contains decaying entities. There is a special kind of freedom for creatures in such a cosmos. And because he prizes freedom, himself being perfectly free as part of (or identical with) his goodness, he permits sin. But in this he does not strictly speaking will sin. By such arguments, in which in part Aquinas follows Augustine, Aquinas seeks to avoid the consequences of adopting the doctrine of the creation of the world out of nothing.

Aquinas' psychology is an adapted version of that of Aristotle. The soul is the form of the body, but the rational soul, because it is capable of knowing all bodies, is not pinned down to a special material type. It is not like the eye which is pinned down to the perception of colors. It does not depend intrinsically on a particular bodily organ. So it is a spiritual entity and so immortal, incorruptible. Moreover, human beings have a natural desire to go on existing, and this natural desire would be in vain if we were not immortal, and would not have been implanted in us by the Creator. Naturally, in all this Aquinas takes a stance against the Averroist doctrine of non-personal immortality. Each soul for him is distinct.

All this is relevant to Aquinas' moral theory. He follows Aristotle in eudaemonism – that is, in interpreting ethics in the context of agents' pursuit of happiness. But he makes a huge change to Aristotle. For the highest happiness according to Thomas is not the imperfect happiness of this temporal world, but the vision of the divine essence: the beatific vision. This has three consequences. First, Aquinas produces an otherworldly *summum bonum*. Aristotle's emphasis is shifted from here to there, from earth to heaven. Indeed, all you can have this side of the grave is a foretaste of the beatific vision (enough though to make Thomas refer to all his writings as so much chaff, when he had this foretaste). Second, it makes Thomas' God a good deal more glorious than that of Aristotle. Third, it makes the highest good depend on divine grace. It also gives a differing slant on the idea of God as final cause, magnetically drawing forth the directions of the cosmos. God as final cause attracts creatures back to himself. This is much more than Aristotle's God ever does.

The whole vision of Aquinas is a hierarchical one, but it is not unnatural that he should integrate into his vision of creation the notion of the State as a natural human institution ruled by a monarch, and indirectly subordinate to the Church, which is concerned with a higher end than the common good of citizens as naturalistically conceived.

The total worldview of Aquinas created opposition partly because of its novelty. There were aspects of his theories which might cause problems related to religious practice. For instance, his theory of the soul–body relation led to his qualifying the view that the body of a dead person is the same substance as the living person, since the soul is withdrawn at death. There were attacks on him for this, as it seemed to undermine the important cult of relics during this part of the Middle Ages. But especially after he himself was canonized as a saint in 1323 such objections did tend to wither away. The majesty of his system, the prestige of Aristotle, the clarity of his exposition gave him a pre-eminent position, especially in his own order, the Dominicans.

It may be added, to jump forward a few centuries, that scholasticism was being revived in the latter part of the nineteenth century within the Catholic Church, having undergone a considerable slump since the early part of the eighteenth century. Thomism and Scotism were for much of the preceding period the primary forms of scholastic theology and philosophy. In the second half of the nineteenth century the drive for revival concentrated on the re-establishment of the Thomistic system. So it was that Pope Leo XIII in his encyclical of 1879 entitled *Aeterni patris* commended the study of Thomas to the Church. The Catholic philosopher should not diverge from Aquinas' views except for reasons which seemed to him to be compelling, nor should he show disrespect for the views of Aquinas. This gave him a semi-official status among Catholics for some eighty years or more. At Vatican II (1962–65) such discipline was dismantled, and a new age of Catholic thinking, and dissent, appeared. The encyclical was part of a broader attempt in the Church to resist the winds of modernity. It could also cause strains. For Thomas in espousing Aristotle was also, in part at least, committed to a system of scientific inquiry which was to become ever more obviously out of phase with modern thinking. Many of the Aristotelian assumptions about motion and change were destined to be eroded and destroyed. But all this should not detract from the remarkable worldview-construction which Aquinas had accomplished. He gave the most impressive and coherent form to Christian philosophy of the period. I use the phrase 'Christian philosophy', not that he used it or would have liked it, but because in fact the synthesis which he evolved injected ideas and layers of reality (for example, the vision of the divine essence) into the Aristotelian framework, thereby effecting vast changes upon it. Aquinas' Aristotle had undergone changes which went well beyond a kind of parallelism: rather, Aquinas had effected a merger between Christian doctrine and the Peripatetic philosophy. This made him, of course, into a highly original figure.

DUNS SCOTUS AND METAPHYSICS

In Latin medieval thought there are, apart from Aquinas, two other towering figures – namely Duns Scotus and William of Ockham. Duns Scotus (1265/6–1308) was born near Edinburgh and studied at Paris and Oxford. A Franciscan, he thought of himself as carrying on the Franciscan tradition, harking back to Augustine. But he was an original thinker who created a synthesis different from, but comparable to, that created by Aquinas. But he was less close to Aristotle, was more Platonist, and owed more to Avicenna.

In his opinion the primary object of the intellect is being. The task of the metaphysician is to explore this concept. He also considered that being must be thought of as a term which can apply equally to transcendent reality, namely God, and the contents of the material world. He did not think there was a difference in the meaning of *being* as between the two levels. Indeed, he considered that the univocal character of the expression is necessary if we are to have any metaphysical knowledge of the Divine Being at all. Those who argued for the opposite doctrine, namely that being used of God and human beings is utterly equivocal, were surely wrong.

Duns Scotus was confident that one could come to understandings of various terms which could be asserted univocally of God and creatures. For instance, being itself can be considered in abstraction from the contrast between infinite and finite. What is is not nothing. In this abstracted sense it can be said univocally of both the transcendent and the creature. Scotus applied similar reasoning to such an attribute as wisdom, once we abstract, again, and remove from it the imperfections which may pertain to finite or human wisdom. Scotus was particularly interested in those categories which he called 'disjunct' – such as finite or infinite, contingent or necessary. They figured in his supposed proofs of God's existence. Indeed, he considered such metaphysical arguments to be probative, as opposed to arguments drawn from the physical world. Such alleged proofs from physics cannot strictly take you beyond physics. On the other hand, metaphysical arguments take you to the heart of the infinite. Disjunct categories are such that they apply disjunctively to all beings. Thus not every being is contingent (for instance, God is not contingent), but every being is either contingent or necessary. And so on with the others.

So it is that from the fact that there are contingent beings we can infer a first necessary being, for a vertical chain of contingencies cannot be infinite, but must find a resting place in what is necessary. Or to put it much more informally, a contingent cosmos presupposes a necessary being to bring it into being. From this he argues that it must be unique, infinite, intelligent, and so on. But he did not consider that all God's attributes can be proven. For some one would have to rely upon revelation – for instance, God's omnipotence and mercy. There are other areas too where revealed theology has to be brought in. You cannot, he thought, demonstrate the immortality of the soul. Aquinas' version, for instance, simply begs the question, for it begins from the thesis that the soul is a form subsisting by itself, which is the point to be proved. As for the thought that the rational soul does not use a bodily organ, the way vision does, and so is incorporeal, such an argument does not sufficiently recognize that the soul may holistically depend on the body, which is certainly destined for decay. He is also critical of the argument from the natural desire for beatitude. In such ways Scotus combines a rather dense and interestingly worked out metaphysics with a skeptical stance.

WILLIAM OF OCKHAM: A RADICAL CRITIQUE OF ARISTOTLE AND OTHERS

William of Ockham (in Surrey, not far from London) (c.1285–1349) was perhaps the most radical and original of the medieval philosophers and theologians. He studied at Oxford, but before receiving his license as a professor, he was summoned to the Papal court at Avignon to face charges of heresy and the like. Later he migrated to Bavaria, where he received the protection of King Ludwig. He died in Munich of the Black Death (it is surmised). The latter scourge carried away many leading European intellectuals of the time.

The radicalism of his views came from his sweeping challenge to realism and the whole Aristotelian scheme of essences. The whole apparatus of thinking of a term like 'falcon' as standing somehow for a form which inheres in particular birds was challenged by him. Scientific generalizations about the world are to be confirmed on the basis of empirical observations, that is, by intuitive cognitions of individual instances. They are at best hypothetical, since they depend on the prior assumption of the uniformity of nature.

From his empiricist perspective it follows that theology is not a science. Science should be based on what is evidently known: this would be something which is a necessary truth or which is known by immediate experience. Neither of these requirements can be met in regard to matters of faith. He made the highly important observation that the articles of faith are by no means evident to infidels and pagans, who are no less intelligent than Christians. Consider for instance the great philosophers of the Hellenistic and Islamic worlds. So you simply have to accept the articles of faith on faith. Ockham was critical of so many of his fellows for trying to clarify theology with the obscurities of philosophy. It was part of his task, therefore, to demolish many of the assumptions and arguments of his time. In this connection his insistence on the free omnipotence of God stood him in good stead, lending a skeptical edge to this thought.

Thus at the physical level he was critical of various Aristotelian assumptions – notably that celestial bodies are immaterial and are not subject to decay, that action at a distance is impossible, and that there cannot be plurality of worlds. In the latter connection, he criticized the argument that you cannot have an infinite chain, going backwards, of efficient causes. Maybe you could not have an infinite vertical chain of conserving causes, but even here, though you might think that you have established a necessary being or first cause, you cannot show that that is unique. There might be many such conservers. All this pointed to what may be called a 'positivist theology'. You accept the divine order as it is revealed. That God acts through sacramental grace is a postulate you acknowledge.

Since for Ockham there is no viable natural theology, this means the breakdown of the whole edifices of Thomism and Scotism. Ockham's epistemology is tied to earthly particulars and we can have no abstract knowledge of unseen divine entities or essences. All this opened up fresh vistas for later thinkers. His refreshing empiricism was supplemented by his famous razor: plurality is not to be assumed without necessity, or, as it is sometimes put (but probably not by Ockham himself), entities are not to be multiplied beyond necessity. In his logical and linguistic writings he made much of the way in which the doctrine of universals and its attendant confusions sprang from linguistic and logical entanglements. For this reason there was a considerable revival of interest in Ockham after World War II in the heyday of linguistic philosophy.

Ockham's insistence on the freedom of God matches his special regard for liberty in individuals. This free will is known by us in experience, and cannot be proved by reasoning. It is also implied in the fact that we are praised and blamed for our actions, which supposes that we could have, had we so willed it, done something other than what we did. But Ockham does not draw from this a Pelagian conclusion. God is supremely free, and if he wishes he can grant eternal life to those who have not obeyed him, and withhold it from those upon whom he has bestowed his grace. In line with his theological positivism he regards what is good and bad as being what is commanded and forbidden by God. If God chose to command us to commit fornication, then fornicating would be a good deed. There is some obscurity at this point in Ockham's position, since he evidently thinks of God as having commanded a moral law which humans can strive to know even if they do not have the benefit of the knowledge of the positive theology of the Christian Church.

OCKHAM'S INFLUENCE

Ockham's influence spread in Oxford and Paris, since his critical views offered an exciting alternative to traditional metaphysical approaches. His empiricism offered avenues for the critique of Aristotle and helped prepare the way for later scientific developments. One of his most radical followers, Nicholas of Autrecourt (c.1300–c.1341), was condemned to death by burning, but recanted in time. He took the view that the only things we can have knowledge of are what we perceive through the senses, the contents of our minds and logically evident propositions (to deny which would offend the law of non-contradiction). This led him to skepticism about substances as depicted by Aristotle: indeed, the greater part of Aristotle's whole system fell apart under his critique. Even Ockham's own worldview was thought by him to be insufficiently empirical.

More moderate was the position of Jean Buridan (c.1295–1356). He was among other things a notable contributor to medieval modal logic. In physics he held to a theory of impetus which was contrary to Aristotle's notion that a projectile's motion is kept going by the supporting agency of the medium.

A severe critic of Ockham was his contemporary Thomas Bradwardine (c.1290–1349), a follower of Duns Scotus. He was disturbed by Ockham's overconfident view of human freedom. On the other hand, he undermined the Thomist notion of secondary causes, thus ascribing directly to God power over casual sequences. He considered Ockham's position to be a modern version of Pelagianism. He thought that he had philosophical reasons for his position, and thought that God was the cause of sin and evil: such consistency led him to suppose that future contingent events, which some philosophers wished to exclude from the range of divine knowledge, were known to God because of his causal activity. His general worldview harked back strikingly to Islamic occasionalism.

Probably the most important contribution of the Ockhamist stream of thought to the ongoing development of thought, including science, was its skepticism towards Aristotle. The grip of his physics upon the medieval imagination was slackened somewhat, and so the way was prepared for the scientific revolutions of the Renaissance and beyond.

Another strand of worldview-construction in the fourteenth century and beyond was that supplied by the mystics. It was a great period of renewal in this kind of religion, with such figures as Eckhart (1260–1327), Tauler (c.1300–61), Ruysbroeck (1293–1381), Catherine of Siena (1347–80) and John Gerson (1363–1429).

THE RELATION OF MYSTICISM TO PHILOSOPHY

As in the case of Sufism, mysticism or the contemplative life led to new ideas on the nature of the universe. The mystics are important in that they stretched the concept of experience. The inner light revealed in Christian contemplative exploration had something to say which was not contained in the rather drier formulas of technical philosophy, as it became increasingly ramified during the period we are looking at. To some extent, the experientialism of the mystics was encouraged by the critical flow of Ockhamism.

The mystics were drawn to depict human psychology in certain ways because of their felt need to take account of the higher experience of knowledge of the divine (or, by a paradox, the cloud of unknowing). While they were not much interested in matters of cosmology, they did have motives to emphasize a negative way in regard to the description, or non-description, of God, since, as we saw earlier, very often the urge for a Neoplatonic type of philosophy has its roots in the ultimate ineffability of the mystical state. Further, mystics, in having a kind of direct access to the divine, have a knowledge which is parallel to, but extra to, revelation. And so they had what may be described as an 'alternative natural theology'. Some of the dryness of scholastic analysis was replaced by something which in their eyes was much warmer and more existential.

MEISTER ECKHART AND SOME RELATIONS TO INDIAN PHILOSOPHY

Perhaps the most interesting of all the mystical writers of the period was Johannes Eckhart, usually referred to as Meister Eckhart. Born in Thuringia, he pursued theological studies in Cologne and Paris. A Dominican, he came to be Superior-general for the whole of Germany. Despite this, some of his statements, drawn both from his more philosophical writings and his sermons, were condemned either as rash or as plain heretical.

He appears to have held what may be called a double-decker theory of God. At the higher level, God is *Deitas* or the Godhead, from which emanates the personalized God, *Deus,* of the Trinity. The Godhead is the ground of the Divine and is ineffable. From it emanate the Three Persons. Out of God there issues the universe, and here some of Eckhart's language suggests the idea of emanation rather than a time-bound act of creation. The reason is that according to him everything for God, being eternal, is in a timeless now. So God acts in such a 'now' in creating the cosmos. But the cosmos itself contains things in time, so the creation can be dated backwards from now. So we naturally talk in a time-bound way about the coming into being of the cosmos.

Though he emphasizes, especially in his later writings, that God's nature is being, *esse*, he also wrote that God's nature is primarily not *esse* but *intelligere* or understanding. This assimilates the Godhead to the nature of the soul. Here his language is sometimes unorthodox. He held that the soul consists in a complex system of layers. At the bottom level it operates through such powers as digestion, assimilation and sensation. To perform these acts it has need of a body. But there is a further level, manifested in various feelings or emotions, such as anger and love, and in the *sensus communis* or 'common sense' which synthesizes the different reports of the senses. At the next level again the soul manifests itself as the memory, will and the higher intellect (the 'common sense' being a sort of lower intellect). Then there is a still higher level at which it can know things in complete abstraction, that is, as pure forms. This is to know them as they exist in God's intellect. We may note that this is an important hangover from Platonist thought. Then finally, the soul is something which transcends all the above-mentioned faculties. It is the ground or *scintilla* – the divine spark. This spark unites with God in the highest form of mystical experience. Does such union spell identity? Eckhart is ambiguous. Sometimes it seems that the spark is uncreated, and sometimes he talks of God's birth in the soul.

Another source of unease about the way he wrote, from an orthodox Catholic angle, was his remarks about creatures. In one of his sermons he said, 'All creatures are a pure nothing. I do not say that they are little or something; they are a pure nothing.' The reason for saying this seems to be as follows: a creature may have a form (which is eternally present in the divine intellect), but it is nothing until existence or being is conferred on it. But this comes from God. Without God, therefore, the creature is nothing.

Eckhart's statements about the mystical experience itself were bound to arouse hostility. They are reminiscent of the language of al-Ḥallāj. So he said, 'God and I, we are one.' He drew a parallel between the way food gets assimilated into me when I eat it and the way I get absorbed into God when I undergo a mystical experience. He also referred to an element in the soul which is uncreated.

The explanation of all this is no doubt that Eckhart was aware of something which many other mystics have said, namely that in the highest experience the subject–object distinction, which is pervasive in most experiences, such as perception, just disappears. Now whether this says anything ontologically about the relation of the soul to God, in those cases where the mystic has a God, is open to question, but it is not unnatural for the mystic to assume that some kind of identification takes place, or is realized in experience. In other words the distinction between God and the soul is washed away. There is, then, a certain symmetry in Eckhart's picture. On the one hand, at the upper level of reality (so to speak) there is an ineffable Godhead beyond God. At the lower level, there is a *scintilla* or spark which lies beneath the regular conscious levels of the soul.

The fact that a number of his statements were condemned is testimony to the strictness with which the Church tried to keep reins upon freedom of thought in theology. There was a terror of heresy. It is also interesting to note, as a number of writers have, that there are places where Eckhart's worldview converges with that of Advaita Vedanta in the Indian tradition, but without benefit of any relevant culture content. So for Advaita there is divine Reality without qualities, corresponding to *Deitas*. There is also at a lower plane of truth *Iśvara*, or the Personal Lord who is creator of the world. Among living beings there exists an empirical soul but beyond or beneath it there is the one Self or *Atman* which is the higher truth to be identified with the non-personal Reality. When viewed from a higher level, creatures are merely illusory; they do not strictly speaking exist at all. They are a mere nothing. The highest mystical experience comes when the individual realizes the essential identity of his underlying Self with the divine Reality.

The parallel is suggestive, and it reinforces the thesis that the primary reason for Eckhart's worldview lies in a tension between his everyday sacramental and pious view of the universe, as ruled over by a personal Creator or *Deus,* and his mystical awareness of the disappearance of the subject–object distinction. He could resolve the tension by his double-decker view of the Divine Being, but not completely. The phenomenology of worship and of mysticism diverges at this point. Hence Eckhart's language is sometimes completely orthodox, and this he did wish to be, for he thought of himself as a loyal son of the Church. But sometimes his language would appear to his contemporaries to be wildly unorthodox. He himself conceded that some of his utterances were indeed mistaken and cast in misleading form.

Eckhart influenced some famous followers, such as Tauler and Suso (whom we shall come to shortly), as well as a seminal thinker, Nicholas of Cusa, who stood on the watershed between the Middle Ages and the Renaissance. Moreover, with the revival of interest in the mystics in the early nineteenth century he had some effect upon some signal figures of that period, notably Hegel and Schelling.

Tauler (?1300–61) of Strasbourg continued with Eckhart's language of the *scintilla*. But he regarded this element in the soul as being God-given. He was able to interpret mystical experience in the light of the doctrine of grace. He also postulated as a vital aspect of the soul *das Gemüt* or the heart. If this is turned towards the divine spark or apex (as he also called it – *das Punkt*), then God will approach the soul and draw it to him. But the way of mysticism is also one of suffering, like that of Christ. The return to God is painful and self-sacrificial. But it is also a way of love: the union between an individual and God is seen as the deepest love.

Heinrich Suso (?1295–1366) used Eckhartian language about the Godhead, but held that the difference between the two aspects of the Divine Being is one created by the human intellect in trying to understand God. He was influenced, as were other Rhineland mystics, by Neoplatonism and Pseudo-Dionysius' negative path. He was also consciously Christocentric in his contemplative life, and referred to the birth of Christ in the soul.

These and other mystics in the general area of the Rhineland were, then, a vital spiritual movement whose ideas had some philosophical shape. The comparative freedom of their language prepared the way for some developments in the Renaissance.

NICHOLAS OF CUSA AND THE COINCIDENCE OF OPPOSITES

Nicholas Cusanus (1401–64) came from Kues on the Mosel River in Western Germany, and played a prominent role in negotiations aimed at healing the gap between the Eastern and Western Churches (which were temporarily at least successful). His writings covered the theory of knowledge, the nature of the Divine, cosmology, the relations between religions and other matters. His works had a wide circulation and a long vogue. They represent a revival of the Platonist tradition, but much more besides. Some of his ideas are startlingly original and surprisingly modern.

First of all, he held a theory of knowledge which underlined the finitude of the human intellect. We can approximate to the truth but not really get to it. Part of the reason lies in the fact that we are stuck with logic and the law of non-contradiction, and this inhibits us from recognizing that in God above all contradictories coexist. This is Cusa's famous idea of the *coincidentia oppositorum* or coincidence of opposites. This was primarily applicable to God, who is simultaneously the absolute maximum and the minimum. Our logic resists this, but Cusanus uses various similes to illustrate how the coincidence of opposites is realistic. As a circle expands so its circumference flattens: at the extreme the straight line and the circle will be identical. So, then, our knowledge is limited, and recognizing why is that learned ignorance which formed the title of one of his writings.

Nicholas of Cusa's cosmology was highly original. He saw the universe of creatures as a kind of contraction of God who is mirrored in them. Indeed, every one thing mirrors everything else (here is a conception close to that of Huayan). Further he held that the universe, while not actually infinite, is without bounds and has therefore no circumference. It follows from this that it has no center, or if you prefer, everywhere is the center. There are in the world no absolutes such as up and down, and Cusanus also denied the difference in substance, postulated by traditional Aristotelianism, between the heavenly bodies and the sublunary world.

The idea that the earth is not at the center and relatively is in motion might be thought of as a metaphor for his view of the religion. He was modern in the sense of taking the comparative study of religions seriously. He considered that beneath the contradictions exhibited by various doctrines there could be discerned a basic harmony. In many ways he was remarkably unorthodox, seeing that he was created a cardinal.

In part he was a reviver of the Platonic tradition. This was something which in any event had a new vogue during the Renaissance. With his critical and revolutionary views, then, Cusanus stood between two worlds.

SOME REFLECTIONS ON MEDIEVAL CHRISTIAN PHILOSOPHY

We have in the foregoing contemplated a number of the more important of the philosophers of what we classify as the Middle Ages. I have not adverted to the surprising and complex developments in medieval logic and theory of language – and these were important, though for a long period later forgotten or neglected. In other ways too the period displayed great vitality. If there is a case for looking at the Middle Ages as a section, so to speak, of Western intellectual history, it lies in the fact that the vast weight of discussion followed similar patterns to those established in Islamic civilization and among Jewish philosophers. It followed a form which was already well adumbrated in the work of Augustine and Pseudo-Dionysius – the synthesis between classical philosophy and Christian belief. In Islam and Jewish theology of course the particularities of the respective theisms were different, but not all that much so. It is not surprising if Aquinas, while most original in his mode of putting together Aristotle and theism, should be seen to be playing in the same league as ibn Rushd and Maimonides. In the three differing cultures (or four if you count the Greek East as another) there were very strong pressures towards a rough conformism at least; and in all three or four mysticism played a role in providing a somewhat maverick alternative tradition.

But we are on the verge of that whole movement starting (let us say rather arbitrarily) in the fourteenth century and sweeping on until, and beyond, the Reformation in the early years of the sixteenth century. This Renaissance saw a breakdown of the previous worldview partly because it began to experience the disintegration of the prevailing Aristotelian physical cosmology. The very power of the latter had been its bugbear: it was plausible enough to take a strong grip on the imagination of intellectuals. But already we have seen the demolition beginning to happen in the 'medieval' period – with the nominalism and empiricism of Ockham and the revolutionary thinking of Cusa. Thomas Aquinas, though possibly the most gifted and constructive philosopher of the whole period, was nevertheless not on the side of the newly conceived angels. The demolition of the medieval worldview was assisted too by the Reformation, which undermined the traditional authority of the Church, and in substituting a paper Pope, ultimately drove authority back to individual interpretation and inner experience.

The fruitful rise of science in the West has been partly ascribed to the notion of God: because God is rational it is easy to think that the patterns underlying the functioning of the material world are rational. There may be something in this, especially with the revival of the mathematization of science, so that rationally describable processes could be looked on as mathematically describable. On the other hand, the large and admittedly fairly comfortable strait-jacket in which thought was held so long as Western Europe was dominated by a single and relatively unified Church was not perhaps so conducive to new critical thinking, such as was demanded by the growth of science. At any rate, with the Renaissance came new freedoms of thought. And this was due to a kind of inner dialectic in Western civilization.

For the great revival of excitement about Hellenism and in general Classical civilization – the new humanism – was not placed against a background of prior ignorance about the ancient world. In its own way Classical values had been quite well served by Arab and Latin translators, commentators and philosophers. But the scale of the new concern with the Classics was great. It was as though pagan civilization had hit back from its grave, and in a new key. Classical philosophy had already made one synthesis with Christianity, and the result had been Neoplatonist and in due course Aristotelian forms of theism. But now another wave rolled into the West, inspiring the arts as well as philosophy. The old contradictions in Western civilization gained a new life. It was the very contradictoriness and relative anarchy of the new culture emerging from the fourteenth century onwards that help to account for its being a matrix of science. In turn the new science could not fail to stimulate philosophy and the construction of new worldviews. How could the Copernican revolution not leave thinkers feeling disoriented? How could Galileo's telescope not leave the whole of Aristotelian physics in ruins? How could new paintings in perspective not begin to affect the whole of optics, and how could this not fail to throw a different light upon the whole process of seeing?

Education also had its role to play. The collection of texts proceeded apace during the Renaissance. The emergence of the printing press began to bring their price down, and to favor the swifter circulation of ideas. The examples of Cicero and Seneca could stimulate the ideal of the urbane and cultivated gentleman. Education was privatized and became an aristocratic pursuit, thus drifting away from the clerics who had previously been the prime educated class. From this time on the intellectuals were predominantly the *kṣatriyas* rather than the brahmins of the Western world.

Nor should we forget that the Renaissance period was also the beginning of that huge expansion of Europe into Asia and the New World. This was anthropologically suggestive, and the existence of diverse other cultures was gradually to make its impact upon Europe. But it also brought a period of new wealth, which was to help to transform European economics, and supply a new class, the bourgeoisie, even more vigorous than the *kṣatriyas* in developing education and ideas.

The influence of mystical and esoteric ideas upon the formation of the Renaissance may also be mentioned. Not only was the work of Nicholas of Cusa influential, but the revived Platonism brought with it new interest in Neoplatonism. Moreover, the rediscovery of the old Hermetic texts – the so-called *Corpus Hermeticum,* composed and assembled between about 100 CE and 300 CE – stimulated new forms of esotericism which came to be combined with a refreshed Kabbalah.

In looking at the philosophy of the Renaissance I shall look first to Italy, its greatest mother, and to the work of four thinkers who illustrate something of the freer atmosphere of the times, namely Marsilio Ficino, Pico della Mirandola and Girolamo Cardano, together with the more cynical Niccolò Machiavelli. Later we shall look to the burning of Giordano Bruno in 1600, which perhaps marks the end of an era. Some of the more interesting action had begun to move to Northern Europe.

MARSILIO FICINO AND THE FLORENTINE ACADEMY

Marsilio Ficino (1433–99) was more than a typical product of the Renaissance: he was a major symbol of it. Patronized by Cosimo de Medici, he with his help founded the Florentine Academy, which for many summed up the new spirit of the times. It was a kind of spiritual community of like-minded people interested in the revival of Platonism. There were banquets in honor of Plato, readings of dialogues, lectures by well-known visitors and so forth. Ficino himself was a clergyman and not at all disloyal to the Church, but he had a wide-ranging and outward-reaching mind. He was well acquainted with many classical works, from Aristotle and Lucretius to Porphyry and Proclus. He also knew the Hermetic corpus, and had some nodding acquaintance with Zoroastrianism. He thought that the Hermetic tradition was ancient and going back to a similar period to that of the Hebrew Bible. So he saw Zoroaster and Hermes as parallel forebears to the Hebrew ancestors of the Christian faith. Thus Platonism and philosophy, on the one hand, and Christianity, on the other, were two parallel streams which could commingle. As one who translated all of Plato's dialogues and issued the first complete edition of them, his Platonism was brighter and more well-informed than many earlier interpretations, and he placed especial emphasis upon Plato's treatment of love and friendship. The love of friends is itself a prelude to the love of God.

His most celebrated writing was his *Platonic Theology on the Immortality of Souls* which was printed in 1482, though it was written about a decade earlier. For him the issue of immortality was central. This was in part because in his hierarchical vision of the cosmos, ranging down from God through angels to minerals and qualityless matter, the human soul stood at the midpoint. It is the center of the universe. And this universe is dynamic, being bonded by love, and the soul's love is in the end to find its true expansion in union with God. For this ultimate satisfaction humans were created. Now for many the chance to ascend through the contemplative life to union with the divine is limited. We need immortality to realize our destinies.

Ficino, with his generous view of other religions, his positive attitude to the philosophical tradition, his esotericism, his love of love, his integration of astrology into his thinking, and so forth, displayed himself to be a Renaissance figure *par excellence*. His *Theologia Platonica* continued to have influence even after scientific knowledge cut at the roots of the hierarchical cosmos he envisaged. He was one of the originators of the tradition of 'perennial philosophy', which sees a convergence between philosophy and religion largely through the mystical traditions.

PICO DELLA MIRANDOLA AND UNIVERSALISM

Count Pico della Mirandola (1463–94) was the younger son in a princely family from Mirandola and Concordia in Northern Italy in the Po valley. He was remarkably fruitful in his writings and learning, considering that he died rather young. He studied not just the Classics, but Hebrew and Arabic as well. When he was 23 he rather boldly assembled 900 theses which he offered publicly to defend in Rome. Some were ecclesiastically condemned and he was in due course arrested in France, where he had fled, but the intervention of Italian princes secured his release. His last days were spent in Florence. His most important work was his *Oration on the Dignity of Man,* which he had prepared as the start of his defense of the 900 theses.

In this work he most eloquently affirmed human freedom. Because of human liberty humankind does not exist in a fixed place in the cosmic hierarchy, but occupies a world which differs from the other orders (the divine, angelic and elementary levels of being). But more important than anything for Pico was his universalism or syncretism. He tried to bring together all the major traditions. He thought that Plato and Aristotle were essentially compatible. But more than that he wove Kabbalism, which he saw as being with Christian belief, into his scheme, and took great pains to interpret ancient mythology in allegorical and figurative senses. He was influenced in his interpretation of the scriptures by the esoteric number symbolism of the Hebrew Kabbalah. And so he perceived himself as a kind of universal philosopher and religious teacher, drawing on all traditions. Perhaps he never assembled his various ideas into a thorough system because of his early death, so that he is more syncretistic than a successful perennial philosopher or universalist. But universalism was what he strove for. He was thus an important figure in helping to create a Renaissance ideology, which would not be afraid to find truth and insight anywhere. Because of his stress on freedom Pico attacked astrology, since it implied some kind of determinism; he showed himself very much *au fait* with a variety of astrological theories. He did believe in the interconnectedness of the cosmos; however, inside this unified structure human beings were free agents. And through the sacrifice of Christ they had access even to the highest level, to God himself. But here we go beyond philosophy, into mystical religion, beyond thought.

CARDANO AND AMBIGUITIES IN RENAISSANCE THOUGHT

Like a number of other prominent thinkers of the period, Girolamo Cardano (1501–76) was a medical man, being professor of medicine at Pavia. He had an interesting holistic philosophy, seeing the world as an organic system. Empty space comes to be filled with animated beings through the operation of the World Soul. All objects in the world have souls, and so have relationships of sympathy and antipathy. The mortal souls of various beings including human beings can be distinguished from the immortal soul with which God has endowed humanity. It is involved in the process of reincarnation.

Unlike Pico, Cardano believed in astrology and natural magic. The idea of the interconnectedness of things in his hylozoic organicism helped to produce a theory of why magic and indeed alchemy could work. So it was that Cardano illustrates another trend in the Renaissance; the acceptance of a range of ideas not destined to have much scientific future, and a fascination with some of the preoccupations with the occult which came down from the ancient and the medieval world. But his restless search for an alternative to official Aristotelianism also illustrates a general uneasiness and critical attitude to the dominant scientific tradition which would soon burst forth in the new science.

MACHIAVELLI – LOOKING AT POLITICS WITH A COOL EYE

Niccolò Machiavelli (1469–1527) was not a general philosopher, and dealt primarily with political arts and the theory of war. He was not quite a systematic political philosopher even. If his work has wider relevance it is because he was empirical about an important area of human experience. After serving the Republic in Florence he found himself without a job in 1512 when the regime was overthrown and the Medicis returned. It was partly to attract attention from the new rulers that he wrote *The Prince* and *The Discourses*. He was not as clear-sighted in his empiricism as ibn Khaldūn, but he did help prepare the way for the establishment of the modern study of politics.

The reason was his lack of sentimentality. He wanted to look at the State and the management of diplomacy and war from the point of view of the most efficient methods. He was not taken up with issues of right and wrong, though he had his private opinions, naturally enough. He also considered that it was natural that states should be concerned with growth and aggrandizement. Force was thus an integral part of what politics was about.

Machiavelli also stressed the importance of history. Any experience that individuals or groups may have is of necessity limited. One should look to the broader sources of history for lessons on how political organisms work. He thought the history of the Roman republic particularly instructive, for it was during that time that Rome succeeded in conquering so much of the known world.

In looking at politics and war with a cool eye Machiavelli showed his liberation from abstract theory or mere moralizing. On the other hand, his empiricism could also be seen as cynicism and there is no doubt that his works for a long time excited hostility and the simplistic judgment that Machiavelli was simply amoral. It is of course the dark interpretation of his writings which has caused the word 'Machiavellian' to enter the English language.

While he was preoccupied with the possible defense and unification of Italy, events of the greatest significance for Western civilization and philosophy were unfolding north of the Alps – namely the Reformation.

THE EFFECTS OF THE REFORMATION UPON PHILOSOPHY

The Protestant Reformation, conventionally dated from 1517, had various effects relevant to philosophy and the formation of worldviews. First, it generally speaking lessened the influence of philosophy in the Church, because it sought a return as far as possible to the Bible, or, in the case of some Churches, such as the Church of England, the teaching of the Bible and of the Church Fathers. It tended to cut away the accretions of Scholasticism.

Second, because it favored the use of the vernaculars, it tended to devolve cultures and therefore the philosophy growing out of them – in that sense it was indirectly encouraging to German, French, English and other forms of philosophy.

Third, the Radical Reformation, associated above all with the Anabaptists, prepared the way for non-conforming groups which, intentionally or not, contributed to the growth of individualism. The notion that infant baptism should be rejected, a prime element in the Radical Reformation, was based on the idea that the adult had to choose, or if you like, recognize that he or she had been chosen. This in turn suggested that there should be a division between religion and the State. The Radicals were therefore looked upon as very threatening and subversive. In Europe for so long the right faith was seen as ideologically necessary. The Anabaptists and others subverted the idea of an official Christianity. Then, again, in the search for the truth merely in revelation, the Reformers often encouraged individualism of interpretation, even if they may not have willed this.

Fourth, the Reformation, in dividing Europe, weakened ecclesiastical authority, and this was helpful to the emergence of new philosophers and worldviews, which became increasingly difficult to prescribe. Generally speaking, the Reformers themselves shared a particular set of beliefs, however much they might have divided on certain issues. These were: the authority of the Word, interpreted to mean the biblical revelation but also extended to cover the Word as preached; the priesthood of all believers, which involved a kind of Church 'democracy', in that every faithful Christian partakes in the governance and the sacramental life of the community; and justification by faith alone

– or to put it another way, by the grace of God, of which faith is a sign. Nothing you do gives you salvation: God alone is the true source of holiness and of salvation.

Among the main Reformers the most philosophical was John Calvin (1509–64), with his doctrine of predestination. This arose from the notion that it is by God's grace alone that a person is saved, and not in any way by his or her good works. God's power is absolute, moreover: and so foresees and indeed predetermines, in an inscrutable way, who is to be saved and who is not.

In returning to the Bible and cutting away the growth of scholastic commentary, the Reformers were preparing for conflict, for the biblical cosmology, even when you remove the overlay of Aristotelian and other ideas, was not that of the new science. While the Reformers had some grasp of the difference between religion and science, they ultimately had no means of warding off the tensions which were bound up between biblical cosmology and that of the modern world.

Maybe such tensions were fruitful. We have already noted a kind of dialectic in European civilization, in which the revival of Classical learning brought in new forces to challenge the various forms of medieval synthesis. So now with the Reformation another struggle in European culture emerged, which was sometimes stormy and bloody, but helped in the onward march of the critical mentality.

Of course there was a backlash. It helped to make Catholicism even more authoritarian, and it allowed States and princes to attain a high measure of ideological power. But in the long run, these forces were counterbalanced by the fragmentation of the Western world.

SCIENCE, PHILOSOPHY AND RELIGION

Nicolas Copernicus (1473–1543) studied in Cracow and in Italy, and was best known as a physician. But it was his new system in astronomy that brought him lasting fame. His heliocentric theory had many advantages, computationally, over the dominant Ptolemaic system. While some earlier thinkers had played with the idea that the earth went around the sun, Copernicus put the idea on a mathematical basis. His revolutionary view was not published until shortly before his death, but he had already expressed it widely, so that, at about the same time as the Protestant Reformation, here was another upheaval in thinking which was to have a profound impact spiritually, since it displaced humanity from the center of the cosmos. It was the symbolic and metaphysical effect of Copernicus that brought clashes between his worldview and that of the Churches. The Reformers were as much, maybe more, anti-Copernican as many Catholics, because they saw in it a challenge to a range of biblical texts.

The symbolic effects of Copernicus can be seen perhaps most plainly in the work of Giordano Bruno (1548–1600), burnt at the stake for heresy, and some of its metaphysical effects in the thinking of Galileo Galilei (1464–1542), who also ran into problems with the Inquisition. Bruno drew much of his inspiration from the Hermetic writings, and while he thought that this ancient alternative religion might flourish within the structures of Catholicism, his vision was not primarily a Christian one. He saw the cosmos as a boundless living thing, somewhat after the manner of Cusanus, and he considered that there were innumerable other worlds. The whole he saw as in motion. He was thus greatly attracted by Copernicus' theory, though he rather despised Copernicus as being a mere mathematician who did not see the secret and mysterious significance of his theory. On his return to Italy in 1591, from extensive travels in England, Germany and other parts of Europe, he was arrested by the Inquisition. Though after his first trial in Venice he recanted, he was transferred to prison in Rome and in due course tried again. This time he would not recant and was burnt.

Galileo was quite a different kind of person. He saw mathematics as a useful tool in astronomy and other sciences, and his various discoveries in mechanics led him to be highly critical of Aristotelianism. His use of the telescope revealed the mountainous character of the moon and four satellites around Jupiter. This destroyed the Aristotelian distinction between celestial and sublunary substances. He stressed the importance of empirical observation, and broke free from the opposition between Platonism and Aristotelianism: a true appraisal of the nature of physical nature could not be arrived at either by authority or by deductive metaphysics. He considered that religion and science should be kept apart – they had differing languages. He was thus critical of those who tried to settle questions in science by appeal to the Bible. In due course he was tried by the Roman Inquisition and was confined to house arrest. Even so he managed to complete and smuggle out his last work *Two New Sciences,* which was published in Holland (here, by the way, we see one of the positive consequences of the fragmentation of Europe: it was not possible, especially with the printing press, to keep anyone universally censored).

Probably the greatest theorist of science, as it was beginning to emerge, was Francis Bacon, Baron Verulam (1561–1624). Much of his life was spent as a statesman, serving Elizabeth I and James I with some distinction and some duplicity. His greatest contributions were his various writings on philosophy and science, notably his *The Advancement of Learning* and the *Novum Organum.* He realized that a new age of scientific knowledge was dawning, with various discoveries and techniques, especially the work of Copernicus and Galileo, the use of the telescope, printing and so forth. He was highly critical of much of the procedures of the learned world: philosophers were like spiders, spinning forth wonderful systems out of their own bodies with no contact with reality; alchemists such as even the great Paracelsus (1493–1541) and other crudely empirical inquirers were like ants, acquiring bits and pieces, but not within a systematic framework. Rather, humans should work together with system in order to create knowledge. Bacon ambitiously wished to create a complete classification of existing sciences, a whole new inductive logic, and a new philosophy of nature. He saw humanity as too much dominated by various idols, which could distort and undermine their knowledge. There are the idols of the tribe, that is to say views which seem to have a commonsense basis, but often represent wishful thinking, inherent in the human condition. There are the idols of the den (or cave: he drew the metaphor from Plato), in which we are fooled by our own individual quirks: we ought to be especially suspicious of views which we find congenial. There are the idols of the marketplace, arising from our taking language too seriously – often it creates the illusion of 'real entities' out there when they are linguistic projections. And there are the idols of the theater, in other words notions which are basically fictional but are given wide currency, because they arise from varying viewpoints, which may have little bearing on reality.

Bacon wanted to see science separated from philosophy and both from religion. The inductive logic he sketched was rich, and part of it was used in the nineteenth century by J.S. Mill (1806–73). Several of his suggestions were taken up after his death through the foundation of the Royal Society, devoted to scientific research and development.

Bacon's thought breathes a new air. For all the glories of the Renaissance, it was also in part backward-looking. The fascination with the Classical past and with such phenomena as the Hermetic corpus could be stultifying. The renewal of religion through the Reformation had its anti-intellectual side. The Roman backlash tended to encourage recourse to the Inquisition. But Bacon pointed the way forward to the systematic and practical development of scientific knowledge. For him the bee, not the spider or the ant, was the right model. He also swung interest towards epistemology. The methods whereby we come to know things became one of the preoccupations of the modern period in philosophy in the West.

Although human knowledge of geography (through the accounts of Marco Polo, the voyages of discovery and so on) and of medicine (through discoveries such as that of the circulation of the blood, and the new interest in anatomy, both in art and in surgery, etc.) and some other areas expanded greatly during this period, it was in the fields of astronomy and mechanics that the largest advances were being made. This had its effects on natural philosophy, where the dominant picture of the physical cosmos was that of the machine. All this raised the issue of the relation of the human soul or mind to the body. This in turn stimulated thinking about how our senses and thoughts can successfully understand what lies 'out there'. Mind–body dualism could create severe problems in the theory of knowledge. And so it was in the seventeenth century that there was something of a sea change in the direction and emphasis in philosophical thinking. This is a major reason why Descartes (1596–1650) is often looked upon as the father of modern philosophy. He looked to a method which would create certain foundations for scientific knowledge.

DESCARTES: THE TRANSITION TO A NEW WORLD

René Descartes came from La Haye in Touraine and was educated at the Jesuit school of La Flèche. He considered that he gained a fine education. In particular he became enamored of mathematics, and was later the chief founder of coordinate geometry. He served for a while in the military, following Maurice of Nassau. For twenty years or so he retired to Holland, and in 1649 was attracted to the court of Queen Christina of Sweden, who was building up a circle of *savants* in Stockholm. He died the next year. He was a cautious person: his book on *Le monde*, expressing his cosmology and endorsing the Copernican heliocentric theory, was withdrawn by him and not published until more than a quarter of a century after his death (in 1677), because he had learned of Galileo's condemnation.

In line with his mathematical interests he wished to propound a cosmology which contains only matter and mathematics. The idea of matter is that of a plenum. Each part of matter excludes every other. Descartes denies the possibility of a void. But in addition to the basic physical matter there are thinking substances, that is to say minds or souls. Of these there are many. But the physical cosmos, as Descartes' theory of matter implies, is one infinite and continuous body in three dimensions. It is strongly analogous to the notion of *prakṛti* in the Sāṅkhya tradition, peppered as it were with *puruṣas* or souls. Now because of his denial of the void, Descartes sees that motion has to involve the circular displacement of matter: in brief, it occurs in a whole series of vortices. This is the basis of his dynamics.

The very abstraction of Descartes' cosmology implies of course that our perception of the outside word is distorted. We see colors, but that is not how things really are. He conceived that there are minute particles which give off from the surface of bodies the stimuli to the senses.

He has a problem with mind, according to this cosmology. As we shall see, the mind plays a crucial part in the building up of the edifice of certainty which Descartes wishes to achieve. He is not keen on appeals to authority, nor in general to what the Indian tradition treats as a source of knowledge, namely testimony. His method of doubt as laid forth in his *Meditations* and the *Discourse on Method* leads inwards to the individual, trying to figure things out for himself. This became a pervasive feature of Western epistemology. But because it was reflective and inward-looking it gave a central part to the mind. But – and this was partly because Descartes was a good Catholic – he saw the mind as being immortal. As for animals, they do not have souls and are machines. In regard to humans the soul is mysteriously joined to the body through the pineal gland; Descartes wrongly thought that this gland did not occur in animals.

The method of doubt was an analytic one. Descartes cannot be thought to be a real skeptic. He postulates the possibility that we are everywhere deceived by a malicious demon as a kind of thought experiment so that we can test out which of our thoughts is after all certain. Is there anything we cannot doubt? Yes: first of all there is the thought 'I think, so I exist' – the famous *Cogito ergo sum,* or *Je pense donc je suis.* By 'thinking' here Descartes means not just understanding, reflecting and so on, but also willing, imagining and feeling. So Descartes considers that he must be certain of his existence as a thinking thing or thinking (willing, etc.) substance.

But though he has now a distinct and clear idea of himself as thinking substance, there is the problem of the external world. Does it really exist, and how can I be certain of it? Descartes arrives at the outer world by taking a roundabout path which runs through heaven. He proceeds to try and prove God's existence, who then becomes the guarantor that the outer world is not at bottom deceptive. And he finds in his mind the idea of a Perfect Being. But a cause must have as much reality as its effect. So it must exist. Moreover, reflection about my existence would indicate that I must have been brought into being by a God and not just by my parents, who also entertain in their minds the idea of a perfect Being. Finally, there is Descartes' version of the ontological argument. God's existence is one of his perfections: so a perfect Being must exist.

Of course there are objections to Descartes' taking of the high road through God to certainty. There are numerous philosophical objections to using 'existence' as standing for some kind of perfection. This seems to be a hangover from scholastic philosophy. Then again, the idea that a less perfect cause cannot produce a more perfect effect seems to us shaky, to put it no more strongly. Moreover, the notion that there is some kind of inner idea of a perfect God may be thought to be culture bound.

God, being perfect, cannot be a deceiver, so we can rely on the existence of the outside world. And we can be assured that provided we proceed deliberately and only accept clear and distinct ideas we can build up a sure system of knowledge.

There are three ways in which Descartes did not set modern philosophy and science on a sound path. First, he was not primarily interested in empirical investigations and had too abstract and mathematical a vision of the outside world. Second, his method was unadventurous and solipsistic. Third, he hoped to avoid uncertainty while at the same time inviting philosophical debate, for instance on the ontological argument. This would seem to have a strange status, if equally acute people disagree as to whether it is valid or not. If it were valid it would bring certainty, but if not, not. And so we would say that pragmatically it is uncertain. Perhaps this is part of what Pascal had in mind when he wrote in his *Pensées* (2, 78, p. 361): 'Descartes useless and uncertain.'

Descartes revolutionized philosophy in various ways. First in starting again freshly with reflection he was not highly dependent on tradition. His anti-authoritarianism was refreshing. Second, he was committed to discovering a method in philosophy, and so is the major progenitor of a systematic epistemology. Third, he set European philosophy along the path to introspection.

MALEBRANCHE AND OCCASIONALISM

Nicolas Malebranche (1638–1715) was considerably influenced by Descartes, and his theory of occasionalism, while serving much wider ends, helped to make sense of the supposed interaction between soul and body opened up by Descartes' work. His most important book, in two volumes, *De la recherche de la vérité,* was inspired by Descartes, though he was also an original thinker. He had a particular vision of God, which harked back to the Islamic occasionalists.

Because he sees necessity in causation, but only regular correspondence, he takes it that bodies do not in fact influence one another, as most people conceive. In fact God is the direct cause of all events, and the idea that one thing causes another is the product of human confusion. So a supposed cause is no more that an occasion for God to produce a particular effect. Now this vision of divine activity was highly useful in explaining how animate bodies work. The trouble is that a spiritual substance cannot affect material bodies. On Malebranche's view there is no need at all to suppose that the spiritual substance affects or is affected by bodily changes.

Malebranche also had a special place in his system for the ideas which are in God. Our minds are passive, and must receive from somewhere general ideas, the concept of extension or matter, and eternal moral truths. They are according to Malebranche given to us by God, in the sense that we can have a vision of such ideas as they exist in the mind of God.

Malebranche's kind of psychophysical parallelism obviously helps to resolve Descartes' problem of how souls affect bodies. By having them not affect bodies the problem is removed. It is in this way that Malebranche adapted Cartesian thought. But in the main the direction of Malebranche's interest is different from that of Descartes. In a sense he was producing an up-to-date version of an older medieval synthesis. It is Neoplatonism modified by occasionalism and given a Cartesian flavor. It was thus attractive to adventuresome traditionalists, and it enjoyed a considerable vogue.

SPINOZA TAKES THE GEOMETRICAL METHOD IN A DIFFERENT DIRECTION

Baruch de Spinoza (1632–77) lived in Amsterdam and made his living as a grinder of optical lenses. But philosophical reflection was his chief joy. Though he was raised a Jew in the Portuguese community in Holland, he was excluded from the community in his twenties, because of his unorthodox view of the scriptures. His most important work the *Tractatus Theologico-Politicus* was published anonymously in 1670. An earlier expounding of Descartes' *Principles of Philosophy* set forth in geometrical form showed something of his debt to Descartes. A collection of posthumous works came out not long after his death and a short treatise on God, man and his well-being was discovered in 1851.

Spinoza was moved by the Cartesian mathematical model; however, the outcome of his system was utterly diverse from that of Descartes. He may have been influenced by Crescas, whom he mentions; and some have seen the imprint of the Kabbalah, which is doubtful, upon his thinking. He was not in his own age a very important thinker, but his rediscovery by Goethe and others gave him a retrospective fame which he still enjoys as one who belongs prominently in the canon of 'rationalist' philosophers, safe between Descartes and Leibniz. In fact, despite the influence of Descartes, he is nearer to Leibniz, in that his whole system is a free-ranging 'sport' in the history of European philosophy.

In fact, he reacted against two kinds of dualism and one kind of brute fact. He rejected the God of Maimonides and of mainstream Jewish belief, primarily because there was something thoroughly inexplicable in the creation. It turned out to be a brute fact, an arbitrary act of will, that God should create the cosmos. On the other hand, attempts to give creation a kind of necessity by a system of emanations did no good in relation to dualism. If spirit and matter differed basically, no amount of emanating gradations in between would properly plaster over the divide. Also, and here he reacted against Descartes, the dualism between mind and body, almost inevitable if you begin in a solipsistic position, leads to unattractive consequences and in particular the lack of intelligibility of the relation between minds and bodies. So Spinoza invented a radical monism.

In one sense it all follows from the definition which Spinoza gives of substance, namely that which is conceived in itself and through itself, so that it does not depend on the conception of another thing from which it must be formed. It does not take long to see that substance must be the cause of itself, and existence belongs to its essence. There cannot be other substances since they would limit it, and substance as unlimited must be infinite. It must also possess infinite attributes, and it must be indivisible and eternal.

Now if you add up a lot of the above epithets you get a typical medieval definition of God – the necessary being who is infinite and so forth. But of course God is outside of the cosmos which he creates. This is impossible from Spinoza's standpoint. If there is to be a nature, that nature has to be God. And this is why he comes to call his monistic substance *Deus sive natura*, that is 'God or Nature'.

One can see this entity under two aspects (and here Spinoza owes something to Descartes), namely as thought and as extension. Under the latter heading Nature is a spatial system which intrinsically contains matter-and-rest. It consists in one vast system. Smaller bodies within the whole are complex and contain particles. Through loss of or addition of particles a body changes, but within a context in which we can think of the loss or addition as internal changes, while the whole remains the same. By analogy the one Nature undergoes a myriad of internal changes but conserves its total of matter-and-rest. Though we think of it as made up of a myriad of bodies this picture in the last resort is mistaken. The cosmos is really a single entity or individual which Spinoza refers to as 'the face of the whole universe' or *facies totius universi*.

Spinoza does not quite explain why amid all the attributes of the *Deus sive natura* it is only thought and extension which we can grasp. Anyway, just as the physical world is a highly complex hierarchy of bodies, made up of tiny packets of energy, so there is a hierarchy of ideas, under the heading of thought, culminating in the infinite idea of God.

Spinoza's theory of knowledge is relevant to his conception of the good life. A human being is subject to various causal processes which physiologically affect him in relation to his central drive for self-preservation. Those that contribute to it give him general pleasure; those that undermine him bring about pain. The causal processes bring about in him ideas, which at this level are confused. The ordinary person is, as it were, buffeted by the processes, even though confusedly he may consider himself an agent. But as bodies interact, humans come to form more general ideas, which are what Spinoza calls adequate ideas, which are necessary and clear, such as those involved in geometry. All bodies have extension, and once this is realized then geometry becomes a crucial part of understanding the world and the wise person is one who replaces the confused, physiological, ideas with adequate ones. These basically are the ideas of Spinoza's whole system. It is easy in this context to understand why it is that Spinoza likes to set forth his system in geometrical fashion. Having clear ideas means also having greater control. It involves therefore an increase in human freedom. In so far as we come to understand the total infinite system we approach the condition of God. Moreover, not only does understanding give us greater control, it replaces the confused ideas which are, or produce in us, passions, and so we simply replace passions with rational desires which conform to the goals of all humans. In short, we are delivered both from the passions and from competitive struggles with others. True freedom resides then in knowledge, and the free person leaves behind her the confusions of ordinary moral discourse, with its illusions of freedom and its use of praise and blame. The free person ultimately will achieve the love of God and become united with God.

This last language sounds of course rather orthodox, no doubt tinged with the language of mysticism. Spinoza sees the Hebrew Bible as interpretable as allegory. The enlightened person cannot accept it literally, though the language was suitable for a relatively primitive people. Human beings, in their generally confused state, need religious discourse. But in the best polity there is freedom and variety of opinion, and false views should not be imposed by the State. So though in some ways Spinoza comes close to Hobbes in thinking that we should hand over our welfare through a social contact, he does not opt as Hobbes did for monarchy as the safest system, but rather for a bourgeois mercantile democracy, with its openness and tolerance, which he himself experienced in Amsterdam.

As I have said above, there is a thoroughly maverick aspect of Spinoza's system. It is a system which hangs together, even though the language of *Deus sive natura* is somewhat misleading (for the God of his philosophy is only in a rather Pickwickian sense divine).

There is a pleasing logic to the whole network of notions which he presents. But it of course begins from that old idea of substance. The hand of Aristotle is visible. What if we were to discard the idea? Again, it is not an easy thing to move from the *Deus sive* just to *natura* alone. A monistic materialism is an obvious invitation. Still, it is a highly original construction. Its puzzlement lies in the *sive*: there is something brutal in the division of aspects between the thought side and the extension side, between the divine and the natural.

Spinoza's influence was slight after his death, but he became fashionable in the nineteenth and twentieth centuries. His notion of the drive for self-preservation had some effect on Freud's *libido*. Russian materialists took him up, and together with Hegel he became a popular philosopher during the early years of the Soviet Revolution, being seen as a materialist before Marx. His pantheism or supposed pantheism appealed to the German Romantics.

THOMAS HOBBES: FROM POLITICS TO PHILOSOPHY

Hobbes had influenced Spinoza somewhat, at least in political thinking. Hobbes (1588–1679) had an extraordinarily long life by the standards of his day. Born near Malmesbury and educated at Oxford, he served the Cavendish family over two major periods. During the Civil War he withdrew for a time to Paris, where he wrote his famous *Leviathan,* and also served as tutor to the future Charles II. After the Restoration of the monarchy he was granted a pension, and had access to the King. His philosophical and controversial writings continued. Even in his eighties he was active, composing among other things an autobiography in Latin verse.

Hobbes' most influential writing was on political philosophy, but his general attitudes to philosophy itself are of interest. First, he wanted rigorously to exclude theology from its purview. Reasoning about God does him no honor, and the proper scope of philosophy is geometry, physics and morals (including politics). He was much impressed with his discovery of geometry, both Euclidean and Cartesian, when he was first in Paris. He considered therefore that a great part of philosophy had to do with behavior of bodies as extended things. Indeed for all practical purposes he was a materialist. Sometimes his remarks about God, whom he did not deny, though some considered him to be an atheist, were ambiguous. But even there, he wrote at one point that God is a pure and simple corporeal spirit. This meant that he regarded spirit as a most ethereal sort of fluid – something like the Indian notion of the subtle body. As for God, we can know that he exists, but we cannot say anything about him seriously on the basis of reason. Ultimately it is for the sovereign in a State to declare the attributes of God: the sovereign after all has the contract for keeping the peace in his realm, and agreement among his subjects in matters of religion is important in this connection.

Hobbes was a nominalist, and saw no merit in the idea of a universal concept or idea. Rather, we wield universal names for sets of individual things which resemble one another. He liked the rationalist idea of science and indeed more generally philosophy as a deductive system: such deductions begin with definitions, in which somewhat arbitrarily we assign precise meanings to basic names. But he was also an empiricist, of a sort. Science he considered to be based on sense-experience, yet on the other hand he thought that secondary qualities, such as sounds, are caused in the head by motions of bodies and do not inhere in bodies themselves. But he was not unduly worried by the epistemological consequences of this position. For Hobbes the investigation of causation boiled down to that of motions of bodies. This applies even to psychology, so that pleasure is nothing but motion about the heart, as he said, as conception is nothing but motion in the head. (But he was a bit traditional: something which is at rest will always be so unless it is moved by some other body; and following Descartes he excluded the void and action at a distance.)

His materialism enabled Thomas Hobbes to take a dispassionate view of politics. This he considered from the perspective of human nature, as he understood it. Thus, roughly speaking, all humans are equal, in that a weakness can be compensated for by some strength elsewhere, so that humans do not back away from competition with others on the grounds that they are not equal to it.

Each person struggles for his own conservation. But humans also worry about self-esteem, so conflict arises between them out of competition, mutual mistrust and the desire for glory. This leads to conflict, either actual or feared – the war of all against all. Unless something is done about it, the life of the human is 'solitary, poor, nasty, brutish and short'. In this primordial state of war there is no law and without law no justice, and without that no morals. Morals have to await civilization, namely a reordering imposed on this basic state of struggle. Hobbes thought he detected this state in contemporary accounts of the American Indians. From this we can judge that he considered his account to be a historical one, not just a theoretically postulated basic scenario to guide his development of political philosophy.

Though the basic passions for self-preservation and self-esteem incline humans to war, other passions have a countervailing effect – the fear of death, the desire for ample goods, and so forth. So reason inclines people to do something about the basic state of war. Enlightened egoism suggests the forming of a government which will regulate civil society. Various laws of nature impel humans: that they will seek peace; be willing to sacrifice a certain amount of liberty against others – each as much as he would allow against himself; and hold to contracts which are made (or contracts become worthless). In making covenants with one another people constitute themselves into a commonwealth in which their power is assigned to a sovereign. Or, alternatively, a sovereign simply takes over this power by acquisition. In either case the commonwealth is formed out of fear, a basic feeling in politics. Once formed it becomes, so to speak, a mortal god, Leviathan.

The sovereign would not have to be a monarch. Various options, clearly enough, are possible. But on the whole he considered monarchy the best option, because the sovereign is then undivided and is more likely to be strong and rule with sagacity. But the option is open, and the best system would be a matter for empirical determination. In the context in which he wrote, his book was an envious defense of the English monarchy, which had been temporarily overthrown because of the Civil War. One can also look on Hobbes' work as a stage in the development of the sovereign national State, which was to become the standard model through which the world is now governed. Religion in his view should be entirely subordinated to the sovereign, and he attacked the Papacy with great vitriol, describing it as 'the ghost of the deceased Roman Empire'. That empire was being replaced by national polities.

Indeed, it is worth remarking that social contract theorists are remarkably silent about who is to do the contracting, as though it is obvious which body of human beings are getting together to determine their organization. Part of the reason is that the idea is abstract and theoretical – meant to give a formal account of the logic of political power. The other reason is that intuitively the reader is supposed to think of a people, and a people is an emerging nation.

Hobbes' whole work was challenging to this contemporaries – on the State, on free will (which he denied), on language, the nature of science, on official religion, and so on. He was a major figure in the evolution of British philosophy and the empiricist outlook. But he also had his connection with the French, and especially the Cartesian movement.

LORD HERBERT OF CHERBURY AND DEISM

A contemporary of Hobbes, Lord Herbert of Cherbury (1583–1648) was the author of a number of works including *De veritate* (*On Truth*), *De causis errorum* (*On the Causes of Errors*) and *De religione gentilium* (*On the Religion of the Gentiles*). He is commonly called the father of deism, that is to say of a general belief in God who is not, however, the God of revelation or one with whom believers have an intense personal relationship. Deism is thus distinguished from what is generally called 'theism'. Eventually his thesis attracted widespread opposition and debate. He complements in certain ways Hobbes' rather offhand treatment of revealed religion. He is also important for his notion, later criticized by Locke, that the human mind is not a *tabula rasa* but has imprinted on it or implanted in it certain universal and necessary conceptions or Common Notions. These he took to be universal and necessary.

In saying that there are such Notions he does not exclude that some human beings might not acknowledge them, for instance because of mental obtuseness or madness. In the religious sphere, they are as follows – first, that there is one supreme God; second, that he ought to be worshiped; third, that the chief part of worship is constituted by the practice of virtue and piety; fourth, that we ought to feel sorry about our sins and repent of them; fifth, that providence will assign punishments and rewards for our actions both in this life and the next.

This, then, is natural religion (this idea came to have increased vogue in Europe) as distinguished from revealed religion. Herbert did not dispense with the latter completely, since he could accept the historical aspect of the Bible. Cherbury was cheered at his discovery of the five principles, which could be defended in the then state of knowledge of religions in the world, but as is obvious from our treatment of Asian civilizations his claim that these ideas are universal is worthless. But the concept of *a priori* notions was an important one in later philosophical history, notably of course in the work of Kant, while deism became quite fashionable in the eighteenth century, and was a vital ingredient in the formation of the values of the American revolution and the Constitution of the United States. Deism there came to be a sort of civil religion which stood above the particular revealed religions, and stressed the importance of toleration. Cherbury's idea of Common Notions stands over against the empiricist tradition. In this connection, we ought to glance at one or two of the school known as the Cambridge Platonists of the same period.

RALPH CUDWORTH AND SOME OTHER CAMBRIDGE PLATONISTS

Some of the thinking of that group of idealist thinkers commonly known as the Cambridge Platonists was highly critical of Hobbesian materialism, as also of Cartesian mechanistic dualism. The case for calling the group Platonist is open to question, but they stressed the contemplative side of religion, and saw knowledge as relating to eternal truths, both Neoplatonic themes.

The most prominent of the group was Ralph Cudworth (1617–88), Head of Clare College for a while and later of Christ's College. His chief work was *The True Intellectual System of the Universe* (1678). His approach to the problem of criticizing materialism and hylozoism was surprising. He invoked atomic theory against them. According to his account, matter consists in nothing but inert atoms, and in this case this proves a sort of dualism. For colors as perceived are not just atomic pressures. Moreover, the mind is experienced as active. For these reasons atomic theory, by its very inability to account for mental objects and activities, proves the separate existence of minds. Atomism also helps to dispose of Aristotle and scholastic applications of his philosophy, which could easily descend into hylozoism. As an extra quirk, Cudworth believed that atomism was originally theistic (he would have been at home in India, with Vaiśeṣika).

Knowledge is not to be gained through sensations, but comes when the mind grasps eternal truths. Here he uses a Cartesian criterion – a person knows she has achieved such a grasp when she has clear and distinct ideas. Another Platonist motif is the idea that the universe consists in a spiritual hierarchy: from this point of view Cartesian dualism involves too brutal a fissure in the fabric of the universe.

The Cambridge Platonists as a group were strongly opposed to Calvinism, which they saw as making God's decrees arbitrary. The rational person is governed by his conscience, and reason itself is the voice of God within us, as Benjamin Whichcote (1609–83) argued. Moreover, Calvinists were too keen on imposing their doctrines on the Church: the Cambridge Platonists stood for a much more tolerant and open attitude. They were critical too of Hobbes, who shared with the Calvinists the error of identifying morality with God's will, not seeing that God chooses what is right because it is right. Their morality – having a contemplative flavor – was that of love, and at its highest it was observed out of the love of God. It was not a matter of stern duty. In general they were against the more empiricist philosophers, and represent an interesting, rather old-fashioned, strain in British thought, which as we know came to be dominated by empiricism. One reason for this dominance was the clarity and power of the ideas of John Locke. We shall proceed to delineate his worldview and then go back to the rationalists in the shape of Leibniz, since Leibniz was critical of Locke's *Essay*.

JOHN LOCKE: EMPIRICISM AND LIBERALISM

John Locke (1632–1704) was educated at Oxford and taught there for a while. He studied philosophy but also took a degree in medicine. He served as secretary to a diplomatic mission to the Elector of Brandenburg, and held posts under Lord Shaftesbury, the Lord Chancellor. He lived abroad for a while, and returned after William of Orange came to the throne in 1688. He held minor offices in London, and eventually died in 1704. His main writings were his *Essay Concerning Human Understanding* and *Two Treatises of Civil Government* (1690), *Some Thoughts Concerning Education* (1693), *The Reasonableness of Christianity* (1695) and from 1689 his various *Letters on Toleration*.

Locke's *Essay* is an ambitious and wide-ranging attempt to establish an empiricist epistemology. To prepare the way for this he set forth in the first book (or major section) of the *Essay* to attack the doctrine of innate ideas, which was to be found implicitly in Descartes, in Lord Herbert of Cherbury and other writers. Every idea (by which Locke meant an object of awareness) springs from experience. Innate ideas or principles can be argued against on a number of counts – the failure of all human to agree on what they are; the fact that we have natural faculties of reasoning not being a basis for belief in particular innate mental contents; the great variety of moral views in the history of the human race, etc. Some ideas become, it is true, established in the minds of children very early, but they are the product of early experience, such as the difference in taste of bitter and sweet.

Our knowledge, then, is not in any way innate, but derives from sensation, on the one hand, and reflection, on the other. Some ideas are simple, such as colors, and others derive from more than one sense, such as number and shape. Others are the product of reflection, such as the idea of thinking. Other ideas again derive from both sensation and reflection, such as existence and power. In such ways Locke rather painstakingly built up a whole empiricist structure. In one respect he made a most fateful distinction, between primary and secondary qualities. The former are inseparable from the body which produces the ideas: such qualities as solidity, extension, figure, motion or rest, and number. Secondary qualities, on the other hand, are powers to produce various sensations in us, such as color and taste. He also makes mention of tertiary qualities, namely the powers in bodies to produce changes in other bodies. But the primary–secondary distinction is the more crucial. Locke evidently thought that the new science propounded by Descartes, Galileo and others required the distinction. In making his distinction Locke affirms his realism, but was it justified? To say that solidity and extension really belong to bodies, but that there is no resemblance between secondary ideas and the bodies which give rise to them was to raise the Berkeleian question as to how we can compare our ideas of solidity or color to bodies themselves as if we can get behind our sensations and see bodies as they are in themselves. And Locke holds that we also conceive as the support for clusters of qualities something 'we know now what' which serves as the support for such accidents (that is, qualities). So we have a whole array of substances or unknown Xs which lie behind the perceptible world.

Locke's realism occasions quite a lot of trouble, for he ends up with two or three ideas which seem to lie beyond the empirical: that of substance; that of power; and that of causation. He also devoted some discussion to other rather troublesome topics (from the standpoint of his commonsense rendition of empiricism), such as identity.

There was also some qualification of his empirical approach in his theory of knowledge, in that he allowed as important for the very idea of demonstration the central part played by intuition: in this the mind sees the agreement or otherwise of two ideas immediately. Also he thought that there was something between bare probability and the certainty of demonstration and intuition, namely sensitive knowledge, concerning the existence of finite beings outside ourselves. He claimed in this the support of common sense.

Locke thought that we could know that God exists, not by some perceptual means, but on the basis of a demonstration, which in fact is a variation on the cosmological argument. In addition we can have faith in (though no demonstration of) the truths of revelation, provided they do not run contrary to reason.

Locke advocated, within certain bounds, toleration in matters of religion. This is in part because you cannot force belief: all you do in trying it on is to breed hypocrisy. Torture is no way for the Church to attempt to enforce conformity, and it is a mark of the true Church that it is tolerant. The only means of conversion should be by persuasion. However, Locke did not extend his tolerance as far as atheists, as he thought that they would not think that promises and contracts are binding. Similarly, it is impossible to tolerate those whose very religion puts them at the service of a foreign power. Here we observe Locke denying rights to Catholics.

These are in effect limitations upon his political theory, to which we now turn. Like Hobbes he postulates a state of nature and a social contract. But his picture of the original human position is very different from that of Hobbes. In the state of nature human beings have an understanding of the moral law which arises quite independently of the State. Every person has certain rights and duties which are, so to speak, 'presocial'. Thus every person has the right to defend herself, and to freedom. Moreover, in a broad sense a person has a right to property: this broad sense is connected with the idea of labor. Human beings create possessions by mixing their labor with things. By mixing the labor of picking apples with those apples, a person acquires a title to them.

But though such rights may be in general recognized, it does not in fact follow that they will actually be respected. Inequalities and injustices are possible and typically actual in a presocial condition. And so it is that the social contract comes about. Humans freely give up their legislative and executive rights to one another, in order to create a sovereign power. But this is a very different situation from that envisaged by Hobbes. Sovereignty ultimately resides in the people, and issues in general are to be decided by majority vote. If a sovereign turns against the people and so becomes a tyrant, then the people have the right of rebellion. All this constitutes a scheme for the justification of democratic forms of government.

Locke's general political theory became a major basis for the justification of democratic government, even if he also produced an argument for slavery, of a rather feeble kind. He saw slaves as people who had been wrongfully at war, so that those who captured them had a right to keep them in captivity. In general he was a major figure in the development of British empiricism and equally in the evolution of democratic political theory, despite his defects (which may be pinpointed as substances and slaves). Locke's endorsement of common sense is problematic, seeing that as science advanced it drew further and further away from our ordinary ways of thinking and talking.

LEIBNIZ AND THE IDEA OF UNIVERSAL HARMONY

Gottfried Wilhelm Leibniz (1646–1716) was a person of dazzling achievements, among them the discovery of the infinitesimal calculus in 1676. He studied philosophy at Leipzig, mathematics at Jena and law at Altdorf. He was for a while in Paris, and was in the service of the House of Hanover, for whom he compiled a history of the Brunswick family. In 1700 he became founding president of what was to become the Prussian Academy of Sciences. He took a strong interest, mainly abortive, in trying to reunite Christian denominations, and argued for a league of Christian States. But in the last few years of his life he somewhat fell from fame and died neglected. His systematic philosophy can be discovered in a wide variety of documents and correspondences, including his *Discourse on Metaphysics* (1686), the *New System of Nature and of the Interaction of Substances* (1695) and the *Monadology* (1714), as well as in his one large book, the *Theodicy* (1710).

The picture which Leibniz paints of the cosmos is a startling one. The whole universe is a system of enclosed or, as Leibniz says, windowless monads, each of which reflects the state of every other, according to a pre-established harmony. This radical pluralism is highly different from the monism of Spinoza (whom Leibniz visited in Holland on his way back from Paris to Germany). The underlying motivation for Leibniz to have painted this picture is to render, in effect, all truths as necessary. This is a paradox, since he sets out by distinguishing necessary truths or truths of reason and truths of fact. The former are such that they cannot be denied without contradiction. For Leibniz every proposition is of subject–predicate form, so the predicate of a truth of reason is contained in its subject. But truths of fact are not like this. You can deny them without contradiction. But still on a deeper analysis they have their own necessity. First of all let us note that all the truths of fact in a given universe are mutually reflective, and they together define this universe. But God must have a sufficient reason for creating this universe and not some other. Now it is certain that God will choose the best cosmos, though he does so freely (there is some tension of course in Leibniz's position here).

The inner necessity, not available to finite knowledge, of all truths of fact helps to explain Leibniz's monadology. Each ultimate entity in the cosmos has to contain within itself the predicates that describe its history. The only predicate which has no necessity, at least at first sight, is existence. Its existence is to the finite observer contingent. But on the other hand, God has to have sufficient reason to bring this cosmos, which contains each monad, into existence, because it is for the best. So from Leibniz's perspective there is a kind of necessity in everything that does exist. All this seems to flow from the desire to model all truths on necessary truths and to treat the latter as those which cannot be denied without offending against the law of contradiction. It may also be noted that Leibniz operates with the notion of substances, which had such a strong grip on the Western philosophical tradition from Aristotle and beyond.

The picture of a vast number of monads which do not interact but yet reflect individually the total state of the universe is one which needs God to act as the creator who pre-establishes the harmony and actually creates this universe. The implication has to be that this is the best of all possible worlds – an optimistic point of view which called down much criticism upon Leibniz. He pondered the issue in some depth, and devoted his *Theodicy* to supplying a defense. First of all, metaphysical evil, which must attach inherently to the creature, is essentially a privation. God has to produce limited beings, and they inherently suffer from their limitations. So any cosmos which God produces must contain such metaphysical evil. Consequently the fact that defects exist in our world does not show that it is not the best of all possible worlds. There is of course a problem which he has to resolve about human freedom. For on his view all the predicates of a subject are contained in it, so that the moral actions of a given individual should be deducible by the divine mind from the fact that that individual exists. Now of course it is God that decides that the individual will come into existence. Does this not preclude real freedom in the individual? Given that Caesar is going to exist, then it is necessary that he crosses the Rubicon. Whether, however, there is room here for any freedom is open to debate.

The pluralism expressed in the innumerable monads of Leibniz is a reflection in another tradition of the Dvaita position in India. It also echoes the net of Indra and the Huayan vision. It is commonly categorized as a 'traditionalist' position – but one cannot help but feel that its attractions lie in more than logic. It has a certain fascinating beauty, and has some interesting spin-offs. One is the motion that space and time are phenomenal, that is, based in reality, but yet subjective – a view which influenced Kant. The vision of harmony enables Leibniz to look upon moral spirits as constituting a kind of heavenly city; and since no finite monad can attain to full knowledge of the cosmos, even in the life after death the beatific vision is not complete, so that souls can progress indefinitely towards perfection.

Both Leibniz and Spinoza in their different ways produced maverick visions: it is ironic that these pictures of the world should be dubbed 'rationalist', except in so far as they represent reason run riot, each taking a different path of deduction from root pieces of reasoning. Leibniz's extravagant cosmology did have an important influence on Kant, however, in his evolution of the contrast between analytic and synthetic judgments, and, as we have just noted, in his heavenly gradualism, as we might call it.

SOME ETHICAL THEORIES IN BRITAIN

Locke began the utilitarian tradition which ultimately saw its apogee in the nineteenth century. Since he defined good as the object of desire, it seemed reasonable to see it also as that which is liable to produce pleasure and reduce pain, since these evidently are desirable consequences. But there came to be greater interest among a number of writers in moral psychology, notably Anthony Ashley, Third Earl of Shaftesbury (1671–1713), Francis Hutcheson (1694–1747) and Joseph Butler, Bishop of Durham (1692–1752). Shaftesbury did not deny the obvious self-interest which humans possessed, which nature compels people to pursue. But there is also an outward-looking benevolence and altruism, because humans are social animals. They have a perception of what is normally admirable which is analogous to esthetic judgments. There is a natural beauty of figures, and likewise a natural beauty of actions. An inward eye sees the amiable and the admirable as well as the odious and despicable. Shaftesbury had a big influence on Hutcheson and through him Hume, Adam Smith, Voltaire and Herder. But he was amusingly criticized by Bernard de Mandeville (1670–1733) in *The Fable of the Bees or Private Vices Public Benefits,* published first in 1714 with a second edition nine years later. He considered there was no real evidence that humans have natural altruistic feelings, and plenty of evidence against. Anyway, a virtuous society would stagnate. It is because people seek their own enjoyment and demand luxuries, thus promoting the circulation of capital and the invention of new machines and so forth, that society flourishes. Mandeville's ideas prefigured some later views about the development of capitalism.

Francis Hutcheson was Professor of Moral Philosophy in Glasgow and an important figure in a chain of famous Scots who created what is sometimes called 'the Scottish Enlightenment' (including such men as David Hume, Thomas Reid and Adam Smith – indeed it could be argued that Scotland was at the core of the development of the industrial revolution, with Smith's foundation of economics and James Watt's invention of the steam engine). He postulated a moral sense which is there independently of education or custom, though it can be strengthened by these forces, as well as by good example. Primarily it sees benevolence as giving pleasure, but it also includes the sense of sympathy, honor and decorum. Hutcheson anticipates utilitarianism in saying that in judging virtue we might consider the amount of happiness in others it produces – the greatest happiness for the greatest numbers.

Hutcheson's emphasis on benevolence and his incipient utilitarianism were criticized by Butler, who saw dangers in subordinating justice to a headcount of happiness. He thought that cool self-love was compatible with altruism, but saw conscience as the higher arbiter of morality. Other important thinkers included Adam Smith (1723–90) whose *Wealth of Nations* not only laid the basis for capitalist thinking, but used Mandeville's ideas in the development of economic theory. He emphasized the importance of an impartial view in looking at our own and others' conduct. Richard Price (1723–91) argued against consequentialism and postulated an intellectual intuition which we possess and which can perceive self-evident moral principles.

The various strands of moral thinking issued in two differing streams – one of which had as its fountain head Immanuel Kant, and the other issuing in nineteenth-century utilitarianism.

THE PROGRESS OF BRITISH EMPIRICISM, ESPECIALLY IN BERKELEY AND HUME

By the second part of the eighteenth century the world had changed. The discoveries by Robert Boyle (1626–91) and Isaac Newton (1642–1727) and others had revolutionized science, setting it apart from the main stream of philosophy but at the same time more or less wiping out the earlier Aristotelian framework, as well as theories such as those of Descartes. The early beginnings of the capitalist era, helped by the Protestant ethos, were giving thinkers a greater interest in the management of human affairs on a new basis. Nationalism, stimulated by the increased use of vernacular languages, leaving Latin behind, caused tensions against the old feudalism and absolute monarchies. Religion was fragmented, and deism was fashionable among intellectuals. In the surge towards a new intellectual framework for Europe, a significant role was played by the further development, beyond Locke, of British empiricism (sometimes misleadingly called English empiricism – Locke was English, but Berkeley Irish and Hume Scottish).

George Berkeley (1685–1753) was educated at, and later taught at, Trinity College, Dublin. In 1728 he set out to found a college in America, in Bermuda or as he later thought, in Rhode Island. The plans came to naught. For a while he was Bishop of Cloyne, and later settled in Oxford, where he died. His most important philosophical writings were *A Treatise Concerning the Principles of Human Knowledge* (1710) and *Three Dialogues between Hylas and Philonous* (1713). His *An Essay Towards a New Theory of Vision* (1709) which analyzed our judgments on the distance, position and size of objects laid some of the foundations of his idealism (or immaterialism).

Negatively, what Berkeley had to say was profoundly important. The glaring weakness of Locke's system was his belief in substances which lie unseen and unseeable behind the sensations, etc., which present themselves as arising from the substances. This Berkeley attacked, as well as the questionable distinction between primary and secondary qualities. He considered himself to be on the side of common sense.

If we wipe out secret substances behind what we perceive, we are left with perceiving as the essence of perceptible objects. *Esse est percipi:* to be is to be perceived. But what of continuities? The rosemary bush outside my window I cannot now see but I can go out and see it: it is still there. Berkeley had to get God into the act to safeguard continuities in the 'outside' world. God sees my rosemary bush when I am not looking at it.

This idea of a Mind (a divine Mind) to guarantee the objective existence of the world was a forerunner of some Absolute Idealist notions in the nineteenth century. Berkeley thought it conduced to piety, in that our perceptions become so to speak a divine visual (and tactile, etc.) language and a common reminder of the presence of God. But it was viewed as a peculiar paradox by many of his contemporaries. Berkeley showed that Locke's substances were an Achilles' heel of his empiricism. Kant's eventual proposed solution of the problem, in the shape of things-in-themselves, turned out to be no better, and the collapse of the notion led into such systems as those of Hegel and Schopenhauer.

David Hume (1711–76) was born in Edinburgh, but spent parts of his life in France. On his first visit he published his *A Treatise of Human Nature* (1738–40), later reshaped as *An Enquiry Concerning Human Understanding* (1751), and in *An Enquiry Concerning the Principles of Morals* (1751). A successful book was *Political Discourses* (1752). From 1752 he was librarian to the Faculty of Advocates in Edinburgh and during the next few years he wrote widely successful historical books on England, from Caesar to Charles I. In France, at the embassy, from 1763, he encountered the French Encyclopedists. His *Dialogues Concerning Natural Religion* came out after his death.

Hume's *Treatise* sets forth the ambitious attempt to create what may be called a scientific psychology. It was based on a strictly empirical model. Ideas are less vivid copies of impressions or sense-impressions as we might call them. All simple ideas come from impressions. General ideas are merely a disposition to bring up similar ideas. We can be certain about immediate impressions, and also about some relations of ideas, as in geometry, but most of our beliefs go well beyond current impressions and typically relate to what is causally connected to impressions. It is at this point that Hume's skepticism becomes prominent. The trouble with causation is that it is usually interpreted as involving some necessity. If A brings about B then A has to be prior and it has to be contiguous. Both these properties are accessible to our senses. But the third ingredient, necessity, is not. So all we are left with is a customary expectation that whenever we get A we will get B. Moreover, though we think that every event has a cause, there is no contradiction in denying this, just as there is no contradiction in denying that the sun will rise tomorrow. So necessity boils down to custom, and the regularity of the empirical world rests on feeble foundations. Somewhat similar arguments apply to the notion of identity through time. A thing supposedly persists in between the times we are perceiving it. This is not empirically justifiable, but we feign an identity because of the natural belief in it. The existence of persisting bodies is something which we imaginatively construct, but is not finally rational.

Hume not only cast a skeptical eye upon causes and persisting things but also upon spiritual substances or selves. He found by introspection nothing but a passing and shifting kaleidoscope of impressions and ideas, and no separate self. When I look inside myself all I stumble upon is some perception or other and nothing but a perception. I never catch *myself* as a separate entity. So though there is a strong natural inclination to look upon the self as something simple and unitary it is not a belief which is at bottom justified.

So Hume's general position is one which, though it begins from a more or less scientific approach to psychology, provokes skepticism: custom has to supplant reason. This in turn is disturbing for those who want a more solid basis for scientific inquiry. Underneath the fine edifice of Newtonian mechanics there lies a philosophical swamp. No wonder Hume roused Kant from his dogmatic slumber. The net effect of Hume's empiricism was deep unease.

Even his famous conclusion to his *Enquiry* (12, 3, 132, p. 165) might be clouded by his previous arguments:

If we take in hand any volume, of divinity or school metaphysics, for instance, let us ask 'Does it contain any abstract reasoning concerning quantity or number? No. Does it contain any experimental reasoning concerning matter of fact and existence? No. Commit it then to the flames: for it can contain nothing but sophistry and illusion.'

Hume was more particularly skeptical, namely about religion, in his *Dialogues* and his famous essay 'On Miracles'. In the former he showed what he had already argued elsewhere, that no *a priori* argument for God's existence would work. We must proceed by analogy from effect (the universe) to cause. But the closer the analogy, the more anthropomorphic the God, while actually the universe has no greater an analogy to a machine than to a vegetable. Moreover, why not postulate many gods rather than one? The conclusion at best is that the universe has cause which has some remote analogy to human intelligence. Moreover, since we proceed back from the universe to its supposed cause, we can get nothing further out of the hypothesis by reversing the direction. We can infer nothing which we do not know already, so the hypothesis of a divine intelligence is in effect empty. As for miracles, they are by definition breaches of laws of nature. To believe one you have to go against a huge weight of evidence. In view of the record of religious deceptions and of the fact that miracles occur in contradictory religions, it is always the presumption that they did not happen. In his *The Natural History of Religion,* Hume traces back the roots of religion to the fear of death, the desire for security and the tendency to personify things. So if Hume had a religion it was a faint one. The Christian story seems to have been, for him, superstition.

In ethics, Hume held a subjectivist position. It is true that we can reasonably and objectively calculate the utility of actions, but in the end moral judgments express sentiments. Fortunately agreement is generally possible because of the pleasure and approbation we tend to feel in contemplating actions directed towards the well-being of others.

Hume's position was responded to principally by the Scottish philosophers of common sense, above all by Thomas Reid (1710–96), Professor at the University of Glasgow. His *Inquiry into the Human Mind* (1764) saw Hume as having produced a clear refutation of Locke by what was a *reductio ad absurdum* of the skeptical position. Reid considered that common sense could yield some fundamental principles such as that every event has a cause and that memory is on the whole reliable, which stand up to any arguments that can be brought against them: in regard to perception, he believed in direct realism. Dugald Stewart (1753–1828) restated Reid's position, and attempted to show that those who reject the above principles in practice make use of them (we may compare the Indian argument that those who are skeptical about causation nevertheless know how to start a fire).

THE FRENCH *ENCYCLOPÉDIE* – HELPING THE ENLIGHTENMENT

The creation of the French *Encyclopédie* in the middle of the eighteenth century was a major publishing event, and brought together a number of vital philosophers, primarily under the leadership of Denis Diderot (1713–84), and including Holbach, Rousseau and Voltaire among others (we shall come to them shortly). Because of its freethinking and challenging character the publication of the *Encyclopédie* was suspended in 1759, but eventually was finished in 1772, in seventeen volumes of letterpress and a further eleven of plates.

Diderot was a most interesting materialist. He saw the universe as matter in motion, which was inherent in it. It was atomic in structure, and sensitive. He also considered higher organisms as acquiring properties, rather like a swarm of bees which functions like a single organism: the unity of the organism in effect derives from the life of the whole. Thought is a property of the brain.

The *Encyclopédie* was deliberately created in a manner designed to stir up the *ancien regime*. Diderot boldly proclaimed that sovereignty rests with the people, and in various ways stated principles upon which the revolution was to be based.

Paul-Henri Thiry, Baron d'Holbach (1723–89) was much more polemical than Diderot. His atheistic materialism was stated in his *Système de la nature* (1770). Though his position was cruder than Diderot's he was nevertheless a staunch believer in freedom of thought and of the press, the separation of Church and State, and constitutionalism. He described his own political outlook as ethocratic, in which the State nurtures the virtues through which people help one another. If the people are unhappy they have the right to overthrow the rulers, since the social contract is based on the mutual usefulness of individuals and the State, and the State is a means, not an end.

François-Marie Arquet de Voltaire (1694–1778) was a passionate and gifted critic of intolerance and of the outmoded institutions of the *ancien regime*. But his plans for tolerance were not anti-religious, since he proclaimed himself a theist (though most classified him as a sort of deist). His awe before the Divine in a vast universe was tempered by the thought that God is not benevolent – and indeed his theism was considerably out of accord with the Christian revelation and the Church. He was appalled by the cruelty of the Inquisition, the backwardness of the Church and the disaster of the close alliance between Church and State. He was a powerful campaigner for the reform of the law, the abolition of torture and so forth: many of these ideas were incorporated in the Declaration of the Rights of Man in 1789.

Jean-Jacques Rousseau (1712–78) gave eloquent expression to the idea of an idealized nature, partly as a means of criticizing existing society. The savage knows how to live with his own needs and is spontaneous in his expression of self-love. This is very different from the false *amour-propre* that modern – and especially the larger – societies inculcate. Rousseau's views on education, expressed in *Emile,* stress the natural progress of the human heart, towards a moral life in society in union with fellow-humans. Rousseau in his *Contrat social* introduced the idea that in civil society humans achieve freedom through the total alienation of each associate with all his rights to the community. He will obey the general will, and will thereby achieve true freedom by obeying a law which he has laid upon himself. In this Rousseau prepared the way, unwittingly, for nationalism and totalitarianism. It would prove easy to manipulate the notion of the general will.

Many of the ideas of the *Encyclopédie* were to explode refreshingly on the scene during the French Revolution. They had their influence too on the earlier American revolution and the formation of the United States Constitution. They also influenced Germany. If the eighteenth century was the great period of British philosophy and of French thought, it was more a period of preparation in Germany, with the refounding of the Berlin Academy by Frederick the Great in 1750, and the significant creation of the University of Göttingen, destined to be an important center of the German Enlightenment, in 1737. French ideas had a considerable impact in Germany, and to a lesser extent British ones, partly through Gotthold Ephraim Lessing (1729–81) and English connections with Göttingen. It was a time of remarkable cultural stimulus, which was to have its philosophical culmination in Germany's most powerful philosopher, Immanuel Kant. Here we come to a watershed, since weaknesses in Kant's general worldview prepared the way for the rather different idealist movement of the nineteenth century and the move into romanticism. Part of Kant's influence lay in the fact that he was very much alive, through Hume, to the threat posed to knowledge and to Newtonian science in particular, by empiricism, while at the same time he was able to make good use of elements drawn from the rationalist tradition. While he was concerned to construct a worldview which had a place for science, morals and religion, he also wished to solve the epistemological problems posed by the subjective starting point of Descartes and the empiricism of Hume. Meanwhile, let us note briefly some developments in religion.

LESSING, MENDELSSOHN AND OTHERS

The increased interest in history in the eighteenth century had its philosophical consequences. The deist Hermann Samuel Reimarus (1694–1768) had begun in effect that search which came to be known as the quest of the historical Jesus. He was followed by the influential playwright Lessing (1729–81) who published a pioneer essay called, 'New Hypothesis about the Gospel-writers Regarded as Human Historians', printed in 1784. He was impressed with the untidiness and uncertainty of history, so that it became a poor vehicle for transmitting the necessary truths of reason. He was therefore inclined towards toleration and a liberal deism, which he expressed in his famous play *Nathan der Weise* of 1779, in which the eponymous hero was supposedly based on the figure of his friend Moses Mendelssohn (1729–86). The latter was the first great figure of the Jewish Enlightenment, and argued for an ethical deism which he identified with the mainstream Jewish tradition. He was also a prominent advocate of religious toleration. In his last years he entered into a public debate about Spinoza's pantheism: it was alleged by a mutual friend of Lessing that the latter in his final years had declared himself a Spinozist. This led to a reconsideration of Spinoza, and this had some influence on the great Johann Wolfgang von Goethe (1749–1832). He defended Spinoza passionately, though his own philosophy of nature was more organicist. He believed among other things in primary plants or basic patterns *(Urpflanze)*; and in general in basic phenomena such as the antipathy of light and darkness *(Urphänomena)*. It was a sort of Platonism migrating towards the theory of evolution.

IMMANUEL KANT AND THE CRITICAL PHILOSOPHY

The power and complexity of Kant's thought gave him a nodal position in the evolution of German and more generally Western philosophy. Born in Königsberg in what was then Prussia (after World War II the city was absorbed into the USSR and renamed Kaliningrad) he lived there all his life (1724–1804). From 1770 he occupied the Chair of Logic and Metaphysics at the university of Königsberg. In 1794 he was forbidden to publish more on religion, as his book on the subject had caused turbulence; no controversy ensued, since he complied with the royal order. His metronomic and quiet life was punctuated by a series of major publications – the *Critique of Pure Reason* (1781), the *Critique of Practical Reason* (1790), the *Critique of Judgment* (1790), the *Religion Within the Bounds of Reason Alone* (1793) and the *Metaphysics of Morals* (1797), together with other important works.

Kant, though he did not have firsthand knowledge of Hume's *Treatise,* was aware of his main positions, and this by his own testimony shook him out of his dogmatic slumber. He sought to evolve a critical philosophy which would show the bounds of reason or metaphysics, and at the same time indicate the role of reason in empirical inquiry. There were two scandals. One was that elucidated by Hume: it seemed that belief in universal causation and the like was based merely on custom or psychological expectation, so it looked as if the foundations of science had crumbled; the other scandal was that metaphysicians came up with such wildly differing conclusions, and had such inconclusive arguments for establishing such central claims as that God exists. Kant's critical philosophy could explain why the latter scandal occurred, for it was brought about primarily by reason's trying to operate outside its legitimate sphere, that is in relation to phenomena. And he hoped to solve the Humean scandal by his Copernican revolution.

This Copernican revolution meant giving a dynamic role to the human mind. There were two ingredients to knowledge, one supplied by phenomena and the other by the mind itself. The one sort is given to us through our sense or sensibility *(Sinnlichkeit)* and the other through our understanding *(Verstand)*. Various *a priori* categories (as he called them) are brought to bear upon phenomena. Problems only arise when we play with such concepts beyond their proper bounds, which are set by phenomena. This is why you get contradictions or antinomies from such over-general argument – for instance that the universe is both finite and infinite. Moreover, the fallacious character, according to Kant, of the argument or proofs of God's existence arise from their transphenomenal character. He thought that the cosmological argument, for instance, in arriving at a necessary being, involved of necessity the ontological argument, which is itself not valid because judgments or propositions asserting existence can always be imagined to be false without contradiction. Such judgments are what he called synthetic, and they cannot be analytic.

In the contrast between analytic and synthetic, Kant was following precedents from earlier philosophers. A judgment is of a subject–predicate structure, and either the predicate or its meaning is contained in the subject or it is not. A bachelor is an unmarried person – this is by definition true and an analytic judgment, because the very meaning of bachelor includes the notion that a bachelor is unmarried. On the other hand, bachelors exist in large numbers in New York: this is a synthetic judgment, because neither existing nor living in New York is contained in the idea of being a bachelor. Generally speaking, synthetic judgments can be true or false, while necessary ones have to be true. But Kant's originality here consisted in interposing a category of *synthetic a priori* propositions. What is known prior to all experience is *a priori*. All *a posteriori* propositions are synthetic, but Kant proposed, contrary to the previous tradition, that some synthetic propositions are necessary or *a priori*. For instance the propositions of mathematics are of this type; there are also some synthetic *a priori* truths, such as that events are causally determined according to constant laws – truths that provide the structural basis of physics and the natural sciences.

In addition to the categories there must be rules whereby we connect them to phenomena, and these are called schemata: these are ways in which they are represented through the imagination. Thus if the category of substance is to be applied to perceptions it must be represented as a permanent substratum of change in time. In general, experience is only possible through the representation of a necessary connection of perceptions. Objective experience is also only possible through a synthesis of perceptions which is given through the unity of the self. The contribution of the *a priori* supplied by the human mind is to make science necessarily applicable to the world 'out there'.

It is a correlate of Kant's whole picture of the way understanding works that the attempt to use categories such as that of causation beyond its proper sphere leads to antinomies or mutually contradictory 'proofs'. This means that we cannot show that God is First Cause, for instance. The idea of God, however, may be useful to us as a regulative idea, which functions as a limiting concept always drawing on our research into the indefinite chain of causes in nature. And as we shall see, the idea of God may have a more positive moral use. Another limiting concept which Kant introduced was the correlative 'out there' of phenomena. Thus underlying phenomena are things-in-themselves or *noumena,* so to speak (he sometimes also referred to God and the self as *noumena*). This notion caused a lot of criticism of Kant, and this criticism could be said to have formed a main basis for the idealist developments of German philosophy in the nineteenth century.

If a substantive God disappears from the *Critique of Pure Reason* he comes back again as one of the three postulates of practical reason. Kant had an original approach to questions of moral sense and the like. It was to consider whether the motive of an action or the principle on which I am acting can be generalized without contradiction. If I think it is all right for me to lie under such-and-such circumstances, then we have to consider what would happen if everyone lied. Language would break down. So there is a contradiction in the universalization of the maxim of my action. This yields the notion of what Kant referred to as the categorical imperative, which he formulated in differing ways, such as 'Act as if the maxim of your action were to become through your will a Universal Law of Nature'. There are two points to notice. First, this imperative is categorical. The moral law has no hypothetical character, like 'If you want to make money, go into the law', which would be merely prudential advice. Morality is absolute, but prudence depends on prior inclinations. Second, morality is conceived by Kant as something categorically laid by the individual on himself. He is his own legislator. In other words morality is autonomous, and not heteronomous or laid on us by others. From all this, a certain psychology of morals emerges: the individual, finding his inclinations liable to be overruled by the categorical imperative, develops for it a special reverence.

Certain postulates emerge from considerations of morality as thus described. One is that I am free to obey it: ought implies, that is, presupposes, can. As a self in an unknowable way I am free, poised as it were timelessly above the flow of nature in which every event necessarily has a cause. As a phenomenon I am determined, as noumenon I am free. Second, we have to recognize, for it is a synthetic *a priori* judgment, that virtue should be accompanied by happiness. The perfect match is the *summum bonum.* To make progress to this ideal possible we must therefore postulate the immortality of the soul. This does not, however, mean that we should corrupt our maxims by being virtuous in the hope of a future reward. Third, the match between perfect virtue and happiness can come about only if nature is organized by an intelligent and benevolent being, namely God. So religion becomes a postulate of morals. Kant, in postulating freedom, immortality and God made these the standard subjects of Western philosophy of religion (largely a Protestant pursuit) during the following century. But an Indian might think that karma and rebirth are as much apposite postulates as immortality and God. And the postulate of freedom might be held by some to be contrary to a naturalistic view of human beings. So either determinism in nature is false, or if it is true there must be something wrong with Kant's moral theory. He himself was raised a Pietist, a sort of *bhakti* or Pure Land Protestant. He was obviously greatly influenced by his own tradition. Yet both in the second Critique and in his 1793 book he is far from orthodoxy. He there saw that original sin can be interpreted as the radical evil in human nature which arises from necessary conflicts between the moral imperative and human inclinations. Christ stands as a symbol of the possible perfection of the individual, and the triumph of moral reason. Kant gave a wholly moralistic account of religion. Oddly, he had no place for religious experience. He carved the world up between perception, morality and esthetics. Religion rode on the back of morals.

His third Critique deals with esthetic judgment (including an analysis of the notions of both beauty and the sublime). He also there deals with teleology. He is anxious to avoid the idea that esthetic judgments have any kind of objectivity in case speculative theology based on the teleological argument were to re-arise. But esthetic judgments do claim to be universal. How can this be? The universal side arises not from the application of some concept but in the delight arising from the free play of the understanding and sensibility, which we ascribe as occurring in all humans.

Altogether the edifice of Kant's system is tremendous. His wide-ranging synthesis was greeted on the whole with admiration. At any rate he established himself as the leading German philosopher of his day, perhaps of all time. He towered above his predecessors, and he set in train many fruitful moves in the nineteenth century. He could appeal to philosophers of differing traditions, and could connect with English-speaking debates in particular.

IDEALISM: FICHTE AND SCHELLING ON THE ROAD TO HEGEL

Johann Gottlieb Fichte (1762–1814) was of a poor family in Saxony but through a local nobleman obtained an education, and eventually became Professor of Philosophy at Jena (though he was driven from there in 1799 on suspicion of atheism). At his death he was Rector of the University of Berlin. His most important publication was his *Basis of the Entire Theory of Science* (1794). As well as developing an idealist philosophy he was an important proponent of pan-German nationalism, and a pioneer of socialist thinking. The heart of his interest was morals, but he set this in the context of a kind of absolute realism.

He was impressed with Kant, but saw that his own critique of the master had drastic consequences. He considered that there was an instability at the core of the Kantian worldview, which was the concept of the *ding-an-sich*. If one wanted seriously to tread the path of things one would end up a materialist; if not, then one would end up an idealist. This path he himself took, and criticized Kant for the noumena which in no way, according to Kant's own principles, could give rise to (that is cause) phenomena. They were superfluous, but their removal meant that the explanation of the world lies on the near side of the subject–object distinction. But to explain the world via an ego it is impossible to identify this with the individual. So we call on the notion of an Absolute Ego (later he wrote of an Absolute Being). Such a Being is not God, in that the latter has to be a person and a person is finite. This is why Fichte was attracted to Spinoza, and why he was accused of atheism. But at the heart of the Absolute there lies ethical concern, and reverence for what could for Fichte substitute for God. The Absolute Ego creates the non-ego as the field for its moral activity: however, if both are unlimited they will tend to blot each other out. So there is a third proposition to be affirmed (a synthesis of the prior thesis and antithesis), namely the positing of a divisible non-ego as opposed to a divisible ego. In other words, the Absolute produces finite self-consciousness which arises through its perception of the resistance of the natural world.

Friedrich Wilhelm Joseph von Schelling (1775–1854) was raised in Württemburg and went to Tübingen University where he was close to Hegel and Hölderlin. At 23 he was appointed to a Chair at Jena. Eventually he taught at Berlin and among those who attended his lectures were an unlikely constellation – Kierkegaard, Burckhardt, Engels and Bakunin. In his earliest philosophy, published in 1800 as his *System of Transcendental Idealism,* his ideas were a stepping stone between Fichte and Hegel. His absolute idealism, similar to Fichte's, had a much warmer conclusion, since he saw the philosophy of art as the culmination of his metaphysics. In nature the Absolute partially manifests the fusion of the real and the ideal through the production of organisms, but it is in the free creative world of art that we can find the intuition of the infinite in the finite product of the intelligence. The artist is not, however, thereby a philosopher, since he may not have the self-understanding to appraise the significance of his achievement. Schelling later developed his work in various ways, partly in response to Hegel, who had in effect broken with him when he published his *The Phenomenology of Spirit* in 1807. Schelling was upset by Hegel's criticisms of his philosophy and become envious of Hegel's rise to become Germany's best-known philosopher, having previously not been well known.

Looking back to Kant, we can see the Absolute Idealists as moving in the direction of the 'hither side' of the creative mind. The reason is that the outer side – the objective world as manifested through phenomena – is hitched by somewhat weak ropes, the ropes of the noumena, to reality. Cut those ropes and the result is Absolute Idealism. There could be other criticisms of Kant, of course: his division of spheres to the spheres of the natural world, morals and esthetics might be thought too restrictive. This was a preoccupation of Friedrich Schleiermacher (1768–1834), who delineated the sphere of what he took to be normative religious experience, namely the feeling of absolute dependence. He wished to create a space between metaphysics and morals for religion. To some degree he was following Pascal (1623–62) and was anticipating Kierkegaard, whom we shall come to later as a major critic of Hegel. Most of all, however, he was anticipating the more historically-grounded work of Rudolf Otto's *The Idea of the Holy* (1917).

HEGEL, THE GIANT OF NINETEENTH-CENTURY GERMAN PHILOSOPHY

If Fichte and Schelling are a bit dry in the rather unwieldy maneuvering of absolutes and egos, they prepared the way for Hegel's moving Absolute Idealism, which itself drew together strands from the criticism of Kant, the emergence of romanticism, the greater conclusiveness of history and the flowering of the intellectual life as systematized in the German universities, the leaders in their day. His huge synthesis helped to stimulate intellectual development, especially in the humanities, and of course he was a powerful shaper of Marx, who in turn had a huge effect on the emerging social sciences.

Georg Wilhelm Friedrich Hegel (1770–1831) was born at Stuttgart and educated at Tübingen. He cooperated with Schelling in publishing a critical journal of philosophy, taught at a school in Nuremberg, and in due course (1818) became a Professor of Philosophy in Berlin. His two most important works were the *Phenomenology of Mind* (1807) and *The Encyclopedia of the Philosophical Sciences* (1817). Also important was *Philosophy of Right* (1821); and after his death his writings were edited by a group of friends and came out in eighteen volumes (1832–34). Various other writings have been published since by Dilthey and others.

If Fichte established the Absolute, Hegel gave it motion. The Absolute is the totality, which is a process, and this process tends towards self-understanding. Like Aristotle's God it is self-thinking thought, but unlike Aristotle Hegel saw the totality as tending towards self-understanding. He wants to set this process forth as a dialectical one. And he does this in three parts (Hegel is in love with triads), in regard to logic, nature and spirit *(Geist)*. From a logical point of view we start with the judgment that the Absolute is Being. But pure Being has within itself a kind of instability. In being completely indeterminate it is equivalent to Nothing. In flickering from Being to Nothing and back again it exhibits something which can be understood by a third notion, which rises beyond the first two, but 'takes them up' in a synthesis, namely the notion of Becoming. This helps to illustrate Hegel's dialectical method. He did not think of contradictions as signs of the breakdown of thinking. Rather he saw it as a stimulus to a higher stage, a synthesis, in which the contradiction is taken up and for the time being resolved. He considered that the limited nature of our concepts is bound to give rise to contradictions (there is a reflection here of Kant's antinomies, or contradictory conclusions arrived at when concepts are used beyond the realm of phenomena).

The final and most important part of Hegel's encyclopedic work deals with the philosophy of *Geist* or Spirit (some prefer the translation Mind, and we have so translated it in the title of the *Phenomenology* cited earlier). First of all we have the spirit as a sensing and feeling subject, which is actual as embodied. It is sunk in a kind of slumber, for so far it has not gained consciousness. But now consider it as aware of outer objects: it has, so to speak, something to push against. This inevitably leads to a third phase in which the duality between subject and object is overcome, namely self-consciousness. But the ballet of triads goes on, because the self-conscious individual comes to recognize a universal self-consciousness in which he perceives other selves. Hegel goes on to examine at a higher level the nature of finite spirit, and stresses the importance of free will seen as a combination of the theoretical and the practical spirit.

He remarks, by the way, that the concept of the rational will is something distinctively Western: it does not exist in Africa and the East, he avers, nor did it among Greeks and Romans. It came into the world through Christianity which conferred infinite value on the individual.

The Totality objectifies itself through nature, which as it were provides resistance for finite spirits and so self-consciousness and then a sort of universal consciousness. But this is not any regular doctrine of creation, though Hegel does have a role for religious language as expressing philosophical insights imaginatively. The Spirit objectifies itself through the ethical substance of human life, which Hegel characterizes as the family, civil society and the State. Civil society is something of an abstraction since it is typically or always developed as a State, but it stands for the network of economic relationships and organizations through which individuals mesh with one another. But the State is the highest manifestation of the objective Spirit, in which human beings submit their wills to rules and their feelings to the control of reason. It incorporates individual freedom, but this is nevertheless subordinate to a higher freedom (there is a strong influence from Rousseau here).

It is through the history of States that the World Spirit comes to self-realization. Hegel did not seemingly look forward to a world government. The struggle of States was in its way good in maintaining competition and ethical health. War itself was natural and rational in keeping the dialectic of history in motion. Hegel saw freedom being most fully realized in the Germanic States in which the Reformation played a vital role. The supreme expression of the onward progress was the Prussian State. Hegel's dialectical account of history of course had a profound effect on the young Marx. It also had a big influence on the Christian scholars in the German universities who tried to unravel the question of the historicity of the Bible. It was easy to see Jesus as thesis, Paul as antithesis, Patristic Christianity as synthesis, and so on.

Philosophy itself, properly understood, is the coming into full self-consciousness of the Absolute, so the philosopher has a spearhead role in the whole evolution of the universe as it thinks itself. This lofty view of the role of philosophy, combined with the huge sweep of Hegel's interests and concerns, gave him a formidable inspirational role in the German culture of the period, and stimulated work in varied and manifold directions – in history, in esthetics, in the philosophy of religion and the philosophy of law, to name a few. It was not a lucid system but it was imposing. In carrying forward the story of European philosophy I shall first say a word about Absolute Idealism in the English-speaking context. Then I shall return to the stimulus Hegel gave to Marxism.

THE BRITISH IDEALISTS – GREEN, BOSANQUET, BRADLEY

Various strands went into the fabric of British Idealism. One was from outside of philosophy proper in the work of men such as Coleridge (1772–1834), who had been influenced by Kant and Schelling, and Thomas Carlyle (1795–1881), who like Fichte, had propounded a Great Man theory of history which reflected a similar theme in Hegel. Influential was James Hutchison Stirling's book of 1865 *The Secret of Hegel*. Stirling (1820–1909) considered that Kant led straight to Hegel. Hume epitomized the Enlightenment; Kant fulfilled and transcended Hume; and Hegel was the result. He also gave a Christian slant to Hegel's thinking. T.H. Green (1836–82) was critical of the (for him) rather shallow theories of the empiricists, and gave some vogue to the deeper approach of Hegel. It was chiefly though the work of B. Bosanquet (1848–1923) and F.H. Bradley (1846–1924) which gave British Idealism a position in the forefront of metaphysical thinking.

Bradley spent most of his life at Merton College, Oxford, writing. His most important works were *Ethical Studies* (1876), *Principles of Logic* (1883) and *Appearance and Reality* (1893). While Green and Bosanquet were liberals in politics, Bradley was highly conservative. Consequently he was highly critical of utilitarianism which starts with bare individuals who strictly are a fiction. In a famous essay in the first collection listed above, 'My Station and its Duties', he argued that individuals are logically dependent on communities, which he saw as concrete universals. Similarly he attacked J.S. Mill's theory of induction because it began from atomistic individuals. No inference is possible apart from the universals which link one fact to another. All this he explored in his *Principles of Logic,* but the full metaphysical implications of his position were set forth in his *Appearance and Reality*.

Here he argued that various commonsense ideas are contradictory, such as time, thing and self. The very idea of a relation is self-contradictory and this reduces the whole world of phenomena to mere appearance, since such pervasive ideas as causation depend upon relations. The reason the concept of relation is problematic is simply as follows. If A is related to B, there must be some relation between A, B and the relation (which we shall call R). But the same problem recurs with A, R and B: we have to have S between A and R and R and B and so on *ad infinitum*. The ultimate must be a single reality or Absolute. In the end truth has to consist in coherence, for particulars, which we might try to compare with judgments, will contain contradictions. There is then a kind of natural hierarchy in the world in the sense that some things are more holistic than others (organisms than minerals, for instance, and minds than organisms). Evil and error contribute somehow to the harmonious whole though we can only get a partial vision of this.

Bradley brought out what is implied in Hegel. It is a kind of identity-in-difference theory. From one point of view Reality and appearances are one, and from another they can be differentiated. So both thinkers have similarities to the Vedanta, especially *bhedābhedavāda*. But Bradley, whose vision is more static and unhistorical, is closer than Hegel to that model, because Hegel sets the Absolute in motion in a way that the others do not.

It was the striking critique of the obscurities of Bradley on time and other matters by G.E. Moore (1873–1958) which set in train the commonsense and linguistic philosophy revolution of the twentieth century in England and the United States. G.E. Moore's appeal to common sense was in consonance with the recurrent empiricism of the British philosophical tradition.

Bernard Bosanquet was a social reformer and prolific writer. From 1905 to 1908 he held the Chair of Moral Philosophy in the University of St Andrews in Scotland. His metaphysics was somewhat nearer to Hegel's than Bradley's, but he did not place the high evaluation on history which Hegel did. There are basically only individuals, and the biggest of them all is the Absolute: indeed, this is the only individual in the primary sense. Human individuals are only so in a secondary sense. In his *The Philosophical Theory of the State* he delineates the State as a macrocosm of which individuals are microcosms. But the resemblance is analogical. The State may be involved in war, not possible strictly for an individual: conversely, the latter can commit theft but not the State (it can do such things as confiscate goods, at a differing logical level). The moral ideal is self-mastery, but this can only occur fully within a social milieu. Bosanquet revived Rousseau's conception of the General Will.

It is interesting that both Hegel and Bosanquet should give metaphysical expression to a set of values which at a less exalted level could be called nationalism. There were obvious dangers in the holistic style of political philosophy espoused with varying degrees of liberalism and conservatism by the idealists, from Hegel to Bosanquet. But the model sometimes helped to stimulate thinking in the social sciences, for obvious reasons.

EMPIRICISM AND MATERIALISM IN THE NINETEENTH-CENTURY BRITISH TRADITION

Essentially, the empiricist tradition was revived in Britain by J.S. Mill (1806–73). Since a significant element in his output had to do with utilitarianism it is worth saying a few words on its antecedents. We have noted that Hutcheson had already written of the greatest happiness of the greatest number. Another important writer who used a similar idea was the famous criminologist Cesare Beccaria (1738–94), who in his persuasive and epoch-making *On Crimes and Punishments (Dei delitti e delle pene)*, talked of the greatest happiness divided among the greatest possible number. But it was above all Jeremy Bentham (1748–1832) who in formulating a hedonistic form of utilitarianism (an action is right if it maximizes the pleasure and minimizes the pain of those affected), made the theory central in debates on such matters as reform of the law. John Stuart Mill sought a deeper way to express the theory.

He was intensively educated and precocious in achievement due to his upbringing by his father James Mill (1773–1836), an ardent defender of Benthamism. In due course he obtained a position in the East India Company and rose high in the office. His major works were *System of Logic* (1843), *Principles of Political Economy* (1848), *On Liberty* (1859), *Utilitarianism* (1863) and *Essays in Religion* (1874). Also illuminating is his *Autobiography* (1873). His chief innovation in regard to utilitarianism was to introduce the notion that some pleasures are qualitatively superior to others, thus rejecting Bentham's idea that, pleasure being equal, pushpin is as good as poetry. He was also committed to the importance of personal self-development. On the matter of individual liberty he well realized that majority rule can produce its own tyrannies, and advocated proportional representation, which he considered would act to protect minorities. But people also need to be educated to respect individual liberties. On the whole he was committed to *laissez-faire* economics, but leaned more in the direction of socialism in his later years.

In his book on logic, Mill turned the tables on many critics of empiricism or the philosophy of experience. Because of Hume, they thought that it issued in skepticism, but Mill argued, by drawing a more detailed picture of methods of induction, that you could achieve certainty by using these methods. He sketched four (or five) methods – that of agreement, that of difference, that of residues, and that of concomitant variations (also the joint method of agreement and difference). For instance, the method of concomitant variations states that whatever phenomenon varies when another phenomenon varies is either the cause or the effect or is connected with the other phenomenon through some causal fact. The method of agreement states that if two or more instances of the phenomenon under investigation have only one circumstance in common, the circumstance in which alone all the instances agree is the cause or effect of the given phenomenon. These methods do not of course contain a recipe for discovery so much as a means of checking on or of proof of hypotheses. But they are enough, he would hope, to dispel skepticism: they also provide a sensible approach by using experience to find the truth – as distinguished from the *a priori* and intuitive ways of much contemporary philosophy especially in Germany. With his distrust of intuitionism Mill wants to see the basis of science, supposedly in such dicta that every event has a cause, essentially based on induction. (His critics argued that without the principle of the uniformity of nature you could not prove by induction the uniformity of nature.)

With regard to religion, Mill thought that only the argument from design had any cogency, and he played with the idea of a limited deity. But his main sympathy lay with a 'religion of humanity' or what came to be called humanism. He was highly critical of Dean Mansel (1820–71), who propounded an interesting form of positive agnosticism, reminiscent of some Islamic philosophical positions. There is, in this doctrine, an unknowable Absolute, namely God, to whom by revelation we ascribe various attributes such as goodness, but in an unknowable way, since God's goodness must be different in kind from human goodness. Mill found such a view incomprehensible: it is equivalent to saying that God is not good in any sense which we use meaningfully. (In this Mill anticipated some logical empiricist objections to theism in the twentieth century.)

In effect Mill proved to be an important bridge between the eighteenth and twentieth centuries. In the twentieth century the very considerable revival of an empirical approach could look back upon Hume and Mill among others as important predecessors.

HERBERT SPENCER AND AGNOSTICISM

As science developed in the nineteenth century, so it had a greater influence on popular thinking. One reaction was adopt a stance of agnosticism in regard to religion, faced as intellectuals were with conflicts between literalist beliefs in the Bible and the new theories, notably that of evolution as propounded by Charles Darwin (1809–92). The word 'agnosticism' was invented by T.H. Huxley (1825–95). Much more famous as a philosopher, though later greatly neglected was Herbert Spencer (1820–1903). His massive *System of Synthetic Philosophy* (1862–93) brought him considerable fame, and his views on education and the need to defend against the State won him wide support in libertarian and progressive circles. He held that knowledge essentially belongs to the phenomenal world, and was keen to set forth principles of biology, psychology and sociology. But behind the knowable lies the Absolute or Unknowable. A sense of mystery here lies at the heart of religion, but he did not accept either theism or pantheism, and he ruled out atheism. So he had a kind of floating agnosticism, which paid heed to religious feelings, but not to any creeds or systems. His evolutionary views in biology and society were in accord with the mood of nineteenth-century popular science. There were some parallels to these British developments in France, to which I shall come back. Meanwhile it is best to return to the aftermath of Hegel, and to see something of the formation of Marxism.

FROM FEUERBACH TO MARX

Ludwig Feuerbach (1804–72) forms a necessary stepping-stone for some highly important figures in Western culture, notably Marx and Freud. For he pioneered the theory of projection, which became a tool for the analysis of religion and of certain elements in personal and social psychology. He studied at Erlangen and taught there for a while, but was sacked when his authorship of an anonymous work attacking Christianity became known. He lived off a small pension and royalties for much of his life. His most vital works were his *Essence of Christianity* (1841) and his *Essence of Religion* (1846). His critique of Hegel was important for the group known as 'left Hegelians', of whom the most important product was Marx.

Feuerbach saw a contradiction nesting in Hegel's thought. Secretly there lay a hidden religious spirit in a system which claimed to be rational. It was the culmination of modern rationalism and yet it quietly degraded the material world. Once this was exposed, the way could be prepared for a humanist ethic. The consciousness which was in effect deified by Hegel is nothing other than our consciousness. Idealism does have a contribution to make, namely its analysis of human consciousness, even if it is in the alienating mode of the analysis of absolute being. It is possible in the light of this thought to see that religion itself is a projection of humanity on to the cosmos. God is a disguise for ideal humanity. The Christian doctrine of the incarnation is nothing other than a projection of the desire to become divine by the ultimate love of our fellow human beings. Feuerbach altered the direction of Hegel. In no way is matter somehow the creation of the Absolute Spirit, but on the contrary, spirit arises out of the material world. If we wish to deify humanity, let us do it through a humanistic ethics.

Karl Marx (1818–83), born at Trier in the Rhineland and an exile for much of his life in Britain, belonged to the circle of the left Hegelians. He early on took up the view expressed in the slogan 'Criticism of religion is the beginning of all criticism'. He thought this had been successfully achieved by Feuerbach, save that we can see the slogan also in economic and political terms. Marx was greatly influenced, of course, by Hegel's dialectical view of history. The new ingredient he added to Feuerbach and Hegel was economic analysis. So he evolved a dialectical view of historical processes based upon materialism interpreted through economic theory. It was a highly potent synthesis. Marx's doctrines were often worked out in cooperation with, and through the financial support of, Friedrich Engels (1820–95), who spent much time in England working in the family firm in Manchester. Their first work together was *The Holy Family* (1845), which was an attack on current idealism. Their most famous joint work was the *Communist Manifesto* (1848). Marx's *Economic and Philosophic Manuscripts of 1844* are important, and of course his most famous book is *Das Kapital* (1867; the second and third volumes were brought out by Engels in 1885 and 1894). Various books were published after Marx's death by Engels, notably his *Dialectics of Nature* (published posthumously in 1925). Mention should also be made of his *Anti-Dühring* (1878), directed against a German socialist writer.

Marx and Engels recognized that their conception of the dialectic came from Hegel. So it was not a question of their going back to some static form of materialism. For them, human beings were essentially active beings whose production changed nature and themselves. The key to understanding history was through consideration of the forces of production and their changes. Other aspects of life (cultural, social and so forth) were essentially secondary, though they could have important reflex effects on the basic economic situation. At a given point the growth of the forces of production might be inhibited by aspects of the economic and social order – this would involve a contradiction which was to be resolved by a revolutionary situation in which a transition would be made to a higher level of activity (for instance, contradictions in the feudal order giving rise to a new bourgeois order, in turn leading to problems resolved by a socialist revolution and the emergence of the proletariat as the leading class). As an active being the human will be alienated from his product by the capitalist system: the worker adds value to matter by his labor, but that surplus value is in effect taken by the capitalist, who thus of necessity exploits his workers. This sense of alienation is reinforced by the fact that it is in the interest of the capitalist to increase as far as possible the exploitation of his workers, leading to a revolutionary situation.

Eventually a socialist system will be established, including the dictatorship of the proletariat. In due course this will be replaced by a classless society, and the State will wither away. The struggle henceforth will be against nature. This ideal picture of the future depicts, so to speak, a heaven upon earth. For Marx and Engels class warfare, and eventually supreme class peace, replace the war of the States in Hegel's scheme. All this was a wonderful vision, and helps to underline the judgment that Marxism was in effect a new religion. It is, that is to say, an inspiring worldview with strong practical implications.

It is worth adding a footnote on Lenin (1870–1924), who somewhat altered certain emphases in the system of Marxism. He was keen to defend materialism, as in his *Materialism and Empirio-Criticism* (1909), against those who tried to incorporate phenomenalistic notions from Marx. He held to a copy theory of perception in which sensations mirror reality. In his *Imperialism, the Highest Stage of Capitalism* (1916) he analyzed the world situation, and foresaw the uneven development of socialism because of the difference in stages of economic development in the world. It was of course Marxism–Leninism that came to be the official doctrine in Marxist countries, though China went further because of the writings of Mao in adapting the underlying themes of Marxism. It is this system which in 1989 largely collapsed amid disillusionment. One main reason for this is that Marx's own devaluation of legal institutions and democratic values paved the way for a ruthless State machinery and a command economy which created a vast amount of human suffering. I shall return to Mao in the chapter on modern China.

One of the themes, especially of Lenin, was the importance of praxis for understanding. The way to the truth lay through Marxism. This doctrine made Marxism virtually unfalsifiable.

OTHER RESPONSES TO HEGEL – SCHOPENHAUER AND KIERKEGAARD

Two other responses to Hegel can be regarded as somewhat maverick, but of wide interest none the less. Arthur Schopenhauer (1788–1860), son of a Danzig (now Gdansk) merchant, was for a time in his father's business, but studied thereafter at Göttingen, publishing his doctoral dissertation: *On the Fourfold Root of the Principle of Sufficient Reason* (1813). His biggest and most famous work was *The World as Will and Idea* (1819), better translated as *The World as Will and Representation*. He lectured briefly and unsuccessfully in Berlin, setting himself up as a rival to Hegel. In the last years of his life he became famous, but he felt himself generally to be an outsider. His rudeness in print about the giants of his day, such as Fichte and Hegel, surely did not help.

Unfortunately, though I have quoted the usual translation of Schopenhauer's title above, the word 'idea' is not well suited to stand for *Vorstellung* in the German. Better would be 'representation'. Schopenhauer's notion of representations gears in with the Kantian distinction between phenomena and noumena. Basically we perceive the world in the guise of representations. He criticized Kant for suggesting, however, that things in themselves give rise to phenomena. On his principles he should not have done so. On the other hand, Schopenhauer pointed to the fact that in a way we do have direct experience of noumena, but in an unexpected way. We are embodied beings who experience our activity from within. So by an analogical leap Schopenhauer used this notion to interpret the world. Likewise the world which lies 'behind' phenomena, or rather the screen of representations, is Will. It is maybe unfortunate that he used the word 'Will' *(Wille)*. Maybe he would have been better off with some word such as Energy – we could see his title as 'the world as energy and representation', which would make it seem much easier to accept. But Schopenhauer saw that primordial drive behind outside things as brutal and without defined purpose.

Given his basic model (which has some likeness to the Vijñānavādin doctrine in Buddhist philosophy, where too the screen of representation is emphasized), Schopenhauer has some very shrewd things to say: about the effective subordination of the understanding to the will; the fact that consciousness is just the surface of our minds; his anticipations of Freud in the notion that the will stops things from coming to the surface of our minds; his distrust of mechanistic models of the mind (and even of nature); his emphasis on the non-rational aspects of decision-making; and so on. He was in many ways a highly modern figure. The escape from slavery to the will was for Schopenhauer esthetic contemplation. He had a notion of patterns or forms in the world, something like Plato's ideas, which we perceive in esthetic experience but are not tied into the network of cause and effect through which we so often interpret the world in order to make it manageable.

While it has been common to compare Schopenhauer's theory to the doctrines of the Upanishads (he had from 1813 onwards taken an interest in Indian philosophy and religion and in the Upanishads in particular), in fact the resemblance is much closer to those motifs in Buddhist philosophy which see that the world as presented to us always occurs as representation. But the roots of his system do not in fact reach to India: they are explicable through his extension of and critique of Kant. He thought of himself as Kant's true heir, and indeed his is quite as plausible a reconstruction of Kant as any of the Idealists'. His solution to the problem of how to get at the noumena is of great interest and originality. Despite his highly potent ideas, which have influenced later thinkers from Freud to Wittgenstein, he has generally been thought of as a 'sport' in the history of philosophy, a maverick.

Very different was the angle from which Søren Kierkegaard (1813–55) came at the problems of philosophy. His highly personal style and his strong concern for a burning Christian faith were out of the mainstream of the philosophy of the period. He had a bitter view not only of Hegel but also of the established Lutheran Church: he did not think much of the spiritual life of an organization where pastors were civil servants. In 1838 he experienced a religious conversion, but three years later he called off his decision to enter the Church, and broke off his engagement to Regina Olsen to devote himself to philosophical and spiritual writing. His writings were published under various pseudonyms as well as under his own name, a literary technique whose meaning is not altogether clear. His most important books are *Either–Or* and *Fear and Trembling* (1843), *The Concept of Dread* and *Philosophical Fragments* (1844), *Concluding Unscientific Postscript* (1846) and *Sickness unto Death* (1849).

Kierkegaard had, like Hegel, his dialectic, but it was not one of synthesis. There are stages on life's way which need to be transcended. The first stage is the esthetic stage, of sensuousness, of emotion, of poetry. But the person plunged in this life comes to realize that his self is dispersed. He lives in the cellar of a building which has as its culmination the spiritual life. The esthetic person is hit by despair, and now comes the either–or. He must commit himself to rise above the esthetic level to the next, the ethical. It involves heroism, and the ethical person thinks that he can achieve perfection, but does not reckon with sin. The consciousness of sin eventually induces a new sense of darkness, corresponding to the esthetic person's despair. He can overcome this only by a new act of commitment – to faith. If the tragic hero sacrifices himself for the universal (like Socrates), the religious person stands as an individual before the Absolute. Truth here is subjectivity – faith is an objective uncertainty held fast in an appropriation-process of the most passionate inwardness. This also is real 'existence'. A man who sits in a cart letting the horse plod along without guidance exists, but the one who guides the horse and directs the cart really *exists*. It is this loaded and pregnant sense of *existence* that was later taken up by the so-called existentialist philosophers of the twentieth century: it was in that century that Kierkegaard was really discovered, being thought a crank by his contemporaries. In all this, Kierkegaard saw system, and the system of Hegelianism, as the enemy. It pantheistically reduced the gulf between the individual and the Absolute. It washed away faith in a deluge of tepid reasoning. It did not make space in the world for the subjective passions of the individual.

Kierkegaard was taken up not just by existentialists but by Christian theologians in the twentieth century, especially during the period before and after World War II when Karl Barth (1886–1968) was fashionable. He argued that the Fall affected reason as well as other aspects of humanity, that projectionism was true, and that only a vertical giving of revelations and faith by God can express the Christian position. The deep irrationalism of both positions blended, and Kierkegaard and Barth could as brothers suggest that it is the leap of faith which counts. (But which faith? From one point of view the two of them were simply cultural tribalists.)

One could leap in quite a different direction from Kierkegaard's; witness the vivid example of another kind of 'existentialist', Nietzsche.

NIETZSCHE – A DIFFERENT KIND OF REBEL

Friedrich Nietzsche (1844–1900) was a Classical scholar at the universities of Bonn and Leipzig, but was appointed to the Chair of Philosophy at Basel before even finishing his doctorate. There he was close to Richard Wagner, with whom, however, he later broke. In 1879 he left his Chair and lived at Sils-Maria and elsewhere in Switzerland and Austria in search of good health. He developed madness towards the end of his life and was treated in clinics in Basel and Jena. His major works were *Human, All-too-human* (1878–79), *Thus Spake Zarathustra* (1883–85), *Beyond Good and Evil* (1886), *On the Genealogy of Morals* (1887), *The Twilight of the Idols* and *Ecce Homo* (1888). His book *The Antichrist* (1895) was part of a larger work he planned on the will to power, which he did not finish.

To some degree Nietzsche was indebted to Schopenhauer: his 'will to power' is an adaptation of Schopenhauer's *Wille*. But he was most eager to reject the split between the phenomenal and the noumenal. Above all he wished to reject the idea of the transcendent or the 'other world'. The will to power was not therefore a dark force living on the other side of the light of this world: it was rather an interpretation of the mode in which the universe manifests itself. Moreover, he thought that the development of philosophy in the nineteenth century had begun to show a most important thing, that God is dead. If God is dead then the morality of God needs to be rejected too. He perceived two forms of ethics – the ethos of the elite and liberated person (whom he called the superman or superior human being) and that of the masses. There is the master morality and the slave morality. The latter seeks as its criterion the conduciveness of virtues and rules to the preservation of the weak. The weak express fear and resentment of the strong, and through Christian morality cut them down to size. Because of belief in what lies beyond, Christianity comes to disvalue this world and the body. What is needed is a transvaluation of values in which human powers are integrated together. The superior human being can go beyond good and evil without collapsing into decadence. The danger is that when God is dead, men will turn to an active nihilism and precipitate wars and destruction on a hitherto unknown scale. It was as if Nietzsche anticipated Nazism (and he was of course falsely linked to the Nazi message, as if Goebbels and Goering and the like could possibly be mistaken for Nietzsche's classically inspired idea of the superior human being).

A subsidiary motif in Nietzsche's thinking is the idea of the eternal return or recurrence. The universe shuffles its pack again and again so that events will replicate themselves exactly over a long enough period. In this way the cosmos is completely closed in on itself. It seemed an idea which haunted Nietzsche and gave him yet a kind of satisfaction.

NINETEENTH-CENTURY DEVELOPMENTS IN FRANCE

Meanwhile, let us glance back at some of the developments in France, especially three rather differing 'moments' in the development of French thought, seen in the writings of Maine de Biran, Auguste Comte and Henri Bergson.

François-Pierre Maine de Biran (1766–1824), was a moderate royalist who served on the Council of Five Hundred from 1897, and was later under the Restoration a member of the Chamber of Deputies and an administrator. He published rather little, but some prize essays made his name as a philosopher. His writings were brought out in various incomplete editions in 1841 and 1859. In some degree he was influenced by the movement known as 'the Ideologists' stemming from Condillac (1715–80) and represented most prominently by Destutt de Tracy (1754–1836), who in 1801 began to publish his *Elements of Ideology*. The term at that time meant the study of ideas – the way they function in psychology, are expressed in language and so on. It only later took on that nest of meanings which assimilate it to the meaning of 'worldview'. Maine de Biran is important in introducing new dimensions into phenomenology, that is, the scrutiny of experiences as they present themselves to us. In particular he was interested in some of our perceptions having an active aspect. While he rejected the notion of innate ideas, he stressed the fact that previous writers tended to neglect the evident fact that the subject has appetites and instincts and is in some degree an active agent even in sensation. He distinguished, however, between passive sensations and what he called perception, where we are aware of our own activity – say, hearing ourselves speak. His emphasis on the self as active agent led him to prefer the formula *Volo ergo sum* to *Cogito ergo sum*.

This picture of individuals, based on scrutiny of one's inner sense, had an effect on the problem of the self. For Maine de Biran the continuous consciousness of active will and the resistances to it made it plausible to postulate a continuous self, not chopped up into the fragmentary outer impressions which Hume relied on. Moreover, our perception of willed effort and its effects gives us a concept of causation and the necessary connection of cause and effect which is realistic. In short, for Maine de Biran we can look to our will and the consciousness of being embodied to resolve some of the problems posed by Hume. Maine de Biran also paid close attention in his writings to speech as a voluntary activity. In brief, he anticipated in many ways later phenomenologists. He influenced also Bergson, to whom we shall return later.

Meanwhile, the growth of social philosophy in France through such figures as the utopian and slightly mad François-Marie Charles Fourier (1772–1837), a grand critic of civilized society, and the forerunner of socialism, Claude-Henri de Rouvroy, Comte de Saint-Simon (1760–1825), who hoped that after the eighteenth-century's critical work in the *Encyclopédie* the nineteenth century could make a new one which would prepare the new industrial and scientific system, prepared the way for the systematic positivism of Auguste Comte (1798–1857). He studied science in Paris, and became secretary to Saint-Simon, though the two men quarreled after seven years. Comte lived somewhat marginally thereafter, tutoring and lecturing. His lectures on positivism were published as a *Course of Positive Philosophy* (1830–42). Various other works followed, including his *Positivist Catechism* (1852). In effect he was founding his own religion of humanity, which he outlined in his *Discourse on Positivism as a Whole* (1848).

One of his most influential ideas was his theory of three stages of human development. This he applied both to human history and to individual growth (less plausibly). The first stage is the theological – beginning with a rather vague endowment of material beings and forces with wills and feelings somewhat analogous to human ones. There are three substages – animism (or fetishism), polytheism (when the gods are more personalized) and theism or monotheism. The next stage Comte described as the metaphysical, when gods and Gods are transformed into abstractions: an inclusive Nature is postulated, along with such forces as ether or gravitation. The third stage is the positive one. Henceforth people give up the search for the real, and confine themselves to phenomena and descriptive laws, enabling prediction. Comte coordinated these stages to forms of society – the first involves the imposition of order by the warrior class and issues in militaristic authoritarianism. Next we have a critique of the preceding era, and the evolution of the idea of the rule of law. Finally, in the positive period there is the growth of a scientific and industrial society, dominated by a scientific elite. This period also needs the development of a new study, namely sociology. Both nature and society will be under human control. Comte divides the new science into two branches, namely social statics, to do with the structure of society at a given time, and social dynamics, which deals with the evolution and progress of society. He thought that the age of science and industry would naturally tend to peace and love, since these are unifying ideas. To reinforce this he proposed a positivist religion, to worship the Great Being – not God but Humanity itself. (This attracted fierce criticism from John Stuart Mill.)

What Comte probably did not foresee was the huge role of nationalism in the era of industrialization. The French Revolution had prepared the way for a new bourgeois order in which sizeable chunks of humanity were reorganized in nation-states, typically based on language, and so too on cultural achievements created and presided over by the bourgeoisie and helped by the universal education which was a necessary ingredient in training people for the new order. So Comte was too optimistic. Perhaps he could have learned more from Johann von Herder (1744–1803), whose monumental *Ideas on the Philosophy of the History of Humankind* (1784–91) helped to form the thinking of Hegel in these matters, and who foresaw some of the developments of modern nationalism. It is of course a common problem that writers refer to 'society' without context, and so secretly suppose the national society (there are analogous problems about 'sociology': as the quip has it, sociology is about us, anthropology is about them). Comte was creative and perspicuous in his view of the possibilities of social science, but his model of the progress of knowledge was insufficiently conflictual.

Henri Bergson (1859–1941) bridges the world of the nineteenth century to the conquest of France by the Nazis. He was raised in Paris, and became a student and then later professor, at the École Normale. From 1900 to 1924 he taught at the College de France, and received the Nobel Prize for Literature in 1928. He was Jewish, though attracted by Catholicism. Among his books were *Time and Free Will* (1889), *Matter and Memory* (1896), *Laughter* (1900), *An Introduction to Metaphysics* (1903), *Creative Evolution* (1907), *The Two Sources of Morality and Religion* (1932) and *The Creative Mind* (1934). The last was a collection of essays.

Bergson was influenced by Maine de Biran, but also by the need to put our understanding of ourselves and of nature in an evolutionary context. The world had had time to digest Darwin by the time he became a student. He saw consciousness as something continuous, not a series of atomistic impressions in the style of British empiricism. As such, we are conscious of time as something dynamic and not as a series of discrete events. We are also aware of our own activity. So deterministic models of the human psyche are inappropriate and we are immediately and intuitively aware of our freedom in the process of coming to a decision. Bergson had interesting things to say about memory. He rejected central state materialism (identifying the brain and consciousness), and thought of it as a mechanism for simplifying consciousness and preventing all our memories from flooding back: a person who is active needs only a selection of what is available. As for evolution, he saw behind the real duration which we experience as *élan vital,* or living impulse, and he projected this drive upon the whole process of evolution, seeing that too as being God's way of creating creators (he identified God with the *élan vital*). He appealed here to mystics whom he thought had an intuitive experience of the living force. The mystical spirit is typically hindered by the struggle of live, but its spread will be vital to the progress of the human race. He also made an interesting distinction between the closed and open societies. This had some influence later upon Popper. The closed society has dogmatic religion and a cohesive morality, the sort of thing indeed praised by the followers of Durkheim (1858–1917). The open society is richer, freer, more fluid, plural. It is full of freedom and spontaneity and expresses the mystical spirit. So the *élan vital* flowers there most manifestly.

Bergson had great influence in his time. He tried to put evolution at the center of his worldview, and had a great number of suggestive ideas related to time, memory, will, introspection and morality. But his work has since faded.

AN INTERLUDE ON RUSSIAN PHILOSOPHY

Because Russia was for much of its history only half interested in Europe and was culturally often inclined to look South, to Constantinople, and East, to its growing North Asian empire, its philosophies were not fully engaged in the mainstream of European thought. Nevertheless, there was much of interest which began to develop during its literary renaissance in the nineteenth century. One of the main issues parallels those which concerned non-Western cultures, namely the question of Russian identity. There developed a polarization between the Westerners and the Slavophiles. This in some degree was tied to issues of religion: for the Slavophiles Eastern Orthodoxy was integral to Slav civilization, and Moscow came to be thought of as the Third Rome. The first Rome had as it were defected (for Roman Catholicism was seen as schismatic and degenerate); the second Rome had been conquered by the Turks in 1453; Moscow stood out as the new center of Christian civilization.

Much of the nineteenth-century debate was heralded by Peter Chaadaev (1794–1856), particularly because of his first *Philosophical Letter,* published in 1829. It brought on him the attention of the censors, who forbade him to write further. In that work he harshly criticized Russia for cutting herself off from Western society. Her isolationism he perceived as a kind of egoism. He emphasized the importance of love and social solidarity both as between individuals forming a given society or nation and between societies. So Russia was implicated in collective egoism. He also considered Russia to be virtually historyless, like a blank sheet of paper. True history belongs to a nation when it is gripped by an idea: in the West – in large measure through Catholicism's role in carrying Europe through its post-Roman disintegration – societies had involved themselves in social progress and the development of science. In all this Chaadaev could be said to be taking a Western line. Yet on the other hand, there were Slavophile elements in his thinking. Each nation has its separate destiny: Russia had both open-mindedness and an ideal which had once been enshrined in village communities. Now we could look forward to a future utopia in which the kingdom of God is realized on earth, in a new solidarity. Chaadaev saw his ideal as universal, but it of course spoke directly to those who were looking for Russia's destiny. Russia's mission might lie in Russia's openness, so that she could become a leader in the historical movement of the future. Chaadaev's ideas thus incorporated differing motifs which were taken up in the subsequent Westerner–Slavophile debate. In this sense he is the father of Russian philosophy.

Among the most influential Slavophiles was I.V. Kireevsky (1806–56), who was influenced by the theologian A.S. Khomyakov (1804–60) who was a factor in his conversion to Orthodoxy. Khomyakov was hostile to both European rationalism and materialism and emphasized the Russian notion of *sobornost* or intimate community. He also held that knowledge is a communal affair. Without *sobornost,* which had religious implications, the pursuit of knowledge only separates human beings. Kireevsky was especially severe on Western rationalism, which he perceived as stemming from Aristotle's abstract characterization of, and exaltation of, reason. From this came scholasticism in Western Christianity, then reform and finally non-religious rationalism. Rather, he favored an epistemology (which he did not spell out very clearly) where the whole human being is integrated into the act of understanding.

Alexander Herzen (1812–70) was a somewhat ambiguous Westerner. The Decembrist rebellion in 1825 led him to vow to avenge the dead in that affair. His radicalism meant that much of the period between graduating in 1834 from Moscow University to his decision to leave Russia in 1847 was spent in exile in the provinces. From abroad he had quite a lot of influence through the journal *The Bell* which he published. While his general position was liberal, his disillusion with the failure of the revolutions of 1848 led him to advocate something other than a purely Western solution to Russia's problems, advocating a kind of commune-based socialism (and in this he anticipated later populist ideology). But Herzen was also a strong individualist and opponent of views of history as rational and teleological. Thus he wove liberal and socialist strands together in his worldviews.

Influenced by him was a major theoretician of the Populist movement, Peter Lavrov (1823–1900). He pursued an army career and for over twenty years taught at the Artillery School. But his radical views landed him with arrest and exile to Vologda, from where he escaped to Paris in 1870. He settled there after a period in Zurich. He was close to Marx and Engels for a while, but he did not subscribe to the idea of laws of historical development, which he thought conflicted with human freedom. He distinguished history and psychology on the one hand from natural science on the other hand. An introspective method is needed for them. He called this idea 'anthropologism'. Out of it he developed a worldview which denied religion and the transcendent, but averred that the human being is free and defines ideals from out of his own subjectivity. Such a philosophy he held had to be practical – hence his own engagement in revolutionary activities. All this went with his thought that anthropology and sociology, as human disciplines, have to be normative. In general his position can be seen as a kind of liberal socialism, but oriented towards Russian Populism. He hoped that Russia would be spared the harshness of the industrial revolution and socialist dictatorship.

Meanwhile, another strand of Russian thought was important, namely anarchism. The prime mover was Mikhail Aleksandrovich Bakunin (1814–76), who spent most of his life abroad, though for a few years he was imprisoned in Russia, then exiled to Siberia. In 1865 he started the International Brotherhood, a major conspiratorial organization, whose influence persisted in Spain during the civil war. He was a major challenger of Marx, considering that a communist State would simply amplify the evils of existing States. In a similar vein, the nihilist position was enunciated by Nikolai Chernyshevsky (1828–89), notably in his novel *What is to be Done?* (1863). Dostoevsky's *Notes from Underground* of the following year is considered to be a reply to this. Fyodor Mikhailovich Dostoevsky (1821–81) expressed fragments of a worldview in the complexities of his novels, incorporating a Slavophile outlook, distrust of the West and a strong commitment to freedom as the central human value, modified by faith in Christ, a rejection of materialism and Western-style humanism, and a vision of goodness in the world's underclass.

Another novelist, Leo Tolstoy (1828–1910) is worth mentioning here, again not because of a systematic presentation of ideas, but because he set forth some notions which have been influential. Notable in his latter-day conversion to a form of the Christian faith (but not Orthodoxy) he espoused pacifism, and had a considerable influence on Mahatma Gandhi, who named one of his farms (or communes) in South Africa after him. In his novels he is most interesting perhaps in *War and Peace* which decisively rejects the idea of patterns and determinism in the historical process. He gives vivid sense to his position, which rejects Hegelian and Marxist interpretations of history among others. History is a swirl of individual events, feelings and processes. The actors do not understand what is going on, and still less do they foresee the consequences of what they are doing. Some try, but fail, to control events. So Tolstoy argues for a highly contingent account of history, which emerges from the chaotic summation of a vast swarm of contingencies. Nevertheless in his Epilogue to *War and Peace* he plays with the idea of a scientific approach to history: but this would have to be merely in principle, since it could never accomplish the task in practice.

Of religiously oriented thinkers in the nineteenth century the most systematic was Vladimir Sergeyevich Solovyev (1853–1900). To his life and influence we now turn.

SOLOVYEV, BERDYAEV AND OTHERS

Solovyev came from an academic background, and after a period of youthful atheism, which, though passing, imbued him with ideals of social reform, he attended first Moscow University and then the Theological Academy at Zagorsk. He taught in Moscow and St Petersburg; traveled widely, and pioneered ecumenical contacts with Catholicism. While his values were up to a point Slavophile, he did not approve of the excessive criticism typically leveled, in a chauvinistic way, at the West. He was also an influential poet.

As a young man he was strikingly influenced by Spinoza: he was indebted to the German idealists from Hegel onwards, and especially to Schelling. But he was also inspired by some of the classical Christian mystical writings, not unnaturally. What he tried to express in his metaphysics is something of a synthesis between traditional Christian thought and a worldview derived from Western philosophy. One can compare his task to that, say, of Swami Vivekananda or Radhakrishnan, though he was probably a deeper student of Western idealism than either of these two.

Solovyev begins from the notion that there is a single reality or total unity. This is God or the Absolute, and Solovyev's full schema could be characterized as panentheism. As things emerge the Absolute appears as nature and as human beings, which form a bridge, as it were, between the divine life and material life. Solovyev attempts to show that human beings are necessary to the unfolding of the Absolute into nature. He also tries to exhibit the necessity of the Trinity doctrine. On his account the First Absolute posits its own essence, the Second Absolute, which is the *Logos*. The relationship between the First and Second is something else again, and is to be described as the Spirit. All these moments of the One coexist and their unfolding is not to be seen in any way as a temporal process. Some of all this Solovyev owes to Schelling. The ballet of the Trinity is followed as it were by the ballet of creation in which nature and human beings make their appearance.

The idea of total unity or the one reality has an effect in epistemology. Since it is not given in experience and cannot be deduced by reason alone, it is known by intuition or direct mystical experience. This he thinks of as interior. He was therefore critical of empiricism, rationalism and positivism. The former shrinks the world to what is phenomenal in the sense of being apprehended by the external senses. The second ends in abstraction. The third excludes metaphysics. It is right to suppose that science's scope of activity is the phenomenal world, but this does not warrant excluding any world beyond. Indeed, to perform this exclusion it has itself in its own way to become metaphysical.

Solovyev held, in the manner of Schelling, that the emergence of individuals, though necessary in the scheme of things, is a kind of Fall. The original unity becomes differentiated. The task of religion is to guide people towards a reunion between human beings and the one reality. There needs to be a harmonization of science, metaphysics and faith. But this is more than an intellectual matter: it has to be practically understood. Conversely, as he stressed in his *Lectures on Godmanhood,* religion is not just pragmatics: religious thought is an inescapable ingredient in the progress of human beings towards the ultimate reconciliation. But this is not just theology, at least as traditionally conceived, because it does not properly allow the free exercise of reason (which Solovyev of course holds leads to a synthesis with religion), and it does not properly take into account the findings of science and so forth.

Interestingly, Solovyev also included in what I have called the ballet of the Trinity the figure of Sophia or Wisdom. His account of her varies: at one time he viewed her as the soul of the cosmos, and later identified her with the Holy Spirit, and also with the Virgin Mary. He had vivid visions of her. At any rate the concept injects a feminine aspect into the Divine Being, for which there are precedents in the Hebrew Bible.

Of modern ideologies, he was much opposed to nationalism and socialism, and hence considered Slavophile chauvinism with disfavor. This was one of the sentiments behind his favorable view of Catholicism. He came to have considerable influence on later Russian Christians, though his general philosophical influence faded after World War I. It was not an era when Absolute Idealism was much in fashion.

Nikolai Berdyaev (1874–1948), scion of a high-class family in Kiev, became for a short period Professor of Philosophy in Moscow during the early years of the Revolution, but was expelled from Russia because he rejected Marxism. He lived much of his life in exile, mainly in France. Many of his most important writings date from his time in exile. He followed Solovyev in positing a reality beyond the phenomenal world, but his picture of the whole was somewhat different, since he saw the phenomenal and noumenal world in a kind of dualistic relationship. He also, while indebted to Kant, had a more Nietzschean outlook, emphasizing the fluidity of creativity. He saw human freedom as of primary importance, beyond the phenomenal world of determinism. His emphasis on freedom gave him an anarchistic tinge: he spoke of the sacred duty of lawlessness. The human being displays freedom in relation to God, and has sacred worth, which rejects the regimentations of theocracy, Marxism, capitalism and other systems. He called for humans to live in expectation of a transformed future, which would transfigure and dissolve present institutions such as the State. His emphasis on freedom gave him a highly liberal ethos, for example in regard to sexual relations and the status of women.

A somewhat more systematic thinker in the Christian tradition was Nicholas Lossky (1870–1965), exiled by the Soviets in 1922: he taught in Czechoslovakia and then for a long period from 1946 in the United States. He counted himself an intuitivist or intuitionist, holding that we intuit objects of perception directly (he therefore rejected the causal theory of perception). He also held that we have intellectual intuitions of non-spatiotemporal objects, such as numbers and mystical intuitions of the Absolute. While the cosmos is composed of a myriad of interacting substantival agents, arranged in a hierarchy, its unity is guaranteed by the Absolute which embraces it and stands behind it. Humans experience the latter as the living God. Another prominent exiled theologian and philosopher was Sergei Bulgakov (1871–1944), who like Solovyev emphasized the role of Sophia and taught a form of panentheism.

RUSSIAN MARXISM: STALIN AND THE AFTERMATH

Meanwhile, of course, Marxism was destined to have a supremely powerful effect in Russia. We have had occasion to advert to Lenin's thought, coming as it did on top of a number of debates about Marxism among Russian scholars, since the time of Georgi Valentinovich Plekhanov (1856–1918), who founded the first organization of Marxists in 1883 (in Geneva, among exiles). While basing his thinking on the work of Marx and Engels and indeed regarding himself as highly orthodox, he developed Marxism in realistic directions, and had an effect on Lenin's philosophy. But as things turned out, what really counted was power in the Soviet Union, and from 1927 that reposed chiefly in the hands of Stalin (1879–1953). His writings on philosophy and related matters do not display great originality, save that he is keen to stress the importance of ideas in sustaining change (even if he had an orthodox notion of their origin). He also emphasized his practical doctrine of socialism in one country, and how the State would not wither away until a global revolution was accomplished. He thus neatly postponed the timetable for the withering away of the State. If there were creative developments in Marxism, they were naturally taking place outside the regimented and necessarily uncritical atmosphere of the Soviet Union.

Probably the two most original thinkers in the main stream of Western Marxism in the aftermath of the October Revolution were Georg Lukács (1885–1971) and Antonio Gramsci (1891–1937). The former played a ministerial role in the short-lived revolutionary regime of 1956, but reverted to conformity to the Communist Party thereafter; Gramsci founded the Italian Party, but spent much of the rest of his life in jail, dying shortly before his destined release. Lukács did not agree with Lenin's over-wide application of the idea of contradiction (in nature), and he held that subject and object become one in society, so that the proletariat in attaining self-knowledge at the same time has knowledge of the whole of society. But Lukács also realized that the relativism which Marxism postulated in regard to all other theories and ideas applies to itself: Lukács hopes for truth in the future, as history and the progress of knowledge attain a finality. This eschatological theory scarcely resolves the problem of relativism but is an interesting way of treating Marxism. It involves an analogy to Hegelianism.

Gramsci had a similar sympathy for idealism, and while he criticized Benedotto Croce (1866–1952) he nevertheless wished to create a new philosophical synthesis with latter-day idealism which would give space for philosophical reflection as well as practical action. As such his writings, which were done mostly during his long prison term under Mussolini, became influential among Western Marxists and Euro-Communists after World War II.

Returning to the Soviet scene: the years succeeding Stalin's death in 1953 were scarcely better for intellectuals. Hence it was mainly abroad that Russian intelligentsia maintained their life and impetus.

Probably the most important theme of the Russian philosophical scene in the late nineteenth and early twentieth centuries, despite its current unfashionability, was that of a synthesis between the Russian tradition and Western Absolute Idealism (itself in some harmony with Neoplatonism, so vital among the Fathers of the Church towards whom Orthodoxy looked back). This was a way of trying to express a position which would make sense of Russia's history. It was a move similar to that taken in other cultures outside the main European orbit. But it was overtaken by Marxism and weakened by its inability to face up to the implications of science and liberalism.

SOME DEVELOPMENTS AFFECTING PHILOSOPHY UP TO WORLD WAR I

The work of Nietzsche, the coming of Sigmund Freud (1856–1939), the expansion of socialist thinking, evolutionary theory and the rapid development of European nationalisms, all took the mood of thinking away from the rational ideals of the Enlightenment. But on the other hand the Victorian age saw the heyday of liberalism, which took up some parts of the earlier concerns, such as the rights of man. The explosive impact of the new discoveries of irrationality in the very fabric of the human psyche had greater effect between the two World Wars than they did before 1914. Meanwhile, though, a large change had been effected as a result of post-Enlightenment social and political changes. This was the increasing concentration of philosophy upon the universities. Increasingly philosophers were university professors, and the art became more and more professionalized. Knowledge in the nineteenth century was getting to be much more specialized. The scope for such wide-ranging thinkers as Descartes or Leibniz was lessening. The tendency was, too, for sub-branches of philosophy to get hived off – into political science, psychology, sociology, and so forth.

Some discoveries were likely to make traditional philosophers pause. Notably, there was the work of Nikolai Ivanovich Lobachevski (1793–1856) and Georg Friedrich Bernhard Riemann (1826–66) in creating non-Euclidean geometry, which was bound to affect the whole post-Kantian tradition. There were new developments in logic, for instance the publication in 1879 of the *Begriffsschrift* of Gottlob Frege (1848–1925) which marks the start of modern logic, with devices such as quantification. There was the work of Giuseppe Peano (1858–1932) of Turin, who foreshadowed the *Principia Mathematica* of Bertrand Russell and A.N. Whitehead (whose philosophies we shall shortly consider), assimilating mathematics and logic. There were other remarkable advances in logic, which assisted in the emergence of technical ways of doing philosophy, especially after World War II, and which helped along the process of professionalization in philosophy.

There were developments, too, in religion which are of some interest. The post-Hegelian period became a fertile one in the self-critical examination of Christianity, through the use of historical methods on the texts and through attempts to reconcile traditional religion and modern science. Evolutionary theory and psychoanalysis called in question uncritical views of the biblical message. Liberal Protestantism emerged as a viable movement; Catholicism, however, resisted modernism. In 1879 an encyclical of Pope Leo XIII, called *Aeterni Patris* laid down the normative character of Thomas Aquinas' thought both in the training of priests and the thinking of philosophers, who should only diverge from Thomism for the most serious and well-considered reasons.

I shall deal with the differing patterns of religious and traditional response to changes in science and philosophy in the context of American philosophy in the next chapter, since it is convenient to discuss both Jewish and Christian responses together, and this is more natural in relation to the American environment.

Meanwhile, the non-Western world, especially Asian religions and philosophies, was slowly beginning to percolate into Western consciousness. A notable Western philosopher who took this seriously was Paul Deussen (1845–1919). He was indeed the first person to incorporate Eastern philosophy into a systematic history of philosophy. He had edited Schopenhauer and in his early years was a friend of Nietzsche. He held that the Divine Being is non-personal, and synthesized the work of Kant, Christian values and Upanishadic teachings.

The period up to World War I was relatively optimistic. The huge changes in human production and the surge of inventions combined with evolutionary theory and its themes to induce a confident sense of progress. In Britain, meanwhile, there were the first signs of that revolt against idealism which prepared the way for the dominance of a humanistic, largely science-oriented ideology.

MOORE AND RUSSELL: COMMON SENSE AND SCIENCE

C.E. Moore (1873–1958) published a striking paper called 'A Refutation of Idealism' in 1903. Arguing that the essence of all idealist positions is the principle *esse est percipi* (taken in a broad sense), he tried to show that already being aware of blue, say, as an object of consciousness, is already to have got out of the circle of our sensations. It anticipated his 1925 essay 'A Defence of Common Sense' in which he held that there are propositions which we know with certainty, e.g. that this is my hand, that I have a body, that there are other living bodies, that the earth has existed for many years, and so on.

A philosopher neither has to prove nor disprove what we know thus. He held also, as argued in his *Principia Ethica* (1903) that good is a non-natural (and objective) property. We can recognize what things are good. In his stress on common sense, his espousal of a form of conceptual analysis and his attempt to dissolve some basic philosophical problems, Moore was an influential player in the development of linguistic philosophy. His worldview was not alarming, or exciting, but very British.

Bertrand Russell (1872–1970) was a much larger and more adventurous figure. Not only did he do remarkable work in mathematics, but published on a huge range of philosophical topics, from Leibniz to pacifism, and from logic to marriage. His most important books are *Principia Mathematica,* with A.N. Whitehead (1910–13), *The Analysis of Mind* (1910), *Our Knowledge of the External World* (1914), *An Inquiry into Meaning and Truth* (1940) and his *Collected Papers,* in 7 volumes (1983–84), edited by Kenneth Blackwell and others. He was educated at Cambridge and in Berlin, and spent most of his career teaching in Cambridge. But he was in prison for pacifism in World War I, and taught in the US during part of World War II. He devoted the latter part of his life to anti-nuclear campaigning. He shared the Nobel Prize for literature in 1950 with William Faulkner.

Various views of Russell came to have very wide influence. One was his and Whitehead's derivation of mathematics from pure logic. Another was his theory of types, in which he tried to avoid logical paradoxes, and his theory of descriptions. The paradoxes seemed to wreck the basis of mathematics. Consider the class of all classes which are not members of themselves. The class in question must, it seems, both be and not be a member of itself. Russell thought the problems could be solved by a hierarchy of types. The notion of a class being a member of itself does not make sense. Later this idea was used in linguistic analysis: Ryle thought that the difference between mind and body was of this rough general kind. Russell's theory of descriptions was invented to avoid such ghostly entities as the king of France. In the sentence 'The king of France is bald' we have to see that there is an implicit claim 'There is a king of France'. In other words, the grammatical form of a sentence does not correspond to its logical form.

In metaphysics Russell, partly under the influence of Wittgenstein, adopted a form of what was called 'logical atomism'. He tries to build the world and scientific knowledge out of elementary propositions describing simple sense-data. This was the reappearance of Hume in modern guise, and did not work either. Simple particulars were built into molecular propositions by logical connectives, such as 'and' and 'or'. All this connected up with another doctrine, later fashionable, that truths are either analytic (tautologies) or synthetic (contingent propositions). The truths of logic give the bare structure of the tautological realm. As noted, Russell was influenced by the earlier Wittgenstein, of the *Tractatus Logico-Philosophicus* (1922 in its English, 1921 in its German, edition). We shall return to Wittgenstein later. Meanwhile, let us note the development of the Vienna Circle, which had some affinity with Russell. Russell was a humanist and wanted a philosophy which was highly consonant with the state of science. He was the leading scientific humanist of his day. The Vienna Circle was a group of philosophers, who through the work of A.J. Ayer (1910–89), became well known and fashionable in Britain, especially after World War II.

THE VIENNA CIRCLE, LOGICAL POSITIVISM AND LINGUISTIC PHILOSOPHY

The Vienna Circle was a group of philosophers round Moritz Schlick (1882–1936), himself a successor to the scientifically-oriented Ernst Mach (1838–1916), who wished not just to find a scientific basis for philosophy but to find a means of banishing metaphysics, or what they took to be metaphysics. It included such figures as Rudolf Carnap, Friedrich Waismann and Otto Neurath. Their chief move was to formulate a criterion of meaning, namely the verifiability principle, often called the verification principle, which stated that the meaning of a sentence lies in its method of verification. That verification was usually thought of in terms of reports of sense-data. It follows that any statement which cannot be verified by sense-data is meaningless. The Logical Positivists thought that this would dispose of all metaphysics, including God. Some, such as Carnap, built up impressive edifices out of the bricks of sentences about sense-data. The chief publicist for this iconoclastic worldview in the English-speaking world was A.J. Ayer, through the publication of his *Language, Truth and Logic* (1936). But Positivism, so brashly anti-metaphysical, broke down. For one thing, what was the status of the verification principle itself? Merely a stipulative definition that tells us how it is best to use 'meaning'? In that case, other paths can be taken. How, too, can universal claims ever be verified? You cannot count all electrons. Or should we take it in a weak form as proposed by Ayer: sense-data are relevant to the truth of meaningful utterances but need not be able to prove or establish them? But God could creep back here on the weak criterion. Then again, sense-data takes us back to Hume and Berkeley. How do we break out of phenomenalism, which looks suspiciously like idealism? Ayer and Russell both looked as if they had walked in from the eighteenth century. As it happened, though, empiricism of this kind blended in with ordinary language philosophy, which became dominant in Oxford after World War II, and Oxford itself became for two decades dominant in English-speaking philosophy.

TWO WITTGENSTEINS AND THEIR EFFECT ON LINGUISTIC PHILOSOPHY

Ludwig Wittgenstein (1889–1951) came from a well-known Vienna family. He studied natural sciences in Linz, and engineering at Manchester. From there in 1912 he moved to Cambridge to work with Russell. He served in the Austrian army in World War I, and afterwards became a primary teacher in Austria. He taught in Cambridge from 1930, and took up hospital portering during the war. In 1939 he had succeeded to Moore's Chair, and he resumed teaching after the war until 1947. He lived in Ireland for a time and returned to Cambridge, where he died. The only book published during his life was the *Tractatus Logico-Philosophicus* (1922). The *Philosophical Investigations* (1953) is the most important of the many manuscripts published after his death. The latter work was in effect a critique of the *Tractatus*.

The *Tractatus* has an analogy to the thinking of the Vienna Circle with whom Wittgenstein was in contact. But it is a delineation of the world as seen through the medium of propositions and logic. It was an attempt to create a structure of propositions on the assumption that every proposition can be analyzed into simple propositions (they are bound together by logical connectives). Every proposition, whether simple or complex, pictures reality. He considered that there must be elementary propositions which show their sense immediately. Apart from tautologies (and mathematical equations), all propositions are only contingently or accidentally true. There can then be no necessity outside of logic and mathematics.

Ethics and the self lie outside the world, which is simply everything that is the case. Similarly, though Wittgenstein emphasized at the end that the unsayable somehow exists, it is the mystical and cannot be spoken. In giving his structure of the world Wittgenstein could have been interpreted in a positivist way; he did not in the work prescribe such an interpretation.

From 1929 onwards he underwent conversion to a different point of view. His later view was that language is already all right and does not need explication in the ideal or logical way he tried in the *Tractatus*. The logical atomism of the latter was replaced by a more empirical ranging through forms of language. He took up a pluralist position: there are many differing language games. He came to a much more elaborate view than Moore's, but one which was somewhat similar. Philosophy results from diseases of language, and can be cured by going back through language to see where the mistakes giving rise unnecessarily to philosophical problems have been made. Philosophy became a kind of therapy turned in upon itself. All this gave impetus to ordinary language philosophy as practiced at Oxford after World War II, especially in the work of Gilbert Ryle (1900–76) and J.L. Austin (1911–60). The former was chiefly noted for his attempt in *The Concept of Mind* (1949) to dissolve away Cartesian dualism by a detailed and often very illuminating examination of the language of mind and body, seeing a lot of mental notions as analyzable through behavior and disposition. Thus for instance, knowing how to do something does not involve internal theorizing: so Ryle hoped to drive the ghost from the machine (but it wouldn't quite leave, and other tougher measures, such as central state materialism, identifying mental with brain processes, were tried out). J.L. Austin's elaboration of the notion of performative utterances which do things with words, as in his *How to Do Things with Words* (1962), made a major contribution to linguistics. But this was taking Wittgensteinian ideas beyond the point where Wittgenstein would have been interested in them.

Wittgenstein's great influence was in part due to his guru-like effect on his circle of disciples. The mystique of his apothegms and of secret manuscripts had a curious influence upon philosophy, which at the same time was heir to Enlightenment motifs of the appeal to reason and the rejection of revealed authority. But linguistic philosophy, as it emerged out of an amalgam of commonsense philosophy, empiricism, analytic philosophy and the later Wittgenstein had some strong contributions to make in the elucidation of different areas of language and life, from ethics and religion to the philosophy of science. Its consequences became more pluralistic, moving away from the attempt to impose a strait-jacket, as in the days of the Vienna Circle.

KARL POPPER: CRITICISM AND THE OPEN SOCIETY

Karl Popper (1902–97) was in touch with the Vienna Circle, but not of it. He has proved to be perhaps the most fertile and original of the philosophers of this ambiance. He used the notion of falsification or refutability to characterize scientific hypotheses: the best stick their necks out, challenging the evidence, so to speak, to rebut them. He did not have much use for a criterion of *meaning,* however, and thus for two reasons distrusted the verifiability principle. His wide range of writings had much to say about society and politics. His famous *The Open Society and its Enemies* (1945) involved a sustained onslaught on historicism (i.e. the view that there are laws of history), and on totalitarian trends as exemplified in the writings of Plato, Hegel and Marx. He became a major theorist of social democratic views and of the need for piecemeal social engineering (as opposed to holistic and utopian policies). His theory of science, as exhibited in his *The Logic of Scientific Discovery* (1959; the German edition came out first in 1935), blended with his defense of the open society: if science advances by refutations and conjectures, then free speech and open attitudes are a necessary ingredient in onward development of knowledge.

SOME SOUTHERN PHILOSOPHERS: UNAMUNO, ORTEGA, GENTILE AND CROCE

A number of Spanish and Italian philosophers played a significant part in the intellectual life of their cultures (including, in the case of Spain, in Latin America) without impinging so greatly on the main stream of European philosophy (so much dominated by Germany, France and Britain). In Spain, Miguel de Unamuno (1864–1936) foreshadowed aspects of existentialism. He was Professor, then Rector at Salamanca University from 1891. His most vital work was undoubtedly *Del sentimiento trágico de la vida* (1913), translated as *The Tragic Sense of Life*. He was also a novelist and poet. For a while he was a politician, opposing the dictatorship of Primo de Rivera, for which he was exiled to the Canary Islands for a number of years, but escaped to France and was after Rivera's fall a member of the Spanish parliament.

In his writings he stressed the central value of integrity. This authenticity applies both to one's own self-understanding and the wider pursuit of truth. The philosopher's task therefore is to keep people honest, in the tradition of Socrates. For Unamuno, life was necessarily problematic. The human longs for immortality, and yet reason casts doubt on its possibility. He thought of reason as forever on the side of skepticism; so there is a perpetual struggle between faith and reason. He considered that in this life of sorrow and despair a commitment is necessary – something like Kierkegaard's leap of faith. Human beings must live as if God exists, since God is the guarantor of immortality, but there can be no proof of God, only at best the assurance that it is possible that God exists.

Unamuno's individualism, his advocacy of commitment, his pursuit of philosophical insights from the realm of emotions, his sense of the collision between faith and reason – all these mark him as an existentialist. This was in part why he did not frame his general position in any systematic way. Since his commitment was irrational, and leads to (and from) a sense of the mysteriousness of the anguish which arises in our experience of existence, a systematic exposition of his position would probably itself be irrational. But he certainly stimulated philosophical reflection in Spain and had some influence in the wider world.

Like Unamuno, Ortega y Gasset (1883–1955) played a part in the Republic as a Deputy in the constituent assembly of the Second Republic and as Governor of Madrid. He taught in the University of Madrid from 1910 onwards, but in 1936 had to leave Spain for Argentina. He went back to Madrid in 1948. His general philosophical position included two or three motifs. He started as a vitalist, but whereas most vitalists were anti-rationalists Ortega gave prominence (increasingly so as his thought progressed) to the rational aspect of life. Moreover, his more biological interest gave way more and more to life in the sense of individual life. Here he held that both idealism and realism are misleading. He saw the individual as the self with the circumstances in which it finds itself. But he also (how consistently is a question) adhered to perspectivism, namely that reality can only be known from a specific point of view, a perspective.

As Ortega shrank his vision to embrace individual lives, he saw morality as related to a person's freedom and potential. The moral person is one who concerns himself to choose and embrace a life project. The inauthentic person is the drifter. Individuals can have rational and sensitive relations with one another, in love and friendship. But such relationships are not what constitutes society: the latter comprises the State, the legal system, tradition and custom. Although it has its uses, of an obvious sort, society in this sense is not fully human: it mechanizes humanity. And so we need, in making society human, to give it a communal project. Ortega was an elitist. He did not see the masses as capable of such thinking through of their destiny. This had to be done by an intellectual aristocracy.

There are of course many elements in this vision which relate to existentialism. Ortega considered not that he had become an existentialist, but that the existentialists had caught up with his thought.

Ortega rejected Catholicism: it represented that sort of weight of custom which imposes upon free individuals. But in his own way, despite his elitism, Ortega was a liberal. Since human beings have no fixed essence, but make themselves up, so to speak, as they go along, it is inevitable that inequality should abound. But Ortega's position had of course to be antithetical to the notion of a fixed or inherited hierarchy.

Curiously, Ortega's best-known disciple, Julián Marías (1914–2005), who cofounded with Ortega the Institute of Humanities in Madrid in 1948, rejected Ortega's anti-Catholicism. He considered that vitalism leads to belief in God, since a spiritual ultimate fulfils an important living need of the person, and disposes of uncertainty and confusion. Although truth is itself powdered into countless perspectives, beyond this lies a kind of certainty. Perhaps in any case Ortega's perspectivism was self-defeating, and so Marías' disposal of it is not altogether irrational.

Generally speaking, though Unamuno and Ortega contributed importantly to thinking in the Hispanic world, their influence was rather slight elsewhere. Spanish philosophy was only just beginning to emerge from a period of relative isolation. There is no doubt, however, that their outlooks corresponded to important motifs in existentialism. There is some truth in the claim that they did not join that movement, but, as Ortega quipped, it was the other way round.

Italian philosophy in the early part of the twentieth century also led something of an isolated life. Leaving aside Gramsci (whom we have dealt with elsewhere), the two major philosophers in Italy were Croce and Gentile, both of whom were idealists at a time when the idealist tradition was fading elsewhere. Benedetto Croce (1866–1952) also approached the world from a less than fashionable direction, underplaying the value of science and making esthetics central to his system. A person of substantial means, he existed outside of the academy, though he exerted great influence upon it. One main instrument of this influence was the journal *La critica* which he founded in 1903.

Esthetics is the basis of his system, because it is in creating and appreciating works of art that we have intuitions. Because most philosophers have tended to deal with logical and conceptual thought, they have ignored the intuitive aspect – the most basic – of mental functioning. It is the awareness of an external or internal image. Croce held that the differing levels of mental activity, beginning with intuition and pure concept, represent not opposites, but 'distincts'. The mind in moving between them is not involved in a dialogue of opposites, and so he does not accept the Hegelian pattern of the dialectic as fundamental. Nor does he look to a conclusion, a final system. The mind makes progress, but it is the progress which counts, not any ultimate conclusion. Despite Croce's rejection of a holistic system, he identifies reality with what the mind finds in itself. There is nothing outside of this: no noumenon and no God. In the final volume of his *Philosophy of the Spirit,* namely the *Theory and Practice of Historiography* (1917), the function of philosophy is simply to trace out the principles involved in the movements of mind, whether dialectical between opposites, or cyclical between 'distincts'. But such a tracing is necessarily historical: the actual way in which mind functions can only be seen in history. So philosophy is in effect a kind of philosophy of history, but looking back at the esthetics which deals with the intuitions on which concepts feed. All this involved Croce in some devaluation of the philosophy of the (natural) sciences. The sciences are essentially forms of practical activity, not of knowledge. Their concepts have a mythic character, being abstractions which are useful rather than descriptive. So Croce reversed some of the major assumptions of much modern philosophy, placing esthetics and history at the center of epistemology. His views on these two branches of inquiry had some influence on Collingwood, probably the most important Northern philosopher to be deeply influenced by historical idealism as articulated by Croce.

Croce was friendly with Gentile, and helped to formulate the educational reforms which the latter promulgated in 1923–4 during the first fascist government. But once the dictatorship was established in 1925 he came to criticize Mussolini and to separate from Gentile. He became the most prominent anti-fascist intellectual in Italy, and after the fall of the regime he served briefly in the cabinet in 1944.

Giovanni Gentile (1875–1944) by contrast remained loyal to fascism, and was ultimately killed by partisans. His most famous book, published while he was Professor of Philosophy at Pisa, was *Teoria generale della spirito come atto puro* (1916). He was later an educational reformer, self-styled philosopher of fascism and editor of the *Enciclopedia italiana*. In his theory, a central role is assigned to the idea of self-affirmation or self-constitution. A sensation is an act of self-awareness, though we often picture it in a bifurcated way, as a subjective feeling which has an objective cause. But in reality, seen as a whole, it is an act of self-awareness in which the subject relates the present sensation to its past. To do this we use language, but this itself has a public or communal character. So my reflective awareness, which is necessary to me as an individual, at the same time introduces me into a world in which nothing can belong to me personally. And so in creating the self I, as it were, create society. Thus there exists a spiritual system of meanings which is the pure act or transcendental Ego. The founding of the Ego is the founding of an ideal community, which Gentile identifies with the state. It is of course not a long step between this idea and the defense of fascism.

Gentile's conception of self-constitution gives the key to his merging of theory and practice. He sought to weave his philosophy into a theory of education and morality, which he closely linked to politics. Political life is the expression of the wider community's ideals. Religion he fitted into his scheme in various ways, as being interpreted practically in the concreteness of the life of the transcendental Ego.

The idealisms of Croce and Gentile did not much succeed in expressing the new feelings and perceptions of the post-World War II period. But they represent an interesting variation on the themes of European philosophy. The deeper problem with Gentile's actual idealism lay with both his view of language and with his identification of the State. Much fallacious thinking has proceeded from the generalization that humans are linguistic animals: they are, but they have particular languages. To assign absoluteness to the particular is the error: so with Gentile his interesting notion of an ideal community becomes menacing when that community is identified with the nation-state.

FROM PHENOMENOLOGY TO EXISTENTIALISM: HUSSERL TO SARTRE

Much of Western philosophy since Descartes has started from inwardness. With Maine de Biran there was perhaps a movement towards being realistic about introspection. Edmund Husserl (1859–1938) tried to purify introspection in order to create a phenomenological method in which the philosopher would only look at what is presented to consciousness. For instance, in examining time we suspend our judgment or, as he said, practice *epoché* concerning theories of time, but look at time as it presents itself to consciousness. On the whole his successors as phenomenologists did not practice *epoché* very thoroughly, but rather presented views of the nature of consciousness from within the framework of a philosophical theory (I am thinking particularly of Sartre and Heidegger, whose 'phenomenology' appears within the ambit of existentialist views). But Husserl's general point about *epoché* is very important in the social sciences – it is necessary for us to suspend our own values in trying to see what values and perceptions animate others, whether groups or individuals. This links up with the ideas of Wilhelm Dilthey in his advocacy of understanding or *Das Verstehen* as distinguishing the social from the physical sciences – a point put in a different way, but importantly, by the English philosopher R.G. Collingwood in his *The Idea of History* (1946). But for the existentialist tradition, phenomenology involved novel analyses of the self.

COLLINGWOOD AND DILTHEY

Collingwood, as has been noted elsewhere, was under the influence of Benedetto Croce. He developed a theory of history which remains significant. But in some respects there is overlap with the thought of Wilhelm Dilthey (1833–1911), and I shall deal with the latter first.

Dilthey's career was an exclusively academic one, culminating in his teaching at the University of Berlin from 1882 until 1905. Although he was an empiricist, wishing to banish both the noumenon and the Divine Being, he was one with a difference, since he was much concerned with meanings and understanding the inner life of humans. He had a keen sense of the richness and variety of life, and was interested in much more than sensations and perceptions, but with the interpretations made consciously and unconsciously of the content of our experience. He was as much concerned with religion and the genesis and function of legal systems as he was with perceptual knowledge. He became a vital theorist of the human sciences. He was especially concerned therefore with the philosophy of history, since human cultures manifest themselves at both the macro and the micro level in historical processes. Not only is history vital in this way, but it displays an epistemological characteristic of importance: in understanding an era or an individual we need to enter into their point of view – to consider what was taken to be of importance, etc. He also recognized that the historian is limited by the horizons of his own time. The meaning of the past is suspended, as it were, between its own time and the present.

The notion of entering into a point of view is the most important here. Of course, doing history employs a lot of the general techniques of the natural sciences. But in addition there is the method of *Das Verstehen,* in which we understand some mental content. A major component of this is what may now be called empathy: to understand rage we need to have experienced it, and we bring that knowledge to bear in entering into another person's experience (we of course learn to read the behavioral signs of rage). In addition it is vital to place a person's experience, or the means of expression of it, into particular context. This in turn implies knowledge of the cultural systems in which actions and feelings are embedded (for instance, the rules of football, or whatever: how can you understand 'He was overjoyed to have scored a goal' without knowing what a goal is, and the significance of the game in a given social context, such as the passion for football in Honduras?).

Dilthey's animadversions on method in history and therefore throughout the human sciences had a vital influence on Max Weber among others, and have an analogy to the later ideas of Collingwood.

R.G. Collingwood (1889–1943) also had a highly academic career, except for a short period with Admiralty intelligence during World War I: he was Professor of Metaphysics from 1934 until his retirement in 1941. He worked both in ancient history and archaeology and in philosophy. Early on he was an idealist, but though he retained the important insights gained from idealism about both the importance of historical method and the need to understand the mental content of what occurs in the historical unfolding of human life, he rejected the absolutist superstructure of idealism. But especially in his theory of art he was greatly indebted to Croce, whose article on esthetics he had translated for the 1929 edition of the *Encyclopedia Britannica.* Because of the expressive character of much language – for it expresses feelings in an imaginative way, bringing them to the surface of consciousness – esthetics becomes the frame for a theory of language. He accepted too from Croce a wider view of language than the conventional one, including all forms of expression (so babies have a language from their earliest times, and before they learn any 'language' as seen from a conventional angle).

In his *Autobiography* he added a new layer to his method. He proposed a question and answer logic. To know something, he claimed, is to get the answer to a question. The question is singularly important. He felt that Russell's propositional logic, for instance, detaches answers from questions. So Collingwood tried to combine a Diltheyan empathetic entering into historical events with a question and answer method. In the period between the two World Wars he was one of the more important figures taking an interest in the philosophy of history, aided by the fact that he was himself also a distinguished practitioner of history.

THE PHILOSOPHY OF MARTIN HEIDEGGER AND JEAN-PAUL SARTRE

Martin Heidegger (1889–1976) taught chiefly in Freiburg, with an interlude at Marburg. In 1933 he became Rector of Freiburg and expressed his adherence to Nazism, which he never expressly repudiated. He had his own sort of cultural nationalism, thinking that philosophy could only be done in German (though once it could be done in Greek). Like Wittgenstein he was something of a guru. His phenomenology of the individual is, though obscure and full of neologisms, interesting. First he sees the individual as thrown into his world – not the cosmos but the world for him, where things are 'to hand', to be used and treated. He is a maker rather than primarily a thinker. The Cartesian picture of us being inside a cabin looking out with interest is not Heidegger's. A person is a temporal being, reaching out beyond himself, but recognizing his finitude, for we are bounded by death. Dread of death and nothingness calls us towards authentic existence: only the individual in silence can come face to face with his nothingness and create destiny for himself. While Heidegger's analysis, especially in his *Being and Time* (1927), sees the individual ineluctably made of time, it is not very much interested in history in the wider sense, though Heidegger looks on himself as in continuity with such a philosopher of history as Dilthey.

Heidegger's use of such locutions as Nothing and his interest in the immediacy of personal existence have made some see affinities with D.T. Suzuki and the Zen tradition. Heidegger seemed to accept the comparison. Yet there is something so rooted in the West about his attitudes, with his harking back to Greece and his use of the poet Hölderlin, that it may be that we have to take his nationalism seriously. Zen has a more universal quality, for all its Japanese austere style and light touch.

326

Philosophically, perhaps what will live on in Heidegger is his phenomenology of being in the world with it 'to hand'.

Jean-Paul Sartre (1905–88) was born in Paris and studied there and later at Freiburg with Heidegger. He taught at high schools before World War II. After capture and release by the Germans he lived in Paris during the war and completed his major philosophical work *Being and Nothingness* (1944). He emerged as the leader of existentialism after the war, and with his novels, plays and philosophical writings became the most brilliant intellectual of his day. He tied in his existentialist ideas with Marxism, but with no great consistency.

While he accepted Heidegger's time-bound view of the individual he added new qualities to the concept of authenticity. The human being is characterized by 'being-for-itself', while things have 'being-in-itself'. So the individual is forced to think of himself as free, beyond the world of things into which he is projected, and beyond any definitions which may be imposed upon him by others (for instance, he might be thought by others to be essentially a waiter). Authenticity means not accepting these external definitions or roles, but by the same token decisions cannot be laid out in advance by criteria of rationality. Such stark choices as we authentically make, then, are non-rational. Sartre's existentialism is atheistic, but God's absence is positive. We expect him to be there, but he is not. In this he takes a different path from that of Gabriel Marcel (1889–1973), who while stressing many existentialist themes, like starting from the fact that we are embodied, sees ourselves as *we* rather than *I* and God as a *thou*.

Perhaps the most successful blend of phenomenology and existentialist motifs – together with a certain positive use of certain Marxist ideas – was the work of Maurice Merleau-Ponty (1908–61). His most important work was *The Phenomenology of Perception* (1945), in which he strongly criticized sense-datum theory. He emphasized the importance of the body in perception; he followed Heidegger in thinking of subjectivity as localized in the world, and so perception comes from a particular perspective. He thought that a true application of Husserl's *epoché* would reveal not structures of pure consciousness, but our 'body-in-the-world'. From this angle, he was critical of Sartre's analysis of consciousness, which he considered to be Cartesian. Moreover, he stressed the role of those given meanings, which yet are alterable, through which embodied beings see their world: freedom consists in our capacities not to be determined wholly by our given social situation (he was critical of Marxism, illuminating in its relentless emphasis upon the social and material milieu, for its neglect of the individual). Merleau-Ponty's perception theory owed much to *Gestalt* psychology and he realistically emphasized the ways we are active in perception, seeing buildings, not façades. Probably Merleau-Ponty was the most realistic of the phenomenologists, building on the insights of Maine de Biran and Bergson among others, and taking up some of the insights of Heidegger.

In surveying some of the existential and phenomenological motifs of French and German philosophy, I have left one important figure on one side, that of Karl Jaspers

(1883–1969). Apart from his noble way of standing up to the Nazis (he was saved from a concentration camp by the arrival of American forces at the end of World War II), he is notable in his interest in world-wide worldviews. His volumes on *The Great Philosophers* (1962–6) incorporate treatments of Confucius, Laozi, Nāgārjuna and the Buddha, as well as Western figures. He was critical of attempted identifications of philosophy with science, and his justification for including sages among the philosophers lay in the fact that worldviews are ways of interpreting the signs of the Transcendent in the world around us, rather than theories of a scientific nature to explain particularities.

CRITICAL THEORY IN GERMANY

The Institute for Social Research was founded in Frankfurt in 1923 and became identified with the Frankfurt School of philosophers, who wished to evolve a critical theory of Marxism. This group of thinkers included Theodor Adorno (1903–69) and Herbert Marcuse (1898–1984), who settled in the United States and became a leading figure during the student movement of the 1960s. The school was critical of Marxism for its tendency to dogmatic materialism. Its tendency therefore to reductionism needed to be corrected. Adorno helped to refound the school after the war, when it took on a more social democratic and rationalist character, especially under the leadership of Jürgen Habermas (1929–), who infused linguistic philosophy into the critical tradition.

SOME REFLECTIONS

In our somewhat selective survey of Western philosophy we have left on one side North American philosophy, which will be dealt with in the next chapter, and some very recent developments, which will be traced in our concluding chapter. In looking at the main trends of Western philosophy, I have left the question of the adaptation of religions to the modern scene to the next chapter also.

There are some wider contextual matters which need to be thought about. The twentieth century has seen the persistence of the older religious traditions, and at the same time in the West the solidification of humanism as a worldview, very often through the efforts of philosophers such as Moore, Russell, Schick and Habermas. But undoubtedly the major force in the twentieth century has been nationalism. This managed in Nazism to combine with racial theories, and in fascism, for instance in Italy, with certain corporatist motifs. Nationalism has retained its impetus because of the late emergence of so many peoples from the colonial era. Often Marxism has been used on its behalf, because it could provide discipline in fighting and a rough way of remaking societies in ways necessary for the successful prosecution of national struggles. The high degree of personalism in existentialist thinking created ambiguities towards the State, and depressions, both psychological and economic, caused by World War I, halted for a while the successful progress of liberal and social democratic ideals. Perhaps because of its internal conflicts, and no doubt too because of the conservatism of higher education, which takes a long time to adapt, especially in the humanities, European thought has been remarkably self-centered.

Of all that we have surveyed, it is difficult to resist the thought that the fourth century BCE and the nineteenth century CE have been the richest and most stimulating, and here the nineteenth century is, naturally, fuller and more exciting for us than the ancient world. But we see there too a divergence. Kant, John Stuart Mill and some others took humanity in the direction of individualism and human rights. But Hegel and Marx took us towards differing forms of collectivism.

Meanwhile in America we see the evolution of a more technical philosophy, and we can perceive there rather more clearly than in Europe the shape of the struggles to adapt traditional religions to the modern world, and the presence of psychoanalysis as a vital movement too. It has been an area of great pioneering which has affected Europe and the wider world – forms of mass air transport, the universality of the automobile, supermarkets, personal computers as a norm, agribusiness: these and many other commonplaces of modern living have been developed there. Will America also export its thinking? To the evolution of North American philosophy and religion I now turn.

10

NORTH AMERICA

NORTH AMERICAN WORLDVIEWS AND VALUES

North American civilization, dominated by the United States, was made up of a number of differing strands. Two of these I shall deal with in other chapters – namely the African strand, and the other the Latino strand. The other ingredients can be summarized as follows. There is the Puritan or left-wing Protestant ingredient, founded in the desire of many to start a new life and even a heavenly city on the Western shore of the Atlantic. There was the emerging set of values of the Enlightenment, so important in framing the American constitution. There were the various kinds of Christianity, most notably Roman Catholicism. During the nineteenth century and early twentieth century these were amplified by the inpouring of so many migrants from Europe. The meld of varying sorts of Protestantism with the earlier Puritanism produced the forces of American Protestantism. Out of these also came the new religions of the US, such as Mormonism and Christian Science. Then there were the influences of European philosophy which stimulated a largely original indigenous set of American philosophies – we can think of such names as Emerson, Thoreau, Royce, James, Peirce, Dewey and Santayana. In the most recent times there has been a knitting together of European and American philosophy through the emergence of a technical philosophy, influenced by science, from Carnap and Quine to Davidson. Another ingredient in American culture has been the Jewish tradition, which has undergone various adaptations and transformations in this new milieu. Finally one can mention the renewal of Indian, that is to say Native American, tradition.

It is convenient to begin with the religious question, namely how it was that Christianity and Judaism (in particular) adapted to the modern age. It is often forgotten in analyses of world mentalities that the Christian and Jewish traditions, while belonging

330

substantially within Western civilization, unlike Islam, Hinduism and so forth that had to cope with the various forces of modernity as coming to them from the outside, and in a colonialist manner (thus amplifying the problems), also had to adapt to modern science, historical probings of revealed sources, new forms of the State and notably nationalism and the changing values of developing capitalism. I wish therefore to generalize about these intellectual and other problems from the American experience – partly because it was in America above all that Protestantism was successful, and Judaism also was able to acquire considerable vitality.

INDIVIDUALISM AS A MAIN CHARACTERISTIC OF AMERICAN PROTESTANTISM

The Radical Reformation had its representation in America – that is, those influences stemming ultimately from the Anabaptists, who prized adult faith, and so disapproved of infant baptism, and who in prizing inwardness emphasized conversion and individual experience of God. It is true that often radical movements stressed ideal communities, as if fearing the atomism of faith. In the Congregationalists and Quakers particularly there was a strongly democratic flavor in the Protestantism of the American North-east. Not surprisingly, American religious life has been punctuated by revivals, such as the Great Awakening, set off by Jonathan Edwards' preaching, in the 1730s. In a sense intensity of feeling came to replace ecclesiastical authority. But Edwards (1703–58), who became President of Princeton, was in the forefront of trying to combine the Reformed tradition with the new philosophy emanating from Britain, notably that of Berkeley. We may say that one response to the challenge of new ideas was for Christianity to combine with them. This may be called the 'liberal' reaction, though as in Edwards' case the theology produced may not be very liberal-seeming.

It was an ingenious conflation, in Edward's case, of Calvinism and idealism. Space, for instance, exists within the divine spirit. The world is really immaterial, though nature exists as appearance, to finite spirits. Because God controls the world of appearance in a regular manner, laws of nature can be described, and this is the job of science. Edwards sees the world somewhat in the manner of Islamic occasionalists. God is the direct cause of the patterns of appearance. There is then no necessity in the uniformity of nature: it is an arbitrary decision by God. Though Edwards believes in a multiplicity of human spirits, he does not ascribe to them genuine freedom. In this he follows the Calvinist path. We always act according to the prevailing motive. Though we are not free, we bear responsibility for bad actions which are bad in themselves. Edwards also had room for the notion of a direct sense of the divine holiness. He thus enshrined in his philosophical theology the principle later fleshed out by Schleiermacher and Rudolf Otto.

If one option was to combine biblical religion and modern philosophy, another was to see philosophical religion as a replacement for revealed religion. This was in general the position of deism. There were a number of prominent American deists who had a vital effect on the new nation because their views were woven into the Constitution. Benjamin Franklin (1706–90) was one of these, though he continued tactfully to attend church (deists were regarded by the orthodox with great suspicion, though orthodoxy itself was greatly loosened by revivalism itself). He espoused, and indeed wrote, a kind of creed which followed much the same lines as the worldview of Lord Herbert of Cherbury.

Another and even more influential figure was Thomas Jefferson (1743–1826). He was a true Enlightenment figure, being involved in politics, agriculture, architecture, new inventions, music and arts. In philosophy and scientific thought he followed Bacon, Locke and Newton; and was a deist, thinking of Jesus as a good moralist (he compiled a filleted version of the Gospels which cut out supernaturalism and emphasized ethics). George Washington (1732–99) was also a deist and keen on the separation of Church and State. In view of the subsequent history of the United States – its blooming through the migration of such diverse peoples of various traditions, including large numbers of non-Protestants, the separation of religion and the State was a singular blessing.

In general deism was associated with toleration. There were factors in American society which favored this – the strand in Puritanism that was in flight from persecution, the fluidity of society which led to blendings of religious conditions, especially on the frontier, the importance of Enlightenment ideas among the elite. But of course there was another response to the challenges of modernity as it then was, and that was a reaffirmation of biblical orthodoxy. This was often heightened by revivals, for the glue of inner conviction was used to bind together the Bible itself as a source of revelation, despite such serious attacks upon it as that of Thomas Paine (1737–1809) in his *The Age in Reason* (1794–6). A succession of conservative backlashes has occurred in American history, the last being during the Reagan presidency. The most important of these came to be known as fundamentalism, named after a series of pamphlets published before World War I on the fundamentals of religion, sparked by nineteenth-century liberal theology and the theory of evolution, an emotional focus for strict adherents to the literal truth of the Bible.

Liberal theology in the nineteenth century was influenced by the optimism of the period, especially in the second half. The rapid and astonishing economic development of the United States and Canada, with the railroads reaching West, the prairies coming under the plow, the enlargement of great industries in the Midwest and the opening up of golden California, promised great human advance. It was not unnatural to combine the ideas of the promised land, evolutionary progress, the Protestant ethic and the coming millennium. But liberal theology had also to cope with the German scholarship which had created the critical examination of biblical texts. It also had to deal with the unevenness of progress. There were severe social problems in the cities. So a couple of themes in liberal theology were the need to temper enthusiasm with a recognition of the human aspect of revelation, and the social gospel, wherein Christian faith saw itself engaged with raising up the poor.

Roman Catholicism had revitalized itself after the Reformation through the Council of Trent. It entered a fairly flourishing Baroque phase. But in migrating to the United States it faced in acute form some problems which had already arisen in Europe. In living in a plural society with separation of Church and State it could benefit from freedom, even though it was highly suspect to many traditional Protestants. Freedom had its penalties. It became interestingly evident that something had to be done about liberal penetration of its intellect. In 1879, Pope Leo XIII issued an encyclical to revitalize Catholic philosophy through a revised and modernized Thomism. This was just about strong enough to fend off some sophisticated contemporary philosophies. But it also served as a framework for clamping down on Catholic modernism, that is to say, liberal theology. Severe constrictions were put upon biblical scholarship, for instance. On the other hand, Catholicism in non-intellectual ways adapted well to the new milieu, being in some modes more American than Americans. In brief, the first major response of Catholicism was intellectually a neo-medievalism. This was something other than the more primitive fundamentalist 'back to the Bible' response of the Protestant backlashes. But it was hard to maintain discipline, and while one or two interesting neo-Thomist thinkers emerged, eventually *aggiornamento* had to occur. The best known Thomist philosopher was Jacques Maritain (1882–1973), who claimed to give an existentialist interpretation of Thomas Aquinas, but was not otherwise very original, though he was a modernizer of Thomistic language for the modern era, and brought Thomism into discussion with contemporary non-Catholic philosophy. Another notable figure was Etienne Gilson (1884–1978), who founded the distinguished Pontifical Institute of Medieval Studies in the University of Toronto, Canada. When Vatican II (1962–5) finally broke the intellectual crust of Catholicism, various new forms flourished. By and large, Catholics adopted variants of the Protestant liberal theology, though liberation theology (which we shall enter into in the chapter on Latin America) was also influential.

Another response to modernity is to turn away from Christianity. Perhaps some deists were already doing this in effect, though usually deism lived uneasily within the customs of the Protestant tradition. But a major movement in the nineteenth century was New England Transcendentalism, led by Ralph Waldo Emerson (1803–82). He was a Romantic, influenced by Wordsworth and Coleridge, but also by Fichte and Hegel. For him nature was something organic, not the cold machines of Newtonian physics, and he saw the world as the product of a Spirit. His general position bore a resemblance to Indian panentheism (such as that of Rāmānuja, with the cosmos as God's body). He stressed self-reliance and the importance of great men in history. Generally he was more a literary figure than a systematic philosopher, but he had influence both upon Nietzsche and Bergson. He was a forerunner of those who in the twentieth century turned to oriental philosophy and religion in turning away, dissatisfied, from the

Christian tradition. Notable among these were Aldous Huxley (1894–1963) and Alan Watts (1915–73), both influential in the 1960s.

To sum up so far: sometimes the Christian tradition blended with current philosophical and scientific thought, to yield what may be called liberal theology. Sometimes it took an emotional and conservative turn, towards fundamentalism and biblical authority, rejecting certain aspects of modern knowledge (though it could be very inventive in practical terms). Sometimes a philosophical religion replaced Christianity, as in the case of eighteenth-century deism, and other forms, such as New England Transcendentalism. To some extent we can see the same patterns in regard to Judaism, but they need separate treatment, especially because it turned out that in America the Jewish tradition found its new and most secure home for a wide cultural renaissance. The case of Judaism is also complicated by the incidence of Zionism.

JUDAISM EMERGES INTO THE MAIN STREAM

It can be imagined how dazzling was the light of European civilization when Judaism was allowed out of the ghettos. Jewish emancipation for the most part occurred during the Enlightenment and into the nineteenth century. Certain trends which were marked in Europe flowered even more in the United States. The uncertain conditions of Jewry in Europe, especially in Russia and a dismembered Poland helped to stimulate a strong exodus to America.

The Jews of Europe were already deeply influenced by Enlightenment thinking, especially in Germany. This was one factor in preparing the way for Reform Judaism. Another factor, on the American scene, was the realization that here Jews would play a very different role from the one they were forced into before migrating. Isaac M. Wise (1819–1900), from Czechoslovak territory, played a large part in developing Reform Judaism in America. He set up the Hebrew Union College in Cincinnati, which came to be the training pivot of Reform rabbis. This kind of Judaism shed a large part of the Torah. It adopted a liberal theology and a critical attitude to the scriptures and the Talmud. Judaism's task, in its view, was to be the main teacher of ethical monotheism, which was seen as the essence of Judaism. So it adapted the faith to fit well with the still predominant ethos of America. This was the one main reaction to the modern scene.

But it did not attract many of the new and more traditionalist migrants. The Reform Jews were to many of these shocking in their cavalier dismissal of so much of the Torah. Orthodoxy, a self-conscious stand in the face of modernity, involves meticulous attention to the Law, but it does not necessarily or at all despise education in a broad sense. Nevertheless, in its very strong defense of traditional behavior it also tends to take an ultra-conservative stance in intellectual matters. Many of its members come from Hasidic backgrounds, that is to say, from the mystical pietism of Eastern Europe.

It is not naturally attracted to philosophical worldviews, whereas Reform Judaism was open to such philosophies as that of Martin Buber (1878–1975), whose existential and personalistic approach to the question of God was for a time highly influential. But Orthodox Judaism is undergoing a revival, because of some Jews' disillusionment with secular life.

Third, there was in America a *via media,* intellectual, much more liberal and scholarly than the Orthodox, but more traditionalist in life and worship than Reform Judaism. A major figure was Solomon Schechter (1847–1915), who presided over the Jewish Theological Seminary, which became the flag-bearing institution of Conservative Judaism.

Another, fourth, motif was retreat from considering Judaism as a religion narrowly considered: Jewishness contains religion, but is a civilization. So the synagogue should contain or be supplemented by social and educational services which would help the Jew to lead a fuller Jewish life. The proponent of this view, commonly called Reconstructionism, was Mordecai Kaplan (1881–1983). Kaplan was influenced by pragmatism, and considered that the meaning of the God-idea could be seen in the behavior and human creativity which are exhibited by those who follow him and conceive themselves to have experience of him. In effect he emphasized phenomenological force.

All these developments were complicated by the emergence of Zionism and in the end by the creation of the State of Israel in 1948. Because in the meantime Judaism and Jewishness had become woven into the fabric of American life, partly because of the disproportionately great prominence of Jews in so many aspects of American cultural life, from Hollywood to philosophy, and from popular songwriters to physics and philosophy, America had to do something about Israel, and it became a vigorous client-state. Zionism was chiefly founded by Theodor Herzl (1860–1904). In 1897 the name was formally adopted by the first Zionist Congress. It was not long after that that the first migrations back to Israel began. Zionism was largely a secular, that is non-religious, movement, and it caused some turmoil among Jews. Many Orthodox Jews thought of the faith as essentially rooted in the Exile (which indeed it had been). Israel was a far-off dream awaiting the Messiah, and one should not try to force God's hand. It was a movement, of course, born in response to European nationalism, and its accompaniment, anti-Semitism. The rising tide of anti-Jewish behavior only helped to stimulate the forces behind the birth of the Jewish State.

Apart from these movements in the US there is also the phenomenon of the widespread secularization of many Jews, who in varying degrees affirm their Jewishness, but reject belief in God and the discipline of the Torah. At any rate Jewishness and Judaism became a characteristic part of the American scene.

One may also briefly mention some other phenomena, namely the creation of American religions on the fringe of Christianity. Among these, two are of some philosophical interest. Mormonism (or, strictly, the Church of Jesus Christ of Latter-day Saints) was founded in 1830, and included not just a narrative account of Jesus' visit to the Western world, but a doctrine of a corporeal God (and also the notion that a God over one area of the cosmos is a former human). Some of the early beliefs have been toned down, however, in later Mormonism.

Christian Science, which owes something to New England Transcendentalism, has a view of reality reminiscent of Advaita Vedānta. Our troubles, notably illness, stem from ignorance that the cosmos we perceive is spiritual and not material. The fundamental fault of humans lies in their misperception of the world as being material. Founded by Mary Baker Eddy (1821–1910), the movement is also of interest as being founded by a woman, despite male dominance in the mainstream Christian tradition.

All these movements and varieties of response to modern knowledge and new life in America may serve as background for our further exploration of American philosophy. For it was in the latter part of the nineteenth century that a flourishing tradition of academic philosophizing began to emerge.

I mentioned at the end of the last chapter that psychoanalysis is a movement which functions like a religion. It is probably in America that it has had its greatest success, and it does indeed function as a spiritual therapy for many people for whom it helps to resolve some of the problems of isolation. Moreover, Sigmund Freud (1856–1939) and later psychoanalysts and theorists of the unconscious supplied something which is a bit like Indian theories of the internal functioning psychology of the individual. I mean that in the Indian case, for instance in Buddhist analysis and in Sāṅkhya theory, there are detailed inventories of internal forces, such as the *buddhi* (intellect), *ahaṃkāra* (the sense of ego), and so on. The Indian who was at all educated in these matters no doubt had an awareness of these forces (just as you find Italians today who can give you a blow-by-blow account of their digestive systems). Such a mythic sort of inner psychology has largely been wanting in the West. It is doubtful whether people really 'feel' Hume's psychology or that of Kant. But Freud, in his dynamic theory of the relation between the *id*, the instinctual aspect of the inner, the *superego* or conscience, that is, the internalized values of the parents and so on, and the *libido,* in interaction with the 'reality-principle' or outside reality and its demands, provided a drama of the inner which people could feel and respond to. In brief, Freud created an existentially meaningful inner psychology. He of course also related this to other dramas: the narrative of one's life and above all one's childhood; infant sexuality; the mechanisms of repression and suppression; the view (also important, naturally) that there is an unconscious life, lying like a dark maelstrom below the rational and conscious surfaces of consciousness, which reveals itself in accidental or seemingly accidental ways. Not only this, but of course there is a practical aim of the theory, to help in curing or relieving people, through a process which is initiatory and revealing, like a mystery religion, but performed in the doctor's office. For those disillusioned with traditional religion (and Freud himself was one of these), he offered a seemingly practical soteriology. Moreover, all this could be presented as scientific, despite some bitter rejoinders on this score by behaviorists and others. For those who preferred other maps, there were alternative views such as that of C.G. Jung (1875–1961), more compatible with traditional religion. But it was above all in America that psychoanalysis had real vogue, and functioned as a worldview which could be combined with or could replace some traditional values. To repeat a point made above, Freud's popularity in part arose from supplying a credible inner worldview, or a map of the psyche.

Such maps are singularly weak in the West, and despite the strong attention to phenomenology and epistemologically-oriented psychology, such as do exist often want concreteness or realism.

THE DISTINCTIVE DEVELOPMENT OF AMERICAN PHILOSOPHY BEYOND EMERSON

The late nineteenth century saw the emergence of some very notable American philosophers – Josiah Royce, C.S. Peirce, William James, John Dewey. Of these, Royce (1855–1916) was an early graduate of the University of California. He used the money from a prize essay to study in Germany, where he was influenced by Schopenhauer and Schelling. He took a doctorate in Johns Hopkins, and taught successively in California and at Harvard. Among his important works are *The Religious Aspect of Philosophy* (1885), *The World and the Individual* (1901–2), *The Philosophy of Loyalty* (1908) and *The Problem of Christianity* (1913).

Royce was, at least in the first part of his career as a thinker, an Absolute Idealist. Later he came to stress more the notion of a community of interpreters, partly under the influence of C.S. Peirce. His Absolutism was highly original. First, he accepted the skepticism about Kant's noumena. Yet beyond phenomena, we are yet convinced, there is something. But the only way to break out of the constriction of phenomena is not vertically, as if we can go behind them, but sideways, that is by extending our purview to the whole system: there is an absolute experience which gives coherence and system to the whole. That is the preliminary conclusion. But it is greatly strengthened by Royce's highly original argument from error. What had been for Absolute Idealists a blot became an advantage. About error there can be no doubt, since the denial of error is the affirmation that thinking error exists is an error. He argues that an error is an incomplete thought that fails in its intention, and to know that it does this we must postulate a higher thought. Ultimately we are driven to the idea of an Absolute experience, which is also an Absolute will. Error, incidentally, is not something which is as it were an accident: it is intrinsic to the quest for truth. All this was an original way of approaching epistemology (it has a more commonsense counterpart in Popper's later emphasis on falsifiability).

In his *The World and the Individual,* partly again because of some criticisms from the pragmatists, Royce lays more stress upon the will, in that he looks upon ideas as not just pure representations but related through intentions to projects. It is absurd to look on the outside world as just given: suppose I am counting ten ships in the bay; how is it that I count just those ships, and then again do not count the number of masts? I already have my own net, so to speak, on what I see.

Since Royce was much concerned with religious, and Christian, belief, he sought to measure it by the results of his metaphysics. In his later writings he was much taken up with the process of interpretation, and with the way our knowledge is mediated through sins. So the self, for instance, is not known by intuition but is the goal of a whole chain of interpreting. This itself requires the community (signs are communal). The individual knows herself through the social world. The Beloved Community is the religious or Christian community, which helps us to overcome our sin and treachery through loyalty. The Spirit is the great Interpreter who links together individuals in the bond of love. Royce, with his imaginative ideas and wonderful mellifluous style (it was thought of as the Californian style), in these ways gave new slants and life to idealism, and had a lasting effect through his writings on a further generation of American philosophers. But his work was already being elbowed aside by pragmatism, which was an American alternative to the common sense and empiricism of Moore and Russell in Britain.

AMERICAN PRAGMATISM: PEIRCE AS THE FOUNDER

C.S. Peirce (1839–1914) was a physicist, astronomer, logician and philosopher. He wrote no books on philosophy, but some influential papers: his works are found in eight volumes, his *Collected Works* (1931–58). Since his death his influence has greatly grown. From 1861 to 1891 he served on the US Geodetic Survey, but was also doing observational work at Harvard University Observatory. He taught for short periods at Harvard, and for a while at Johns Hopkins. Mostly he was poor, and earned money by writing.

He made some important contributions to logic, notably to the logic of relations, a field he virtually invented. Changes in logic forced him into revising his system of ideas, since he was given to an architectonic approach to philosophy. He anticipated some important later ideas, e.g. of Karl Popper (fallibilism and the central role of falsifiability, and evolutionary epistemology). His work was soaked in science, but he at the same time had belief in God. He used the word 'pragmatism', but Williams James, he thought, took it in directions he did not want to go, so he later invented the term 'pragmaticism', remarking that the ugliness of the expression would be an insurance against its being kidnapped.

Peirce's system is highly complex and underwent various changes. Three or four motifs can be stated at the beginning, and then we shall present his final evolutionary worldview as a whole. First, he held a pragmatic theory of meaning according to which the concept of an object is the set of all habits of that object. Or to put it another way, the concept of an object is the set of all those conditional statements relating test conditions to experiences. This permits us to translate ideas which refer to theoretical constructs in science, such as gravitation or charm, into statements about observable behavior. A second motif was his theory of categories. What he called Firstness is a monadic relation: a phenomenal quality given in perception. Secondness is dyadic, and is the 'upagainstness' of experience when we encounter the other, which Peirce referred to as *haeceitas* or 'thisness', borrowing a term from Duns Scotus. Thirdness is a triadic relation, typically the way the sign relates the object and the interpretant. Peirce considered all thought triadic in character. Another motif was his doubt–belief theory of inquiry. Beliefs are habits; doubts are unsettled and unsettling and so unpleasant. So organisms like to replace doubts by further beliefs. Methodology clarifies ways in which we can the more easily replace doubt by beliefs which will survive a long time. Another motif was his claim that there are real continua in the cosmos, a doctrine which he referred to as synechism.

These and many other subtleties were woven into an evolutionary cosmology and worldview. He saw the progress of knowledge in the context of evolution. This involved him in the view that evolution itself must have given the human being the capacity to create likely hypotheses. But we of course have to view them critically and test them. He argued that a law is itself a habit, so in acquiring a true belief, also a habit, we assimilate ourselves to the cosmos. Conversely we can look upon the cosmos itself as an organism. It does not have doubts, but something like them, pure chance. The universe is a progress from chaos to order. It has a certain teleology, which Peirce called agapism. This together with tychism (the occurrence of pure chance) and synechism make up the fabric of the cosmos. They give rise to what Peirce calls musement, a kind of reflection which does not amount to a rigorous argument, but relies on instinct, which considers that belief in God is required to account for these features of the cosmos.

Peirce's discoveries and thoughts in the area of logic and linguistics were important. For instance he attacked the traditional distinction between terms and propositions as arising from an accident of Western language that so many words are common nouns (terms). In fact a term is an incipient proposition. We have already mentioned Peirce's work in the logic of relations, and he has an important place in the development of modern logic. He is also relevant to the whole flowering of modern hermeneutics or the theory of the interpretation of signs and texts.

Although William James regarded himself as a disciple of Peirce, at least to some extent, the way he developed what he called pragmatism was quite different from Peirce's attention. Though they were good friends, and James was most generous in trying to help Peirce, the latter was often exasperated with what he saw as the slapdash ways of James. Part of the latter's popularity came from his wonderful writing style, but this could easily supply a fine surface to underlying discontinuities of thought.

WILLIAM JAMES AND THE DEVELOPMENT OF TRUTHPRAGMATISM

William James (1842–1910) was educated in Europe and at Harvard. He studied painting and medicine and for a time wished to become a painter. He took his doctorate in 1869, and thereafter taught medical subjects and psychology. But in 1885 he became Professor of Philosophy, and most of his subsequent writing was in this field. His principal works are *Principles of Psychology* (1890), *The Will to Believe and Other Essays* (1897), *Varieties of Religious Experience* (1902), *Pragmatism* (1907), *A Pluralistic Universe* (1909) and *The Meaning of Truth* (1909). Among influences upon him the most vital was that of the French Neokantian, Charles Renouvier (1815–1903), notably through his defense of free will in his *Essays in General Criticism* (1859).

James described his position both as radical empiricism and as pragmatism. The two of course do not mean the same thing. His empiricism based knowledge on experience, but it was experience seen realistically. Here he was helped by his work in psychology. He was critical of the prevailing paradigms of experience found in academic works and previous philosophy (e.g. British empiricism). This was often too selective, while James was vigorous in saying that we need to look at all experience (this was one strand in his tackling religious experience in an empirical manner in his *Varieties*). He was particularly hostile to the use of the spectator paradigm. In his chapter on the stream of thought in his *Principles of Psychology* he noted how thought is personal, *mine,* is ever-changing, is continuous, deals with things other than itself and is selective. His picture is continuous with Bergson's and that of Maine de Biran. So we can say that James' radical empiricism is among other things phenomenological in character. To all this he added pragmatism, but for him it is not merely a theory of meaning, though he presents it that way in *Pragmatism* in order to show that certain metaphysical disputes are vacuous. Beyond that, James held that pragmatism is a theory of truth: the truth of an idea is the process of its verification or validation. Ideas are incipient projects. So if I am lost, finding a path back to the main road involves the project of finding my way back, and the belief that such-and-such a path will lead me home. If in following it I do so find my way, then my belief that this is the right path is validated. In his *The Will to Believe* he argues that when faced with a genuine option you have the right to believe one thing rather than another, for instance because it satisfies our moral nature better. Pragmatically, belief in free will means belief in novelties in the world: it is much more fruitful than determinism in encouraging us in improving life.

His examination of religious experience suggested to him that the believer 'is continuous, to his consciousness at any rate, with a wider self from which saving experiences flow in' (*Varieties*, p. 109). But evil exists, and so it is probable that the God or higher self is finite in power or in knowledge or both. The future is not fixed: if humans cooperate with God, the cosmos will become better (note that belief in materialism would not have the same pragmatic consequences).

It may be noted that James was strong in arguing that a religious empiricism is superior to a non-religious one. The non-religious form unnecessarily and unnaturally restricts the scope of experience. James' position won him a lot of support, partly because pragmatism seemed to be both common sense and optimistic, and because James took an interest at least in traditional religion, even if his philosophy of religion looked decidedly heterodox. He had a lasting influence, for his pragmatism if not for his religious worldview. In England his line of thinking was carried on by F.C.S. Schiller (1864–1937) of Oxford, who had taught for a while in Cornell University. It was chiefly carried on, though, in America. The other main figure in this tradition whom we have to consider is that of John Dewey.

JOHN DEWEY: PRAGMATISM BECOMES INSTRUMENTALISM

John Dewey (1859–1952) was educated at the University of Vermont. After a spell as a high-school teacher he took a doctorate at Johns Hopkins, and taught at Michigan and Chicago. He published a large amount, on ethics, education and epistemology. Important among his philosophical writings are *Essays in Experimental Logic* (1916), *Experience and Nature* (1935) and *The Quest for Certainty* (1929).

He attacked the spectator theory of knowledge, which he saw as prevalent in classical philosophical writings. Thought or consciousness is not something which stands apart from the world. It is just a highly evolved form of the way an organism responds to its environment. In the course of its flow of life the human organism meets something which is problematic: it stops its other activities in order to resolve the problem, and this is how thought typically occurs. The problem is resolved when a course of action becomes defined. Let us put all this a bit more formally. A felt difficulty occurs, and then we attempt to articulate the problem or problems. Once this is done, we formulate various hypotheses on how to resolve the problem. Finally, we engage in experimental testing, to confirm or disconfirm the suggested hypotheses. When we come to what appears to be the right answer, then provided we have followed the norms and methods of inquiry, we can call this knowledge 'warranted assertibility'. For all this we do not need foundations, that is, indubitable truths in the manner of Descartes. The process of building up knowledge is a self-corrective one, and it is cumulative. Dewey hoped to supply the outline of a logic or inquiry which would be realistic, and would occur within a naturalistic setting.

Natural transactions, as Dewey saw them, occur at three levels – the physicochemical, the psychophysical, and that of human experience. Within this setting, human beings have values of various kinds, from esthetic to ethical. A somewhat similar picture is given of the moral life to that of inquiry. So a person faces a problem or conflict of values. He has to deliberate, and examine the relative consequences of diverse courses of action. A choice is reasonable in reflecting our developed habits of intelligence.

All this implies that Dewey must set a high appraisal on education. For intelligence is as evident in moral as intellectual action. Schools should be the setting for encouraging and inculcating good habits (Dewey of course set great store by habits), including those which conduce to open and critical inquiry, the enjoyment of esthetic experience and ethical reasonableness. His theories of education, which became tremendously influential, stressed the connection between learning and doing. The child is an active being, and not to be regarded as the passive receptor of 'knowledge'.

SOME FURTHER DEVELOPMENTS IN AMERICA: CRITICAL REALISM AND A.N. WHITEHEAD

The naturalistic tradition was perhaps best represented in the inter-war period by critical realism. A volume of *Essays in Critical Realism* appeared in 1920, and among its contributors were A.O. Lovejoy (1873–1962), who had been a keen analyst and critic of pragmatism, as well as an important contributor to the history of ideas – as in his *The Great Chain of Being* (1936); R.W. Sellars (1880–1973), an evolutionary materialist; and George Santayana (1863–1952), a Spaniard who taught at Harvard, chiefly noted for his esthetic theory and flowing style, and his somewhat fluid naturalism.

But though A.N. Whitehead (1861–1947) was British, he can justly be called an American metaphysician. For his strikingly original, but not easily understood, system dates from after the time he settled into a Harvard Chair in 1924. He had previously collaborated in *Principia Mathematica* (1910), a pathbreaking work, and had then taught in London, where he did a lot of work in the philosophy of science. His most important book was *Process and Reality* (1929), but we can also mention *Religion in the Making* (1926), *Adventures of Ideas* (1933) and *Nature and Life* (1934).

To a great degree he was influenced by science and wished to create a system which would meld with the latest advances in physics and cosmology. On the other hand, he did not feel that laws of nature were unchanging, so that there can be diverse cosmic epochs with differing laws. He wanted to have a smoothed-out view, however, of our cosmos, not making it dualistic, say, as between experience and non-experience. This is why he talked about feelings belonging to molecules and the like, for the response of any event to the rest of its environment is like a perception – he talked here of 'prehensions' or graspings. He held that actual entities are minimal events, that is, having minimal duration. They are then replaced by other events, whose similarity secures their continuity (so 'feelings' are contagious so to speak, and give rise to persisting objects, from our point of view, lasting over time). Actual entities or events cluster together in concrescences: we might look on his picture of things as organisms, and thus see the whole cosmos as a kind of super-organism. There are reminiscences in much of this of Buddhist philosophy. He found room in his picture for God or perhaps 'God', for in using traditional language he was perhaps being misleading. God is the principle of concretion. The whole process of the cosmos involves the move into creativity, as new concrescences make their appearance. God changes with the rest, in this dynamically operative interplay of events. This notion was later taken up by so-called process theologians, Christian thinkers who wanted to emphasize that God is not as classical theology would have it, impassible and changeless. The obscurity of Whitehead's terminology and so of his thought have limited his influence, but he wrestled with finding a system which would express the homogeneity of reality, including consciousness; the interconnectedness of events; the obsolete character of traditional substance-talk; and an event ontology.

LOGICAL POSITIVISM AND ANALYTIC PHILOSOPHY IN AMERICA

Meanwhile, because in part of the affinity between logical positivism and American naturalism, the two flowed together in America. C.I. Lewis (1883–1964) worked in logic in ways which had affinity to the thought of Schlick, of the Vienna Circle, and European positivists such as Rudolf Carnap, Carl Hempel and Ernest Nagel found a welcoming environment in the United States.

Ernest Nagel (1901–85) in his *The Structure of Science* (1961) and elsewhere formulated a naturalistic position which covers both the physical and biological sciences, on the one hand, and the social sciences, on the other. He holds to a view of logic without ontology (to quote the title of a famous paper); and sees human inquiry as unavoidably fallible. Hence he embraces an open and critical stance. He is also a materialist of a sort – not a reductionist one, but one who holds that all psychological events, etc., are dependent on material objects, which are spatially and temporally located. He is on the side of Einstein in denying that quantum theory entails indeterminism in physics. It is not necessary to hold to determinism in the social sciences, but whether it obtains here or there is itself an empirical question. Nagel supports atheism, but considers that tragedies are to be faced rather than evaded: so atheism becomes a noble moral position.

Rudolf Carnap (1891–1974) was born in Germany and after service in World War I he taught in the University of Vienna from 1926, where he associated closely with the Vienna Circle. In 1928 he published his *Der logische Aufbau der Welt* or *The Logical Construction of the World*. In 1935, because of the Nazis, he went to America and after a while taught at the University of Chicago and later (1954–61) at UCLA. His was an ingenious and broad-ranging attempt to build a theory both of language and reality constructed in the terminology of modern logic. He saw the world as composed of four types of objects: sociocultural objects, other minds, physical objects and one's own experiences. Epistemologically, we begin with the last (in this respect Carnap stays in the Cartesian tradition). Metaphysical issues have nothing to do with the answering of scientific questions. A little later Carnap shifted from this neutral stance towards metaphysics to an outright rejection. Metaphysics is the alleged solution to pseudo-problems. Metaphysical claims are unverifiable or (more moderately) not subject to confirmation or disconfirmation. However, the *Aufbau* position had its own problems: it started from epistemology and ended up as a sort of phenomenalism. In 1934, Carnap published *The Logical Syntax of Language*. Among other consequences of this work he saw the structure of science in terms of the logical syntax of the language of science. This defined the scope of philosophy proper. In his onslaught on pseudo-problems Carnap wanted to get rid of meanings, so that his classification of all possible sentences could hold – viz. syntactical sentences (about language), object sentences and pseudo-object sentences. Consequently: 'Yesterday's lecture was about Babylon' is translated by him as 'In yesterday's lecture the word "Babylon" occurred (seventeen times, or whatever).'

Carnap's empiricism was a severe one, but there remained real doubts as to whether his methods of technical analysis, ingenious as they were, could really work. Moreover, he softened his position on matters such as verifiability. It became harder to maintain the scientism of the Vienna Circle. With the slide from hard verification (or falsification) towards the concept of confirmability as consigning meaningfulness to scientific claims, there was a need for work on the logic of confirmation. The principal person to undertake this was C.G. Hempel (1905–97), who studied in Germany, went to America after leaving Germany in 1934, and taught at Yale from 1948 and Princeton from 1955. He also devised the covering law model of explanation, where an event is explained when it is deducible from prior conditions and certain general laws. His use of this model to treat of historical and social science explanations was ambitious. While he exhibited a gentler positivism, he contributed to the general stream of scientistic naturalism in the United States.

Positivism and naturalism tended to merge with linguistic analysis, often referred to as 'Oxford philosophy' in the period immediately after World War II, because of its strength in England. Now things have changed; the center of gravity has shifted to North American language philosophy, and its cousins have since, because of changes in ease of transportation and the increase of exchange between English-speaking universities, largely joined together in many ways. It is no longer apposite to talk separately about American and British and European and Australian philosophy. I shall leave until my concluding chapter a discussion of more recent trends in Western philosophy.

In concluding this section on American naturalism it is appropriate to finish with Willard Van Orman Quine (1908–2000), who perhaps was the most influential and the clearest thinker to adopt a scientistic outlook. Born in Ohio, he worked on his doctorate at Harvard. He had very broad language interests and was a philosopher of language as well as a logician. But he believed that it is useful to go beyond natural languages and introduce a degree of regimentation through logic. Apart from his contributions to logic itself, he is notable for certain philosophical positions which have stimulated a lot of controversy. For one thing, he attacked the analytic–synthetic distinction which underpinned so much in the usual formulations of logical positivism. Further, as part of this critique he expressed doubts, to put it no more strongly, about synonymy. In part because he had a behaviorist view of language, he held to the thesis of the indeterminacy of translation. It is possible to create alternative manuals of translation from one language to another which will fit the observed behavior of the users of the languages. All this underpins his revisionary view of the subject matter of philosophy. If the notion of synonymy is in any case open to question we should not worry about his regimentation of language – that is, the use of logic to reformulate our conceptual schemes. This might allow us to change our presupposed ontology. In any case the sharp distinction (which the synthetic–analytic distinction did something to sustain) between philosophy and science can be abandoned. In the end, of course, Quine was a naturalist. For him, science is a kind of religion. Anything which in principle is outside science lies outside of his worldview.

In surveying elements of the North American scene there are a number of influential philosophers during the inter-war and early post-war periods whom I have left on one side. Among them are Max Black, Brand Blanshard, Morris Cohen, C.J. Ducasse, W.E. Hocking, Norman Malcolm, Paul Tillich (really a Christian theologian) and Arthur Pap. Some of these explored in very different directions from the predominant naturalism and positivism which came to loom large in the 1950s and 1960s.

REFLECTIONS ON THE AMERICAN SCENE

We can see a growing split in the American worldview between what became dominant in the academy under the heading of philosophy and the prevailing ethos in the country. The 1960s for instance saw a reinforcement, but in a new key, of the older concerns for religion – a new quest for spiritual enlightenment to go alongside the older norms of Christian and Jewish loyalty. There were too new patterns of study in the academy: not just the great growth in sociological studies, but more particularly the creation of pluralistic and multidisciplinary religious studies. These quests to some degree fulfilled the traditional functions which philosophy courses had had: the search for deeper values. Philosophy had become highly preoccupied with the nature of science, and had often come to use logic as its key to the analysis of problems. It was thus very technical and often conceived of itself as highly professional in character. These themes are relevant to the conclusions of this book, as we shall see. We shall note how in the next chapter.

Enterprises in philosophy in North America

No single thread binds together the diverse religious, scientific, political, and social commitments that inform the intellectual tradition of North American thought, and various emergent philosophical inquiries, likewise, cannot be cut from whole cloth. Some enterprises will be left out, such as continental philosophy, since it will be given attention in another chapter; others will be given too short a shrift, due to the broad sweep of a very far-ranging landscape. If there are a plurality of enterprises in philosophy on the North American continent today, the ways in which these inquiries are conducted will be framed here according to two distinct emphases: one, which seeks to separate the activity of philosophy from the history of philosophy, in view of formulating and resolving problems; and the other, which recognizes its own philosophical trajectory as arising from a tradition of thought to which it responds, critiques, and reconstructs in view of the questions and concerns specific to the context of its own era. Philosophy in the ahistorical mode began in the Modern period and continues today, especially within the range of philosophical enterprises that fall under the rubric of Anglo-American analytic philosophy, itself the predominant field in the professional world of philosophy today.

Anglo-American analytic philosophy

It was Willard Quine (1908–2000), as reported by Richard Rorty (1931–2007), who described the ahistorical/historical divide, saying 'some are interested in the history of philosophy and some are interested in philosophy', suggesting that the real subject matter of philosophy, properly speaking, is the study of problems arising from the consequences of empirical science (Rorty, *Consequences of Pragmatism,* p.211). While the philosophical enterprises of Anglo-American analytic philosophy are in fact quite diverse, and not without proponents who emphasize the historical component of various inquires, the history of analytic philosophy emphasizes formulation and resolution of problems as a technical and/ or scientific endeavor. The common historical locus of the analytic approach to philosophy is the work of two British philosophers, Bertrand Russell (1872–1970) and G.E. Moore (1873–1958), whose arguments against idealism early in the twentieth century served to jumpstart a philosophical movement rejecting any split between the actual and appearing worlds, asserting instead that the empirical world is one to which human beings have direct access, depicted in the correspondence of words or logical signs to objects. At least two other thinkers were of seminal import here, as well: German philosopher Gottlob Frege (1848–1925), whose complex logic and mathematical logic schemas were incorporated in Russell's work, and Austrian philosopher Ludwig Wittgenstein (1889–1951), who was Russell's student, although eventually surpassing his teacher in philosophical import.

In the United States, an influential movement called logical positivism gained a strong foothold due to the influence of a group of philosophers comprising the Vienna Circle, whose members emigrated after the rise of Hitler's Weimar Republic. The philosophers of the Vienna Circle saw their work as following the precepts set out by Wittgenstein's early work, *Tractatus: Logico-Philosophicus* (although Wittgenstein disagreed), and set out to delimit problems of philosophical merit and set the standards for their resolution through science and the rejection of metaphysics. Otto Neurath (1882–1945), a prominent member of the Vienna Circle, rejected any conception but a scientific view of the world, and viewed any non-verifiable statement as not philosophical. Rudolph Carnap (1891–1970), the most influential proponent of logical positivism in the United States, set the standards for verifiability: propositions could be only of two types: analytic (problems resolved by definition or logic) or empirically verifiable (problems of science). Although the most important doctrine of logical positivism was the principle of verifiability, which demanded that every proposition be tested according to an empirical criterion of meaning, this principle itself failed to adhere to the standards of logical positivism: it was itself neither an analytic proposition nor empirically verifiable. Thus the insinuation of metaphysics weakened the logical positivists' project. Today, there are two leading ideas in analytic philosophy, both arising from Wittgenstein's later work, *Philosophical Investigations*. The first idea is that philosophical problems arise solely due to the misuse of language, and thus the problem-solving work of philosophy requires exposing linguistic confusions. The second idea is that meaning itself can be discerned only through attention to language use. Quine, whose work in philosophy would surpass in import the work of his teacher, Carnap, significantly and influentially elaborates this latter idea, rejecting incipient claims of positivism, finding no direct relation, much less correspondence, between language and objects in the world. According to Quine, reference is not transparent due to the fact that meanings of words are inter-linguistically indeterminate; that is, no well-defined fact corresponds in the same way to different words, which puts into question the legitimacy of analyticity. This allows Quine to postulate his thesis of indeterminacy of translation, which paves the way for what he names semantic holism as the idea that words have no meaning apart from the context in which they are used, and that the quest for understanding must be pursued holistically. In a related and also suggestively pragmatic move, Hilary Putnam (1926–) also rejects what is now referred to as the externalist position – that there is an objective, real world about which we can make verifiable truth claims – in favor of an internalist position – that conceptual schemas map descriptive if not absolutely determinative meanings on the world; there is no objective world independent of conceptual frameworks. Thomas Kuhn (1922–96), a philosopher of science and science historian, conceptualized these frameworks as paradigms, claiming that the history of scientific research does not show linear growth, as would be expected if purely stated facts map onto the objective world. Rather it is the case that revolutionary shifts in ways of conceiving the world make certain research projects absolutely incommensurable with others whose paradigms – conceptual schemas – are different. Richard Rorty, whose philosophical enterprise lies within the analytic-neo-pragmatist framework, also rejects direct correspondence between words or symbols and what they reference, and instead emphasizes interpretation as a fundamental component of understanding. Rorty also rejects the possibility of philosophy solving social problems, since conceptualizing these problems is a matter of interpretative contingency (and bad metaphysics), and since concepts do not mirror reality at all the best philosophy can do is ease the pain of everyday life.

American pragmatism

Thinkers in the tradition of classical American philosophy include philosophers as diverse as Ralph Waldo Emerson (1803–82), Charles Sanders Peirce (1839–1914), William James (1842–1910), Josiah Royce (1855–1916), George Santayana (1863–1952), George Herbert Mead (1863–1931), and John Dewey (1859–1952), and in varying contexts and to differing degrees these thinkers have significant import in the world of philosophy today, and in some cases, particularly those whose thought is grounded in the tradition of pragmatism, their influence is very far reaching and enjoying resurgence in its own right, as well as how it has been taken up by Anglo-American analytic philosophers. Neo-pragmatists embrace a fundamental component of the tradition's rejection of an objective correspondence between objects and signifiers, but ignore or do not take as seriously the socially contextual, historically rooted aspect of classical pragmatism. Inquiries and analyses generated by those in the latter tradition arise out of the whole cloth of human experience, because human life is itself socially constituted and thus in some fundamental sense the ground upon which disagreement and convergence erupt in the first place. This ground is not arbitrary, even lacking an objective backdrop, for if there is no ultimately unifying perspective to be gained human beings embark on contestation in the first place because there is some irreducible ground of the mere possibility of disagreement: the shared world. But outcomes of the most careful inquiry are held to be fallible. Knowledge claims are hypotheses, in the very best sense of scientific inquiry; such claims may justify action and fortify belief, yet as they give rise to new questions such claims might be shown to be inadequate or false; they are truths along the way and products of inquiry guided by the possibility of achieving truth, at least in the very long run. Pragmatic inquiry is therefore ongoing and inextricably bound to the multitudinous contexts from which it arises, contexts irreducibly social and pluralistic.

Arguably the originator of pragmatism and perhaps its most brilliant proponent is Charles Sanders Peirce, who renamed his philosophy pragmaticism in order to distinguish it from what he took to be the too free interpretation of it found in the work of Peirce's own most loyal friend, William James. Peirce's logic and theory of semiotics

– his own classification for a triadic theory of signs – brings rich complexity to questions of reference, for these three elements (and simplifying greatly): the sign, the object, and the interpretant must be considered together and thus are inextricably temporal and situated, that is, contextually rooted. One of the many important contributions of William James, psychologist and philosopher, is his radical empiricism, much more inclusive than that which could be counted as experience according to science or by traditional philosophical empiricism. Precisely in view of the pragmatic rejection of subject/object dualism – as if an observer of the world can be extricated from his or her place within it, naming and categorizing objects from afar, an Archimedean point beyond the world, perhaps – James' radial empiricism is modal, relational, since experience is marked out and designated as such in the first place by one who experiences. Subsequent analyses and understanding of experience must include affective impact as well as cognitive concern, both in view of perspective and desire, that is, how what we might want to be the case or not want to be the case also influences what we perceive and how we experience the world. The most internationally influential American philosopher is John Dewey, whose commitment to pluralism is reflected in his pluralistic undertakings in philosophy and in his role as a public thinker. Addressing concrete as well as philosophical concerns in education (Dewey founded what is known as the 'laboratory school' where the aim of education would serve as means – education as a vehicle of active involvement and social inquiry – as opposed to education structured by means of social control acclimating children to the boredom they would experience in their work-lives later), Dewey saw the nature and activity of philosophy to be fundamentally critical, and from the broadest purview: experience and those aspects of experience that alert us to problematic situations. Critical inquiry requires thoughtful analyses of issues, but more importantly, a careful formulation of specific problems in view of considering meaningful outcomes. Reconstruction of belief and action in view of desired outcomes demands a rethinking of means to attain them, and Dewey's instrumentalism evokes the irremediably relational aspect of a process from which experience is parsed and considered. No operative dualism between subject and object, but always a context in which something takes place whose meanings are constituted by experience as it is undergone and at the same time the extenuations of experience – that which is not noticed or lacks immediate impact – define and delimit what constitutes the experience itself. Thus to analyze an experience is through and through an instrumental enterprise, dependent upon what tools or instruments are utilized, that is, what factors are considered, from whose point of view, and in what context. Which pieces of information will be used and what will be left out? What ends are desired or feared? Context – the historical claims made upon present circumstances in view of future expectations – is inseparable from philosophical and practical analysis of problems, in other words.

Other philosophical enterprises in North America

Classical American thought owes a debt not only to the history of philosophy since Plato, but also in context of its own specific traditions, to the early Puritan thinker John Winthrop (1588–1649), whose notion of the covenant between the individual human being and God would influence the emphasis on individuality and the religious panentheism of Ralph Waldo Emerson, as well as idealists Josiah Royce and George Santayana. Likewise, Calvinist Jonathon Edwards (1703–58), whose harsh sermons emphasizing the contingent aspects of life and the essential nature of human depravity, gave efficacious voice to affectivity as the locus of the right-directed will, as opposed to granting that power solely to the rational mind. Edwards' emphasis on embodiment and the wisdom of the heart would certainly bear significant fruit in the thought of Emerson and James, who in turn would influence the work and thought of early feminist activist Jane Addams (1860–1935), whose Hull House grounded philosophical commitment in real life action. Emerson's elucidation of the difficulties of expressing ourselves as individuals, the necessity of courage and the willingness to not conform to social expectations in that enterprise influenced W.E.B. Dubois (1868–1963), whose conceptualization of *double consciousness* describes the difficulty of being in specific context of a world in which being black meant subscribing to a set of norms that would delimit possibilities of becoming from the outset. Current work in African American philosophy is also influenced by Alain Locke (1885–1954), who argued against the universality of social values, and who saw in the Harlem Renaissance the possibility of promoting a new social type: the New Negro, whose consciousness would be liberated from the constraints of racism by recognizing such assumptions as having no objective basis. Locke sought to undermine assumptions of cultural hierarchy as well; so-called high culture was different from but not better than the 'folk' culture given vital representation in Harlem through new musical forms, such as jazz, the visual arts, dance, and literature. Locke saw in this a renaissance of the indigenous African spirit, and he urged the embrace of a difficult dialectic: the freedom of the inner creative self with the outer world of politics and cultural life, specifically through creative participation in and the celebration of black culture, whose extant context was, at least for a time, Harlem.

Questions about meaning, purpose, place in the world, and about responsibility and the extent of our obligations to and for others arise in every human context. Historically these fundamental philosophical questions are not always separable from religious views, such as in the work of Emerson and Royce. American Indian thought is fundamentally grounded in spiritual life, the philosophical articulation of which was first developed by Vine Deloria, Jr. (1933–2005), of Lakota descent. Indigenous American thought takes up the philosophical conversation and debate within a broadly pluralistic context informed by the theological and cultural traditions of Europe, as well as by the diverse religious views and political organization of other tribal cultures.

Social and political enterprises

Leading thinkers in social/political thought today are analytic philosophers John Rawls (1921–2002) and Robert Nozick (1938–2002), from the United States, and the more historically oriented – sometimes referred to as 'post-analytic' – philosopher Charles Taylor (1931–), from Canada. Rawls' early work, *A Theory of Justice*, captured the attention of theorists across academic disciplines; his resolution to social inequities through the formulation of two principles, the liberty principle and the difference principle, results in his theory of justice as fairness, which urges the consideration of wealth and services distribution on the basis of self-interest – but with the caveat that this self might be the least advantaged member of society. Robert Nozick's *Anarchy, State, and Utopia* also captured widespread interest, and like Rawls' framework, Nozick focuses on the efficacy of the rational individual actor. But unlike the upshot of Rawls' position, which would lead to a more liberal society, Nozick's political leanings were not liberal, but libertarian. Nozick argues that the role of the state should be severely limited and not interfere with the life of individuals or the business of business, not merely on the basis of the merits of free market capitalism, but that a libertarian defense of persons as self-owners is fundamentally a moral defense advocating respect for individual rights. Charles Taylor, in contrast, argues against the emphasis on abstract individualism as the ground of moral social life, insisting on the intractable fact of social life as the basis for individuality in the first place. Taylor's communitarianism emphasizes the importance of social and communal arrangements and institutions as the context in which acquisition of meaning and sense of identity occurs. Human beings are not isolated individuals who might freely and arbitrarily choose one good over another, but make decisions in the first place against the backdrop of the social world – what Taylor calls the horizons of meaning – where communal norms and values already obtain and where real relationships inform choices with tangible meaning. Taylor's communitarian philosophy draws from pragmatist George Herbert Mead's idea of significant others, to whom the self is accountable and for whom the self is responsible.

Enterprises in feminism

If the social world is the locus of meaning and constitutive of the individual self, one crucially significant factor in individual development is sex, or, politically speaking, gender. Although feminist philosophy and gender studies can only be given cursory mention here, it is important to mention its influence. The work of attorney Catherine MacKinnon (1946–) continues to impact social consciousness even as her insights on the instantiation of pornography in advertising, entertainment, fashion, and everyday life grow but remain largely ignored. On the other hand, her work in civil rights and women's rights on the national level has made sexual harassment in the workplace a crime and, on the international level, MacKinnon was the first to adjudicate the war crime of rape as an act of genocide. Carol Gilligan (1936–) drew attention to the philosophical import of a different moral framework, that of the ethics of care. Current enterprises in feminist philosophy examine subject matter such as the phenomenon of dependency, work and women's labor, not only in view of women's place in society but also metaphysically. Helen Longino (1944–) critiques assumed objectivity in 'pure' disciplines, such as science and found sexist biases in scientific research and theories of knowledge. The feminist philosophical enterprise provides yet another angle from which to critique modernist notions of objectivity, autonomy, and the disembodied rational mind. Donna Haraway (1944–) also critiques science as biased but focuses on the biases of scientific researchers, male and female, whose narratives about the animal world mimic cultural stereotypes of masculinity and femininity. Haraway argues against gender essentialism – the view that behavioral differences between men and women mirror biological differences. According to Haraway, there is nothing about being female that naturally binds women to a particular set of behavioral norms; she promotes instead her theory of the Cyborg, which does not require a stable 'feminine' identity, but allows women to create coalitions against sexism and patriarchal attitudes through chosen affinities rather than on the basis of sex.

11

LATIN AMERICA

SOME GENERAL PATTERNS

Because Latin American cultures were heavily imprinted with Iberian civilization, the philosophy of the region is in large measure derivative from that of Europe. Nevertheless, there are variations, caused by differing factors. First, there remain underlying impulses originating in pre-Colombian values. I shall here say something about the major such cosmologies. More importantly, the race relations in Latin America did create in some areas, especially Mexico, the ambition of creating in modern times a new kind of civilization, distinct from both pre-Colombian patterns and those of the White world. Second, the movements of Liberation in the early part of the nineteenth century likewise stimulated ambitions of difference, while the growth during the nineteenth and early twentieth centuries of North American dominance could nurture an anti-Yanqui and antimaterialistic ideology. Third, the role of the Church and other religious organizations and movements has always been important in the area: for instance, the strand of thinking and of action as Liberation Theology during the latter half of this century has counted for more than its equivalent movements elsewhere. Fourth, to some extent, as in Africa, a lot of discussion has occurred about the identity of Latin American civilization (consequently I shall pay quite of a lot of attention to the worldview known as Arielism, flowing from the book *Ariel* by the Uruguayan philosopher Rodó, which perhaps gave the most coherent expression to an 'alternative identity', that is, alternative to the European and North American identity). Because the Church came rapidly to be in control of higher education in Latin America, naturally philosophy was deeply influenced by the emergent patterns of reformed teaching after the Council of Trent (1545–63). But before we explore this period, we can glance briefly at the Inca and

Aztec worldviews, representing the most fully developed systems encountered in the New World by the Spaniards.

INCA AND AZTEC WORLDVIEWS

The Inca civilization in an important sense inherited its predecessors, for its ideology incorporated a federation of gods and cults in which the various peoples were integrated into the one central system. Presiding over the whole in the heavenly sphere was Viracocha, the supreme creator and leader of the *huaca* or spirits – gods controlling various spheres of the cosmos as well as various human groups. The doctrine emphasized the importance of a polarity in the cosmos, between male and female, Sun and Moon, and so forth. The polarity could breed conflict, but the aim of religion was to induce ultimate harmony. On earth this was a primary function of the emperor, who was not just an earthly ruler but a kind of mediator. The ceremonial at Cuzco, the capital (literally the 'Navel' of the earth and of the cosmos), must have been most grand and glittering. Cuzco was seen (probably) as the confluence not only of its two earthly rivers, but of the Milky Way as well, seen as a celestial river flowing both in heaven and beneath the earth. It was the extraordinary centralization of the Empire that led to its collapse, since Pizarro and a few companions could strike so easily at its jugular. With that the ideology collapsed, though the local cults subsumed under Inca ideology would persist and blend with official Catholicism. If Inca cosmology reminds us of the yin–yang dialectic of Chinese cosmology, so also there are echoes of China in the worldview of the Aztecs, whose empire was based in Tenochtitlan, later Mexico City. Aztec cosmological geography had five directions, as did China; namely the four quarters plus the 'central direction', vertically through the center, conceived as being located in the capital. Above the city rise thirteen levels of heaven and below it nine underworlds (also reminiscent of Asian systems of cosmology). Aztec thinking was much preoccupied with issues of time. The world divides into different epochs, related to the different directions. Humans are in the fifth age, a period of great instability. The sun has to be given energy to keep on going, and such energy supposedly was imparted by sacrifices. Indeed at the start of the fifth age, when the sun failed to rise, it had to be powered through a collective self-sacrifice of the gods. The need to energize the sun (central organ of the universe) justified the sacrifice of victims through the emperor in the great temple (Templo Mayor) in Tenochtitlan. There were various dramatically depicted deities, such as the awe-inspiring Omoteotl, a blend of male and female, and ultimate creator, the female Coatlicue (Snake Skirt), strong in fertility, and like Kālî decorated with skulls, and Quetzalcoatl, recreator and inventor of the human arts, who died and came to life again, ruled and fell, and will return from exile in the East (he was not just a pattern for understanding Cortez in the mind of Montezuma, his unwilling host, but in some degree expressed values important in the native acceptance of Christ). The Aztec empire was a great military complex, requiring battle to capture sacrificial victims. This and its centralization proved its downfall. But its civilizational achievements were considerable and it is looked back upon with some pride by those who wish to interpret Mexico's special history and genius. There were of course plenty of other cultures, both large and small, scattered throughout the whole region. They were in due course integrated into Latin civilization. Two events were of some importance in this, which may be mentioned briefly. One was the occurrence of a vision to an Indian (the Spanish, for better or worse, called the aborigines indios, thinking the New World was the Indies), outside Mexico City, of a Nahuatl-speaking Virgin, the Virgin of Guadalupe, who became a kind of bridge between cultures and spiritual values. The other was the struggle of Bartolomé de las Casas (1474–1566), a priest, on behalf of the indios, arguing vigorously that they had souls, against those who denied it so as to be justified in the harshest modes of exploitation and killing. He helped to persuade the imperial monarchy to impose laws in the New World to protect the Indians, though even so the number of deaths was enormous, because of harsh conditions and European diseases.

THE EARLY AND INTERMEDIATE PERIOD: SCHOLASTICISM

Between the conquista and the period of liberation, beginning in 1810, the interest of the Church was paramount in education. Nevertheless the currents of thought present in the New World did not exclusively represent orthodoxy. The first bishop in Latin America was Juan de Zumárraga whose Short Doctrine (*Doctrina breve*) contained the influence of the humanism of Erasmus. Naturally too the importance of science was not neglected, and the work of Descartes was known in Latin America, both in Mexico and in Argentina, where it had a defender in José Elias del Carmen Pereira (1750–1804). On the other hand, much of the science taught in the New World was seen under the stamp of Aristotelianism and scholastic developments therefrom. One can say that over the first two and a half centuries the scene in Central and South America was not creative philosophically. But in the latter half of the eighteenth century and also in the early nineteenth century important European influences came to bear. These helped to prepare the way for the middle-class revolts which led to independence from Spain (and Portugal). These were deeply influenced by the ideals of the French and American Revolutions, themselves permeated by differing aspects of the Enlightenment. Important were ideas of individual liberty and the hope of social progress, of course. Elements of the Scottish Enlightenment, including the thought of Thomas Reid (1710–96), had an impact on the liberation movement in Venezuela. But also vital in the Latin American scene were variations on materialism, as derived from the French milieu. Thus the works of Destutt de Tracy (1754–1836) and of Pierre-Jean George Cabanis (1757–1808) were significant. These ideologues could appeal to the rising liberal intelligentsia precisely because their materialist and positivist stance was the opposite of Church teaching. The orthodox stream in the universities was deeply indebted to the scholasticism of Suarez (1548–1617), a schema that went beyond Aquinas in its system and coherence. But the scholastic tradition was not only uncreative in the eighteenth century, it was also disadvantaged by its political placement. The Church's alliance with the imperial government helped to call in question its worldview. The attractions of positivism therefore lay in its polar opposition not just to the methods of scholasticism but also to its content. Important too in the period of the Latin American revolution were the theories of the utilitarians, especially Jeremy Bentham. They set forth ways of conceiving law and government which did not depend upon any eternal verities, but could be employed in both a pragmatic and a critical manner. If one side of the liberation movement was the replacement of the older elite, itself heavily entangled in the institution and outlook of the Church, by a new one, dominated by various Enlightenment ideas and exemplars, the new revolution also exhibited aspects of nascent nationalism. It was therefore not surprising that during the mid-nineteenth century positivism lived somewhat uneasily alongside strains of romanticism. Nevertheless the materialist emphasis continued to grow, reinforced by the discovery of the evolutionary process, and by new theories of history. From this point of view the theories of Auguste Comte had wide appeal. It was indeed on the basis of Comtean theory that the Mexican education system was thoroughly reformed by Gabino Barreda in 1867 and succeeding years, under the patronage of Benito Juárez (1806–72). The fashionability of positivism (or naturalism, as some preferred to call it) lasted well into the twentieth century. We shall note some of its variations shortly. But meanwhile, the project of framing a progressive (as it was seen) metaphysics to replace the older Spanish thought-world was seen as insufficient, in the sense that the identity of the New World culture had to be diagnosed. What was the nature and destiny of this whole new culture? One sort of answer was given by the Uruguayan writer and philosopher, José Enrique Rodó (1871–1917). In 1900 he published a curious, highly rhetorical book, which came to have immense appeal on the Latin American scene.

THE THEORIES OF ARIEL

The Ariel of Rodó is of course the Ariel of *The Tempest*, a light and spiritual, esthetic creature, as over against the brutish Caliban. The latter stood for the materialism and utilitarianism of modern civilization as represented by the United States. Actually, the image is much, much too negative. For Rodó admires a great deal of North American civilization. For instance he is deeply appreciative of its giving dignity to labor, its democratic institutions, its thirst for knowledge, its investment in education, its individualism in association, its love of philanthropy, its inventiveness, its capacity to improvise, and so forth. Nevertheless, he wrote at a period when the new North was becoming in effect a new empire. Had Latin America thrown off the empires of Iberia only to be subjugated by a new imperial power? The defeat of Spain two years before the publication of *Ariel* naturally stimulated a certain sympathy. Rodó was also above all conscious of the European aspect of Latin American culture. Could old Europe be brought in somehow to counterbalance the brash new North? Rodó was curiously uninterested in various aspects of Latin American culture – for instance the pre-Colombian elements, and strands of scholastic and Catholic philosophy, mysticism, piety, art, and so forth. He is a modern and a romantic, and quintessentially a White man. Maybe this is because he came from one of the countries in the continent which are White in culture, not containing any serious indio strand. He could not have written in the same manner, one suspects, in Mexico. So he is in the upshot a sort of neo-European, who sees a new estheticism as possible in the translatlantic world. At the same time his model is France, rather than Spain. His argument seems to run as follows: we represent a new life, which will complement North America. But we are born of Europe. The new Europe cannot, however, be built upon our old parent, Spain (hence Rodó's relative lack of interest in Spanish models), so it has to be built on a transformation of the essence of Europe, which is French. The effect of Arielism was to promote a kind of elitist, spiritual estheticism as a counterpoise to the robust 'materialism' of the North. It is not that Rodó suggested that the Protestant and democratic philosophy of the North was literally materialistic. But nevertheless, he saw in the creation of material wealth only a partial step towards true civilization. This critique of the United States could be appealing, and hence the popularity of his book. On the other hand, Rodó was not in a strict sense anti-democratic, despite his elitism. He argued that a true elite cannot arise by force, but must arise from within the willing recognition of higher values in a democratic environment.

OTHER RESISTANCE TO POSITIVISM

Apart from Arielism, two worldviews, approaching from a different direction from that of Christianity, expressed positions which challenged the orthodox pieties of scientistic positivism. One of these was Krausism, which had an influence partly because of its relative popularity in Spain. In 1843, Julian Sanz del Rio (1814–69) was influentially elected as Professor of the History of Philosophy at Madrid, and went off to study in Germany. It was here that he became acquainted with and persuaded by the work of Karl Christian Friedrich Krause (1781–1832). He promulgated these ideas in Spain, and up until World War II Krausism became extraordinarily influential. Krause followed a panentheism in which the universe is seen as part of, or contained by, God. Both

Reason and Nature participate in God, and the human being is a synthesis of these on a microcosmic scale. In effect Krause's philosophy was a religion, and one in which reason predominates. The aim of human beings is to achieve maturity, having passed through a stage of self-definition which can lead to various evils. Taken together, human beings constitute the sphere of Reason. In an early stage of history you have polytheism, wars, slavery, tyrannies, and so forth. At the next higher stage we recognize the one infinite Being, but monotheism itself fosters theocracy and censorship. At the highest or panentheistic stage, humanity as it were returns to harmony with both itself and the divine, and this fosters toleration, republicanism, freedom and the ideal of world citizenship. Krausism, though expressed by its author in formidably obscure terms, was an appealing new religion for intellectuals, and a powerful alternative worldview to that of the existing Catholic hierarchy. It had elements of Kant, Fichte, Comte and Hegel. It was a major strand of Spanish-speaking liberalism. The other movement worth commenting on was more important in Brazil. It was based on the thought of the French thinker Allan Kardec (1804–69). It had a sort of positivistic framework, since its chief tenets were supposedly based on scientific inquiry. Its chief doctrines affirm the existence of God, who is the origin of innumerable spirits seen as in the process of reincarnation. It has a Christian ethos, since the central virtue is love. In some degree Kardecism also coalesced with earthier movements such as Umbanda, which flourishes especially among Afro-Brazilians, infused with West African Yoruba ideas and practices. Both these movements express a desire to have a religious worldview which is alternative to orthodox Catholicism. The scholastic tradition in the Catholic Church remained remarkably vital, partly because of the encyclical of Pope Leo XIII of 1879, *Aeterni patris*. This recommended powerfully the use of Aquinas' system of thought in a modern context to reaffirm traditional Catholic intellectual values. As the Church also took steps to suppress modernism at the turn of the century, it was not until well after World War II, and after the reforming Council of Vatican II (1962–5) that radical new thought was to emerge – most notably Liberation Theology, one of the major intellectual creations of Latin America.

Alejandro Deustea

An example of a philosopher who was influenced by Krause, though also by Henri Bergson (who exerted a powerful magnetism in Latin America), was Alejandro Deustea (1849–1945), Rector of the University of San Marcos in Peru. He saw esthetics as a supreme value, and he might be looked on as a Krausean estheticist. His concept of civilization is that it brings together the two sides of life, summed up as liberty and natural order. Art manages to harmonize the two through the use of the imagination, but a merely internal reconciliation is inadequate, since nature, for one thing, is external and material. So it is that the artist materializes her or his product, and similarly with a civilization. Deustea had various theories about the nature of harmony, which brings unity in variety, through rhythm and symmetry. Liberty is relevant to all this, since it implies essentially the absence of resistance. This allows the play of the emotions and the imagination, which is a creative force within human beings. Since it is only in the esthetic sphere that liberty is absolutized, while there are various constraints operative in other spheres such as economics (where desire becomes paramount), morality (where duty is supreme) and religion (where the divine will rules), Deustea's system becomes a kind of esthetic spirituality. This has some affinities to the general position of Rodó. It drives a middle path between Catholic tradition and the prevailing positivism.

Varona in Cuba

By contrast, the leading Cuban intellectual of the latter part of the nineteenth century, bridging the period to independence after the war of 1898, was Enrique José Varona y Pera (1849–1933), who became Vice-President of the Cuban Republic during World War I. He was influenced by British empiricism and especially by the work of J.S. Mill, as well as by French positivism. He was a physiological determinist, though humans have escaped being automata precisely because they have knowledge of causal patterns, and capitalizing on this have a certain plasticity of action (though not true freedom). He was also sensitive to the social dimension of existence, and argued that human personality itself is importantly derivative from society. But again, knowledge of this dependence gives humans a plasticity of behavior which is the sphere of morality. Such minimal notions of freedom and solidarity were enough to satisfy Varona's patriotism in the struggle against Spain. His materialist outlook helped to make him a radical critic of tradition.

SOME OTHER LATIN AMERICAN PHILOSOPHERS OF THE LATE NINETEENTH AND EARLY TWENTIETH CENTURY

Probably the most important positivist in the Argentine tradition was José Ingenieros (1877–1925), whose main training was in medicine and psychiatry, but who also studied philosophy. He rejected traditional religious formulations of problems, such as the issue of the existence of God, as being falsely posited. The true metaphysical questions arise out of, yet beyond, the sciences. But because they concern matters of which we have no present experience, they are of the nature to generate hypotheses rather than dogmas. Ingenieros was much gripped by the vision of evolution and saw the possibility of human perfectibility. Ideals themselves are hypotheses for the improvement of human nature.

In his work *El Hombre mediocre* of 1913 he saw ideal values as being the production of a creative elite, which is typically thwarted in its moral ambitions by *el hombre mediocre*, the mediocre human being. One major philosopher in the trend away from positivism was Bergson, with his evolutionary intuitionism. In the Argentine, Alejandro Korn (1860–1936) took up some of Bergson's motifs, as well as ideas drawn from Schopenhauer. Korn postulated a two-decker intuitionism. On the one hand, there was ordinary, experiential intuition. The idea here was to see an active role for consciousness in the discovery of knowledge. At another level, there are intellectual, religious and esthetic intuitions. They do not produce any certainty. Since Korn was left with two halves to reality, one external and the other arising out of consciousness, he had to create some synthesis in one direction or the other, which he did by fashioning a kind of absolute idealism. A more colorful and syncretic intuitionist was the Mexican philosopher José Vasconcelos (1882–1952), whose work was influenced not only by Bergson, but also by Plotinus, Schopenhauer and Nietzsche. He held to a form of dynamism, postulating energy as the key concept; this was an adaptation of Schopenhauer's key notion of *Wille*. Energy, however, was not homogeneous but occurred in three modes – atomic, organic and spiritual. So there was a psychic aspect to the energy of the cosmos: this somewhat pantheistic account was changed in Vasconcelos' later life, when he had gone back to the Catholic Church and to a form of theism (how orthodox is open to some question). Like so many other Latin American philosophers, he placed great weight upon esthetics, and was also critical of capitalism, though his socialism was anti-Marxist. He was also one of the few philosophers to take non-Christian religions seriously and praised Buddhism for its emphasis on infinite love and compassion. In the reaction against positivism it is clear that certain themes came to predominate in Latin American philosophy. One was the notion of intuition, and with it a broader view of knowledge than that contained in the positivistic or empiricist model of science. Another was the importance of esthetic values as being allied to or alternative to traditional religious values. Another notion was the fluidity of change, as expressed especially by Bergson. Probably both Bergson and Schopenhauer had greater impact on the Latin American scene than they did back in Europe. Positivism cleared the way for an acceptance of evolutionism which could be given an esthetic and ethical flavor to chime in with the desire to transcend North American positivism and pragmatism. However, much of Latin American philosophy in the twentieth century can be considered just as an extension of European and North American philosophical debate. The most original wave of thought which has worked in the opposite direction has been so-called Liberation Theology, and to that I now move, with some brief preliminary reflections on the cultural and political milieu which gave rise to it.

THE BACKGROUND TO LIBERATION THEOLOGY

Liberation Theology, briefly, is a movement chiefly within the Catholic Church which makes use of Marxist tools of analysis in expressing a radical position. Its genesis coincided with certain changes in Catholicism following upon Vatican II (1962–5). The new flexibilities aroused Catholic imaginations. But there were deeper reasons why it was in Latin America that the new rather revolutionary ideas fermented. The Church had an ambiguous position. In much of Latin America it tended to be allied with government forces which, while inheriting the results of the early nineteenth-century liberation, were also allied to often repressive economic and political arrangements. Moreover, Latin America retained in some degree a racist aspect: the peasants and working class in many countries were indios and in Brazil especially blacks, whose presence was a consequence of the slave trade. Color of skin was an index of social position. In such societies (outside of all-white countries such as Argentina, Uruguay, and Chile) the concept of class struggle could have a more obvious instantiation. Further, the mid-twentieth century saw a large number of countries where militarism and right-wing politics held sway. Caudillismo had in any case been a major Latin American tradition. In all these circumstances the conditions were ripe for the appeal of Marxist analysis. This was doubtless why Liberation Theology first took root in Latin America and was indeed a major intellectual product of the continent. In the 1970s it had a major impact on Christian thought, both in the North and in other parts of the South, despite reactions against the movement from governments and some Church authorities. The conference of bishops which took place in Medellín in 1968, representing the Churches of Latin America, had expressed the need to struggle against the social injustices which 'keep the majority of our peoples in dismal poverty, which in many cases becomes inhuman wretchedness' (cited in Gremillion (ed.), *The Gospel of Peace and Justice*, p. 471). This gave the impetus to new thinking about economic and social development. In 1969, Gustavo Gutiérrez, the Peruvian theologian, reflected that the term development is already theory-and value-laden. Why not talk about liberation? Out of that reflection came the title of his highly influential book which he published in 1971: *A Theology of Liberation*. Various themes emerged in the formulation of Liberation Theology through such writers as Gutiérrez, Leonardo and Clodovis Boff, Juan Segundo and Hugo Assmann. I shall begin here with a crucial notion which underlines much of Liberation Theology's critique of capitalism, and reinforces some of the factors listed earlier which make for the use of Marxist tools of analysis. This notion is dependency theory. It is the view that peripheral countries in the world system, which is capitalist, have their economies conditioned by others, namely those countries which form the center of the system. It is a theory which in another form occurs as the thesis of neo-colonialism. But not only is the periphery conditioned by the center: its growth is actually impeded (some theorists think) by the center. In short, capitalism is actually a system which helps to contribute to the poverty of the Third World. Moreover, the evolution of the world into a single and synergistic system means that it is unlikely or even impossible to think that the poorer countries' growth could ever replicate that of the advanced countries. One consequence of these positions is that the theory of orthodox development, as preached by the World Bank and other such 'Northern' organs and theorists, is actually used by many liberationists in effect as a pejorative notion: it was called *desarrollismo* in Spanish, i.e. developmentalism, and critiqued strongly. The theory paves the way for an identification, in effect, of the Third World with the suffering working class: now class theory can be expounded in terms of international relations, international economics and of course politics. Now we can move towards the more intimate themes of Liberation Theology as conceived in Latin America.

THEMES IN LIBERATION THEOLOGY

First, while liberation theologians have embraced Marxism, this is seen as the taking up of a set of tools of analysis: it is claimed that Marxism is used instrumentally, rather than substantially. Still, while of course liberation theologians are Christians first and Marxists second, it is not unreasonable to see their position as a kind of synthesis. Since Marxism itself propounds certain diagnoses of the human tradition, and dependency theory might be one of these, it is not easy to see how Marxism as incorporated into Liberation Theology can be purely instrumental. Questions of fact do make their presence felt. But liberation theologians are not uncritical Marxists, out of the very nature of their commitments. Still, Marxist analysis is very far away from mainstream Catholic philosophizing. There is therefore in Liberation Theology a certain sort of Protestant flavor. The writers of this movement are deeply concerned with presenting the God of the Bible. Their movement does represent a variation on the theme of 'back to the Bible'. Here in particular they take up a theme which is difficult to avoid in the Gospels – Jesus' support for and concern for the poor. So the major valuational starting point of Liberation Theology is the Christian 'option for the poor'. From this angle, God is not the impartial creator of rich and poor alike. He loves the poor (I here, by the way, use the non-inclusive language that characterizes much of the relevant literature) and takes their side in the struggles of history. God suffers with the poor, but not as one who surrenders to the cruelty of the world: rather, he struggles against it. In this he joins in the class struggle, which liberationists tend to see as a reality. In this analysis use is made of the concept of praxis. This embraces various thoughts. First of all, the understanding of the world has to be tied to the historical situation in which human beings find themselves. One's position in the socioeconomic classes and on the historical stage is vital. This in turn means that any theory of knowledge needs to locate that knowledge. Moreover, in being tied to practical reality knowledge arises in an intersubjective way, and also has a role in helping to create new realities – to create history, in short. In various ways liberationism tends to reject older notions drawn from the Enlightenment of objectivity and of disengaged reason. This helps also to explain the large-scale rejection of the Neothomist heritage of the Catholic tradition, which had in any case become somewhat superseded by the decisions of Vatican II. It also helps to determine how liberationists read the New Testament. There is in all this a tendency towards making human decisions, and behind that consciousness, the determining factor in what counts as knowledge. This is reinforced by new readings of the Old Testament, where to know God is to love God (so knowledge becomes the analogy of sexual intercourse and conversely). But to love God is to act with him, on behalf of justice. So knowledge of God immediately plunges us into the world of action. There is of course a problem with the liberationists' view of the temperament of God, as suffering activist. How is it that if God created the world, there is so much suffering which he himself needs to combat? The answer has to do with sin. Liberationists are unlike liberals, who have tended to water down sin to individual acts, and who indeed tend to take an optimistic view of human nature. For the liberationists, sin is woven deeply into the structures of the world. It is not just an individual condition (though it does have its individual and group dimensions), but is a suprapersonal reality. All this no doubt leaves the question of the ultimate genesis of sin as mysterious. But it is a view wholly consistent with another theme of the movement, namely that of the solidarity between sacred and secular history. Liberation theologians tend to be highly critical of an idea which had quite a lot of vogue after World War II, that of salvation history – as though a thread or a stream of divine history runs within the broader stream of total human history. For liberationists all history is to be seen as the area of God's activity, and our activity. That is why we have to tackle problems in the concreteness of actual events and actual structures. Because of this the picture of God has to be modified from the transcendent Being who stands outside the concreteness of the social and historical facts of human life. God is not to be thought of as an omnipotent, omniscient Being 'out there'. He is the poor God, suffering with the poor and striving, with and through the faithful who are joined to him, to establish human justice. Hence God is a liberator and we in being with him are liberators too. Where does this leave the theme of Christ? First of all of course, the story of the incarnation is the narrative of how God becomes poor. Jesus' life was one of relative poverty, and he preached often against the rich. He saw himself as poor in spirit. But he also saw himself as ushering in a new age, one of liberation in which the historical reality of the world starts to be transformed. Liberationists see importantly the political side of Jesus' ministry. He critiqued deeply the power groups of his day – the Romans, the Sadducees (orthodox rulers of the Jewish community who cooperated with Rome), the Pharisees, fashioning a new piety, and others. The rulers of his day did not appreciate the criticism and responded with persecution: it was not surprising that he was put to death. Naturally, liberationists also speculate on what

Jesus' attitude would have been to today's sociopolitical structures, including those of the Church. Another theme of liberationism has to do with Marx's analysis of religion. The movement is often critical of Marx's consistent denial of the importance of the superstructure, of human consciousness and institutions as having a causative role to play in the ongoing transformations of history. For liberationism of course envisages a highly creative role for religion and the Church in particular: moreover, they see liberation as a spiritual as well as simultaneously a material and social process. They perceive the Church as the community of those who work in solidarity with God in the task of freeing humans. The Church must take the option for the poor, and go down into the hell of suffering in the world in order to help raise the poor up from the depths to a higher life. It has to proclaim liberation and so be a sacramental sign of the new life: it must at the same time be an instrument of liberation and so help in the struggle against the structures of the world which prevent liberation. In all this Gutierrez and others affirm a real role for the Church which was different from the location assigned to it by Marx. For Marx the Church had to be part of the oppressive system: its fairytales of heavenly life were designed to assist in the pacifying and oppression of the lower classes. But for liberationists a Christian mission holds itself forth for the Church if she can but be clear about the true message of Jesus which it is her duty both to proclaim and to act out. An important theme of liberationism is not just the rejection of developmentalism as conceived according to capitalist criteria. It looks, obviously, to a liberated society. But what is that? It is not basically a movement of amelioration, in the sense of trying to reform present society, since it considers that present society is itself oppressive. It has a thoroughly negative view of capitalism, which it associates with the colonial and exploitative processes which do so much harm to the poor of the Third World. What is needed is a social order which is qualitatively different: hence the movement tends to postulate a new form, indigenously grown, of socialism. By this they mean a Latin American version of socialism: there is in liberationism a sort of regional nationalism. Theirs is a more politically expressed hope corresponding to the more elitism doctrine of Arielism. The Boff brothers in their *Introducing Liberation Theology* (1987) think of the liberated society as one of cooperation which reflects something of the nature of the Trinity, itself of course, since relatively early in the Church's history, a model of Christian love. But on the whole liberationists are fairly vague about the future. On the other hand, they reject those mythologically expressed eschatologies which foresee the consummation of history as involving divine and spectacular intervention. They are highly resistant to the miraculous here: God works within history for them, rather than as a *deus ex machina* descending with clouds of glory to save and transfigure the human race. They are adamant on the necessity of looking at the world and at the Christian's task from within history. Important to Liberation Theology is the notion of raising consciousness. It was an important part of the diffusion of the central tenets of the new worldview that it should draw in the poor themselves. Indeed, the intellectuals of the movement hoped to be able to learn from the oppressed. One of the mechanisms for raising consciousness was the Base Ecclesial Community – groups at grass-roots level who discussed the ideas of Liberation Theology, studied the Bible, held house church meetings, set about remedying local problems and so forth.

REFLECTIONS ON LIBERATION THEOLOGY IN RELATION TO PHILOSOPHIES

While Latin American Liberation Theology has been attractive to many both inside and outside the region, it of course arises as an expression of a religious worldview. Still, it fulfils a function not unlike some of the philosophies we have looked at here – namely, helping to define a uniquely Latin American system of values. Other regions of the world, such as Africa, have been stimulated to create parallel worldviews. As a set of ideas it is probably the most original contribution that Latin America has so far made to world thinking. Much of the philosophical thought in the area is derivative from European and in particular Spanish models, as I have already noted. Unlike alternatives to traditional Catholic thinking, however, Liberation Theology comes from within the Church, while systems such as those we have examined, whether positivistic or idealistic, have arisen among a partially alienated middle class, often hostile to the Church. Liberation Theology is consciously anti-elitist as well, a contrast to Rodó, Ingenieros and others. The direction that Latin America will probably take as a region is to be sucked more and more into a global philosophical debate still dominated by the thought of North America and Europe.

IDENTITY AND LIBERATION

Yet it is not only contemporary Latin American theologians who have been concerned with liberation. From the wars of independence to the present, a number of feminist theorists and social and political philosophers have reflected on this topic. But here it is raised in connection with another issue of foremost importance to Latin American philosophy: identity, understood as either gender identity, ethnic-group identity, or philosophical identity. Each of these can be treated separately.

Gender identity, feminism, and liberation

When feminist theorists worldwide address the topic of gender identity, they standardly endorse equal rights for both women and men. Although Latin American feminists are not an exception to this, they have distinguished themselves from their European and North American peers by also insisting from the start on fundamental differences between men and women – a view that has now become mainstream among feminists in the West. Another distinctive aspect of Latin American feminism concerns its struggle with the prevalence of *machismo* (from 'macho', literally 'male'). For Latin Americans, this is the term of choice for the notorious prejudice affecting their society and culture that consists in a social and individual tendency to underestimate women's achievements and capabilities and to overrate those of men. Even women of unquestioned ability often face obstacles due to machismo. The bitter legacy of male dominance is often explained by reference to the Spanish conquest, which conferred a tacit entitlement to Iberian conquerors in failing to stop their common abusive practices toward native women. The relationship between the Spanish conqueror Hernán Cortez (1495–1547) and Doña Marina or 'La Malinche', one of the twenty Indian women presented to him as human 'gifts', symbolizes such practices. Although an Indian herself, she was forced to travel with Cortez as his companion and his translator of the native languages – thus becoming instrumental in the fall of the Aztecs and ultimately of Mexico itself. As a result of machismo, Latin American women have been assigned subservient roles for centuries.

Even so, in Latin America there is also a long tradition of women reacting vigorously against machismo. A pioneer among them was Sor (Sister) Juana Inés de la Cruz (1651–95). Still referred to as 'the Tenth Muse' and 'the Phoenix of Mexico', Sor Juana was a Mexican nun of considerable accomplishments as a poet and a playwright whose scientific and philosophical interests, unusual for a woman at the time, gained her a wide reputation in colonial Mexico. Her knowledge and artistic talents impressed the participants of animated *salons* which often included prominent intellectuals and leaders of the local society. The Church's official criticism of her intellectual activities, at the time judged inappropriate for a woman, were rejected by Sor Juana in her *Reply to Sor Philothea*. This modern feminist manifesto offers biographical details of how her passion for learning developed, and is perhaps the earliest modern vindication of both women's rights to knowledge and women's distinctive intellectual competence.

Today, independent-minded women in Latin America continue to feel stifled in a machista society that refuses to recognize their capacity for achievement and restricts them to subservient roles. But an increasing number of Hispanic philosophers, both in the United States and south of the border, are now denouncing machismo. For 'liberation philosophers' such as Enrique Dussel (Argentinean, 1934–), there can be no liberation of society without the liberation of women.

Hispanics' ethnic identity

From the time of their revolt against Iberian rule to the present, Latin Americans and their descendants abroad have often raised the question of their identity as an ethnic group. Is there something common to all of them that distinguishes them from other groups? In fact, they have in common no one religion, no single view of history, no unified perception of the Other, no agreed set of moral norms, or other qualities. Some are Roman Catholics, but others are Protestants, Jews, Buddhists, and other faiths. Some are of European ancestry (which may or may not be Spanish), but others of Amerindian, African, Middle Eastern, or East Asian descent. Some speak European languages, mainly but not uniquely, Spanish, Portuguese, and English; others, Amerindian ones such as Quechua and Guaraní. Some have dark skin, others light. In sum, they are of diverse racial backgrounds, cultural practices, and social preferences. To Jorge Gracia (Cuban-born American, 1942–), this is not an obstacle to their having a common ethnicity. For although there is no property at all that Hispanics share, their ethnic identity consists in a 'family resemblance' they have in common. Whether or not this account is correct, Hispanics clearly share a wealth of communal experiences, including the legacy of some historical events, that make them the people they are.

The issue of the 'name'

What, then, should members of this ethnic group be called? In US English the most common non-derogatory words to refer to them are 'Hispanics' and 'Latinos'. The first of these, though never entirely accepted by those to whom it is applied, has become accepted usage in spite of persistent attempts to replace it with 'Latinos'. US philosopher Linda Alcoff advocates use of the latter, a proposal not surprising in light of the history of 'Hispanics', which was introduced with its present meaning during the Nixon administration (to stop public officials from using 'Chicano' to refer to anyone of Latin American ancestry, whether or not of Mexican descent). A further problem is that, although 'Hispanics' applies to anyone of Hispanic ethnicity or descent, the term appears to derive from, 'hispanos', a Spanish word denoting anyone fundamentally related to either Spain or its former colonies overseas. But if this were part of the meaning of 'Hispanics', then the word might be inappropriate on moral grounds (compare calling North Americans 'Britons'). A case could be made, however, that 'hispanos' and 'Hispanics' are false cognates. In the early part of the twentieth century, the Peruvian Marxist thinker José Carlos Mariátegui (1895–1930) noted that 'Hispanics' leaves out the indigenous peoples of Latin America, and so he coined the substitutes, 'Indo-Ibero Americans' and 'Indo-Hispanic Americans'. Unfortunately, these have never caught on.

THE EXISTENCE OF A CHARACTERISTICALLY LATIN AMERICAN PHILOSOPHY

From the mid-twentieth century to the present, there has been a noticeable interest among Hispanic philosophers in whether their culture, so rich in all other ways, has produced *philosophy* that is original and concerns the Latin American context. In other words, is there a characteristically Latin American philosophy? An influential view on this question is that of Leopoldo Zea (Mexican, 1912–2004). For him, no philosophical work is *perspective-less*, and philosophers invariably show their characteristic cultural perspectives, whatever their favorite topics and methods. As a result, any work by a Latin American philosopher constitutes characteristically Latin American philosophy. Prominent among those who reject Zea's view is Augusto Salazar Bondy (Peruvian, 1927–74), for whom the historical dependence of Latin America on major Western powers has precluded the development of original philosophical traditions in Latin America. But his position is only that there is at present no characteristically Latin American philosophy, not that there *couldn't be one*, since such a philosophy may flourish once dependence is overcome.

A similarly skeptical conclusion based on an entirely different argument is that of Risieri Frondizi (Argentinean, 1910–85). Acknowledging that there is a characteristically Latin American philosophy in a *broad sense*, Frondizi denies that there is one *in a strict sense*. In the broad sense, 'philosophy' might include the work of anyone who raises philosophical questions, even though they are subordinated to an interest in another discipline. In the narrow sense, or 'philosophy as such', it includes only the work of those who raise philosophical questions for their own sake, as most professional philosophers at universities do today.

On this view, although Latin American thinkers such as las Casas, Sor Juana, Rodó and many others produced characteristically Latin American work, none of it would count as characteristically Latin American philosophy in the narrow sense. But it is important to remember that in Latin America, philosophy *as such* began only in the twentieth century, when professional philosophers achieved an academic and social status similar to that of their colleagues in Europe and the United States. This was due in great part to the work of the so-called *fundadores* (founders) of the early twentieth century, who were a diverse group of Latin American philosophers who reacted against positivism and strove to develop a practice of philosophy in the subcontinent more like what their peers were doing at the time in major universities in the northern hemisphere. Through the efforts of the *fundadores*, standard forms of professional interaction among philosophers were created, such as journals and learned societies. These developments, together with the new status thereby achieved for philosophy within the community, earned the founders credit for having established philosophical 'normalcy' in Latin America.

Heavily influenced by European philosophers of the time, however, the founders failed to produce truly original philosophical work. If we focus exclusively on their

368

work, then, we are bound to agree with Frondizi's skepticism about the existence of a characteristically Latin American philosophy. But Frondizi is led to this skepticism only because his conception of philosophy in the narrow sense is too severe: under it, many of the greatest works of the philosophical canon – from Hobbes and Locke to Mill, Marx, and Rawls – would not count as philosophical! Since there is no good reason to accept such a limited conception of philosophy, we can conclude that there is a characteristically Latin America philosophy: that made up of the work of many thinkers of original philosophical insights, whether or not they thought of themselves as philosophers, and even though many of them did not have the rigorous training philosophers are expected to have now.

12

MODERN ISLAM

THE DECLINE OF THE ISLAMIC WORLD AND EUROPEAN DOMINATION

For diverse reasons the three great Islamic empires, the Ottoman, the Persian and the Mughal were in decline by the eighteenth century. After Sulayman the Magnificent in Turkey, Shah 'Abbas among the Safavids in Iran and Aurangzib in India, the political and cultural life in these dynasties went into decline: meanwhile Europe was becoming technically powerful and culturally dynamic. In due course, India was conquered by the British in the nineteenth century, and somewhat earlier the Dutch established dominance in Indonesia, itself a relatively recent convert to Islam; by the nineteenth century the whole area was under Dutch control. At the end of the nineteenth century France came to dominate most of North Africa, and the Italians took Libya (1911). Egypt meanwhile had succumbed to British domination, and later the Sudan. World War I saw the collapse of the remainder of the Ottoman empire, and protectorates were established by the British and French over much of the Arab areas east of the Mediterranean. Iran was eyed by the Russians and the British and partially penetrated. There was little of the Islamic world which was not directly or indirectly controlled by the West. It was after World War II that the whole crescent from Indonesia to West Africa was liberated, though economically the West remained dominant, especially in the oil-rich regions of the Middle East. The penetration of outsiders and infidels into the region led to a revival of Islamic thought and culture, but in a somewhat new form. By reaction to the West, nationalism of various sorts was stimulated. Sometimes this was highly regionalized and somewhat identified with colonial boundaries, such as Algerian and Sudanese nationalism. Sometimes it took on a Pan-Arab character – this in part because it was nationalism on the main European model, based on language and therefore literary culture. Sometimes it was Pan-Islamic, based for instance after the fall of the Ottomans on the vision of a restored Caliphate. These aspirations in very recent times maintain an existence through such organizations as the Arab League and the Organization of the Islamic Conference.

If nationalism was one form which a restimulated Islam took, another factor was Western orientalism, which helped to make available in modern editions many of the classics and brought new methods and slants to scholarship: it provided also another way into the past, circumventing the highly traditional teachers of the mosque schools and traditional universities. Notable, for example, was the foundation of the American University of Beirut (originally a Presbyterian College started in 1866). Such endeavors wed Islamic and Western scholarship together in a new and vital interplay. The introduction of Western-style education in countries such as Egypt and India (partly later Pakistan) not only forced Muslims to think about the relations of religion and science, it also injected new literary and philosophical ambitions. It was also greeted by a fair degree of enthusiasm for practical reasons. If the conquered peoples were ever to fight back against the West, they needed modern methods of warfare, which involved the learning of new technologies, which in turn meant science. All this implied social changes and the rooting out of what were perceived as decadent aspects of Islamic civilizations. So Western-style culture was more than a source of ideas: it was a means of creating national strength. It was also an opportunity for a new middle class. In brief, Western culture was both a stimulus and a weapon. But it also posed a question: how much of it was needed to blend with Islamic and national values? And how much of the old could be retained? It was no help if in trying to defend Islam you had to destroy it. Naturally, among the new middle class were those who in effect abandoned tradition and became humanists. There were also Marxist-style revolutionary movements. But on the whole the Muslim world set about trying to revive the faith while incorporating some or all features of modernity. Here Western-type institutions of higher education played an important role.

Before we see something of the emergence of modern Islamic thinking, under the impact of these forces, it is worth noting that as at other places and times the Islamic world experienced a few new religious movements, which presented new or revived worldviews. We shall glance at these briefly before we get on to the whole rainbow of the Islamic revival. The ones we shall contemplate are the Wahhābī movement in Arabia, forerunner of a number of revivalist phenomena; the Baha'i out of Iran, a new religion, though coming out of an Islamic milieu; and the Ahmadiyyah movement in India.

THE WAHHĀBĪ MOVEMENT IN ARABIA: VIBRANT FUNDAMENTALISM

Essentially the Wahhābīs, who came to set the pattern for Arabian (Saudi Arabian) religion, were premodern fundamentalists. They desired to return to a pristine Islam and thereby to cut out what they saw as degenerate and un-Islamic elements in prevailing Arabian Islam. Their name derives from the founder and leader of the movement, Muhammad ibn 'Abd al-Wahhāb (1703–92). He was particularly critical of popular Sufism: the cult of the tombs of popular saints and the veneration of mystics led to a screen of fragmented popular devotion arising between the individual and God. In 1744 'Abd al-Wahhāb formed an alliance with a ruler of central Arabia, Muhammad ibn Sa'ūd. Eventually, though Sa'udi rulers using Wahhābī ideology came to control most of Arabia, this stimulated the Ottomans to order the governor of Egypt to restore Ottoman rule. But in the middle of the nineteenth century the Sa'udis ruled part of central Arabia, though in the 1890s they were forced into exile by internecine strife in the peninsula. But in the period after World War I, 'Abd al-'Azīz ibn Sa'ud re-established the Sa'udi monarchy and rule, and imposed a somewhat pragmatic version of Wahhābism on his kingdom.

The Wahhābī worldview wished for revived pristine Islam. It allowed *ijtihād* or analogical reasoning, long frozen out in the traditionalist schools of *Sharī'ah*, but strictly on the basis of the early faith. Emphasis was placed on the unity of God, and this should be applied to political and economic life: anything which is not traced back to God's revealed will counts as polytheism. The interpretation of Law is relatively strict, according to the Hanbali school. Most of medieval interpretation is rejected, together with Shi'i practices and Sufism. This ideology has come to rule Arabia, and to surround the way the holy places are administered. Though the movement is Neofoundationalist or fundamentalist, it was, as we noted, a pre-modern fundamentalism, which was itself subject to pragmatic reinterpretation during the latest period of the monarchy, since the 1920s.

THE BAHA'IS: BEYOND ISLAM

The Baha'is are so called because they are followers of a faith proclaimed by Mirza Husayn 'Ali Nuri (1817–92) of Teheran, known as 'Glory of God' or Baha'ullāh. He is thought by the Baha'is to be the messianic figure proclaimed by the earlier prophet known as the Bab or 'Gate' (1819–43). Baha'ullāh ended up in Palestine, after imprisonments and exile; Palestine is therefore the holy land of the Baha'is and the site of their headquarters. The religion became a worldwide mission, since it is strongly missionizing. It sees truth as relative, so that in due course Baha'ism itself will be superseded: previous faiths have had missions which have been accomplished, so that now we move on to a higher stage. The Baha'i have varying tenets, including the need for a world language, the imperative for the whole of humanity to share in a common sanctity, beyond the divisive religions. Its prayer life is private, but followers are expected to pray daily. It proclaims the equality of men and women, and teaches monogamy. In some ways it is a sort of simplified Islam, but in its emphasis on world values it is unifying in intent, and has a brotherly view of the other major religions. It has substantial appeal, as a minority movement, in the West, and has always taken its mission seriously. But because it came from an Islamic milieu it is regard as apostasy and heresy in many Muslim countries, and has been severely persecuted in Iran. It is the most vigorous new religion to have come out of the Islamic world.

THE AHMADIYAHS: A VERSION OF PRACTICAL MODERNISM

A vigorous group arising in the Punjab in the 1880s was the following of a charismatic leader Mirzā Ghulām Ahmad (1835–1908). On the whole their teachings are orthodox Muslim, except that Ahmad considered himself a prophet (a thing no Muslim would recognize, since Muhammad is the last and the seal of the Prophets), as well as an incarnation of Vishnu and Messiah (he hoped to appeal to adherents of all three religions). But the movement came to be highly modern in its methods, generally adopting Western missionary techniques and sending missions around the world, where, in America, it was one of the ingredients in the formation of Black Islam. But it has been declared in Pakistan to be non-Muslim, and so not entitled to the benefits of the established religion.

The three movements we have noted indicate indirect effects of the interplay between Western culture and the Muslim heartlands. One is a fundamentalist *sunna* which retains strong influence in Islam because of its control of the Holy Places; another is a new universalist faith with some of the flavor of Islam; the third is a heretical modernism. But more important than any of these are the various forms of modernism which have arisen in various regions of Islamic culture.

AL-AFGHANI: THE PRECURSOR OF ISLAMIC MODERNISM

Jamal al-Din al-Afghani (1838/9–97) came from Iran, though he claimed to be Afghan. Traditionally educated, he came to see the impact of the modern world through a visit to India, and subsequent travels – to Cairo, Istanbul, London and Paris. In India he learned something of European methods and the bad consequences of Muslims submitting themselves to Western rule. In philosophy, he adopted a position like that of ibn Sīnā. Reason can demonstrate the existence of God, but the masses need to have the truth given to them in symbolic form, and this is the task of the Prophet. But naturally, he lived at a particular time: in so far as times have changed, it is needful to interpret afresh the teachings of the Qur'an. But there can ultimately be no question of a conflict between science and religion.

He stressed the vitality of a religious sense, and saw in religion the very substance of nations and the higher source of the happiness of humanity. True civilization is based on morality. While the Islamic *jihad* was a struggle to spread the faith, Western imperial wars were aimed at economic and political subjugation. But only a revived Islam could successfully struggle against foreign domination.

Al-Afghani was a modernist in the sense that he perceived the necessity of finding and using the secrets of Western power, notably scientific endeavor. As a rationalist, he was open to the acceptance of modern Western ideas. But at the heart of his teaching was the need for a revived Islam. Moreover he joined with this the hope of a Pan-Islamic recovery under a renewed Caliphate. Most important, however, was his effect on others and the influence in particular he had on the most famous of Arabic modernists, Muhammad 'Abduh.

MUHAMMAD 'ABDUH: THE PRIMARY EXPONENT OF ISLAMIC MODERNISM

Muhammad 'Abduh (1849–1905) was raised in the Nile Delta, and went to al-Azhar University. As we have seen, he came under the influence of al-Afghani. He was involved in a revolt against the British (1881–2) and was exiled for six years, where he cooperated with al-Afghani in a popular and revolutionary journal. On his return to Egypt he became a judge and in due course in 1889 the Grand Mufti of Egypt, that is the highest interpreter of Islamic Law. As such, he engaged in various legal reforms, especially in the matter of the training of traditional lawyers. His most important publications were *The Theology of Unity* and an interpretation of the Qur'an.

Like other reformers he noted the decay of Islam in contemporary society, which he attributed in large measure to the blind reliance upon tradition and the failure to use personal judgment in *ijtihad*. In a sense he was a Neofoundationalist, in that he wanted to go back to beginnings. Indeed, his theory of history reinforced the necessity of this, since there are three ages – one of reliance on the senses, when humans are preoccupied with survival; this is the age of animism. The second involves learning more from experience; it is also the age of the prophets. Their teachings have to be related to their times: in a cruel age Christ taught love; in a period of sloth, Muhammad brought a vivid and unifying message to dynamize humankind. But there is a third age, which is that of error, as we get further away from the time of the prophets. But reason and our conscience, if aroused, will lead us back to the true path. After all, human nature is at its basis good, and everyone shares reason and the impulse to associate together. 'Abduh held to a sort of human universalism, holding that our primary obligation is to humanity as a whole. The diversity of languages, nations and races is quite secondary.

In accord with his educational and moral concerns, 'Abduh was keen to affirm free will. He strongly resisted Western caricatures of Islam, including the idea that it is fatalistic. He was keen to reaffirm Mu'tazilah values. He argued that though God has foreknowledge of our actions this is neither a curb upon our freedom nor indeed relevant to motivation. Various points seemed to him important. First, without freedom the divine commandments would be meaningless. Second, there is the testimony of common sense. Third, even apart from divine commands there is conscience, which we experience, but which should vanish if our acts were not in some sense free. Maybe our freedom is not absolute, for we indeed find that when we try to do something we fail: our ideals outrun our nature. But there is some freedom, within limits. This means that the idea of necessity or predestination refers merely to the laws of nature and maybe to some aspects of social science, but not totally to our actions. The whole 'fatalistic' motif of Islam is foreign to the Qur'an, which exhibits vigorous men and women of action. It is merely a sign of that sloth and false other-worldliness which Islam had descended into: indeed, it furnishes a further argument for the decayed state of Islam from which 'Abduh's Neofoundationalist reforming hopes to rescue the religion. Incidentally, because 'Abduh saw humans as good, he considered them to have a natural knowledge of good and evil (which compares somewhat with an esthetic judgment). So God chooses this and that as part of the Law because these things are good. The *Sharī'ah* is in effect a means of guiding the mass of humans who do not reason much and who are easily led astray. Thus for 'Abduh there is a solidarity between natural morality and revealed religion.

Because of all this 'Abduh considered that jurists should use their reason and common sense, and not always feel constricted by a very narrow idea of analogy. He was, thus, going back to Mu'tazilah thinking from the early days of Islam, before the religion got too encrusted with legal judgments and tradition. His espousal of reason made space for modern science and other advances in knowledge. In his commentary on the Qur'an 'Abduh affirms that its primary aims are spiritual: it is not a textbook in astronomy or geography.

On the other hand, he repudiated the division between God and Caesar. He wrote a polemical reply to some strictures by the then French Foreign Minister, G. Hanotaux, who had commended Christianity precisely because it made a distinction not made in Islam, allowing Europeans space for advance. 'Abduh defended the organic unity of the Islamic outlook, integrating social, political and religious life. On the other hand, 'Abduh did himself have to struggle against the actual Islam of his day: the fact that *Sharī'ah* is so integral to it involves the philosopher not just in creating a worldview which will help to reform life and education, but also in jurisprudence and the reconsideration of Islamic Law. In this the integralism of Islam is a mixed blessing. Consequently 'Abduh was himself much taken up with certain social causes, especially the education of women; this impinged dramatically on the *Sharī'ah* as it was understood by many conservatives. Still, it is in no small measure due to 'Abduh's example and stimulus that Egypt has become the country that has best put Islamic modernism into practice.

Muhammad 'Abduh founded a school which included a number of social and religious reformers. Among their achievements were the foundation of the Egyptian University, the reform of al-Azhar University under Mustafa 'Abd al-Rāziq (1885–1960) and strong progress in the liberation of women. Other ingredients to 'Abduh's thought were added in the process, such as Arab socialism.

SECULAR REFORM: ANOTHER ALTERNATIVE

There was an alternative to modernization of the tradition, and that was simply to abandon the tradition. This was the course taken, essentially, by Turkey under Kemal Atatürk (1881–1938), who was founding dictator of the Turkish State from 1923, after its disastrous break-up after World War I, and the bitter war fought against Greece. The Caliphate, which had survived as a rather hollow symbol of Islamic unity, was abolished in 1924, thus torpedoing the so-called Caliphate Movement, a Pan-Islamic quest. In due course Turkey was declared a secular State; religious instruction in schools was abolished; the fez was banned as a symbol of Islam; polygamy was forbidden; Sufi orders were suppressed; Arabic script was replaced by Roman; and, among other things, a largely European philosophy was introduced into the universities. But in the long run some of the problems of Islamic modernism remained. As Islam has persisted in Turkey and Sufi schools have belatedly come back, the main issues of trying to reconcile the tradition of belief in God and revelation with the practice of a modern society and scientific education remain.

REFORM AND NEW THINKING IN SOUTH ASIA

One of the major figures in modernizing Islam in South Asia was Sir Sayyid Ahmad Khan (1817–98), educationalist, reformer and historian. He was drawn into the philosophical questions of his community because, after a visit to England in particular in 1869, he saw the necessity for Muslims to learn from Western thinking. This in turn posed questions of traditionalist Islam. It was the usual story – Western ideas and techniques to combat the imperial arrogance of the West. He was something of a bridge person, in that he not only wrote studies such as *The Causes of Indian Revolt* (1859) shortly after the revolt of 1857, to fight against the anti-Muslim feelings of the British at the time, but he also founded the Scientific Society in 1864 to acquaint Muslims with the riches of new scientific knowledge.

Sayyid Ahmad Khan has some interesting things to say about prophethood, prayer and the origin of humanity in the course of laying forth a scientifically based worldview. In expounding these views Ahmad Khan adopts a rigorous Neofoundationalist outlook, confining authority to the Qur'an and rejecting or sidestepping the Hadith and other aspects of the tradition (this allows him to repudiate slavery, religious warfare and the subjugation of women, which he ascribes to these later sources). Regarding prophecy, he thought that capacity for it exists in all human beings to a greater or lesser degree. This constitutes an openness in experience to respond to the call of the Divine Being. So the distinguishing feature of the great prophets is their religious genius – this is true above all of the Prophet Muhammad. Also, once there was a full clarification of the meaning of monotheism, there was no need for any further prophet. Because it is difficult for people to arrive correctly at the moral and spiritual truth, they need prophets, but essentially natural and revealed religion are one.

This means in turn that there is not or need not be any conflict between religion and science. Ahmad rejected belief in miracles and therefore the efficacy of prayer (at least in the sense that praying for something could significantly affect whether it would happen or not). God was author of nature and the laws which we detect are his fixed habits and promises: a law of nature is a practical promise by God that things will happen so. It should be noted that in the Qur'an there is a repeated refusal of the Prophet to bolster his claims by miracles, when people demand this of him. But the book does contain reference to the miraculous accomplishments of earlier prophets. But by and large Islam does not seem to depend on miracles, in the way that Christianity, because of the Resurrection in particular, seems to focus on such divine intervention. Prayer's importance lies of course in great part in the recognition which it gives of God's majesty, but this recognition is not something, by the same token, that God needs. Rather, prayer helps humans to express that recognition and helps them in strengthening their resolve and comforting them in the face of the troubles and anxieties of life.

Sayyid Ahmad Kahn faces the issue of evolution (coming to the fore in the 1860s) head on. Humans are indeed evolved. The universe, through its physical and chemical processes, gave rise to life and life to humanity. What then of Adam? Ahmad Khan is remarkably modernist: the dramatic story in the scriptures is a way of putting vividly before us certain deep truths about human nature. There is of course the language of angels and of Satan used in and about the narrative. It is wrong to take this language in a highly literal fashion. Angels stand for God's powers, including the physical powers which are manifested in the cosmos, such as the solidity of mountain ranges and the growth of vegetation. Satan is nothing other than the power of evil in the world, and that lies inside of us. So humans are figuratively a fusion of angelic and Satanic qualities. The demonic power of Satan is an indication of the way our passions rage despite our reasoning. They are hard for humans to control. The fruit of the forbidden tree in the garden stands for reason and self-consciousness.

It is not surprising in view of all this if Sayyid Ahmad Khan argues for genuine freedom of the will. Humans have bad and good tendencies and an inner light capable of redirecting our evil motives and insufficient attention to the moral law. Salvation will depend on our sincere use of our capacities to improve our natures. It is the reward for doing our best to overcome our lower and evil impulses. Moreover, our freedom is quite compatible with God's omniscience and hence prescience. The fact that an astrologer correctly predicts that someone will drown does not entail at all that the astrologer is the cause of the drowning.

From the facts of freedom, the inner light and reason we can conclude that humans have souls. Sayyid Ahmad Khan thought that since scientifically the quantity of matter in the world (it was supposed) remains the same, nothing is destroyed, so the soul is immortal (a rather weak argument). But he saw paradise and hell as being sensuous and symbolic representations of essentially psychological states.

Not only was Sayyid Ahmad Khan modernist in his treatment of revelation, but he was also forthright about the need for reform. This meant in effect the reform of the *Sharī‘ah*. Here he had an interesting position. Religion itself or *dīn* is changeless and is what the Prophet is concerned with. Islam is the perfect religion. But our needs in society are changeable: as historical conditions change, so we require new laws and new developments of morality. A special ethic will arise in relation to every important technological development. And so if there is the necessity for changing the *Sharī‘ah*, we would, according to orthodox assumptions, need a new prophet from time to time. But since Muhammad is the last of the Prophets, it follows that the *Sharī‘ah* has to be adapted by us. The trouble is that the jurists have tried to present a changeless Law which really depends on their own consensus and decisions. Ancient jurists had of course to devise a framework for society in accord with the teachings of the Qur'an, but it does not follow that we need to adhere to those ancient and in many ways obsolete patterns. This is partly why he repudiated the *Hadīth* as authoritative. There is a need for a critical appraisal of tradition.

It was in accord with his modernist views that Sayyid Ahmad Khan played a central role in the setting up of the first institution of higher education on the Western model for Muslims at Aligarh. Sayyid Ahmad Khan is, then, a major exponent of liberal Islamic theology, and ultimately through his writings and work in education he had a large effect on the Indian scene. One person he inspired was Muhammad Iqbal.

MUHAMMAD IQBAL: A ROMANTIC AND BERGSONIAN WORLDVIEW REINFORCED BY SUFISM

Undoubtedly the greatest figure of the Muslim renaissance in India was Sir Muhammad Iqbal (1873–1938). Born in Sialkot in the Punjab and son of a tailor, he showed early brilliance, and eventually he went to college in Lahore, and to Cambridge and then Germany to study philosophy. The thinker who had the greatest influence upon him was Bergson. He had through this period already been prolific in writing Urdu poems.

He came to be recognized as one of the greatest poets in that language. But his best-known book is a work of philosophy, *The Reconstruction of Religious Thought in Islam*. In this he attempted to fuse Western and Eastern elements, together with traditional and Sufi motifs, into a single worldview, which could represent a revitalized Islam. His experience of Europe impressed him, but also depressed him. The dynamism was exhilarating, and the scientific and technical achievements were considerable. The cultural and philosophical richness was exciting. But the effects of capitalism were inhumane, he thought, and this convinced him of the superiority of Islamic values for the creation of a balanced civilization. If his metaphysics were between East and West, this was right, because the combination of human achievement and the revelation of God in human experience was needed. (Incidentally he saw the achievements of Western science as being in part due to Islam, since it was Islamic thought which in reaction to much in Greek philosophy had emphasized concrete reality and had in this way given birth to the 'inductive intellect'. Through the Muslim universities of Spain this penetrated into northern Europe and was expressed by Roger Bacon and others.)

One aspect of the Europe of his day which he opposed was its nationalism. On his return to India he preached a universalist Islam, beyond national sentiments, and oriented towards the whole of humanity. But he had plenty of evidence of the divisions of Islam and the narrowness of traditional dogma. He became something of an iconoclast.

His book, setting forth his main ideas, is highly eclectic. He shows huge reading but often a sloppiness in putting different intellectual figures together. Nevertheless, the total edifice is original and interesting. He was much influenced by Bergson, but criticized the idea of the *élan vital* as being unteleological. He saw consciousness as Bergson described it but as having forward impulse through our purposes. God, whom he identified with vital impulse, works with purposes, because that is the nature of a rational consciousness. But Iqbal saw creativity in a very modern and artistic way. The true poet like Shakespeare or musician like Mozart has open-ended purposes. He does not create according to a predetermined plan. So Iqbal objected to that so-pervasive picture in theism, of the predetermined plan. This had been reinforced by the effect of Greek philosophy. Plato after all had seen the pattern of ideas as static. According to Iqbal it was only with Hegel that this fixed mold is broken, but even here there is a sort of mechanistic flavor to the operation of the dialectic. So Iqbal took Bergson as his model and then theized it. What he arrived at has affinities with Whitehead and a lot in common with the movement known as 'process theology' (itself following Whitehead).

In seeing the world as unfolding through the continuous creative power of God, Iqbal is led to deny God's omniscience. That is to say, God does not have a fixed knowledge in advance of the whole range of cosmic history. This would imply some version of the pre-planned cosmos. Not only is there God's own creative thrust, which has unforeseen possibilities in it, but God has also freely out of his own substance created free selves. Humans share the creative life of the Divine, and so human history is intrinsically unpredictable.

Without resistance you cannot have freedom, Iqbal believed. And so it is that in the onward thrust of God's creativity there appear many things which involve suffering and moral evil. Those who think that it is possible to have life without suffering have an unrealistic grasp of the nature of life. So it is that even immortality is not static. The soul graduates after death to higher forms of struggle. Satan is the mythic figure who stands for resistance, and so you should never ask for a life without Satan. In accord with such notions Iqbal saw the Fall as the awakening from simple consciousness to a new self-awareness. It is a rise. In this he reflected in an Islamic context a view which has sometimes made itself felt in modern Christian theology. It also relates to his notion of grades of selves. For Iqbal was also a monadologist, in thinking of the universe as composed of atomic selves. In this he reinterprets the picture presented by Ash'arī theology. But the more self-conscious a self is, the nearer it is to the Divine. In this he in part drew upon the Sufi tradition.

Because of his mystical leanings, Iqbal criticized the empiricism so strong in the West, as leaving religious experience out of account. After all, it has played a most vital part in human history. Why should the evolutionist place more weight upon the instinctive knowledge of animals than on the higher experiences of saints and prophets? If some religious claims based on intuitive experience are inadequate, so what? It is also true that 'scientific' accounts based on sense-perception have turned out to be false. It is the nature of all our sources of knowledge to be corrected as human understanding progresses. So in his interpretation of the onward creative process Iqbal draws upon the Sufi heritage.

As it happened, events were not kind to Iqbal, for after his death came World War II and with it negotiations for the independence of India. As is well known, the notion of Pakistan became reality, and with it, at least by counterposition to predominantly Hindu India, Pakistani nationalism was nourished. This ran contrary to Iqbal's ideal. Bergson and evolutionary philosophy lost their attractions, and other fashions became more vital. Religious orthodoxy was somewhat received, as Pakistan evolved towards a Muslim State. Elsewhere Arab and other nationalisms flourished. Modernism was also less potent, with the revival of fundamentalisms. Many of the forces, therefore, to which Iqbal had been opposed were revitalized. Nevertheless, he remains a highly interesting figure, with an attractive worldview, which was reinforced by his poetical creations, themselves often the vehicles for his philosophy. He must be reckoned as maybe the most original of the Islamic modernists.

POSTMODERN DIRECTIONS IN ISLAMIC COUNTRIES

Though modernism continued to leave its imprint on Muslim countries, perhaps especially Indonesia and India, other trends became more vigorous. Arab nationalism often took a secular form after World War II, under the leadership of Nasser (1918–70), and under the influence of the Ba'ath parties in Syria and Iraq, which espoused a strongly non-religious ideology with some socialist elements (though both subserved rigorous dictatorships later on). After the establishment of the State of Israel this became the focus of a pan-Arab national spirit. Socialism itself had quite an appeal in the Muslim world, as it also did in Africa and elsewhere, for fairly obvious reasons: one was that the challenge and oppression by the West came into the Islamic world in capitalist clothes; another was that socialism was contrary to individualism, which, partly because of its very attractiveness, was seen as a threat to traditional society. For some intellectuals moreover, socialism in its more full-blooded form, as Marxism, was appealing because, while being modern, it was so strongly anti-Western. It is true that al-Afghani had written vigorously against it in his *Refutation of the Materialists*. But nevertheless there were quite a number of intellectuals willing to turn their back on traditional religion. Others again sought ways to combine Marxist analysis with Islamic loyalty. But in many ways the most significant postmodernist move was so-called fundamentalism, which was expressed most influentially through the Muslim Brotherhood.

This movement was founded in Egypt in 1928 by Ḥasan al-Bannā (1906–49). It became the pattern for a variety of such groupings in a wide range of Muslim parties. The main aspects of the outlook of such movements are as follows. First, it is necessary to restore Islam and that means above all Islamic Law or *Sharī'ah*. Second, this in turn means that modernist and liberal attempts to separate mosque and State are invalid: the purpose of the State is to subserve true religion, and religion helps to guide the State. Third, the Brotherhood uses modern and often Western means of propaganda and teaching. Fourth, on the whole the movement wants to go back to essentials, namely the Qur'an and the values of early Islam. Much that lies between then and now is to be swept away as corruption. Sometimes it is argued that the reason why Islam has fallen into its bad state, dominated by the unspiritual and decadent West, is that it itself became decadent, through the overlay of many unnecessary cultural elements. Though Ḥasan was at one time deeply drawn to Sufism, it is usual among these neo-traditionalist Islamic groups to attack Sufism as drawing bad elements into Islam, such as the cult of saints and other perverse and blasphemous items. So it is that the Brotherhood and other analogous parties tend to make a clean sweep of intervening Islamic culture and to go back to beginnings.

But the movement was modern in its methods of education, and was convinced of the up-to-date and scientific character of Islam itself. There is no question here of any serious conflict between Islam and science, to parallel some of the tensions and contradictions between Christian fundamentalism and a scientific outlook. Still, there are of course problems between the typical highly committed follower and contemporary humanistic interpretations of Islamic scholarship.

The larger tension is a pragmatic one, between modernizing attitudes towards the law and the reaffirmation of traditional *Sharī'ah*. There are thus conflicts with, for instance, feminist Muslims, and difficult questions about how to organize a modern economy given older Islamic views about the impropriety of charging interest. Often the fundamentalist movements, despite successes here and there, and above all in Iran, with the Ayatollah Khomeini's revolution of 1979, are suppressed harshly by modernist and socialist regimes (they were drastically put down in Syria in 1976, at Mecca in 1979, in Algeria in 1992, etc.).

While fundamentalists draw on early Islamic concepts to sketch out a political philosophy, they tend to look upon philosophy itself as having a corrupt influence, partly because in older days it brought various Greek ideas into play, which were not traditionally Islamic, and partly because modern philosophy was an open attempt to borrow Western ideas, often at the expense of traditional religious loyalty. This was especially true of atheistic systems such as Marxism and logical positivism and its aftermath. So in a certain way fundamentalism is anti-intellectual, though it often appeals to those who have some education, without having attained to anything like a deep understanding of modern humanistic scholarship. Often the universities of the Islamic world, themselves rather woodenly putting into practice Western models of learning, are apt places for the recruitment of radical Islamic fundamentalists. And as we have noted already, the Brotherhood, for instance, is up to date in trying to blend modern concerns with economics and politics, on the one hand, and traditional religious values, on the other.

While most of the movements are Sunni, the successful Iranian revolution arose from a Shi'a context. The leader of this transformation of Iran, the Ayatollah Khomeini (1900–89) could not strictly be called a philosopher, but he did fashion the original idea of blending a modern conception of the State with a traditional Islamic ideology of theocratic rule. The conception of an Islamic republic envisages the institutionalization of Islamic Law and of the domination of Islamic lawyers and clerics in the process of interpretation and governance. This then is a modernizing of Islamic political philosophy.

There remain a number of unresolved questions about the continuance of Islamic philosophy. One concerns the future of Sufism. While it is largely under a cloud as a result of the resurgence of Islamic reform movements, it does have excellent potential to form a framework of a scientific outlook with religious values in the ongoing dialog between Islamic values and the new physics. It also forms a bridge between Islam and other religions, which plainly the new fundamentalism does not. Then, at the level of political thinking, there is the question of the role of Islam within the new global order.

While it is possible to establish important Islamic enclaves, the pluralism of global civilization and of pervasive capitalism needs facing, and a revival of traditional *Sharī'ah* does not seem to do this. Finally, there is the issue of whether Islamic philosophers can be players in a basically religiously neutral conception of philosophy, such as is likely to dominate the global religious scene.

Meanwhile we note that the modern period, since the colonial era brought such rude humiliations to the Islamic cultural and political scene, has experimented in differing directions to overcome the disadvantages of being dominated by Western ideologies.

13

MODERN SOUTH AND SOUTH-EAST ASIA

THE IMPACT OF EUROPE ON THE REGION

Gradually during the eighteenth and nineteenth centuries Britain consolidated its grip on India, from the Himalayas to Sri Lanka (then Ceylon). South-east Asia, comprising such countries as Burma, Laos, Cambodia, Vietnam and Thailand, as well as predominantly Muslim Malaya and Indonesia, were also taken over by European powers. Of the Buddhist countries – namely the first five of the above, Burma was conquered by the British, Thailand retained its independence, and the rest became French. It is the predominantly Hindu and Buddhist countries which we shall be considering in this chapter. I shall begin with India itself (and here I use the term to cover the region which later evolved into the Republic of India, Pakistan and Bangladesh), and from there move on to the Buddhist cultural milieu.

British rule brought with it a number of challenges to traditional values. One was a new system of education and of universities in particular, often founded and run by Christian missionaries. I put this first because it had the profoundest effect on intellectual life, since it brought into being an English-speaking elite in India and an English-speaking way of doing philosophy. Second, there was the challenge of the content of education, above all, new scientific ways of looking at the world. Third, the new imperial bureaucracy, itself largely staffed by Indians, was guided by certain principles, influential among which was utilitarianism as an ethic. Fourth, Christianity itself was highly critical, on the whole, of the Hindu tradition – of child marriage, the use of images, of caste, of *suttee* (widow-burning), etc. Evangelical clergy in particular decried the confusing mass of 'superstitions'. Fifth, new technology and industries were introduced into India, above all the railroad network, which was significant for the process of the unification of India. Sixth, new political notions came into the subcontinent, including, towards the end of the nineteenth century, the nationalist ideal. All these challenges had direct or indirect effects on Indian philosophy. And since Indian culture was suffused by religion, philosophical reflection and reaction to the new forces were predominantly religious in flavor. It may be noted by the way that though similar influences applied in British-controlled Buddhist areas, the effects were somewhat different, owing to the different intellectual character of the religion.

The most important of the movements of response in the nineteenth century and the early part of the twentieth were: the Brahmo Samaj; the Arya Samaj; the Ramakrishna Vedānta movement; the philosophy of Aurobindo; and the political–religious worldview of Gandhi. I shall consider these first, and then move on to some other thinkers and motifs of the twentieth century. We have noted some concurrent Islamic reactions, including the thought of Iqbal, which runs parallel to some of the Hindu worldviews we shall be considering.

THE BRAHMO SAMAJ: A FIRST ATTEMPT TO BRIDGE TWO WORLDS

It is generally recognized that the first of the Indian reformers of the modern period was Ram Mohan Roy (1772–1833). During his life the paramount power in Northern India and influential elsewhere was the East India Company: it was only in 1858 that Britain took over direct imperial rule. Roy, a Bengali, was good at languages, and knew Arabic, Persian and Sanskrit: he then learned English and got a job with the Company in 1803. A Persian book of his in 1804 was critical of Hindu polytheism. He later translated five of the Upanishads to demonstrate that at core Hinduism is not polytheistic. His *Precepts of Jesus* (1920) tried to show that the essence of Jesus' message was ethical, and need not be overlaid with the heavy and complex doctrinal interpretations typical of the Churches. In these various works he put forward in effect a simplified version of the Vedānta. In a certain sense he was 'fundamentalist', going back to the fundamentals of the Hindu tradition as he saw them: as basic scriptures. In this he was influenced both by Islam and Christianity. For orthodox Brahmins the Hindu revelatory tradition was essentially oral. To print and translate the Vedas was to broadcast them in a mode which escaped the close control of the Brahmins. Indeed he himself fell outside the sacred castes who had tended to control Bengali religion. So he was a significant agent in bringing in an age when Hinduism was to be expressed in English or written Sanskrit rather than in the premodern way. This was to mean various things: it liberated Hindu writings from Brahmin control; it made them accessible to people of other religions; and it stimulated subsequent gurus and other preachers to treat Hinduism as a universal, that is a world religion. This culminated as we shall see in Swami Vivekananda's appearance and impact at the World Parliament of Religions in 1893.

Roy's critique of Hindu ritual and polytheism was strong. It closely matched the charges leveled at the religion by Christian missionaries. On the other hand, his view of Christianity stirred up controversy and opposition. While he admired the Christian ethic, he opposed what he saw as unnecessary accretions to the faith. He did not see the value of miracles, and he found the Trinity doctrine to be a quite unnecessary complication. His *Precepts of Jesus* demolished the doctrinal dimension of Christianity. He tended to explain it much as he explained the bad aspects of Hinduism, as being growths and corruptions which had gathered on the more austere pure Hinduism which he found in the Upanishads. Hence his desire to go right back to fundamentals. In pursuance of these ideals he founded the Brahmo Samaj (Divine Society) in 1828, together with some disciples. What it expressed was a rationalistic Hindu unitarianism. It was heir both to Roy's new vision of one Deity, but also to a version of late eighteenth-century rationalism. As such it was not likely to become popular; however, it did have a striking influence on the literate and growing middle classes of Bengal. From there it had some pan-Indian importance.

In 1830 Roy went to England, and died there, in 1833, in Bristol. His chief significance in the philosophical context is as a trailblazer in bringing together the paths of European and Indian thought, and in loosening up traditional attitudes to the Sanskrit heritage. He made it easier for later writers to explore ways of adapting Indian ideas to the new conditions in which India found itself. He indicated a mode in which Hinduism itself could both receive – and adapt to – criticism and mete it out. He was thus a precursor of a kind of universal protestant Hinduism, which saw beyond the forms of religion to the direct relations with the Ultimate lying at the heart of every faith. He was highly committed to new forms of education and struggled for women's rights. He left his imprint on later important figures, such as Debendranath Tagore and Keshab Chandra Sen (on whom more below), who helped to make the Brahmo Samaj flourish for a while, as well as on Vivekananda and Gandhi. He is considered by many to have been the 'father of the modern Hindu renaissance' – that general movement which synthesized Indian and English ideas, and led to a revival of the spirit of Hinduism, which had been dampened by the Muslim and then the British conquests. He also pioneered a non-Brahmin and secular leadership in a spiritual movement, to set something of a pattern in the nineteenth and twentieth centuries.

Debendranath Tagore (1817–1905) carried on the organization. He helped to give it a doctrinal shape, espousing belief in a single personal God. Though his religion was devotional it did not have, however, that flowery and mythically focused fervor of much Hindu *bhakti*. He was father of the even more famous Rabindranath Tagore (1861–1941), who won the Nobel Prize for Poetry, large on the basis of his verses 'Song Offerings' or *Gītāñjalī*. He carried on the tradition of reverent rationalism, but with a warmer and more artistic touch.

Keshab Chandra Sen (1838–84) was another significant leader in and beyond the movement. He was influenced by the elder Tagore but also claimed – influentially –

that Christ was the greatest of religious teachers. He thought of the Samaj as lying outside of Hinduism proper, and looked for a new synthesis which would combine the spirituality of both Hindu and Christian living. He thus helped to move India further in the direction of a universalist interpretation of Hinduism itself. The whole Brahmo Samaj movement and its breakaway aftermaths represent the first phase of the modern Hindu renaissance.

DAYANANDA SARASVATI AND A DIFFERENT REACTION TO THE WEST

A somewhat divergent reaction to the Western impact on Indian civilization is associated with the Gujarati leader Dayananda Sarasvati (1824–83), who founded a movement known as the Arya Samaj (Noble or Aryan Society) in 1875. He had at first been a largely intra-Hindu yogi, who had been turned off image-worship, but contact with the Brahmo Samaj led him to see a broader landscape for reform and better, more Westernized, methods of spreading his message. His doctrines appealed to a new class of professionals and business people, who wanted to defend their Hindu roots, though they recognized the force of Christian and government criticisms of some of the features of the tradition. He was in a stronger sense than Ram Mohan Roy a fundamentalist, identifying eternal revelation with the Vedic hymns, which he interpreted in his own way, as expressing monotheism. He was convinced that everything later than the four collections of hymns, which went back to the *ṛṣis* (seers) of old, contained false teachings, so he came to abandon the monism of the Upanishads and the worship of Śiva and Viṣṇu. Though the form of his belief was fundamentalism, his interpretation of scripture was imaginative, and resisted by virtually all orthodox teachers. He rejected caste and thought that Brahmin control of sacred scripture was wrong. Religion is to be open to all. Moreover, he had a ritual method for receiving Hindus who had left the fold back into the religion (as interpreted by him). He saw God as coeval with the myriad souls or *puruṣas* inhabiting the material cosmos (this aspect of his doctrine came from the Sāṅkhya system). Souls might be saved by the efforts of individuals following the guidance of the *dharma* or divine law revealed in the scripture, but salvation was itself temporary and souls would re-enter the world again. The openness of the Arya Samaj was appealing to the new middle class and also to Indians in the overseas diaspora in such places as South Africa and Fiji.

Dayananda was traditional to the extent that he thought of the four classes (Brahmins and so on) as corresponding to divisions of labor in society: they represented something of a Vedic sociology. He did not think of them as determined by birth, however, and was a notable social reformer, defending untouchables and pressing for women's rights. His movement met some of the challenges from the West, though its lack of real concern with scientific thinking could be a weakness (Dayananda considered that basic truths of modern physics, such as atomic theory, were present in the Vedas). In general, the Arya Samaj was not very philosophical, but it did open up a new path to modernity to reforming Hindus. Dayananda was an early nationalist, and the Arya Samaj had some influence on the militant Hindu Mahasabha movement.

A DEEPER SYNTHESIS: RAMAKRISHNA AND VIVEKANANDA

Undoubtedly the most important figures in the Hindu renaissance were Ramakrishna and Swami Vivekananda. The first (1836–86) was not a philosopher but a saint. The latter (1863–1902) was an intellectual, following the saint, but translating his worldview into a viable philosophy which had a large effect on Indian thought, partly because it provided a good theoretical underpinning to the emergent Indian nationalism. Ramakrishna was a remarkably colorful individual and teacher, who was open to varying powerful influences. One of these was that of a woman guru who initiated him into tantric play and reinforced his sense of devotion to the divine Mother (he was himself employed as the priest of Kālī, outside Calcutta). Another was that of an Advaitin who instructed him in absolute monism: he was for several months plunged in identification with the One. Another was the Hindu tradition of *līlā* or play. His position was a kind of pious synthesis, which brought together both ineffable mysticism and fervent *bhakti*. His teachings were full of images and parables.

In addition, Ramakrishna claimed to have had Islamic and Christian experiences. He devoted himself for short periods to the worship of Christ and Allah, resulting in visions of these spiritual foci. He therefore considered that all religions pointed to the same truth, which could be tasted intimately in experience.

Vivekananda was a well-educated young Bengali who came under the spell of Ramakrishna while at college. In due course, under pressure from Ramakrishna, he consented to take up the spiritual life as a successor and disciple of the older man. Taking on the name of Vivekananda, he became a highly influential teacher, in part because he attended the World Parliament of Religions in Chicago in 1893, where his speech caused a sensation; in it he expounded his view of the nature of the deeper Hindu beliefs, consonant with the (at that meeting) popular idea of a truly universal or world religion.

Vivekananda took up Ramakrishna's themes, but in a much more systematic fashion. He in general subscribed to a newly formulated version of Non-dualistic Vedānta (*Advaita Vedānta*). He formed the organization of the Ramakrishna Math and Mission: that is the monastic and missionary institution which would carry on the teaching of Ramakrishna (and Vivekananda). This was strongly devoted both to educational and social enterprises, including medical work. Because the new philosophy was pan-religious in scope the Math and Mission is to be found established in many Western and other countries as well as in the Republic of India itself.

Vivekananda's ideology began from the point that Hinduism had since early days had a pluralistic aspect. This was evident already in the Vedas, where reality is at one point seen as one, even if sages name it variously. Hence the many gods all really stand for the One Brahman or Holy Power. This motif was used to explain the essential unity of all religions. Differing ways of symbolizing and conceiving God conceal the essential unity of religions, and of levels of religion. This approach to a monism or unitarianism (in a sense Vivekananda's system was both) was much more persuasive than what may be called the negative unitarianism of the Brahmo Samaj. For it meant that different believers could hold on to their existing allegiances to Śiva or Viṣṇu or Christ or whoever, while affirming their ultimate unity. At the same time, in accordance with a certain interpretation of Vedānta, Vivekananda wished to affirm the unity of diverse kinds of religion, notably those of *bhakti* and yogic meditation. This distinction was also a clue as to how it is that religions could seem to differ while concealing their ultimate unity. For varying religious experiences could give rise to differing conceptual schemes: devotion is personalized and visionary; while meditation loses itself in pure consciousness rather than in colorful divine visions.

Thus, while Vivekananda, true to the Advaita–Vedāntin spirit, saw the pure Brahman as higher than the Lord (who is the focus of devotion), he did not emphasize the idea of the world as *māyā*. The world is God's play and ultimately not as real as the One, but it is a vital sphere for humans to act in. Vivekananda stressed the importance of social and medical work. But the only Holy Power is also identical with the Self. A highly important motif of Vivekananda's is the immanence of the Divine within, or as the soul or self. The Upanishadic formula 'That art thou' meant that Vivekananda was keen to affirm the divinity of human beings within. It happened that this notion chimed in well with the thrust of absolute idealism, which was a vital worldview during the last years of the Victorian era and the time which was still to expire before World War I.

This framework enabled Vivekananda to meet the objections and challenges then being leveled at Hinduism highly effectively. It also incidentally helped to create the modern idea of Hinduism as a unified system rather than as a congeries of diverse religious movements and cults, overlapping but also variegated; basically a loose federation at best of often rival movements and the pieties of half a million villages and a plethora of regions and towns. First, his formulation of the neo-Hindu ideology in an English medium had its appeal among those educated in the new British-style system of higher education. It was also sufficiently articulate and plausible to be persuasive. Second, the new Advaita dealt with the problems of the relation of religion and science well: science had its range over the world of *māyā* or this world. Neither myth nor the details of scripture were that important to the new Hinduism, which did not have to fight the old, tired battles of Christian scripturalism. Third, Vivekananda could enter meaningful debate about the ethics of utilitarianism. While the notion that ethics should cause society to flourish through the formula of providing happiness for the greatest possible number and the least suffering of the least number, there remained the deeper question as to what is the true nature of happiness (and suffering). For Vivekananda the self or soul is divine, is eternal; so the spiritual life (which turns inwards) is what brings and reveals true happiness. The way was open towards the realization of a deep utilitarianism. Fourth, while Christianity was critical of various practices, so was reforming Hinduism; indeed it could be a powerful force for a new and vigorous Indian society. Fifth, there was nothing in Vivekananda's ideology which was inimical to the development of new industries and so on; Vivekananda could combat a crass materialism with his appeal to some of the deeper values of the Advaitin quest. And as with other movements of the time, notably Arya Samaj, it might be possible to expand it greatly by using Western methods of preaching and missionizing. And so the Ramakrishna Mission could be seen to be modern in its endeavors. It became a major player in the rapidly expanding field of Hindu proselytization.

In all this, then, Vivekananda put his stamp on a thoroughly modern movement. Yet it was one which ingeniously could underpin Indian nationalism (as remarked above) and present itself as relevant to adherents of all religions. The two points were connected. The divide between Muslims and Hindus in particular could threaten the new national movement. There were other faiths too which were important in the Indian scene, especially in regard to the intelligentsia – there were Christians, the Parsees, Jains, Sikhs, some Buddhists, and so on. The emerging India had to focus the loyalty not just of Hindus but all these others as well. Even with the subsequent partition of India and its split into India, Pakistan and Bangladesh, Hindu India nevertheless has about a hundred million Muslims (in the last decade of the twentieth century). India needed an ideology which could express a wider loyalty and promote harmony in a volatile subcontinent. So Vivekananda's theme of the unity of religions, though not original, was very important to the process of forming an Indian patriotism.

Vivekananda's scheme also helped to give a new slant on the history of Indian philosophy. By putting Śankara in the middle of the picture it encouraged a neo-Vedāntin lens with which to view the history of thought in the subcontinent. Already the opening up of India to British influence had greatly stimulated attempts at a general understanding of Indian philosophy and religion. Sir William Jones (1746–94) had laid the foundations of a new English-speaking science of Sanskrit learning. There was considerable interest in Indian philosophy in the early twentieth century, at the end of the period of British idealism, since the similarities between absolutism in the West and Advaitin and Upanishadic thought were noticed. Earlier there had been a like synthesis between Śankara's thought and that of German idealism through the work of Paul Deussen (1845–1919). He wrote two books noteworthy in connection with the significance of Indian philosophy: his relatively early *The System of the Vedānta* and his later and massive *Universal History of Philosophy*. His general view of truth was not unlike that of Vivekananda, in that he saw his job as being to strip away the outer husks of religion and thought to reveal the inner truth lying within all of the systems. Such books as Deussen's and Vivekananda's gave an impetus to a new revisionary history of Indian thought. This saw the perennialism of an updated Śaṅkara as running through the story of Indian philosophy. It became the fashionable view among English-speaking educated Indians during much of the twentieth century. One can see some of Vivekananda's themes running through the thought of both Gandhi and Radhakrishnan. I shall return later to this point when dealing with Surendranath Dasgupta. At any rate, Indian philosophy as seen from a Neo-Advaitin perspective could benefit from the dominance of Hegel, Bradley, Bosanquet and others of the idealist stream in British universities. The analogies between them and Advaita greatly stimulated comparative studies, but was another reason why Indians could see Vivekananda's system of thought as thoroughly modern (such a perception was to fade after the revolution caused by Moore and Russell, in turning their backs on the absolute idealism of the period).

The Neo-Advaitin casting of the history of Indian thought had, of course, its problems: what was to be made of the *nāstika* systems, such as Cārvāka materialism, Jainism and Buddhism? The tendency was to view Buddhism through the lens of Mahāyāna and the *Śūnyavāda,* which could look very like Śaṅkara's philosophy. It might be noted that as far as the religious aspect of the systems was concerned, emphasis was placed on the mystical path and experience, which favored the language of the *via negativa* pointing to a non-personal Absolute.

BEYOND VIVEKANANDA: GANDHI'S WORLDVIEW

While Mohendas Gandhi (1869–1948) was not exactly a philosopher, his outlook had a great impact on India because of his influential political activity. His methods of non-violence became vital first in his organizational work among Asians in South Africa, from 1893 to 1914 (he returned to India in 1915), and then in his long struggle with the Congress Party against British rule and social evils such as, above all, untouchability, communalism and the degradation of humanity (here he saw perils in industrialization). Gandhi's general position owed something to diverse strands: one was Christianity as he encountered it among followers of Tolstoy and others in the London of his young manhood; another was the Jain tradition, which was influential beyond its numbers in his native region (Kathiawar, in northern Gujarat); a third was the main drift of the Hindu tradition of religious thought. His favorite book was the *Bhagavadgītā,* which he interpreted in his own way.

The general shape of his worldview was roughly consistent with the philosophy of Vivekananda, but it was a good deal more vaguely stated. He equated Truth with God, and there was an ambivalence about this, which echoed perhaps the typical Vedāntin distinction between *nirguṇam and saguṇam* Brahman, that is, between God or the

Ultimate without and with qualities, that is between the non-personal and the personal Ultimate. But while Gandhi crossed religious boundaries with ease, he does not seem to have been greatly attracted by the polymorphous character of traditional Hindu *bhakti* and its colorful mythology. He nevertheless took the personal side of God or Truth seriously, as his prayer-meetings and hymn-singing testified. Moreover, he wanted to see the varying religions as legitimate vehicles of true religion. This view was reinforced by his antipathy to communalism, which he perceived as a great curse in India. His own piety was unmediated by priests or icons, and in this he may have been influenced by Islam.

Gandhi's chief originality lay in his reinterpretation of the ideal of *ahiṃsā* that it became a virtue which could be used politically, through mass action (or rather non-action). He shrewdly perceived that non-violent means of political agitation and struggle would be very difficult for the British to combat and so in using it he was able to redress the inequality of power between the two sides. But it was not for him a mere tactic: it was also a vital ethical ideal to be adopted by his followers. He rightly saw that unless his followers were trained in true non-violence, that is a kind of love of the enemy, *ahiṃsā* could easily turn sour and vicious. Similarly he held that truly non-violent people would be hospitable to differing faiths as diverse expression of human spirituality. Yet such diversity has to be controlled by reason and morality, which he saw as the twin criteria of 'good' religion. His general notion that the paths of the different faiths were merely methods of approach through which humans could gain their way to God was a neo-Hindu one. He had little contact with Buddhists, though his closeness to the Jain tradition might have alerted him to the reality of non-theistic religions. He did not quite think through the ambivalence of his idea of God as Truth. While it had its resemblances to Neo-Advaita, as we have seen, he also in part negated this analogy through proclaiming his adherence to *anekāntavāda,* which, as we have seen, is a Jaina doctrine. It is the doctrine of relativism or what may be called perspectivalism.

Gandhi saw a close solidarity between the Christian concept of love and the ideal of non-violence. He could thus combine motifs from the Christian tradition, especially as interpreted by Tolstoy in his latter days, and the Hindu. His major emphasis was on social and individual reform: this was for him the true basis of religion. He was not, therefore, much moved by theological and philosophical debates, and this helps to account for the looseness and vagueness of his thinking on these matters. But he was an important reformer.

His inconsistencies could be creative: through many years of his struggle for *swaraj* he was allied with the aristocratic, British-trained, agnostic, socialist Jawaharlal Nehru (1889–1964). The latter had no great interest in religion, set India on a course of heavy industrialization of which Gandhi would have disapproved, was Westernized (while Gandhi was so to speak 'Easternized') and scarcely kept India to any path of absolute non-violence. Perhaps Nehru was more realistic. However, it is still of interest that an alliance between the two men could have been formed and could have proved ultimately to be so successful.

Anyway, Gandhi's worldview helped to reinforce the tendencies set in train by Vivekananda and his vision of the unity to religions. Gandhi was always vigorous in his advocacy of the unity of all human beings, which he squared with the particularity of Indian nationalism by averring that the latter would be in the service of the whole of humanity. His universalism and his belief in Truth have left their imprint on Indian philosophy, even if he was never a precise or systematic thinker. Like other members of the Hindu renaissance he was critical of some aspects of traditional society, especially of untouchability (he renamed untouchables *harijans* or 'offspring of God' and sought their integration into the caste-based system of social organization). His example spread in the world, and he helped to inspire the work of Martin Luther King (1929–68), among other reformers and peace workers.

SRI AUROBINDO: A DIFFERENT KIND OF METAPHYSICS

Aurobindo Ghose (1872–1950) had a highly interesting life, and fashioned out of both European and Indian elements a metaphysics which had some analogy to the spiritual evolutionism of Teilhard de Chardin (1881–1955), though the two thinkers were not consciously influenced by one another. Aurobindo was the son of a highly Anglophile father, who wished to bring up his children as English, and screened them from Indian culture. As a boy of seven he was sent to England for his education, and did well at school in Classics and other languages, including French. He went on to Cambridge. There he associated with radical and other Indian students dedicated to independence for the motherland. When he went back to India to teach, first at a college in Baroda and then as Principal of the National College in Calcutta, his revolutionary impulses came to the fore. He was arrested in 1908 for supposedly taking part in a bombing conspiracy. He had already taken up the practice of yoga, but he developed this when in jail. He underwent a religious experience, and seemed to hear a call from God, which led him to give up politics and revolutionary action. On leaving prison he moved to Pondicherry, then an enclave under French control (to get out from under British rule), and there founded an *ashram* or spiritual center. A few years later a French lady, Mme Richard, looking for a guru, found him and brought energy and organizational ability to administering and expanding the Sri Aurobindo Ashram, which gained world-wide fame in due course, attracting both Indian and non-Indian disciples. Aurobindo sought to serve his motherland now by preaching doctrines and giving examples in practice of a movement to re-energize traditional spiritual practice but in the light of modern knowledge, especially that of evolutionary theory. His background and interests gave him special opportunities to form a synthesis between Eastern and Western thought.

Various influences show in his work. First, there was the general effect of English culture, including poetry, upon him (he himself wrote extensive poetry, including an epic). Second, though it was not part of his original education, the Upanishads and other major ancient Indian works attracted his deep attention. Third, he was impressed by modern evolutionary philosophy, especially that of Bergson. Fourth, he learned from Vivekananda's self-confident poise in preaching to the West from the standpoint of Indian spirituality. His synthesis was an interesting one. He took a version of Upanishadic absolutism and set it in motion – that is, he saw it in the light of an evolving universe. At the same time he rejected the Advaitin doctrine of illusion or *māyā*: evolution itself was both a spiritual and material phenomenon.

Aurobindo held that a materialistic account of evolution was not possible because of the manifest existence of consciousness. He thus saw the cosmos as mixed, having both material and conscious aspects. He also considered creation to be an evolutionary process, so that somehow God draws the world upwards, from a state where the material forces predominate to one in which the divine life becomes possible here on earth. Consequently (and here is a major analogue with de Chardin) consciousness has to be contained within matter. Aurobindo had a problem with the mechanisms of progress, which he saw as the progressive emergence of society from a materialistic, barbarous phase, in which human beings identified themselves with their bodies. As civilization advances, humans come to a realization of their mental life. Beyond that they recognize their spiritual potential. How does all this relate to the creative work of the Absolute, which Aurobindo described in traditional Advaitin terms as *Saccidānanda,* i.e. Being, Consciousness and Bliss? Here he interposed an intermediary which he called (perhaps unfortunately, since it led him also to use the expression Superman) Supermind. This acts, like grace in other systems, in drawing humans upwards. As humans emerge, under the influence of Supermind, from their present stage, they can begin to realize the divine life. And so we may create a kind of kingdom of heaven on earth.

Another aspect of Aurobindo's synthetic approach is his desire to overcome the gulf between individuals and society. He perceived traditional Indian yoga as being individualistic. He preferred a form which had its social side. Indeed he saw the society which was set up in Pondicherry as being a kind of harbinger of the next stage in human civilization. Since the process of evolution is slow, it follows that the new divine life of humanity will not come immediately. But it can be helped along by example, and by the teaching of enlightened leaders whose consciousnesses have reached out beyond the restricted life of humanity hitherto. Part of the secret of speeding up the development of humanity lies in the spread of enlightenment. So he advocated an integral yoga which he himself had pioneered. This opens up the human psyche to the higher force of Supermind. It, as it were, descends into the soul and raises it up. It is integral because it is supposed to bring about both a spiritual and material change: a new life, both individual and social. And from there it is supposed to help with the transformation of the whole of humanity.

If the Absolute draws out of the material an ascending degree of spiritual perception and awareness, it also in the first instance brings itself into the depths of the material world it creates: thus Aurobindo postulates a preceding involution, in which the divine involves itself in the cosmos.

All this makes for an interesting metaphysical picture. As I said, it sets the old Indian Absolute in motion, both inwards and outwards. Aurobindo's greatest book, *The Life Divine,* is florid and in many ways attractive. He makes strong use of his rhetorical gifts in the English language. Since he thought of his work as being both practical and theoretical, much will depend, for its future, on the continuing health of the Pondicherry and other communities. In some ways his schema lies at a tangent from the main drive of much modern Indian thought. But it sets India in a wider world, since he was keen to stress the importance of his ideas for the whole of humanity. He was a strong advocate of world union (in which differing cultures would freely contribute).

SOME EFFECTS OF THEOSOPHY

Although the Theosophical Movement, as started primarily by Mme H.P. Blavatsky (1831–91) was predominantly a religious movement, the work of some of its leaders had an effect on the subcontinent which stimulated a more philosophical side of both Hinduism and Buddhism. Colonel Henry S. Olcott (1832–1907) made a visit to Ceylon which helped to invigorate a Theravādin revival, while Annie Besant (1847–1933) was one of the forces behind the establishment of Banaras Hindu University, and was a notable feminist advocate. She played a vital part in Indian nationalist politics and was President of the Indian Congress. She was scarcely a systematic thinker, but she did nurture the intellectual growth of Jiddu Krishnamurti (1895–1986), whom she adopted, hoping he would be the messiah. Instead he became an independent-minded philosopher of education. He rejected his religious role, and indeed rejected religion and religions. His charming personality and sincerity gave him a wide audience, and though he attacked the idea of the guru, he himself, no doubt against his inclinations, became a guru. It was as if people need a guru to tell them that they don't really need a guru. At any rate, he advocated an attractive kind of humanism, in which he urged that people should give up all ideologies and -isms, and learn to be free and spontaneous. He attacked the prevalence of imitation in education, and the overdependence on book-learning. Some of his teachings have strong analogies to Zen Buddhism. While we have to use concepts in dealing with everyday life, we should not be beguiled by them, but learn to experience life as it is and not filtered through the various intellectual modes which traditions have handed down. In short, he was a powerful philosopher of spontaneity.

SURENDRANATH DASGUPTA AND SARVEPALLI RADHAKRISHNAN

Undoubtedly the greatest of modern historians of philosophy has been S.N. Dasgupta (1885–1952). His five-volume work on Indian philosophy was a masterpiece, based on his own wide researches on primary sources. From 1924 he taught in the University of Calcutta, and made a strong impression before that when from 1920 to 1922 he was a research student at Cambridge, England. He did not espouse the fashionable theory of the unity of Indian philosophy put forth by Vivekananda, and adopted in a modified way by Radhakrishnan (1888–1975).

Radhakrishnan, from South India near Madras, and educated at the University of Madras and Madras Christian College, taught in Madras and was later Vice-Chancellor (President) of Andhra and Banares Hindu Universities. Still later he was Spalding Professor of Eastern Religions and Ethics at Oxford, Indian Ambassador to Moscow and President of India. Much of his intellectual effort was spent in exploring the Hindu and more generally the Indian tradition in relation to the West. His writings also involved commenting on Indian philosophical texts and history. In this category the most influential were his *Indian Philosophy* in two volumes (1923, 1926), and his *The Principal Upaniṣads, The Brahma Sūtra, The Bhagavadgītā* and *The Dhammapada*. In all of these he was comparative in approach; he would display parallel ideas from other traditions, notably Christianity. While not all the comparisons are of equal value or all well founded, they created a climate of comparative understanding which helped Westerners gain a better insight into the major motifs of Indian religion and philosophy. In his book on the *Brahma Sūtra* he included a long defense of the doctrine of reincarnation, deploying the arguments used in the Indian tradition plus some from the West. This fundamental belief was under some challenge from modern science (notably genetics).

His history of Indian thought was in part a defense of an idealistic position not unlike that of Vivekananda, but done more systematically. The problems of his scheme relate primarily to his attempts to assimilate Buddhism and materialism to an overall non-dualist position. Radhakrishnan set the tone for those who interpret Buddhism as not really denying the eternal self, which exists ineffably behind or below the empirical self. In this way, the Buddha can be represented as affirming that same *ātman* that appears in the Upanishads. By this route Mahāyāna Buddhism, especially as expressed in the Mādhyamaka philosophy, and Advaita become more or less identical. Materialism for Radhakrishnan becomes a partial view. As we shall see, Radhakrishnan did not take a radical position in relation to the reality of the world, so for him materialism had something positive to affirm. But Radhakrishnan's general view seems much too irenic, and takes the sting, and a lot of the interest, out of traditional Indian debates.

Radhakrishnan declared his main position to be an idealist one. This he expounded in 1932 in his *An Idealist View of Life,* following six years on from his *The Hindu View of Life* which involves an irenic response to narrower views of religion. He was critical of some major forms of Western philosophy, e.g. that of Bertrand Russell, for rejecting religion somehow in the name of science. Since the divine is transcendent to the cosmos as materially understood and presented, there should be no clash between religion (which rests on intuitive experience) and science. His appeal to intuition, which includes contemplative or yogic experience, as well as ethical and scientific insight, is the main ground of his criticism of naturalism. Other reasons for his skepticism of naturalism are his acceptance of grounds for belief in God, and of a creative, intelligent explanation of the universe, as well as the arguments he deployed on behalf of rebirth – which if accepted would imply a wider naturalism than customary views. Otherwise, however, he is not greatly interested in the detailed relations between science and religion.

While Radhakrishnan borrows his general position from Advaita, there are differences in his interpretation. Like other modern thinkers he plays down the role of *māyā*. He wants to assure the Hindu tradition of a concern with the real social and physical world. He makes impermanence the mark of empirical reality – indeed Śaṅkara had thought of the unreal as the impermanent: but there is no reason why something should not be both real and impermanent (this, for instance, is the position of the Theravāda). Radhakrishnan, it should be noted, held to the traditional notion of the self as transcending the mind, that is, the thoughts and feelings of the empirical ego. Each person's self is a partial manifestation of the one Self (the Divine Being). As selves emerge within the process of the cosmos they can be seen as part of the universe. It is because this whole cosmos including the selves is the product of the one supreme Consciousness that he can describe himself as an idealist. He was somewhat influenced by Bergson and therefore presents a kind of evolutionist picture of the cosmos.

Because of the role which Radhakrishnan assigned to *anubhava* or intuitive experience, as something over and above perception of the ordinary kind, he was especially interested as a comparativist in the relations between mysticism in the different religions. He was one of a number of twentieth-century perennialists – that is, adherents of the view of the similarity between mystical or contemplative experience in the diverse cultural circumstances of the different major traditions. He upheld the Vivekananda insistence on the essentially tolerant position of Hinduism, which had always, he considered, prized pluralism. In so far as he took notice of British and American philosophy during the period of his heyday, Radhakrishnan had a distaste for positivism and subsequent scientistic tendencies in linguistic philosophy. He considered that the denial of religious experience was not justified; and that if it is to be taken seriously it would of course cause a sea-change in epistemology. Because of these unfashionable (by Western standards) views, and also because of his somewhat diffuse method of writing, he had much less impact on Western philosophy than he had at home, where he was seen as a major articulator of the modern Hindu ideology.

OTHER FIGURES WITHIN THE HINDU CULTURAL DOMAIN

Probably the most original thinker of those working roughly within the ambit of the traditional framework of Hindu philosophy was K.C. Bhattacharya (1875–1949). He did not favor old-fashioned methods, however, and did not see much attraction in quoting authoritative texts. Such dogmatism could not cut much ice on the wider stage of modern philosophy. But he still was interested in the notion of spiritual freedom or *mokṣa*, and he saw the path to this as lying through phenomenology. He held that we could, by beginning with an examination of ordinary experience, get to a realization of the self as absolutely free. His examination of the phenomenology of the body anticipates some other modern philosophers (such as Merleau-Ponty). He distinguished between the objective body (as perceived from outside) and the felt body. Already in one's sense of the body 'from within', one has an intimation of freedom from the objective. He proceeds to a description of the next level, which is the psychological, ranging from the relatively unfree arising of images to the relatively free status of rational thought. Beyond this, reflection through introspection can take a person to higher levels of liberation from the world of objectivity. Bhattacharya was also interested in working out updated versions of Jaina theories of perspectivism *(anekāntavāda)* and *syādvāda* or 'maybe-ism'. This is in line with his emphasis on subjectivity.

Of comparativists, perhaps the most significant recent writer was B.K. Matilal (1935–91), whose many works on Indian metaphysics, logic and the philosophy of language, epistemology and ethics attempted to articulate Indian traditions of thought in contemporary categories of analytic philosophy. Bimal Matilal was Spalding Professor of Eastern Religions and Ethics in the University of Oxford and a Fellow of All Souls College from 1976 until his untimely death. Prior to his election at Oxford, he had taught at the University of Toronto for eleven years. He insisted that our understanding appreciation of philosophical problems would be enhanced if the arguments of classical Indian philosophers were introduced into modern discussions. He was concerned to dispel the misconception that Indian philosophy is exotic and mystical, having no regard for reasoned argument. His own philosophical outlook was one of commonsense realism. He eschewed both the relativism which holds that the truth and intelligibility of a philosophical position are relative to a tradition of thought, and the sort of universalism that sees such problems as global and differences between cultures as merely superficial. He was a humanist, believing that there are minimal values shared by all cultures, deriving from basic human needs and capacities. His Harvard doctoral thesis was published as *The Navya-Nyāya Doctrine of Negation* by the Harvard University Press in 1968. *Epistemology, Logic and Grammar in Indian Philosophical Analysis* (Mouton) followed in 1971. *Perception: An Essay on Classical Indian Theories of Knowledge*, was published by the Clarendon Press in 1986. Various collections of articles include *Logic, Language and Reality* (Motilal Banarsidass, 1985), *The Word and the World* (OUP, Delhi, 1990),

Mind Language and World and *Ethics and Epics* (OUP, Delhi, 2002). From 1970, he was the founding editor of the *Journal of Indian Philosophy*.

J.N. Mohanty (1928–) is another influential Indian philosopher who has spent much of his career in North America. He is also a distinguished exponent of Husserlian phenomenology. Like Matilal, he presents classical Indian thought in terms accessible to Western philosophers and is concerned to identify 'deep and significant differences'. He sees Indian philosophy as both analytical in so far as it is the analysis of ordinary usage and phenomenological in that it describes how things are presented to the testimony of consciousness. *Reason and Tradition in Indian Thought: An Essay on the Nature of Indian Philosophical Thinking* was published by the Clarendon Press in 1992.

An increasing number of Indian philosophers have become absorbed in Western and international modes of thinking, often of a refined and technical kind. As we have seen, the main thrust of the modern phase from the early nineteenth century to after independence in 1947 has been the need to pose a response to Western values: in other words, Hindu intellectuals have been greatly exercised with the problem of reconstructing a worldview which might both underpin Indian nationalism and give a modern face to the Hindu experience. Such concerns are parallel to those among Muslims and others in the colonialized world. Meanwhile, Hindu thinking is only a half of the Indian tradition. There is also the Buddhist response to Western domination. Here we shall extend our gaze to Sri Lanka and Greater India, that is, to the Theravādin countries of South-east Asia.

THE WESTERN IMPACT ON BUDDHISM

Challenges to the traditional cultures of South-east Asia and of Theravādin Sri Lanka came chiefly from Western conquest. The British had consolidated their rule over Ceylon by 1815, while they attached lower Burma in 1852 and upper Burma in 1885–90. In the last quarter of the nineteenth century France came to dominate Indo-China (Laos, Cambodia and Vietnam). Thailand managed to exempt itself from the colonial takeover, remaining an independent kingdom, partly because of the farsightedness of King Mongkut (1804–68), who had been a Buddhist monk for 27 years before he became king of Siam. As a monk, he had promoted stricter discipline within the order and this he extended when he became king. State and religion were brought close together, a situation that prevails in Thailand where the Saṅgha is a national institution under state control.

It was not unnatural for nationalism to develop strongly in all these countries and for it to be associated to a greater or lesser degree with the revival and assertion of the indigenous Buddhist heritage – especially in Thailand and Sri Lanka. But in a number of the countries the vicissitudes of the anti-colonial struggle also bred various Marxisms, including the murderous Khmer Rouge ideology in Cambodia. In Laos, Cambodia and Vietnam Buddhism itself was under attack from the official ideologies. It therefore has suffered greatly in the area as a whole. In Burma a military regime came to dominate affairs and to remain in tension with traditionalism, although immediately after independence after World War II a kind of Burmese socialism predominated, before the military coup of 1962. It was in Sri Lanka and Thailand that something of a real Buddhist revival took place, and philosophical ideas played their part here.

Mongkut was perhaps the major progenitor of Buddhist modernism (or what some have called Buddhist Protestantism – I prefer the former locution as being more general and less prone to misinterpretation): namely a form of interpretation of the Theravāda in particular which emphasizes its scientific, ethical, modern and contemplative side, and underplays the role of gods, rituals, old cosmological conceptions and popular religion. It seeks to show that the Buddha's teaching was essentially modern, though overlaid since his time with superstitions and aberrations. In this it has received support from Western scholars and converts who have seen Buddhism as a testable rational morality, untainted by supernatural speculations, offering a solution to life's problems.

Mongkut had been a monk before he eventually assumed the throne. He was interested both in the practice of contemplation and in Pāli scholarship: he indeed acquired considerable learning as well as a desire to reform the monasticism of his day. He founded a new order within the Thai Saṅgha, the Dhammayuttika-nikāya, and later as king used this as an instrument of reform. Importantly too he favored a new look at the Pāli sources: in effect, like a number of reformers all over the world, he used the foundational documents as a basis for the critique of contemporary practice. He commissioned one of his ministers to write a rationalistic text expounding the true and scientific nature of the Buddha's teachings. This was where what he had learned of Western science had a powerful impact on him as an individual and through him as a learned king on Thai culture as a whole. His reshaping zeal had a strong effect on the modernization of Thailand, a factor in its capacity to remain independent of the colonial powers.

His work was carried on during the long reign of his son Chulalongkorn (1868–1910), who set up academies and universities for the better training of monks and other intellectuals. The stress on the scientific nature of the Buddha's teaching was maintained, and the so-called law of dependent origination was often seen as prefiguring patterns of thought in modern physics. At the same time the consolidation of the Saṅgha and the intensification of nationalism gave Buddhism in Thailand a somewhat chauvinist character, yet the reform of the Order also brought with it a raising of the level of spirituality, and some of the more spiritual monks, while living at the periphery of politics, can represent a challenge to the government.

The various challenges to indigenous tradition which I listed earlier in relation to Hinduism obtained in much the same force in Ceylon as Britain developed its rule. But there were differences in their impact, partly because of the rather divergent nature of Buddhism in comparison with Hinduism. The reception of Buddhist ideas in the West was also somewhat different.

Interestingly, Theosophy played a part, as it did in India, in reviving the morale of Buddhism. The movement played a role in the foundation of Ananda College, which is still the top Buddhist school in Ceylon. Buddhists were able in a practical way to use Western-style methods of revival and teaching, including the creation of such organizations as the Young Men's Buddhist Association, consciously modeled on its Christian counterpart. On the other hand, Christian, especially evangelical, criticism of Buddhism was less pointed than that directed towards the Hindu tradition, even if Bishop Heber of Calcutta could write in a famous hymn: 'What though the balmy breezes/Blow soft o'er Ceylon's isle/Where every prospect pleases/And only man is vile.' Though early Western missionaries and commentators on Ceylonese culture thought that Buddhists actually worship the Buddha, they do not conceive themselves this way, and the educated (whether Western-wise or indigenously) elite especially do not. A series of public debates between prominent monks and Christian missionaries in the latter part of the century left the Buddhists with the clear impression that they had won.

Moreover, Ceylon did not have such practices as *suttee*, nor a very marked caste system (there was one, but of a much gentler sort, and Buddhists could claim, not quite truly, that the Saṅgha, transcended it). From an ethical perspective it could be thought that Buddhism had as noble or a nobler morality than Christianity. The demands of compassion were wider than those of love, since they applied beyond the human realm to all living beings. There was also a lot of very practical advice on methods of meditation and the like which could improve individual character. Religiously, since nirvāṇa transcends heaven, which, however blissful, eventually comes to an end, the Buddhist goal could be thought to be higher than ultimate salvation in the Christian framework.

One of the major figures in revivalist Buddhism was Anagārika Dharmapāla (1864–1933), who was keen on the restoration of Buddhist pilgrimage sites in India, such as Bodh-Gaya, where the Buddha gained enlightenment, and Sarnath, where he taught his first sermon. In his work in this direction he also began to promote the cause of Buddhist ecumenism. In 1891, he founded the Mahabodhi Society, the first international Buddhist organization, which received support from other parts of Asia. Conceived as an instrument for the unification of all Buddhists, in 1892 it moved its headquarters from Bodh-Gaya to Calcutta where the conversion of Indians to Buddhism became one of its purposes. Dr B.R. Ambedkar (1891–1956), who was born into the 'untouchable' Mahar caste, had the luck to receive a proper education, culminating in a doctorate from Columbia University, New York, in 1916. On his return to India, he practiced law and worked on behalf of untouchables. He clashed with Gandhi who approved of the caste system as a means of social organization, albeit one in need of reformation through the integration of the outcastes ('harijans'). After independence in 1947, Ambedkar was a member of the government and drafted parts of the constitution. In the face of opposition to his radically reformist views, he resigned in 1951. In 1950, he announced his conversion to Buddhism, although this had in fact happened in 1935. Thereafter he encouraged untouchables to espouse a religion that promoted equality and freedom. He saw the Buddha's message as a means of social reform through personal transformation, and nirvāṇa as the just society. Although there have been mass conversions of members of what are euphemistically called 'scheduled castes', the lack of an inherited infrastructure has posed problems. In addition, relinquishing scheduled caste status involves the forfeiture of some rights and privileges.

Significant in the Western reception of Buddhism was the massive effort of T.W. Rhys Davids (1843–1922), a professor in Manchester, England, who founded and ran the Pāli Text Society. This not only had the Pāli Canon printed and edited in roman script, but also sponsored translations of the whole. In addition Rhys Davids wrote quite a number of books on Buddhism, tending to stress its rational nature. He and other Westerners such as Theodore Stcherbatsky (1866–1942) tended to underline the modern and scientific nature of Buddhism. One of the reasons for a favorable reception for Buddhism in the West was that a number of Westerners were attracted to agnosticism, in the face of somewhat puerile discussions of the biblical texts and the clash between literalism and science in the post-evolutionary nineteenth century; they had a nostalgia for spirituality. Buddhism was a revelation: you could have a spiritual path without God, and a rational ethic which was deeper than utilitarianism. The doctrines of momentariness and the fluid nature of the ephemeral mental and material basic elements of existence fitted in with Western atomic theories, and the denial of permanent identity is concordant with skeptical Western views about enduring selfhood. Somehow such perceptions did not apply in the same way to the Hindu tradition.

A revived Buddhism in Ceylon and South-east Asia could profit from these factors, and reply to possible Western critiques in a double manner. On the one hand, versus theism, there were both traditional and modern Buddhist arguments; but versus positivism and scientism, there were wider perspectives of spiritual orientation provided by Buddhism. It could therefore as usual steer a middle path, contrary to both the wings of Western ideology. It could also make use of, without succumbing to, Western critiques of Western religion – chiefly of course those of Marx and Freud. They could see Marx's 'opium of the people' stance as directed chiefly at Christianity and popular religion. On the other hand, Freud's Father figure had no purchase on Theravāda Buddhism, where there was no Father (or Mother) creator, no God.

Many of these themes came together most perspicuously in the work of such writers as G.P. Malalasekara (1911–68), who launched the Buddhist Encyclopedia, and K.N. Jayatilleke (1911–67), Professor of Philosophy at the University of Ceylon in

Peradeniya. The latter's general philosophy was much the most sophisticated to come out of the Theravādin countries. He was able to combine, with aplomb, motifs from British verificationism, Wittgensteinian linguistic philosophy and the Pāli tradition (of which he had a detailed grasp). What he presented was a highly modern version of the Buddha's teachings, based on canonical sources.

SOME OTHER TRENDS IN BUDDHIST SOUTH AND SOUTH-EAST ASIA

As elsewhere in Asia and more generally in the Third World, Marxism has its attractions. The enemy's enemy can seem a friend, especially where the ideology is much modified to seem like a home-grown variety. Oddly enough two independently arrived at worldviews in the Theravādin sphere have borne a strong resemblance: the Khmer Rouge ideology, articulated by Khieu Sampan (c.1929) and put into effect in 1975, with the fall of Pnomh Penh; and the JVP philosophy, which instigated a powerful uprising in 1971, and nearly twenty years later took an active role in Sri Lanka's complex civil war. Khieu's French doctorate concerned economics, but essentially what he wanted was to withdraw Cambodia from the whole global capitalist system. This required force, and also, it was thought, purging Cambodia of all those who, because of education, had been in effect entangled in global ideology and capitalist practice. The ideal was a purified, isolated Kampuchea (as the Khmer renamed the country). Similarly the Jayantha Vimukthi Peramuna in Sri Lanka wished to create a socialist sort of country isolated from world capitalism, and existing in a state of rural simplicity. Both movements drew on idealism, ruthlessness and patriotism. Perhaps, together with the less striking but analogous case of Burma, they testify to a desire for a secularized and collectivized nirvana: a wish to have national hermit status. Whatever else that they indicate, they certainly are far removed from Buddhist modernism or genuine intellectual sophistication.

SOME CONCLUSIONS ABOUT BUDDHISM

There remain some thoughts about where Theravāda Buddhism goes from here. A greater ecumenical sense means that Theravādin scholars are more interested in wider debates: for instance, there is greater concern with Mādhyamaka philosophy, with its interesting critical stance. There is also further concern with problems of personal identity, in the light of rebirth; with the unconscious and the application of Freudian ideas to Buddhist psychology; with the relation of Buddhist epistemology to Western ideas; and with Buddhist ethics and applied psychology. It would seem that there is quite a lot which Buddhism could offer to global debate. By and large the Theravādin countries have not made much of a contribution to a theory of religions, from a Buddhist perspective, nor to the dialogue between religions. In view of most of the countries of the area having substantial Muslim and Christian, not to mention Hindu, minorities, this seems to be an important desideratum. Here there is a vital contrast to Hindu intellectual life, which has been greatly preoccupied with the perennialist theory. Since Buddhism does not have a one Reality for religions to revolve round, its general approach to alternative faiths has to be of quite a different, probably a much subtler kind.

But Buddhist modernism, though it may not have too much credence among anthropologists, who perceive the richer 'religion on the ground', and though it does not recognize clearly enough that modern nationalism, particularly in Sri Lanka, depends on chronicles of former, classical glory rather than on the austerer banner of a scientific Neofoundationalism, looking back to purged scriptures, nevertheless remains attractive to intellectuals, and is largely the type of Buddhism making its way in the West, where there are no local gods to patronize except perhaps Jesus, who likes to stand apart. As a response to Western ideologies, whether missionary or scientist, it has so far proved reasonably effective.

I have not dealt here either in the Hindu or the Buddhist part of this chapter with those scholars from Greater India who have participated simply in Western philosophy debates. It is obvious that much of the energy of indigenous intellectuals has been devoted to thinking about the equations involved in reviving older intellectual traditions in the face of imperialism and the challenge of a vigorous, both economically and culturally, Western world. Despite the fact that there has been a somewhat lukewarm counter-response, the situation is that the twentieth century, building on beginnings made in the nineteenth century, has seen a vast flourishing of the activities of rescuing and making available the great philosophical resources of the region. We are now in a position to understand the philosophical past, and it may be that Indian philosophy will take on new forms as we move into a global civilization. Already perhaps the differences between it and other forms of philosophy, e.g. Chinese and European, will give scholars pause for reflection. It is for instance, interesting that people built the same way should have such differing models of human psychology.

I have emphasized too in this chapter the importance of religion in the story of modern adaptations to the colonial experience and to the consequent reformulation of worldviews. This emphasis on religion may not be to everyone's taste, but it is realistic.

Finally, it is important to say something about Tibetan Buddhism. The fact that the major center for Tibetans is in North India and that the great resources of texts and knowledge which the Tibetan diaspora is helping to make available to the wider world are highly relevant to classical Indian Buddhism, means that India is beginning a new phase of the rediscovery of its Buddhist heritage. It may also be mentioned that in so far as he expresses a philosophical position, the worldview of the Dalai Lama is a form of Buddhist modernism, from a Mādhyamaka point of view. One can expect new ideas to emerge from the Tibetan traditions, as its diaspora has longer and longer experience of the West.

14

CHINA, KOREA AND JAPAN IN MODERN TIMES

THE WESTERN CHALLENGE IN THE FAR EAST

The defeat by the British of the French in the Seven Years' War (1756–63) brought the East India Company wonderful opportunities for trade with China. In the eighteenth century China was highly prosperous and well run. Tea and luxury household items were increasingly traded for opium. The attempt by China to resist this import led to the Opium War, settled in 1842, with the opening up of China to trade concessions, unequal treaties and territorial rights for foreigners. From then on there was a crisis which posed both practical and intellectual questions. In particular, was it possible to learn enough of modern ways to resist the foreigners? Could such technical knowledge be combined with Confucian tradition (since this was the ideology of the government and the bureaucracy)? The Taiping Rebellion of the mid-century sparked by the visions of Hung Hsiu-ch'üan (Hong Xiuquan) (1813–64) posed the issue in a crude form. His new religion demanded the smashing up of traditional temples. It incorporated certain Christian ideas. It promised a new harmony when various reforms would be realized: equality for women; the use of colloquial rather than classical language; land redistribution with communes; the suppression of Confucianism – it was like the future Maoist worldview in its promises. It failed ultimately after huge suffering. One of the reasons it failed had to do with philosophy: its worldview, despite the forward-looking nature of many of its proposed reforms, was highly mythic, somewhat crude and could not command the loyalty of the educated. Could China produce a worldview which would help it with the reconstruction that the incursion of powerful foreigners indicated was necessary? This, rather than theoretical and refined issues in technical and traditional philosophy, was what most of the debate was about over the next hundred years and more. It began at a conscious level with the foundation of the so-called 'Self-strengthening Movement' by Feng Kuei-fen (Feng Guifen) (1809–74) in the 1860s: it used the slogan 'Learn the superior barbarian techniques in order to control the barbarian'. It led to a certain piecemeal modernization: sending people abroad for training, etc. The Taipings had had a different instinct: you really need to modernize society itself, rather than graft a few new methods onto the fabric of an old-fashioned society.

The situation in Korea and Japan was rather different. The Japanese realized early that there was urgent need for reform. The visit of Admiral Perry to Tokyo Bay in 1853 was ominous. In 1867 the Tokugawa regime, which had done more than a little to anticipate reform, was overthrown and the new imperial Meiji era started, with tremendous social and other changes. This enabled Japan to modernize at some cost but at great speed, and to embark on its own colonialist path, after the defeat of Russia at the decisive naval victory of Tsushima in 1905. This led to the conquest of Korea in 1910, strangling its indigenous modernization and imposing a foreign one. This made Korea's recent history quite different from that of its neighbors.

But all these events had the same precipitating force: the intrusion of the powerful and seaborne Western powers into the region, armed with cannon, modern science, new forms of education, missionary ambitions, liberal ideology, capitalist power and colonialist arrogance. How could these countries cope with such intruders?

In China, as already indicated, the question at first related to the role of Confucianism. Its literary flavor, its position as the worldview of the imperial bureaucracy, its subservience to the Manchu dynasty (still perceived as rather foreign), its conservative social nature, its philosophical strengths – all these were obstacles to modernization. But there were stirrings of a new approach. The first major attempt to reformulate a modern Confucianism was that of K'ang Yu-wei (Kang Youwei) (1858–1927).

KANG YOUWEI'S THOUGHT

As a young man, Kang, though dedicated primarily to Confucian scholarship, immersed himself in a consideration of other systems – Western thought, Mahāyāna Buddhism, Taoist philosophy. What emerged from his intense reflections was a new syncretic Confucianism, which later became important when he persuaded the Emperor in 1898 to undertake extensive changes, known as the Hundred Days Reform (the program was, however, defeated by conservative forces). His system of ideas centered on a reformulated notion of the main Confucian moral ideal, that of *ren* or human-heartedness. This he saw in both cosmic and egalitarian terms. In other words he perceived a future state in which *ren* would be all-penetrating and all-encompassing, so that all human beings would share the blessings of life equally. He even boldly projected the sharing of men and women, a kind of free love. These ideas he expressed in his *Book of Great Concord*. He saw history as unfolding in three stages: the first is the period of disorder, comprising the dominance of egoism, nationalism and capitalism; the second sees countries uniting under the banners of nationalism and internationalism; and finally there emerges a period of global civilization. In this great concord humans would be united in egalitarianism, liberty and hedonism, gaining, therefore, within a new moral framework the benefits of material abundance. All this looks rather far removed from traditional Confucian morality: but Kang held that the older values were relevant to the ages preceding the final concord, which could only come about after some time and the gradual evolution of human values. His radical vision of a new sense of *ren* applied to the final stage. *Ren* was not only intensely compassionate, so refusing to see suffering in others (in some ways Kang was influenced by the bodhisattva ideal of Buddhism, though his account of *ren* also owes much to Mencius), but it was also a kind of magnetic force which would penetrate the new world and hold humanity together. His system was a curious mixture, in some respects naive: however, his practical attempt at reform gave him wide historical influence, and he set a powerful example of reformulating Confucianism. His representation of Confucius himself as a reformer was bold, and left its mark on the Chinese intellectual scene.

Kang's vision was carried on by his disciples, notably by Liang Ch'i-ch'ao (Liang Qichao) (1873–1928), who synthesized Buddhist and Confucian ideals with modern Western values. However, he was much disillusioned as a result of a visit to the West in 1919. As a result of this he published a book called *Recollections of a Trip to Europe*, in which he heavily criticized the modern West, both because of the mechanized life imposed by industry and because of the awful destruction brought about by World War I. Recoiling from industrialization, he advocated a political economy based upon rural development. Once rural prosperity is assured, it will be possible to build up industries on a saner basis. For him, Chinese civilization is a mean between Western materialism and the world-renunciation of the Hindus. It is on a Chinese model that the world civilization of the future will be constructed. He was highly critical of the utilitarian ethic, which was in his view a poor basis for developing a scientific worldview. He considered that the values of Wang Yangming formed a better platform for scientific endeavor. His views, as expressed above, proved to be controversial, since so many young Chinese intellectuals of the period were captivated by Western approaches and the achievements of modern science.

QUESTIONS OF MODERNIZING BUDDHISM

Naturally the Western challenge posed similar problems to both Buddhism and Taoism, but in a less sharp form, since these traditions had less to do with official government ideology, and more to do with individual spirituality. Taoism of course had had long associations with anarchism and rebellion. But if modern Chinese philosophers interpreted it, it was in the light of early philosophical Taoism rather than in the light of the later and somewhat different religious tradition. However, it was among Buddhist thinkers that systematic attempts to represent the faith occurred. The most influential of writers and organizers was T'ai Hsü (Tai Xu) (1889–1947), who set up a modern academy for training monks at Wu-ch'ang, and was involved in various educational and political enterprises, giving support to Chiang Kaishek and helping to win support in neighboring countries for China during World War II. What he did in his various writings, such as *The New Realism* (1940) was to use the language of modernity in presenting Buddhism. He was insistent that Westerners should see that at heart Buddhism is atheistic, that the cult of Buddhas is commemorative and inspirational, and that gods and spirits, while not denied in Buddhism, are peripheral. Indeed he tried to show that traditional Buddhist metaphysics is compatible with modern physics. Probably Tai Xu's importance lies less in any originality, for in essence he presented the traditional doctrines of Consciousness Only, but in his modernizing tone and recognition that it was not difficult to combine scientific and Buddhist ideas. He was, importantly, a practical reformer, though he encountered quite a lot of opposition from conservative Buddhists. He was also ecumenical in spirit, not just in relation to world Buddhism (being somewhat before his time in this, since the international organizations he founded did not survive in their original form), but also in regard to world religions. At least, he appreciated the existential and practical side of the religious quest, though he was highly critical of both religions and ideologies, including Communism, for causing divisions between people.

A more original figure was Hsiung Shih-li (Xiong Shili) (1885–1968) whose *New Exposition of the Pure Idea* appeared in 1944. He was perhaps only partially a Buddhist, since he incorporated into his scheme of thought some ideas both from the Neoconfucianist Wang Yangming and from Bergson. The presence of the former was not too difficult since he himself had in turn been influenced by Buddhism. He considered that the cosmos or nature is a single process of transformation, arising from a primordial blind spirit. This is a kind of noumenon or original substance which manifests itself in an evolving way, as change. At differing phases of change the original spirit manifests itself as spirit or mind and as matter. Xiong's system is Buddhist in so far as the distinction between mind and matter turns out to be unreal, and since the original substance is in some sense spiritual, it is possible to classify his scheme as being idealist. It is Bergsonian in that not only is the primordial substance constantly evolving, but its nature is known by intuition. It is Neoconfucian in that his system incorporates something of the distinction between *li* and *qi*. It represents an up-to-date way of presenting both Confucian and Buddhist metaphysics in a mode which harmonizes with the scientific outlook.

But the future of Buddhist intellectuals was not to be bright. Soon after World War II the Marxists came to dominate, and scholarly life among Buddhists (and Confucians) was largely suppressed, not only in mainland China but also in Tibet.

SOME FURTHER DEVELOPMENTS IN CONFUCIANISM

As in India the impact of the West revitalized concern for the history of Chinese philosophy. Hu Shih (Hu Shi) (1891–1962) wrote a history from the angle of pragmatism, which he had studied with John Dewey. But more influential were the volumes of Fung Yu-lan (Feng Youlan) (1895–1990), published in 1931 and 1934, entitled *History of Chinese Philosophy*. Feng was also a philosopher in his own right, and espoused a modernized version of Neoconfucianism, blending in some Taoist elements. He revived the Neoconfucian concept of principle (*li*) but considered it to be transcendent, and not immanent within the material universe. Its nature is, however, reflected in material things and this is why the scientific and logical study of beings is important. One can through knowledge grasp things as systematically interrelated: in this the wise person participates in *ren*. So in scientific inquiry one learns to go beyond the senses; and beyond that the wise person can leave egoism behind.

While the history of Chinese philosophy has undergone a great revival in this century, other and more political issues have had a greater impact. One of the problems posed during and after the revolution of 1911 was whether anything of the Confucian tradition could survive into the new ideology which might be needed in the reconstruction of the Chinese nation. Here the thought of Sun Yat-sen (1866–1925) was of some importance.

THE PHILOSOPHY OF THE KUOMINTANG: SUN AND CHIANG

Sun Yat-sen was educated in Hawaii and Hong Kong, in missionary schools (he was a Christian), and so was one of the earliest Western-trained Chinese intellectuals. In due course he became leader of the Revolutionary Alliance in Tokyo, the predecessor of the Kuomintang, the party headed by him and later by Chiang Kai-shek (1887–1975).

In his political outlook Sun tried to combine the best of the West and the best of traditional China. In Chinese history the three powers separated in some modern constitutions were combined under the emperor, namely the executive, legislative and judicial branches of government. These are best, as in the West, kept separated. But in ancient China two further powers were kept out of the emperor's control, namely the examination system and the censorate. Sun therefore advocated a five-power constitution (which, however, was never properly put into practice in post-revolutionary China).

410

Sun's ideology also prominently included the Three People's Principles – Nationalism, Democracy and Popular Livelihood. His espousal of nationalism, however, left him haunted with a sense that eventually there should be practiced the brotherhood of all human beings. This was the ideal of the Great Harmony which had long been an eschatological concept of importance in Chinese history and which now might illuminate the world stage. Here there was some influence of Kang Youwei who had so vividly revived it. Another Confucian element in Sun's thought, and about which he debated in his own mind, was the supposed close relation between knowledge and action, a primary plank in Wang Yangming's philosophical platform. While Sun accepted the conjunction, he was disappointed by people's passivity during the takeover and as he saw it perversion of the Revolution by Yüan Shih-k'ai (Yuan Shikai) (1859–1916). Sun concluded that Wang's linkage had to be modified: the emphasis now was on knowledge itself – to flow into action it had to be real knowledge, and Sun diagnosed some of the problem of passivity to be mere ignorance.

But though Sun was important, obviously, in the history of China, it cannot be claimed that he was a very acute or systematic thinker. Similarly, Chiang, his successor, was more a person of action than a thinker, but helped in the New Life Movement, which he launched in 1934, to reassert some of the traditional Confucian ethical values.

THE NEW CULTURE MOVEMENT AND MARXISM

The fact is, however, that a large number of the intellectuals after the revolution of 1911 and through the chaotic period between the world wars, marred in China by warlordism, civil war, economic dislocation and Japanese invasion, were disillusioned with the Confucian tradition. As early as 1916 Ch'en Tu-hsiu (Chen Duxiu) (1879–1942) had launched a very strong attack on the tradition. He castigated Confucius' ethics as being feudal and so unsuited to the modern age. At the same time intellectuals were affected by new attitudes towards the literary enterprise. This was more revolutionary than might be expected among those used to a Western appraisal of literary activity. The fact is that in writing in the colloquial language and in advocating this with passion, Chinese writers were moving against the old, arcane literary culture. In freeing writing and reading from the classical language, pioneers of the literary movement were undermining respect for both the vehicle and the content of the old Confucian past. All this went with new modes of education, based on Western models. This introduced young intellectuals to the ideals and results of science. There were thus attractions for young Chinese in positivism and a scientifically based worldview. Such figures as Dewey and Russell were appealing. Wu Chih-hui (Wu Zhihui) (1865–1953) wrote a highly pungent essay, hailed as significant by Hu Shi, in which he declared boldly that all things in the universe can be explained by science. Although there were others preferring a middle path synthesizing

411

Western and Chinese values, materialistic conceptions drawn from the West remained popular among the elite, and helped to prepare the way for the acceptance of Marxism. From a Chinese point of view there happened to be foretastes of various Marxian ideas, such as the yin–yang oscillation as the forerunner of the dialectic. But more important was the widespread disillusion with a tradition which had failed to ward off the Western intrusions and had collapsed as an educational force. It was not therefore surprising if a certain portion of Chinese intellectuals should be attracted to Marxism. As it happened, the struggle within the Chinese Communist Party resulted in the increasing dominance of Mao Zedong (1893–1976), and it was largely his theoretical opinions which came to form Marxist orthodoxy in China.

MAO ZEDONG THOUGHT

Certain practical experiences helped to shape Mao's reflections. One was his perception after the massacre of leftists in 1927 by Chiang's forces in Shanghai that it was unlikely that by itself the Chinese proletariat could win. Mao's work in the countryside led him to realize increasingly that the peasants needed to be mobilized. This in turn led him to be skeptical of the orthodox theory that it was necessary for China to go first through the bourgeois phase before being ready for revolution. Stalin, retaining a more traditional view, came to support Chiang during the war, as the person able to lead China through a bourgeois and nationalist phase of her history. Further, Mao became an adept at war and was an important theoretician of war. As a successful and thoughtful guerrilla leader he could envisage a form of revolution which was conceived in terms of civil war rather than the anarchic overthrow of an existing regime. In these ways he adapted Marxism to Chinese conditions, as he saw them.

Mao also, somewhat influenced not just by Western anarchism but by Taoist strands in Chinese culture, saw the revolution as something which would continue over the years. This was one reason why at differing periods, most notably during the Cultural Revolution, he wished to stir up society and not let it settle back into a new bureaucratic order.

There was a strong voluntarism inculcated by Mao: perhaps we might call it a kind of faith. Faith could move mountains. Because he placed so much importance on the will he tended to undervalue the mind. Indeed he felt that in reshaping human nature it was as well not to have to encounter too many ideas which were learned from books, even Marxist ones. The mind of a peasant was seen by him as like a blank sheet of paper: on it one could write such beautiful characters. This was why he appears to have been largely unworried during the 1960s by the assaults made on the whole educational system. In this attitude, however, he failed to meet the challenges to traditional learning. China came to be very short of skilled people to work in the various sophisticated industries which were indispensable to economic health. His rather romantic view here of the possibilities of human nature owed something to the Taoist tradition. He was strongly anti-Confucian, especially in its treatment of women. From a boy he had been keen to see rights for women, and a kind of feminism informed his vision. There are one or two elements of Buddhism in Mao's thinking too, especially in so far as he encouraged faith in the leadership. When, during the Cultural Revolution, some of his sayings were put together in the 'Little Red Book' it was treated as a sacred scripture in effect – something like the *Lotus Sūtra*. The fideism of some strands of the Mahayana was revived in the cult of Mao.

However, the theoretical basis of Mao's Marxism is displayed more fully in one or two important essays. One of these is his 'On Practice', which deals among other things with a problem we have touched on already, namely the relation between knowledge and practice, as debated by Wang Yangming and Sun Yat-sen. Mao held to a double connection between theory and practice. On the one hand, ideas, which themselves arise from fragmentary perceptions, have to be tested through social practice. On the other hand, ideas or theories at which we arrive, having tested them in practice, have to be reapplied in practice. Theories which are merely contemplated are useless. Empiricists, relying on perception and being skeptical of theory, would not, he avers, be suitable to direct a revolution, since theory can give a person or a group a much wider vision, of the situation of a whole society. The cyclical process of moving to theory and modifying it in the light of practice is also important for Mao, because when the theory is first formulated it will not have disclosed itself completely. This notion forms the basis of Mao's critique of conservative Marxists, whose ideas lag behind the onward process of society, driven forward by the dialectical processes inherent both in nature and history.

In his essay 'On Contradiction', Mao sets forth a general view of Marxism and of the operation of the processes of the dialectic in particular. He introduced flexibility into his analysis by noting that contradictions are or can be qualitatively different. The consequence is that the methods of resolving them are also different. Such flexibility should also apply to what is counted the principal aspect in any one contradiction. For instance, in the contradiction between the productive forces and the relations of production, the former is principal, as in the contradiction between the economic foundation and its superstructure the former is dominant. But to apply these estimates universally is what Mao castigates as being 'mechanistic' Marxism. He already hints at the voluntarism he came to apply when in the 1950s and 1960s he encouraged the Great Leap Forward and the Cultural Revolution. He noted that while in the development of history as a whole it is material things which determine spiritual things, nevertheless the spiritual superstructure reflects upon and affects the economic foundation. This he holds is a view which does not run counter to materialistic philosophy, but merely against a mechanistic interpretation of it. Mao also adds a distinction between contradiction and antagonism, designed to soften struggles within and outside the party and to lend tactical mobility to Communist policy. Such flexibility enabled Mao to distinguish between potential allies and those inevitably committed to the other side (such as the comprador class among the bourgeoisie, tied to external imperialist forces).

Mao's voluntarism became marked during the Cultural Revolution, which can be seen as an attempt to reshape the Chinese world and to break down bureaucratic Communism through the mobilization of spiritual forces, overcoming varied material obstacles. The fact that Mao himself was venerated with a passion worthy of Pure Land devotionalism blended in with his emphasis on the will. Mao's position also had as its background the successful prosecution of armed struggle, often against material odds, such as the survival of the Long March, and the successful conclusion of the civil war in 1949.

But though Mao showed himself to be a successful military leader, a dynamic force in rebuilding China's national strength and an interesting theorist and stimulator of change, his rule was remarkably unsuccessful in the fields of economics and education. As to the latter, he held to a strongly anti-Confucian view, which led to his wishing to remove traditional learning: on the other hand, the initial successes of his philosophical and practical pragmatism, together with his inspirational voluntarism, led to his undervaluing technical and scientific expertise. Both in military and in other matters he thought that the resources suitable for guerrilla warfare and for early industrial development were enough. Consequently he presided over a crippling of the educational system (which in any case would have the disadvantage of the discouragement of criticism). As to economics, his largely agricultural view of China's strength and his experimentation with collectives and communes had a stultifying effect. It was only after Mao that China began to move forward to more imaginative and semi-capitalist measures which stimulated the process of strong economic development. China's troubles had substantially been due to Mao's worldview – a good illustration no doubt of the effect of the superstructure on the economic base!

China remained largely a closed society, so that there was not much room for independent philosophizing, free of the Marxist strait-jacket during Mao's time, and it will be interesting to see how an opening to more varieties of philosophy than in the past will change the nature of Chinese philosophy during the recent period of rapid economic growth and change.

CHINESE PHILOSOPHY AFTER MAO'S DEATH

Deng Xiaoping's return to power after Mao's death brought a period of liberalization which, although not completely free of the Marxist straight-jacket, provided enough space for intellectual effervescence that some discerned a new Enlightenment. Officially, there was a turn to a 'pragmatic' position of allowing practice to determine truth, to find better means to build 'socialism with Chinese characteristics'. Attempts to renovate Maoist orthodoxy to justify reforms soon led to more fundamental re-examination of Marxism. Party theoreticians and academics debated humanism, alienation, subjectivity, and praxis materialism. A reform movement developed in Chinese Marxism defending humanism, involving thinkers such as Wang Ruoshui, Su Shaoqi, Gao Ertai, Feng Lanrui, and Li Zehou. Li was also the central figure in a lively revival of aesthetics in the early 1980s – he reassessed Kant and expounded the view that aesthetics was determined by the moral category of freedom. Li later became interested in Confucianism and some even consider him a New Confucian. Towards the end of the 1980s, some Chinese intellectuals such as Yan Jiaqi, Fang Lizhi and Liu Xiaobo began to oppose Marxism openly.

A growing interest in Western Enlightenment ideas accompanied a vibrant debate over the future of Chinese culture. At the height of 1980s 'culture craze', the television series, *River Elegy* (*Heshang*), attacked Chinese tradition for obstructing modernization and advocated turning to the West completely. Like the 'complete Westernizers' of an earlier era, the main interest of these cultural iconoclasts was liberal democracy as the political counterpart of free market economy. During the 1989 Democracy Movement which ended so tragically, a 'Goddess of Democracy' statue (an obvious mimicry of the Statue of Liberty) was erected in Tiananmen square, and demonstrators wore T-shirts with 'Science and Democracy', the slogans of the earlier New Culture movement.

Since the 1990s, Enlightenment ideals came under strong attack by conservatives, nationalists, and those who adopted various Western critical methodologies criticizing modernity. Paradoxically, this led to the emergence of a liberal discourse in China, with Hayek as the main influence. Some liberals and neo-conservatives hoped that marketization of economy would nurture the growth of a middle class to lead a peaceful transition to democracy, but the 'marketization of power' or accumulation of 'power capital' and corrupt 'money politics' prevented the widespread devolution of power to individual citizens and significantly reduced the chances of such a transition. Thinkers identified as the 'New Left' criticized reforms and argued that China should not follow Western models slavishly, but must aim for a 'deep' democracy with arrangements capable of increasing political mobilization, constitutional arrangements for breaking intra-governmental deadlocks by the electorate through referendums or early elections, a social system that fosters the self-organization of civil society and its spontaneous participation in collective discussion and problem-solving. This requires 'institutional innovation' which could benefit from 'reasonable elements' of past institutions, including some experiments of the Mao era. New Left philosophy draws from post-modernist, post-colonial, post-structuralist, and other critical methodologies (collectively known as post-isms or *houxue*) to criticize (Western) modernity.

Pragmatic attitudes resonate in many Chinese intellectual discussions, and Dewey's followers look forward to a revival of Pragmatism; but generally the Chinese understanding of 'pragmatic', even in intellectual discourses, is different from Dewey's Pragmatism. For example, neo-authoritarians and neo-conservatives are credited with being 'pragmatic' when they argue that a strong state, even authoritarian political control, was necessary to facilitate liberal economic policies during the transition from traditional authoritarianism to democracy. Some neo-conservatives would like to see positive elements of traditional culture, especially those conducive to social harmony and stability, preserved and transformed for the modern age. While neo-conservatives may also see Chinese culture playing a role in creating a new global civilization, cultural nationalists generally have a narrower concern in their championing of Chinese culture, viewing it as a matter of asserting 'Chineseness' against a hostile world. Both domestic development and international environment since 1989 have contributed to the rise of nationalism in China. The Chinese Communist Party (CCP) has made moves to use Confucianism as the basis of a state nationalism that is replacing Marxism as the party's ideological prop. Intellectuals generally look toward the 'mainstream Chinese culture', usually understood as Confucian, for the basis of nationalism; but most Chinese nationalists focus on the (Han) Chinese nation, and do not accept the CCP's claim that the party represents the nation's will and interest.

The 1990s witnessed a 'return to traditional culture' linked to the rise of neoconservatism–neoauthoritarianism and the generally more critical attitudes toward Western cultural–intellectual imports. A 'national studies craze' (including a revival of Taoism) developed from the tentative efforts of the 1980s to rediscover 'national essence' which philosophically means a revival of Confucianism, initially focusing on overseas New Confucianism. Despite its association with nationalism, such cultural revivals may yet play an important role in connecting China to the world.

NEW CONFUCIANISM AND LATE TWENTIETH-CENTURY REVIVALS OF CONFUCIANISM

In the last two decades of the twentieth century, some Chinese scholars recognized New Confucianism or *Dangdai Xin Rujia* as one of three main currents of thought in modern China (besides Marxism and liberalism). To others, New Confucianism is very much retrospectively constructed and includes too diverse a group of thinkers to be considered a movement. New Confucian thinkers, most of whom resided outside the People's Republic of China until the 1980s, are all preoccupied with the problems of China in modern times, although what constitutes 'China' is increasingly problematic and contested. As a broad trend of thought that arose in defense of Chinese culture, especially Confucianism, in response to a crisis of meaning brought on by the New Culture movement, it attempts to modernize Confucianism with the aid of Western ideas such as democracy and science, without succumbing to scientism or cultural iconoclasm.

Xiong Shili, Liang Shuming, Ma Yifu, and Zhang Junmai (Carsun Chang), Fung Yu-lan, He Lin, Qian Mu and Fang Dongmei (Thomé Fang) have been identified as first-generation New Confucians; Mou Zongsan, Tang Junyi and Xu Fuguan as the second generation, and Liu Shu-hsien, Tu Wei-ming, Cheng Chung-ying, A.S. Cua and Yu Ying-shih as the third generation. These thinkers differ in which period of Confucianism they chose to emphasize and which Western philosophical traditions they drew on for comparison or resources to modernize Confucianism.

Liang Shu-ming's highly influential 1922 *Eastern and Western Cultures and their Philosophies* argues that cultures, as peoples' respective ways of life, are valuable in their distinctive differences arising from different characteristic 'wills'. Although Western-type culture with its 'forward seeking' will has dominated, Chinese-type culture with a will that characteristically 'side steps', highly adaptive and accommodating, valuing contentment and endurance, represents future world culture. It will in turn give way eventually to Indian (Buddhist) type culture, which emphasizes eliminating desires and transcending this world, with a will that looks back to itself. However, both China and India have suffered by being 'pre-mature' in their cultural development and would have to Westernize first, before their own respective culture types gain dominance.

Following Liang, Carsun Chang sparked off one of the most important intellectual debates of Republican China over 'Science and Philosophy of Life' when he argued at a lecture at Qinghua University in 1923 that, for all its usefulness, science has limitations and cannot provide a philosophy of life. Chang argued that the future of Chinese culture lay in creating a national culture based on spiritual freedom. Chang's political philosophy proposes democratic socialism based on British liberalism and constitutionalism – it values social justice as much as individual freedom and integrates them through the Confucian idea of *datong*, or great unity. Chang was convinced that the ethical focus of Confucianism renders its revival necessary and inevitable, for the Western tendency to subordinate the ethical to epistemological cannot adequately deal with the problems of the age. In his view, the accommodating nature of Confucianism facilitates and necessitates learning from the West, and only with such 'new blood' will Confucianism gain global new life.

During the 1940s, many Chinese intellectuals sought the answer to the question of national salvation in some kind of cultural revival that integrated Chinese and Western cultures. Fung Yu-lan advocated a form of new Learning of Principle (*Xin Lixue*) that modernizes Neoconfucianism with the conceptual tools of Western New Realism and Logical Positivism. In contrast, He Lin believed that the development of Confucianism in the twentieth century had mainly followed the path of the Learning of Mind, which had achieved a new integration with the Learning of Principle. He Lin's article, 'New Development of Confucian Thinking' suggests that the future of Chinese philosophy lies in the development of such 'New Confucian philosophy' and argues that cultural comparisons lack depth unless grounded in metaphysics and philosophy of culture (which turned out to be the emphases of second-generation New Confucians). Most commentators view He Lin as an advocate of a new Learning of Mind that borrows from Western Idealism.

Thomé Fang was influenced by both Dewey and Bergson early in his career, but later turned to Idealism and was also influenced by S. Radhakrishnan. His philosophy begins with aesthetic experience, and presents a philosophy of life embedded in an organicist cosmology emphasizing creativity and comprehensive harmony. He identified three modes of metaphysics – transcendent, transcendental and immanent. Chinese metaphysics is 'transcendental–immanent', and views the world or cosmos as something to be transformed, and constantly transforming itself. Human nature is correspondingly dynamic and can progress from lower to higher forms of existence and corresponding spiritual horizons: from *homo faber* to *homo creator, homo sapiens* (knowing being), *homo symbolicus, homo honaestatis* (moral being), and finally to *homo religiosus.* Fang described the ideal personality collectively represented by Chinese philosophers as 'poet–sage–prophet'. He believed that the core of Chinese wisdom may be found in pre-Qin early or *yuanshi* Confucianism, as well as the philosophies of Lao Zi, Zhuang Zi, and Mozi. He maintained that Confucius was able to thoroughly comprehend and combine the other philosophies and 'attain the middle path'. For him, being truly Chinese is being Confucian.

Although Xiong Shili was not as influential as Liang Shuming in the 1920s and Fung Yu-lan in the 1940s, his personal influence on the second-generation New Confucians was more significant. He was credited with dissolving Xu Fuguan's long-held hostility to Confucianism. Both Tang Junyi and Mou Zongsan shared his belief that philosophy is primarily metaphysics and were influenced by his non-reductionist holism. Despite differing in the details of their understanding of the history of Chinese philosophy, Tang and Mou both maintained that Confucianism is the legitimate mainstream of Chinese thinking and the Learning of Mind-and-Nature of the Song and Ming Neoconfucians, with its central notion of unity of heaven and humanity (*tianren heyi*), represents the tradition's true transmission of the way (*daotong*). Both employed Western philosophical concepts and methods, especially those of German Idealism (Mou preferring Kant, and Tang, Hegel), to elucidate traditional Chinese philosophy, and brought it into modern philosophical discourse.

Tang's idealist philosophy of life reflects on 'building the moral self': the development of the mind, the expansion and enrichment of the inner self to encompass the outer world, so that inner and outer interpenetrate, and the mind becomes one with the cosmos. All moral activities are to realize the metaphysical self, or original mind/original nature in Neoconfucian terms, by transcending the actual or phenomenal self immersed in and limited by time and space. All cultures are human spiritual expressions; cultures become bad and harmful when they are no longer governed by the moral self, when they fail to express moral order-and-nature (*daode lixing*, sometimes translated as 'moral reason'). Most of Tang's works are devoted to affirming the value, or 'replanting the spiritual root' of Chinese culture, which he poignantly compared to the scattered and dwindling fruits and flowers of a fallen tree. He believed that the survival of Chinese culture in the contemporary world and its contribution to world philosophy depends on rebuilding its 'humanistic spirit', which 'affirms and respects, in their entirety without deliberate neglect, and certainly does not obliterate or distort, humanity, human relations, human way, human character, human cultures, their values and historical existence, in order to avoid reducing human beings to the non-human'. This requires affirming also the 'supra-humanistic world' of religion that people aspire to, the value of investigating the science of 'non-humanistic nature', and the value of protecting human rights and expressing equality of persons through free society and democratic politics. Besides engaging in cross-cultural comparative philosophy throughout his life, Tang constructed a comprehensive philosophical system of the nine spiritual horizons that incorporates the philosophies of various Eastern and Western traditions, which suggests that Confucianism offers superior solutions to problems left unanswered or inadequately handled in other philosophies. Despite this ethnocentric undercurrent in his thinking, Tang subscribed to a humanistic cosmopolitanism that values cultural diversity and asserts equality of all cultures.

Mou transformed Confucianism with Kantian concepts and methods, but at the same time challenged Kant's conclusions. Mou considered Neoconfucian teachings on 'actualizing humanity (*ren*) and fully realizing human nature (*xing*)' equivalent to Kant's 'metaphysics of morals' concerned with the *a priori* ground of morality. Neoconfucianism goes further than Kant in its moral metaphysics, going beyond explicating the *a priori* nature of morality to ontological–cosmological statements about all existence. While metaphysics of morals focuses on morality, moral metaphysics focuses on metaphysics, which is approached not theoretically but through personal testimony of moral practice, in the actualization of the human mind, the realization of original mind or mind-substance (*xinti*) and original nature or nature-substance (*xingti*). Such moral doing-knowing attains a creative reality that is absolutely universal, leaving out nothing, connecting the finite with the infinite, so that moral metaphysics is also moral religion.

Mou maintains, *contra* Kant, that human beings, as finite beings, nevertheless have intellectual intuition or intuitive understanding, which proceeds from the synthetically universal that supplies its own particulars, and constitutes its own objects as complete, as things-in-themselves not mere appearances. Mou employed the concept of intellectual intuition giving direct access to noumena to explain Neoconfucian moral doing–knowing which realizes original substance/original mind. The personal testimony involved is intuitive and non-conceptual. The possibility of human intellectual intuition offers more rational ways of uniting phenomena and noumena, thereby achieving the highest good, than Kant's anthropomorphic God. Mou insisted that uniting the noumena and phenomena does not require a third

419

being but requires holistically apprehending their mutual implication and paradoxical oneness.

Mou divided the development of Confucianism into three periods: the first from Confucius to Dong Zhongshu in the early Han, the second during the Song and Ming dynasties, and the third in the contemporary world, when a new flourishing of Confucianism is needed to meet the challenges of China's cultural and national survival. In this third period, China needs to expand its cultural horizon to include science and democracy – establish an independent academic tradition (*xuetong*) and reconstruct its tradition of politics (*zhengtong*) – without sacrificing its strengths in ethics and religion, its tradition of the way. Mou suggested that this cultural renewal requires self-negation of original knowledge (*liangzhi*, which is also used to translate 'conscience'), a move from an ontology of non-grasping (*wuzhi*) to an ontology of grasping (*zhi*). The idea of '*liangzhi*'s self-negation' is controversial and has attracted considerable criticisms.

The value and function of Confucianism for Mou is global. It could save the West from self-destruction brought on by its narrow materialistic focus and being trapped between empty individualism and degrading collectivism. Confucianism is committed to transform and complete the world with humaneness or *ren*, 'the reason determined by human nature continuous with divine nature', the universal principle driving human society.

Xu Fuguan co-signed with Tang and Mou (and Carsun Chang) the 1958 'Manifesto on Chinese Culture to the World', which has become a landmark document in New Confucianism. However, Xu rejected metaphysics as unproductive, devoting his efforts instead to a critical examination of Confucianism and its role in Chinese history. He argued for building democracy and science on the basis of Confucianism while criticizing other aspects of Western culture. He maintained that humans are distinguished from animals by their moral nature, which is the basis of human equality. Instead of seeking ultimate value elsewhere, nurturing one's moral responsibility guarantees the meaning of one's life in the world.

The international dimension of New Confucianism has become more prominent in the third generation. Tu Wei-ming has been very influential in promoting Confucianism world-wide. His visit to Beijing was seen as the beginning of the 'return of New Confucianism to its homeland'. Tu draws on Western Enlightenment ideas to elaborate Confucianism in contemporary terms, and in the process also criticizes those Western ideas. He argues that modernization is culturally differentiated so that there are multiple modernities rather than a singular modernity defined by the West, and suggests that European and American intellectuals should 'appreciate what Confucian humanism, among other rich spiritual resources in Asia, has to offer toward the cultivation of a global ethic'. Liu Shu-hsien has also promoted a global ethic for the twenty-first century, in response to Hans Küng's call to develop a global consciousness. Liu suggests that the Neoconfucian concept of 'one principle, many manifestations' (*liyi feshu*) offers a way to unity in diversity, a third way beyond absolutism and relativism. Cheng Chung-ying also advocates creative development of Chinese philosophy to contribute to world philosophy and culture. His idea of onto-hermeneutics refers to an intellectual art of understanding ontology of another culture without reducing it to nonsense, through conceptual and textual dialogue among different cultural traditions. For Cheng, the dialogue between Chinese and Western philosophies is crucial for China's future.

The meaning of being Chinese has been changing in the modern world. As it enters a new millennium, China now has a chance to change the meaning of being modern.

REFLECTIONS ON THE MODERN CHINESE INTELLECTUAL HERITAGE

There has, in the last twenty-five years or more, been a genuine revival, outside of China, in the history of Chinese philosophy. Favorable attitudes to the Confucian heritage have been cultivated in part because of some perception of the link between its values and the development of modern Asian capitalism and of the remarkable welfare state in Singapore. The journal *Philosophy East and West* has helped to stimulate a reappraisal of the Chinese tradition. The time is ripe for such a going-back: it was notable that even before the Marxist' revolution there were forces in China, even in the attitudes of Sun Yat-sen, which wished to leave traditional reflection behind. The Marxist period has been singularly barren, since the chief reason for taking Maoism seriously was its pragmatic success, and that has burnt itself out. On the other hand, the Maoist totalitarian system had a blighting effect. Some contemporary writers are reviving an interest in Confucian moral values – writers such as Tu Wei-ming (Du Weiming). There is also a recognition of the attractions of Huayan holism, a theory of course drawn from the Buddhist heritage. And so in varying ways there are movements of recovery. I shall leave to the last chapter my reflections on the relations between new Chinese thought and Western philosophy as we move into a global civilization.

NOTES ON KOREA

The modern period in Korea has been problematic. Because it was controlled so early by Japan, basically from 1905 onwards, and then formally annexed in 1910, it scarcely had the opportunity to react against Western colonialism. Moreover, the West had in many ways a stronger appeal because in Korea non-Western colonialism was experienced. At any rate, Western and in particular American missionaries made substantial conversions, and Korea now is the most Protestant country in Asia. After World War II, the country was split and the North has had a highly eremitical and totalitarian regime, which has not permitted the development of alternative philosophical thought. The South, while over a long period heavily controlled by right-wing dictators, has had good contacts outside, and this has led to some revival of historical appraisal of Korean thought, notably Korean Neoconfucianism. Some new religious movements, in particular Won Buddhism, a revived and modern form of Buddhism, and so-called *minjung* theology among Christians – a form of doctrine emphasizing solidarity with the poor and exploited, the *minjung* – have made their appearance.

Juche, the thought of Kim Il-Sung (1912–1994), has developed over time from a Koreanized version of Marxism to a Korean philosophy that has come to resemble a religion rather than a Marxist system of belief. North Koreans are encouraged to think of Kim Il Sung as immortal, a state that his followers can participate in through their participation in *Juche*, the community. The North Korean system of thought then can be seen as fitting in closely with the tradition in Korean thought of looking for a savior. Juche philosophy stressed its difference from Marxism–Leninism after 1972, and quotations from Marx and Lenin are almost totally replaced by those from Kim Il-Sung and Kim Chong-il. 'Juche' means subject, and the subject of this system of thought is supposed to be the mentality of the working people in Korea. Its supporters argue that it is superior to the materialism of Communism since it stresses by contrast the ability of the community to lift itself up and take independent charge of its destiny.

THE JAPANESE RESPONSE TO THE WEST

By the time China got into a position to respond to the West it was already largely too late. Western influences and Western power were already creating dislocation along the coasts and up the rivers of the Empire. The Japanese, by contrast, foresaw the dangers approaching them and began of their own accord the process of reshaping society and learning from the West. Among the reforms made was the creation of Western-style universities, and with it the concept of philosophy as understood in Europe. To some degree Western philosophy came to live alongside Japanese traditional reflective concerns. A new term for philosophy was coined in the Japanese language, *tetsugaku*, in the first instance in the early 1870s. In the 1980s Westerners came to Japan to teach philosophy.

The Meiji era saw the birth of Japanese nationalism in its modern form. Part of the reform was the separation of Shinto from Buddhist, referred to as *shinbutsu bunri*, as well as a differentiation between State Shinto (*kokka shintō*) and Sect Shinto (*shuha shintō*). State Shinto was considered a secular ideology. This rhetorical sleight of hand allowed Meiji Japan to pretend that it had embraced the separation of religion and state, while using the Shinto mythology to justify the emperor system. State Shinto culminated in the reverence for the emperor, a symbol of Japanese nationhood and the incarnation of the *kokutai* or national substance. This indicates how Japan was driven simultaneously in two directions: on the one hand, it struggled to embrace the achievements of modernity and economic prosperity promised by a global trade and, on the other, to define its national but also cultural identity in an increasingly pluralistic world. The Japanese referred to this dual attitude as 'Japanese soul – Western genius' (*wakon yōsai*). To some extent such a polarity was reflected in Japanese thought.

The primary exponent of the Western idea in early Meiji times was Nishi Amane (1829–97). In pre-Meiji times he had already been sent to the West to study, under the shogunate, and after the Meiji restoration he was influential in the new educational system and in the circle of intellectuals who were pro-Western. It was he who brought in the word *tetsugaku,* and he wrote encyclopedic and other works which introduced Western thought systematically to the Japanese. He was an advocate of both positivism and utilitarianism. There have been, of course, quite a few modern Japanese who have essentially carried on Western philosophy, following the example of Nishi. The absorption of Western science tended to favor materialism and various forms of evolutionary philosophy.

In addition, one cannot discuss the first generation of philosophers after the Meiji restoration without mentioning Fukuzawa Yukichi (1835–1901). In his most famous work, *An Outline of the Theory of Civilization* (*Bunmeiron no gairyaku*), Fukuzawa listed the benefits of civilization such as hospitals and electricity for Japan, the obstacles that could prevent civilization in Japan such as feudalism and the belief in the moral superiority of one's nation, and the dangers Western civilizations bring to Japan such as colonialism. He propagated equality with regard to class and nationality in slogans such as 'heaven did not create some people above others and some below others' and emphasized the importance of education and independence, personal and national – another one of Fukuzawa's famous slogans was 'national independence through personal independence' – as the key to prosperity. More precisely, he believed that universal education, a functioning and just government, and a prosperous economy constitute the pillars of civilization. At the same time, he could not hide a certain intellectualist snobbism insofar as he suggested that the ignorant masses would have to be forced to their own happiness. In the end, however, his appreciation for 'Western civilization' did not result in a rapprochement of Japan and Europe but rather in the call to construct such a civilization on the foundation of Japanese culture and tradition – a call that reflected the Meiji slogan of '*wakon yōsai*' and that lent itself to be co-opted by nationalism and imperialism.

A second group of Meji thinkers rejected mainstream academic, that is, 'Western', philosophy in favor of the Japanese intellectual tradition. The reasons for this rejection can be found in a reaction to Western claims of intellectual superiority and a turn to the wealth of the Japanese tradition as well as in philosophical arguments. The two main representatives of this group were Inoue Enryō (1859–1919) and Inoue Tetsujirō (1855–1944). The former argued for a 'middle way in philosophy' that received its inspiration from Buddhist philosophy and partly from Hegelian dialectics. He rejected all kinds of philosophical dualism as well as exclusive philosophical positions such as materialism and spiritualism or realism and idealism. In their stead, he proposed alternately a 'philosophy of nothingness' (*mu no tetsugaku*), a 'mind and yet matter theory' (*bussoku shin ron*), and an 'identity realism' (*genshō soku jitsuzai ron*). Central to his argument was the use of the phrase '*soku*' as a dialectical principle that overcomes dualism. Inoue Tetsujirō suggested, along the same line of thought, that identity realism constitutes the purest philosophy and accommodates various categories developed in the philosophical traditions of East and West. He argued for the complexity of identity realism and suggested that it presupposed two layers: phenomena and the real are differentiated in abstract thought, in one sense, and unified, in another. His philosophy anticipated the non-dualism that Nishida Kitarō and the members of the Kyoto school developed later. On a different note, Inoue Tetsujirō expressed a strong national ethic, including a pungent attack on Christianity for putting loyalty to Christ above everything else (notably above devotion to the emperor). He also contributed a philosophical dictionary, Japan's first, and thus helped in the evolution of an indigenous technical vocabulary for the subject.

A number of Japanese writers were keen to reject the individualism of the West, as they perceived it. While this rejection of individualism was inspired and nurtured by Buddhist and Confucian ideas, it was frequently put in the service of the national revival. For instance Watsuji Tetsurō (1889–1960), whose most famous book was *Ethics as Study of Humanity*, depicts human beings as essentially relational and as social in nature. Human beings, Watsuji argued, were inherently spatial and not independent from their geographical context, as he tried to show in his second famous work, *Climate* (*Fūdo*). He contrasted his philosophical approach to the concept of the self with the Heideggerian emphasis on the self's temporality and its implicit preoccupation with an individual that persists through time, yet is seemingly untouched by the social relationships it engages in. Watsuji suggested that a study of what it means to be human and especially ethics cannot ignore the social dimension of human beings and requires as its fundamental concept the notion of inbetweenness (*aidagara*). After World War II he revised his work to remove some of the more nationalist parts from it. But he was also a notable historian of Japanese ethics and his work on this had more lasting influence.

Marxism also of course left its mark on Japanese thinking in the period between the wars. Some of its major exponents were imprisoned during the nationalist period, because of their opposition to what they perceived as fascist policies. There was some revival of such leftwing thinking after World War II. Needless to say, there were other Western streams of influence on Japanese philosophy, dominated as it tended to be by Western influences – streams such as phenomenology and existentialism, as well as empiricism and American pragmatism. There has also been as interest in the project of comparative philosophy, under the leadership of Nakamura Hajime among others. Such an interest spills over into comparative religion. In this connection it is not easy to place D.T. Suzuki, but he was surely influential, both inside Japan and in the West.

D.T. SUZUKI AND COMPARATIVE STUDIES

Suzuki had an unusual life. He was a lifelong friend of Nishida Kitarō. While he was studying at Waseda University he became a close friend of the Zen abbot of a Zen monastery in Kamakura, Shaku Sōen, who was one of those chosen to go to the famous World Parliament of Religions in Chicago in 1893. As a consequence of the latter's contact with the orientalist Paul Carus (translator among other things of the *Daodejing*), Suzuki went to work as his assistant in Illinois. He thus gained good experience of the Western world, and indeed he married an American. His translations and editions of Chinese and Japanese texts were important, but more vital were his various writings, both of an expository and a comparative nature in English. He perceived affinities between Buddhist mysticism and that of Westerners, especially that of Meister Eckhart.

Suzuki promoted Buddhism and documented its vigorous effect on the evolution of Japanese culture. At the time he was writing Buddhism was under some degree of official disapproval. Its outlook was not highly conducive to nationalism, and it had suffered somewhat in the previous century from the forcible and often damaging separation from Shinto. But he did not just see Buddhism as a cultural force: it was also scientific in its spirit and teachings. His later writings also underlined the vital importance of direct experience. This experience could be seen as spiritual. And so while the conceptual and philosophical side of Buddhism might be important in various ways, Suzuki wished to present insights drawn from Zen Buddhism and Zen practice. His delineations both of Mahayana Buddhism in general and Zen in particular made a very deep impression in the West, so that Suzuki came to be a key interpreter of his religious tradition.

His greatest philosophical contribution was the so-called 'logic of *sokuhi*' (*sokuhi no ronri*). Suzuki claimed that the Diamond Sūtra employed the Chinese characters for '*sokuhi*', literally 'is not', to express a logic that is unique to and characteristic of Mahāyāna Buddhism. This logic, Suzuki argued, was in direct contrast with the logical principle of non-contradiction developed by Aristotle and disclosed the transrational character of Mahāyāna Buddhism in general and Zen Buddhism in particular. More specifically, Suzuki believed that this logic was indicative of the Zen experience of *satori* and necessary to describe reality as it is disclosed by intuition unadulterated by reflection.

He also had some influence on Nishida, just as Nishida influenced him – notably in regard to religious experience. Suzuki, because of his wide travels in the West and the success of his books, was a primary figure, especially after World War II, in translating aspects of Japanese culture to the West and in the sense of domesticating Buddhism for

Western consumption. A factor in all this was his independent-mindedness during the first part of this century and his lack of association with Japanese nationalism during its aggressive phase. At any rate he built important bridges between Japanese and Western thinking.

NISHIDA KITARŌ AND THE KYOTO SCHOOL

Because of the fact that philosophy, though potentially universal – or at least global – is also culturally particular, those who followed the path of importing philosophy wholesale from the West had their own particularism, and this differed from the particularism of the Japanese tradition itself. Suzuki took the path of comparison, by and large. More interesting, however, than any of the Japanese positivists or existentialists or Marxists or traditionalists were those who attempted in effect a new synthesis. Of such thinkers there is no doubt that the most famous in modern Japan was Nishida Kitarō (1870–1945). He was deeply influenced by Zen Buddhism. While teaching at a junior college over a number of years he engaged in both Zen meditation and the history of Western philosophy. He published the result of his prolonged reflection as *Zen no kenkyū,* translated as *A Study of Good:* it was published in 1911 (the translation in 1960). It struck many readers as the first truly creative work by a Japanese that did not merely repeat Western ideas, and yet made use of modern thinking and terminology. From 1910 until 1928 he taught at Kyoto University, where he formed a retinue of excellent students. Tosaka Jun (1900–64) coined the label 'Kyoto school' to refer to the philosophical approach of Nishida and his students; however, it was not a simple school in the sense of complete agreement. His most outstanding follower came to be an important critic, namely Tanabe Hajime. Nishida had a highly original way of dealing with the opposition between subjectivity and objectivity. He considered pure experience to be prior to either. In this way he hoped to overcome some of the persistent problems of philosophy, such as the question of how the self, beginning with experience, can proceed outwards to know anything about the outside world. He thought that pure experience is, so to speak, the matrix from which both subjectivity and objectivity emerge. He went on to struggle with the notion of self-consciousness as another way of rendering pure experience. He went on from there to identify it with absolute free will, at the heart of which lies the absolute self. The difficulty of his thinking in these matters in part arises from the fact that reflection itself is a product of a distinction to which the will or self-consciousness or pure experience is prior. It is like a hand trying to grasp itself.

Nishida, in trying to transcend subjectivity (since even the above description of his thought veers towards the subjective), had some recourse to Kant. He rejected Kant's notion of transcendental subjectivity, since he believed, not unlike Hegel, that subjectivity cannot be conceived of without its opposite, objectivity. However, to avoid a bad infinity, on the one side, and Hegel's absolute spirit, on the other, Nishida developed a kind of field-theory or logic of place *(basho no ronri)*. Pure experiences occur, so to speak, in a framework or system of places. Notions of things or selves are posterior to this network. If he made some use of Neokantian suggestions, Nishida also had recourse, quite naturally, to Buddhist philosophy and Zen ideas in particular. In pure experience the distinction between subject and object has not arisen. However, the field in which pure experiences occur is itself neither being nor non-being but functions as the ground of both. Thus, the field functions as a third term and is described as 'absolute nothingness' *(zettai mu)*. While his early formulations of the logic of *basho* in the mid-1920s still had the taste of transcendentalism, Nishida insisted in the later years of his career (1934–45) that this field does not constitute a transcendental ground but has to be manifested and realized concretely in the historical world. Nishida's use of nothingness as that which transcends, grounds, and yet is manifested in the relativity of being and non-being seems to overcome the problems inherent in Kantian noumena or things-in-themselves. They should neither be singular nor plural, like nothingness in the Buddhist tradition. To describe the historical world Nishida borrowed the term one-and-yet-many (Chinese: *yijiduo*; Japanese: *issokuta*) from Huayan (Japanese: *Kegon*) Buddhism. Thus Nishida's scheme welds some Western thoughts into an Eastern frame, but without artificiality. In his later work there was also a greater affinity with Hegel and the dialectic, since Nishida saw contradictions as arising from human experience as it develops out of pure experience. At the end of his career in 1945, Nishida identified the dialectical principle he saw at work in the historical world with religious experience as it was expressed in Zen literature.

Ultimately, his goal was to deconstruct the subject–object dualism he believed was foundational for European philosophy. Nishida suggested that traditional philosophy provided two positions to each philosophical problem, objectivism and subjectivism, neither of which is satisfactory. He then proposed a third position, non-dualism, whose terminology seems, when looked at from the perspective of objectivism, self-contradictory *(jiko mujunteki)*. Nishida described reality as that which constitutes the 'subject-and-yet-the-object' *(shukan soku kyakkan)* as well as the 'many-and-yet-one' *(tasokuitsu)*. The reason Nishida proposed this non-dualism is twofold. First, Nishida insists that reality is neither exclusively subjective nor objective; these standpoints are artificial and can be compared to the audience and the performers in a play. In real life, however, humans constitute neither a disengaged observer nor an unreflective performer; on the contrary, human beings should be conceived of as engaged observers or observing agents. However, there is a second dimension to Nishida's non-dualism. Nishida points out that human cognition depends on the standpoint of the observer and is thus necessarily perspectival and incomplete. This common sense notion has far-reaching implications. It means that, depending on one's necessarily incomplete vantage point, concepts change their meaning and may even be contradictory. Nishida's terminology thus does not only disclose the ambiguous nature of reality but also exposes the fallibility of conceptual language itself. This means that his infamous phrase 'self-identity of the absolute contradictories' (*zettai mujunteki jiko dōitsu*) does not evoke a mystical or transcendental reality as is often assumed by commentators but rather indicates the limitations of human cognition and of conceptual language. In his last work, Nishida not only defines the 'religious heart' as the existential attitude that faces the ambiguity of the human predicament but also evokes similarities between his philosophy and the iconoclasm characteristic of Zen literature.

The most famous of Nishida's followers and his successor and critic, was Tanabe Hajime (1885–1962), who studied in Freiburg in the early 1920s and whose first book was on Kant's teleology. His most famous works were, however, *Suri testsugaku* on the philosophy of mathematics, which made him the best-known philosopher of science in Japan; and *Shu no ronri* (*The Logic of the Specific*), published in 1939. This involved a criticism of Nishida's field theory. On his view Nishida's position was a kind of shadowy individualism. Indeed, Buddhism does encourage an individualism: it is the individual's compassion which promotes solidarity rather than an intrinsic or substantial link to fellow-beings. This is in line with its non-substantialism. While Nishida tried to ground the opposites, being and non-being, many and one, in an all-encompassing field, Tanabe sought to mediate them and to address their inherent historical nature. He introduced the concept of the specific (*shu*) to mediate the abstract universal and the always elusive individual. Tanabe identified the specific, which he conceived of as radically historical, with the nation state. While this line of thinking of course coincided with the nationalism of his time, Mutai Risaku (1890–1974) re-conceived of this idea after the war. Mutai argued that as the mediation of the opposites the specific not only comprises the concrete reality of the historical world but also provides the philosophical foundation of a humanism that reconciles peace, which expresses the universal principle of humanity, and freedom, which is indicative of individualism. Mutai disavowed nationalism and suggested that it committed the fallacy of arbitrarily privileging one particular specific over the others by universalizing and absolutizing it. Even the totality of the historical world is incomplete and subject to an infinite process of transformation. Mutai thus showed that Tanabe's concept of the specific had the potential of supporting the vision of an egalitarian and democratic society. Tanabe himself realized the fallacy of nationalism at the end of World War II and turned towards what he called a philosophy of metanoetics. This philosophy is based on the notion of 'absolute critique' (*zettai hihan*). Following the rhetoric of Shinran and Søren Kierkegaard, Tanabe renounced what he conceived to be the hypocrisy of reason and proposed a turning away from a philosophy based on self-power (*jiriki*) to one rooted in the reliance on an other-power (*tariki*). Identifying the fallibility and unreliability of the subjective self as his most fundamental standpoint, Tanabe constructed what James Heisig calls a 'philosophy-in-religion'.

It is possible to observe two general tendencies among the philosophers of the Kyoto school. First there are those who employ the non-dual paradigm developed by Nishida Kitarō to develop a 'Zen philosophy'. The most accomplished of these philosophers is Nishitani Keiji (1900–90), who introduced the philosophical 'standpoint of Zen' (*zen no tachiba*). In short, the standpoint of Zen outlines a philosophy of self-awareness. In an essay with the same title, Nishitani argues that the third and fourth of the so-called 'four principles of Zen' – 'directly pointing to one's mind and becoming Buddha upon seeing one's own nature' – share with the Cartesian *cogito* the basic interest in self-consciousness, but disclose realms more foundational than the *cogito*. These depth layers of the human psyche are hinted at by the concept of the *ālaya vijñāna* of Yogācāra Buddhism and can only be articulated by the infamous formula of the Heart Sūtra 'form is emptiness, emptiness is form'. In his most famous work, *What is Religion (Shūkyō wa nani ka)*, Nishitani chooses the Mahāyāna Buddhist conception of emptiness (Sanskrit: *śunyatā*; Japanese; *kū*) over Nishida's 'absolute nothingness' as his fundamental paradigm. Nishitani takes pains in emphasizing that his conception of emptiness is fundamentally different from the 'non-being' of nihilism. The latter is opposed to 'being' and thus negative in an ontological and an existential sense: it is indicative of a relativist worldview and the experience of alienation. The standpoint of emptiness, on the contrary, essentially comprises self-awareness and thus not only cures the problem of nihilism but also, due to its non-dual nature, overcomes the antagonism between religion and science that characterizes modernity. It also radically transforms our understanding of ethics, science, and religion: ethics has to be grounded in a non-dual conception of self and other, science has to be conceived of from a standpoint that transcends science itself in order to avoid the mechanization and dehumanization of our world, and religion has to shift its focus from a transcendent other with respect to embodied self-awareness. His student, Ueda Shizuteru (born 1926), developed Nishitani's standpoint of Zen into a full-fledged philosophy of self-awareness. His greatest achievements are the careful formulation of a Zen philosophy, which is fundamentally different from mysticism – he suggests the term 'non-mysticism' (*hishinpi shugi*) – and a systematic philosophy of the self in the sense of the Buddhist conception of no-self (Sanskrit: *anātman*; Japanese: *muga*). To illustrate Zen philosophy, Ueda himself provides many philosophical analyses of Zen texts and the famous ten ox-herding pictures. More importantly, however, he distinguishes Zen discourses that take as their basis 'pure experience' or the 'practice of non-thinking' from Zen philosophy, which is based on an 'analysis of the highest reflection' or on the 'reflection on reflection' and thus paves the road for a Zen philosophy in the academic sense. Ueda's philosophical formulation of the no-self culminates in the conception of the 'self that is not a self' (*ware naki ware*) and the 'self of no-self' (*muga no ware*). These phrases envision a self that transcends the *cogito*, encompasses the *I and Thou* as developed by Nishida, and eschews the binary opposition of self and not-self. In other words, Ueda rejects the belief that the self possesses an essence and constitutes a self-contained system; on the contrary, he envisions a self that is dynamic and interacts with its environment. Ueda's philosophy also portrays a self that embodies a self-awareness beyond the dichotomy of subjectivity and objectivity. Both Nishitani and Ueda devoted their careers to employing Nishida's most fundamental paradigm in the service of the introduction of Zen ideas into the academic discourse of philosophy and are thus extremely faithful to the vision developed in Nishida's last completed book, *The Logic of Basho and the Religious Worldview* (*Basho no ronri to shūkyōteki sekaikan*).

On the other side, there are the thinkers usually referred to as the leftist wing of the Kyoto school. However, they focused their philosophical inquiry on historical and social realities rather than on a class analysis usually characteristic of Marxism. In contrast to philosophers such as Nishitani and Ueda, they steered, for the most part, clear of the religious themes that made Kyoto school philosophy famous in the 'West'. The first philosopher to take Nishida to task for neglecting historical reality in his philosophy was Takahashi Satomi (1886–1964), who due to his affiliation with Tōhoku University is not counted as member of the Kyoto school in the narrow sense of the term. Takahashi criticized the subjectivism of 'pure experience' as it is found in Nishida's *Study of the Good* as too psychological and rejected Nishida's attempts to balance the notion of linear time characteristic of objectivism with that of circular time indicative of subjectivism. Subjectivism, so Takahashi argues, distracts from the linearity of history. By the same token he rejected Nishida's conception of the absolute in favor of the notion of 'totality'. This concept of totality, he claimed, is without the religious overtones of Nishida's 'absolute' and constitutes a limit concept. To be exact, Takahashi maintained that totality is constituted only at the end of time. Takahashi's philosophy thus ended up promoting an awkward dualism of an atemporal totality infinitely deferred to the end of time and the temporality of history. While Takahashi's sharp criticism forced Nishida to rethink his notion of 'pure experience' and to give up the unbridled subjectivism of his early period, Takahashi himself failed to appropriate Nishida's greatest achievement, the formulation of the non-dual paradigm *vis-à-vis* 'Western' philosophy, and to employ this paradigm to develop a coherent philosophy of history. The two most prominent philosophers to fill this lacuna and to develop a unique political and social philosophy more or less in the tradition of the Kyoto school were Tosaka Jun and Miki Kiyoshi (1897–1945). The former adopted a 'radical criticism' (*konponteki na hihanshugi*), that is, an 'ideological criticism' (*ideologii hihan*), to argue the unity of the natural and social sciences. Regardless of whether the subject of an inquiry is an individual 'thing' (*mono*) or a 'spirit' (*seishin*) such as the 'spirit of technology', neither discipline can escape its own historicity and necessarily reveals the material nature of the world. When Tosaka argues for materialism, he implies a notion of 'matter' as energy akin to that of quantum theory rather than that of Newtonian physics. In analogy to the unity of the natural and social sciences, he also proposed that the acts of 'knowing' and 'making' are not separate but indicative of the creative process. Ultimately, Tosaka argues, the spirit of science and technology are, appearances to the contrary, not distinct but the same. Miki developed a humanism (*ningen shugi*) insofar as he makes the concept of 'human person' (*ningen*) the center of his philosophy. Following the thought of Nishida rather closely, he defined the human person as the intersection of 'infinity' (*mugen*) and 'vanity' (*kyomu*) and more generally as the 'center space' (*chūkansha*). By the same token, Miki conceived of human creativity, that is, imagination, as that which combines subjective and objective expression, of the 'fact' as the unity of 'action' and 'objects', and of technology as the synthesis of regularity and *telos*. These formulations reflect, according to Miki, the structure of the concrete and of history. The concept of technology is important to Miki since it marks the difference between humans and animals and, at the same time, discloses the structure of the human subject's interaction with the environment. In doing so, Miki was not only able to expand Nishida's paradigm but also to apply it to an analysis of economic and social issues. In the end, despite their rhetoric, the thinkers associated with the leftist wing of the Kyoto school did not disavow Nishida's non-dualism but rather employed it to construct a social philosophy beyond nationalism and imperialism.

Finally, there is Yuasa Yasuo (1925–2005). A student of Watsuji and professor at Tsukuba University for most of his career, Yuasa does not belong to the Kyoto school proper. Not unlike the Kyoto school philosophers, however, Yuasa introduced insights from Buddhist philosophies in the discourse of mainstream philosophy. In particular, he was interested in developing a philosophy of the body based on Buddhist and Daoist theories of self-cultivation. To develop such a philosophy of the body, Yuasa applied Maurice Merleau-Ponty's phenomenology and C.G. Jung's Analytical Psychology to Buddhist and Daoist meditation and martial arts manuals. To Yuasa, self-cultivation constitutes systematized practices such as meditation, martial arts, and the so-called 'Zen arts' such as tea ceremony and Nō that are designed to forge what Nagatomo Shigenori calls an attunement of the subject to the environment, and of the mind to the body. Self-cultivation thus defined overcomes the dualistic structure of everyday consciousness, which constitutes itself as separate from its environment and from its own body, and habituates an awareness of the otherwise unconscious regions of human existence. Yuasa thus rejects the popular assumption common to most of European philosophy that the self is separated from its environment and the mind from the body. Rather he follows Dōgen's doctrine of the 'oneness of body and mind' (*shinjin ichinyo*) as well as Merleau-Ponty's notion of the *somatic cogito* and argues that the self interacts with the environment by means of a bilateral intentionality. Yuasa proposed that such a conception of intentionality corresponds to the concept of *qi* (Japanese: *ki*) as it can be found in Daoist meditation manuals, treatises on traditional Chinese medicine, and selected Buddhist texts of the Edo period. Yuasa goes one step further and denies any essential differences between self and the environment. He identifies various circuits of interaction between self and environment, the external sensory–motor circuit, the circuit of kinesthesis, the emotion–instinct circuit, and the unconscious quasi body. The latter circuit corresponds to the meridians in which *qi* flows. This understanding of the human body penetrates all of Yuasa's thought and is most visible in his discussion of ethics. Ethics, Yuasa argues, cannot be the intellectual pursuit of an individual subject but must involve practice that attunes one's intellect and emotion and that discloses the deeper reality that Shingon Buddhism identifies as the cosmic sun Buddha (Sanskrit: *Mahāvairocana*; Japanese: *Dainichi nyorai*) and is mapped out in the Womb World and Diamond World Mandalas. Only such an ethics can reconcile the human aspirations of happiness and morality and is able to conceive of a social good that is not external, that is, alien, to the self.

Today, philosophy in Japan is highly diverse and covers the whole spectrum of philosophical methodologies and areas including philosophy of science and feminist philosophy in addition to the philosophies that evoke the Japanese tradition more explicitly and that were discussed in this section.

REFLECTIONS ON THE PHILOSOPHIES OF THE FAR EAST

As elsewhere beyond the West, a main preoccupation for Far Eastern thought has been how to integrate tradition into a new form of culture which can deal, on a nationalist basis and through social reconstruction, with the menace of foreign domination. None of the Far Eastern cultures have had a long period for working out such an agenda in the philosophical context. The failure of a middle path in China led to a time of extreme intellectual and spiritual repression under the domination of Maoism. Korean culture was distracted first by foreign conquest by the Japanese, then a division of the country into a hermetically sealed North and (for much of the time) an authoritarian South. Japan suffered from its strong nationalism, verging on fascism during the inter-war period. But despite this some of the most creative work was done then. Japan's experience, because it was so successful in taking over the methods of Western education, posed most sharply the challenge of synthesis: how could past philosophy be successfully integrated into the many fertile ideas on show in the West? So far no doubt the most fruitful integrator has been Nishida. But Japanese culture has certainly made a strong showing in this area, and new younger thinkers are developing an aftermath to the powerful Kyoto school.

15

AFRICAN PHILOSOPHIES

WHAT IS AFRICA?

To the south of Europe, between the Atlantic and Indian oceans, lies Africa, the hottest and second-largest continent. While culturally sub-Saharan Africa, the major part of the continent south of the Sahara, has been very rich in resources including art, music, religion, narrative and oral tradition, it has only recently entered the period of systematic written philosophy or formal worldview construction. On the other hand, traditional African religions have expressed a series of worldviews of great interest. Before we come to look at these, however, we first need to be clearer as to what Africa is.

Africa is an extensive landmass, much bigger than Europe or North America, with many languages and ethnic groups. For the purposes of this book I shall focus on sub-Saharan Africa as the major cultural area. Most North Africans, currently, since the days of ancient Egypt, are of Arab or Berber background and they are woven firmly by the strands of Islam into Middle Eastern culture. Islam has made deep penetrations into sub-Saharan Africa, of course, but the basic styles and physiognomies of the region are not Arab. The history of philosophy in North Africa, particularly after the ancient Egyptian civilization, is closely affiliated with the history of Islamic thought. Sub-Saharan Africa has its own and often very different creativities. Secondly, we have to note that there is a region which might be known as Greater Africa, including those areas and strands of African culture on the other side of the Atlantic, largely but not exclusively a result of the slave trade, most notably in the Caribbean, North America and Brazil. These areas have been influential and creative. When I refer to Africa, here, I shall mean sub-Saharan Africa and, when I refer to Greater Africa, I shall include the transatlantic portion of that culture.

Even so, there remain some other questions about Africanness. The consciousness of being African is a modern development. The fact is that Africa is a mosaic of relatively small-scale societies. There have been empires in West Africa, Zimbabwe and elsewhere, but currently many of the groups in Africa are relatively fairly small. Thousands of languages flourish. In the old days a given society might look on itself as the world, at least existentially: other humans were outsiders, barbarians. True humanity would be identified as one's own group. Some of the same sentiment exists among modern nations, as in war, when there may be little compunction about killing an enemy. Africa remained such a mosaic until modern times. Three forces helped to raise consciousness of being different. There were the two slave trades – the European operation, largely from the sixteenth to the nineteenth centuries, and the Arab operation, which went on until towards the end of the latter century. Then, vitally important, was the scramble for Africa. This basically continued from the 1850s to World War II. Before that there had been European and Arab colonizations up and down the coasts. Portuguese settlements had flanked the Cape and nibbled at the West Coast. The Dutch had settled the Cape, to be superseded there by the British. Boer or Afrikaner settlers had penetrated northwards. But, thereafter, the big rush was on, spurred by many explorers' reports and dreams of wealth and imperial pride. France, Britain, Germany, Italy, Belgium – these became the principal players. With the conquest of the whole continent (except for Ethiopia), Africa became more than a geographical expression. European rule brought with it new customs, new styles of education, new technologies, new sufferings, as well as new opportunities. Perforce Africans had to come to terms with the new realities.

Nationalism was itself a spur to empire and a potent force in Europe. Wherever empire went it stimulated the reaction of counternationalism. But, on the whole, Africa was not divided up by nations, but arbitrarily. Hardly any African state in the postcolonial era is anywhere nearly nationally homogeneous. Moreover, the colonialists hardly recognized indigenous national entities: the preferred word was 'tribes'. As a result of such factors it was not surprising that a major form of nationalism in Africa was pan-African. Under the impact of these alien forces the sense of Africanness was born, and it was reciprocated by Europeans.

Among the by-products of the pan-African feeling was the notion of African religion, in the singular. Actually, though there are analogies and similitudes between the many religions of the African continent, each regional or ethnic group expressed its own sacred values in its own way, at least according to the classical tradition. From the point of view to be perceived on the ground, there are numerous African religions. Nevertheless there is a growing perception of a unified African religion. This embodies themes which became important in pan-African consciousness.

Some of these themes persist overseas, in the African diaspora. Moreover, an important degree of Africanness has permeated Christianity, both in the New World (with variations such as Vodun or Voodoo) and Africa proper, where during the twentieth century in particular more than ten thousand new religious movements and independent churches, blending indigenous values and Christian messages, have arisen.

Other sources of the sense of pan-African identity were the need for wider forces in the struggle against imperialism in the twentieth century, the movement known as Negritude, partly inspired by Sartre's dialectic, Marxist thinking, especially in relation to the need to indigenize socialism, the ideology of Nyerere as expressed in the Arusha Declaration (1967), transatlantic searches for roots, the continuation of racism among Whites and others and transnational languages and literatures, notably English and French. Over the period from 1948 until 1990 in particular, the fight against apartheid in South Africa formed a pan-African and Greater African focus for action. In general a sense of loyalty to Africa as a whole could mean much more, especially to the educated, than narrow loyalty to a rather artificial nation-state.

AFRICAN RELIGIOUS WORLDVIEWS: THEMES

Various important themes emerge in African religions. Among them we can pay special attention to the reverence for ancestors, healing rituals, the idea of a Supreme Being, and ideas of possession.

The focus, in many societies, upon ancestors indicates a different and broader conception of society from what is normally entertained in much of today's Western world. The dead remain alive, in a sort of limbo and can be appealed to for help. This wider feeling for a society which includes both visible and invisible members impels a stronger sense of tradition. It also reinforces the sense of family solidarity. Misfortunes which befall the family are often attributed to the displeasure of the ancestors and are taken as a warning that relatives should reflect about the appropriateness of their behavior to one another. The ancestors represent one class among a cloud of invisible beings and forces which populate the African realm. These may be anything from influences to entities: so, for example, healing rituals, sometimes linked to ancestors, can help to deal with unseen powers which bring about disease and which may or may not be due to deliberate actions on the part of others. The role of healing is of course central in much pre-modern society, and often new African Churches see it as a vital ingredient in the Christian gospel: indeed, the New Testament and above all the Gospels hold it to be central to Jesus' mission in the early days.

The fact that specialists are adept at healing links human society and nature; for it is implicit in the whole range of African ritual procedures that it is possible through ceremonies, formulas, sacrifices, etc. to establish communication between ourselves and the living environment, whether it be the living dead, the gods or ultimately the Supreme Being.

It is common in African traditional religion to find an ultimate focus in a Supreme God. But often the Supreme Being is regarded as too exalted to deal with the rather petty concerns of human beings. There are, in any case, typically many intermediates between the One and the lower world. It is more modest and appropriate to turn to lesser functionaries if we want help. For the purposes of creation, including the formation of human societies and skills, God may often use an intermediate figure – maybe a culture hero or a lesser god. For some cultures, God is basically the only force operative behind the world; in others, the creation is highly populated with supernaturals. Moreover, the gods and spirits can be malevolent, and so may be in need of ritual treatment to ward them off and neutralize their effects. In some schemes of belief, God also creates each person's destiny – a notion somewhat akin to *karma*.

God is conceived as immense: indeed some exponents of traditional African religion see Christian conceptions (or at least Western Christian ones) of the Deity as narrow and somehow overindividualized. There are, of course, elements of negative theology in traditional African discourse, and it is true that this has often been neglected in modern Western theology. The immensity of the Divine is reinforced by the perception that God is distant, which is in part a reflection of the inadequacy of humans: consequently, a recurrent theme in African traditional discourse is how the first man or woman made some grievous, sometimes unintentional error, which caused God to withdraw to a more distant heaven or to raise up the sky where he lived. This symbolizes the alienation of the human race from God. There are, naturally, analogies between such myths and the narrative of the Garden of Eden. But though the Divine Being may be distant and hard to approach, it is not uncommon for folk on earth to experience possession by a divine spirit. 'Shamanism' is a common phenomenon in Africa as among many other milieus. It links, among other things, with the healing process; because the 'shaman' can lead the sick through the valley of the shadow of death and rise up on the other side. African religion is also profoundly intrigued by the meaning of dreams. Such encounters with the supernatural in private experience become important in the selection of sacred specialists.

SOME CLASSICAL WORLD-PICTURES

It may be useful to glance at some traditional worldviews which represent differing examples of African values. I shall later describe some new Christian movements which absorb classical values, up to a point, into a Christian framework.

Let me begin with the Lele (described by Mary Douglas in Daryll Forde (ed.) *African Worlds*). Here is a people living in very small-scale conditions, in separate villages, with trading connections to outside peoples, on the edge of the equatorial forest in South-west Zaire. As in many African systems, as we have already indicated, there is a Supreme

Being – creator and master of the world and of living beings – and a whole host of spirits, dwelling above all invisibly in the deep forest, especially in the sources of the streams. They are typically active at night, hence it is important for the village not to generate unharmonious noises at night (such as the sound of pounding grain, a daytime activity). Some objects are especially associated with the spirits, for instance the banana, because when it is cut it sprouts again, exhibiting the immortality associated with spiritual beings. The moon is highly spiritual, because though it too appears to die it always comes back again: moreover, it is associated with fertility. A high value is placed on harmony in the village, which tends to be very decentralized in its operation, so solidarity in atmosphere goes with lack of strong authority. This, together with rituals such as the hunt in the forest (a communal activity), helps to determine good relations with the spirits and with God. It shows that the ancestral traditions have been rightly carried out, for in addition to the spirits (who have never been human and are not anthropomorphically represented) there remain the invisible ancestors, another factor in the equation whereby the villagers calculate the prosperity and peaceful fruitfulness of their life.

A very different milieu surrounds the Dinka of the Sudan (whose life has rather recently been disrupted by the ferocious civil war in that country) and the Nuer. The latter were the subject of a famous monograph called *Nuer Religion* (1956) by the famous British anthropologist E.E. Evans-Pritchard. This gave a new impetus to the study of African religion, partly through taking it seriously as a framework of spiritual and ethical belief, and partly through seeing religion as a force in its own right in society and not merely as a dependent variable. The supreme God of the Nuer is Kwoth, and the experience of this universal, omnipotent, all-creative Being is numinous, awe-inspiring. But there are also a cloud of other spirits, some foreign and many hostile, some associated with the sky above (these being the more important) and others with the realm below. The latter are often petty and malevolent. Very often people become polluted by their own and others' actions, and need helping by specialist priests. Prophets have also arisen, frequently enough in the last hundred years, especially with the impact of colonial rule and other outside interferences, to lead the people on hopeful, though sometimes destructive, paths.

More complex are the patterns of Yoruba religion, itself quite important in the Western world, because the Yoruba region in Nigeria was one of the main areas of slavery. The chief divinity (there are over four hundred in the pantheon) is Olorun, a High God remote from immediate dealings with humans (so there are rarely shrines to him). The rest of the gods are thought of as his family, and in consequence offerings made to them will ultimately be passed on to him. The creation of the world was entrusted to the god Obatala and was finished off by the original ancestor and culture hero Oduduwa. While the complexity of the pantheon testifies to the fragmentation of Yoruba society and religion, mostly in relatively recent times, the uniqueness of Olorun signifies how the universe itself is a unity under the one Spirit. Still, in many ways the most influential god is Ogun, deity of iron, war and hunting – a great god of weaponry. The dog is sacrificed to Ogun, human beings' great companion in killing. The meaning of Ogun to us is that our security and welfare ultimately depend on the destruction of other living beings. Sacrifice itself has power, for the rituals have the power to draw the gods into human presence and so to channel power.

Other systems of belief are even more complex, most notably the elaborate cosmology of the Dogon in the Western Sudan and the vast mythic corpus of the Fon of Dahomey. And so we move from the relatively simple world-picture of the Lele to the creations of the priestly classes of rich and widely organized West African states. A question to ask is how far modern Africa can build upon some of the conceptions and experiences of the past. Here we may turn to the controversial case of Placide Tempels' interpretation of Bantu philosophy (*La Philosophie bantoue*, 1949) and its aftermath. This work, like Griaule's on the Dogon, gave impetus to a reappraisal of the issue of African philosophy. For he gave philosophical clothing to the body of indigenous assumptions. Sometimes this 'method' is referred to as ethnophilosophy. I would prefer to call it the construction of worldviews on a traditional or classical basis. Tempels' book was also controversial in that the philosophical filter was the systematic theology which he had learned, in effect, at seminary. He was a Catholic missionary and overtly concerned with building up the Christian faith on what he saw as an indigenous basis.

BANTU, OR AFRICAN, ONTOLOGY

Placide Tempels wrote a bit vaguely about who he was talking about: sometimes it was Bantu-speaking people, sometimes more widely it was Africans. He also expressed himself in a highly paternalistic (some might say patronizing) way. He saw himself, and White men more generally, as able to do something which, unless aroused, Africans would not do of their own accord. In short, Bantu philosophy is implicit, and it is only in response to questions self-consciously arrived at (out of Western culture, in effect) that it reveals itself. In accord with much of Western philosophical tradition Tempels averred that the Bantu philosophy is at bottom an ontology, but it contrasts with the Aristotelian tradition. In European languages the verb 'to be' can be used both as copula and as the term for 'to exist'. So it comes about that 'being' is a substantive, and that the Greek present participle can help to form the expression 'ontology', but in Bantu languages there is no existential use of 'to be'. The ontology of the Bantu relates to the key root *ntu,* and signifies force. To put it another way, force and being are ineluctably coupled together. If Western philosophy tends towards an ontology of being, the Bantu tend towards a dynamism. It is not exactly, however, that the energy displayed by reality is a kind of single ocean of power, but that each entity displays its own particular and appropriate force.

Certain consequences flow from this ontology: one person can diminish the force of another person; she can also influence lesser force-beings, and through the intermediacy of such force-beings can influence other persons. Force-beings may be spirits, persons and ancestors, but they may also be things. Indeed, *ntu* in effect belongs or relates to four basic categories: there are rational or conscious beings, *muntu;* things or inanimate force-beings, *kintu;* time and place, *hantu;* and other modalities such as possession, action, passion, etc., *kuntu*. These terms refer to classifiers used in Bantu languages. Tempels' followers and critics, Alexis Kagame (author of *La Philosophie bantu-rwandaise de l'être,* 1955/6), V. Mulago (*La Religion traditionelle des Bantu et leur vision du monde,* 1973) and E.N.C. Mujynya (*L'homme dans l'univers des Bantu,* 1972) among others, consider that they place his theory on a sounder basis by appealing to the analysis of language on a more systematic basis.

About the status of God there is some debate and disagreement. For some authors, God is not a *ntu* but is the pre-existing, originating Creator, somehow belonging to a different category; for others, he is the supreme and primordial force-being. In either case, however, the cosmos is perceived as dynamic and composed of vast numbers of force-beings, with humans at the center, having animals and inanimate beings at their disposal, but being influenced by ancestral force-beings, gods and finally God above them.

Perhaps the most articulate and wide-ranging of the post-Tempels intellectuals is Kagame. He sees his work as revealing not so much a systematic Bantu philosophy as an intuitive scheme containing philosophical principles. The creation of this scheme he ascribed ultimately to the founding fathers of the Bantu languages and cultures.

Although the Tempels hypothesis (as he himself saw it – that is, a hypothesis about the deeper structures of Bantu thought) was paternalistic, as I have remarked, and emerged within the ambit of a missionary enterprise, and thus had negative attributes from an African point of view, it caused a stir because it was also relatively positive: it gave a new dignity to the conceptual patterns of African thinking. It lifted that thinking above the mythic to the metaphysical. It conjured the ghost of an African alternative to Aristotle. The periods of slavery and imperialism had created a Western ideology of racism and superiority, and had fostered anthropological ideas which were very questionable. It is useful for us to pause here to consider the impact of these in relation to thinking about Africa and within Africa.

PATTERNS OF WESTERN ANTHROPOLOGY

Partly because of developmental systems, for instance those of Hegel and Comte, and partly because of the theory of animal evolution propounded by Darwin and others, the pattern of human life was seen in a certain way in the nineteenth century, and this led to profound effects on social sciences. Above all it made the model of evolution a powerful one. At the same time colonialism and above all the scramble for Africa bent Western consciences in the direction of justifying aggrandizement by the theory that Westerners had a duty to bring the benefits of civilization (usually conceived as Christian civilization) to the conquered peoples. Science and paternalism could be blended by thinking of human history in evolutionary terms. Thus the conquered peoples could be thought of as 'primitive', that is, poised at an earlier stage of evolution. From this various schemes emerged – interpreting animism, for instance, as an early stage in the development of human religion, to be succeeded by other stages, of which pure monotheism or maybe atheism is the highest. Indeed, anthropology often defined itself as the study of so-called primitive peoples. This redoubled the disadvantage of those being studied: they tended to belong to small-scale societies with no large organizational development, while being confronted by scholars drawn from large-scale societies; and they were also being studied, typically, by their conquerors. It is partly for this reason that some modern accounts of religion, which do not speak from above to below, and which have a sensitive appreciation of the meanings and depths of indigenous beliefs and practices, have made a strong impact over against the often trivializing and sometimes ideologically slanted accounts of primitive religions: I am thinking, in regard to the former, of such works as *Nuer Religion,* already mentioned, and in its own way Tempels' book.

Very often a sharp sense of difference between Africans and Europeans was generated by the very use of language: the primitive mentality supposedly studied and revealed by Levy-Bruhl did not correspond to the higher logic of civilized thinking – the English title of Lévi-Strauss' most famous work could be *The Savage Mind*. Anthropology also was and in some degree still is a scholarly field supported because of its aptness in the control and administration of subjugated populations. It was a highly useful adjunct to general training in imperial administration, and after that in development economics and the like, perhaps conceived somewhat in a neocolonialist milieu. At any rate, such characterizations of the peoples of Africa, coming in the aftermath of the slave trade, were bound to stimulate a critique of Western social sciences as biased and insufficiently self-reflective about the irrationalities and accidentalities of Western culture and with it Western learning. In this African criticisms have been reinforced by recent emphases on hermeneutics, deconstruction, Marxist thinking and postmodernism, even though these have often arisen out of the same rather smug milieu that created earlier evolutionary theories. At any rate, philosophical ideas that encourage self-criticism should be important within academic circles which have often fostered senses of differences (e.g. through such notions as 'primitive') which are ill-founded. This is not of course to say that differences of scale in society are without significance, or that literacy does not create profound changes, and so on. Nevertheless, a perception of the distorted views of Africa often held by Westerners and projected through Western intellectual life helped to stimulate new African perceptions. One such movement was that of Negritude.

NEGRITUDE AND E.W. BLYDEN

Negritude was a movement of thought which was particularly influential after World War II, though it originated under that name in the 1930s and is especially associated with the name of the West African intellectual and statesman Leopold Senghor (1906–2001). It was given added dynamism by the support of Jean-Paul Sartre, who wrote an extensive introduction called *Black Orpheus* to an anthology edited by Senghor in 1948. But some aspects of the ideology can be found earlier in the thought of the noted writer E.W. Blyden (1832–1912). He originated in the West Indian Danish-controlled island of St Thomas, but, denied education in North America, he settled in West Africa (in Liberia) in 1851. He was a Christian minister, but his life was substantially devoted to public affairs – he was for a time Liberian Secretary of State and then Minister of the Interior, as well as being Minister to London. He was concerned to preach the notion of a positive African personality. This led him into a sort of counter-racism, yet one wholly understandable. He considered of course that the usual images of Africans were colored by grave distortions, in part consequent upon the slave trade. Even the concept of the noble savage was a fanciful device for European self-scrutiny. Blyden wanted to put forward the picture of an African personality which was peculiar to Africans and to transatlantic Blacks (he got into hot water over derogatory opinions about people of mixed race descent). The idea of African personality in effect stood for the 'sum of values of African civilization, the body of qualities which make up the distinctiveness of the people of Africa' (E.W. Blyden, *Christianity, Islam, and the Negro Race*). He was clear in his critique of imperialism and colonization as exploitative and ultimately ineffective: Africans would have to absorb elements of progress on their own. Blyden recognized the importance of European classical culture and indeed advocated its incorporation (as did Senghor ninety years later) into West African educational systems. But he thought that many of the effects of White interference were highly negative. Likewise a distinction had to be made between Christian spirituality and the culture in which it had become embedded. He thus advocated the study of the pure New Testament without commentary. He thus foreshadowed notions of an African interpretation of the Gospel. At the same time he had a profound regard for Islam, which he saw as a thoroughly benign influence (he appears simply to have ignored its entanglement with the slave trade). About 'paganism' rather than traditional African religion, his attitudes were ambiguous. But overall his positions were prophetic of the ideas of African personality, Negritude, Black Consciousness, Black Theology, political liberation and the sense of a Greater Africa stretching on both sides of the Atlantic.

Negritude as it arose in the 1930s, mainly through a group of Martinican intellectuals including Aimé Césaire together with Léopold Césaire, combines a kind of celebration of traditional African values, stressing the harmony of earlier, undisturbed society, with a weighting of the forces of feeling and intuition over against Westernized reason. (There are interesting overlaps, as it happens, with a strand in later feminist thinking.) It has a pan-African basis, and so is very diverse from the appeal to the particularities of differing African ethnicities. Because, as with Blyden, it expresses a kind of counter-racism, it is somewhat indebted to figures such as Levy-Bruhl and Gobineau, more favored by the political right than the left, even though in its anti-colonialist aspect it is distinctively left-wing. These tensions remained with it in the continuing political debate after the end of World War II and during the run up to independence and beyond.

Negritude made much of the esthetic dimension of African culture (which of course had become both influential and fashionable in Western artistic circles since, roughly, the start of the twentieth century). In an essay Senghor wrote that:

> The Negro is a man of nature ... He is first of all sounds, odours, rhythms, forms and colours ... He is touch before he is sight, unlike the White European. He feels more than he sees: he feels himself. It is within himself, within his flesh, that he receives and senses the radiations that any existing object emits. Aroused, he responds to the appeal and lets himself go, moving from subject to object, from me to thou, on the waves of the Other ... This is not to say that the Negro is traditionally devoid of reason as one would have me believe. But his reason is not discursive; it is synthetic. It is not antagonistic but sympathetic.
>
> (R. Betts, ed., *The Ideology of Blackness*, pp. 110–11)

The emphasis upon cultural and esthetic matters in the Negritude movement may have attracted criticism from those who saw a more direct political path (one critic said that the tiger does not reflect upon his tigritude – to which a reply was that the man can catch the tiger, no doubt because of his reflective capabilities). Senghor attempted to place his esthetics in a wider political structure, indeed a kind of metaphysics of civilization. He absorbed Marxian theory of knowledge, though he refused to regard the pattern of class struggle as universal: he saw a coming world civilization, in part based on the evolutionary philosophy of Teilhard de Chardin, in which Negritude would mark an important ingredient and preparation. It would be a world culture in which certain traditional African values, notably harmony between humans, and the vision of a unitary universe under God, would be central. (He rejected Marxist atheism.) Despite the fact that Senghor has become controversial and for many out-dated, he remains a powerful figure in the development of modern African thought.

SOME OTHER CONTRIBUTIONS TO PAN-AFRICANISM

While much of the emerging political philosophy in anti-colonial Africa was Marxist, and of strictly Western provenance, there were other, religious, roots of the pan-African movement. For instance, Marcus Garvey (1887–1940) founded the Universal Negro Improvement Association in 1914, which pioneered a millennialist aspiration for a return to Africa. Hopes came to be pinned on Ethiopia, and through that on its Emperor Ras Rafari (Haile Selassie) (1892–1975) who ascended the imperial throne in 1930. Ethiopia, as the long-unconquered section of Africa and as an ancient Christian region, became a symbol of heaven, as opposed to the hell of slavery. Naturally such yearnings for a Zion, inspired by Christian images, came more easily to those with a sense of exile through slavery. They are an instance of the effects of diaspora values upon the center, since the focus of a single Africa seen from afar could be transformed into the ideal of a single nationalism. There had also been in the nineteenth century those well-meaning attempts, consequent upon the abolition of slavery, to resettle Blacks in West Africa, in the freed slave states of Sierra Leone and Liberia.

If the most pervasive effect on African self-consciousness has been due to the rapid colonization of the continent in the latter half of the nineteenth century and the bringing of the area decisively within the capitalist system, an added strand has been the fact that racism naturally enough operated on a pan-African basis. Indeed racism, as distinguished from nationalist groupism (for instance), can be defined roughly as any form of prejudice which extends beyond the national and racial group. Thus, we do not refer to, say, anti-Polish prejudice as racism, but we do think of anti-East-Asian prejudice as racist. If prejudice against a people on account of their wider 'racial' classification exists, then that can be thought of as racist, so hostility to Japanese or Koreans on the part of White Americans can be seen as racist. Basically, then, racism is just a term for transethnic hostility. On this basis, racism itself helps to form pan-Africanism. Thus, even after the demise of political colonialism, an extra life was given to anti-African racism by the example of apartheid. Generally speaking, the anti-apartheid movement has had universal backing from Black African states (even if Malawi and one or two others were, for special reasons, less forward in the movement). Some words about the genesis of apartheid are in order, since it represents a political ideology with theological underpinning.

Basically, the ideology arose from Afrikaner nationalism, and this in turn arose through the disaffection of Dutch-speaking settlers under British rule. During the latter part of the nineteenth century and the early twentieth century the Afrikaans language was developed as a literary and bureaucratic language, under the leadership above all of the Calvinist minister and poet G.J. Du Toit. At the same time, the history of the emerging nation was worked up into a powerful myth – for instance the story of the Great Trek of the 1830s and the Battle of Blood River against the Zulus, with its attendant Covenant between the people and their God, was celebrated through a huge monument in Pretoria and through annual rituals. The British had formed the Union of South Africa in 1910, uniting the provinces of the Cape and Natal with the former Boer (Afrikaner) republics of the Orange Free State and the Transvaal. All this was part of the consolidation of large swathes of South and East Africa under British domination during and after the scramble for Africa. The Boers, bitterly defeated by the British in 1901, worked, under the new constitution, to achieve political power, which came to them in 1948. The philosophy of apartheid was designed to preserve their power indefinitely. At one level it drew upon the newly formed Afrikaner nationalism. At another level it drew on Calvinist theology, as expressed in the Dutch Reformed and other Churches. According to this, election was ineluctable: you were saved because God chose you (indeed, from the beginning of the world). This doctrine of individual salvation was collectivized into the election of a whole people (the Afrikaners drew for inspiration on their reading of the Old Testament). At still another level it drew upon the Nazi ideology of between the wars. The Afrikaners actually attempted, so far as possible, to ensure separateness: apartheid was probably the most elaborate practical attempt to put into force the values of racism. For this reason it rapidly became a symbol not only of evil, among anti-racists, but inversely of Africanism. Although its values were directed against Asians and people of mixed race, it was primarily anti-African.

Moreover, South Africa was the most industrially developed part of Africa. As such it pioneered large urban cities, and here the importance of particular ethnicities diminished. Not surprisingly, the main opposition to apartheid, which was the African National Congress, had a pan-South-African, anti-racist ideology, heavily under the influence of Marxism. It is, incidentally, a tribute to the power of nationalism that such an artificial construction as South Africa, put together so recently, and ruled for so long under imperial and racist auspices, should still attract such a high degree of loyalty as an entity.

BEYOND TRADITIONAL WORLDVIEWS: NEW MOVEMENTS

In looking to the mythic worldviews which characterized traditional Africa we have seen one set of patterns. But equally important, in fact more important as time goes on, are those worldviews expressed through new independent Churches and other movements. These result from the impact of Christianity, both Catholic and Protestant, on indigenous Africa, through the very vigorous and very successful missionary endeavors of the last hundred years and more. But though Christianity has taken a powerful grip throughout Africa, its mainstream versions did not always attract loyalty from Africans because during the main missionary period its administration was in the hands of Whites who not only retained power but tended often to ally themselves with the colonial authorities and usually too with colonial-style thinking. The missions admittedly caused various revolutions: by introducing indigenously written scriptures throughout Africa they sowed powerful seeds of education and self-consciousness; by bringing in Western-style medicine they expanded indigenous horizons; by providing schools they inevitably began to raise economic and political expectations. But their very success in supplanting much of traditional religion and altering the terms of indigenous society, notably by controlling marriage and the family in new ways and 'domesticating' women, also stimulated strong nostalgia for the old classical ways and powerful desire for religious ways to express African dignity. African societies had been so unnerved and disoriented by the experiences of conquest, redeployment and conversion that it is not surprising that many people became attracted to a third way, between the mainstream and the traditional, namely the path of new independent Churches and new religious movements. Various themes can be discerned: first, a reappraisal of the meaning of the newly-found scriptures; second, and connectedly, an identification of charismatic leaders with the prophets of the Bible; third, a connected emphasis on various underlying themes of classical society, such as healing, polygamy, 'shamanism', and so on. It will be useful, therefore, to look at a few examples of these new movements, now experiencing such vigorous growth. I shall follow this brief sampling with a similar tasting of new movements in Greater Africa, in the Caribbean and elsewhere. We have already noted how this world has had reflexive influence upon Africa itself.

KIMBANGUISM

The movement started by and around Simon Kimbangu in Zaire is perhaps the independent movement which has come closest to the mainstream – indeed in 1969 it was admitted to the World Council of Churches. Simon Kimbangu (1889–1951) spent much of his life imprisoned by the colonial authorities, who typically saw an indigenous movement as being implicitly a threat. As a result of prophetic, visionary experiences, Kimbangu took up a life of preaching and healing. His followers multiplied, and in 1921 he was arrested, sentenced to death, reprieved and imprisoned until his death in 1951. The religion spread in part because the government tended to exile his prominent followers, who spread his message. Important in the worldview of the Church of Jesus Christ through the Prophet Simon Kimbangu is the power of the Spirit, and the possibility therefore of direct empowerment by God. In many ways Kimbangu was seen as a messianic figure, second only to Christ.

This example of a prophetic religion opens up a question which is not much discussed philosophically, but is pertinent. As with the case, for instance, of Isaiah Shembe among the Zulus, the prophet is seen as – of course – receiving his commission and indeed revelation from God. Mainstream Christianity had in theory sealed off its revelations during the apostolic period. Could the new prophets of Africa be considered to have revelatory experiences? There was something of a tension between written scripture and living vision.

But another and more disturbing implication of new religions of prophecy and healing related to the interpretation of the New Testament. Africans could view the revelation afresh and against their traditional culture. It is obvious that a great part (about a third) of the Gospel narratives are about healing and related miracles. It is clear that polygamy occurs in the Old Testament. It is equally strange that Christian missionaries could see the New Testament through such a strong filter of European presuppositions, such as that Africans need civilizing, are pagans and savages, etc. African thinkers could thus easily begin to make the crucial distinction between the Christian essence and its fortuitous Western cultural clothing. A new debate about religion and culture was set in train. Such a debate finds, for instance, scholarly expression in the thinking of V.Y. Mudimbe (in *The Invention of Africa* and elsewhere). For him, a theology of incarnation would involve taking embodiment in a culture seriously, but the effect would be to relativize, in that an incarnated African Christian worldview would incorporate specifically African motifs. A modern African civilization could emerge, taking up not only African classical as well as Islamic and European themes, but also assimilating intellectually and culturally the traumatic experiences of slavery, exploitation and colonization.

A somewhat similar theme to that of the Kimbangu worldview is to be found in the Zulu Zionism founded by the prophet Isaiah Shembe (1870–1935). The term 'Zionism' in this context has reference to the influence of the Christian Catholic Apostolic Church in Zion, founded in 1896 in Zion, Illinois, near Chicago. The notion was that Zion should be a pure community unpolluted by the surrounding and evil world. This ideal represented one solution to the existential problem facing people in a changing and menacing world. The fact is that Shembe's preaching received a warm reception from the Zulu people because of their vicissitudes. In 1879 they had been finally defeated at the Battle of Ulundi. The kingdom had been split up. In 1906 they had rebelled and again been defeated. In 1913 the Native Land Act in Natal had deprived them of much of their land. What the Prophet did was to give them, through their Nazarite Church, an alternative life, which was not predicated upon hostility to the Whites or to the government, but which offered a pure way of life and healing for both their spiritual and bodily ailments. Since the framework of Shembe's thinking was broadly speaking Christian, he was not an enemy of the Whites, who had brought the Christian message to Africa. While the movement has a nationalist dimension, it concentrates on the spiritual life. Shembe, who had a call as prophet through his visions, proved also to be a masterly hymn-composer, and the Nazarite hymnal is a major spiritual document. The movement tended to be opposed by the government during the inter-war period. More recently it and other independent church movements have been growing in numbers, and attract attention because collectively they are statistically important players in the emerging South Africa, yet they have steered a course between the opposing political factions.

It is also worth mentioning two movements founded by women: religion here gives women important roles to play, as opposed to their relatively subordinate status (until recently) in mainstream Christianity. In 1954 a new Church called the Lumpa (or Excellent) was formed in what was to become Zambia, by the prophetess Alice Lonshina (c.1919–78), who promised her followers a new and deeper life if they were to give up magic and witchcraft. It is fairly characteristic of new movements that they should steer a middle path between classical healing and ritual practices, on the one hand, and the repudiation in much mainstream Christianity of the missionaries (and medical missionaries) on the other. Another woman-generated movement is that associated with Mai Chaza Jesus (d. 1960), who had in 1954 fallen seriously ill, appeared to die and revived: she compared herself to Moses and Jesus, and was looked upon by her followers in Zimbabwe and Malawi as a savior. Such movements represent intuitive ways of affirming women's leadership role.

While new religions tend not to be systematic in their articulation of philosophy and theology, they do provide a matrix which in due course is leading to reflection upon the crucial question of the distinction between message and culture: that is, the question of how Christianity or Islam can be distinguished essentially from the Western or Arabic culture in which they appear in Africa as incoming forces.

NEW WORLDVIEWS IN THE NEW WORLD

Parallel in some ways to the independent Churches in Africa are the various new ways in which African culture has expressed itself in the Americas, sometimes in new syntheses between Catholicism and African-style motifs. The best known of these, probably, is Haitian Voodoo. Basically this is a system which reflects a major feature of much African religion, namely belief in the one High God (called Bondye, i.e. Bon Dieu), in our separation from him in practical day-to-day living, and the occurrence of numerous spirits who act as intermediaries. These are often blends between Catholic saints and West African, mainly Yoruba and Fon, deities. The god of serpents is identified with St Patrick and that of thunder with Santa Barbara (who is in Western lore the patroness both of thunder and of artillery). Much Voodoo ritual connects with possession by spirits, and so there is a strong shamanistic motif running through the religion. Most Voodoo participants count themselves as regular Catholics, go to mass and confession and attend festivals. Probably we should think of it as a religious system which, having for its adherents a broader significance than Catholic Christianity, has in effect taken the latter over and effectively absorbed it. Much ritual centers on cemeteries and the dead: issues of survival are important and affect Voodoo's conception of psychology. This holds that we each have more than one soul or spirit, the most vital notions being those of the *gro bonanj* or consciousness and the *ti bonanj* or conscience. When a spirit or *lwa* takes possession the *gro bonanj* is displaced and may go wandering.

Another not dissimilar system is the Santeria of Cuba, and because of a million or more refugees, of Venezuela, Puerto Rico and the United States. This blends belief in Yoruba deities and Yoruba methods of divination and medicine with Catholicism: identifications between saints and gods account for the name. Its initiates are known as *santeros* and *santeras*. Again, while superficially it is a syncretism between Catholicism and African elements, it involves to a great extent the takeover of Catholic myth and practice by a predominantly African strain of faith. It dates essentially from the establishment of the Cuban sugar plantations in the nineteenth century, with the strong importation of West African slaves. It does not seem to have been greatly affected by the Marxist takeover in Cuba. Conversely, Voodoo was used politically by the Duvalier dictatorship in Haiti.

We may see the new African religions of the Americas as extensions of the same phenomena exhibited in the independent churches of Africa: the attempt to reassert African identity. But the new world religions were played out in much harsher and more disturbed conditions. They involve in effect the attempt to reconstruct the Old World faiths, but in a situation of ethnic mixture and chaos, suffering, racism and slavery. They are intended both to deal with the day-to-day problems of disadvantaged people and to give meaning to the African inheritance. They are thus intuitive discussions, so to speak, of the problem of identity, and so also have something to say in the debate about Africanness, Negritude and political power.

NEW THEOLOGIES

At a different level, because it is involved in the intellectual quest within the framework of Western-style higher education, is the evolution of new patterns of Christian theology. A major trend is indigenization or what may be called African theology. This, in some degree, draws on the Negritude theme; but, more particularly, it expresses a new evaluation of traditional African culture and religion. It thus involves a reaction against some of the implicit negativities already touched upon in the enterprise of Western anthropology and against the main thrust of the judgments of most missionaries. It draws upon some of the scholarly work done by both Western and African scholars in rediscovering some of the deeper themes of traditional religion. Important here in rebutting a lot of the anthropological attitudes was the work of Father Wilhelm Schmidt, the Austrian anthropologist, in his interesting and challenging series of volumes *Die Ursprung der Gottesidee* in which he argued for a primordial monotheism in human societies, an *urmonotheismus*. His data were drawn from all over the globe and not just from Africa, but his argument focused attention upon the phenomenon of the High God as typical. His was one of the influences giving a more profound significance to traditional religious ideas and practices. While Christian theologians, African or not, could not simply rest content with pre-Christian values, the concept of African culture and religion as containing useful depths could pave the way for the treatment of the traditional heritage as being something like the 'Old Testament' to Christianity's 'New'.

But though the positive use of pre-Christian themes was revolutionary in one way, since it removed any simplistic use of such notions as 'paganism' (and queried other allegedly 'scientific' concepts such as animism), it was in certain respects a conservative move, and could not always come to terms with the new conditions of urban living, which already moved people, literally, away from their traditional heritage. Consequently, while the African theology movement has promising aspects, it is also in part overtaken by events, and there are other alternatives emerging. Still, it does help to open up a broader debate about the role of Africa in an evolving world civilization. In effect, new African theologies are modes of rewriting African history. That history, like all history, functions as a myth, a narrative which both highlights ancestral values and retells the past in ways which give a sense of identity to African culture as a whole. We have seen that the philosophy of pan-Africanism is crucial to the whole modern period of African thinking. Also, we may note that the concept of African theology is parallel to other instances of indigenization, for instance in Indian thought in relation to the Christian message, and so on.

Part of the conservatism of African theology had to do with the issue of individualism. African theologians perceived Western culture as ineluctably individualist, in ways that clearly diverged from the values both of the Old Testament and of the early Church. In harking back to a warmer more collective or social view of personhood, African theology could easily be too rurally oriented, while the growing new form of existence in the continent is and was, as elsewhere in the world, urban. Moreover, the issues of village life were not those of wider political life nor of the whole framework of neocolonialism. Here notions of Negritude and African personality represented a halfway house: they emphasized the warm, social milieu of African personal existence without necessarily reaffirming some of the particularities of rural religious life. Something of a synthesis between Negritude and Marxism was also possible, and the Marxist ingredient in African thinking in the modern period has remained important for various reasons (which we shall come to shortly). That synthesis had in some degree been achieved in the book *Consciencism* (1970), by Kwame Nkrumah (1902–72), which blended pan-African and socialist motifs. Marxism was scarcely easy to synthesize with traditional values. Marxism indeed generally has been more hostile to 'paganism' than even evangelical missions. It has absorbed some of the negativities of anthropological 'science' as well.

For obvious reasons South Africa as been an important milieu for working out the various options for thought. Perhaps the most significant writer in what may be thought of as the transition from African theology to liberation thought was Anton Lembede (1914–47), of Catholic upbringing. He was a warm advocate of a kind of pan-Africanism, looking in fact to an African nationalism. This should not be racially conceived, but based on the relativism of national contributions: each nation has its special gift to civilization as a whole. But the nation's past needs reconstructing. Lembede wanted to transcend tribal particularities, and to recreate an African past, with its heroes and great events. But because the solidarity of groups was vital in earlier Africa, Lembede saw the new nationalism as being socialist in emphasis. (In this he echoed many nationalists of the period, who often thought of socialism as reflecting better the ethos of traditional life.) On the other hand, the new nation should be democratic, just as older societies saw a person's worth often in his courage or participation in public life. The ethics of the older times, crowned and criticized by the Christian morality, could help the new nation transcend various temptations to narrowness.

The effect of this new kind of Black Theology was to give a new vitality to pan-Africanism. Of course, since Lembede and other such writers were operating within the South African context, the effect was to produce not so much pan-Africanism strictly as pan-South Africanism, itself invisibly resting on the irony of an imposed order of four provinces united under British imperial policy – a true definition by the Other. Nevertheless, there is an important degree of pan-Africanism here, which itself rests, as we have noted, on a theory of civilizational blocs, each with its special offering to make to the ultimate world order.

Black Theology also tended to draw a line between itself and the generally repressive example of White theology. Even when the latter is well-meaning and pious, by its apolitical stance it may effectively favor repression. Hence Black Theology tended towards a theory of struggle. The debate was whether this should be non-violent (as argued for instance by Archbishop Desmond Tutu, first African head of the Anglican Church in South Africa) or should use force. The African National Congress, whose ideology tended to overlap with that of Black Theology, had felt obliged to take up armed struggle. In all this, especially during the 1980s, Black Theology was under some influence from Latin American Liberation Theology, with its Marxist and in some degree revolutionary ideology. It was also influenced by the Black Consciousness movement, itself a variation on the theme of Negritude. Elsewhere also in Africa, one can see the influences of liberation thinking – notably in F. Eboussi-Boulaga's 1981 book: *Christianisme sans fétiche: révélation et domination,* which urges and involves a deconstruction of accumulated Christian ideas and practices, with a view to converting it into a religion which here and now liberates the human being.

REFLECTIONS ON AFRICAN THOUGHT

As we have seen, the preponderant issue about Africa is Africa itself. Much of the Western conception of African thinking has, moreover, been tied to religious issues rather than secular philosophical issues. It has necessarily also been tied to political issues, so that Marxist thinking has often been dominant in African thinking. The issues about ethnophilosophy have opened up a question as to whether there is anything that in a strict sense is both philosophical and African as such. In a famous speech in

1965, F. Crahay argued that for philosophy proper to exist in Africa you would need a group of intellectuals working within an intellectual tradition together with critical and cross-cultural thought, together with a repertoire of concepts, values, etc., drawn from the African heritage which would stimulate reflection (the text was published in *Diogenes* as 'Le "décollage" conceptual', 1965). But this model envisages virtually that philosophy would be a world activity, and African philosophy would simply bring some applications to the African scene and be 'done' by Africans. This of course is all part of a wider debate as to whether all the variety of philosophies will not simply merge in a world activity. Crahay and other critics of African ethnophilosophy draw a fairly clear distinction between expressing worldviews and doing philosophy. But as the latter gets to be critical and technical, it may of course lose contacts with the value-questions and metaphysical speculations which have formed so much of the substance of traditional philosophy in so many cultures. If African thought displays less of the complex metaphysical thought which has gone on elsewhere, it is largely because of differing material conditions, including very importantly limitations upon the medium of writing, which has often proved critical elsewhere.

Much of the discussion, in the twentieth century, among Africans about philosophy rather than religion, has been metaphilosophical. It has been a debate about the definition of philosophy and the characteristics of an African philosophy. One view of African philosophy is backward-looking; the other, forward-looking. On the first view, African philosophy is contained in, found in, or constructed out of the proverbs, folklore, art, aphorisms, fragments, rituals, traditions and collective wisdom of the African people; and African philosophy so discovered or constructed is comparable to Western philosophy. On this view, the lack of writing in large areas of traditional Africa is not sufficient for denying the existence of a traditional African philosophy that is comparable to Western philosophy. The general reasoning for this traditional approach to African philosophy seems to be that the post-colonial African society has been so Westernized that any authentic African philosophy must be rooted in the pre-colonial society.

On the second view, African philosophy consists of the post-colonial, literary works of individuals connected to the African continent. According to those who adopt this view, the reason for this approach to African philosophy is that real or serious philosophy is not a collective activity by the whole society as is apparently suggested by the first view. On this view, as expressed by Kwame Anthony Appiah for example, philosophy is an individual and literary activity; hence, writing is necessary for philosophy. Until writing was introduced on a mass scale in Africa, much of Black Africa lacked a tradition of writing and, hence, the absence of traditional African philosophy.

According to Kwame Gyekye of Ghana, for example, 'a distinction must be made between traditional African philosophy and modern African philosophy'. He adds, 'the latter, to be African, and have a basis in African culture and experience, must have a connection with the former, the traditional'. 'African philosophy as distinct from African traditional world-view,' Kwasi Wiredu writes, 'is the philosophy that is being produced by contemporary African philosophers.' John Mbiti of Kenya believes that 'philosophical systems of different African people have not yet been formulated, but some of the areas where they may be found are in the religion, proverbs, oral tradition, ethics and morals of the society concerned'. According to Kobina Oguah, many Western philosophical doctrines are expressed in Africa 'not in documents but in the proverbs, ritual songs, folktales and customs of the people'. Odera Oruka of Kenya, like W. Emmanuel Abraham of Ghana, denies that literacy or writing is necessary for philosophy but, at the same time, dissociates himself from the works of Gyekye and Olubi Sodipo as being 'unable to get out of the anthropological fog'. According to Abraham, one 'can find all over Africa specimens of what might be called a public philosophy, usually tracing out the theoretical foundations of the traditional society' and 'also the private philosophy which is more the thinking of an individual than a laying-bare of the communal mind'. V.Y. Mudimbe prefers to call traditional thought *gnosis*, on the grounds that 'it is only metaphorically, or, at best, from a historicist perspective, that one would extend the notion of philosophy to African traditional systems of thought, considering them as dynamic processes in which concrete experiences are integrated into an order of concepts and discourses'.

This debate among contemporary African philosophers has led to two kinds of projects. The first is the attempt to document, capture or re-create the traditional philosophy of Africa. Sodipo, Oruka and Gyekye, for examples, have attempted to do that in their analyses of concepts such as time, causation and logic. On the other hand, others such as Wiredu have tried to philosophize about issues from metaphysics through ethics to epistemology with an African conscience or a comparative approach, being mindful of their African heritage and experience.

16

CONCLUDING REFLECTIONS

SOME NOTES ON THE GLOBAL SCENE

In this chapter I shall start by sketching the global scene, so far as it is relevant to worldviews and philosophies. Then I shall briefly look at some particular developments, notably in the West. I have taken the story up to about the 1960s, and I do not wish to try to cover in any full way what has happened since then. It is appropriate to let the dust settle before coming to a judgment. Still, some sketches of certain trends may be helpful. Finally I want to set out my own feelings about the future directions of worldview construction and philosophy, in the light of what I have attempted in this book.

At the beginning let me notice a lacuna which I hope briefly to fill here. My division of the material has been continental: large areas of history have been tackled, from Latin America to the Far East, and from Africa to the Islamic world. But I have not devoted separate space to a string of smaller societies which collectively perhaps represent three hundred million inhabitants of our planet: the peoples of Oceania (or the South Pacific), the Native Americans, the smaller cultural groups of North Asia, tribal folk in South and South-east Asia. Though they are, taken together, significant, they are only beginning to realize this fact and to organize together. They are starting to be politically and therefore intellectually self-conscious. But because of their diversity they find it difficult to be a single cultural force. Who quite knows what they will make of their identity? They are beginning to establish their credentials, though on aliens' terms. There are Hawaiian studies in Hawaii, Maori studies in New Zealand and so on. In some areas they are amalgamating, as in North America, where a single identity of Native American peoples is beginning to be fashioned, and in Oceania, where appeal to something called 'the Pacific Way' is being made. All this creates some questions about the future. Let me turn first, in my global stocktaking, to such matters.

SMALL-SCALE PEOPLES AND IDENTITY

The challenge of external forces has been taken up in some measure by a series of small-scale new religions in which new elements are borrowed from Christianity. But in many cases the smaller groups convert substantially; so that most Pacific communities, for instance, are Christian. The incoming religion helps to reshape society without letting it disintegrate. Nevertheless, in many areas the problem of traditional culture can reassert itself: for many such groups, the nature of the old is questioned through considering its religious relevance – can it be a kind of substitute for the Old Testament?

There has been in some degree a revival of values, in so far as modern environmentalism can create an important space for traditional practice: in the nature of the case, all the societies we are here considering live (as we say) close to nature. An adaptation of classical ideas can move them in the direction of modern ecological consciousness. This not only chimes in with Western notions and sympathies, but also latches on to a whole swathe of newer philosophical interests in the rights of animals, etc.

Regarding the diversity of values in such societies, a logic of universalism begins to apply. The reply to universal movements such as Christianity, modern secularism, etc., as they move in on the particularities of small-scale societies must be of the following form: peoples should be allowed to continue their separate cultural heritages, so far as feasible. But the implication of this, so far as claims to truth or value go, is that every tradition embodies an aspect of truth or value. The result is something like Vivekananda's universalism. There emerges as it were a federal principle, which affirms the validity of each culture for each group. On the face of it another principle might also emerge: that every group has something distinctive to offer to world culture. There is plausibility in this since each tribal entity has had long experience in varied conditions, so it would not be surprising that there was something distinctive that they had discovered either about their environment or about the means of coping with it. This principle of 'distinctive contribution', as we may call it, already is evident in larger groups. It is the practical assumption of each national group: that the Finns, or the Mauritians, for instance, have something to offer the global community as a distinctive offering. It is a way of effecting a compromise between national consciousness and the sense of belonging to humankind as a whole.

Exchange, of course, is not confined to material inventions but to ideas and pieces of behavior as well. We are entering a time of world history when such mental and practical exchange is greatly accelerating. Contributions of such items to world culture will in due course result in a general diffusion of human values on the world scene, not necessarily held in a consistent manner. One of the themes that I shall return to is this: whether items drawn from differing world philosophies can enter into the same global debate and dialogue. In part I intend this book as an instrument of trade, so that knowledge of the different traditions of philosophy can help to fuse them into a single area of, if not agreement, then at least discussion.

SOME GENERAL FEATURES OF INTELLECTUAL AND OTHER CHANGES IN THE SECOND HALF OF THE TWENTIETH CENTURY

The backcloth of the period since the early 1960s has been variegated. The most dramatic series of events has been the collapse of the old Eastern European system: the throwing off of Marxist regimes in the ex-Soviet satellites, the break-up of the old Soviet Union into constituent nationalist republics and the emergence throughout the area of more or less vigorous attempts to establish multi-party democracies and market economies. All this has led to greater intellectual interest in social democratic theory, notably in the writings of Karl Popper. Marxian influence remains fairly strong in Western universities, but Marxist philosophers in the East are turning increasingly to new ideas. Historians of atheism, for instance, are turning to the history of religions.

Such collapse has not, however, overtaken Marxism in the East. China remains attached to one-party rule, as the events of Tiananmen Square in May 1989 demonstrated. Similarly in North Korea and Vietnam orthodoxy persists. However, there is a kind of loosening in China, because market forces are being allowed, successfully on the whole, to operate. Especially in South China, in the region adjacent to Hong Kong and Macao, new prosperity is tacitly weakening the grip of conformity. But at the time of writing China is a long way from an intellectual revolution.

There is, however, a renewed interest, in the Chinese diaspora, in Confucianism. A revived variety is being seen as a genuine possibility for ordering the lives of Chinese cultures abroad. Meanwhile, in the Islamic crescent, from Indonesia across to West Africa, the resurgence of Islam continues. Among other areas where significant revival is taking place is that of the new states of ex-Soviet Central Asia and Afghanistan. The Islamic revival, however, does not help to foster philosophical thinking, because it tends to be 'fundamentalistic'. That is, in its revivalism it goes back to the primary sources, as it conceives them, and bypasses both the history of philosophical thought in Islam and the productive Sufi movement. It tends therefore to be inimical to modern speculative tendencies in Islam and new-found flexibilities in understanding the world.

Such Islamic response to modernity and to continuing neo-colonial factors is understandable. It is exacerbated in the Indian subcontinent by a resurgence of Hinduism, in which political parties as well as public sentiment have taken a part. It involves a reaction against the pluralism of the classical modern period of Indian nationalism. Such resurgence is beginning to reject the old modern Hindu ideology of Vivekananda, Gandhi and Radhakrishnan. It again is not so favorable to philosophical thinking and has some affinities to Islamic fundamentalism. The old myths and epics are taken literally and concretely. This can lead to conflicts over sacred sites, as at Ayodhya (in 1991–2).

Buddhism has its nationalist impetus in Sri Lanka in the growing conflict with Tamil resistance groups, notably the Tamil Tigers. Nevertheless, overall Buddhist modernism still flourishes, and with it a continuance of its fruitful dialogue with the West. Indeed, in North America it is getting thoroughly embedded and has become a modest yet important addition to the array of religions available.

We have noted the way in which Africa is forming itself and preparing for a more vigorous and distinctive role in world civilization. Philosophically, these are early days: we have seen how much intellectual effort is being spent on the question of self-identity. This is a necessary part of a process which, hopefully, will produce a new super-nation. No doubt, in this an increased role will be played by Africans beyond the Atlantic, in Greater Africa, including Brazil, Central and Caribbean societies, and North America.

Meanwhile, Latin America also is evolving its own identity. So far its contributions to world literature are immense, but philosophically it has produced less. But both Arielism and Christian Liberation Theology are indications of distinctiveness. During the 1980s the most significant developments have involved the wider demise of Caudillismo and the introduction of democratic government through nine-tenths of the region. Similar changes have been stirring in Africa.

Both Europe and America remain vigorous on the philosophical front. We shall discuss changes below. The fabric of the Cold War has largely perished, but we have seen the amazing revival of nationalism. Just when Western Europe is softening its ethnic identities, Eastern Europe reveals the power of old ethnic identities which have come out from under the disintegration of totalitarian rule. Such new ethnic rivalries should stimulate thinking in political philosophy on how to establish a just order which does not stimulate wars over territory and resources, above all civil wars.

Another, countervailing tendency in the contemporary globe is the rapid development or reinforcement of transnational entities: for instance, transnational corporations (which now tend to dominate the world); transnational intellectual and practical organizations (for medicine, philosophy, cricket, fish-farming and what have you); international political entities (UN, European Community, ASEAN and so forth); new means of travel; electronic and other global communications networking of individuals on a global scale; and so on. It tends to mean the end of separate traditions. They are all interpenetrative.

However, it is the case that Western institutions are often dominant. This is the case with universities and so with intellectual work. The Western pattern of higher education has more or less taken over the world, and with it often Western categories, including the category 'philosophy'. In some cases a range of study such as physics becomes sufficiently well-defined and culture-free that this does not matter: indeed what you have is an international neutral subject called physics, and what they teach in California, Japan, Sierra Leone, Russia or Beirut under this head is the same. It might be better done in one place rather than another, but what is done is recognizably and transculturally the same. But it is not easy to apply this satisfaction to cultural subjects, either in the social sciences or the humanities and arts. The assumptions of anthropology are sometimes colonialist or culturally determined. There is no absolutely right and easily defined way of doing philosophy, for the subject not only has its particular Western history, but is in its nature essentially debatable. So if Western models dominate such a field, there are real problems for those whose deep tradition goes by different questions and methods. We shall reflect further on this matter later on. But meanwhile let us note that Western domination of the subject is not necessarily healthy, even when it may be felt that modern Western philosophy has been remarkably dynamic and productive. But it is a fact of life that the global world is shrinking in thought and communication. In the future none of the traditions will stay apart but all will become more or less mutually interpenetrative.

This global shrinkage is the single most important cultural fact which has occurred in the last thirty years or more. Since the relations – economic, political, cultural, ideological, and so on – between differing regions and cultures of the world are unequal, this shrinkage itself generates various dynamics of interaction and response which help to account for some of the changes I have briefly described earlier.

It may also be noted that shrinkage generates, for obvious reasons, a heightened sense of the finitude of the planet, and with that two reactions: one is a curbing of the ambitious horizons typical of the West in the previous century and in the early part of this century; another is an increased awareness of environmental issues.

All the above patterns of change in recent times – the emerging self-consciousness of small-scale societies; the collapse of orthodox Marxism; the growth of non-Marxist Far Eastern societies and a growth of interest in their traditions; the Islamic revival; the fading of Hindu federalism; the spread of Buddhist ideas; the creation of the concept of Africa and of Greater Africa; the evolution of Latin American identity; the spread of social democratic thinking; the eruption of new nationalisms; the growth of transnational entities and relations; the domination of Western higher education and the creation of world intellectual institutions; global interpenetration and responses to unequal power relations; the heightened sense of finitude on our planet – all these changes have philosophical implications and need to be addressed in the varying branches of reflection. For instance, political philosophy needs to create imaginatively better models for dealing with ethnically mixed areas of the world; the philosophy of religion has to deal with the ultimate relations between differing worldviews; the philosophy of the social sciences needs to be critical of culture-bound values brought into the assumptions behind the pursuit of disciplines such as sociology and anthropology.

457

Meanwhile, it may be useful to look at some of the recent directions of European and American philosophy, before we comment on the possible global developments of philosophies.

SOME NEW DIRECTIONS IN EUROPE

One of the major developments in Europe has been a variety of forms of structuralism, which have had their philosophical effects. In many ways the most important figure here has been that of Claude Lévi-Strauss (b. 1908). His work on the 'savage mind' has a certain armchair quality: he is not so greatly concerned with ethnographic fieldwork, but rather with creating a theory of how 'primitive' myths work. This will throw light in general on the role of mythmaking. He was attracted by relatively isolated societies which had not been affected (infected perhaps) by European conceptions and values, notably the Western bent to see life historically. Such 'cold' societies, as he called them, reflect very clearly certain permanent patterns of human thinking. Lévi-Strauss was influenced both by Marxism and psychoanalysis, being attracted to them because they contain the notion of depth or unconscious structures which are not evident on the surface. He wished to bring out the logic of culture (which he loosely identified with language) by an examination of myths and their relation to wider aspects of a given society. In doing so he wanted to put anthropology on a scientific basis. While his methods of analysis have a wide application and have influenced ways of looking at mythology, his doctrines have only an oblique relationship to philosophy. But structuralism has left its mark on the field. Moreover, Lévi-Strauss's account of the 'savage mind' represents a thesis about the nature of human thought which is of philosophical interest.

His most incisive successor is Michel Foucault (1926–84). If structuralism is summed up as involving synchronic rather than diachronic studies, his approach is rather more historical than Lévi-Strauss's, since, especially later in his career, he tended more towards history. His most important observation is that we should look at the investigation of past epochs in human knowledge as a kind of archeology. That is, there are separate strata, or epistemic epochs, which are largely incommensurable with one another. So for instance the whole idea of the human sciences incorporates the notion of man: this notion, though, belongs to a particular epistemic epoch which is starting to fade. Man is a construct invented by science. But it is not a *necessary* concept. The underlying structure of a given age which shapes what we regard as knowledge Foucault calls an episteme: we as individuals do not create it, but it helps to determine the way in which we proceed. Moreover, Foucault holds that there are discontinuities between one epoch and another. So he rejects the smoother and progressive accounts of history which have become the normal ways to treat of the development of epistemology. This is a challenge, then, to the way most history of philosophy is thought about and practiced.

As we have seen, Lévi-Strauss was heavily influenced both by Marxism and by psychoanalysis. Both these are evident too in the work of Louis Althusser (1918–90). His account of Marxism as scientific is interesting. For him the later Marx involved the true discovery of history, and is scientific. For him there is a rupture (there is an analogy here with Foucault) between ideology and science. All prior philosophies and worldviews count as ideology. Marx's writings, on the other hand, can be read in a certain way which brings out their structure. Marx was the first theoretician to note that class struggles cannot be understood subjectively but as the interplay of forces which operate as items within a structural system. But the operation of the forces of history is not something which goes in a linear fashion; it involves dialectical and structural links. Althusser wedded his structuralist account of Marxism to the radical reinterpretation of Freudianism of Jacques Lacan (1901–81).

We may note that mostly these structuralists were indebted to Marx. While such a stream of thought may be healthy in that it involves a critique of assumptions not otherwise questioned, the collapse of Eastern European Marxism and with it much of the fabric of European Communist parties is bound to have an effect in diminishing the appeal of Marxian thought. Moreover, Freudianism, whose evidence is overwhelmingly drawn from Western society, is under question when it is thought about from the perspective of alternative psychologies (and family relations) in other societies beyond the West.

But the questioning of intellectual categories in these writers is helpful, in that it would be somewhat optimistic to think of the patterns of Western universities and subject distinctions as set in stone.

On the other hand, we may note the irony of Althusser's distinction between ideology and science. It reminds one of the line drawn by early Christianity between its own stories (true) and those of others (myths). 'Ideology' now can play a similar role to the old 'myth'. But as we shall see, the recognition that one's own point of view is to be challenged by others creates hermeneutical and theoretical problems of some magnitude, which are dealt with in one way or another by some of the figures we now turn to.

We have already looked at Jürgen Habermas. He attempts to deal with the problem of relativism by looking to the notion that genuine human discourse aims at the ideal of unrestricted communication. This is habitually distorted by ideology, that is, by the systematic distortion of communication by force. If we have a critical comprehension of cultural tradition it will help to reveal the systematic distortions and ideological clouding which stop social groups from attaining their emancipatory aims. Habermas postulates an ideal speech situation which would involve a free and equal exchange between social actors. He thinks that all this needs supplementing by a psychoanalytic criticism of the means by which we repress the knowledge of social strategies of power, such as censorship. All this critical theory should bring about freedom from a dogmatic past. Knowledge becomes emancipatory, so that the social sciences themselves become emancipatory and critical. For Habermas, however, the human subject is central: in this he is unlike some other Marxists in being genuinely a humanist.

Often the French structuralists have had a more noted effect on literature than philosophy in the English-speaking world, notably Roland Barthes and Jacques Lacan. They have been ineluctably Western in approach. It would seem however, that testing theories against the history of alternative societies would be wise.

Another strand of modern thinking in Europe has been phenomenological, via Martin Heidegger. We have touched on some of this history already. Two important figures are those of Paul Ricoeur (1913–2005) and Jacques Derrida (1930–2004), a student of Ricoeur's.

Ricoeur has made major contributions to hermeneutics, but starting from phenomenology. This he sees as 'the art of deciphering indirect meaning'. He is consequently greatly interested in the interpretation of myths and symbols, for which reason he worked for a number of years at the University of Chicago in parallel with Mircea Eliade. With Marx he believes in false consciousness, and this is why the hermeneutics of suspicion is important in trying to unmask what is false. In all this, as having a critical method of interpretation, Ricoeur wishes to proceed to something positive. This emerges as an eschatology of the sacred. This cuts the self down to size, ridding it of the illusion that it can exist in self-sufficiency.

Derrida is a more radical figure. He applies his deconstructive method to his hero Heidegger. He absorbed Heidegger's project in *Being and Time* to overcome what he saw as the ontotheological bias of Western philosophy. But Derrida saw in Heidegger nevertheless a nostalgia for Being. This criticism linked up with his attack on what he called logocentrism. This is the notion that all the terms relating to ultimates in Western metaphysics designate a presence, but that this is a kind of illusion. In another sense of logocentrism (not at all Derrida's) he is logocentric, since he argues that there is no *hors texte*. All signifiers are metaphors for what is signified, since the signified becomes a signifier itself. So everything exists as it were within a magic circle of language.

Another thesis of Derrida's is that the West prizes spoken language over written – this is phonocentrism. He refers especially to Plato. He has also introduced various neologisms, perhaps the most important of which are *différance* and *alterity*. The former word rests on a near-pun: it means both difference (for each sign differs from each other) and deferment, because the presence is always deferred: it is a kind of eschatological postulate. There are problems no doubt here, since there is no need for us to accept Derrida's analysis of logocentrism as involving presence. Alterity is a kind of otherness of play. It is engaged with desire, for every text in the very incompleteness of its meaning exhibits desire for its completion.

It is hard to see how Derrida provides much of a framework for discovering new things. He seems to involve the end of philosophizing. The ultimate victory of language over thought is that philosophy becomes enthralled with what cannot break out of its own linguistic circle to reality. In general, Derrida has had more influence in literary analysis in the English-speaking world than he has in philosophy itself.

In general, one may say that Marx, Freud and to some degree Nietzsche have had a great effect on continental European philosophers. Anglo-Saxon philosophers have paid less attention to these figures, partly because the empiricist mentality has tended to question the viability of Freudian and Marxist theories. Less attention has also been paid perhaps to the philosophy of the social sciences in Britain and America than has been the case on mainland Europe. The technical bent of analytic philosophy has leaned towards logic, mathematics and the 'hard sciences'.

NOTES ON RECENT ISSUES IN NORTH AMERICAN AND BRITISH PHILOSOPHY

The dominant motif in Anglo-Saxon philosophy has been a blend and a debate between different strands of the congeries of linguistic philosophy, analytic philosophy, empiricism and scientism. The fashionable worldview has been a version of scientific humanism.

Not surprisingly a large part of the effort of English-speaking philosophy has been tied in to the philosophy of science. The initial post-war dominant views were variants of empiricism and positivism, together with Popper's maverick theory which emphasized the use of the hypothetico-deductive method and the central importance of falsifiability. Something of a revolution in thinking was effected by Thomas S. Kuhn's 1970 book *The Structure of Scientific Revolutions*. He argued that theories and facts have a more ambiguous relationship than had previously been supposed. They occur within broad theoretical frameworks or paradigms. This situation helps, among other things, to determine what counts as evidence and confirmation or their opposites. They are incommensurable gestalt-like ways of looking at the world. In some degree Kuhn's picture is like that of Foucault in his notion of the archeology of knowledge. Kuhn's observations stimulated a rethink on the objectivity of science and seemed to introduce relativism into the fabric of science. Could we go on any more talking of the progress of science? Kuhn's position has been criticized from different directions, partly on historical grounds (was the Newtonian 'revolution' that sudden and cataclysmic?) and partly on analytic grounds (for the notion of a paradigm is difficult to define and flesh out). But his position helped to open the way to more anarchistic views of knowledge and science. It also encouraged deeper studies in the sociology of science. All this, however, seems to reinforce a Popperian insistence on the necessity of a continuing critical attitude in science, fostered hopefully by its institutional framework and the need for the use of the imagination in framing new hypotheses. But the notion that science makes progress seems ineluctable.

These issues are linked to issues about subjectivity of another sort. Ever since Descartes and beyond there has in the West been a quest in epistemology for a good way of proceeding from conscious states to a real outer world. Similar questions arise about realism in science. If hypotheses and theories are creations of the human imagination, it leads us to suppose that there is not a one–one correlation between theoretical concepts such as *electron* and what lies 'out there'. Such concepts come trailing clouds of theory. It is too simple to suppose that theories are mirrors of nature 'out there'. All this inhibits an easy foundationalism, namely a theory of knowledge which exhibits foundational beliefs which are certain and evident. For the relation between human perception and reality out there will be a complex and hazardous one. Indeed, as Richard Rorty (1931–2007) has argued in *Philosophy and the Mirror of Nature* (1979), the metaphor of 'mirroring' nature is open to many objections. He has taken up pragmatism as a mode of resolving the problems created by the issue of realism. But his wide critique of classical epistemology and much of what passes for philosophical activity has led him into seeing the philosopher's task as a fruitful conversation with other disciplines, notably literature.

Meanwhile there remains a vigorous activity in analytic and technical philosophy, making use of logic and the analysis of concepts to try to resolve old problems. The central one, partly because it relates to so many epistemological issues, is the question of the relation of mind and body. A powerful lobby is seen in modern materialism which identifies mental goings-on with brain processes. The issues here can be presented in a logical manner, as turning on such issues as to whether there are contingent identity statements (for materialism, to be an empirical hypothesis, would claim that the identification referred to above is a contingent one). A main basis for the claim is evolutionary theory, although that is compatible with an intermediate position, namely that there are emergent (mental) characteristics arising out of the complexity of material arrangements. Debates about mind–body relationships abut on the development of artificial intelligence, arising chiefly from the evolution of computers.

Various strands of thinking in relation to ethics and politics can be discerned. Important was *A Theory of Justice* (1971), by John Rawls (1921–2002), concerned with answering the question as to what rules humankind would contract to obey if they were to establish a social order in conditions where none of them could take advantage of their fellows. But while his general theory has plausibility, a particular, and according to critics, unnecessary aspect of it was to the effect that the least well off in a given society should have a maximum minimum. Rawls and others have encouraged a general impulse towards applied ethics, in which philosophers embark on the substantive task of sketching ethical approaches in such areas as business, medicine, animal rights and so forth. This is a turn away from the predominant analytic, conceptual and supposedly neutral approach of much of the tradition.

Some of the work of modern philosophers in moving towards relativism, hermeneutics and deconstruction ought to have been more keenly aware of the culture-bound character of many of the vital major concepts and assumptions brought to bear in Western culture. On the other hand, it is clear that despite prejudices and narrowness, Western philosophy is still dynamic. In general, the history of the last three hundred years – from the early eighteenth century say – has been tremendously fecund. No other culture has produced the variegation represented by Hume, Kant, Hegel, Marx, Kierkegaard, Freud, Nietzsche, Russell, Wittgenstein, Sartre, James and Peirce. Nevertheless, there are some traditional tasks of philosophy which remain to be resumed, and I hope to sketch some of these in the following reflections on the relation between the West and other philosophical traditions.

As I have said before, a dominant motif in Anglo-Saxon philosophy is a kind of scientism, while European philosophy on the Continent has been much soaked in Marxist presuppositions. Both traditions tend to be skeptical of religion, but it appears to me that all worldviews, including these too are to some extent fragile. At any rate it is good to take seriously some of the questions posed by other cultures. To this I now turn.

REFLECTIONS ON THE RELATIONS OF PHILOSOPHIES: SOME CONCEPTUAL ISSUES

I shall begin with some more particular conceptual issues which are raised by non-Western philosophies. I am assuming here that we are entering a period of global debate in which the varying streams will feed one another.

First, and very importantly, to my mind, we need to take seriously the facts of comparative psychology. Thus, and notoriously, it is difficult to translate some of the major pieces of terminology in the analysis of the human inner world. Startling, for instance, is the Buddhist account of persons as constituted by the *skandhas* – bodily events, sensations, feelings, dispositions and conscious states. This is very different from the scheme deployed by Plato or by modern Western commonsense psychology. Another diverse scheme is that of Sānkhya. It seems to me that these divergent pictures are ground for radical criticism of some of the counters often used in the West, such as the will, or reason. Admittedly linguistic philosophy gave these a skeptical going-over, especially in Ryle's *The Concept of Mind*. But the existence of alternatives also raises doubts about the project of philosophical phenomenology. It may be noted that all the social sciences may be under a similar skeptical threat in so far as it is not merely in psychology that other cultures' human classifications are very different. We might ask, in the case of Marxist analysis, whether the Western account of class struggle is a necessary one, or whether it is secretly influenced by the old tripartite classification in Indo-European cultures.

Second, Indian epistemology contains some ideas which could be of deeper interest to Western philosophers. One is the question of how perception works and whether the subject plays a more active role than has often been assumed in the West. There is also the problem of the limits of perception: Indian notions on the perception of absence and of non-sense-bound perception (yogic perception, religious experience) are interesting. Again, Indian ideas of verbal communication as a source of knowledge might reinforce investigations into the social nature of knowledge.

Third, the Buddhist ontology should be examined more seriously in today's world, since it presents a view which is not only in accord with modern science but it also much less muddy than the parallel attempt by Whitehead to create a process-oriented metaphysics.

While rebirth theory is pervasive in India and countries deeply affected by Buddhism, there is a question as to the compatibility of the belief with evolutionary biology and with that modern genetics. Still, there are interesting issues to explore: whether a 'metaphysical' rebirth theory is possible; and whether a Vaihinger-type rebirth belief (a kind of model) would not greatly refresh and illuminate ethics. On the more general front of the philosophy of religion, it is obvious that the diversity of models to be found in non-Western countries would greatly enrich the material to be dealt with. Some Indian and Chinese philosophies (for instance Rāmānuja's qualified non-dualism and Huayen) would help in explicating alternative philosophical and religious cosmologies.

There are also some novel relations which can be sketched between the notion of the noumenal and Buddhist emptiness. Buddhist linguistics has much to offer in modern reflections, perhaps in part because it is less immediately concerned with deceptive problems of interpretation. Another area for rethinking is in concepts of nature, which have a divergent development in India, China and the West, not to mention in small-scale societies.

On the front of ethics, the attitudes of other traditions are illuminatingly different. The four *brahmavihāras* or great virtues in Buddhism paint a very different picture from typical Western ones, whether religious or not. Again, the Chinese concept of *li* can be seen anew from the perspective of performatives. Reflection on the cult of ancestors, from China and Japan to Africa, may enlarge our discussion of the composition of societies. Do societies actually include their pasts? And if so, how? Do we have obligations to our predecessors as well as to our descendants? The answers to these questions have relevance both to sociology and political theory, as well as to the scope of utilitarianism. Similarly with non-Western views of animals and other living beings: they alter the calculus of maximized happiness and minimized suffering.

REFLECTIONS ON PHILOSOPHIES IN THE WORLD ORDER

Above all during the modern period we have noted how greatly questions of identity and tradition have loomed, in the face of largely Western colonialism and domination. It is not fashionable for modern philosophy to conceive itself in the business of supplying a worldview which will help to integrate knowledge and identity. Nevertheless, we are surely arriving at an epoch in world history in which a theory of how to live together needs to be articulated. There are conflicting points of view, and contradictions perhaps in this task. They need to be overcome. I believe that certain desiderata are to be realized.

First, we need to have a myth to guide us, and these being modern times, such a myth becomes history. World history should not only tell the human story in a whole and comprehensive way (hitherto it has tended to be partial in at least two senses). It should also illuminate our ancestors in ways that will allow people of differing cultures to share meaningfully in each other's pasts.

Second, we need to avoid a homogenized globe. Differences should be preserved. This is so for two reasons, one cultural and the other intellectual. Differing peoples are aware of their pasts and feel somewhat at home in them. We should not, even if we could, bulldoze cultures in the service of some global goal. And just as important, variety will itself preserve the means of cross-cultural criticism and evaluation – keeping the global world open (as in the sense of the Open Society).

Third, we need to have an intellectual theory which will give differing parts of a global civilization a meaningful role together in contributing to the whole. This cannot be imposed from above, but must well up from dialogue. In this connection, conflicts between worldviews must be dealt with. It is often religions that pose the sharpest problems, in so far as they depend on contradictory revelations. This makes the philosophy of religion – or more generally the philosophy of worldviews – vital in the process of continuing cross-worldview arguments.

Fourth, where there are single-globe issues, such as those arising in the planetary environment, and those which concern global resources and their equitable distribution, it is necessary to evolve a world ethic, which might be created out of a synthesis of ideas from differing cultures – African, Chinese, Indian, Buddhist, Islamic and so forth. Already we are beginning to see a consensus developing on human rights, though these are approached from differing angles in the major traditions.

Fifth, we could really begin to evolve a world vocabulary, drawing on differing philosophical and cultural traditions, for use in the social sciences. At the moment the terminology is much too Western and so faces the danger of being culture-bound.

Sixth, by drawing on differing great segments of human cultural creations we are likely in general to become more self-critical, and sensitive to other points of view. I consider that cross-cultural exploration is itself a highly fruitful ingredient, for many different purposes, in education. But there are forces which resist it: nationalism; narrow and frightened religious perceptions; ideological arrogance; and the exclusions created by institutionalized subject-disciplines.

From all these angles, it seems desirable that we should know more about the variety of cultures: this book in essence is meant as a small contribution to cross-cultural knowledge in one of the most vital fields of human activity, namely the construction and defense of worldviews.

BIBLIOGRAPHY

1. THE HISTORY OF THE WORLD AND OUR PHILOSOPHICAL INHERITANCE

Audi, Robert, ed. *The Cambridge Dictionary of Philosophy*. Cambridge, UK: Cambridge University Press, 1995.

Bartley, Christopher. *Indian Philosophy A–Z*. New York: Palgrave Macmillan, 2005.

Becker, Lawrence C., ed. *A History of Western Ethics: Survey Articles from the Encyclopedia of Ethics*. New York: Garland Publishing, 1992.

Blaauw, Martin and Duncan Pritchard. *Epistemology A–Z*. Edinburgh: Edinburgh University Press, 2005

Blackburn, Simon. *The Oxford Dictionary of Philosophy*. New York: Oxford University Press, 1994.

Borchert, Donald M. *The Encyclopedia of Philosophy: Supplement*. New York: Macmillan Reference USA, 1996.

Borchert, Donald, ed., *Encyclopedia of Philosophy* 2nd edn, Vol.8. Detroit, MI: Macmillan Reference, 2006.

Bunnin, Nicholas and E.P. Tsui-James, eds. *The Blackwell Companion to Philosophy*. Malden, MA: Blackwell, 1995.

Carr, Brian and Indira Mahalingam eds. *Companion Encyclopedia of Asian Philosophy*. New York: Routledge, 1997.

Collins, John J., ed. *The Encyclopedia of Apocalypticism*, Vol. 1: *The Origins of Apocalypticism in Judaism and Christianity*. New York: Continuum, 2000.

Collins, Randall. *The Sociology of Philosophies: A Global Theory of Intellectual Change*. Cambridge, MA: Belknap Press of Harvard University Press, 1998.

Cooper, David E., ed. *A Companion to Aesthetics*. Malden, MA: Blackwell, 1993.

Cooper, David Edward. *World Philosophies: An Historical Introduction*. Cambridge, MA: Blackwell, 1996.

Copleston, Frederick C. *A History of Philosophy*. Westminster, MD: Newman Press, 1946–53 (Vols. 1–3); 1959–60 (Vols. 4–6); 1963–74 (Vols. 7–9). 9 Vols published in 3 Vols: Garden City, NY: Image Books/Doubleday & Company, 1985.

Copleston, Frederick C. *Philosophies and Cultures*. New York: Oxford University Press, 1980.

Cottingham, John. *Western Philosophy: An Anthology*. Oxford, UK: Blackwell, 1996.

Craig, Edward, ed. *Routledge Encyclopedia of Philosophy*. New York: Routledge, 1998.

Dancy, Jonathan and Ernest Sosa , eds. *A Companion to Epistemology*. Malden, MA: Blackwell, 1994.

Deutsch, Eliot, ed. *Culture and Modernity: East–West Philosophic Perspectives*. Honolulu, HI: University of Hawaii Press, 1991.

Deutsch, Eliot and Ron Bontekoe, eds. *A Companion to World Philosophies*. Malden, MA: Blackwell, 1997.

Edwards, Paul. *The Encyclopedia of Philosophy*. 8 Vols/4 Vols. New York: Macmillan, 1972 (1967).

Eliade, Mircea, ed. *The Encyclopedia of Religion*, 16 Vols. New York: Macmillan, 1987.

Ellwood, Robert S., ed. *The Best in the Literature of Philosophy and World Religions. The Reader's Adviser,* Vol. 4. New Providence, NJ: R.R. Bowker, 1994, 14th edn.

George, Alexander ed. *What would Socrates say?* New York: Random House, 2007.

Goodin, Robert E. and Philip Pettit, ed. *A Companion to Contemporary Political Philosophy*. Malden, MA: Blackwell, 1995.

Grimes, John. *A Concise Dictionary of Indian Philosophy*. Albany, NY: State University of New York Press, revised edn, 1996.

Guttenplan, Samuel, ed. *A Companion to the Philosophy of Mind*. Malden, MA: Blackwell, 1995.

Hale, Robert and Crispin Wright, ed. *A Companion to the Philosophy of Language*. Malden, MA: Blackwell, 1997.

Honderich, Ted, ed. *The Oxford Companion to Philosophy*. New York: Oxford University Press, 1995.

Hutchinson, John A. *Living Options in World Philosophy*. Honolulu, HI: University of Hawaii Press, 1977.

Kenny, Anthony. *Philosophy in the Modern World: A New History of Western Philosophy*. Oxford, UK: Oxford University Press.

Kim, Jaegwon and Ernest Sosa, ed. *A Companion to Metaphysics*. Malden, MA: Blackwell, 1995.

Lacey, A.R. *A Dictionary of Philosophy*. 3rd edn. London: Routledge, 1996.

Lamarque, P., ed. *Concise Encyclopedia of Philosophy Language*. New York: Elsevier Science, 1997.

Leaman, Oliver. *Key Concepts in Eastern Philosophy*. London: Routledge, 1999.

Leaman, Oliver, ed. *Encyclopedia of Asian Philosophy*. London: Routledge, 2001.

Machamer, Peter and Michael Silberstein, eds. *The Blackwell Guide to the Philosophy of Science*. Malden, MA: Blackwell, 2002.

Malachowski, Alan, ed. *A Companion to Logic*. Malden, MA: Blackwell, 1996.

Mautner, Thomas. *A Dictionary of Philosophy*. Cambridge, MA: Blackwell, 1996.

McEvilley, Thomas. *The Shape of Ancient Thought: Comparative Studies in Greek and Indian Philosophies*. New York: Allworth Press, 2002.

McGinn, Bernard, ed. *The Encyclopedia of Apocalypticism*, Vol. 2: *Apocalypticism in Western History and Culture*. New York: Continuum, 2000.

Newton-Smith, W.H., ed. *A Companion to the Philosophy of Science*. Malden, MA: Blackwell, 2001 edn.

Parkinson, G.H.R., ed. *An Encyclopedia of Philosophy*. London: Routledge, 1988.

Pike, Jon. *Political Philosophy A–Z*. Edinburgh: Edinburgh University Press, 2007.

Plott, John C. *Global History of Philosophy, 5 Vols.* Delhi: Motilal Banarsidass, 1977–89.

Popkin, Richard. *The History of Scepticism: From Savonarola to Bayle.* New York: Oxford University Press, 2003 edn.

Quinn, Philip L. and Charles Taliafesso, eds. *A Companion to the Philosophy of Religion.* Malden, MA: Blackwell, 1997.

Rakova, Marina. *Philosophy of Mind A–Z.* Edinburgh: Edinburgh University Press, 2006.

Scharfstein, Ben-Ami, ed. *Philosophy East/Philosophy West: A Critical Comparison of Indian, Chinese, Islamic and European Philosophy.* Oxford, UK: Oxford University Press, 1978.

Schumacher, Stephan and Gert Woerner, eds. *The Encyclopedia of Eastern Philosophy and Religion.* Boston, MA: Shambhala, 1989.

Singer, Peter, ed. *A Companion to Ethics.* Cambridge, MA: Blackwell, 1993.

Smart, Ninian. *The World's Religions: Old Traditions and Modern Transformations.* Cambridge, UK: Cambridge University Press, 1989.

Solomon, Robert C. and Kathleen Higgins, eds. *From Africa to Zen: Essays in World Philosophy.* Lanham, MD: Rowman & Littlefield, 1993; 2nd edn. 2003.

Stein, Stephen J., ed. *The Encyclopedia of Apocalypticism,* Stephen J. Stein, ed., Vol. 3: *Apocalypticism in the Modern Period and the Contemporary Age.* New York: Continuum, 2000.

Tierney, Helen, ed. *History, Philosophy and Religion. Women's Studies Encyclopedia,* Vol. 3. Westport, CT: Greenwood Publishing Group, 1991.

Turner, Bryan S., ed. *The Blackwell Companion to Social Theory.* Malden, MA: Blackwell, 1996.

Zeyl, Donald J., ed. *Encyclopedia of Classical Philosophy.* Westport, CT: Greenwood Press, 1997.

Ziman, John. *Real Science: What it is, and what it means.* Cambridge, UK: Cambridge University Press, 2000.

2. SOUTH ASIAN PHILOSOPHIES

Anacker, Stefen. *Seven Works of Vasubandhu: The Buddhist Psychological Doctor.* Delhi: Motilal Banarsidass, 1984.

Apte, V.M., trans. *Brahma-sūtra Shānkara-bhāshya: Bādarāyaṇa's Brahma-sūtras with Shankarāchāryā's Commentary.* Bombay, India: Popular Book Depot, 1960.

Atharva-veda. See: Whitney, W.D.

Bādarāyaṇa *Brahma-sūtra. See:* Apte, V.M.; Radhakrishnan, S., 1961.

Bartley, Christopher J. *The Theology of Ramanuja.* London. Routledge Curzon, 2002.

Bartley, Christopher J. *Indian Philosophy: A–Z.* Edinburgh: Edinburgh University Press, 2005

Barz, Richard Keith. *The Bhakti Sect of Vallabhacarya.* Faridabad (India): Thomson Press, 1976.

Basham, A.L. *History and Doctrines of the Ajivikas: A Vanished Indian Religion.* London: Luzac, 1951.

Basham, A.L. *The Wonder That Was India: A Survey of the Culture of the Indian Sub-Continent Before the Coming of the Muslims.* New York: Grove Press, 1954.

Basham, A.L. *A Cultural History of India.* Oxford, UK: Clarendon Press, 1975.

Bhagavad-gītā. See: Zaehner, R.C., 1973; Edgerton, F., 1944; Buitenen, J.A.B.van.

Bhaktivedanta, A.C., Swami Prabhupada. *Sri caritāmṛta of Kṛṣṇadāsa Kavirāja Gosvāmi,* 17 Vols. Los Angeles, CA: Bhaktivedanta Book Trust, 1973–75.

Bhandarkar, R.G. *Vaiṣṇavism, Śaivism and Minor Religious Systems.* Reprint. Varanasi (India): Indological Book House, 1965.

Bhattacharyya H., ed. *The Cultural Heritage of India,* 4 Vols. Calcutta, India: Ramakrishna Mission Institute of Culture, 1957–62.

Bist, Umrao Singh. *Jaina Theories of Reality and Knowledge.* Delhi: Eastern BookLinkers, 1984.

Blumenthal, James. *The Ornament of the Middle Way: A Study of the Madhyamaka Thought of Śantaraksita.* Ithaca, NY: Snow Lion, 2004.

Bodhi, Bhikkhu. *The Connected Discourses of the Buddha: A Translation of the Samyutta Nikāya.* Boston, MA: Wisdom Publications, 2000.

Bowes, Pratima. *The Hindu Religious Tradition: A Philosophical Approach.* London: Routledge & Kegan Paul, 1977.

Brahma-sūtra. (Vedānta-sūtrās.) See: Apte, V.M.; Radhakrishnan, S., 1961.

Brown, Norman. *Man in the Universe: Some Cultural Continuities in Indian Thought.* Berkeley, CA: University of California Press, 1970.

Buddhaghosa (Bhikkhu Nyanamoli, trans.). *The Path of Purification: Visuddhimagga.* Berkeley, CA: Shambhala, 1976.

van Buitenen, J.A.B. *Ramanuja's Vedarthasamgraha.* Poona, India: Deccan College Postgraduate and Research Institute, 1956.

van Buitenen, J.A.B., trans. *The Bhagavadgītā in the Mahābhārata.* Chicago, IL: University of Chicago Press, 1981.

Buswell, Jr., Robert E. and Robert M. Gimello, eds. *Paths to Liberation: The Mārga and Its Transformations in Buddhist Thought.* Honolulu, HI: University of Hawaii Press, 1992.

Caitanya, Śri. *See:* Bhaktivedanta, A.C.

Candrakirti (Karen C. Lang, trans.). *Four Illusions: Candrakirti's Advice to Travelers on the Bodhisattva Path.* Oxford, UK: Oxford University Press, 2003.

Carman, John B. *The Theology of Rāmānuja: An Essay in Interreligious Understanding.* New Haven, CT: Yale University Press, 1974.

Carman, John and Vasudha Narayanan. *The Tamil Veda: Pillan's Interpretation of the Tiruvaymoli.* Chicago, IL: University of Chicago Press, 1989.

Carpenter, J. Estlin. *Theism in Medieval India.* London: Constable, 1921.

Carr, Brian and Indira Mahalingam, eds. *Companion Encyclopedia of Asian Philosophy.* New York: Routledge, 1997.

Chandrakirti (Padmakara Translation Group, trans.). *Introduction to the Middle Way: Chandrakirti's Madhyamakavatara.* Boston, MA: Shambhala, 2002.

Chapple, Christopher and Yogi Anand Viraj, trans. *The Yoga Sūtras of Patañjali* With analysis of the Sanskrit. Delhi: Sri Satguru Publications, 1990.

Chari, S.M.S. *Vaisnavism.* Delhi: Motilal Banarsidass, 2000.

Chattopadhyaya, Debiprasad. *Cārvāka/Lokāyata.* New Delhi: Indian Council of Philosophical Research, 1990.

Chennakesavan, Sarasvati. *Concept of Mind in Indian Philosophy.* Delhi: Motilal Banarsidass, 1980.

Collins, Steven. *Selfless Persons: Imagery and Thought in Theravāda Buddhism.* Cambridge, UK: Cambridge University Press, 1982.

Conze, Edward. *Buddhism: Its Essence and Development.* New York: Harper Torchbooks, 1959.

Conze, Edward. *The Prajñāpāramitā Literature.* The Hague: Mouton, 1960.

Conze, Edward. *Buddhist Thought in India.* Ann Arbor, MI: University of Michigan Press, 1967.

Conze, Edward. *The Short Prajñāpāramitā Texts.* London: Luzac, 1974.

Conze, Edward, trans. and ed. *The Large Sutra on Perfect Wisdom.* With the divisions of the *Abhisamayālākāra.* Berkeley, CA: University of California Press, 1975.

Coward, Howard G. and Raja, K. Kunjunni, eds. *The Philosophy of Indian Grammarians. Encyclopedia of Indian Philosophies,* Vol. V. Princeton, NJ: Princeton University Press, 1990.

Dasgupta, Surendranath. *A History of Indian Philosophy,* 5 Vols. Cambridge, UK: CambridgeUniversity Press, 1922–55.

Dasgupta, Surendranath. *Yoga as Philosophy and Religion.* New York: E.P. Dutton, 1924. Delhi: Motilal Banarsidass, (Reprint) 1973.

Dasgupta, Surendranath. *Yoga Philosophy in Relation to Other Systems of Indian Thought.* Calcutta, India: 1930. Delhi: Motilal Banarsidass, (Reprint) 1974.

Datta, Dhirendra Mohan. *Six Ways of Knowing: A Critical Study of the Vedanta Theory of Knowledge.* London: George Allen & Unwin, 1932.

Dayal, Har. *The Bodhisattva Doctrine in Buddhist Sanskrit Literature.* London: Kegan Paul, 1932. Delhi: Motilal Banarsidass, (Reprint) 1975.

De, Sushil Kumar. *Early History of the VaiṣṇavaFaith and Movement in Bengal.* 2nd edn. Calcutta, India: Firma K.L. Mukhopadhyay, 1961.

Deussen, Paul (Charles Johnston, trans.). *The System of the Vedānta.* Chicago, IL: Open Court, 1912.

Deussen, Paul, ed. (V.M. Bedekar and G.B. Palsule, trans.). *Sixty Upaniṣads of the Veda,* 2 Vols. Delhi: Motilal Banarsidass, 1980.

Deutsch, Eliot. *Advaita Vedānta: A Philosophical Reconstruction.* Honolulu, HI: University of Hawaii Press, 1969.

Deutsch, Eliot and J.A.B. van Buitenen. *A Source Book in Advaita Vedānta.* Honolulu, HI: University of Hawaii Press, 1971.

Dhavamony, Mariasusai. *Love of God According to Saiva Siddhānta: A Study in the Mysticism and Theology of Saivism.* Oxford, UK: Clarendon Press, 1971.

Dīgha Nikāya (Long Discourses of the Buddha). See: Walshe, M.

Dumont, Louis. (Mark Sainsbury, Louis Dumont and Basia Gulati, trans.). *Homo Hierarchicus: The Caste System and Its Implications.* Chicago, IL: Chicago University Press, revised edn, 1980,

Dutt, Sukumar. *The Buddha and Five After-Centuries.* London: Luzac, 1957.

Dyczkowski, Mark S.G. *The Doctrine of Vibration: An Analysis of the Doctrines and Practices of Kashmir Shaivism.* Albany, NY: State University of New York Press, 1987.

Dyczkowski, Mark S.G., trans. *The Stanzas on Vibration.* Albany, NY: State University of New York Press, 1992.

Eckel, Malcolm David. *Buddhism: Origins, Beliefs, Practices, Holy Texts, Sacred Places.* New York: Oxford University Press, 2002.

Edgerton, Franklin, trans. *The Bhagavad Gītā,* 2 Vols. Harvard Oriental Series vols. 38–39. Cambridge, MA: Harvard University Press, 1944.

Edgerton, Franklin, trans. *The Beginnings of Indian Philosophy: Selections from the Rig Veda, Atharva Veda, Upanisads, and Mahabharata.* Cambridge, MA: Harvard University Press, 1965.

Eliade, Mircea (Willard R. Trask, trans.). *Yoga: Immortality and Freedom.* Bollingen Series LVI. Princeton, NJ: Princeton University Press, 2nd edn, 1969.

Evans-Wentz, W.Y. *Tibetan Yoga and Secret Doctrines.* London: Oxford University Press, 1958, 2nd edn.

Feuerstein, Georg. *The Yoga-Sūtra of Patañjali: A New Translation and Commentary.* Rochester,VT: Inner Traditions International, 1989.

Frauwallner, Erich. *Geschichte der indischen Philosophie,* 2 Vols. Salzburg, Austria: Otto Muller, 1953, 1956.

Frauwallner, Erich (V.M. Bedekar, trans.). *History of Indian Philosophy*, 2 vols. Delhi: Motilal Banarsidass, 1973.

Ganeri, Jonardon. *Semantic Powers: Meaning and the Means of Knowing in Classical Indian Philosophy*. Oxford, UK: Clarendon Press, 1999.

Ganeri, Jonardon. *Philosophy in Classical India*. London: Routledge, 2001.

Ganeri, Jonardon. *Artha: Meaning*. New Delhi: Oxford University Press, 2006.

Ganeri, Jonardon. *The Concealed Art of the Soul: Theories of the Self and Practices of Truth in Indian Ethics and Epistemology*. New York: Oxford University Press, 2007.

Ganeri, Jonardon, ed. *The Collected Essays of Bimal Krishna Matilal: Mind, Language and World*. New Delhi: Oxford University Press, 2002.

Ganeri, Jonardon, ed. *Indian Logic: A Reader*. London: Curzon Press, 2001.

Ganeri, Jonardon, ed. *The Collected Essays of Bimal Krishna Matilal: Ethics and Epics*. New Delhi: Oxford University Press, 2002.

Gaṅgeśa (Stephen H. Phillips and N.S. Ramanuja Tatacharya, translit. and trans.). *Epistemology of Perception – Gaṅgeśa's Tattvacintāmani: Jewel of Reflection on the Truth (about Epistemology), The Perception chapter (pratyaksa-khanda)*. New York: American Institute of Buddhist Studies (with Columbia University's Center for Buddhist Studies and Tibet House US), 2004.

Gautama. *Nyāya-sūtra. See:* Jha, G., 1912–19.

Gethin, Rupert. *The Foundations of Buddhism*. Oxford, UK: Oxford University Press, 1998.

Gethin, Rupert. *The Buddhist Path to Awakening: A Study of the Bodhi-Pakkhiya Dhamma*. Oxford, UK: Oneworld, 2nd edn, 2001.

Glasenapp, Helmuth von (Shridhar B. Shrothri, trans. and K.T. Pandurangi, ed.). *Madhva's Philosophy of the Visnu Faith*. Bangalore, India: Dvaita Vedanta Studies and Research Foundation, 1992.

Gnoli, Raniero, trans. *Essenza dei Tantra (Tantrasāra)*. Turin, Italy: Boringhieri, 1960.

Gnoli, Raniero, trans. *Luce delle Sacre Scritture (Tantrāloka)*. Turin, Italy: Unione tipografico-editrice torinese, 1972.

Gombrich, Richard. *Theravada Buddhism: A Social History from Ancient Benares to Modern Colombo*. London: Routledge, 1988.

Gonda, Jan. *Die Religionen Indiens*, Vol. 1. *Veda und älterer Hinduismus*, Vol. 2. *Der jüngere Hinduismus*. Stuttgart, Germany: Kohlhammer, 1960–63.

Gonda, Jan. *Change and Continuity in Indian Religions*. The Hague: Mouton, 1965.

Gonda, Jan. *Visṇuism and Śivaism: A Comparison*. London: Athlone Press, 1970.

Gonda, Jan. *Vedic Literature (Samhitas and Brahmanas). A History of Indian Literature*, Vol. 1. Wiesbaden, Germany: Harrassowitz, 1975.

Goudriaan, Teun. *Māyā Divine and Human*. Delhi: Motilal Banarsidass, 1978.

Griffiths, Paul J. *On Being Mindless: Buddhist Meditation and the Mind–Body Problem*. LaSalle, IL: Open Court, 1986.

Guenther, Herbert V. *The Life and Teachings of Naropa*. Oxford, UK: Clarendon Press, 1963.

Guenther, Herbert V. *Philosophy and Psychology in the Abhidharma*. Berkeley, CA: Shambhala, 1976.

Gupta, S., D.J. Hoens and T. Goudriaan. *Hindu Tantrism*. Leiden, Netherlands: E.J. Brill, 1979.

Halbfass, Wilhelm. *Tradition and Reflection: Explorations in Indian Thought*. Albany, NY: State University of New York Press, 1991.

Halbfass, Wilhelm. *On Being and What There Is: Classical Vaiśeṣika and the History of Indian Ontology*. Albany, NY: State University of New York Press, 1992.

Hardy, Friedhelm. *Viraha-Bhakti: The Early History of Kṛṣṇa Devotion in South India*. Delhi: Oxford University Press, 1983.

Hardy, Friedhelm. *The Religious Culture of India: Power, Love, and Wisdom.* Cambridge, UK: Cambridge University Press, 1994.

Hariharānanda Shaṇkara, Swami (P.N. Mukerji, trans.). *Yoga Philosophy of Patañjali.* Albany, NY: State University of New York Press, 1983.

Harris, Ian. *Cambodian Buddhism: History and Practice.* Honolulu, HI: University of Hawaii Press, 2005.

Harvey, Peter. *An Introduction to Buddhist Ethics: Foundations, Values and Issues.* Cambridge, UK: Cambridge University Press, 2000.

Hirakawa, Arika (Paul Groner, trans. and ed.). *A History of Indian Buddhism: From Śākyamuni to Early Mahāyāna.* Honolulu, HI: University of Hawaii Press, 1990.

Hiriyanna, Mysore. *Outlines of Indian Philosophy.* London: George Allen & Unwin, 1932.

Holt, John Clifford, Jacob N. Kinnard and Jonathan S. Walters, eds. *Constituting Communities: Theravada Buddhism and the Religious Cultures of South and Southeast Asia.* Albany, NY: State University of New York Press, 2003.

Hume, Robert Ernest, trans. *The Thirteen Principal Upanishads.* Delhi: Oxford University Press, 2nd edn, 1983.

Indich, William M. *Consciousness in Advaita Vedānta.* Delhi: Motilal Banarsidass, 1980.

Isayeva, Natalia.*Īśvarakṛṣṇa and Indian Philosophy.* Albany, NY: State University of New York Press, 1993.

Jacobsen, Knut A. *Prakriti in Sāmkhya-Yoga: Material Principle, Religious Experience, Ethical Implications.* Delhi: Motilal Banarsidass, 2002.

Jaini, Jagomandar Lal (F.W. Thomas, ed.). *Outlines of Jainism.* Cambridge, UK: Cambridge University Press, 1916.

Jaini, Padmanabh S. *The Jaina Path of Purification.* Berkeley, CA: University of California Press, 1979.

Jayatilleke, K.N. *Early Buddhist Theory of Knowledge,* London: George Allen & Unwin, 1963.

Jayatilleke, K.N. *The Message of the Buddha.* New York: Free Press, 1974.

Jha, Ganganatha. *The Yogadarśana (Comprising the Sūtras of Patañjali with the Mīmāṃsā of Vyāsa).* Madras, India: Theosophical Publishing House, 1934, 2nd edn.

Jha, Ganganatha. *Prābhākara School of Pūrva Mīmāṃsā.* Allahabad: 1911. Delhi: Motilal Banarsidass, (Reprint) 1978.

Jha, Ganganatha, trans. *The Nyāya-sūtra of Gautama.* With the commentaries of Vātsyāyana and Uddyotakara, 4 Vols, 1912–19. Delhi: Motilal Banarsidass, (Reprint) 1984.

Johansson, Rune E.A. *The Psychology of Nirvana.* London: George Allen & Unwin, 1969. Johansson, Rune E.A. *The Dynamic Psychology of Early Buddhism.* Copenhagen: Scandinavian Institute of Asian Studies, 1979.

Kalupahana, David J. *Causality: The Central Philosophy of Buddhism.* Honolulu, HI: University of Hawaii Press, 1975.

Kalupahana, David J. *Buddhist Philosophy: A Historical Analysis.* Honolulu, HI: University of Hawaii Press, 1976.

Kalupahana, David J. *A History of Buddhist Psychology.* Honolulu, HI: University of Hawaii Press, 1992.

Keith, Arthur B. *Indian Logic and Atomism.* Oxford, UK: Clarendon Press, 1921.

Keith, Arthur B. *The Karma Mīmāṃsā.* Calcutta, India: Association Press, 1921.

Keith, Arthur B. The *Sāṃkhya System.* Calcutta, India: YMCA Publishing House, 2nd edn, 1949.

Keith, Arthur B. *The Religion and Philosophy of the Veda and Upanishads,* 2 Vols. Cambridge, MA: Harvard University Press, 1925. Reprint, Delhi: Motilal Banarsidass, 1976.

King, Richard. *Early Advaita Vedanta and Buddhism: The Mahayana Context of the Gaudapadiya-Karika*. Albany, NY: State University of New York Press, 1995.

Klostermaier, Klaus K. *A Survey of Hinduism*. Albany, NY: State University of New York Press, 1989.

Krom, N.J., ed. *The Life of Buddha on the Stupa of Barabudur, According to the Lalitavistara-Text*. Varanasi, India: Bhartiya Publ. House, 1974.

Kumar, Shiv and D.N. Bhargava, trans. *Yuktidīpikā,*. 2 Vols. Delhi: Eastern Book Linkers, 1992.

Lalitavistara. See: Poppe, N.; Krom, N.J.

Lamotte, Etienne (S. Webb-Boin, trans.). *History of Indian Buddhism*. Louvain, Belgium: Peeters Press, 1988.

Larson, Gerald J. *Classical Sāṃkhya: An Interpretation of Its History and Meaning*. Delhi: Motilal Banarsidass, 1979, 2nd revised edn.

Larson, Gerald J. and Ram Shankar Bhattacharya, eds. *Sāṃkhya: A Dualist Tradition in Indian Philosophy. Encyclopedia of Indian Philosophies,* Vol. IV. Delhi: Motilal Banarsidass, 1987.

Leggett, Trevor, trans. *The Complete Commentary by Śaṅkara on the Yoga Sūtras: A Full Translation of the Newly Discovered Text*. London: Kegan Paul, 1990.

Lester, Robert C. *Rāmānuja on the Yoga*. Madras, India: Adyar Library and Research Center, 1976.

Ling, Trevor. *The Buddha: Buddhist Civilization in India and Ceylon*. Baltimore, MD: Penguin, 1976.

Lorenzen, David N. 'The Life of Śaṅkarācārya. In Frank E. Reynolds and Donald Capps, eds., *The Biographical Process: Studies in the History and Psychology of Religion*. The Hague: Mouton, 1976.

Lott, Eric J. *God and the Universe in the Vedāntic Theology of Rāmānuja*. Madras, India: Ramanuja Research Society, 1976.

Macy, Joanna. *Mutual Causality in Buddhism and General Systems Theory: The Dharma of Natural Systems*. Albany, NY: State University of New York Press, 1991.

Mahadevan, T.M.P. *Vaiśeṣika A Study in Early Advaita*. Madras, India: University of Madras, 1952.

Majumdar, A.K. *Caitanya: His Life and Doctrine*. Bombay, India: Bharatiya Vidya Bhavan, 1969.

Makransky, John J. *Buddhahood Embodied: Sources of Controversy in India and Tibet*. Albany, NY: State University of New York Press, 1997.

Marcaurelle, Roger. *Freedom Through Inner Renunciation: Śankara's Philosophy in a New Light*. Albany, NY: State University of New York Press, 2000.

Marfatia, Mrudula I. *The Philosophy of Vallabhacarya*. Delhi: Munshiram Manharlal, 1967.

Matilal, Bimal Krishna. *The Navya-Nyāya Doctrine of Negation*. Cambridge, MA: Harvard University Press, 1968.

Matilal, Bimal Krishna. *Nyāya-Vaiśeṣika*. Wiesbaden, Germany: Otto Harrassowitz, 1977.

Matilal, Bimal Krishna. *Perception: An Essay on Classical Indian Theories of Knowledge*. Oxford, UK: Clarendon Press, 1986.

Matilal, B.K. and Robert D. Evans, eds. *Buddhist Logic and Epistemology: Studies in the Buddhist Analysis of Inference and Language*. Boston, MA: D. Reidel, 1986.

McDermott, Charlene, ed. *Comparative Philosophy: Selected Essays*. Lanham, MD: University Press of America, 1983.

Mohanty, J.N. *Upaniṣads Theory of Truth*. Delhi: Motilal Banarsidass, 1989.

Mohanty, J.N. (Purushottama Bilimoria, ed.). *Essays on Indian Philosophy, Traditional and Modern*. Delhi: Oxford University Press, 1993.

Moore, Charles A., ed. *The Indian Mind: Essentials of Indian Philosophy and Culture.* Honolulu, HI: University of Hawaii Press, 1967.

Muller-Ortega, Paul Eduardo. *The Triadic Heart of Śiva: Kaula Tantricism of Abhinavagupta in the Nondual Shaivism of Kashmir.* Albany, NY: State University of New York Press, 1989.

Murti, T.R.V. *The Central Philosophy of Buddhism: A Study of the Mādhyamika System.* London: George Allen & Unwin, 1960, 2nd edn.

Nāgārjuna (Jay L. Garfield, trans. and commentary). *The Fundamental Wisdom of the Middle Way: Nāgārjuna's Mūlamādhyamakakārikā.* New York: Oxford University Press, 1995.

Nakamura, Hajime. *Indian Buddhism: A Survey with Bibliographic Notes.* Delhi: Motilal Banarsidass, 1987.

Nyāya-sūtra. See: Jha, G., 1912–19.

O'Flaherty, Wendy Doniger, trans. *The Rig Veda: An Anthology.* Harmondsworth, UK: Penguin Books, 1981.

Olivelle, Patrick, trans. *Upaniṣads* New York: Oxford University Press, 1996.

Otto, Rudolf. *The Idea of the Holy: An Inquiry into the Non-Rational Factor in the Idea of the Divine and its Relation to the Rational.* New York: Oxford University Press, 1973.

Padoux, André. (Jacques Gontier, trans.). *Vāc: The Concept of the Word in Selected Hindu Tantras.* Albany, NY: State University of New York Press, 1990.

Pandey, Kanti Chandra. *Abhinavagupta: An Historical and Philosophical Study.* Varanasi, India: Chowkhamba Sanskrit Series Office, 2nd edn, 1963.

Panikkar, Raimundo, trans. *The Vedic Experience: Mantramañjarī.* Berkeley, CA: University of California Press, 1977.

Parekh, Manilal Chhotalal. *Sri Vallabhacharya: Life, Teachings and Movement.* Rajkot, India: Sri Bhagavata Dharma Mission, 2nd edn, 1943.

Patañjali. *Yoga-sūtra. See:* Chapple, C. and Yogi Anand Viraj; Feuerstein, G.; Hariharānanda Araṇya; Jha, G., 1934; Woods, J.H.

Poppe, Nicholas, trans. *The Twelve Deeds of Buddha: A Mongolian Version of the Lalitavistara.* Mongolian text [in transcription], Wiesbaden, Germany: Harrassowitz, 1967.

Potter, Karl H. *Presuppositions of India's Philosophies.* Englewood Cliffs, NJ: Prentice-Hall, 1963.

Potter, Karl H., ed. *Indian Metaphysics and Epistemology: The Tradition of Vaiśeṣika up to Gangeśa. Encyclopedia of Indian Philosophies.* Vol. II. Princeton, NJ: Princeton University Press, 1977.

Potter, Karl H., ed. *Advaita Vedānta up to Saṃkara and His Pupils. Encyclopedia of Indian Philosophies,* Vol. III. Princeton, NJ: Princeton University Press, 1981.

Potter, Karl H. *Bibliography. Encyclopedia of Indian Philosophies,* Vol. I. Princeton, NJ: Princeton University Press, revised edn, 1983.

Potter, Karl H. and Sibajiban Bhattacharyya, eds. *Nyāya- Vaiśeṣika from Gangeśa to Raghunātha Śiromaṇni. Encyclopedia of Indian Philosophies,* Vol. VI. Princeton, NJ: Princeton University Press, 1992.

Potter, Karl H. (with Robert E. Buswell, Jr., Padmanabh S. Jaini and Noble Ross Reat). *Abhidharma Buddhism to 150 AD. Encyclopedia of Indian Philosophies.* Vol. VII. Delhi: Motilal Banarsidass, 1996, 1st edn.

Radhakrishnan, Sarvepalli. *Indian Philosophy,* 2 Vols. London: George Allen & Unwin, 1948.

Radhakrishnan, Sarvepalli, trans. *The Principal Upaniṣads.* London: Allen & Unwin, 1953.

Radhakrishnan, Sarvepalli. *The Brahmasūtra.* London: Allen & Unwin, 1961.

Radhakrishnan, Sarvepalli and Charles Moore. *A Sourcebook in Indian Philosophy.* Princeton, NJ: Princeton University Press, 1957.

Raghavendrachar, H.N. *The Dvaita Philosophy and its Place in the Vedanta*. Mysore, India: University of Mysore, 1941.

Rahula, Walpola. *What the Buddha Taught*. New York: Grove Press, 1974, 2nd revised edn.

Raju, P.T. *Structural Depths of Indian Thought*. Albany, NY: State University of New York Press, 1985.

Rāmānuja. *Vedantasara of Bhagavad Ramanuja*. (Krishnamacharya, ed. and M.B. Narasimha Ayyangar, trans.). Wheaton, IL: Theosophical Publ. House, 2nd edn, 1979.

Ram-Prasad, Chakravarthi. *Knowledge and Liberation in Classical Indian Thought*. New York: Palgrave, 2001.

Ram-Prasad, Chakravarthi. *Advaita Epistemology and Metaphysics: An Outline of Indian Non-Realism*. London: RoutledgeCurzon, 2002.

Rastogi, Navjivan. *The Krama Tantricism of Kashmir: Historical and General Sources*, Vol. 1. Delhi: Motilal Banarsidass, 1979.

Reat, N. Ross. *The Origins of Indian Psychology*, Berkeley, CA: Asian Humanities Press, 1990.

Renou, Louis. *Religions of Ancient India*. London: Athlone Press, 1953.

Reynolds, Frank E. and Donald Capps, eds. *The Biographical Process: Studies in the History and Psychology of Religion*. The Hague: Mouton, 1976.

Ṛg-veda. See: O'Flaherty, W.D.

Riepe, Dale. *The Naturalistic Tradition in Indian Thought*. Seattle, WA: University of Washington Press, 1961.

Rizvi, S.A.A. *The Wonder That Was India*, Vol. II. *A Survey of the History and Culture of the Indian Sub-Continent from the Coming of the Muslims to the British Conquest, 1200–1700*. London: Sidgwick & Jackson, 1987.

Robinson, Richard H. and Willard L. Johnson. *The Buddhist Religion: A Historical Introduction*. Belmont, CA: Wadsworth, 3rd edn, 1982.

Rukmani, T.S., trans. and ed. *Yogavārttika of Vijñāabhikṣu*, 4 Vols. New Delhi: Munshiram Manoharlal, 1980–89.

Saksena, S.K. *Nature of Consciousness in Hindu Philosophy*. Delhi: Motilal Banarsidass, 1971.

Sāṃkhya-kārikā. See: Larson, G.J.

Sāṃkhya-kārikā Bhāsya. See: Larson, G.J.

Śaṅkara. *Commentary on the Brahma-sūtra. See:* Apte, V.M.

Śaṅkarācārya (Swami Prabhavananda and Christopher Isherwood, trans). *Shankara's Crest-Jewel of Discrimination (Viveka-chudamani)*. Hollywood, CA: Vedanta Press, 3rd edn, 1978,

Śaṅkarācārya (trans. with notes, Sengaku Mayeda). *A Thousand Teachings: The Upadesasahasri of Śaṅkara*. Tokyo: University of Tokyo Press, 1979.

Sarma, Candradhara. *The Advaita Tradition in Indian Philosophy: A Study of Advaita in Buddhism, Vedanta and Kashmira Shaivism*. Delhi: Motilal Banarsidass, 1996, 1st edn.

Sarma, Deepak. *An Introduction to Mādhva Vedānta*. Burlington, VT: Ashgate, 2003.

Sarma, Deepak. *Epistemologies and the Limitations of Philosophical Inquiry: Doctrine in Mādhva Vedānta*. London: RoutledgeCurzon, 2005.

Schopen, Gregory. *Bones, Stones, and Buddhist Monks: Collected Papers on the Archaeology, Epigraphy, and Texts of Monatic Buddhism in India*. Honolulu, HI: University of Hawaii Press, 1996.

Shambhala Publications Staff, eds. *Encyclopedia of Eastern Philosophy and Religion*. Boston, MA: Shambhala Publ., 1994.

Sharma, B.N.K. *A History of the Dvaita School of Vedānta and its Literature*, 2 Vols. Bombay, India: Booksellers Publ., 1960–61.

Sharma, B.N.K. *Madhva's Teachings in His Own Words*. Bombay, India: Bhavan's Book University, 1961.

Sharma, Jagdish S. *Encyclopaedia Indica,* 2 Vols. Delhi: S. Chand, 1981.

Shastri, D.R. *A Short History of Indian Materialism, Sensationalism, and Hedonism*. Calcutta, India: The Book Company, 1930.

Shastri, Hara Prasad. *Lokayta and Vratya*. Calcutta, India: Firma K.L. Mukhopadhyay, 1982.

Shastri, Pashupatnath. *Introduction to Pūrva Mīmāṃsā*. Varanasi, India: Chaukhambha Orientalia, 2nd edn, 1980.

Sherburne, Richard, S.J., trans. *The Complete Works of Atīśa, Śrī Dīpamkara Jñāna, Jo-Bo-Rje. The Lamp for the Path, the Commentary, with Twenty-five Key Texts*. New Delhi: Aditya Prakashan, 2000.

Siderits, Mark. *Buddhism as Philosophy: An Introduction*. Indianapolis, IN: Hackett, 2007

Silburn, Lillian (Jacques Gontier, trans.). *Kuṇḍalinī: The Energy of the Depths*. Albany, NY: State University of New York Press, 1988.

Sinha, Jadunath. *Indian Psychology,* 3 Vols. Delhi: Motilal Banarsidass, 1996 (1969).

Smart, Ninian. *Beyond Ideology: Religion and the Future of Western Civilization*. London: Collins, 1981.

Smart, Ninian. *Doctrine and Argument in Indian Philosophy*. Leiden, Netherlands: E.J. Brill, 2nd edn, 1992.

Smith, Bardwell L., ed. *Hinduism: New Essays in the History of Religions*. Leiden, Netherlands: Brill, 1976.

Snellgrove, David. *Indo-Tibetan Buddhism: Indian Buddhists and their Tibetan Successors,* 2 Vols. Boulder, CO: Shambhala, 1987.

Snellgrove, David L. and Hugh E. Richardson, *The Hevajra Tantra: A Critical Study,* 2 Vols. London: Oxford University Press, 1959.

Snellgrove, David L. and Hugh E. Richardson, *A Cultural History of Tibet*. New York: F.A. Praeger, 1968.

Sopa, Geshe Lhundub, Roger Jackson and John Newman (Beth Simon, ed.). *The Wheel of Time: The Kalachakra in Context*. Ithaca, NY: Snow Lion, 1985.

Srinivasa Chari, S.M. *Advaita and Visiṣṭādvaita: A Study Based on Vedanta Dasika's Satadusan*. Delhi: Motilal Banarsidass, 2nd edn, 1976.

Srinivasachari, P.N. *The Philosophy of Bhedabheda*. Madras, India: Adyar Library, 2nd edn, 1950.

Stcherbatsky, Theodore. *The Central Conception of Buddhism and the Meaning of the Word 'Dharma'*. London: Royal Asiatic Society, 1923; Delhi: Indological Book House, 4th edn, 1970.

Streng, Frederick J. *Emptiness: A Study in Religious Meaning*. Nashville, TN: Abingdon Press, 1967.

Strong, John S. *The Experience of Buddhism: Sources and Interpretation*. Belmont, CA: Wadsworth, 2nd edn, 2001.

Suzuki, Daisetz Teitaro. *The Lankavatara Sutra: A Mahayana Text*. London: Routledge & Kegan Paul 1932.

Taber, John. *A Hindu Critique of Buddhist Epistemology: Kumārila on Perception*. New York: RoutledgeCurzon 2005.

Tandon, S.N. *A Re-Appraisal of Patañjali's Yoga-Sūtras in the Light of the Buddha's Teaching*. Igatpuri, Maharashtra: Vipassana Research Institute, 1995.

Tatia, Nathmal, trans. *That Which Is: Tattvārtha Sūtra. Umāsvāti/Umāsvāmī*. With commentaries of Umāsvāti/Umāsvāmī, Pūjyapāda and Siddasenagni. San Francisco, CA: Harper Collins, 1994.

Thomas, E.J. *The Life of the Buddha as Legend and History*. London: Routledge & Kegan Paul, 1927.

Thomas, E.J. *The History of Buddhist Thought*. London: Routledge & Kegan Paul, 1933.

Tucci, Giuseppe. *Linee di una storia del materialsmo indiano*. Rome: Tipografia della R. Accademia nazionale dei Lincei, proprieta del dott. Pio Befani, 1924–29.

Udayanācārya. (Swami Revi Tirtha, trans.). *The Nyāya-kusumañjali of Udayanācarya: A Presentation of Theistic Doctrines According to the Nyaya System of Philosophy*. Adyar, India: Adyar Library, 1946.

Upanisads. *See:* Deussen, P., 1980; Hume, R.E.; Olivelle, P.; Radhakrishnan, S., 1953.

Urquhart, W.S. *The Vedanta and Modern Thought*. London: Oxford University Press, 1928.

Varma, Chandra B. *A Concise Encyclopedia of Early Buddhist Philosophy: Based on the Study of the Abhidhammatthasangahasarupa*. Delhi: Eastern Book Linkers, 1992.

Walker, Benjamin. *The Hindu World: An Encyclopedic Survey of Hinduism*, 2 Vols. New York: Frederick A. Praeger, 1968.

Walshe, Maurice, trans. *Thus Have I Heard: The Long Discourses of the Buddha (Dīgha Nikāya)*. London: Wisdom, 1987.

Warder, A.K. *Indian Buddhism*. Delhi: Motilal Banarsidass, 2nd edn, 1980.

Wayman, Alex. *The Buddhist Tantras: Light on Indo-Tibetan Esotericism*. New York: Samuel Weiser, 1973.

Wayman, Alex. *The Yoga of the Guhyasamājatantra: The Arcane Lore of Forty Verses, A Buddhist Tantra Commentary*. Delhi: Motilal Banarsidass, (1977) (Reprint) 1980.

Whitney, William Dwight, trans. *Atharva-veda Samhita*. With a critical and exegetical commentary by W.D. Whitney. Delhi: Motilal Banarsidass, (Reprint) 1962.

Williams, Paul. *Mahāyāna Buddhism: The Doctrinal Foundations*. London: Routledge, 1989.

Williams, Paul (with Anthony Tribe). *Buddhist Thought: A Complete Introduction to the Indian Tradition*. London: Routledge, 2000.

Wiltshire, Martin G. *Ascetic Figures before and in Early Buddhism: The Emergence of Gautama as the Buddha*. Berlin: Mouton de Gruyter, 1990.

Woods, James Haughton, trans. *The Yoga-System of Patañjali*. Harvard Oriental Series, Vol. 17, 1914; Delhi: Motilal Banarsidass, (Reprint) 1983.

Yamunacharya, M. *Ramanuja's Teachings in His Own Words*. Bombay, India: Bharatiya Vidya Bhavan, 1963.

Yoga-sūtra. See: Chapple, C., and Yogi Anand Viraj; Feuerstein, G.; Hariharānanda Aranya; Jha, G., 1934; Woods, J.H.

Zaehner, R.C. *Hinduism*. London: Oxford University Press, 1962.

Zaehner, R.C. *The Bhagavadgītā with a Commentary Based on the Original Sources*. Oxford, UK: Oxford University Press, 1973 (1969).

Zimmer, Heinrich (Joseph Campbell, ed.). *Philosophies of India*. Princeton, NJ: Bollingen Foundation, 1951.

3. CHINESE PHILOSOPHIES

Allinson, Robert E., ed. *Understanding the Chinese Mind: The Philosophical Roots*. New York: Oxford University Press, 1989.

Ames, Roger T. and Henry Rosemont, Jr., trans. (with intro.). *The Analects of Confucius: A Philosophical Translation.* New York: Ballantine Books, 1998.

Ames, Roger T., and David L. Hall, trs. *Daodejing: "Making This Life Significant." A Philosophical Translation.* New York: Ballantine, 2003.

Avatamsaka Sutra. See: Cleary, T., 1984–87.

Berthrong, John H. *Transformations of the Confucian Way.* Boulder, CO: Westview Press, 1998.

Birdwhistell, Anne D. *Transition to Neo-Confucianism: Shao Yung on Knowledge and Symbols of Reality.* Stanford, CA: Stanford University Press, 1989.

Birdwhistell, Anne D. *Li Yong (1627–1705) and Epistemological Dimensions of Confucian Philosophy.* Stanford, CA: Stanford University Press, 1996.

Bishop, Donald H., ed. *Chinese Thought: An Introduction.* Reprint, Columbia: South Asia Books, 1994.

Bloom, Irene, trans. *Knowledge Painfully Acquired: The K'un-Chin Shi of Lo Ch'in-Shun.* New York: Columbia University Press, 1987.

Bloom, Irene, ed. *Meeting of Minds: Intellectual and Religious Interaction in East Asian Traditions of Thought.* New York: Columbia University Press, 1996.

Broughton, Jeffrey L. *The Bodhidharma Anthology: The Earliest Records of Zen.* Berkeley, CA: University of California Press, 1999.

Bruce, E. and A. Taeko Brooks. *The Original Analects: Sayings of Confucius and His Successors.* New York: Columbia University Press, 1998.

Bruce, J. Percy. *Chu Hsi and His Masters.* London: Probsthain, 1923.

Burnouf, Eugène, trans. *Le Lotus de la Bonne Loi.* Paris: A. Maisonneuve, 1973.

Chai, Ch'u and Ch'ai, Winberg, eds. *The Humanist Way in Ancient China: Essential Works of Confucianism.* New York: Bantam Books, 1965.

Chai, Winberg, and Ch'u Chai, eds. *Li Chi: Book of Rites.* New York: Carol Publ. Group, 1966.

Chan, Alan K.L. *Two Visions of the Way: A Study of the Wang Pi and the Ho-shang Kung Commentaries on the Lao-Tzu.* Albany, NY: State University of New York Press, 1991.

Chan, Alan K.L, ed. *Mencius: Contexts and Interpretations.* Honolulu, HI: University of Hawaii Press, 2002.

Chan, Wing-tsit. *An Outline and an Annotated Bibliography of Chinese Philosophy.* New Haven, CT: Far Eastern Publications, Yale University, 1961.

Chan, Wing-tsit. *The Way of Lao Tzu (Tao-te Ching).* Indianapolis, IN: Bobbs-Merrill, 1963.

Chan, Wing-tsit. *A Source Book in Chinese Philosophy.* Princeton, NJ: Princeton University Press, 1963.

Chan, Wing-tsit, trans. *The Platform Scripture.* New York: St John's University Press, 1963.

Chan, Wing-tsit. *Instructions for Practical Living and Other Neo-Confucian Writings by Wang Yang-ming.* New York: Columbia University Press, 1964.

Chan, Wing-tsit, ed. *Chu Hsi and Neo-Confucianism.* Honolulu, HI: University of Hawaii Press, 1986.

Chan, Wing-tsit. *Chu Hsi, Life and Thought.* New York: St Martin's Press, 1987.

Chang, Carsun. *The Development of Neo-Confucian Thought,* 2 Vols. New York: Bookman Associates, 1957–62.

Chang, Chung-yüan. *Creativity and Taoism.* New York: Julian Press, 1963.

Chang, Tsai. 'Western Inscription.' *See:* Chan, Wing-tsit, 1963b, pp. 497–500.

Chappell, David, ed. (Buddhist Translation Seminar of Hawaii, trans.). *T'ien-t'ai Buddhism: An Outline of the Fourfold Teachings.* (Recorded by Korean Buddhist Monk Chegwan). Honolulu, HI: University of Hawaii Press, 1983.

Chen, Jo-Shui. *Liu Tsung-yuan and Intellectual Change in T'ang China, 773–819*. New York: Cambridge University Press, 1992.

Ch'en, Kenneth. *Buddhism in China: A Historical Survey*. Princeton, NJ: Princeton University Press, 1972.

Ch'en, Kenneth. *The Chinese Transformation of Buddhism*. Princeton, NJ: Princeton University Press, 1973.

Chen, Liu F. (Shih S. Liu, trans.). *The Confucian Way: A New and Systematic Study of the Four Books*. New York: Routledge, Chapman & Hall, 1986.

Cheng, Chung-ying. *New Dimensions of Confucian and Neo-Confucian Philosophy*. Albany, NY: State University of New York Press, 1991.

Cheng, Hsueh-li, ed. *New Essays in Chinese Philosophy*. New York: Peter Lang, 1997.

Ch'ien, Edward T. *Chiao Hung and the Restructuring of Neo-Confucianism in the Late Ming*. New York: Columbia University Press, 1986.

Ching, Julia. *To Acquire Wisdom: The Way of Wang Yang-ming*. New York: Columbia University Press, 1976.

Ching, Julia. *Mysticism and Kingship in China: The Heart of Chinese Wisdom*. New York: Cambridge University Press, 1997.

Chong, Kim-chong. *Early Confucian Ethics: Concepts and Arguments*. Chicago, IL: Open Court, 2007.

Chong, Kim-chong, *et al.*, eds. *The Moral Circle and the Self: Chinese and Western Perspectives*. La Salle, IL: Open Court, 2003.

Chow, Kai-Wing. *The Rise of Confucian Ritualism in Late Imperial China: Ethics, Classics, and Lineage Discourse*. Stanford, CA: Stanford University Press, 1994.

Chu Hsi (J. Percy Bruce, trans.). *The Philosophy of Human Nature*. London: Probsthain, 1922.

Chu, Hsi (Wing-tsit Chan, trans.). *Reflections on Things at Hand: The Neo-Confucian Anthology*. New York: Columbia University Press, 1967.

Chuang Tzu. *See:* Fung Yu-lan; Graham, A.C., 1981; Mair, V.; Palmer, M. and Breuilly, E.; Watson, B., 1968.

Cleary, J.C., ed. and trans. *The Art of Worldly Wisdom: Confucian Teachings of the Ming Dynasty*. Boston, MA: Shambhala, 1991.

Cleary, Thomas F. *Entry into the Inconceivable: An Introduction to Hua-yen Buddhism*. Honolulu, HI: University of Hawaii Press, 1983.

Cleary, Thomas F. *The Flower Ornament Scripture: A Translation of the Avatamsaka Sutra*, 3 Vols. Boulder, CO: Shambhala, 1984–87.

Cleary, Thomas F. *The Essential Tao: An Initiation into the Heart of Taoism through the Authentic Tao Te Ching and the Inner Teachings of Chuang Tzu*. San Francisco, CA: Harper, 1992.

Cleary, Thomas F. *The Essential Confucius*. San Francisco, CA: Harper, 1993, revised edn.

Confucius. *Analects (Lun-yü). See:* Bruce, E. and Brooks, A.T.; Dawson, R.; Lau, D.C., 1992; Legge, J., 1971; Waley, A., 1938.

Cook, Francis D. *Hua-yen Buddhism: The Jewel Net of Indra*. University Park, PA: Pennsylvania State University Press, 1977.

Cook, Scott, ed. *Hiding the World in the World: Uneven Discourses on the Zhuangzi*. Albany, NY: State University Press, 2003.

Coutinho, Steve. *Zhuangzi and Early Chinese Philosophy: Vagueness, Transformation and Paradox*. Aldershot, UK: Ashgate, 2004.

Creel, Herrlee G. *Chinese Thought from Confucius to Mao Tse-tung*. Chicago, IL: University of Chicago Press, 1953.

Creel, Herrlee G. *Confucius and the Chinese Way*. New York: Harper Torchbooks, 1960.

Csikszentmihalyi, Mark. *Material Virtue: Ethics and the Body in Early China*. Leiden, Netherlands: Brill, 2004.

Cua, Antonio S., ed. *Encyclopedia of Chinese Philosophy*. London: Routledge, 2002.

Cua, Antonio S. *Human Nature, Ritual, and History: Studies in Xunzi and Chinese Philosophy*. Honolulu, HI: University of Hawaii Press, 2005.

Cutler, Joshua W.C. and Guy Newland, eds. Lamrim Chenmo Translation Committee. *The Great Treatise on the Stages of the Path to Enlightenment by* Tsong kha pa, Vol. 1. Ithaca, NY: Snow Lion, 2000.

Davenport, John T., trans. *Ordinary Wisdom: Sakya Pandita's Treasury of Good Advice*. Boston, MA: Wisdom, 2000.

Dawson, Raymond. *Confucius*. Oxford, UK: Oxford University Press, 1981.

Dawson, Raymond, trans. *The Analects*. New York: Oxford University Press, 1993.

Day, Clarence Burton. *The Philosophers of China: Classical and Contemporary*. Secaucus, NJ: Citadel Press, 1978.

De Bary, William Theodore. *The Message of the Mind in Neo-Confucian Thought*. New York: Columbia University Press, 1988.

De Bary, William Theodore. *Learning for One's Self: Essays on the Individual in Neo-Confucian Thought*. New York: Columbia University Press, 1991.

De Bary, William Theodore. *The Trouble with Confucianism*. Cambridge, MA: Harvard University Press, 1996.

De Bary, William Theodore (and the Conference on Seventeenth-Century Chinese Thought). *The Unfolding of Neo-Confucianism*. New York: Columbia University Press, 1975.

De Bary, William Theodore, Wing-tsit Chan and Burton Watson. *Sources of Chinese Tradition*, 2 Vols. New York: Columbia University Press, 1960.

De Groot, J.J.M. *Sectarianism and Religious Persecution in China*, 2 Vols. Amsterdam, Nethrlands: J. Muller, 1903–4.

De Groot, J.J.M. *The Religious System of China*. Taipei: Literature House, 1964.

Dreyfus, Georges B.J. *The Sound of Two Hands Clapping: The Education of a Buddhist Monk*. Berkeley, CA: University of California Press, 2003.

Dreyfus, Georges B.J. and Sara L. McClintock, eds. *The Svātantrika-Prāsangika Distinction*. Boston, MA: Wisdom, 2003.

Dubs, Homer H. *Hsuntze: The Moulder of Ancient Confucianism*. London: Arthur Probsthain, 1927.

Dubs, Homer H., trans. *The Works of Hsuntze*. London: Arthur Probsthain, 1928.

Dumoulin, Heinrich. *Zen Buddhism: A History*, Vol. 1: *India and China*. New York: Macmillan, 1994.

Ebrey, Patricia B. *Confucianism and Family Rituals in Imperial China: A Social History of Writing about Rites*. Princeton, NJ: Princeton University Press, 1991.

Eliade, Mircea, ed. *The Encyclopedia of Religion*, 16 vols. New York: Macmillan, 1987.

English, Elizabeth. *Vajrayoginī: Her Visualizations, Rituals, and Forms*. Boston, MA: Wisdom, 2002.

Eno, Robert B. *The Confucian Creation of Heaven: Philosophy and the Defense of Ritual Mastery*. Albany, NY: State University of New York Press, 1990.

Fa-tsang. 'Treatise on the Golden Lion.' *See:* Chan, Wing-tsit, 1963b, pp. 409–13.

Fingarette, Herbert. *Confucius: The Secular as Sacred*. New York: Harper & Row, 1972.

Fogel, Joshua A. and Irene Bloom, eds. *Meeting of Minds: Intellectual and Religious Interaction in East Asian Traditions of Thought: Essays in Honor of Wing-Tsit Chan and William Theodore De Bary*. New York: Columbia University Press, 1996.

Forke, Alfred. *Geschichte der neueren chinesischen Philosophie*. Hamburg, Germany: Friederichsen, De Gruyter, 1938.

Fung Yu-lan (Derk Bodde, trans.). *A History of Chinese Philosophy*, 2 Vols. Princeton, NJ: Princeton University Press, 1952–53, 2nd edn.

Fung Yu-lan. *Chuang-tzu: A New Selected Translation with an Exposition of the Philosophy of KuoHsiang*. New York: Paragon Book Reprint Corp., 1964, 2nd edn.

Gardner, Daniel K. *Chu Hsi and the Ta-hsueh: Neo-Confucian Reflection on the Confucian Canon*. Cambridge, MA: Harvard University Press, 1986.

Gardner, Daniel K. *Chu Hsi: Learning to be a Sage*. Berkeley, CA: University of California Press, 1990.

Gardner, Daniel K. *Zhu Xi's Reading of the Analects: Canon, Commentary, and the Classical Tradition*. New York: Columbia University Press, 2003.

Geaney, Jane. *On the Epistemology of the Senses in Early Chinese Thought*. Honolulu, HI: University of Hawaii Press, 2002.

Giles, Herbert A. *Chuang Tzu: Textual Notes*. New York: Routledge, Chapman & Hall, 1980.

Giles, Lionel, trans. *Sayings of Confucius: A New Translation of the Greater Part of the Confucian Analects*. Boston, MA: Charles E. Tuttle, 1993.

Girardot, N.J. *Myth and Meaning in Early Taoism: The Theme of Chaos (Hun-tun)*. Berkeley, CA: University of California Press, 1983.

Goldin, Paul Rakita. *Rituals of the Way: The Philosophy of Xunzi*. La Salle, IL: Open Court, 1999.

Goldin, Paul R. *After Confucius: Studies in Early Chinese Philosophy*. Honolulu, HI: University of Hawaii Press, 2004.

Goodman, Steven D. and Ronald M. Davidson, eds. *Tibetan Buddhism: Reason and Revelation*. Albany, NY: State University of New York Press, 1992.

Graham, A.C. *Later Mohist Logic, Ethics and Science*. London: School of Oriental and African Studies, University of London, 1978.

Graham, A.C., trans. *Chuang-tzu: The Seven Inner Chapters and Other Writings from the Book of Chuangtzu*. London: Allen & Unwin, 1981.

Graham, A.C. *Disputers of the Tao*. La Salle, IL: Open Court, 1989.

Graham, A.C. *Studies in Chinese Philosophy and Philosophical Literature*. Albany, NY: State University of New York Press, 1990.

Graham, A.C. *Two Chinese Philosophers: Ch'eng Ming-tao and Ch'eng Yi-ch'uan*. La Salle, IL: Open Court Press, 1992.

Hall, David and Roger Ames. *Thinking Through Confucius*. Albany, NY: State University of New York Press, 1987.

Han Fei Tzu. *See:* Watson, B., 1967.

Hansen, Chad. *Language and Logic in Ancient China*. Ann Arbor, MI: University of Michigan Press, 1983.

Hartman, Charles O. *Han Yu and the T'ang Search for Unity*. Princeton, NJ: Princeton University Press, 1986.

He Zhaowu *et al. An Intellectual History of China*. Beijing: Foreign Languages Press, 1991.

Henricks, Robert G., trans. *Lao-Tzu: Te-Tao Ching: A New Translation Based on the Recently Discovered Ma-wang-tui Texts*. New York: Ballantine Books, 1989.

Herbert, Edward and Arthur Waley. *A Confucian Notebook*. Reprint, Boston, MA: Charles E. Tuttle, 1992.

Hinton, David, trans. *Chuang Tzu: The Inner Chapters*. Washington, DC: Counterpoint, 1997.

Hopkins, Jeffrey. *Reflections on Reality: The Three Natures and Non-Natures in the Mind-Only School.* Berkeley, CA: University of California Press, 2002.

Hopkins, Jeffrey. *Maps of the Profound: Jam-yang-shay-ba's Great Exposition of Buddhist and Non-Buddhist Views on the Nature of Reality.* Ithaca, NY: Snow Lion, 2003.

Hsiao, Kung-ch'uan (F.W. Mote, trans.). *A History of Chinese Political Thought.* Princeton, NJ: Princeton University Press, 1979.

Hsu, Shie L. *The Political Philosophy of Confucianism.* Albuquerque, NM: American Classical College Press, 1992.

Hsün Tzu. *See:* Dubs, H.; Knoblock, J.; Watson, B., 1963b, 1967.

Hu, Shih. *The Development of Logical Method in Ancient China.* New York: Paragon Book Reprint Corp., 1963, 2nd edn.

Huang, Hsiu-Chi. *Lu Hsiang-Shan: A 12th Century Chinese Idealist Philosopher.* Reprint, Westport, CT: Hyperion Press, 1976.

Huang, Tsung-hsi. (Julia Ching and Chaoying Fang, eds.). *The Records of Ming Scholars.* Honolulu, HI: University of Hawaii Press, 1987.

Hui-neng. *The Platform Scripture. See:* Chan, Wing-tsit, 1963c; Yampolsky, P.

Hui-neng. *Sutra of the Sixth Patriarch. See:* Hui-neng, *The Platform Scripture.*

Hurvitz, Leon. *Chih-I (538–597): An Introduction to the Life and Ideas of a Chinese Buddhist Monk.* Bruges, Belgium: Imprimerie Sainte-Catherine, 1962.

Hurvitz, Leon, trans. *Scripture of the Lotus Blossom of the Fine Dharma.* New York: Columbia University Press, 1976.

Hymes, Robert. *Way and Byway: Taoism, Local Religion, and Models of Divinity in Sung and Modern China.* Berkeley, CA: University of California Press, 2002.

Ivanhoe, Philip J. *Ethics in the Confucian Tradition: The Thought of Mencius and Wang Yang-ming.* Atlanta, GA: Scholars Press, 1990.

Ivanhoe, Philip J. *Confucian Moral Self Cultivation.* Indianapolis, IN: Hackett, 2nd edn, 2000.

Ivanhoe, Philip J. *Ethics in the Confucian Tradition: The Thought of Mengzi and Wang Yangming.* Indianapolis, IN: Hackett, 2002.

Ivanhoe, Philip J., trans. *The Daodejing of Laozi.* New York: Seven Bridges, 2002.

Ivanhoe, Philip J. and Bryan W. Van Norden, eds. *Readings in Classical Chinese Philosophy.* New York: Seven Bridges, 2001.

Jamgön Kongtrül, III (Tina Drasczyk, Alex Drasczyk and Richard Gravel, trans.). *Cloudless Sky: The Mahamudra Path of the Tibetan Buddhist Kagyü School.* Boston, MA: Shambhala, 2001.

Journal of Chinese Philosophy. (Special issue on Chu Hsi.). Vol. 5, No. 2, June 1978.

Kaltenmark, Max. (Roger Greaves, trans.). *Lao Tzu and Taoism.* Stanford, CA: Stanford University Press, 1969.

Kapstein, Matthew T. *The Tibetan Assimilation of Buddhism: Conversion, Contestation, and Memory.* New York: Oxford University Press, 2002.

Kern, Hendrik, trans. *The Puṇḍarīka.* Oxford, UK: Clarendon Press, 1884. Reprint, Delhi: Motilal Banarsidass, 1965.

Kirkland, Russell. *Taoism: The Enduring Tradition.* New York: Routledge, 2004.

Kjellberg, Paul and Philip J. Ivanhoe, eds. *Essays on Skepticism, Relativism, and Ethics in the Zhuangzi.* Albany, NY: State University of New York Press, 1996.

Kline, T.C., III, and Philip J. Ivanhoe, eds. *Virtue, Nature, and Moral Agency in the Xunzi.* Indianapolis, IN: Hackett, 2000.

Knoblock, John. *Xunzi, 3 Vols.* Stanford, CA: Stanford University Press, 1988, 1990, 1994.

Kohn, Livia. *Early Chinese Mysticism: Philosophy and Soteriology in the Taoist Tradition.* Princeton, NJ: Princeton University Press, 1992.

Kohn, Livia, ed. *Daoism Handbook*. Leiden, Netherlands: Brill, 2000.

Kohn, Livia. *Cosmos and Community: The Ethical Dimension of Daoism*. Cambridge, MA: Three Pines Press, 2004.

Kohn, Livia and Michael Lafargue, eds. *Lao-Tzu and the 'Tao-Te-Ching'*. Albany, NY: State University of New York Press, 1998.

Lai, Whalen and Lewis Lancaster, eds. *Early Ch'an in China and Tibet*. Berkeley, CA: Asian Humanities Press, 1983.

Lao Tzu. *Tao Te Ching. See:* Chan, Wing-tsit, 1963a; Henricks, R.G.; Lau, D.C., 1963, 1994; Lin, P.; Mair, V., 1990; Wilhelm, R.

Lau, D.C., trans. *Lao Tzu: Tao Te Ching*. New York: Penguin Books, 1963.

Lau, D.C., trans. *Mencius*. New York: Penguin Books, 1970.

Lau, D.C., trans. *Confucius: The Analects (Lun Yü)*. Ann Arbor, MI: University of Michigan Press, 1992, 2nd edn.

Lau, D.C., trans. *Lao-tzu: Tao Te Ching*. New York: Alfred A. Knopf, 1994.

Lee, Janghee. *Xunzi and Early Chinese Naturalism*. Albany, NY: State University of New York Press, 2004.

Legge, James. *The Chinese Classics*, 5 Vols. Oxford, UK: Clarendon Press, 1893–95, 2nd edn.

Legge, James. *Mencius*. New York: Dover Books, 1970 (1895).

Legge, James. *Confucian Analects, the Great Learning, and the Doctrine of the Mean*. New York: Dover Books, 1971 (1893).

Legge, James, trans. *The Chinese Classics: With a Translation, Critical and Exegetical Notes, Prolegomena, and Copious Indexes*. Set. New York: State Mutual Book & Periodical Service, 1982.

Lenk, Hans and Gregor Paul, eds. *Epistemological Issues in Classical Chinese Philosophy*. Albany, NY: State University of New York Press, 1993.

Li, Chenyang, ed. *The Sage and the Second Sex: Confucianism, Ethics, and Gender*. La Salle, IL: Open Court, 2000.

Li, You-Zheng. *The Constitution of Han-Academic Ideology: The Archetype of Chinese Ethics and Academic Ideology*. New York: Peter Lang, 1997.

Lin, Paul J., trans. *A Translation of Lao Tzu's Tao Te Ching and Wang Pi's Commentary*. Ann Arbor, MI: University of Michigan, 1977.

Liu, James T. *Ou-yang Hsiu: An Eleventh-Century Neo-Confucianist*. Stanford, CA: Stanford University Press, 1967.

Liu, JeeLoo. *An Introduction to Chinese Philosophy: From Ancient Philosophy to Chinese Buddhism*. Malden, MA: Blackwell, 2006.

Liu, Ming-Wood. *Madhyamaka Thought in China*. Boston, MA: Brill Academic Publishers, 1994.

Liu, Wu-Chi. *A Short History of Confucian Philosophy*. (Reprint) Westport, CT: Hyperion Press, 1987.

Liu, Xiusheng and Philip J. Ivanhoe, eds. *Essays on the Moral Philosophy of Mengzi*. Indianapolis. IN: Hackett, 2002.

Lotus Sutra. See: Burnouf, E.; Hurvitz, L., 1976; Kern, H.

Lovin, R. and F. Reynolds, eds. *Cosmogony and Ethical Order*. Chicago, IL: University of Chicago Press, 1985.

Lowe, Scott. *Mo Tzu's Religious Blueprint for a Chinese Utopia*. Lewiston, NY: Edwin Mellen Press, 1992.

Machle, Edward J. *Nature and Heaven in the Xunzi*. Albany, NY: State University of New York Press, 1993.

Mair, Victor, ed. *Experimental Essays on Chuang-tzu*. Honolulu, HI: University of Hawaii Press, 1983.

Mair, Victor. *Tao Te Ching: The Classic Book of Integrity and the Way*. New York: Bantam Books, 1990.

Mair, Victor. *Wandering on the Way: Early Taoist Tales and Parables of Chuang Tzu*. Honolulu, HI: University of Hawaii Press, 1998 (1994).

Makeham, John, trans. *Balanced Discourses: A Bilingual Edition*. New Haven, CT: Yale University Press, 2002.

Makeham, John. *New Confucianism: A Critical Examination*. New York: Palgrave Macmillan, 2003.

Makeham, John. *Transmitters and Creators: Chinese Commentators and Commentaries on the Analects*. Cambridge, MA: Harvard University Press, 2004.

McNaughton, William, ed. *The Confucian Vision*. Ann Arbor, MI: University of Michigan Press, 1974.

Mei, Yi-pao. *The Ethical and Political Works of Motse*. Westport, CT: Hyperion Press, 1973 (1929).

Mencius. *See:* Lau, D.C., 1970; Legge, J, 1970.

Michael, Thomas. *The Pristine Dao: Metaphysics in Early Daoist Discourse*. Albany, NY: State University of New York Press, 2005.

Moeller, Hans-Georg. *Daoism Explained: From the Dream of the Butterfly to the Fishnet Allegory*. Chicago, IL: Open Court, 2004.

Moeller, Hans-Georg. *The Philosophy of the Daodejing*. New York: Columbia University Press, 2006.

Mo Tzu. *See:* Graham, A.C., 1978; Mei, Yi-pao; Watson, B., 1963a, 1967.

Moore, Charles A., ed. *The Chinese Mind: Essentials of Chinese Philosophy and Culture*. Honolulu, HI: University of Hawaii Press, 1974 (1967).

Mou, Bo, ed. *Two Roads to Wisdom? Chinese and Analytic Philosophical Traditions*. La Salle, IL: Open Court, 2001.

Mou, Bo, ed. *Comparative Approaches to Chinese Philosophy*. Aldershot, UK: Ashgate, 2003.

Munro, Donald J. *The Concept of Man in Early China*. Stanford, CA: Stanford University Press, 1969.

Munro, Donald J. *Images of Human Nature: A Sung Portrait*. Princeton, NJ: Princeton University Press, 1988.

Needham, Joseph. *Science and Civilisation in China*, 6 Vols. Cambridge, UK: Cambridge University Press, 1954–94.

Nivison, David S. *The Life and Thought of Chang Hsüeh-ch'eng, 1738–1801*. Stanford, CA: Stanford University Press, 1966.

Nivison, David S. (Bryan Van Norden, ed.). *The Ways of Confucianism: Investigations in Chinese Philosophy*. Chicago, IL: Open Court Press, 1996.

Nivison, David S. and Arthur F. Wright, eds. *Confucianism in Action*. Stanford, CA: Stanford University Press, 1959.

Nylan, Michael, trans. *The Elemental Changes – The Ancient Chinese Companion to the I Ching: The T'ai Hsuan Ching of Master Yang Hsiung*. (Text and Commentaries). Albany, NY: State University of New York Press, 1994.

Nylan, Michael. *The Five "Confucian" Classics*. New Haven, CT: Yale University Press, 2001.

Oldstone-Moore, Jennifer. *Confucianism: Origins, Beliefs, Practices, Holy Texts, Sacred Places*. New York: Oxford University Press, 2002.

Oldstone-Moore, Jennifer. *Taoism: Origins, Beliefs, Practices, Holy Texts, Sacred Places*. New York: Oxford University Press, 2003.

Palmer, Martin and Eliszabeth Breuilly, trans. *The Book of Chuang Tzu*. New York: Viking Penguin, 1996.

Paper, Jordan. *The Spirits are Drunk: Comparative Approaches to Chinese Religion*. Albany, NY: State University of New York Press, 1995.

Paul, Gregor. *Aspects of Confucianism: A Study of the Relationship Between Rationality and Humaneness*. New York: Peter Lang, 1991.

Peerenboom, R.P. *Law and Morality in Ancient China: The Silk Manuscripts of Huang-Lao*. Albany, NY: State University of New York Press, 1993.

Poo, Mu-Chou. *In Search of Personal Welfare: A View of Ancient Chinese Religion*. Albany, NY: State University of New York Press, 1998.

Pound, Ezra, trans. *The Stone Tablet Inscriptions: or The Great Digest by Confucius*. Albuquerque, NM: Catholic Art Society, 1991.

Puett, Michael J. *To Become a God: Cosmology, Sacrifice, and Self-Divinization in Early China*. Cambridge, MA: Harvard University Asia Center for the Harvard-Yenching Institute, 2002.

Queen, Sarah A. *From Chronicle to Canon: The Hermeneutics of the Spring and Autumn Annals, According to Tung Chung-shu*. New York: Cambridge University Press, 1996.

Ray, Reginald A. *Secret of the Vajra World: The Tantric Buddhism of Tibet*. Boston, MA: Shambhala, 2001.

Rickett, W. Allyn, trans. *Guanzi: Political, Economic, and Philosophical Essays from Early China*. Princeton, NJ: Princeton University Press, 1985.

Robinet, Isabelle (Julian F. Pas and Norman J. Girardot, trans.) *Taoist Meditation: The Mao-shan Tradition of Great Purity*. Albany, NY: State University of New York Press, 1993.

Rosemont, Henry, ed. *Chinese Texts and Philosophical Contexts*. La Salle, IL: Open Court, 1991.

Roth, Harold D. *A Companion to Angus C. Graham's Chuang-tzu: The Inner Chapters*. Honolulu, HI: University of Hawaii Press, 2002.

Rubin, Vitaly A. (Steven I. Levine, trans.). *Individual and State in Ancient China*. New York: Columbia University Press, 1976.

Rump, Ariane and Wing-tsit Chan, trans. *Commentary on the Lao Tzu by Wang Pi*, Honolulu, HI: University of Hawaii Press, 1979.

Schipper, Kristofer. *Le Corps Taoiste*. Paris: Fayard, 1982.

Schwartz, Benjamin I. *The World of Thought in Ancient China*. Cambridge, MA: Belknap Press, 1985.

Shankman, Steven and Stephen Durrant. *The Siren and the Sage: Knowledge and Wisdom in Ancient Greece and China*. London: Cassell, 2000.

Shankman, Steven and Stephen W. Durrant, eds. *Early China/Ancient Greece: Thinking through Comparisons*. Albany, NY: State University of New York Press, 2002.

Shaughnessy, Edward L. *Before Confucius: Studies in the Creation of the Chinese Classics*. Albany, NY: State University of New York Press, 1997.

Shun, Kwong-loi. *Mencius and Early Chinese Thought*. Stanford, CA: Stanford University Press, 1997.

Shun, Kwong-loi and David B. Wong, eds. *Confucian Ethics: A Comparative Study of Self, Autonomy, and Community*. Cambridge, UK: Cambridge University Press, 2004.

Shyrock, John K. *The Origin and Development of the State Cult of Confucius*. New York: Paragon Book Reprint Corp., 1966 (1932).

Sivin, Nathan. *Chinese Alchemy: Preliminary Studies.* Cambridge, MA: Harvard University Press, 1968.

Sivin, Nathan. *Medicine, Philosophy and Religion in Ancient China: Researches and Reflections.* Brookfield, VT: Ashgate, 1995.

Slingerland, Edward. *Effortless Action: Wu-wei as Conceptual Metaphor and Spiritual Ideal in Early China.* Oxford, UK: Oxford University Press, 2003.

Slingerland, Edward, trans. *Confucius: Analects.* Indianapolis, IN: Hackett, 2003.

Smith, D. Howard. *Chinese Religions.* London: Weidenfeld & Nicolson, 1968.

Sommer, Deborah, trans. and ed. *Chinese Religion: An Anthology of Sources.* New York: Oxford University Press, 1995.

Suzuki, D.T. *Essays in Zen Buddhism.* New York: Grove/Atlantic, 1989.

Swanson, Paul (James A. Heisig, ed.). *Foundations of T'ien-T'ai Philosophy: The Flowering of the Two-Truth Theory in Chinese Buddhism.* Fremont, CA: Asian Humanities Press, 1989.

Tanaka, Kenneth K. *The Dawn of Chinese Pure Land Buddhist Doctrine: Ching-ying Hui-yuan's Commentary on the Visualization Sutra.* Albany, NY: State University of New York Press, 1990.

Taylor, Rodney L. *The Way of Heaven: An Introduction to the Confucian Religious Life.* Boston, MA: Brill Academic, 1986.

Taylor, Rodney L. *The Religious Dimensions of Confucianism.* Albany, NY: State University of New York Press, 1990.

Thompson, Laurence G. *Chinese Religion: An Introduction.* Belmont, CA: Wadsworth, 1979, 3rd edn.

Thurman, Robert A. *The Central Philosophy of Tibet.* Princeton, NJ: Princeton University Press, 1991.

Tillman, Hoyt C. *Utilitarian Confucianism: Ch'en Liang's Challenge to Chu Hsi.* Cambridge, MA: Harvard University Press, 1982.

Tillman, Hoyt C. *Confucian Discourse and Chu Hsi's Ascendancy.* Honolulu, HI: University of Hawaii Press, 1992.

Tillman, Hoyt C. and Stephen H. West, eds. *China under Jurchen Rule: Essays on Chin Intellectual and Cultural History.* Albany, NY: State University of New York Press, 1995.

Tsong-Kha-Pa (The Lamrim Chenmo Translation Committee). *The Great Treatise on the Stages of the Path to Enlightenment.* Ithaca, NY: Snow Lion, 2000.

Tsongkhapa (Gavin Kilty, trans.). *The Splendor of an Autumn Moon: The Devotional Verse of Tsongkhapa.* Boston, MA: Wisdom, 2001.

Tu Wei-ming. *Neo-Confucian Thought in Action: Wang Yang-ming's Youth (1472–1509).* Berkeley, CA: University of California Press, 1976.

Tu Wei-ming. *Humanity and Self-Cultivation: Essays in Confucian Thought.* Fremont, CA: Asian Humanities Press, 1980.

Tu Wei-ming. *Confucian Thought: Selfhood as Creative Transformation.* Albany, NY: State University of New York Press, 1985.

Twitchett, Denis, and John K. Fairbank, eds. *The Cambridge History of China.* Multiple Vols. Cambridge, UK: Cambridge University Press, 1978–91.

Van Norden, Bryan W., ed. *Confucius and the Analects: New Essays.* New York: Oxford University Press, 2002.

Verdu, Alfonso. *Dialectical Aspects in Buddhist Thought.* Lawrence, KS: University of Kansas, 1974.

Verdu, Alfonso. *The Philosophy of Buddhism: A 'Totalistic' Synthesis.* The Hague: Martin Nijhoff, 1981.

Wagner, Rudolf G., trans. *A Chinese Reading of the Daodejing: Wang Bi's Commentary on the Laozi with Critical Text and Translation*. Albany, NY: State University of New York Press, 2003.

Waley, Arthur. *The Way and its Power: A Study of the Tao Te Ching and its Place in Chinese Thought*. New York: Grove Press, 1958.

Waley, Arthur D., trans. *Analects of Confucius*. New York: Vintage Books, 1989 (1938).

Wang Yang-ming. *Inquiry into the Great Learning*. See: Chan, Wing-tsit, 1963b, 1964.

Watson, Burton, trans. *Mo Tzu: Basic Writings*. New York: Columbia University Press, 1963.

Watson, Burton, trans. *Hsün-tzu: Basic Writings*. New York: Columbia University Press, 1963.

Watson, Burton, trans. *Basic Writings of Mo Tzu, Hsün Tzu, and Han Fei Tzu*. New York: Columbia University Press, 1967.

Watson, Burton, trans. *The Complete Works of Chuang Tzu*. New York: Columbia University Press, 1968.

Weber, Max (Hans H. Gerth, trans. and ed.). *Religion of China*. New York: Free Press, 1968 (1951).

Welch, Holmes. *Taoism: The Parting of the Way*. Boston, MA: Beacon Press, 1966, revised edn. (1965).

Welch, Holmes and Anna Seidel, eds. *Facets of Taoism: Essays in Chinese Religion*. New Haven, CT: Yale University Press, 1979.

Wilhelm, Richard (H.G. Ostwald, trans.). *Tao Te Ching: The Book of Meaning and Life*. London: Arkana, 1985.

Wilson, T.A. *On Sacred Grounds: Culture, Society and the Formation of the Cult of Confucius*. Cambridge, MA: Harvard University Asia Center, 2002.

Wright, Arthur F. *Buddhism in Chinese History*. Stanford, CA: Stanford University Press, 1959.

Wright, Arthur F. and Denis Twitchett, eds. *Perspectives on the T'ang*. New Haven, CT: Yale University Press, 1973.

Wu, Kuang-Ming. *The Butterfly as Companion: Meditations on the First Three Chapters of the Chuang-Tzu*. Albany, NY: State University of New York Press, 1990.

Yao, Xinzhong. *An Introduction to Confucianism*. Cambridge, UK: Cambridge University Press, 2000.

Yampolsky, Philip, trans. *The Platform Sutra of the Sixth Patriarch: The Text of the Tun-huang Manuscript with Translation, Introduction, and Notes*. New York: Columbia University Press, 1967.

Yates, Robin D. *Five Lost Classics: Tao, Huan-Lao, and Yin-Yang in Han China*. New York: Ballantine Books, 1997.

Yu, David C., trans. *History of Chinese Daoism*, Vol. 1. Lanham, MD: University Press of America, 2000.

Zhang, Dainian (Edmund Ryden, trans.). *Key Concepts in Chinese Philosophy*. New Haven, CT: Yale University Press, 2002.

Ztircher, Erik. *The Buddhist Conquest of China*, 2 Vols. Reprint, Leiden, Netherlands: Brill, 1972.

4. KOREAN PHILOSOPHIES

Bartz, Patricia M. *South Korea*. Oxford, UK: Clarendon Press, 1972.

Buswell, Robert E. *The Formation of Ch'an Ideology in China and Korea: The Vajrasamadhi-Sutra, A Buddhist Apocryphon*. Princeton, NJ: Princeton University Press, 1989.

Buswell, Robert E. *The Zen Monastic Experience: Buddhist Practice in Contemporary Korea.* Princeton, NJ: Princeton University Press, 1992.

Chappell, David, ed. (Recorded by Korean Buddhist Monk Chegwan; Buddhist Translation Seminar of Hawaii, trans.). *T'ien-t'ai Buddhism: An Outline of the Fourfold Teachings.* Honolulu, HI: University of Hawaii Press, 1983.

Chinul. *The Korean Approach to Zen: The Collected Works of Chinul.* (Robert Evans Buswell, Jr., trans.). Honolulu, HI: University of Hawaii Press, 1983.

Chinul. (Robert Evans Buswell, Jr., trans.). *Tracing Back the Radiance: Chinul's Korean Way of Zen.* Honolulu, HI: University of Hawaii Press, 1991.

Chung, Chai-Sik. *A Korean Confucian Encounter with the Modern World: Yi Hang-No and the West.* Berkeley, CA: University of California, Institute of East Asian Studies, 1995.

Chung, Edward Y. *The Korean Neo-Confucianism of Yi T'oegye and Yi Yulgok: A Reappraisal of the 'Four-Seven Thesis' and its Practical Implications for Self-Cultivation.* Albany, NY: State University of New York Press, 1995.

Cleary, Thomas F., trans. *Entry into the Realm of Reality. A Translation of the Gandavyuha, the FinalBook of the Avatamsaka Sutra.* Boston, MA: Shambhala, 1989.

De Bary, William Theodore and Jahyun Kim Haboush, eds. *The Rise of Neo-Confucianism in Korea.* New York: Columbia University Press, 1985.

Deuchler, Martina. *The Confucian Transformation of Korea: A Study of Society and Ideology.* Cambridge, MA: Harvard University Press, 1993.

Eckert, Carter J. *et al. Korea, Old and New: A History.* Seoul: Published for the Korea Institute, Harvard University by Ilchokak; Cambridge, MA: Harvard University Press, 1990.

Grayson, James Huntley. *Early Buddhism and Christianity in Korea: A Study in the Emplantation of Religion.* Leiden, Netherlands: E.J. Brill, 1985.

Han, U-gun (Woo-Keun Han) (Lee Kyung-shik, trans. and Grafton K. Mintz, ed.). *The History of Korea.* Seoul: Eul-Yoo, 1970.

Hardacre, Helen. *The Religion of Japan's Korean Minority: The Preservation of Ethnic Identity.* Berkeley, CA: University of California, Institute of East Asian Studies, 1985.

Kakhun, Sok (Peter H. Lee, trans.). *Lives of Eminent Korean Monks: The Haedong kosung chon.* Cambridge, MA: Harvard University Press, 1990 (1969).

Kalton, Michael C., trans. *To Become a Sage: The Ten Diagrams on Sage Learning by Yi T'oegye.* New York: Columbia University Press, 1988.

Kalton, Michael C. *The Four-Seven Debate: An Annotated Translation of the Most Famous Controversy in Korean Neo-Confucian Thought.* Albany, NY: State University of New York Press, 1994.

Kang, Wi J. *Christ and Caesar in Modern Korea: A History of Christianity and Politics.* Albany, NY: SUNY Press, 1997.

Keel, Hee-sung. *Chinul: Founder of the Korean Son Tradition.* Berkeley, CA: University of California at Berkeley, Institute of Buddhist Studies, 1984.

Kendall, Laurel and Griffin Dix, eds. *Religion and Ritual in Korean Society.* Berkeley, CA: University of California, Institute of East Asian Studies, 1987.

Keum, Jang-tae. *Confucianism and Korean Thoughts.* Seoul: Jimoondang, 2000.

Kusan, Sonsa. (Martine Fages, trans. and Stephen Batchelor, ed.). *The Way of Korean Zen.* New York: Weatherhill, 1985.

Kwon, Ho-Youn, ed. *Korean Cultural Roots: Religion and Social Thought.* Chicago, IL: North Park College and Theological Seminary, 1995.

Lancaster, Lewis R. (with Sung-bae Park). *The Korean Buddhist Canon: A Descriptive Catalogue.* Berkeley, CA: University of California Press, 1979.

Lancaster, Lewis R. and C.S. Yu, eds. *Introduction of Buddhism to Korea: New Cultural Patterns.* Berkeley, CA: Asian Humanities Press, 1989.

Lancaster, Lewis R. and C.S. Yu, eds. *Assimilation of Buddhism in Korea: Religious Maturity and Innovation in the Silla Dynasty.* Fremont, CA: Asian Humanities Press, 1991.

Lancaster, Lewis R. and C.S. Yu, eds. *Buddhism in the Early Choson: Suppression and Transformation.* Berkeley, CA: University of California, Institute of East Asian Studies, 1996.

Lancaster, Lewis R., Kikun Suh and Chai-shin Yu, eds. *Buddhism in Koryo: A Royal Religion.* Berkeley, CA: University of California, Institute of East Asian Studies, 1996.

Lee, Jung Y. *Korean Shamanistic Rituals.* Hawthorne, NY: Mouton de Gruyter, 1980.

Lee, Kwan-Jo. *Search for Nirvana: Korean Monks' Life.* Boston, MA: Charles E. Tuttle, 1984.

Lee, Peter H., ed. *Anthology of Korean Literature from Early Times to the 19th Century.* Honolulu, HI: University of Hawaii Press, 1981.

Lee, Peter H. and William Theodore de Bary, eds. (with Yongho Ch'oe and Hugh H.W. Kang). *Sources of Korean Tradition.* New York: Columbia University Press, 1997–.

Mu, Soeng Sunim. *Thousand Peaks: Korean Zen–Tradition and Teachers.* Cumberland, RI: Primary Point Press, 1991, revised edn.

Nemeth, David J. *The Architecture of Ideology: Neo-Confucian Imprinting on Cheju Island, Korea.* Berkeley, CA: University of California Press, 1988.

Odin, Steve. *Process Metaphysics and Hua-yen Buddhism: A Critical Study of Cumulative Penetration vs. Interpenetration.* Albany, NY: State University of New York Press, 1982.

Palais, James B. *Confucian Statecraft and Korean Institutions: Yu Hyongwon and the Late Choson Dynasty.* Seattle, WA: University of Washington Press, 1996.

Palmer, Spencer J. *Confucian Rituals in Korea.* Fremont, CA: Asian Humanities Press, 1984.

Park, Sung Bae. *Buddhist Faith and Sudden Enlightenment.* Albany, NY: SUNY Press, 1983

Pou Kuksa. (trans. with commentary by J.C. Cleary). *A Buddha from Korea: The Zen Teachings of T'aego.* Boston, MA: Shambhala, 1988.

Setton, Mark C. *Chong Yagyong: Korea's Challenge to Orthodox Neo-Confucianism.* Albany, NY: State University of New York Press, 1997.

Shrobe, Richard. *Don't-Know Mind: The Spirit of Korean Zen.* Boston, MA: Shambhala, 2004.

Yang, Nak-Heong. *Reformed Social Ethics and the Korean Church.* New York: Peter Lang, 1997.

Yi, Ki-baek. (Edward W. Wagner, trans., with Edward J. Shultz). *A New History of Korea.* Cambridge, MA: Harvard University Press, 1984.

Young-chan Ro. *The Korean Neo-Confucianism of Yi Yulgok.* Albany, NY: State University of New York Press, 1988.

Yu, C.S. *Shamanism: The Spirit World of Korea.* Fremont, CA: Asian Humanities Press, 1988.

Yun, Sasoon (Michael C. Kalton, trans.). *Critical Issues in Neo-Confucian Thought: The Philosophy of Yi T'oegye.* Honolulu, HI: University of Hawaii Press, 1992.

5. JAPANESE PHILOSOPHIES

Anesaki, Mahasaru. *Nichiren, the Buddhist Prophet,* Cambridge, MA: Harvard University Press, 1916.

Armstrong, Robert C. *Light from the East: Studies in Japanese Confucianism.* Toronto, Canada: University of Toronto, 1914.

Bellah, Robert. *Tokugawa Religion: The Cultural Roots of Modern Japan.* New York: Free Press, 1985.

Bloom, Alfred. *Shinran's Gospel of Pure Grace.* Tucson, AZ: University of Arizona Press, 1965.

Blum, Mark L., ed. *The Origins and Development of Pure Land Buddhism: A Study and Translation of Gyonen's Jodo Homon Genrusho.* Oxford, UK: Oxford University Press, 2002.

Brinker, Helmut and Hiroshi Kanazawa (Andreas Leisinger, trans.). *Zen Masters of Meditation in Images and Writings.* Honolulu, HI: University of Hawaii Press, 1996.

Brinkman, John T. *Simplicity: A Distinctive Quality of Japanese Spirituality.* New York: Peter Lang, 1996.

Carr, Brian and Indira Mahalingam, eds. *Companion Encyclopedia of Asian Philosophy.* New York: Routledge, 1997.

Chien, Cheng. *Manifestation of the Tathagata: Buddahood According to the Avatamsaka Sutra.* Boston, MA: Wisdom, 1993.

Cleary, Thomas F., trans. *The Flower Ornament Scripture: A Translation of the Avatamsaka Sutra,* 3 Vols. Boulder, CO: Shambhala, 1987 (1984).

Coates, Harper Havelock and Ryugaku Ishikuza, trans. *Honen: The Buddhist Saint,* 5 vols. Kyoto, Japan: Society for the Publication of Sacred Books of the World, 1949 (1925).

Cook, Francis. *How to Raise an Ox: Zen Practice as Taught in Zen Master Dogen's Shobogenzo.* Los Angeles, CA: Center Publications, 1978.

Deutsch, Eliot, and Ron Bontekoe, ed. *A Companion to World Philosophies.* Malden, MA: Blackwell, 1997.

Dobbins, Frank. *An Illustrated Comparative Study of Chinese and Japanese Buddhism,* Albuquerque, NM: American Classical College Press, 1988.

Dogen (Reiho Masunaga, trans.). *A Primer of Soto Zen: A Translation of Dogen's Shobogenzo Zuimonki,* Honolulu, HI: East–West Center Press, 1971.

Dogen. *A Complete English Translation of Dogen Zenji's Shobogenzo (The Eye and Treasury of the True Law).* San Francisco, CA: Daihokkaikaku, 1975.

Dogen (Daizui MacPhillamy, trans.). *The Shobogenzo, or, the Treasure House of the Eye of the True Teachings.* Mount Shasta, CA: Shasta Abbey, 1996.

Dumoulin, Heinrich (Paul Peachey, trans.). *A History of Zen Buddhism.* Boston, MA: Beacon Press, 1969.

Earhart, H. Byron. *Religion in the Japanese Experience: Sources and Interpretations.* Encino, CA: Dickenson, 1973; 1974.

Edwards, Paul. *The Encyclopedia of Philosophy,* 8 Vols (4 Vols.). New York: Macmillan, 1972 (1967).

Eliade, Mircea, ed. *The Encyclopedia of Religion,* 16 Vols. New York: Macmillan, 1987.

Eliot, Charles. *Japanese Buddhism.* Honolulu, HI: University of Hawaii Press, 1993.

Fields, Rick. *The Code of the Warrior: A Way of Personal Development Through Classic Warrior Traditions: Japanese Samurai, Plains Indians, and Medieval Knights.* New York: Harper Collins, 1991.

Furuya, Yasuo, ed. *A History of Japanese Theology.* Grand Rapids, MI: William B. Eerdmans, 1996.

Gardner, James L. *Zen Buddhism: A Classified Bibliography of Western-Language Publications through 1990.* New York: Random House, 1991.

Grapard, Allan G. *The Protocol of the Gods: A Study of the Kasuga Cult in Japanese History.* Berkeley, CA: University of California Press, 1992.

Groner, Paul. *Saicho and the Establishment of the Japanese Tendai School.* Berkeley, CA: Center for South and Southeast Asian Studies, University of California at Berkeley, Institute of Buddhist Studies, 1984.

Hakuin (Philip B. Yampolsky, trans.). *The Zen Master Hakuin: Selected Writings.* New York: Columbia University Press, 1971.

Hakuin (Norman Waddell, trans.). *The Essential Teachings of Zen Master Hakuin: A Translation of the Sokko-roku Kaien-fusetsu*. Boston, MA: Shambhala, 1994.

Hamill, Sam. *Basho's Ghost*. Seattle, WA: Broken Moon Press, 1989.

Hammitzsch, Horst. *Zen in the Art of the Tea Ceremony*. New York: Viking Penguin, 1993.

Hatano, Seiichi. (Ichiro Suzuki, trans). *Time and Eternity*. Westport, CT: Greenwood, 1988.

Heine, Steven. *A Dream within a Dream: Studies in Japanese Thought*. New York: Peter Lang, 1991.

Hisao, Inagaki. *A Dictionary of Japanese Buddhist Terms*. Torrance, CA: Heian International Publishing, 1989.

Holzman, Donald, *et al*. *Japanese Religion and Philosophy: A Guide to Japanese Reference and Research Materials*. Ann Arbor, MI: University of Michigan Press, 1959.

Honen. *Honen's Senchakushu: Passages on the Selection of the Nembutsu in the Original Vow (Senchaku hongan nembutsu shu)*. Honolulu, HI: University of Hawaii Press, 1998.

Honen. *See:* Coates, H. and Ishikuza, R.

Hoover, Thomas. *Zen Culture*. New York: Random House, 1977.

Hyers, Conrad. *Once-Born, Twice-Born Zen: The Soto and Rinzai Schools of Japanese Zen*. Durango, CO: Hollowbrook, 1989.

Itoh, Toshio. *Wisdom at Work: Confucian Ideals and Japanese Business Success*. Santa Barbara, CA: Fithian Press, 1992.

Iwasaki, Chikatsugu. *Nihon kindsei shisōshi josetsu ki zenpen*, 2 vols. Tokyo: Shin nihon shuppansha, 1997.

Kageyama, Haruki (Christine Guth, trans.). *Shinto Bijutsu: The Arts of Shinto*. New York: Weatherhill, 1973.

Kaibara, Ekiken. *Women and Wisdom of Japan*. (Selection from the *Onna Daigaku* by Ekiken Kaibara, transl. by Basil Hall Chamberlain in his *Things Japanese* orig. pub. London: J. Murray, 1905.) Microfilm. Glen Rock, NJ: Microfilming Corporation of America, 1975.

Kashiwahara, Yusen and Koyu Sonoda, eds. *Shapers of Japanese Buddhism*. Boston, MA: Charles E. Tuttle, 1993.

Kasuli, Thomas P. *Shinto: The Way Home*. Honolulu, HI: University of Hawaii Press, 2004.

Kim, Hee-jin. *Dogen Kigen, Mystical Realist*. Tucson, AZ: University of Arizona Press, 1975.

Kitagawa, Joseph N. *Religion in Japanese History*. New York: Columbia University Press, 1966.

Kiyota, Minoru. *Shingon Buddhism: Theory and Practice*. Los Angeles, CA: Buddhist Books International, 1978.

Kodera, T. James. *Dogen's Formative Years in China: An Historical Study and Annotated Translation of the Hokyo-ki*. Boulder, CO: Prajna Press, 1980.

Kraft, Kenneth. *Eloquent Zen: Daito and Early Japanese Zen*. Honolulu, HI: University of Hawaii Press, 1997.

Kukai. (Yoshito S. Hakeda, trans.) *Kukai: Major Works*. New York: Columbia University Press, 1972.

Lotus Sutra. See: Watson, B.

Maruyama, Masao (Mikiso Hane, trans.). *Studies in the Intellectual History of Tokugawa Japan*. Princeton, NJ: Princeton University Press, 1974.

Matsunaga, Alice and Daigan Matsunaga. *Foundations of Japanese Buddhism*. 2 Vols. Los Angeles, CA: Buddhist Books International, 1974.

McCallum, Donald F. *Zenkoji and its Icon: A Study in Medieval Japanese Religious Art*. Princeton, NJ: Princeton University Press, 1994.

McFarland, H. Neill. *Daruma: The Founder of Zen in Japanese Art and Popular Culture*. New York: Kodansha America, 1987.

McGovern, William M. *Introduction to Mahayana Buddhism: With Special Reference to Chinese and Japanese Phases*. Columbia, MO: South Asia Books, 1997.

Mercer, Rosemary, trans. *Deep Words: Miura Baien's System of Natural Philosophy*. Boston, MA: Brill Academic, 1991.

Mochizuki, Kanko. *Nichiren Kyogaku no kenkyu*. Kyoto, Japan: Heirakuji Shoten, 1958.

Motoori, Norinaga (Ann Wehmeyer, trans.). *Kojiki-den*. Book 1. Ithaca, NY: East Asia Program, Cornell University, 1997.

Nagatomo Shigenori. *Attunement through the Body*. Albany, NY: State University of New York Press, 1992.

Nakamura, Hajime. *Ways of Thinking of Eastern Peoples; India-Tibet-China-Japan*. Reprint, Columbia, MO: South Asia Books, 1991.

Nakamura, Kyoko M. (trans.). *Miraculous Stories from the Japanese Buddhist Tradition: The Nihon Ryoiki of the Monk Kyokai*. Honolulu, HI: University of Hawaii Press, 1997.

Nichiren. (Burton Watson *et al., trans.* and Philip B. Yampolsky, ed.). *Letters of Nichiren*. New York: Columbia University Press, 1996.

Nosco, Peter, ed. *Confucianism and Tokugawa Culture*. Princeton, NJ: Princeton University Press, 1984.

Ono, Motonari. *Shinto: The Kami Way*. Rutland, VT: Charles E. Tuttle, 1962.

Payne, Richard, ed. *Re-visioning "Kamakura" Buddhism*. Honolulu, HI: University of Hawaii Press, 1998.

Petzold, Bruno. *Buddhist Prophet Nichiren: A Lotus in the Sun*. Tokyo: Hokke Janaru, 1978.

Saicho (Robert Rhodes, trans.). *The Candle of the Latter Dharma*. Berkeley, CA: Numata Center for Buddhist Translation and Research, 1994.

Sanford, James H., Masatoshi Nagatomi, and William R. Lafleur, eds. *Flowing Traces: Buddhism in the Literary and Visual Arts of Japan*. Princeton, NJ: Princeton University Press, 1992.

Shaner, David Edward. *The Bodymind Experience in Japanese Buddhism*. Albany, NY: State University of New York Press, 1986.

Shoeki, Ando. (Yasunaga Toshinobu, trans.). *Ando Shoeki: Selected Works, Selected Writings*. New York: Weatherhill, 1992.

Stone, Jacqueline I. *Original Enlightenment and the Transformation of Medieval Japanese Buddhism*. Honolulu, HI: University of Hawaii Press, 1999.

Storry, George Richard. *The Way of the Samurai*. New York: Putnam, 1978.

Suzuki, D.T. *Collected Writings on Shin Buddhism*. Kyoto, Japan: Shinshu Otaniha, 1973.

Suzuki, D.T. *Zen and Japanese Culture*. Princeton, NJ: Princeton University Press, 1993 (1959).

Tajima, Ryujun. *Les deux grands mandalas et la doctrine de ésoterisme Shingon*. Paris: Maison Francojaponaise, 1959.

Takenuki, Kenjō. *Nihon zenshūshi*. Tokyo: Daizō shuppan, 1989.

Tamura, Yoshirō. *Hongaku shisō ron*. Tokyo: Shunjūsha, 1990.

Taylor, Rodney L. *The Confucian Way of Contemplation: Okada Takehiko and the Tradition of Quiet Sitting*. Columbia, SC: University of South Carolina Press, 1988.

Totman, Conrad. *Japan before Perry: A Short History*. Berkeley, CA: University of California Press, 1981.

Tsunoda, Ryusaku, William Theodore De Bary, and Donald Keene, eds. *Sources of Japanese Tradition*, 2 Vols. New York: Columbia University Press, 1969 (1958).

Tucker, Mary E., ed. *Moral and Spiritual Cultivation in Japanese Neo-Confucianism: The Life and Thought of Kaibara Ekken*. Albany, NY: State University of New York Press, 1989.

Tyler, Susan C. *The Cult of Kasuga Seen Through its Art*. Ann Arbor, MI: University of Michigan, Center for Japanese Studies, 1992.

Waddell, Normanoth, trans. *The Life of Hakuin: Life Records of the Japanese Zen Master.* New York: Kodansha America, 1994.

Watson, Burton, trans. *The Lotus Sutra.* New York: Columbia University Press, 1993.

Yamaga, Soko. *Yamaga Sokos 'Kompendium der Weisenlehre' (Seikyo yöroku): ein Wörterbuch des neoklassischen Konfuzianismus im Japan des 11. Jahrhunderts.* Wiesbaden, Germany: O. Harrassowitz, 1989.

Yamasaki, Taiko and Carmen Blacker. *Shingon: Japanese Esoteric Buddhism.* Boston, MA: Shambhala, 1988.

Yamashita, Samuel H. *Master Sorai's Responsals: An Annotated Translation of Sorai Sensei Tomonsho.* Honolulu, HI: University of Hawaii Press, 1994.

Yokoi, Yuho (with Victoria Daizen). *Zen Master Dogen: An Introduction with Selected Writings.* New York: Weatherhill, 1976.

Yuasa, Yasuo. *The Body: Toward an Eastern Mind–Body Theory.* (Nagatomo Shigenori and T.P. Kasulis, trans.; T.P. Kasulis, ed.). Albany, NY: State University of New York Press, 1987.

6. PHILOSOPHIES OF GREECE, ROME AND THE NEAR EAST

Ackrill, J.L. *Aristotle the Philosopher.* Oxford, UK: Oxford University Press, 1981.

Ackrill, J.L., ed. *A New Aristotle Reader.* Princeton, NJ: Princeton University Press, 1987.

Ackrill, J.L. *Essays on Plato and Aristotle.* New York: Oxford University Press, 1997.

Anastaplo, George. *The Thinker as Artist: From Homer to Plato and Aristotle.* Athens, OH: Ohio University Press, 1997.

Arieti, James A. *Interpreting Plato: The Dialogues as Drama.* Lanham, MD: Rowman & Littlefield, 1991.

Aristotle. *Metaphysics.* (Trans. with commentaries by Hippocrates G. Apostle). Grinnell, IA: Peripatetic Press, 1979.

Aristotle. Jonathan Barnes, ed. *The Complete Works of Aristotle: The Revised Oxford Translation,* 2 Vols. Princeton, NJ: Princeton University Press, 1984.

Aristotle. J.L. Ackrill, trans. *Aristotle's Categories, and De Interpretatione.* Oxford, UK: Clarendon Press, 1990 (1963).

Aristotle. *Poetics.* (Stephen Halliwell *et al.,* trans.) Cambridge, UK: Harvard University Press, 1995, 2nd edn.

Aristotle. *Nichomachean Ethics.* Lincolnwood, IL: NTC/Contemporary Publishing, 1997.

Armstrong, A.H. *The Architecture of the Intelligible Universe in the Philosophy of Plotinus.* Cambridge, UK: Cambridge University Press, 1940.

Armstrong, A.H., ed. *The Cambridge History of Later Greek and Early Medieval Philosophy.* London: Cambridge University Press, 1967.

Augustine, St *Confessions.* (R.S. Pine-Coffin, trans.) Harmondsworth, UK: Penguin, 1981.

Augustine, St *The City of God.* (H. Bettenson, trans.) Harmondsworth, UK: Penguin, 1984.

Austin, Scott. *Parmenides: Being, Bounds and Logic.* New Haven, CT: Yale University Press, 1986.

Bailey, Cyril. *Greek Atomists and Epicurus: A Study.* Oxford, UK: Clarendon Press, 1928.

Balot, Ryan. *Greek Political Thought.* Malden, MA: Blackwell, 2006.

Balthasar, Hans Urs von. (Mark Sebanc, trans.). *Presence and Thought: Essay on the Religious Philosophy of Gregory of Nyssa.* San Francisco, CA: Ignatius Press, 1995.

Barnes, Jonathan. *The Presocratic Philosophers.* London: Routledge, 1982.

Barnes, Jonathan, ed. *The Cambridge Companion to Aristotle*. New York: Cambridge University Press, 1995.

Barnes, Timothy D. *Constantine and Eusebius*. Cambridge, MA: Harvard University Press, 1981.

Benardete, Seth. *The Rhetoric of Morality and Philosophy: Plato's Gorgias and Phaedrus*. Chicago, IL: University of Chicago Press, 1991.

Bidez, J. *Vie de Porphyrie, le philosophe néo-platonicien: avec les fragments des traités [Peri agalmaton (romanized form)] et De regressu animae*. Hildesheim, Germany: G. Olm, 1964.

Bignone, Ettore. *Empedocles*. Turin, Italy: Fratelli Bocca, 1916.

Blackwood, R.T. and Herman, A.L., eds. *Problems in Philosophy: West and East*. Englewood Cliffs, NJ: Prentice-Hall, 1975.

Blumenthal, H.J. *Aristotle and Neoplatonism in Late Antiquity: Interpretations of the 'De Anima'*. Ithaca, NY: Cornell University Press, 1996.

Bolotin, David. *An Approach to Aristotle's Physics: With Particular Attention to the Role of His Manner of Writing*. Albany, NY: State University of New York Press, 1997.

Bos, E.P. and P.A. Meijer, eds. *On Proclus and His Influence in Medieval Philosophy*. Leiden, Netherlands: E.J. Brill, 1992.

Boyce, Mary. *Zoroastrians: Their Religious Beliefs and Practices*. London: Routledge & Kegan Paul, 1979.

Boyce, Mary, trans. *Textual Sources for the Study of Zoroastrianism*. Totowa, NJ: Barnes & Noble, 1984.

Bradshaw, David. *Aristotle East and West: Metaphysics and the Division of Christendom*. Cambridge, UK: Cambridge University Press, 2004.

Bréhier, Emile. *La philosophie de Plotin*. Paris: J. Vrin, 1961, 2nd edn.

Brentano, Franz. (Rolf A. George, trans.). *On the Several Senses of Being in Aristotle*. Reprint, Berkeley, CA: University of California Press, 1981.

Brown, Peter. *Augustine of Hippo: A Biography*. Berkeley, CA: University of California Press, 1967.

Burkert, Walter. (Edwin L. Minar, Jr., trans.). *Lore and Science in Ancient Pythagoreanism*. Cambridge, MA: Harvard University Press, 1972.

Burnet, J. *Early Greek Philosophy*. London: A. & C. Black, 1952, 4th edn. (1930).

Burnyeat, Myles F., ed. *The Skeptical Tradition*. Berkeley, CA: University of California Press, 1983.

Burnyeat, Myles F. *The Theaetetus of Plato*. Indianapolis, IN: Hackett, (Reprint) 1990.

Burrell, Roy. *The Greeks*. Oxford, UK: Oxford University Press, 1989.

Bussell, F.W. *Marcus Aurelius and the Later Stoics*. Edinburgh: T. & T. Clark, 1910.

Chadwick, Henry. *Early Christian Thought and the Classical Tradition: Studies in Justin, Clement and Origen*. New York: Oxford University Press, 1966.

Chadwick, Henry. *Augustine*. Oxford, UK: Oxford University Press, 1986.

Cohen, S. Marc, Patricia Curd and C.D.C. Reeve, eds. *Readings in Ancient Greek Philosophy: From Thales to Aristotle*. Indianapolis, IN: Hackett, 1995.

Connell, Richard J. *Substance and Modern Science*. Notre Dame, IN: University of Notre Dame Press, 1988.

Cooper, John M. *Reason and Human Good in Aristotle*. Cambridge, MA: Harvard University Press, 1975.

Cornford, F.M., trans. *Plato and Parmenides: Parmenides' Way of Truth and Plato's Parmenides*. New York: Harcourt Brace, 1939.

Dancy, R.M. *Two Studies in the Early Academy*. Albany, NY: State University of New York Press, 1991.

Daniélou, Jean. (Walter Mitchell, trans.). *Origen*. New York: Sheed and Ward, 1955.

Davis, Michael. *The Politics of Philosophy: A Commentary on Aristotle's Politics*. Lanham, MD: Rowman & Littlefield, 1996.

Day, Jane M. *Plato's Meno in Focus*. London: Routledge, 1994.

De Vogel, C.J. "Amor quo caelum regitur." *Vivarium* 1 (1963), 2–34.

Denyer, Nicholas. *Language, Thought and Falsehood in Ancient Greek Philosophy*. London: Routledge, 1993.

Desjardins, Rosemary. *The Rational Enterprise: Logos in Plato's Theaetetus*. Albany, New York: State University of New York Press, 1990.

Dillon, John. *The Middle Platonists 80 BC to AD 220*. Ithaca, NY: Cornell University Press, 1977.

Dilman, Ilham. *Philosophy and the Philosophic Life: A Study in Plato's Phaedo*. New York: Saint Martin's Press, 1991.

Dionysius the Areopagite. *Pseudo-Dionysius: The Complete Works* (trans. Colm Luibheid). New York: Paulist Press, 1987.

Dodds, Eric R. *The Greeks and the Irrational*. Berkeley, CA: University of California Press, 1951.

Dudley, Donald R. *A History of Cynicism from Diogenes to the 6th century AD*. London: Methuen, 1937.

Durrant, Michael. *Aristotle's De Anima in Focus*. London: Routledge, 1993.

Empedocles. (M.R. Wright, ed.). *Empedocles, the Extant Fragments*. New Haven, CT: Yale University Press, 1981.

Empedocles. *Purifications*. *See:* Selections in Wheelwright, Philip, ed. and in *Empedocles, the Extant Fragments,* M.R. Wright, ed.

Everson, Stephen. *Aristotle: The Politics and the Constitution of Athens*. New York: Cambridge University Press, 1996, 2nd edn.

Everson, Stephen. *Aristotle on Perception*. New York: Oxford University Press, 1997.

Farquhar, J.N. *The Crown of Hinduism*. London: H. Milford, Oxford University Press, 1930.

Ferguson, John. *Aristotle*. New York: Twayne, 1972.

Festugière, A.J. (C.W. Chilton, trans.). *Epicurus and His Gods*. Oxford, UK: Blackwell, 1955.

Findlay, J.N. *Plato and Platonism: An Introduction*. New York: Times Books, 1978.

Fine, Gail. *On Ideas: Aristotle's Criticism of Plato's Theory of Forms*. New York: Oxford University Press, 1993.

Frankfort, Henri, H.A. Frankfort and John A. Wilson. *The Intellectual Adventure of Ancient Man: An Essay on Speculative Thought in the Ancient Near East*. Chicago, IL: University of Chicago Press, 1946.

Freudenthal, Gad. *Aristotle's Theory of Material Substance: Heat and Pneuma, Form and Soul*. New York: Oxford University Press, 1995.

Gagarin, Michael and David Cohen, eds. *The Cambridge Companion to Ancient Greek Law*. Cambridge, UK: Cambridge University Press, 2005.

Gerson, Lloyd P., ed. *The Cambridge Companion to Plotinus*. New York: Cambridge University Press, 1996.

Gerson, Lloyd P. *Plotinus*. London: Routledge, 1998.

Gill, M.L., D. Charles and Theodore Scaltsas, eds. *Unity and Identity in Aristotle's Metaphysics*. New York: Oxford University Press, 1994.

Gilson, Etienne (L.E.M. Lynch, trans.). *The Christian Philosophy of St Augustine*. New York: Random House, 1960.

Gosling, J.C.B. *Plato*. London: Routledge, 1983.

Granger, Herbert. *Aristotle's Idea of the Soul*. Norwell, MA: Kluwer Academic, 1996.

Grant, Robert M. *Augustus to Constantine: The Rise and Triumph of Christianity in the Roman World*. San Francisco, CA: Harper & Row, 1990 (1970).

Gregory of Nyssa. *Gregory of Nyssa: Ascetical Works* (Virginia Woods Callaban, trans.) Washingotn, DC: Catholic University of America Press, 1967.

Grene, Marjorie. *A Portrait of Aristotle*. Chicago, IL: University of Chicago Press, 1964 (1963).

Guthrie, W.K.C. *A History of Greek Philosophy,* 6 Vols. Cambridge, UK: University Press, 1962–65.

Guthrie, W.K.C. *The Greek Philosophers: From Thales to Aristotle*. London: Routledge, 1968.

Guthrie, W.K.C. *The Sophists*. London: Cambridge University Press, 1971.

Hadot, Pierre (Michael Chase, trans.). *The Inner Citadel: The* Meditations *of Marcus Aurelius*. Cambridge, MA: Harvard University Press, 1998.

Hadot, Pierre (Michael Chase, trans.). *What Is Ancient Philosophy?* Cambridge, MA: Belknap Press of Harvard University Press, 2002.

Hampton, Cynthia. *Pleasure, Knowledge, and Being: An Analysis of Plato's Philebus*. Albany, NY: State University of New York Press, 1990.

Hankinson, R.J. *The Sceptics*. London: Routledge, 1995.

Heidegger, Martin. *Aristotle, Metaphysics Theta 1–3: On the Essence and Actuality of Force*. Bloomington, IN: Indiana University Press, 1995.

Hintikka, Jaakko. *Time and Necessity: Studies in Aristotle's Theory of Modality*. New York: Oxford University Press, 1973.

Hoitenga, Dewey J., Jr. *Faith and Reason from Plato to Plantinga: An Introduction to Reformed Epistemology*. Albany, NY: State University of New York Press, 1991.

Hussey, Joan M. *Church and Learning in the Byzantine Empire, 867–1185*. London: Oxford University Press, 1937.

Ierodiakonou, Katerina, ed. *Byzantine Philosophy and Its Ancient Sources*. Oxford, UK: Clarendon Press, 2002.

Inge, W.R. *The Philosophy of Plotinus,* 2 Vols. London: Longmans, Green and Co., 1948, 3rd edn.

Inwood, Brad, ed. *The Cambridge Companion to the Stoics*. Cambridge, UK: Cambridge University Press, 2003.

Inwood, B. and Gerson, L., eds. *Hellenistic Philosophy: Introductory Readings*. Indianapolis, IN: Hackett, 1988.

Irwin, Terence. *Classical Thought*. Oxford, UK: Oxford University Press, 1989.

Jaeger, Werner. (Gilbert Highet, trans.). *Paideia: The Ideals of Greek Culture*. New York: Oxford University Press, 1945, 2nd edn.

John of Damascus, Saint. (Frederic H. Chase, Jr., trans.). *Writings*. Washington, DC: Catholic University of America Press, 1970 (1958).

Jones, Howard. *The Epicurean Tradition*. London: Routledge, 1992.

Jordan, William. *Ancient Concepts of Philosophy*. London: Routledge, 1993.

Kahn, Charles H. *Anaximander and the Origins of Greek Cosmology*. New York: Columbia University Press, 1964.

Kahn, Charles H., ed. *The Art and Thought of Heraclitus: An Edition of the Fragments with Translation and Commentary*. Cambridge, UK: Cambridge University Press, 1979.

Kelly, J.N. *Early Christian Creeds*. London: Longman, 1972, 3rd edn.

Kirk, G.S., ed. *Heraclitus: The Cosmic Fragments.* Cambridge, UK: Cambridge University Press, 1954.

Kirk, G.S., J.E. Raven and M. Schofield *The Presocratic Philosophers.* Cambridge, UK: Cambridge University Press, 1983.

Kraut, Richard, ed. *The Cambridge Companion to Plato.* New York: Cambridge University Press, 1992.

Kraut, Richard. *Aristotle: Political Philosophy.* Oxford, UK: Oxford University Press, 2002.

Kraut, Richard, ed. *The Blackwell Guide to Aristotle's Ethics.* Oxford, UK: Blackwell, 2005.

Lear, Jonathan. *Aristotle: The Desire to Understand.* New York: Cambridge University Press, 1988.

Lee, H.D.P., trans. *Zeno of Elea.* Cambridge, UK: Cambridge University Press, 1936.

Lewis, Frank A. *Substance and Predication in Aristotle.* New York: Cambridge University Press, 1992.

Lieu, Samuel N.C. *Manichaeism in the Later Roman Empire and Medieval China: A Historical Survey.* Manchester, UK: Manchester University Press, 1985.

Lloyd, G.E. *Aristotelian Explorations.* New York: Cambridge University Press, 1996.

Long, A.A. *Hellenistic Philosophy: Stoics, Epicureans, Sceptics.* London: Duckworth, 1986.

Long, A.A. and D.N. Sedley, eds. *The Hellenistic Philosophers.* 2 Vols. Cambridge, UK: Cambridge University Press, 1987.

Lossky, Vladimir. *The Mystical Theology of the Eastern Church.* London: J. Clarke, 1957.

Louth, Andrew. *Origins of the Christian Mystical Tradition: From Plato to Denys.* Oxford, UK: Clarendon Press, 1981.

Louth, Andrew. *Denys the Areopagite.* London: Geoffrey Chapman, 1989.

Louth, Andrew. *Maximus the Confessor.* London and New York: Routledge, 1996.

Loux, Michael J. *Primary Ousia: An Essay on Aristotle's Metaphysics Z and H.* Ithaca, NY: Cornell University Press, 1991.

Lucretius. (R. Latharn, trans.). *On the Nature of the Universe.* Harmondsworth, UK: Penguin, 1986.

Lucretius Carus, Titus. (Sir Ronald Melville, Don Fowler and Peta Fowler, trans.). *On the Nature of the Universe (De Rerum Natura).* Oxford, UK: Clarendon Press, 1997.

Lukasiewicz, Jan. *Aristotle's Syllogistic from the Standpoint of Modern Formal Logic.* Oxford, UK: Clarendon Press, 1957, 2nd edn.

Malcolm, John. *Plato on the Self-Predication of Forms: Early and Middle Dialogues.* New York: Oxford University Press, 1991.

Marrou, H.L. (Patrick Hepburne-Scott; trans.; texts of St Augustine, Edmund Hill, trans.). *Augustine and his Influence through the Ages.* New York: Harper, 1962 (1957).

Maximus the Confessor. *Maximus Confessor: Selected Writings* (George C. Berthold, trans.). New York: Paulist Press, 1985.

Mayhew, Robert. *Aristotle's Criticism of Plato's 'Republic'.* Lanham, MD: Rowman & Littlefield, 1997.

Meyendorff, John. *A Study of Gregory Palamas.* London: Faith Press, 1964 (1959).

Meyendorff, John. *A Study of Gregory Palamas.* Crestwood, NY: St Vladimir's Seminary Press, 1974. Originally published as *Introduction à l'étude de Grégoire Palamas.* Paris: Editions du Seuil, 1959.

Meyer, Marvin W., ed. *The Ancient Mysteries, a Sourcebook: Sacred Texts of the Mystery Religions of the Ancient Mediterranean World.* New York: Harper & Row, 1987.

Miller, Fred D. Jr. *Nature, Justice, and Rights in Aristotle's Politics.* New York: Oxford University Press, 1997.

Miller, Mitchell H., Jr. *Plato's Parmenides: The Conversion of the Soul*. University Park, PA: Pennsylvania State University Press, 1991.

Moline, Jan. *Plato's Theory of Understanding*. Madison, WI: University of Wisconsin Press, 1981.

Morenz, Siegfried. (Ann E. Keep, trans.). *Egyptian Religion*. Ithaca, NY: Cornell University Press, 1973.

Nussbaum, Martha. *The Therapy of Desire: Theory and Practice of Hellenistic Ethics*. Princeton, NJ: Princeton University Press, 1994.

Oates, Whitney J., ed. *Basic Writings of St Augustine*, 2 Vols. New York: Random House, 1948.

O'Brien, Denis. *Empedocles' Cosmic Cycle: A Reconstruction from the Fragments and Secondary Sources*. London: Cambridge University Press, 1969.

O'Brien, Michael J. *The Socratic Paradoxes and the Greek Mind*. Chapel Hill, NC: University of North Carolina Press, 1967.

Ophir, Adi. *Plato's Invisible Cities: Discourse and Power in the Republic*. London: Routledge, 1991.

Palamas, Gregory (Nicholas Gendle, trans). *Gregory Palamas: The Triads*. New York: Paulist Press, 1983.

Patrick, Mary Mills. *The Greek Sceptics*. New York: Columbia University Press, 1929.

Pavry, J.D.C. *The Zoroastrian Doctrine of a Future Life: From Death to the Individual Judgment*. New York: Columbia University Press, 1926.

Pelletier, Francis J. *Parmenides, Plato and the Semantics of Not-Being*. Chicago, IL: University of Chicago Press, 1990.

Philip, James A. *Pythagoras and Early Pythagoreanism*. Toronto, Canada: University of Toronto Press, 1966.

Photius I, Saint, Patriarch of Constantinople. (Nigel Guy Wilson, trans.). *The Bibliotheca: A Selection*. London: Duckworth, 1994.

Planinc, Zdravko. *Plato's Political Philosophy: Prudence in the Republic and the Laws*. Columbia, MO: University of Missouri Press, 1991.

Plato. (Edith Hamilton and Huntington Cairns, eds.). *Collected Dialogues*. Princeton, NJ: Princeton University Press, 1961.

Plato. (John M. Cooper, trans.). *Plato, Complete Works*. Indianapolis, IN: Hackett, 1997.

Plotinus. (S. MacKenna, trans.). *Enneads*. London: Faber & Faber, 1962, 3rd edn.

Popper, Karl. *The Open Society and Its Enemies*, 2 Vols. Princeton, NJ: Princeton University Press, 1966, 5th edn.

Prestige, George L. *God in Patristic Thought*. London: SPCK, 1952, 2nd edn.

Price, A.W. *Love and Friendship in Plato and Aristotle*. New York: Oxford University Press, (Reprint) 1990.

Prior, William J. *Socrates: Critical Assessments*. London: Routledge, 1997.

Psellus, Michael. *Fourteen Byzantine Rulers: The Chronographia of Michael Psellus*. Harmondsworth, UK: Penguin Books, 1966, revised edn.

Randall, John H. *Plato: Dramatist of the Life of Reason*. New York: Columbia University Press, 1970.

Raven, J.E. *Pythagoreans and Eleatics: An Account of the Interaction between the Two Opposed Schools During the Fifth and Early Fourth Centuries BC*. Cambridge, UK: Cambridge University Press, 1948.

Reedy, Jeremiah, trans. *The Platonic Doctrines of Albinus*. Grand Rapids, MI: Phanes Press, 1991.

Reeve, C.D. *Practices of Reason: Aristotle's Nicomachean Ethics*. New York: Oxford University Press, 1995.

Rist, John M. *Plotinus: The Road to Reality*. Cambridge, UK: Cambridge University Press, 1967.

Rist, John M. *Stoic Philosophy*. London: Cambridge University Press, 1969.

Rist, John M. *Epicurus: An Introduction*. Cambridge, UK: Cambridge University Press, 1972.

Roochnik, David. *The Tragedy of Reason: Towards a Platonic Conception of Logos*. New York: Routledge, 1990.

Roques, René. *L'univers dionysien*. Paris: Aubier, 1954.

Rorty, Amelie O., ed. *Essays on Aristotle's Rhetoric*. Berkeley, CA: University of California Press, 1996.

Rosan, L.J. *The Philosophy of Proclus*. New York: Cosmos, 1949.

Ross, David. *Aristotle*. New York: Routledge, 1995, 6th edn.

Ross, W.D. *Plato's Theory of Ideas*. Oxford, UK: Clarendon Press, 1951.

Rowe, Christopher and Malcolm Schofield, eds. *Greek and Roman Political Thought*. Cambridge, UK: Cambridge University Press, 2000.

Rudolph, Kurt. *Gnosis: The Nature and History of Gnosticism*. San Francisco, CA: Harper & Row, 1983.

Sandmek, Samuel. *Philo of Alexandria: An Introduction*. New York: Oxford University Press, 1979.

Sayre, F. *The Greek Cynics*. Baltimore, MD: J.H. Furst, 1948.

Schofield, Malcolm. *An Essay on Anaxagoras*. Cambridge, UK: Cambridge University Press, 1980.

Sharples, R.W. *Stoics, Epicureans and Sceptics: An Introduction to Hellenistic Philosophy*. London: Routledge, 1996.

Stough, Charlotte L. *Greek Skepticism: A Study in Epistemology*. Berkeley, CA: University of California Press, 1969.

Stove, David. *The Plato Cult and Other Philosophical Follies*. Malden, MA: Blackwell, 1991.

Stunkel, Kenneth R. *Relations of Indian, Greek and Christian Thought in Antiquity*. Washington, DC: University Press of America, 1979.

Suarez, Francisco. *On Efficient Causality: Metaphysical Disputations 17–19*. New Haven, CT: Yale University Press, 1995.

Tarrant, Harold. *Scepticism or Platonism: The Philosophy of the Fourth Academy*. Cambridge, UK: Cambridge University Press, 1985.

Tatakis, Basil. *Byzantine Philosophy*. Indianapolis, IN: Hackett, 2003. Originally published as *La philosophie Byzantine*. Paris: Presses Universitaires de France, 1949.

Taylor, A.E. *Socrates*. London: Peter Davies, 1951.

Taylor, C.C.W., ed. *From the Beginning to Plato*. London: Routledge, 1997.

Teodorsson, Sven-Tage. *Anaxagoras' Theory of Matter*. Göteborg, Sweden: Acta Universitatis Gothoburgensis, 1982.

Thunberg, Lars. *Microcosm and Mediator: The Theological Anthropology of Maximus the Confessor*. Chicago, IL: Open Court Press, 1995, 2nd edn.

Veatch, Henry B. *Rational Man: A Modern Interpretation of Aristotelian Ethics*. Bloomington, IN: Indiana University Press, 1962.

Vernant, Jean Pierre. *The Origins of Greek Thought*. Ithaca, NY: Cornell University Press, 1982.

Vernant, Jean Pierre. *Myth and Thought among the Greeks*. London: Routledge & Kegan Paul, 1983.

Versényi, Laszlo. *Socratic Humanism*. New Haven, CT: Yale University Press, 1963.

Virgil (W.F. Jackson Knight, trans. and ed.). *The Aeneid*. Baltimore, MD: Penguin Books, 1962.

Vlastos, Gregory, ed. *The Philosophy of Plato and Aristotle*. North Stratford, MH: Ayer, 1973.

Vlastos, Gregory. *The Philosophy of Socrates: A Collection of Critical Essays*. Notre Dame, IN: University of Notre Dame Press, 1980 (1971).

Wheelwright, Philip, ed. *The Presocratics*. Indianapolis, IN: Odyssey Press/Bobbs-Merrill, 1966.

White, Nicholas. *Individual and Conflict in Greek Ethics*. Oxford, UK: Oxford University Press, 2002.

Whittaker, Thomas. *The Neo-platonists*. Cambridge, UK: Cambridge University Press, 1918, 2nd edn.

Widengren, Geo. *Mani und der Manichäismus*. Stuttgart, 1961.

Wiles, Maurice F. *The Making of Christian Doctrine*. London: Cambridge University Press, 1967.

Witt, Charlotte. *Substance and Essence in Aristotle: An Interpretation of Metaphysics, VII–IX*. Ithaca, NY: Cornell University Press, 1989.

Witt, R.E. *Albinus and the History of Middle Platonism*. Cambridge, UK: Cambridge University Press, 1937.

Zaehner, R.C. *The Dawn and Twilight of Zoroastrianism*. London: Weidenfeld and Nicolson, 1961.

Zervos, Christos. *Un Philosophe néoplatonicien du XIe siècle: Michael Psellos*. Paris: E. Leroux, 1920.

Zeyl, Donald J., ed. *Encyclopedia of Classical Philosophy*. Westport, CT: Greenwood, 1997.

7. ISLAMIC PHILOSOPHIES

Abrahamov, Binyamin. *Divine Love in Islamic Mysticism*. London: Routledge, 2003.

Adamson, P. *Al-Kindi*. New York: Oxford University Press, 2007.

Adamson, P. and R. Taylor, eds. *Cambridge Companion to Arabic Philosophy*, Cambridge, UK: Cambridge University Press, 2005.

Affifi, Abul E. *The Mystical Philosophy Muhyid Din-Ibnul 'Arabi*. Cambridge, UK: Cambridge University Press, 1939.

Afnan, Soheil M. *Avicenna: His Life and Works*. London: Allen & Unwin, 1958.

Ahmed, Akbar S. *Discovering Islam: Making Sense of Muslim History and Society*. London: Routledge, 1989.

Ali, Kecia and Oliver Leaman. *Islam: The Key Concepts*. London: Routledge, 2008.

Arnzen, R. and J. Thielmann, eds., *Words, Texts and Concepts Cruising the Mediterranean Sea: Studies on the Sources, Contents and Influences of Islamic Civilization and Arabic Philosophy and Science*. Leuven, Belgium: Peeters, 2004.

al-Ash'ari, 'Ali Ibn Isma'il. (Richard Joseph McCarthy, ed.). *The Theology of al-Ash'ari: The Arabic Texts of al-Ash'ari's Kitāb al-Luma' and Risālat Istiḥsān al-Khawd fi 'Ilm al-Kalām*. Beirut: Impr. Catholique, 1953.

al-Ash'ari, 'Ali Ibn Isma 'il. (Walter Conrad Klein, ed.). *Abu'l-Hasan 'Ali Ibn Isma 'il al-Ash'ari's al-Ibanah 'An Usul Ad-diyanah (The Elucidation of Islam's Foundation)*. New York: Kraus, 1967.

Allard, Michel. *Le problème des attributs divins dans la doctrine d'al-As'ari et de des premiers grands disciples*. Beirut: Impr. Catholique, 1965.

Arberry, Arthur J., trans. *The Doctrine of the Sufis. (Kitāb al-Ta'arruf li-madhhab ahl al-Tasawwuf)* Cambridge, UK: Cambridge University Press, 1935.

Arberry, Arthur J. *Sufism: An Account of the Mystics of Islam*. New York: Routledge, Chapman & Hall, 1990.

Attar, Farid Al-Din. *Muslim Saints and Mystics*. New York: Routledge, 1976.

Averroes. (Simon van den Bergh, trans.). *Tahafut al-Tahafut (The Incoherence of 'The Incoherence')*, 2 Vols. London: Luzac, 1969, 1954.

Averroes. *Kitāb Faṣl al-Maqāl, with its Appendix (Damīma) and an Extract from Kitab al-Kashf' 'an Manāhij al-Adilla [by] Ibn Rushd (Averroes)*. (Arabic text, George F. Hourani, ed.). Leiden, Netherlands: E.J. Brill, 1959.

Averroes. (G.F. Hourani, trans.). *Averroes on the Harmony of Religion and Philosophy*. (A translation, with introduction and notes, of Ibn Rushd's *Kitab Fasl al-Maqal*, with its appendix (Damima) and an extract from *Kitab al-kashf 'an manahij al-adilla*.). London: Luzac, 1961.

Avicenna. *Avicenna's Psychology: An English translation of Kitāb al-Najāt, Book II, Chapter VI*. (With historico-philosophical notes and textual improvements on the Cairo edition by Fazlur Rahman). London: Oxford University Press, 1952.

Avicenna. (Fazlur Rahman, ed.). *Avicenna's De Anima (Arabic Text): Being the Psychological Part of Kitab al-Shifa'*. London: Oxford University Press, 1959.

Avicenna. (Farhang Zabeeh, trans. and ed.) *Avicenna's Treatise on Logic. (A Concise Philosophical Encyclopaedia) and Autobiography*. The Hague: Nijhoff, 1971.

Avicenna. *Avicenna's Commentary on the Poetics of Aristotle*. (A critical study with an annotated translation of the text by Ismail M. Dahiyat). Leiden, Netherlands: Brill, 1974.

Avicenna. (William E. Gohlman, trans. and ed.) *The Life of Ibn Sina: A Critical Edition and Annotated Translation*. Albany, NY: State University of New York Press, 1974.

Baldick, Julian. *Mystical Islam: An Introduction to Sufism*. New York: New York University Press, 1989.

Bello, Iysa A. *The Medieval Islamic Controversy Between Philosophy and Orthodoxy: Ijma' and Ta'wil in the Conflict between Al-Ghazali and Ibn Rushd*. New York: E.J. Brill, 1989.

Black, Antony. *The History of Islamic Political Thought: From the Prophet to the Present*, Edinburgh: Edinburgh University Press, 2001.

Black, Deborah L. *Logic and Aristotle's Rhetoric and Poetics in Medieval Arabic Philosophy*. Kinderhook, NY: E.J. Brill, 1990.

Butterworth, Charles E. and Blake Andree Kessel, eds. *The Introduction of Arabic Philosophy into Europe*. Boston, MA: Brill Academic, 1993.

Calder, Norman, Jawid Mojaddedi and Andrew Rippin, eds. *Classical Islam: A Sourcebook of of Religious Literature*. New York: Routledge, 2003.

Campanini, Massimo. *The Qur'an: the Basics*, London: Routledge, 2007.

Campanini, Massimo. *An Introduction to Islamic Philosophy*. Edinburgh: Edinburgh University Press, 2008.

Chittick, William C. *Imaginal Worlds: Ibn al-'Arabi and the Problem of Religious Diversity*. Albany, NY: State University of New York Press, 1994.

Chittick, William C. *The Self-Disclosure of God: Principles of Ibn al-'Arabi's Cosmology*. Albany, NY: State University of New York Press, 1997.

Cleary, Thomas, trans. *The Essential Koran: The Heart of Islam: An Introductory Selection of Readings from the Qur'an*. San Francisco, CA: Harper San Francisco, 1993.

Conrad, Lawrence I., ed. *The World of Ibn Tufayl: Interdisciplinary Perspectives on Hayy Ibn Yaqzan*. Leiden, Netherlands: E.J. Brill, 1996.

Cook, Michael. *Commanding Right and Forbidding Wrong in Islamic Thought*. Cambridge, UK: Cambridge University Press, 2000.

Corbin, Henry (Willard R. Trask, trans.). *Avicenna and the Visionary Recital.* Princeton, NJ: Princeton University Press, 1960.

Corbin, Henry (Philip Sherrard and Liadain Sherrard, trans.). *History of Islamic Philosophy.* New York: Routledge, Chapman & Hall, 1993.

Corbin, Henry. *Alone with the Alone: Creative Imagination in the Sufism of Ibn 'Arabi.* Princeton, NJ: Princeton University Press, 1998.

Davidson, Herbert A. *Alfarabi, Avicenna, and Averroes on Intellect: Their Cosmologies, Theories of Active Intellect and Theories of the Human Intellect.* New York: Oxford University Press, 1992.

Esack, Farid. *The Qur'ān: A Short Introduction.* Oxford, UK: Oneworld, 2002.

Esposito, John L. and John Obert Voll. *Makers of Contemporary Islam.* Oxford, UK: Oxford University Press, 2001.

Fakhry, Majid. *Islamic Occasionalism, and its Critique by Averroes and Aquinas.* London: Allen & Unwin, 1958.

Fakhry, Majid. *A History of Islamic Philosophy.* New York: Columbia University Press, 1983, 2nd edn.

Fakhry, Majid. *Ethical Theories in Islam.* Kinderhook, NY: E.J. Brill, 1991.

Frank, Richard M. *Beings and their Attributes: The Teaching of the Basrian School of the Mu'tazila in the Classical Period.* Albany, NY: State University of New York Press, 1978.

Friedlander, Shems. *The Whirling Dervishes: Being an Account of the Sufi Order Known as the Mevlevis and its Founder the Poet and Mystic Mevlana Jalalu'ddin Rumi.* Albany, NY: SUNY Press, 1992.

Gardet, Louis, and M.M. Anawati. *Introduction a la théologie musulmane.* Paris: J. Vrin, 1970, (2nd edn. 1948).

al-Ghazālī. (W. Montgomery Watt, trans.). *The Faith and Practice of al-Ghazali.* London: Allen & Unwin, 1953.

al-Ghazālī. (Commentary and index by G.-H. Bousquet). *Ih'ya 'Ouloum ed-din; ou vivification des sciences de la foi.* Paris: M. Besson, 1955.

al-Ghazālī (Fazlul Karim, trans.). *Gazali's Ihya' Ulum-id-din; or, the Revival of Religious Learnings.* Dacca, Bangladesh: F.K. Islam Mission Trust, 1971.

al-Ghazālī (Syed Nawab Ali, trans.). *Some Moral and Religious Teachings of al-Ghazali* (Excerpts from the author's *Ihya' 'Ulum al-Din.*). Lahore, Pakistan: Muhammad Ashraf, 1974, 2nd edn.

al-Ghazālī. (Claud Field, trans.). *The Confessions of Al Ghazali.* Lahore, Pakistan: Sh. Muhammad Ashraf, 1978.

al-Ghazālī. *On the Duties of Brotherhood.* Chicago, IL: Kazi, 1991.

al-Ghazālī. (T.J. Winter, trans.). *Al-Ghazali on Disciplining the Soul and on Breaking the Two Desires.* Chicago, IL: Kazi, 1996.

al-Ghazālī. (Michael E. Marmura, trans.). *The Incoherence of the Philosophers: Tahafut al-Falasifah: A Parallel English-Arabic Text.* Provo, UT: Brigham Young University Press, 1997.

Gibb, H.A.R. *et al. The Encyclopaedia of Islam,* 8 Vols. Leiden, Netherlands: Brill, 1960–97.

Glassé, Cyril. *The New Encyclopedia of Islam.* Lanham, MD: AltaMira Press, 2003.

Goichon, A.M. *La philosophie d'Avicenne et son influence en Europe mediévale.* Paris: Adrien-Maisonneuve, 1944.

Goodman, L.E. *Avicenna.* London: Routledge, 1993.

Goodman, Lenn E. *Islamic Humanism.* Oxford, UK: Oxford University Press, 2003.

Groff, Peter. *Islamic Philosophy A–Z.* Edinburgh: Edinburgh University Press, 2007.

Gutas, Dimitri. *Avicenna and the Aristotelian Tradition: Introduction to Reading Avicenna's Philosophical Works.* Boston, MA: Brill Academic Publishers, 1988.

Hahn, Lewis, Randall Auxier and Lucian Stone, eds. *The Philosophy of Seyyed Hossein Nasr,* Chicago, IL: Open Court, 2001.

Hallaq, Wael B. *Authority, Continuity and Change in Islamic Law.* Cambridge, UK: Cambridge University Press, 2001.

Hallaq, Wael B. *The Origins and Evolution of Islamic Law.* Cambridge, UK: Cambridge University Press, 2005.

Halm, Heinz. *Shi'ism.* Edinburgh: Edinburgh University Press, 2004, 2nd edn.

Heath, Peter. *Allegory and Philosophy in Avicenna, Ibn Sina: With a Translation of the Book of the Prophet Muhammad's Ascent to Heaven.* Philadelphia, PA: University of Pennsylvania Press, 1992.

Heer, Nicholas and Kenneth L. Honerkamp, (intro. and trans.). *Three Early Sufi Texts.* Louisville, KY: Fons Vitae, 2003.

Hermansen, Marcia K., ed. *The Conclusive Argument from God: Shah Wali Allah of Delhi's Hujjat Allah al-Baligha.* Boston, MA: Brill Academic Publishers, 1995.

Hogendijk, J.P. and A.I. Sabra, eds., *The Enterprise of Science in Islam.* Cambridge, MA: MIT Press, 2003.

Hourani, George F. *Islamic Rationalism: The Ethics of 'Abd al-Jabbar.* Oxford, UK: Clarendon Press, 1971.

Ibn al-'Arabi (Reynold Alleyne Nicholson, trans.). *The Tarjumān al-Ashwāq: A Collection of Mystical Odes.* Wheaton, IL: Theosophical Publishing House, 1978.

Ibn al-'Arabi (R.W.J. Austin, trans.). *The Bezels of Wisdom.* New York: Paulist Press, 1980.

Ibn Bājjah, Muhammad Ibn Yahya (Miguel Asín Palacios, trans. and ed.). *El regimen del solitario por Avempace (The Rule of the Solitary Person).* Madrid: 1946.

Ibn Khaldūn (Charles Philip Issawi, trans.). *An Arab Philosophy of History: Selections from the Prolegomena of Ibn Khaldun of Tunis (1332–1406).* London: John Murray, 1963 (1950).

Ibn Khaldūn (Franz Rosenthal, trans. and ed.). *The Muqaddimah: An Introduction to History.* Princeton, NJ: Princeton University Press, 1989.

Ibn Tufayl, Muhammad Ibn 'Abd al-Malik (S. Ockley, trans.). *The Improvement of Human Reason.* London: E. Powell, Reprint, 1929.

Ibn Tufayl, Muhammad Ibn 'Abd al-Malik (Riad Kocache, trans.). *The Journey of the Soul: The Story of Hai Bin Yaqzan.* London: Octagon Press, 1982.

Ibn Tufayl, Muhammad Ibn 'Abd al-Malik (Lenn E. Goodman, trans.). *Ibn Tufayl's Hayy Ibn Yaqzan: A Philosophical Tale.* Los Angeles, CA: Gee Tee Bee, 4th edn, 1996.

Izutsu, Toshihiko. *Sufism and Taoism.* Berkeley, CA: University of California Press, 1984.

Kemal, Salim. *The Poetics of Alfarabi and Avicenna.* Boston, MA: Brill Academic, 1991.

Kennedy-Day, K. *Books of Definition in Islamic Philosophy.* London: Routledge, 2003.

al-Kindi, Ya'qub I. (Alfred L. Ivry, trans.). *Al-Kindi's Metaphysics: A Translation of the Treatise on First Philosophy.* Albany, NY: State University of New York Press, 1974.

al-Kindi. *The Philosophy of the Arabs.* Chicago, IL: Kazi, 1996.

Knysh, Alexander D. *Ibn 'Arabi in the Later Islamic Tradition: The Making of a Polemical Image in Medieval Islam.* Albany, NY: State University of New York Press, 1998.

Kogan, Barry S. *Averroes and the Metaphysics of Causation.* Albany, NY: State University of New York Press, 1985.

Kohlberg, Etan. *Medieval Muslim Scholar at Work: The Life, Sources and Method of Ibn Tawus and his Library.* Boston, MA: Brill Academic, 1992.

Kraemer, Joel L. *Philosophy in the Renaissance of Islam: Abu Sulayman Al-Sijistani and his Circle.* Leiden, Netherlands: E.J. Brill, 1986.

Kraye, Jill, W.F. Ryan, and C.B. Schmitt, eds. *Pseudo-Aristotle in the Middle Ages: The Theology and Other Texts.* London: Warburg Institute, University of London, 1986.

Kretzmann, N. *et al.,* eds. *The Cambridge History of Later Medieval Philosophy.* Cambridge, UK: Cambridge University Press, 1982.

Lameer, Joep. *Al-Farabi and Aristotelian Syllogistics: Greek Theory and Islamic Practice.* Boston, MA: Brill Academic, 1994.

Leaman, Oliver. *An Introduction to Medieval Islamic Philosophy.* Cambridge, UK: Cambridge University Press, 1985.

Leaman, Oliver. *Brief Introduction to Islamic Philosophy.* Oxford, UK: Polity Press, 1999.

Leaman, Oliver. *An Introduction to Classical Islamic Philosophy.* Cambridge, UK: Cambridge University Press, 2nd edn, 2001.

Leaman, Oliver, ed. *The Qur'an: An Encyclopedia.* New York: Routledge, 2005.

Leaman, Oliver, ed. *Biographical Encyclopedia of Islamic Philosophy.* New York: Continuum, 2006.

Lewisohn, Leonard, ed. *The Heritage of Sufism, Vol. I: Classical Persian Sufism from its Origins toRumi (700–1300).* Oxford, UK: Oneworld, 1999.

Lewisohn, Leonard, ed. *The Heritage of Sufism, Vol. II: The Legacy of Medieval Persian Sufism (1150–1500).* Oxford, UK: Oneworld, 1999.

Lewisohn, Leonard and David Morgan, eds. *The Heritage of Sufism, Vol. III: Late Classical Persianate Sufism (1501–1750).* Oxford, UK: Oneworld, 1999.

Mahdi, Muhsin. *Ibn Khaldun's Philosophy of History: A Study in the Philosophic Foundation of the Science of Culture.* Chicago, IL: University of Chicago Press, 1964.

Mahdi, Muhsin, trans. *Alfarabi's Philosophy of Plato and Aristotle.* Ithaca, NY: Cornell University Press, 1969 (1962).

Mallat, Chibli. *The Renewal of Islamic Law.* Cambridge, UK: Cambridge University Press, 2003.

Massignon, Louis. *The Passion of al-Hallaj, Mystic and Martyr of Islam,* 4 Vols. Princeton, NJ: Princeton University Press, 1981.

McAuliffe, Jane Dammen, ed. *The Encyclopedia of the Qur'an,* 5 Vols. Leiden, Netherlands: E.J. Brill, 2001–06.

McAuliffe, Jane Dammen, ed. *The Cambridge Companion to the Qur'ān.* Cambridge, UK: Cambridge University Press, 2007.

McGinnis, J. *Interpreting Avicenna: Science and Philosophy in Medieval Islam.* Leiden, Netherlands: E. J. Brill, 2004.

McGinnis, Jon and David Reisman. *Classical Arabic Philosophy: An Anthology of Sources.* Indianapolis, IN: Hackett, 2007.

McInerny, Ralph. *Aquinas Against the Averroists: On There Being Only One Intellect.* West Lafayette, IN: Purdue University Press, 1993.

Mohammed, Ovey N. *Averroes' Doctrine of Immortality: A Matter of Controversy.* Waterloo, OT: Wilfrid Laurier University Press, 1984.

Morewedge, Parviz. *The Metaphysica of Avicenna (Ibn Sina).* London: Routledge & Kegan Paul, 1973.

Morewedge, Parviz, ed. *Islamic Philosophical Theology.* Albany, NY: State University of New York Press, 1979.

Morewedge, Parviz, ed. *Neoplatonism and Islamic Thought.* Albany, NY: State University of New York Press, 1992.

Nasr, Seyyed Hossein. *Three Muslim Sages: Avicenna, Suhrawardi, Ibn-'Arabi.* Cambridge, MA: Harvard University Press, 1964.

Nasr, Seyyed Hossein. *An Introduction to Islamic Cosmological Doctrines.* Albany, NY: State University of New York Press, 1993.

Nasr, Seyyed Hossein (Mehdi Amin Razavi, ed.). *The Islamic Intellectual Tradition in Persia.* Richmond, UK: Curzon Press, 1996.

Nasr, Seyyed Hossein and Oliver Leaman, eds. *The History of Islamic Philosophy.* New York: Routledge, 1996.

Netton, Ian Richard. *Muslim Neoplatonists: An Introduction to the Thought of the Brethren of Purity, Ikhwan al-Safa.* Boston, MA: Allen & Unwin, 1982.

Netton, Ian Richard. *Al-Farabi and his School.* London: Routledge, 1992.

Netton, Ian Richard. *Muslim Neoplatonists: An Introduction to the Thought of the Brethren of Purity.* London: Routledge Curzon, 2002 edn.

Nicholson, R. *Studies in Islamic Mysticism.* Cambridge, UK: Cambridge University Press, 1921.

Ormsby, Eric L. *Theodicy in Islamic Thought.* Princeton, NJ: Princeton University Press, 1984.

Peters, F.E. *A Reader on Classical Islam.* Princeton, NJ: Princeton University Press, 1994.

Pines, Shlomo. *Studies in the History of Arabic Philosophy.* Jerusalem: Magnes Press, Hebrew University, 1996.

Quadir, C.A. *Philosophy and Science in the Islamic World: From Origins to the Present Day.* New York: Routledge, Chapman & Hall, 1988.

Quadri, G. *La philosophie arabe dans l'Europe médiévale.* Paris: Payot, 1947.

Rahman, Fazlur. *The Philosophy of Mulla Sadra Shirazi.* Albany, NY: State University of New York Press, 1976.

Rahman, Fazlur. *Islam.* Chicago, IL: University of Chicago Press, 2nd edn, 1979.

Rahman, Fazlur. *Prophecy in Islam: Philosophy and Orthodoxy.* Chicago, IL: University of Chicago Press, 1979.

Razavi, Mehdi Amin. *Suhrawardi and the School of Illumination.* Richmond, UK: Curzon Press, 1997.

Reinhart, A. Kevin. *Before Revelation: The Boundaries of Muslim Moral Thought.* Albany, NY: State University of New York Press, 1995.

Renan, Ernest. *Averroès et l'averroisme.* Paris: Michel Levy frères, Revised edn, 1922.

Renard, John. *Historical Dictionary of Sufism.* Lanham, MD: Scarecrow Press, 2005.

Ruthven, Malise. *Islam in the World.* New York: Oxford University Press, 2nd edn, 2000.

Richard, Yann (Antonia Nevill, trans.). *Shiite Islam: Polity, Ideology and Creed.* Malden, MA: Blackwell, 1995.

Riddell, Peter G. *Islam: Essays on Scripture, Thought, and Society: A Festschrift in Honour of Anthony H. Johns.* Boston, MA: Brill Academic, 1997.

Rippin, Andrew. *Muslims: Their Religious Beliefs and Practices.* New York: Routledge, 1993.

Rippin, Andrew. *The Islamic World.* London: Routledge, 2008.

Rosenthal, Franz. *Greek Philosophy in the Arab World: A Collection of Essays.* Brookfield, VT: Ashgate, 1990.

Rowson, Everett. *A Muslim Philosopher on the Soul and its Fate: al-'Amiri's Kitāb al-Amad 'ala L-Abad.* Chicago, IL: Kazi, 1996.

Sartain, E.M. *Jajal Al-Din Al-Suywti.* New York: Cambridge University Press, 1975.

Schimmel, Annemarie. *Mystical Dimensions of Islam.* Chapel Hill, NC: University of North Carolina Press, 1975.

Schimmel, Annemarie. *Islam in the Indian Subcontinent.* Leiden, Netherlands: E.J. Brill, 1980.

Schimmel, Annemarie. *Islam: An Introduction.* Albany, NY: State University of New York Press, 1992.

Sharif, M.M., ed. *A History of Muslim Philosophy,* 2 Vols. Wiesbaden, Germany: Harrassowitz, 1963–65.

Sherif, Mohammed A. *Ghazali's Theory of Virtue.* Albany, NY: State University New York Press, 1975.

Smith, Margaret. *Al-Ghazali the Mystic.* London: Luzac, 1944.

Smith, Margaret, ed. *The Sufi Path of Love: An Anthology of Sufism.* London: Luzac, 1954.

Smith, Margaret. *Readings from the Mystics of Islam: Translations from the Arabic and Persian.* London: Luzac, 1972.

Smith, Margaret. *Rabi'a the Mystic, and her Fellow Saints in Islam.* New York: Cambridge University Press, 1984.

Thackston, Wheeler M., Jr., trans. *The Mystical and Visionary Treatises of Shihabuddin Yahya Suhrawardi.* London: Octagon, 1982.

Trimingham, J. Spencer. *The Sufi Orders in Islam.* Oxford, UK: Clarendon Press, 1971.

Van Donzel, E. *Islamic Desk Reference: Compiled from The Encyclopedia of Islam.* Leiden, Netherlands: E.J. Brill, 1994.

Walbridge, John. *The Science of Mystic Lights: Quṭb al-Dīn Shīrāzī and the Illuminationist Tradition of Islamic Philosophy.* Cambridge, MA: Harvard University, Center for Middle Eastern Studies, 1992.

Walzer, Richard. *Greek into Arabic: Essays on Islamic Philosophy.* Cambridge, MA: Harvard University Press, 1962.

Walzer, Richard, ed. *Al-Farabi on the Perfect State: Abu Nasr al-Farabi's 'The Principles of the Views of the Citizens of the Best State'.* New York: Oxford University Press, 1985.

Wansbrough, John and Andrew Rippin. *Quranic Studies: Sources and Methods of Scriptural Interpretation.* Amherst, NY: Prometheus Books, 2004.

Watt, W. Montgomery. *Muslim Intellectual: A Study of al-Ghazali.* Edinburgh: Edinburgh University Press, 1963.

Watt, W. Montgomery. *The Formative Period of Islamic Thought.* Edinburgh: Edinburgh University Press, 1973.

Watt, W. Montgomery. *Islamic Philosophy and Theology.* New York: Columbia University Press, 2nd edn, 1988.

Watt, W. Montgomery. *Islamic Creeds.* New York: Columbia University Press, 1995.

Wheeler, Brannon M. *Applying the Canon in Islam: The Authorization and Maintenance of Interpretive Reasoning in Hanafi Scholarship.* Albany, NY: State University of New York Press, 1996.

Williams, John Alden A., ed. *The Word of Islam.* Austin, TX: University of Texas Press, 1994.

Wolfson, Harry A. *The Philosophy of the Kalam.* Cambridge, MA: Harvard University Press, 1976.

Yazdi, Mehdi H. *The Principles of Epistemology in Islamic Philosophy: Knowledge by Presence.* Albany, NY: SUNY Press, 1992.

Zedler, Beatrice H., ed. *St Thomas Aquinas: On the Unity of the Intellect Against the Averroists.* Milwaukee, WI: Marquette University Press, 1968.

Zaehner, R.C. *Hindu and Muslim Mysticism.* New York: Schocken, 1969 (1960).

8. JEWISH PHILOSOPHIES

Abelson, Joshua. *Jewish Mysticism: An Introduction to the Kabbalah.* New York: Sepher-Hermon Press, 1981.

Abravanel, Isaac (Menachem Marc Kellner, trans.). *Principles of Faith (Rosh Amanah).* Rutherford, NJ: Fairleigh Dickenson University Press, 1982.

Altmann, Alexander. *Studies in Religious Philosophy and Mysticism.* Ithaca, NY: Cornell University Press, 1969.

Baer, Yitzhak. *A History of Jews in Christian Spain,* 2 Vols. Philadelphia, PA: Jewish Publication Society of America, 1961–66.

Bension, Ariel. *The Zohar in Moslem and Christian Spain.* New York: Hermon Press, 1974.

Buber, Martin. *A Believing Humanism: My Testament, 1902–1965.* Atlantic Highlands, NJ: Humanities Press, 1990.

Buijs, Joseph A., ed. *Maimonides: A Collection of Critical Essays.* Notre Dame, IN: University of Notre Dame Press, 1990.

Cohn-Sherbok, Dan. *Medieval Jewish Philosophy: An Introduction.* Honolulu, HI: University of Hawaii Press, 1996.

Cooperman, Bernard D., ed. *Jewish Thought in the Sixteenth Century.* Cambridge, MA: Harvard University Press, 1984.

Davidson, Herbert A. *Proofs for Eternity, Creation, and the Existence of God in Medieval Islamic and Jewish Philosophy.* New York: Oxford University Press, 1987.

de Lange, Nicholas and Miri Freud-Kandel, eds. *Modern Judaism: An Oxford Guide.* New York: Oxford University Press, 2005.

Epstein, Isidore, ed. *Moses Maimonides.* London: Soncino Press, 1935.

Fackenheim, Emil L. *Jewish Philosophers and Jewish Philosophy.* Bloomington, IN: Indiana University Press, 1996.

Feldman, Syemour. *Philosophy in a Time of Crisis: Don Isaac Abravanel, Defender of the Faith,* London: Routledge, 2003.

Fishbane, Michael. *Biblical Myth and Rabbinic Mythmaking.* Oxford, UK: Oxford University Press, 2003.

Fox, Marvin. *Interpreting Maimonides: Studies in Methodology, Metaphysics and Moral Philosophy.* Chicago, IL: University of Chicago Press, 1990.

Frank, Daniel H. and Oliver Leaman, eds. *The Cambridge Companion to Medieval Jewish Philosophy.* Cambridge, UK: Cambridge University Press, 2003.

Frank, Daniel H. and Oliver Leaman, eds. *History of Jewish Philosophy.* New York: Routledge, 2004 (1997).

Frank, Daniel H., Oliver Leaman and Charles H. Manekin, eds. *The Jewish Philosophy Reader.* New York: Routledge, 2000.

Gershom, Gerhard Scholem. *Zohar: The Book of Splendor: Basic Readings from the Kabbalah.* New York: Schocken, 1995.

Glatzer, Nahum N., ed. *Faith and Knowledge: The Jew in the Medieval World.* Boston, MA: Beacon Press, 1963.

Glatzer, Nahum N., ed. *Modern Jewish Thought: A Source Reader.* New York: Schocken Books, 1977.

Goodman, Lenn E. *On Justice: An Essay in Jewish Philosophy.* New Haven, CT: Yale University Press, 1991.

Goodman, Lenn E., ed. *Neoplatonism and Jewish Thought.* Albany, NY: State University of New York Press, 1992.

Goodman, Martin, with Jeremy Cohen and David Sorkin, eds. *The Oxford Handbook of Jewish Studies*. Oxford, UK: Oxford University Press, 2002.

Gordon, Peter Eli. *Rosenzweig and Heidegger: Between Judaism and German Philosophy*. Berkeley, CA: University of California Press, 2003.

Graupe, Heinz M. *Systematic Nature of Jewish Theology: Two Examples*. Chicago, IL: Academy Chicago Publ., 1995.

Guttman, Julius (David W. Silverman, trans.). *Philosophies of Judaism: The History of Jewish Philosophy from Biblical Times to Franz Rosenweig*. New York: Schocken, 1973 (1964).

ha-Levi, Judah (Hartwig Hirschfeld, trans.). *The Kuzari (Kitab al Khazari): An Argument for the Faith of Israel* New York: Schocken Books, 1974 (1964).

ha-Levi, Judah (N. Daniel Korobkin, trans.). *The Kuzari: In Defense of the Despised Faith*. Northvale, NJ: Jason Aronson, 1998.

Harvey, Steven. *Falaquera's Epistle of the Debate: An Introduction to Jewish Philosophy*. Cambridge, MA: Harvard University Press, 1990.

Heschel, Abraham J. *Maimonides: A Biography of the Great Medieval Jewish Thinker*. New York: Doubleday, 1991.

Hughes, Aaron W. *The Texture of the Divine: Imagination in Medieval Islamic and Jewish Thought*. Bloomington, IN: Indiana University Press, 2004.

Hughes, Aaron W. *The Art of the Dialogue in Jewish Philosophy*. Bloomington, IN: Indiana University Press, 2007.

Ibn Daud, Abraham (Gerson D. Cohen, trans.). *A Critical Edition with a Translation and Notes of the Book of Tradition (Sefer ha-qabbalah)*. Philadelphia, PA: Jewish Publication Society of America, 1967.

Ibn Daud, Abraham (trans. with commentary by Norbert M. Samuelson; Gershon Weiss, ed.). *The Exalted Faith*. Rutherford, NJ: Fairleigh Dickinson University Press, 1986.

Ibn Gabirol (H.E. Wedeck, trans.). *The Fountain of Life*. New York: Philosophical Library, 1962.

Jacobs, Louis. *A Tree of Life: Diversity, Flexibility, and Creativity in Jewish Law*. New York: Oxford University Press, 1984.

Kajon, Irene. *Contemporary Jewish Philosophy: an Introduction*. London: Routledge, 2006.

Katz, Claire Elise. *Levinas, Judaism, and the Feminine: The Silent Footsteps of Rebecca*. Bloomington, IN: Indiana University Press, 2003.

Katz, Steven T. *Jewish Philosophers*. New York: Bloch, 1975.

Katz, Steven T., ed. *Medieval Jewish Philosophy: Original Anthology*. North Stratford, NH: Ayer Co. Publ., 1980.

Katz, Steven T., ed. *Saadiah Gaon: Selected Essays: An Original Anthology*. North Stratford, NH: Ayer Co. Publ., 1980.

Katz, Steven T. *Historicism, the Holocaust, and Zionism: Critical Studies in Contemporary Jewish History and Thought*. New York: New York University Press, 1992.

Kellner, Menachem M. *Maimonides on Judaism and the Jewish People*. Albany, NY: State University of New York Press, 1991.

Kravitz, Leonard S. *The Hidden Doctrine of Maimonides' Guide for the Perplexed: Philosophical and Religious God-Language in Tension*. Lewiston, NY: Edwin Mellen Press, 1988.

Lachower, Yeruham Fishel, Isaiah Tishby and David Goldstein, eds. and trans. *The Wisdom of the Zohar: An Anthology of Texts*. London: Littman Library of Jewish Civilization, 1991.

Landman, Isaac *et al.*, eds. *The Universal Jewish Encyclopedia*, 10 vols. New York: Ktav, 1939–43 (1969).

Leaman, Oliver. *Evil and Suffering in Jewish Philosophy*. Cambridge, UK: Cambridge University Press, 1995.

Leaman, Oliver. *Jewish Thought: An Introduction.* New York: Routledge, 2006.

Leon, Hebreo (F. Friedeberg-Seeley and Jean H. Barnes, trans.). *The Philosophy of Love (Dialoghi d'amore).* London: Soncino Press, 1937.

Levy, Solomon. *Isaac Abravanel as a Theologian.* London: Williams, Lea, 1939.

Lewy, Hans, Alexander Altmann and Isaak Heinemann, eds. *Three Jewish Philosophers.* New York: Meridian Books, 1960.

Maccoby, Hyam. *The Philosophy of the Talmud.* London: Routledge, 2002.

Maimonides, Moses. (trans. and ed., M. Friedlander). *The Guide of the Perplexed of Maimonides (Dalalat al-ha' irin).* New York: Dover, 2nd edn, 1956.

Maimonides, Moses. (Shlomo Pines, trans.). *The Guide of the Perplexed.* Chicago, IL: University of Chicago Press, 1963.

Maimonides, Moses. (Fred Rosner, trans.). *Moses Maimonides' Commentary on the Mishnah.* New York: Feldheim, 1975.

Maimonides, Moses (trans. and commentary, Lenn Evan Goodman). *Rambam: Readings in the Philosophy of Moses Maimonides.* New York: Viking Press, 1976.

Maimonides, Moses (H.M. Russell and J. Weinberg, trans. and ed.). *The Book of Knowledge: From the Mishnah Torah of Maimonides (Sefer ha-mada).* Edinburgh: Royal College of Physicians of Edinburgh, 1981.

Maimonides, Moses (Fred Rosner, trans. and annot.). *Maimonides' Introduction to His Commentary on the Mishnah.* Northvale, NJ: Jason Aronson, 1995.

Malter, Henry. *Saadia Gaon: His Life and Works.* Philadelphia, PA: Jewish Publication Society of America, 1942 (1921).

Matt, Daniel C. *The Zohar (Pritzker Edition), Vol. 1–3.* Stanford, CA: Stanford University Press, 2003–05.

McCallum, Donald. *Maimonides' Guide for the Perplexed: Silence and Salutation.* London: Routledge, 2007.

Meltzer, David, ed. *The Secret Garden: An Anthology of the Kabbalah.* New York: Seabury Press, 1976.

Minkin, Jacob S. *Abarbanel and the Expulsion of the Jews from Spain.* New York: Behrman's Jewish Book House, 1938.

Nadler, Steven. *Spinoza's Heresy: Immortality and the Jewish Mind.* Oxford, UK: Clarendon Press, 2001.

Neusner, Jacob. *The Foundations of Judaism,* 3 Vols. Philadelphia, PA: Fortress Press, 1983–85.

Neusner, Jacob. *Judaism and Christianity in the Age of Constantine: History, Messiah, Israel, and the Initial Confrontation.* Chicago, IL: University of Chicago Press, 1987.

Neusner, Jacob. *Judaism as Philosophy: The Method and Message of the Mishnah.* Columbia, SC: University of South Carolina Press, 1991.

Philo of Alexandria. *The Works of Philo: Complete and Unabridged.* Peabody, MA: Hendrickson, 1993 edn.

Pines, Shlomo. *Studies in the History of Jewish Thought.* Jerusalem: Magnes Press, Hebrew University, 1997.

Poma, Andrea. *The Critical Philosophy of Hermann Cohen.* Albany, NY: State University of New York Press, 1997.

Rose, Gillian. *Judaism and Modernity: Philosophical Essays.* Malden, MA: Blackwell, 1993.

Rosner, Fredann (trans. and ed.). *The Existence and Unity of God: Three Treatises Attributed to Moses Maimonides.* Northvale, NJ: Jason Aronson, 1990.

Roth, Cecil. *The Jews in the Renaissance.* New York: Harper & Row, 1965 (1959).

Rudavsky, Tamar, ed. *Divine Omniscience and Omnipotence in Medieval Philosophy: Islamic, Jewish, and Christian Perspectives.* Dordrecht, Netherlands: Kluwer Academic, 1985.

Sa'adia ben Joseph (Samuel Rosenblatt, trans.). *The Book of Beliefs and Opinions (Amanat wa-al-i'tiqadat).* New Haven, CT: Yale University Press, 1976.

Samuelson, Norbert M. *An Introduction to Modern Jewish Philosophy.* Albany, NY: State University of New York Press, 1989.

Samuelson, Norbert. *Judaism and the Doctrine of Creation.* New York: Cambridge University Press, 1995.

Scholem, Gershom. *Major Trends in Jewish Mysticism.* New York: Schocken Books, 1961(1954).

Scholem, Gershom (Ralph Manheim, trans.). *On the Kabbalah and its Symbolism.* New York: Schocken Books, 1965.

Sirat, Colette. *A History of Jewish Philosophy in the Middle Ages.* Cambridge, UK: Cambridge University Press, 1985.

Sperling, Harry and Maurice Simon, trans. *The Zohar.* London: Soncino Press, 2nd edn, 1984.

Spinoza, Baruch. *Œuvres Completes.* New York: French and European Publications, 1955.

Tirosh-Samuelson, Hava. *Happiness in Premodern Judaism: Virtue, Knowledge, and Well-Being.* Cincinnati, OH: Hebrew Union College Press, 2003.

Twersky, Isadore, ed. *Studies in Medieval Jewish History and Literature.* Cambridge, MA: Harvard University Press, 1979.

Twersky, Isadore. *Introduction to the Code of Maimonides (Mishneh Torah).* New Haven, CT: Yale University Press, 1980.

Twersky, Isadore, ed. *Studies in Maimonides.* Cambridge, MA: Harvard University Press, 1990.

Twersky, Isadore and Bernard Septimus, eds. *Jewish Thought in the Seventeenth Century.* Cambridge, MA: Harvard University Press, 1990.

Wigoder, Geoffrey, ed. *The Encyclopedia of Judaism.* New York: Macmillan, 1989.

Wolfson, Elliot R. *Language, Eros, Being: Kabbalistic Hermeneutics and Poetic Imagination.* New York: Fordham University Press, 2005.

Wolfson, Harry A. *Crescas' Critique of Aristotle.* Cambridge, MA: Harvard University Press, 1971 (1929).

Wolfson, Harry A. *Studies in the History of Philosophy and Religion,* 2 Vols. Cambridge, MA: Harvard University Press, 1973–77.

Wolfson, Harry A. *The Repercussions of the Kalam in Jewish Philosophy.* Cambridge, MA: Harvard University Press, 1979.

Yehudah, ha-Levi. *See:* ha-Levi.

Zonta, Mauro. *Hebrew Scholasticism in the Fifteenth Century: A History and Sourcebook.* Dordrecht, Netherlands: Springer, 2006.

9. EUROPE

Aaron, R.I. *John Locke.* Oxford, UK: Clarendon Press, 3rd edn, 1971.

Abbagnano, Nicola. *Guglielmo di Ockham.* Lanciano: [s.n.], 1931.

Altmann, Alexander. *Moses Mendelssohn: A Biographical Study.* Montgomery, AL: University of Alabama Press, 1973.

Anselm (S.N. Dean, trans.). *Basic Writings: Proslogium, Monologium, Gaunilon's On Behalf of the Fool, Cur Deus Homo.* La Salle, IL: Open Court Press, 1966 (1962).

Aquinas, St Thomas (George Gaines Leckie, trans.). *Concerning Being and Essence (De ente et essentia).* New York: Appleton-Century, 1937.

Aquinas, St Thomas (A.C. Pegis, trans.). *Basic Writings of St Thomas Aquinas*, 2 Vols. New York: Random House, 1945.

Aquinas, St Thomas. *On the Truth of the Catholic Faith (Summa contra gentiles)*. Garden City, NY: Hanover House, 1955 (1957).

Aquinas, St Thomas (T. Gilby, trans.). *Philosophical Texts*. Oxford, UK: Oxford University Press, 1956.

Aquinas, St Thomas (various translators). *Summa theologiae*. 60 Vols. London: Fyre & Spottiswood, 1963–75.

Aquinas, St Thomas (P.E. Sigmund, ed.). *On Politics and Ethics*. New York: Norton, 1988.

Aquinas, St Thomas (Robert W. Mulligan, James V. McGlynn and Robert W. Schmidt, trans.). *Truth (Quaestiones disputatae de veritate)*. Indianapolis, IN: Hackett, 1994.

Armstrong, D.M. *Cambridge History of Later Greek and Early Medieval Philosophy*. London: Cambridge University Press, 1967.

Aune, Bruce. *Kant's Theory of Morals*. Princeton, NJ: Princeton University Press, 1979.

Austin, J.L. *How to Do Things with Words*. Cambridge, MA: Harvard University Press, 1962.

Ayer, A.J. *Language, Truth and Logic*. London: V. Gollancz, 1967.

Ayer, A.J. *Russell and Moore: The Analytical Heritage*. Cambridge, MA: Harvard University Press, 1971.

Bacon, Francis. *Advancement of Learning; Novum Organum; New Atlantis*. Chicago, IL; Encyclopaedia Britannica, 1990.

Bacon, Francis (Peter Urbach and John Gibson, trans.). *Novum Organum; With Other Parts of the Great Instauration*. Chicago, IL: Open Court Press, 1994.

Baker, Gordon and Katherine Morris. *Descartes' Dualism*. London: Routledge, 1996.

Barnes, Jonathan. *The Ontological Argument*. London: Macmillan, 1972.

Bauer, N. *Simone de Beauvoir, Philosophy, and Feminism*. New York: Columbia University Press, 2001.

Baumgardt, David. *Bentham and the Ethics of Today*. Princeton, NJ: Princeton University Press, 1952.

Bayle, Peter (revised, corrected and enlarged by Pierre Desmaizeaux). *Bayle's Dictionary. Historical and Critical*. London: Routledge, 1997.

Beccaria, Cesare. *On Crimes and Punishments*. New York: Marsilio, 1996 (Oxford, UK: Oxford University Press, 1964).

Beck, Leslie John. *The Method of Descartes: A Study of the Regulae*. Oxford, UK: Clarendon Press, 1952.

Beck, Lewis W., ed. *Eighteenth-Century Philosophy*. New York: Free Press, 1966.

Beiser, Frederick C., ed. *The Cambridge Companion to Hegel*. New York: Cambridge University Press, 1993.

Berdyaev, N. (R.M. French, trans.). *The Divine and the Human*. London: G. Bles, 1949.

Bergson, Henri (Arthur Mitchell, trans.). *Creative Evolution*. London: Macmillan, 1911.

Bergson, Henri (R. Audra and C. Brereton, trans.). *The Two Sources of Morality and Religion*. London: Macmillan, 1935.

Bergson, Henri (Nancy Margaret Paul and Mary Emily Dowson, trans.). *Matter and Memory*. London: Allen & Unwin, 1970.

Bergson, Henri (Frank Lubecki Pogson, trans.). *Time and Free Will; An Essay on the Immediate Data of Consciousness*. London: Allen & Unwin, 1971.

Bergson, Henri (Thomas A. Goudge and Thomas Ernest Hulme, trans.). *An Introduction to Metaphysics*. Indianapolis, IN: Bobbs-Merrill, 1975.

Bergson, Henri (Mabelle L. Andison, trans.). *An Introduction to Metaphysics; The Creative Mind.* Totowa, NY: Littlefield, Adams, 1975.

Bergson, Henri. *Laughter: An Essay on the Meaning of the Comic.* London: Macmillan, 1983.

Berkeley, George. *The Works of George Berkeley,* 9 Vols. London: Nelson, 1948.

Berkeley, George. *A New Theory of Vision: And Other Writings.* London: Dent, 1960.

Berkeley, George (David M. Armstrong, ed.). *Berkeley's Philosophical Writings.* New York: Collier Books, 1965.

Berkeley, George. *A Treatise Concerning the Principles of Human Knowledge.* Oxford, UK: Oxford University Press, 1998.

Berkeley, George. *Three Dialogues between Hylas and Philonous.* Oxford, UK: Oxford University Press, 1998.

Berlin, Isaiah. *Karl Marx: His Life and Environment.* Oxford, UK: Oxford University Press, 1978, 4th edn.

Berlin, Isaiah (Henry Hardy and Aileen Kelly, eds.). *Russian Thinkers.* London: Hogarth Press, 1978.

Bett, Henry. *Johannes Scotus Erigena: A Study In Medieval Philosophy.* Cambridge, UK: Cambridge University Press, 1925.

Blaug, Mark. *Economic Theory in Retrospect.* Cambridge, UK: Cambridge University Press, 3rd edn, 1978.

Bonansea, Bernardino M. *Man and his Approach to God in John Duns Scotus.* Lanham, MD: University Press of America, 1983.

Borchert, Donald M. *The Encyclopedia of Philosophy. Supplement.* New York: Macmillan Reference, 1996.

Bosanquet, Bernard. *Politics and Philosophy.* (reprints). London: Routledge/Thoemmes, 1996.

Bowie, Andrew. *Introduction to German Philosophy: From Kant to Habermas.* Cambridge, UK: Polity Press, 2003.

Bradley, F.H. *The Principles of Logic.* Oxford, UK: Oxford University Press, 1928.

Bradley, F.H. *Ethical Studies.* Oxford, UK: Oxford University Press, 1962.

Bradley, F.H. *Appearance and Reality: A Metaphysical Essay.* Oxford, UK: Clarendon Press, 1968.

Brentano, Franz. *Psychology from an Empirical Standpoint.* London: Routledge, 2nd edn, 1995.

Broad, C.D. *Five Types of Ethical Theory.* London: Routledge & Kegan Paul, 1951.

Broad, C.D. *Kant: An Introduction.* New York: Cambridge University Press, 1978.

Broadie, Alexander, ed. *The Cambridge Companion to the Scottish Enlightenment.* Cambridge, UK: Cambridge University Press, 2003.

Brown, Stuart. *British Empiricism and the Enlightenment. Routledge History of Philosophy,* Vol. V. London: Routledge, 1996.

Brown, Stuart C. *Leibniz.* Minneapolis, MN: University of Minnesota Press, 1984.

Buridan, John (Theodore Kermit Scott, trans.). *Sophisms on Meaning and Truth.* New York: Appleton-Century-Crofts, 1966.

Butler, E. Cuthbert. *Western Mysticism: The Teaching of Augustine, Gregory and Bernard on Contemplation and the Contemplative Life.* London: Constable, 1927; New York: Harper & Row, 2nd edn, 1966.

Callinicos, Alex. *Marxism and Philosophy.* Oxford, UK: Oxford University Press, 1985.

Cappuyns, Maieul. Jean *Scot Erigène, sa vie, son œuvre, sa pensée.* Paris: Desclee, de Brouwer, 1933.

Card, C., ed. *The Cambridge Companion to Simone de Beauvoir.* Cambridge, UK: Cambridge University Press, 2003.

Carr, E.H. *Michael Bakunin*. London: Macmillan, 1937.

Carver, Terrell, ed. *The Cambridge Companion to Marx*. New York: Cambridge University Press, 1991.

Cassirer, Ernst (James P. Pettegrove, trans.). *The Platonic Renaissance in England*. Austin, TX: University of Texas Press, 1953.

Cassirer, Ernst (Mario Damandi, trans.). *The Individual and the Cosmos in Renaissance Philosophy*. Oxford, UK: Basil Blackwell, 1963.

Catholic Church. Pope (1878–1903: Leo XIII). (Father Rawes, trans.). *Encyclical Letter of Our Holy Father...Pope Leo XIII on the restoration of Christian philosophy in Catholic universities, according to the mind of St Thomas Aquinas, the angelic doctor (Aeterni Patris)*. London: Burns and Oates, 1879.

Catholic Church. Pope (1878–1903: Leo XIII). (Gerald Carr Treacy, trans.). *Scholastic Philosophy: Encyclical Letter of Pope Leo XIII: Aeterni Patris*. New York: Paulist Press, 1951.

Chaadaev, Peter (R.T. McNally, trans.). *The Major Works of Peter Chaadaev*. Notre Dame, IN: University of Notre Dame Press, 1969.

Chaadaev, Peter (Mary-Barbara Zeldin, trans.). *Philosophical Letters; & Apology of a Madman*. Knoxville, TN: University of Tennessee Press, 1990 (1969).

Chappell, Vere, ed. *The Cambridge Companion to Locke*. New York: Cambridge University Press, 1994.

Chenu, M.D. (A.M. Landry and D. Hughes, trans.). *Towards Understanding Saint Thomas*. Chicago, IL: H. Regnery, 1964.

Chernyshevsky, Nikolay Gavrilovich (Lenin) (Michael R. Katz, trans.). *What Is To Be Done?* Ithaca, NY: Cornell University Press, 1989.

Clark, J.M. *The Great German Mystics: Eckhart, Tauler and Suso*. Oxford, UK: Basil Blackwell, 1949.

Clarke, O.F. *Introduction to Berdyaev*. London: G. Bles, 1950.

Collingwood, R.G. *The Idea of History*. Oxford, UK: Clarendon Press, 1946.

Collingwood, R.G. *An Autobiography*. London: Oxford University Press, 1951.

Collins, Ardis B. *The Secular is Sacred: Platonism and Thomism in Marsilio Ficino's Platonic Theology*. The Hague: Nijhoff, 1974.

Collins, James. *The Mind of Kierkegaard*. Princeton, NJ: Princeton University Press, 1983.

Comte, Auguste. *Catéchisme Positiviste; Appel aux Conservateurs; Discours sur l'esprit Positif*. Paris: Editions Anthropos, 1970.

Comte, Auguste. *Auguste Comte and Positivism: The Essential Writings*. Chicago, IL: University of Chicago Press, 1983 (New York: Harper & Row, 1975).

Comte, Auguste. *Discourse on Positivism as a Whole. See:* Comte, Auguste. *Auguste Comte and Positivism: The Essential Writings*.

Comte, Auguste (Frederick Ferré, trans.). *Introduction to Positive Philosophy*. Indianapolis, IN: Hackett, 1988 (Indianapolis, IN: Bobbs-Merrill, 1970).

Copenhaver, Brian P. and Charles B. Schmitt. *Renaissance Philosophy*. Oxford, UK: Oxford University Press, 1992.

Copleston, Frederick C. *Arthur Schopenhauer: Philosopher of Pessimism*. London: Burns Oates & Washbourne, 1946.

Copleston, Frederick C. *History of Medieval Philosophy*. London: Methuen, 1972.

Copleston, Frederick C. *Aquinas*. Harmondsworth, UK: Penguin, 1975 (1955).

Copleston, Frederick. *A History of Philosophy*. Westminster, MD: Newman Press, 1946–53 (vol. 1–3); 1959–60 (vol. 4–6); 1963–74 (vol. 7–9). Reprint, 9 Vols., Published in 3 Vols.: Garden City, NY: Image Books/Doubleday, 1985.

Copleston, Frederick C. *Philosophy in Russia: From Herzen to Lenin and Berdyaev*. Notre Dame, IN: University of Notre Dame, 1986.

Corpus Hermeticum. See: Hermes, Trismegistus.

Cottingham, John G., ed. *The Cambridge Companion to Descartes*. New York: Cambridge University Press, 1992.

Cottingham, John G., ed. *Western Philosophy: An Anthology*. Cambridge, MA: Blackwell, 1996.

Craig, Edward, ed. *Routledge Encyclopedia of Philosophy*. New York: Routledge, 1998.

Cranston, Maurice. *John Locke: A Biography*. London: Longmans, 1957.

Critchley, Simon and William Schroeder, eds. *A Companion to Continental Philosophy*. Malden, MA: Blackwell, 1998.

Croce, Benedetto. *Filosofia dello spirito*, 8 Vols. Bari, Italy: G. Laterza & Figli, 1912–.

Croce, Benedetto (Douglas Ainslie, trans.). *History, its Theory and Practice*. New York: Harcourt, Brace, 1923.

Croce, Benedetto (R.G. Collingwood, trans.). *Autobiography*. Oxford, UK: Clarendon Press, 1927.

Cudworth, Ralph. *The True Intellectual System of the Universe, 1678*. New York: G. Olm, 1977.

Cushing, Max Pearson. *Baron d'Holbach: A Study of Eighteenth Century Radicalism in France*. New York: B. Franklin, 1971 (1914).

Cutrofello, Andrew. *Continental Philosophy: A Contemporary Introduction*. New York: Routledge, 2005.

Debus, A.G. *Man and Nature in the Renaissance*. Cambridge, UK: Cambridge University Press, 1978.

Descartes, René (A. Kenny, trans.). *Descartes: Philosophical Letters*. Oxford, UK: Oxford University Press, 1970.

Descartes, René (Elizabeth Anscombe and Peter T Geach, eds.). *Philosophical Writings*. Indianapolis, IN: Bobbs-Merrill, 1971.

Descartes, René (J. Cottingham, R. Stoothoff and D. Murdoch, trans.). *Selected Philosophical Writings*. Cambridge, UK: Cambridge University Press, 1988.

Descartes, René (Valentine Rodger Miller and Reese P. Miller, trans.). *Principles of Philosophy*. Boston, MA: Kluwer, 1991 (1983).

Descartes, René (Elizabeth S. Haldane and G.R.T. Ross, trans.). *Discourse on the Method; and, Meditations on First Philosophy*. New Haven, CT: Yale University Press, 1996.

Destutt de Tracy, Antoine Louis Claude. *Élémens d'idéologie* (Facsimile). Paris: V. Courcier, 1970.

Dicker, Georges. *Hume's Epistemology and Metaphysics: An Introduction*. London: Routledge, 1998.

Diderot, D. (Jean Stewart and Jonathan Kemp, trans.). *Diderot, Interpreter of Nature: Selected Writings*. New York: International Publishers, 1943.

Diderot, Denis. (Nelly S. Hoyt and Thomas Cassirer, eds.). *Encyclopedia*. Indianapolis, IN: Bobbs-Merrill, 1965.

Dilthey, Wilhelm (H.P. Rickman, ed.). *Meaning in History: Dilthey's Thought on History and Society*. London: Allen & Unwin, 1961.

Dilthey, Wilhelm (H.P. Rickman, trans.). *Selected Writings*. Cambridge, UK: Cambridge University Press, 1976.

Donagan, Alan. *The Later Philosophy of R.G. Collingwood*. Oxford, UK: Clarendon Press, 1962.

Dostoevsky, Fyodor. *Notes from Underground*. New York: Bantam Books, 1992 (1974).

515

Dreyfus, Hubert L. and Harrison Hall, eds. *Husserl: Intentionality and Cognitive Science.* Cambridge, MA: MIT Press, 1982.

Duncan-Jones, Austin. *Butler's Moral Philosophy.* Harmondsworth, UK: Penguin Books, 1952.

Dunn, John (commentary by Allan B. Wolter). *Locke.* Oxford, UK: Oxford University Press, 1984.

Duns Scotus, John. *Treatise on God as First Principle.* Franciscan Herald Press, 2nd edn, 1982 (1966).

Eckhart, Meister (James M. Clark and John V. Skinner, trans. and notes). *Meister Eckhart: Selected Treatises and Sermons Translated from Latin and German.* London: Faber & Faber, 1958.

Edwards, Paul. *The Encyclopedia of Philosophy,* 8 vols. New York: Macmillan, 1972 (1967).

Elster, Jon. *Making Sense of Marx.* Cambridge, UK: Cambridge University Press, 1985.

Elton, G.R. *Reformation Europe, 1517–1559.* London: Collins, 1963.

Engels, Friedrich (J.B.S. Haldane, trans. and Clements Palme Dutt, ed.). *Dialectics of Nature.* New York: International Publishers, 1971.

Engels, Friedrich (Emile Bottigelli, trans.). *Anti-Dühring: M.E. Dühring Bouleverse la Science.* Paris: Ed. Sociales, 3rd edn, 1977.

Engels, Friedrich. *See also:* Marx, 1975, 1998.

Erigena, Johannes Scotus (Charleen Schwartz, trans.). *On the Division of Nature. Book I (De divisione naturae).* Annapolis, MD: St John's Bookstore, 1940.

Erigena, Johannes Scotus. *Joannis Scoti Erigenæ De divisione naturæ: libri quinque, div desiderati.* (Facsimile). Frankfurt am Main, Germany: Minerva, 1964 (1681).

Fann, K.T., ed. *Symposium on J. L. Austin.* London: Routledge & Kegan Paul, 1969.

Feuerbach, Ludwig A. (G. Eliot, trans.). *The Essence of Christianity.* New York: Harper & Row, 1957.

Feuerbach, Ludwig A. *Lectures on the Essence of Religion.* New York: Harper & Row, 1967.

Fichte, Johann Gottlieb (P. Heath and J. Lachs, trans.). *Science of Knowledge (Wissenschaftslehre): with First and Second Introductions.* New York: Appleton-Century-Crofts, 1970.

Fichte, Johann Gottlieb (G.D. Green, trans.). *Attempt at a Critique of All Revelation.* Cambridge, UK: Cambridge University Press, 1978.

Fichte, Johann Gottlieb (Daniel Breazeale, trans.). *Foundations of Transcendental Philosophy (Wissenschqftslehre nova methodo 1796/99).* Ithaca, NY: Cornell University Press, 1992.

Fichte, Johann Gottlieb (Daniel Breazeale, trans.). *Fichte, Early Philosophical Writings.* Ithaca, NY: Cornell University Press, 1993 (1988).

Ficino, Marsilio (Raymond Marcel, trans.). *Théologie platonicienne de l'immortalité des âmes.* Paris: Société d'édition 'Les belles lettres', 1964–.

Ficino, Marsilio. *Theologia Platonica de Immortalitate Animorum.* New York: Olms, 1995.

Findlay, John N. *Hegel: A Re-examination.* New York: Collier Books, 1962 (1958).

Findlay, John N. *Kant and the Transcendental Object.* Oxford, UK: Oxford University Press, 1981.

Flew, Antony. *Hume's Philosophy of Belief.* New York: Humanities Press, 1961.

Fogelin, Robert J. *Wittgenstein.* London: Routledge, 2nd edn, 1987.

Fowler, Thomas. *Shaftesbury and Hutcheson.* London: Sampson Low, Marston, Searle & Rivington, 1882.

France, Peter. *Diderot.* Oxford, UK: Oxford University Press, 1983.

Frege, Gottlob. *Begriffsschrift und andere Aufsätze.* Hildesheim, Germany: G. Olm, 2nd edn, 1964 (1879).

Frege, Gottlob (Michael Beaney, trans.). *The Frege Reader.* Oxford, UK: Blackwell, 1997.

Galilei, Galileo (Stillman Drake, trans.). *Two New Sciences: Including Centers of Gravity & Force of Percussion*. Madison, WI: University of Wisconsin Press, 1992.

Gargan, Edward T. *Leo XIII and the Modern World*. New York: Sheed and Ward, 1961.

Garin, Eugenio. *Giovanni Pico della Mirandola*. Florence, Italy: F. Le Monnier, 1937.

Garin, Eugenio (Carolyn Jackson and June Allen, trans., revised by Clare Robertson). *Astrology in the Renaissance: The Zodiac of Life*. London: Routledge & Kegan Paul, 1983.

Garrett, Don, ed. *The Cambridge Companion to Spinoza*. New York: Cambridge University Press, 1995.

Gay, Peter. *Voltaire's Politics: The Poet as Realist*. Princeton, NJ: Princeton University Press, 1959.

Gendzier, Stephen J. (Stephen J. Gendzier, trans. and ed.). *Denis Diderot's The Encyclopedia: Selections*. New York: Harper Torchbooks, 1967.

Gentile, Giovanni. *Theory of the Spirit and the Egocentric Propensities of Man*, 2 Vols. New York: 1978.

Gibson, Alexander Boyce *The Religion of Dostoevsky*. Philadelphia, PA: Westminster Press, 1973.

Gilson, Étienne (Illtyd Trethowan and Frank J. Sheed, trans.). *The Philosophy of St Bonaventure*. Paterson, NJ: St Anthony Guild Press, 1965.

Gilson, Étienne (L.K. Shook, trans.). *The Christian Philosophy of St Thomas Aquinas*. Notre Dame, IN: University of Notre Dame Press, 1994.

Gleason, Abbot. *European and Muscovite: Ivan Kireevsky and the Origins of Slavophilism*. Cambridge, MA: Harvard University Press, 1972.

Goldsmith, Maurice. *Hobbes's Science of Politics*. New York: Columbia University Press, 1966.

Gouhier, Henri G. *La Jeunesse d'Auguste Comte et la formation de positivisme*, 3 Vols. Paris: Librairie Philosophique J. Vrin 1933–41.

Grosholz, E., ed. *The Legacy of Simone de Beauvoir*. Oxford, UK: Oxford University Press, 2004.

Guignon, Charles B., ed. *The Cambridge Companion to Heidegger*. New York: Cambridge University Press, 1993.

Gunton, Colin E., ed. *The Cambridge Companion to Christian Doctrine*. New York: Cambridge University Press, 1997.

Gutting, Gary, ed. *The Cambridge Companion to Foucault*. New York: Cambridge University Press, 1994.

Gutting, Gary. *French Philosophy in the Twentieth Century*. Cambridge, UK: Cambridge University Press, 2001.

Guyer, Paul, ed. *The Cambridge Companion to Kant*. New York: Cambridge University Press, 1992.

Halévy, Élie (Mary Morris, trans.). *The Growth of Philosophical Radicalism*. London: Faber, 3rd edn, 1972.

Hallie, P.P. *Maine de Biran, Reformer of Empiricism, 1766–1824*. Cambridge, MA: Harvard University Press, 1959.

Hammond, M., J. Howarth and R. Keat. *Understanding Phenomenology*. Oxford, UK: Blackwell, 1991.

Hampshire, Stuart. *Spinoza*. Harmondsworth, UK: Penguin, 1951.

Hanfling, Oswald, ed. *Essential Readings in Logical Positivism*. Oxford, UK: Blackwell, 1981.

Hankins, James. *Plato in the Italian Renaissance*, Vol. 1. Boston, MA: Brill Academic, 1991.

Hannay, Alastair and Gordon Marino, eds. *The Cambridge Companion to Kierkegaard*. New York: Cambridge University Press, 1997.

Hegel, G.W.F. (J. Sibree, trans.). *The Philosophy of History*. New York: Dover, 1956.

Hegel, Georg Wilhelm Friedrich (T. Knox, trans.). *Philosophy of Right*. Oxford, UK: Clarendon Press, 1962.

Hegel, Georg Wilhelm Friedrich (J.B. Baillie, trans.). *The Phenomenology of Mind*. London: Allen & Unwin, 2nd edn, 1966.

Hegel, Georg Wilhelm Friedrich (A.V. Miller, trans.). *Phenomenology of Spirit*. Oxford, UK: Oxford University Press, 1977.

Hegel, G.W.F. (T.M. Knox and A.V. Miller, trans.). *Introduction to the Lectures on the History of Philosophy*. Oxford, UK: Clarendon Press, 1987.

Hegel, Georg Wilhelm Friedrich (Peter C. Hodgson, ed.) (R.F. Brown, P.C. Hodgson and J.M. Stewart, with H.S. Harris, trans.). *Lectures on the Philosophy of Religion*. Berkeley, CA: University of California Press, 1988.

Hegel, Georg Wilhelm Friedrich (Ernst Behler, ed.). *Encyclopedia of the Philosophical Sciences in Outline, and Critical Writings*. New York: Continuum, 1990.

Hegel, G.W.F. (T. Geraets, W. Suchting and H. Harris, trans.). *The Encyclopaedia: Logic*. Indianapolis, IN: Hackett, 1991.

Heidegger, Martin (P. Hertz, trans.). *On the Way to Language*. New York: Harper & Row, 1971.

Heidegger, Martin (David F. Krell, ed.). *Basic Writings*. New York: Harper & Row, 1977.

Heidegger, Martin (J. Macquarrie and E. Robinson, trans.). *Being and Time*. Oxford, UK: Blackwell, 1980.

Heidegger, Martin (D.F. Krell, trans.). *Nietzsche*. Vol. 4: *Nihilism*. San Francisco, CA: Harper & Row, 1982.

Heidegger, Martin (A. Hofstadter, trans.). *The Basic Problems of Phenomenology*. Bloomington, IN: Indiana University Press, 1982.

Hendel, C.W. *Studies in the Philosophy of David Hume*. Princeton, NJ: Princeton University Press, 1925.

Herbert of Cherbury, Edward Herbert, Baron (Günter Gawlick, ed.). *De Veritate. Ed. 3. De Causis Errorum. De Religione Laici. Parerga*. Stuttgart-Bad Cannstatt, Germany: F. Frommann, 1966.

Herbert of Cherbury, Edward Herbert, Baron. *De Causis Errorum*. London: Cura Philemonis Stephani, 1645. Reproduction of original in Cambridge University Library (Microfilm), Ann Arbor, MI: University Microfilms, 1977.

Herbert of Cherbury, Edward Herbert, Baron. *De Veritate*. London: Routledge/Thoemmes Press, 1992 (Reprint, originally published Bristol, UK: University of Bristol by J.W. Arrowsmith, 1937).

Herbert of Cherbury, Edward Herbert, Baron (John A Butler, trans.). *Pagan Religion: A Translation of De Religione Gentilium*. Binghamton, NY: Medieval & Renaissance Texts & Studies, 1996.

Herder, Johann Gottfried (Frank Edward Manuel, trans.). *Reflections on the Philosophy of the History of Mankind*. Chicago, IL: University of Chicago Press, 1968.

Hermes, Trismegistus (Brian P. Copenhaver, trans.). *Hermetica: The Greek Corpus Hermeticum and the Latin Asclepius in a New English Translation, with Notes and Introduction*. Cambridge, UK: Cambridge University Press, 1995 (1992).

Hobbes, Thomas (C.B. Macpherson, ed.). *Leviathan*. Harmondsworth, UK: Penguin, 1981 (1968).

Hobbes, Thomas. *The Collected English Works of Thomas Hobbes*. London: Routledge, 1997.

Holbach, Paul Henri Thiry, baron d'. *System of Nature (Système de la nature), or, The Laws of the Moral and Physical World*. Philadelphia, PA: R. Benson, 1970 (1979).

Holveck, E. *Simone de Beauvoir's Philosophy of Lived Experience: Literature and Metaphysics*. Lanham, MD: Rowman and Littlefield, 2002.

Hope, Vincent, ed. *Philosophers of the Scottish Enlightenment*. Edinburgh: Edinburgh University Press, 1984.

Hopkins, Jasper. *A Companion to the Study of St Anslem*. Minneapolis, MN: University of Minnesota Press, 1972.

Houlgate, Stephen. *Freedom, Truth and History: An Introduction to Hegel's Philosophy*. London: Routledge, 1991.

Howells, Christina, ed. *The Cambridge Companion to Sartre*. New York: Cambridge University Press, 1992.

Hume, David (Thomas H. Green and Thomas H. Grose, eds). *Philosophical Works*, 4 Vols. London: Longmans, Green, 1875–82.

Hume, David. *Hume's Political Discourses*. London: Walter Scott, 1906.

Hume, David. *A Treatise of Human Nature*. Oxford, UK: Clarendon Press, 1960.

Hume, David. *Essays: Moral, Literary and Political*. Oxford, UK: Oxford University Press, 1965.

Hume, David. *An Enquiry Concerning Human Understanding*. Indianapolis, IN: Hackett, 1977.

Hume, David. *Political Discourses*. Faksimile-Ausg. Frankfurt, Germany: Verlag Wirtschaft und Finanzen, 1987 (Reprint. Originally published Edinburgh: Printed by R. Fleming, for A. Kincaid and A. Donaldson, 1752).

Hume, David. *Principal Writings on Religion, including Dialogues concerning Natural Religion and The Natural History of Religion*. Oxford, UK: Oxford University Press, 1993.

Hume, David. *Political Essays*. Cambridge, UK: Cambridge University Press, 1994.

Hume, David. *An Enquiry Concerning the Principles of Morals: A Critical Edition*. New York: Oxford University Press, 1998.

Husserl, Edmund. *Phenomenology and the Crisis of Philosophy*. New York: Harper & Row, 1965.

Hutchings, Kimberly. *Kant, Critique and Politics*. London: Routledge, 1996.

Hyppolite, Jean. *Genesis and Structure of Hegel's Phenomenology of Spirit*. Evanston, IL: Northwestern University Press, 1974.

Jacoff, Rachel, ed. *The Cambridge Companion to Dante*. New York: Cambridge University Press, 1993.

Janelle, Pierre. *The Catholic Reformation*. New York: Bruce, 1949.

Jaspers, Karl. *The Great Philosophers. The Disturbers: Descartes, Pascal, Lessing, Kierkegaard, Nietzsche; Philosophers in Other Realms: Einstein, Weber, Marx*. New York: Harcourt Brace, 1995.

Jay, Martin. *Adorno*. Cambridge, MA: Harvard University Press, 1984.

Johnson, Oliver A. *The Mind of David Hume: A Companion Book to Book 1 of 'A Treatise of Human Nature'*. Champaign, IL: University of Illinois Press, 1995.

Joll, James. *Antonio Gramsci*. New York: Penguin, 1978.

Jolley, Nicholas, ed. *The Cambridge Companion to Leibniz*. New York: Cambridge University Press, 1994.

Kamenka, Eugene. *The Portable Karl Marx*. New York: Viking, 1983.

Kant, Immanuel (J.H. Bernard, trans.). *Critique of Judgment*. New York: Hafner Press, 1951.

Kant, Immanuel (T.M. Greene, H.H. Hudson and J.R. Silber, trans.). *Religion within the Limits of Reason Alone*. New York: Harper & Row, 2nd edn, 1960.

Kant, Immanuel (L. Infield, trans.). *Lectures on Ethics*. New York: Harper & Row, 1963.

Kant, Immanuel (Lewis White Beck, trans.). *Critique of Practical Reason*. Indianapolis, IN: Bobbs-Merrill, 1976.

Kant, Immanuel. *Fundamental Principles of the Metaphysic of Morals*. New York: Prometheus, 1987.

Kant, Immanuel (H.B. Nisbet, trans.). *Political Writings*. Cambridge, UK: Cambridge University Press, 1991.

Kant, Immanuel (Norman Kemp Smith, trans.). *Critique of Pure Reason*. New York: Palgrave Macmillan, 2007 edn.

Kaufmann, Walter. *Nietzsche: Philosopher, Psychologist, Antichrist*. Princeton, NJ: Princeton University Press, 1950.

Kaufmann, Walter. *Hegel: A Reinterpretation*. Notre Dame, IN: University of Notre Dame Press, 1978.

Keat, Russell. *The Politics of Social Theory: Habermas, Freud and the Critique of Positivism*. Chicago, IL: Chicago University Press, 1981.

Kemp Smith, Norman. *The Philosophy of David Hume*. London: Macmillan, 1941.

Kenny, Anthony. *Wittgenstein*. Cambridge, MA: Harvard University Press, 1973.

Kenny, Anthony. *Aquinas*. Oxford, UK: Oxford University Press, 1980.

Kibre, Pearl. *The Library of Pico della Mirandola*. New York: Columbia University Press, 1936.

Kierkegaard, Søren (A. Dra, trans.). *The Journals 1834–54*. London: Collins, 1958.

Kierkegaard, Søren (Walter Lowrie, trans.). *The Concept of Dread*. (Reprint) Princeton, NJ: Princeton University Press, 1968 (1957).

Kierkegaard, Søren (D. Swenson and W. Lowrie, trans.). *Concluding Unscientific Postscript*. Princeton, NJ: Princeton University Press, 1968.

Kierkegaard, Søren. *Fear and Trembling: and The Sickness unto Death*. Princeton, NJ: Princeton University Press, 1970.

Kierkegaard, Søren (W. Lowrie, trans.). *Either/Or*, 2 Vols. Princeton, NJ: Princeton University Press, 1971.

Kierkegaard, Søren (R. Bretall, trans.). *A Kierkegaard Anthology*. Princeton, NJ: Princeton University Press, 1973.

Kierkegaard, Søren (A. Hannay, trans.). *Fear and Trembling*. Harmondsworth, UK: Penguin, 1985.

Kierkegaard, Søren (H. Hong and E. Hong, trans.). *Philosophical Fragments: Johannes Climacus*. Princeton, NJ: Princeton University Press, 1985.

Kolakowsky, L. (P.S. Falla, trans.). *Main Currents of Marxism: Its Rise, Growth and Dissolution, 3 Vols*. Oxford, UK: Clarendon Press, 1978.

Körner, Stephan. *The Philosophy of Mathematics*. London: Hutchinson University Library, 1960.

Kraft, Victor (Arthur Pap, trans.). *The Vienna Circle: The Origin of Neo-positivism, a Chapter in the History of Recent Philosophy*. New York: Philosophical Library, 1953.

Kretzmann, Norman and Eleonore Stump, eds. *The Cambridge Companion to Aquinas*. New York: Cambridge University Press, 1994.

Kristeller, Paul Oskar. *The Philosophy of Marsilio Ficino*. New York: Columbia University Press, 1943.

Kuhn, Thomas. *The Copernican Revolution*. Cambridge, MA: Harvard University Press, 1957.

Kulstad, Mark, ed. Essays *on the Philosophy of Leibniz*. Houston, TX: Rice University, 1977.

Lavrov, P.L. (J.P. Scanlan, trans.). *Historical Letters*. Berkeley, CA: University of California Press, 1967.

Law, David R. *Kierkegaard as Negative Theologian*. Oxford, UK: Clarendon Press, 1993.

Leff, Gordon. *Medieval Thought from St Augustine to Ockham.* Baltimore, MD: Penguin, 1965.

Leff, Gordon. *William of Ockham: The Metamorphosis of Scholastic Discourse.* Manchester, UK: Manchester University Press, 1975.

Leibniz, Gottfried Wilhelm (George Montgomery, trans.). *Discourse on Metaphysics; Correspondence with Arnauld; Monadology.* La Salle, IL: Open Court Press, 1902 (1991).

Leibniz, Gottfried Wilhelm (Philip P. Wiener, ed.). *Selections.* New York: Scribner, 1951.

Leibniz, Gottfried Wilhelm (G. Montgomery, trans.). *Basic Writings.* La Salle, IL: Open Court Press, 1962.

Leibniz, Gottfried Wilhelm (Austin Marsden Farrer, trans.). *Theodicy: Essays on the Goodness of God, the Freedom of Man, and the Origin of Evil.* La Salle, IL: Open Court Press, 1985 (originally published by London: Routledge & Kegan Paul, 1951).

Leibniz, Gottfried Wilhelm (G. Parkinson, ed.). *Philosophical Writings.* London: Dent, 1990.

Leibniz, Gottfried Wilhelm (R. S. Woolhouse and Richard Francks, trans.). *Leibniz's 'New System' and Associated Contemporary Texts,* Oxford, UK: Clarendon Press, 1997.

Lenin, Vladimir Ilich. *Collected Works.* Moscow: Foreign Languages Publishing House, 1960–.

Lenin, Vladimir Ilich. *Materialism and Empirio-Criticism: Critical Comments on a Reactionary Philosophy.* Moscow: Progress Publishers, 1977.

Lenin, Vladimir Ilich. *Imperialism: the Highest Stage of Capitalism.* Moscow: Progress Publishers, 1978.

Lenin, Vladimir Ilich (Norman Lewis and James Malone, trans.). *Imperialism: The Highest Stage of Capitalism: A Popular Outline.* London: Pluto, 1996.

Leo XIII, Pope. *See:* Catholic Church.

Lessing, Gotthold Ephraim (Henry Chadwick, trans.). *Lessing's Theological Writings: Selections in Translation.* Stanford, CA: Stanford University Press, 1957.

Lessing, Gotthold Ephraim (Christopher G. Trump and Miriam J. Levy, trans.). *Nathan the Wise: A Drama in Five Acts, in Modern American Prose.* New York: McGraw-Hill, 1996.

Locke, John (Peter Laslett, ed.). *Two Treatises of Government: A Critical Edition with an Introduction and Apparatus Criticus.* Cambridge, UK: Cambridge University Press, 2nd edn, 1970.

Locke, John. *Two Treatises of Civil Government.* London: Dent, 1970.

Locke, John (Peter H. Nidditch, ed.). *An Essay Concerning Human Understanding.* Oxford, UK: Clarendon Press, 1975.

Locke, John (William Popple, trans.). *A Letter Concerning Toleration.* New York: Macmillan, 1988 (1689).

Locke, John (John W. Yolton and Jean S. Yolton, eds.). *Some Thoughts Concerning Education.* Oxford, UK: Oxford University Press, 1989.

Locke, John. *Collected Works of John Locke.* New York: Routledge, 1997.

Locke, John. *The Reasonableness of Christianity as Delivered in the Scriptures.* Dulles, VA: Thoemmes Press, 1997.

Lonergan, Bernard (David B. Burrell, ed.). *Verbum: Word and Idea in Aquinas.* Notre Dame, IN: University of Notre Dame Press, 1967.

Losskii, N.O. *History of Russian Philosophy.* New York: International Universities Press, 1951.

Luce, Arthur Aston. *The Life of George Berkeley, Bishop of Cloyne.* London: T. Nelson, 1949.

Lukács, Georg (Rodney Livingstone, trans.). *History and Class Consciousness.* Cambridge, UK: MIT Press, 1971.

Lyons, William E. *Gilbert Ryle: An Introduction to His Philosophy.* Atlantic Highlands, NJ: Humanities Press, 1980.

Macann, Christopher. *Four Phenomenological Philosophers: Husserl, Heidegger, Sartre, Merleau-Ponty*. London: Routledge, 1994.

Machiavelli, Niccolò (Leslie Joseph Walker, trans.). *The Discourses of Niccolò Machiavelli*. New Haven, CT: Yale University Press, 1950.

Machiavelli, Niccolò (George Bull, trans.). *The Prince*. Harmondsworth, UK: Penguin, 1961.

Machiavelli, Niccolò *Discourses on Livy*. (Julia Conaway Bondanella and Peter E. Bondanella, (trans.). New York: Oxford University Press, 1997.

Mackey, Louis. *Peregrinations of the Word: Essays in Medieval Philosophy*. Ann Arbor, MI: University of Michigan Press, 1997.

Macquarrie, John. *Martin Heidegger*. London: Lutterworth Press, 1968.

Magee, Bryan. *Popper*. London: Woburn Press, 1974.

Magee, Bryan. *The Philosophy of Schopenhauer*. Oxford, UK: Clarendon Press, 1983.

Magnus, Bernd and Kathleen Higgins, eds. *The Cambridge Companion to Nietzsche*. New York: Cambridge University Press, 1996.

Makkreel, Rudolf A. *Dilthey: Philosopher of the Human Studies*. Princeton, NJ: Princeton University Press, 1975.

Malebranche, Nicholas (Morris Ginsberg, trans.). *Dialogues on Metaphysics and on Religion*. London: Allen & Unwin, 1923.

Malebranche, Nicolas (Geneviève Rodis-Lewis, ed.). *Œuvres*. Paris: Gallimard, 1979–92.

Malebranche, Nicolas (Thomas M. Lennon and Paul J. Olscamp, trans. and ed.). *The Search after Truth. (Recherche de la vérité)* Cambridge, UK: Cambridge University Press, 1997.

Malia, Martin E. *Alexander Herzen and the Birth of Russian Socialism*. New York: Grosset & Dunlap, 1971.

Mandeville, Bernard. *The Fable of the Bees And Other Writings*. Indianapolis, IN: Hackett, 1997.

Manser, Anthony. *Sartre: A Philosophic Study*. London: Athlone Press, 1966.

Manser, Anthony and Guy Stock, eds. *The Philosophy of F.H. Bradley*. Oxford, UK: Clarendon Press, 1984.

Manuel, Frank E. *The Prophets of Paris*. Cambridge, MA: Harvard University Press, 1962.

Marenbon, John. *The Philosophy of Peter Abelard*. New York: Cambridge University Press, 1997.

Marx, Karl. *Economic and Philosophic Manuscripts of 1844*. Moscow: Progress Publishers, 4th revised ed., 1974.

Marx, Karl (Serge L. Levitzky, trans.). *Das Kapital: A Critique of Political Economy*. Washington, DC: Regnery Gateway, 1993.

Marx, Karl and Friedrich Engels (Richard Dixon and Clemens Dutt, trans.). *The Holy Family, or, Critique of Critical Criticism: Against Bruno Bauer, and Company*. Moscow: Progress Publishers, 2nd revised edn, 1975 (1956).

Marx, Karl and Friedrich Engels (E.J. Hobsbawm, trans.). *The Communist Manifesto: A Modern Edition*. London: Verso, 1998.

McCarthy, Thomas A. *The Critical Theory of Jürgen Habermas*. Cambridge, MA: MIT Press, 1978.

McMurty, John. *The Structure of Marx's World-View*. Princeton, NJ: Princeton University Press, 1978.

Meinecke, Friedrich (Douglas Scott, trans.). *Machiavellism*. New Haven, CT: Yale University Press, 1957.

Merleau-Ponty, Maurice. *Signs*. Evanston, IL: Northwestern University Press, 1964.

Merleau-Ponty, Maurice (C. Smith, trans.). *Phenomenology of Perception*. London: Routledge & Kegan Paul, 1981.

Mill, John Stuart. *A System of Logic.* London: Longmans & Green, 1886.

Mill, John Stuart. *Collected Works.* Toronto, Canada: University of Toronto Press, 1963.

Mill, John Stuart. *Essays on Ethics, Religion and Society.* Toronto, Canada: University of Toronto Press, 1969.

Mill, John Stuart. *Auguste Comte and Positivism.* Ann Arbor, MI: University of Michigan Press, 1973.

Mill, John Stuart. *Three Essays: On Liberty; Representative Government; The Subjection of Women.* Oxford, UK: Oxford University Press, 1987.

Mill, John Stuart. *Principles of Political Economy; and, Chapters on Socialism.* Oxford, UK: Oxford University Press, 1994.

Mill, John Stuart. *Autobiography and Literary Essays.* London: Routledge, 1996.

Mill, John Stuart. *Utilitarianism.* Oxford, UK: Oxford University Press, 1998.

Milne, A.J.M. *The Social Philosophy of English Idealism.* London: Allen & Unwin, 1962.

Moore, F.C.T. *The Psychology of Maine de Biran.* Oxford, UK: Clarendon Press, 1970.

Moore, G.E. *Philosophical Papers.* London: Allen & Unwin, 1959.

Moore, G.E. *Principia Ethica.* Cambridge, UK: Cambridge University Press, 1989.

Neu, Jerome, ed. *The Cambridge Companion to Freud.* New York: Cambridge University Press, 1991.

Nicholas of Cusa (Germain Heron, trans.). *Of Learned Ignorance.* New Haven, CT: Yale University Press, 1954.

Nietzsche, Friedrich Wilhelm (Oscar Levy, ed.). *Complete Works.* New York: Russell & Russell, 1964.

Nietzsche, Friedrich Wilhelm (Walter Kaufmann, trans. and ed.). *Basic Writings of Nietzsche.* New York: Modern Library, 1968.

Nietzsche, Friedrich Wilhelm. *Complete Works.* New York: Gordon Press, 1974.

Nietzsche, Friedrich Wilhelm. *Human, All-too-human: A Book for Free Spirits.* New York: Gordon Press, 1974.

Nietzsche, Friedrich Wilhelm (Walter Kaufmann, trans. and ed.). *The Portable Nietzsche.* New York: Viking Press, 1980.

Norton, David F., ed. *The Cambridge Companion to Hume.* New York: Cambridge University Press, 1993.

Nussbaum, Stephanie Ann, John Canfield and Stephanie E. Lemasters. *Philosophy of the English Speaking World in the Twentieth Century 2: Meaning, Knowledge and Value.* Vol. X: *Routledge History of Philosophy.* London: Routledge, 1997.

O'Meara, Dominic J., ed. *Neoplatonism and Christian Thought.* Albany, NY: State University of New York Press, 1982.

O'Neill, John. *Perception, Expression and History: The Social Phenomenology of Maurice Merleau-Ponty.* Evanston, IL: Northwestern University Press, 1970.

Orsini, Gian N.G. *Benedetto Croce: Philosopher of Art and Literary Critic.* Carbondale, IL: Southern Illinois University Press, 1961.

Ortega y Gasset, José . (Anthony Kerrigan, trans. and Kenneth Moore, ed.). *The Revolt of the Masses.* Notre Dame, IN: University of Notre Dame Press, 1985.

Otto, Rudolf. (Bertha L. Bracey and Richenda C. Payne, trans.). *Mysticism East and West: A Comparative Analysis of the Nature of Mysticism.* New York: Macmillan, 1970.

Otto, Rudolf. *The Idea of the Holy: An Inquiry into the Non-Rational Factor in the Idea of the Divine and its Relation to the Rational.* London: Oxford University Press, 1973.

Pagel, Walter. *Paracelsus: An Introduction to Philosophical Medicine in the Era of the Renaissance.* New York: S. Karger, 1958.

Parkinson, G.H.R. *The Renaissance and Seventeenth-Century Rationalism.* Vol. IV: *Routledge History of Philosophy.* London: Routledge, 1993.

Pascal, Blaise. (A. Krailsheimer, trans.). *Pensées.* Harmondsworth, UK: Penguin, 1980.

Pasnau, Robert. *Theories of Cognition in the Later Middle Ages.* New York: Cambridge University Press, 1997.

Passmore, John A. *Hume's Intentions.* Cambridge, UK: Cambridge University Press, 1952.

Passmore, John A. *A Hundred Years of Philosophy.* Harmondsworth, UK: Penguin, 2nd edn, 1968.

Paton, H.J. *The Categorical Imperative: A Study in Kant's Moral Philosophy.* Chicago, IL: University of Chicago Press, 1948.

Peel, J.D.Y., ed. *Herbert Spencer on Social Evolution: Selected Writings.* Chicago, IL: University of Chicago Press, 1972.

Peltonen, Markku, ed. *The Cambridge Companion to Bacon.* New York: Cambridge University Press, 1996.

Peters, Richard S. *Hobbes.* Harmondsworth, UK: Penguin, 1956.

Phillipson, Coleman. *Three Criminal Law Reformers: Beccaria, Bentham, Romilly.* London: J.M. Dent, 1923.

Pico della Mirandola, Giovanni. *Oration on the Dignity of Man.* Washington, DC: Regnery, 1996.

Pilkington, A.E. *Bergson and his Influence: A Reassessment.* Cambridge, UK: Cambridge University Press, 1976.

Pinkard, Terry. *German Philosophy, 1760–1860: The Legacy of Idealism.* Cambridge, UK: Cambridge University Press, 2002.

Popper, Karl. *The Open Society and its Enemies,* 2 Vols. Princeton, NJ: Princeton University Press, 5th edn, 1966.

Popper, Karl. *Logic of Scientific Discovery.* London: Hutchinson, 1975.

Powicke, Frederick J. *The Cambridge Platonists.* London: J.M. Dent, 1926.

Raphael, D.D. *The Moral Sense.* London: Oxford University Press, 1947.

Raphael, D.D. *Hobbes: Morals and Politics.* London: Allen & Unwin, 1977.

Read, Herbert. *The True Voice of Feeling.* London: Faber and Faber, 1953.

Redpath, Theodore. *Tolstoy.* London: Bowes & Bowes, 1960.

Reid, Thomas (Derek R. Brookes, ed.). *An Inquiry into the Human Mind: On the Principles of Common Sense: A Critical Edition.* University Park, PA: Pennsylvania State University Press, 1997.

Rescher, Nicholas. *G.W. Leibniz's Monadology.* London: Routledge, 1992.

Richter, M. *The Politics of Conscience: T.H. Green and his Age.* Cambridge, MA: Harvard University Press, 1964.

Robb, Nesca A. *Neoplatonism of the Italian Renaissance.* London: Allen & Unwin, 1935.

Romanell, Patrick. *Gentile: The Philosophy of Giovanni Gentile.* New York: S.F. Vanni, 1938.

Rosen, Michael. *Hegel's Dialectic and its Criticism.* Cambridge, UK: Cambridge University Press, 1982.

Ross, G. MacDonald. *Leibniz.* Oxford, UK: Oxford University Press, 1992.

Rossi, Paolo. (Sacha Rabinovitch, trans.). *Francis Bacon: From Magic to Science.* Chicago, IL: University of Chicago Press, 1968.

Rousseau, Jean-Jacques (Barbara Foxley, trans.). *Emile.* London: J.M. Dent, 1993.

Rousseau, Jean-Jacques (Victor Gourevitch, trans.). *The Social Contract and Other Later Political Writings.* Cambridge, UK: Cambridge University Press, 1997.

Rudd, Margaret Thomas. *The Lone Heretic: A Biography of Miguel de Unamuno y Jugo.* Austin, TX: University of Texas Press, 1963.

Ruffo-Fiore, Silvia. *Niccolò Machiavelli.* Boston, MA: Twayne, 1982.

Russell, Bertrand. *The Philosophy of Bergson.* London: Bowes & Bowes, 1914.

Russell, Bertrand. *A Critical Exposition of the Philosophy of Leibniz.* London: George Allen & Unwin, 1958.

Russell, Bertrand. *The Analysis of Mind.* London: Allen & Unwin, 1968

Russell, Bertrand. *The Collected Papers of Bertrand Russell.* Vols. 1–4, 6–14. London: Allen & Unwin, 1983. Later volumes and reprints, London: Routledge, 1992–.

Russell, Bertrand. *Our Knowledge of the External World: As a Field for Scientific Methods in Philosophy.* London: Routledge, 1993.

Russell, Bertrand. *An Inquiry into Meaning and Truth: The William James Lectures for 1940 Delivered at Harvard University.* London: Routledge, Revised edn, 1995.

Russell, Bertrand. *Principles of Social Reconstruction.* London: Routledge, 2nd edn, 1997.

Russell, Bertrand and Alfred N. Whitehead. *Principia Mathematica.* New York: Cambridge University Press, 1927.

Russell, Jeffrey B. *Dissent and Reform in the Early Middle Ages.* Berkeley, CA: University of California Press, 1965.

Ryle, Gilbert. *The Concept of Mind.* Chicago, IL: University of Chicago Press, 1984.

Sartre, Jean-Paul (R.D. Cumming, ed.). *The Philosophy of Jean-Paul Sartre.* New York: Random House, 1965.

Sartre, Jean-Paul. *Being and Nothingness: An Essay on Phenomenological Ontology.* London: Routledge, 1989 (1958).

Schelling, Friedrich Wilhelm Joseph von (Frederick de Wolfe Bolman, Jr., trans.). *The Ages of the World.* New York: Columbia University Press, 1942.

Schelling, F.W.J. (Peter Lauchlan Heath, trans.). *System of Transcendental Idealism (1800).* Charlottesville, VA: University Press of Virginia, 1978.

Schilpp, Paul A. *The Philosophy of G.E. Moore.* New York: Tudor, 2nd edn, 1952.

Schilpp, Paul A., ed. *The Philosophy of Bertrand Russell.* La Salle, IL: Open Court Press, 4th edn, 1971.

Schilpp, Paul A., ed. *The Philosophy of Jean-Paul Sartre.* La Salle, IL: Open Court Press, 1981.

Schilpp, Paul A., ed. *The Philosophy of Karl Jaspers,* Augmented edition. La Salle, IL: Open Court Press, 1981 (1957).

Schilpp, Paul A. and Lewis Edwin Hahn, eds. *The Philosophy of Gabriel Marcel.* La Salle, IL: Open Court Press, 1984.

Schmitt, Charles B. *Aristotle and the Renaissance.* Cambridge, MA: Harvard University Press, 1983.

Schoolman, Morton. *The Imaginary Witness: The Critical Theory of Herbert Marcuse.* New York: Free Press, 1984.

Schopenhauer, Arthur. *The Essential Schopenhauer.* London: Allen & Unwin, 1962.

Schopenhauer, Arthur (E.F.J. Payne, trans.). *The World as Will and Representation,* 2 Vols. New York: Dover, 1966.

Schopenhauer, Arthur (E.F.J. Payne, trans.). *On the Fourfold Root of the Principle of Sufficient Reason.* La Salle, IL: Open Court, 1974.

Schopenhauer, Arthur (Wolfgang Schirmacher, ed.). *Philosophical Writings.* New York: Continuum, 1994.

Scott, Charles E. *The Language of Difference.* Atlantic Highlands, NJ: Humanities Press International, 1987.

Scruton, Roger. *A Short History of Modern Philosophy: From Descartes to Wittgenstein,* London: Routledge, 2nd edn, 1996.

Scruton, Roger. *Kant.* Oxford, UK: Oxford University Press, 1982.

Silver, Philip W. *Ortega as Phenomenologist.* New York: Columbia University Press, 1978.

Singer, Peter. *Marx.* Oxford, UK: Oxford University Press, 1980.

Singer, Peter. *Hegel.* Oxford, UK: Oxford University Press, 1983.

Skorupski, John, ed. *The Cambridge Companion to Mill.* New York: Cambridge University Press, 1998.

Sluga, Hans and David G. Stern, eds. *The Cambridge Companion to Wittgenstein.* New York: Cambridge University Press, 1996.

Smart, Ninian. *Reasons and Faiths: An Investigation of Religious Discourse.* London: Routledge & Kegan Paul, 1958.

Smart, Ninian. *Historical Selections in the Philosophy of Religion.* London: SCM Press, 1962.

Smart, Ninian. *The Religious Experience.* New York: Maxwell Macmillan International, 4th edn, 1991.

Smith, Adam. *Wealth of Nations.* London: Penguin Books, 1986.

Smith, Barry and David W. Smith, eds. *The Cambridge Companion to Husserl.* New York: Cambridge University Press, 1995.

Smith, Norman Kemp. *Studies in the Cartesian Philosophy.* London: Macmillan, 1902.

Solomon, Robert C., ed. *Nietzsche: A Collection of Critical Essays.* Notre Dame, IN: University of Notre Dame Press, 1980 (1973).

Solomon, Robert C. and Kathleen M. Higgins, eds. *The Age of German Idealism.* London: Routledge, 1993.

Solovyev, Vladimir Sergeyevich (Peter P. Zouboff, ed.). *Vladimir Solovyev's Lectures on Godmanhood.* London: Dennis Dobson, 1948.

Solovyev, Vladimir Sergeyevich (S.L. Frank, ed. and Natalie Duddington, trans.). *A Solovyev Anthology.* London: SCM Press, 1950.

Sorell, Tom, ed. *The Cambridge Companion to Hobbes.* New York: Cambridge University Press, 1996.

Southern, Richard W. *St Anslem and his Biographer: A Study of Monastic Life and Thought, 1059–c. 1130.* Cambridge, UK: Cambridge University Press, 1963.

Spencer, Herbert. *A System of Synthetic Philosophy,* 10 Vols. Osnabrück, Germany: Zeller, 1966. (Reprint of 1892–1907).

Spencer, Herbert. *Epitome of the Synthetic Philosophy of Herbert Spencer.* London: Williams and Norgate, 5th edn, 1973 (1901).

Spencer, Herbert. *Herbert Spencer: Collected Writings.* London: Routledge/Thoemmes Press, 1996.

Spinoza, Baruch. *Œuvres Complètes.* New York: French and European Publications, 1955.

Spinoza, Benedictus de. (Edwin Curley, ed. and trans.). *The Collected Works of Spinoza.* Princeton, NJ: Princeton University Press, 1985–.

Spinoza, Benedictus de. (Samuel Shirley and Seymour Feldman, trans.). *Tractatus Theologico-Politicus.* Indianapolis, IN: Hackett, 1998.

Stace, Walter T. *The Philosophy of Hegel: A Systematic Exposition.* London: Macmillan, 1924.

Stern, J.P. *A Study of Nietzsche.* Cambridge, UK: Cambridge University Press, 1979.

Stern, Robert. *Hegel, Kant and the Structure of the Object.* London: Routledge, 1990.

Stirling, James Hutchison. *The Secret of Hegel: Being the Hegelian System in Origin, Principle, Form, and Matter.* Dubuque, IA: Brown Reprint Library, 1971.

Strauss, Leo. *Thoughts on Machiavelli.* Chicago, IL: University of Chicago Press, 1984.

Stroud, Barry. *Hume.* London: Routledge, 1981.

Talbot, Ellen Bliss. *The Fundamental Principle of Fichte's Philosophy.* New York: Macmillan, 1906.

Thompson, Clara. *Psychoanalysis: Its Evolution and Development.* New York: Thomas Nelson, 1950.

Thompson, Josiah. *Kierkegaard.* New York: Knopf, 1973.

Tolstoy, Leo. *War and Peace: The Maude Translation, Backgrounds and Sources, Criticism.* New York: W.W. Norton, 2nd edn, 1996.

Torrey, Norman L. *Voltaire and the English Deists.* New Haven, CT: Yale University Press, 1930.

Tweyman, Stanley. *René Descartes' Meditations on First Philosophy in Focus.* London: Routledge, 1994.

Unamuno, Miguel de (Anthony Kerrigan, trans.). *The Tragic Sense of Life in Men and Nations.* London: Routledge and Kegan Paul, 1972.

Underhill, Evelyn. *Mysticism: A Study in the Nature and Development of Man's Spiritual Consciousness.* London: Methuen, 1912.

Urmson, J.O. *Berkeley.* Oxford, UK: Oxford University Press, 1982.

Van Duzen, Charles H. *The Contributions of the Ideologues to French Revolutionary Thought.* Baltimore, MD: Johns Hopkins Press, 1935.

Voltaire. *Dictionnaire Philosophique.* Oxford, UK: Voltaire Foundation, 1994.

Wallace, William A. *Causality and Scientific Explanation.* Ann Arbor, MI: University of Michigan Press, 1972–74.

Walsh, W.H. *Kant's Criticism of Metaphysics.* Edinburgh: Edinburgh University Press, 1975.

Warnock, G.J. *Berkeley.* Notre Dame, IN: University of Notre Dame Press, 1983.

Warnock, G.J. *J.L. Austin.* London: Routledge, 1989.

Wartofsky, Marx. *Feuerbach.* Cambridge, UK: Cambridge University Press, 1977.

Watts, Pauline Moffit. *Nicholaus Cusanus: A Fifteenth-century Vision of Man.* Leiden, Netherlands: Brill, 1982.

Webb, Clement C.J. *Studies in the History of Natural Theology.* Oxford, UK: Clarendon Press, 1915.

Wendel, François (Philip Mairet, trans.). *Calvin: Origins and Development of his Religious Thought.* London: Collins, 1963.

Wessell, L.P., Jr. *G.E. Lessing's Theology: A Reinterpretation.* The Hague: Mouton, 1977.

Weston, Michael. *Kierkegaard and Modern Continental Philosophy: An Introduction.* London: Routledge, 1994.

White, Stephen K., ed. *The Cambridge Companion to Habermas.* New York: Cambridge University Press, 1995.

Wienpahl, Paul. *The Radical Spinoza.* New York: New York University Press, 1979.

William, of Ockham (Philotheus Boehner, trans. and ed.). *Philosophical Writings: A Selection.* Indianapolis, IN: Bobbs-Merrill, 1964.

Williams, Bernard. *Descartes: The Project of Pure Enquiry.* New York: Penguin Books, 1978.

Wilson, Arthur M. *Diderot.* New York: Oxford University Press, 1957.

Wilson, Margaret Dauler. *Descartes.* London: Routledge, 1983.

Wiltshire, David. *The Social and Political Thought of Herbert Spencer.* Oxford, UK: Oxford University Press, 1978.

Wittgenstein, Ludwig (G.E.M. Anscombe, trans.). *Philosophical Investigations.* Oxford, UK: Blackwell, 1953.

Wittgenstein, Ludwig. *Tractatus Logico-Philosophicus: English Translation.* London: Routledge, 1975.

Wolfson, Harry A. *The Philosophy of Spinoza: Unfolding the Latent Processes of His Reasoning.* Cambridge, MA: Harvard University Press, 1983.

Wood, Allen W. *Karl Marx.* New York: Routledge, 2nd edn, 2004.

Woolhouse, Roger. *Descartes, Spinoza, Leibniz: The Concept of Substance in Seventeenth-Century Metaphysics.* London: Routledge, 1993.

Woolhouse, Roger. *G.W. Leibniz: Critical Assessments.* London: Routledge, 1994.

Yates, Frances. *Giordano Bruno and the Hermetic Tradition.* Chicago, IL: University of Chicago Press, 1964.

Yolton, John W. *John Locke: An Introduction.* Oxford, UK: Blackwell, 1985.

Yolton, John W., ed. *The Blackwell Companion to the Enlightenment.* Malden, MA: Blackwell, 1992.

Zernov, N. *Three Russian Prophets: Khomiakov, Dostoevsky, Soloviev.* London: SCM Press, 1944.

Zernov, N. *The Russian Religious Renaissance of the Twentieth Century.* New York: Harper & Row, 1963.

10. NORTH AMERICA

Albanese, Catherine L. *America: Religions and Religion.* Belmont, CA: Wadsworth, 1981.

Barzun, Jacques. *A Stroll with William James.* New York: Harper & Row, 1983.

Bellah, Robert N. *Habits of the Heart: Individualism and Commitment in American Life.* Berkeley, CA: University of California Press, 1985.

Bernstein, Richard J. *John Dewey.* New York: Washington Square Press, 1966.

Capps, Donald and Jacobs, Janet L., eds. *The Struggle for Life: A Companion to William James's the Varieties of Religious Experience.* West Lafayette, IN: Society for the Scientific Study of Religion, 1995.

Carnap, Rudolf. *Logical Syntax of Language.* London: Routledge & Kegan Paul, 1964.

Carnap, Rudolf (Rolf George, trans). *The Logical Structure of the World and Pseudoproblems in Philosophy. (Der logische Aufbau der Welt)* Berkeley, CA: University of California Press, (Reprint) 1967.

Christian, William A. *An Interpretation of Whitehead's Metaphysics.* New Haven, CT: Yale University Press, 1959.

Cottingham, John. *Western Philosophy: An Anthology.* Cambridge, MA: Blackwell, 1996.

Craig, Edward, ed. *Routledge Encyclopedia of Philosophy.* New York: Routledge, 1998.

Dean, William. *American Religious Empiricism.* Albany, NY: State University of New York Press, 1986.

Delaney, Cornelius. *Mind and Nature: A Study in the Naturalistic Philosophies of Cohen, Woodbridge and Sellars.* Notre Dame, IN: University of Notre Dame Press, 1969.

Dewey, John. *Essays in Experimental Logic.* New York: Dover, 1953.

Dewey, John. *Reconstruction in Philosophy.* Boston, MA: Beacon Press, 1957 (1948).

Dewey, John. *Experience and Nature.* La Salle, IL: Open Court Press, 1958 (1929).

Dewey, John (Jo Ann Boydston, ed.). *The Early Works: 1882–1898.* 5 Vols. Carbondale, IL: Southern Illinois University Press, 1967–.

Dewey, John (Jo Ann Boydston, ed.). *The Middle Works of John Dewey, 1899–1924.* 15 Vols. Carbondale, IL: Southern Illinois University Press 1976–83.

Dewey, John (John J. McDermott, ed.). *The Philosophy of John Dewey.* Chicago, IL: University of Chicago Press 1981.

Dewey, John (Jo Ann Boydston, ed.). *The Later Works of John Dewey, 1925–1953*. 17 Vols. Carbondale, IL: Southern Illinois University Press, 1984–88.

Dewey, John. *The Quest for Certainty: A Study of the Relation of Knowledge and Action*. Carbondale, IL: Southern Illinois University Press, 1988.

Diamond, Malcolm L. *Martin Buber: Jewish Existentialist*. New York: Oxford University Press, 1960.

Diggins, John P. *The Promise of Pragmatism: Modernism and the Crisis of Knowledge and Authority*. Chicago, IL: University of Chicago Press, 1994.

Drake, Durant, Arthur O. Lovejoy and J.B. Pratt, *et al. Essays in Critical Realism: A Co-operative Study of the Problem of Knowledge*. New York: Gordian Press, 1968.

Edwards, Paul. *The Encyclopedia of Philosophy*. 8 vols (4 vols). New York: Macmillan, 1972 (1967).

Eliade, Mircea, ed. *The Encyclopedia of Religion*. 16 vols. New York: Macmillan, 1987.

Ellwood, Robert S. *The Sixties Spiritual Awakening: American Religion Moving from Modern to Postmodern*. New Brunswick, NJ: Rutgers University Press, 1994.

Emerson, Ralph Waldo. *The Collected Works*. Cambridge, MA: Belknap Press of Harvard University Press, 1971–87.

Feffer, Andrew. *The Chicago Pragmatists and American Progressivism*. Ithaca, NY: Cornell University Press, 1993.

Fisch, Max H., ed. *Classic American Philosophers*. Bronx, NY: Fordham University Press, (Reprint) 1995.

Ford, Marcus P. *William James's Philosophy: A New Perspective*. Amherst, MA: University of Massachusetts Press, 1982.

Fox, Richard W. and James T. Kloppenberg,. *A Companion to American Thought*. Malden, MA: Blackwell, 1998.

Gallie, W.B. *Peirce and Pragmatism*. Westport, CT: Greenwood Press, 1975 (1966).

Gaustad, Edwin S. *A Religious History of America*. New York: Harper & Row, 1974.

Glazer, Nathan. *American Judaism*. Chicago, IL: University of Chicago Press, 2nd edn, 1972.

Goldsmith, Emanuel S., ed. *The American Judaism of Mordecai M. Kaplan*. New York: New York University Press, 1992.

Goodman, Russell B. *American Philosophy and the Romantic Tradition*. New York: Cambridge University Press, 1991.

Gottschalk, Stephen. *The Emergence of Christian Science in American Religious Life*. Berkeley, CA: University of California Press, 1973.

Greeley, Andrew M. *The American Catholic: A Social Portrait*. New York: Basic Books, 1977.

Hahn, Lewis and P.A. Schilpp, eds. *The Philosophy of W.V. Quine*. La Salle, IL: Open Court Press, 1986.

Haraway, Donna. "The Bio-politics of a Multicultural Field," in *Primate Visions*. New York: Routledge, 1989, pp. 244–75.

Hart, Richard E. and Douglas R. Anderson, eds. *Philosophy in Experience: American Philosophy in Transition*. New York: Fordham University Press, 1997.

Hartshorne, Charles. *Creativity in American Philosophy*. Albany, NY: State University of New York Press, 1985.

Heller, James G. *Isaac M. Wise*. New York: Union of American Hebrew Congregations, 1965.

Helm, Bertrand P. *Time and Reality in American Philosophy*. Amherst, MA: University of Massachusetts Press, 1986.

Hempel, C.G. *Aspects of Scientific Explanation*. New York: Free Press, 1965.

Herberg, Will. *Protestant, Catholic, Jew: An Essay in American Sociology.* Garden City, NY: Anchor Books, 1960.

Hine, Robert V. *Josiah Royce: From Grass Valley to Harvard.* Norman, OK: University of Oklahoma Press, 1992.

Hook, Sidney. *John Dewey: An Intellectual Portrait.* New York: John Day, 1939.

Hookway, Christopher. *Peirce.* London: Routledge, 1993.

Huyler, Jerome. *Locke in America: The Moral Philosophy of the Founding Era.* Lawrence, KS: University Press of Kansas, 1995.

James, William. *Essays in Radical Empiricism.* Cambridge, MA: Harvard University Press, 1976.

James, William. *A Pluralistic Universe.* Cambridge, MA: Harvard University Press, 1977.

James, William (John J. McDermott, ed.). *The Writings of William James.* Chicago, IL: University of Chicago Press, 1977.

James, William. *Pragmatism and the Meaning of Truth.* Cambridge, MA: Harvard University Press, 1978.

James, William. *The Will to Believe.* Cambridge, MA: Harvard University Press, 1979.

James, William. *Essays in Psychology.* Cambridge, MA: Harvard University Press, 1983.

James, William (Bruce W. Wilshire, ed.). *William James: The Essential Writings.* Albany, NY: State University of New York Press, 1984.

James, William. *The Varieties of Religious Experience.* Cambridge, MA: Harvard University Press, 1985.

James, William. *Principles of Psychology.* Magnolia: Peter Smith, 1990.

Jones, Ernest (Lionel Trilling and Stephen Marcus, eds.). *The Life and Work of Sigmund Freud.* New York: Basic Books, 1961.

Kaplan, Amy. *The Social Construction of American Realism.* Chicago, IL: University of Chicago Press, 1992.

Kasulis, Thomas P. and Robert Cummings Neville, eds. *The Recovery of Philosophy in America: Essays in Honor of John Edwin Smith.* Albany, NY: State University of New York Press, 1997.

Keller, Evelyn Fox and Helen Longino, eds., *Feminism and Science.* New York: Oxford University Press, 1996.

Kraus, Elizabeth and Neville, Robert C. *The Metaphysics of Experience: A Companion to Whitehead's 'Process and Reality'.* Bronx, NY: Fordham University Press, 2nd edn, 1997.

Lawrence, Nathaniel. *Whitehead's Philosophical Development.* Berkeley, CA: University of California Press, 1956.

Levinson, Henry S. *The Religious Investigations of William James.* Chapel Hill, NC: University of North Carolina Press, 1981.

Libowitz, Richard. *Mordecai M. Kaplan and the Development of Reconstructionism.* New York: Edwin Mellen Press, 1984 (1983).

Longino, Helen. *Science as Social Knowledge.* Princeton, NJ: Princeton University Press, 1990

Lovejoy, Arthur O. *The Great Chain of Being: A Study of the History of an Idea.* Cambridge, MA: Harvard University Press, 1936.

Lynch, Michael P. *Truth in Context: An Essay on Pluralism and Objectivity.* Cambridge, MA: MIT Press, 1998.

MacKinnon, Barbara. *American Philosophy: A Historical Anthology.* Albany, NY: SUNY Press, 1985.

McDermott, John J. *Streams of Experience: Reflections on the History and Philosophy of American Culture.* Amherst, MA: University of Massachusetts Press, 1986.

McHugh, Nancy. *Feminist Philosophies A–Z.* Edinburgh: Edinburgh University Press, 2007.

Melton, J. Gordon. *Encyclopedia of American Religions*. Detroit, MI:, MI: Gale Research, 5th edn, 1996.

Mounce, Howard. *The Two Pragmatisms: From Peirce to Rorty*. London: Routledge, 1997.

Murphey, Murray G. *Development of Peirce's Philosophy*. Cambridge, MA: Harvard University Press, 1961.

Nagel, Ernest. *The Structure of Science: Problems in the Logic of Scientific Explanation*. New York: Harcourt, Brace & World, 1961.

Neufeldt, Leonard N. and Nancy C. Simmons, eds. *The Writings of Henry D. Thoreau Journal, Vol. 4: 1851–1852*. Princeton, NJ: Princeton University Press, 1992.

O'Dea, Thomas F. *Mormons*. Chicago, IL: University of Chicago Press, 1963 (1957).

Odin, Steve. *The Social Self in Zen and American Pragmatism*. Albany, NY: State University of New York Press, 1996.

Oppenheim, Frank M. *Royce's Mature Ethics*. Notre Dame, IN: University of Notre Dame Press, 1993.

Paine, Thomas. *The Age of Reason*. Avenal, NJ: Random House, 1993.

Parrington, Vernon L. *Main Currents in American Thought*. Norman, OK: University of Oklahoma Press, 1987.

Parzen, Herbert. *Architects of Conservative Judaism*. New York: J. David, 1964.

Peirce, Charles S. (Charles Hartshorne and Paul Weiss, eds.). *Collected Papers of Charles Sanders Peirce*, 8 Vols. Cambridge, MA: Harvard University Press, 1934–.

Peirce, Charles S. *Reasoning and the Logic of Things*. Cambridge, MA: Harvard University Press, 1993.

Peirce, Charles S. (Patricia A. Turrisi, ed). *Pragmatism as a Principle and Method of Right Thinking: The 1903 Harvard Lectures on Pragmatism*. Albany, NY: State University New York Press, 1997.

Peirce, Charles S. (Morris R. Cohen, ed.). *Chance, Love, and Logic: Philosophical Essays* Lincoln, NE: University of Nebraska Press, 1998.

Perry, Ralph B. *The Thought and Character of William James*. Nashville, TN: Vanderbilt University Press, 1996.

Popkin, Richard H., ed. *Scepticism in the History of Philosophy: A Pan-American Dialogue*. Dordrecht, Netherlands: Kluwer Academic, 1996.

Potter, Vincent G., ed. *Doctrine and Experience: Essays in American Philosophy*. Bronx, NY: Fordham University Press, 1988.

Potter, Vincent G. *Peirce's Philosophical Perspectives*. Bronx, NY: Fordham University Press, 1995.

Psillos, Stathis. *Philosophy of Science A–Z*. Edinburgh: Edinburgh University Press, 2007.

Putnam, Hilary. *Reason, Truth and History*. Cambridge, UK: Cambridge University Press, 1981.

Putnam, Hilary. *Representation and Reality*. Cambridge, MA: Harvard University Press, 1988.

Putnam, Hilary (James Conant, ed.). *Realism with a Human Face*. Cambridge, MA: Harvard University Press, 1990.

Putnam, Hilary (James Conant, ed.). *Words and Life*. Cambridge, MA: Harvard University Press, 1994.

Putnam, Hilary. *Pragmatism: An Open Question*. Malden, MA: Blackwell, 1995.

Putnam, Hilary. *The Threefold Cord: Mind, Body, and World*. New York: Columbia University Press, 1999.

Putnam, Hilary. *The Collapse of the Fact/Value Dichotomy and Other Essays*. Cambridge, MA: Harvard University Press, 2002.

Putnam, Ruth A., ed. *The Cambridge Companion to William James*. New York: Cambridge University Press, 1997.

Quine, Willard Van Orman. *From a Logical Point of View: 9 Logico-philosophical Essays*. Cambridge, MA: Harvard University Press, 1953.

Quine, Willard Van Orman. *Word and Object*. Cambridge, MA: MIT Press, 1964 (1960).

Reck, Andrew J. *Introduction to William James: An Essay and Selected Texts*. Bloomington, IN: Indiana University Press, 1967.

Renouvier, Charles. *Essais de Critique Générale*. Paris: A. Colin, 1912.

Rescher, Nicholas. *Process Metaphysics: An Introduction to Process Philosophy*. Albany, NY: State University of New York Press, 1996.

Rieff, Philip. *Freud: The Mind of a Moralist*. Chicago, IL: University of Chicago Press, 3rd edn, 1979.

Rorty, Richard. *Consequences of Pragmatism*. Brighton, UK: Harvester, 1982.

Roth, Robert J. *British Empiricism and American Pragmatism: New Directions and Neglected Arguments*. Bronx, NY: Fordham University Press, 1993.

Royce, Josiah. *The World and the Individual*. New York: Dover, 1959.

Royce, Josiah. *The Religious Aspect of Philosophy: A Critique of the Bases of Conduct and of Faith*. Gloucester, MA: P. Smith, 1965.

Royce, Josiah. *The Problem of Christianity*. Chicago, IL: University of Chicago Press, 1968.

Royce, Josiah (John J. McDermott, ed.). *The Basic Writings of Josiah Royce*. Chicago, IL: University of Chicago Press, 1969.

Royce, Josiah. *The Philosophy of Loyalty*. Nashville, TN: Vanderbilt University Press, 1995.

Sandel, Michael J. *Democracy's Discontent: America in Search of a Public Philosophy*. Cambridge, MA: Harvard University Press, 1996.

Santayana, George. *The Life of Reason, or the Phases of Human Progress*. New York: Scribner, 1954.

Schilpp, Paul A., ed. *The Philosophy of John Dewey*. Evanston, IL: Northwestern University, 1939.

Schilpp, Paul A., ed. *The Philosophy of George Santayana*. Evanston, IL: Northwestern University, 1940.

Schilpp, Paul A., ed. *The Philosophy of Rudolph Carnap*. La Salle, IL: Open Court, 1963.

Schilpp, Paul A., ed. *The Philosophy of Alfred North Whitehead*. La Salle, IL: Open Court, 1971 (1951).

Scott, Stanley J. *Frontiers of Consciousness: Studies in Classical American Philosophy and Poetry*. Bronx, NY: Fordham University Press, 1991.

Singer, Marcus G., ed. *American Philosophy*. New York: Cambridge University Press, 1986.

Smith, John E. *Royce's Social Infinite: The Community of Interpretation*. New York: Liberal Arts Press, 1950.

Smith, John E. *The Spirit of American Philosophy*. New York: Oxford University Press, 1963.

Smith, John E. *America's Philosophical Vision*. Chicago, IL: University of Chicago Press, 1992.

Stuhr, John J., ed. *Classical American Philosophy: Essential Readings and Interpretive Essays*. New York: Oxford University Press, 1987.

Stuhr, John J., ed. *Philosophy and the Reconstruction of Culture: Pragmatic Essays after Dewey*. Albany, NY: State University of New York Press, 1993.

Superson, Anita and Ann Cudd, eds. *Theorizing Backlash: Philosophical Reflections on Resistance to Feminism*. Lanham, MD: Rowman Littlefield, 2002.

Tanesini, Alessandra. *Philosophy of Language A–Z*. Edinburgh: Edinburgh University Press, 2007.

Tejera, V. *American Modern: The Path Not Taken: Aesthetics, Metaphysics, and Intellectual History in Classic American Philosophy.* Lanham, MD: Rowman & Littlefield, 1996.

Urmson, J. O. and Jonathan Ree. *The Concise Encyclopedia of Western Philosophy and Philosophers.* New York: Routledge, revised edn, 1991.

Weinstein, Michael A. *The Wilderness and the City: American Classical Philosophy as a Moral Quest.* Amherst, MA: University of Massachusetts Press, 1982.

Whitehead, Alfred North. *Alfred North Whitehead: An Anthology Selected by F.S.C. Northrop and Mason W. Gross.* New York: Macmillan, 1953.

Whitehead, Alfred North. *Adventures of Ideas.* New York: Macmillan, 1961 (1933).

Whitehead, Alfred North. *Process and Reality: An Essay in Cosmology.* New York: Free Press, 1969 (1929).

Whitehead, Alfred North. *Nature and Life.* Westport, CT: Greenwood (Reprint) 1970 (1934).

Whitehead, Alfred North. *Religion in the Making: Lowell Lectures, 1926.* Bronx, NY: Fordham University Press, Revised edn, 1996.

Whitehead, Alfred North and Bertrand Russell. *Principia Mathematica.* New York: Cambridge University Press, 1927.

Wilson, Daniel J. *Arthur O. Lovejoy and the Quest for Intelligibility.* Chapel Hill, NC: University of North Carolina Press, 1980.

Wilson, John F. *Public Religion in American Culture.* Philadelphia, PA: Temple University Press, 1979.

11. LATIN AMERICA

Alcoff, Linda co-ed. with Eduardo Mendieta. *Thinking From the Underside of History: Enrique Dussel's Philosophy of Liberation*, Lanham, MD: Rowman and Littlefield, 2000

Alcoff, Linda co-ed. with Eduardo Mendieta. *Identities: A Reader*, Blackwell 2003.

Alcoff, Linda co-ed. with Satya Mohanty, Paula Moya, and Michael Hames-Garcia. *Identity Politics Reconsidered.* New York: Palgrave/MacMillan, 2006.

Aldridge, A. Owen, ed. *The Ibero-American Enlightenment.* Urbana, IL: University of Illinois Press, 1971.

Becker, Marc. *Mariategui and Latin American Marxist Theory.* Athens, OH: Ohio University Press, 1993.

Berryman, Phillip. *Liberation Theology: Essential Facts about the Revolutionary Movement in Latin America – and Beyond.* Philadelphia, PA: Temple University Press, 1987.

Bethell, Leslie, ed. *Ideas and Ideologies in Latin America since 1870.* New York: Cambridge University Press, 1996.

Boff, Leonardo and Clodovis Boff. *Introducing Liberation Theology.* Maryknoll, NY: Orbis Books, 1987.

Brundage, Burr C. *The Fifth Sun: Aztec Gods, Aztec World.* Austin, TX: University of Texas Press, 1979.

Carrasco, David. *Quetzalcoatl and the Irony of Empire: Myths and Prophecies in the Aztec Tradition.* Chicago, IL: University of Chicago Press, 1982.

Catholic Church. Pope (1878–1903: Leo XIII) (Father Rawes, trans.). *Encyclical Letter of Our Holy Father Pope Leo XIII on the restoration of Christian philosophy in Catholic universities, according to the mind of St Thomas Aquinas, the angelic doctor (Aeterni Patris).* London: Burns and Oates, 1879.

Catholic Church. Pope (1878–1903: Leo XIII) (Gerald Carr Treacy, ed.). *Scholastic Philosophy: Encyclical Letter of Pope Leo XIII: Aeterni Patris.* New York: Paulist Press, 1951.

Cavalcanti, Maria Laura Viveiros de Castro. *O mundo invisível: cosmologia, sistema rituel e noção de pessoa no espiritismo.* Rio de Janeiro, Brazil: Zahar Editores, 1983.

Crawford, William Rex. *A Century of Latin American Thought.* Cambridge, MA: Harvard University Press, 1945 (1944).

Dascal, Marcelo. *Cultural Relativism and Philosophy: North and Latin American Perspectives.* Boston, MA: Brill Academic, 1991.

Davis, Harold E. *Latin American Thought: A Historical Introduction.* Baton Rouge, LA: Louisiana State University Press, 1972.

De Mendiola, Marina P., ed. *Bridging the Atlantic: Toward a Reassessment of Iberian and Latin American Cultural Ties.* Albany, NY: State University of New York Press, 1996.

Deustea, Alejandro O. *Estética general.* Lima: Imp. E. Ravago, 1923.

Dobson, Andrew. *An Introduction to the Politics and Philosophy of José Ortega y Gasset.* New York: Cambridge University Press, 1989.

Dussel, Enrique (Alan Neely, trans.). *A History of the Church in Latin America: Colonialism to Liberation (1492–1979).* Grand Rapids, MI: Eerdmans, 1981.

Ferm, Deane William. *Third World Liberation Theologies: A Reader.* Maryknoll, NY: Orbis Books, 1986.

Flannery, Austin, ed. *Vatican Council II: The Conciliar and Post Conciliar Documents.* Grand Rapids, MI: Eerdmans, 1992.

Frondizi, Risieri. *Qué son los valores? Introducción a la axiología.* México: Fondo de Cultura Económica, 1958.

Frondizi, Risieri (Solomon Lipp, trans.). *What is Value? An Introduction to Axiology.* La Salle, IL: Open Court, 1962.

Frondizi, Risieri. *Fuentes de la filosofía latinoamericana.* Washington, DC: Unión Panamericana, 1967.

Frondizi, Risieri. *Los "fundadores" en la filosofía de América Latina.* Washington, DC: Unión Panamericana, 1970.

Frondizi, Risieri. *El yo como estructura dinámica.* Buenos Aires: Paidós, 1970.

Frondizi, Risieri. *La Universidad en un mundo de tensiones: Misión de la universidades en América Latina.* Buenos Aires: Paidós, 1971.

Frondizi, Risieri (Author and E. Rivers, trans). *The Nature of the Self: A Functional Interpretation.* New Haven, CT: Yale University Press, 1953 (reprinted Carbondale, IL: Southern Illinois University Press, 1971).

Frondizi, Risieri. *Introducción a los problemas fundamentales del hombre.* México: Fondo de Cultura Económica, 1977.

Gracia, Jorge J.E., ed. (William Cooper *et al.*, trans.). *Latin American Philosophy in the Twentieth Century: Man, Values, and the Search for Philosophical Identity.* Buffalo, NY: Prometheus Books, 1986.

Gracia, Jorge J.E. and Mireya Camurati, eds. *Philosophy and Literature in Latin America: A Critical Assessment of the Current Situation.* Albany, NY: State University of New York Press, 1989.

Gracia, Jorge J.E. and Elizabeth Millán-Zaibert, eds. *Latin American Philosophy for the 21st Century: The Human Condition, Values, and the Search for Identity.* Amherst, NY: Prometheus Books, 2004.

Gremillion, Joseph, ed. *The Gospel of Peace and Justice: Catholic Social Teaching since Pope John.* Maryknoll, NY: Orbis Books, 1976.

Gutiérrez, Gustavo. *A Theology of Liberation: History, Politics and Salvation.* Maryknoll, NY: Orbis Books, 1973.

Haddox, John H. *Antonio Caso: Philosopher of Mexico.* Austin, TX: University of Texas Press, 1971.

Huescar, Antonio R. (Garcia-Gomez, trans. and ed.). *José Ortega y Gasset's Metaphysical Innovation: A Critique and Overcoming of Idealism.* Albany, NY: State University of New York Press, 1994.

Ingenieros, José. *Obras completas,* 24 Vols. Buenos Aires: Ediciones L.J. Rosso, 1930–40.

Ingenieros, José. *El Hombre mediocre.* Buenos Aires: Editorial Losada, 20th edn, 1994 (1961).

Jaksic, Ivan. *Academic Rebels in Chile: The Role of Philosophy in Higher Education and Politics.* Albany, NY: State University of New York Press, 1989.

Korn, Alejandro. *Obras.* 3 Vols. La Plata, Argentina: printers 'Tomas Palumbo', 1938–40.

Leo XIII, Pope. *See:* Catholic Church.

Lumbreras, Luis G. *The Peoples and Cultures of Ancient Peru.* Washington, DC: Smithsonian Institution Press, 1974.

MacCauley, Clay. *Karl Christian Friedrich Krause, Heroic Pioneer for Thought and Life.* Berkeley, CA: Gazette Press, 1925.

Mackinnon, Catherine. *Toward a Feminist Theory of the State.* Cambridge, MA: Harvard University Press, 1989.

Mendieta, Eduardo, ed. *Latin American Philosophy: Currents, Issues, Debates.* Bloomington, IN: Indiana University Press, 2003.

Nessan, Craig. *Orthopraxis or Heresy: The North American Theological Response to Latin American Liberation Theology.* Atlanta, GA: Scholars Press, 1989.

Novak, Michael. *Freedom with Justice: Catholic Social Thought and Liberal Institutions.* San Francisco, CA: Harper & Row, 1984.

Nuccetelli, Susana. *Latin American Thought: Philosophical Problems and Arguments.* Boulder, CO: Westview Press, 2002.

Peña, Milagros. *Theologies and Liberation in Peru: The Role of Ideas in Social Movements.* Philadelphia, PA: Temple University Press, 1995.

Rodó, José Enrique. *Escritos de José Enrigue Rodó.* Mexico: Imprenta Victoria, 1916.

Rodó, José Enrique. *La Tradición Intelectual Argentina.* Buenos Aires: EUDEBA, Editorial Universitaria de Buenos Aires, 1968.

Rodó, José Enrique. (Margaret Sayers Peden, trans.). *Ariel.* Austin, TX: University of Texas Press, 1988.

Romanell, Patrick. *Making of the Mexican Mind.* Notre Dame, IN: University of Notre Dame Press, 1967.

Rubenstein, Richard and John Roth, eds. *The Politics of Latin American Liberation Theology.* Washington, DC: Washington Institute Press, 1988.

Salazar Bondy, Augusto. *Philosophy in Peru (La filosofía en el Peru).* Washington, DC: Union Panamericana, 1955.

Sanchez Reulet, Anibal. *Contemporary Latin-American Philosophy.* (Willard R. Trask, trans.). Albuquerque, NM: University of New Mexico Press, 1954.

Sanz del Rio, Julian. *K.C.F. Krause: lecciones sobre el sistema de la filosofía analítica.* Madrid: 1850.

Smart, Ninian. *The World's Religions: Old Traditions and Modern Transformations.* Cambridge, UK: Cambridge University Press, 1989.

Smith, Christian. *The Emerence of Liberation Theology: Radical Religion and Social Movement Theory.* Chicago, IL: University of Chicago Press, 1991.

Stabb, Martin S. *In Quest of Identity: Patterns in the Spanish-American Essay of Ideas, 1890–1960*. Chapel Hill, NC: University of North Carolina Press, 1967.

Thorn, Judith. *The Lived Horizon of my Being: The Substantiation of the Self and the Discourse of Resistance in Rigoberta Menchu, M.M. Bakhtin and Victor Montejo*. Tempe, AZ: Arizona State University, Center for Latin American Studies, 1996.

Torchia Estrada, Juan Carlos. *La filosofía en la Argentina*. Washington, DC: Union Panamericana, 1961.

Trueblood, Alan S., trans. *A Sor Juana Anthology*, Foreword by Octavio Paz, Cambridge, MA: Harvard University Press, 1988.

Urton, Gary. *At the Crossroads of the Earth and the Sky: An Andean Cosmology*. Austin, TX: University of Texas Press, 1981.

Varona, Enrique José. *Obras*. 4 Vols. Havana: [Cultural, s.a.] 1936–38.

Vasconcelos, José. *El realismo científico*. Mexico City: D.F., Centro de Estudios Filosóficos, 1943.

Vasconcelos, José. *Obras Completas*. 4 Vols. Mexico City: Libreros Mexicanos Unidos, 1957–61.

Vitier, Medardo. *La filosofía en Cuba*. Mexico City: Fondo de Cultura Económica, 1948.

Weinstein, Michael A. *The Polarity of Mexican Thought*. University Park, PA: Pennsylvania State University Press, 1977.

Woodward, Ralph Lee, ed. *Positivism in Latin America, 1850–1900: Are Order and Progress Reconcilable?* Lexington, MA: Heath, 1971.

Zea, Leopoldo. (Lowell Dunham and James H. Abbott, trans.). *Latin-American Mind*. Norman, OK: University of Oklahoma Press, 1970.

Zumárraga, Juan de. *The Doctrina Breve in Facsimile*. New York: United States Catholic Historical Society, 1928.

12. MODERN ISLAM

Abdul Baha. (Baha'Allah) *Selected Writings of 'Abdul-Baha*. Wilmette, IL: Baha'i Pub. Trust, 1942.

Abdul Baha. *Foundations of World Unity: Compiled from Addresses and Tablets of 'Abdu'l-Baha*. Wilmette, IL: Baha'i Pub. Trust, 1971 (1945).

Abou El Fadl, Khaled. *Speaking in God's Name: Islamic Law, Authority and Women*. Oxford, UK: Oneworld, 2001.

Abu 'Amr, Ziyad. *Islamic Fundamentalism in the West Bank and Gaza: Muslim Brotherhood and Islamic Jihad*. Bloomington, IN: Indiana University Press, 1994.

Abu-Rabi', Ibrahim M. *Intellectual Origins of Islamic Resurgence in the Modern Arab World*. Albany, NY: State University of New York Press, 1996.

Adams, Charles C. *Islam and Modernism in Egypt: A Study of the Modern Reform Movement Inaugurated by Muhammad 'Abduh*. London: Oxford University Press, 1933.

Afghani, Jamal al-Din (trans., intro. and notes, A.M. Goichon). *Refutation des Matérialistes*. Paris: P. Geuthner, 1942.

Ahmad, Aziz. *Islamic Modernism in India and Pakistan, 1857–1964*. London: Oxford University Press, 1967.

Ahmad, Layla 'Abd Al-Latif. *Women and Gender in Islam: Historical Roots of a Modern Debate*. New Haven, CT: Yale University Press, 1992.

Ahmad, Mirza Ghulam. *Teachings of Islam*. Delhi: Inter-India Publications, 1978.

Ahmad Khan, Sayyid, Sir. *The Causes of the Indian Revolt*. Lahore, Pakistan: Book House, 1970.

Ahmed, Akbar. *Postmodernism and Islam: Predicament and Promise*. New York: Routledge, 1992.

Ahmed, Akbar. *Jinnah, Pakistan and Islamic Identity: The Search for Saladin*. London: Routledge, 1997.

Al-Attas, Muhammad Naguib, Syed. *Islam, Secularism, and the Philosophy of the Future*. London: Mansell, 1985.

Amin, Osman (Amin, 'Uthman) (Charles Wendell, trans.). *Muhammad 'Abduh*. Washington, DC: American Council of Learned Societies, 1953.

Arkoun, Mohammed. *Islam: To Reform or to Subvert?* London: Saqi Books, 2006.

Ayoub, Mahmoud M. *Islam and the Third Universal Theory: The Religious Thought of Mu'ammar al Qadhdhafi*. New York: Routledge, Chapman & Hall, 1991.

Berkes, Niyazi. *The Development of Secularism in Turkey*. Montreal, Canada: McGill University Press, 1964.

Boland, B.J. *The Struggle of Islam in Modern Indonesia*. The Hague: Nijhoff, 1971.

Boullata, Issa J. *Trends and Issues in Contemporary Arab Thought*. Albany, NY: State University of New York Press, 1990.

Brown, Daniel W. *Rethinking Tradition in Modern Islamic Thought*. Cambridge, UK: Cambridge University Press, 1996.

Burgat, Francois and William Dowell. *The Islamic Movement in North Africa*. Austin, TX: Center for Middle Eastern Studies, University of Texas at Austin, 2nd edn, 1997.

Caldarola, Carlo, ed. *Religions and Societies: Asia and the Middle East*. New York: Mouton, 1982.

Cragg, Kenneth. *Counsels in Contemporary Islam*. Edinburgh: Edinburgh University Press, 1965.

Eaton, Richard Maxwell. *Islamic History as Global History*. Washington, DC: American Historical Association, 1990.

Ghazali, Aidit and Syed Omar, eds. *Readings in the Concept and Methodology of Islamic Economics*. Selangor Darul Ehsan, Malaysia: Pelanduk, 1989.

Gibb, H.A.R. *et al. The Encyclopaedia of Islam*, 8 Vols. Leiden, Netherlands: Brill, 1960–97.

Habib, John S. *Ibn Saud's Warriors of Islam: The Ikhwan of Najd and Their Role in the Creation of the Sa'udi Kingdom, 1910–1930*. Leiden, Netherlands: Brill, 1978.

Hatcher, William and James D. Martin. *The Baha'i Faith: The Emerging Global Religion*. San Francisco, CA: Harper & Row, 1984.

Hiro, Dilip. *Holy Wars: The Rise of Islamic Fundamentalism*. New York: Routledge, 1989.

Hussain, Sheikh Zafar. *The Reconstruction of Islamic Society: A Comparative Study of Principles and Values of Islam with the Philosophy of Secularism*. Lahore, Pakistan: Ferozsons, 1992.

Iqbal, Muhammad. *The Reconstruction of Religious Thought in Islam*. London: Oxford University Press, 1934.

Irwin, Robert. *Dangerous Knowledge: Orientalism and Its Discontents*. Woodstock, NY: Overlook Press, 2006.

Jansen, Godfrey. *Militant Islam*. New York: Harper & Row, 1980 (1979).

Jansen, Johannes J.G. *The Dual Nature of Islamic Fundamentalism*. Ithaca, NY: Cornell University Press, 1997.

Johansen, Julian. *Sufism and Islamic Reform in Egypt: The Battle for Islamic Tradition*. Oxford, UK: Clarendon Press, 1996.

Johnson, James Turner. *The Holy War Idea in Western and Islamic Traditions*. University Park, PA: Pennsylvania State University Press, 1997.

Keddie, Nikki R. *An Islamic Response to Imperialism; Political and Religious Writings of Sayyid Jamal Ad Din 'al-Afghani', including a translation of the Refutation of the Materialists.* Berkeley, CA: University of California Press, 1968.

Keddie, Nikki R. *Sayyid Jamāl Ad-Dīn 'al-Afghāni': A Political Biography.* Berkeley, CA: University of California Press, 1972.

Keddie, Nikki R., ed. *Religion and Politics in Iran: Shi'ism from Quietism to Revolution.* New Haven, CT: Yale University Press, 1983.

Kepel, Gilles (Susan Milner, trans.). *Allah in the West: Islamic Movements in America and Europe.* Stanford, CA: Stanford University Press, 1997.

Kurzman, Charles, ed. *Liberal Islam: A Sourcebook.* New York: Oxford University Press, 1998.

Lacey, Robert. *The Kingdom: Arabia and the House of Saud.* New York: Harcourt Brace Jovanovich, 1982 (1981).

Landau, Jacob M. *The Politics of Pan-Islam: Ideology and Organization.* Oxford, UK: Clarendon Press, 1990.

Lavan, Spencer. *The Ahmadiyah Movement: A History and Perspective.* New Delhi: Manohar Book Service, 1974.

Lewis, Bernard. *The Emergence of Modern Turkey.* London: Oxford University Press, 1961.

Mahmood, Saba. *Politics of Piety: The Islamic Revival and the Feminist Subject.* Princeton, NJ: Princeton University Press, 2005.

Malik, Hafeez, ed. *Iqbal, Poet-Philosopher of Pakistan.* New York: Columbia University Press, 1971.

Marlow, Louise. *Hierarchy and Egalitarianism in Islamic Thought.* New York: Cambridge University Press, 1997.

Moussalli, Ahmad S. *Radical Islamic Fundamentalism: The Ideological and Political Discourse of Sayyid Qutb.* Syracuse, NY: Syracuse University Press, 1993.

Muhammad 'Abduh (Ishaq Masa'ad and Kenneth Cragg, trans.). *The Theology of Unity.* London: Allen & Unwin, 1966.

Nasr, Seyyed Vali Reza. *Mawdudi and the Making of Islamic Revivalism.* New York: Oxford University Press, 1996.

Nouraie-Simone, Fereshteh, ed. *On Shifting Ground: Muslim Women in the Global Era.* New York: Feminist Press at The City University of New York, 2005.

Saeed, Abdullah. *Interpreting the Qur'ān: Towards a Contemporary Approach.* New York: Routledge, 2005.

Sardar, Ziauddin, ed. *An Early Crescent: The Future of Knowledge and the Environment in Islam.* London: Mansell, 1989.

Schimmel, Annemarie. *Gabriel's Wing: A Study into the Religious Ideas of Sir Muhammad Igbal.* Leiden, Netherlands: E.J. Brill, 1963.

Smart, Ninian. *The World's Religions.* Cambridge, UK: Cambridge University Press, 1989.

Smith, Wilfred C. *Islam in Modern History.* Princeton, NJ: Princeton University Press, 1957.

Sonn, Tamara. *Interpreting Islam: Bandali Jawzi's Islamic Intellectual History.* New York: Oxford University Press, 1996.

Troll, Christian. *Sayyid Ahmad Khan: A Reinterpretation of Muslim Theology.* New Delhi: Vikas, 1978.

Van Donzel, E., *Islamic Desk Reference: Compiled from the Encyclopedia of Islam.* Leiden, Netherlands: E.J. Brill, 1994.

Watt, W. Montgomery. *Islamic Fundamentalism and Modernity.* London: Routledge, 1988.

Winder, R. Bayly. *Saudi Arabia in the Nineteenth Century.* London: Macmillan, 1965.

Wright, Robin. *Sacred Rage: The Crusade of Modern Islam*. New York: Linden Press/Simon and Schuster, 1985.

13. MODERN SOUTH AND SOUTH-EAST ASIA

Ashby, Philip H. *Modern Trends in Hinduism*. New York: Columbia University Press, 1974.

Aurobindo. *Complete Works*. 30 Vols. Pondicherry, India: Sri Aurobindo Ashram, 1972–76.

Aurobindo. *The Life Divine*. Pondicherry, India: Sri Aurobindo Ashram, 1988 (1982).

Baird, Robert D., ed. *Religion in Modern India*. New Delhi: Manohar, 1981.

Balasubramanian, R., ed. *Perspectives in Philosophy, Religion and Art: Essays in Honour of Margaret Chatterjee*. Columbia, MO: South Asia Books, 1993.

Bellah, Robert N., ed. *Religion and Progress in Modern Asia*. New York: Free Press, 1965.

Bharathi, K.S. *The Philosophy of Sarvodaya*. Columbia, MO: South Asia Books, 1990.

Bilimoria, P. and Mohanty, J.N. eds., *Relativism, Suffering, and Beyond: Essays in Memory of Bimal K. Matilal* Delhi: Oxford University Press, 1997.

Campbell, Bruce F. *Ancient Wisdom Revised: A History of the Theosophical Movement*. Berkeley, CA: University of California Press, 1980.

Carr, Brian and Mahalingam, Indira, eds. *Companion Encyclopedia of Asian Philosophy*. London: Routledge, 1997.

Cenkner, William. *The Hindu Personality in Education: Tagore–Gandhi–Aurobindo*. Columbia, MO: South Asia Books, (Reprint) 1995.

Chatterjee, Margaret. *Gandhi's Religious Thought*. Notre Dame, IN: University of Notre Dame Press, 1983.

Chattopadhyaya, Debiprasad. *Philosophy and the Future*. Bangalore, India: Navakarnataka, 1991.

Chattopadhyaya, Debiprasad and Ravinder Kumar, eds. *Science, Philosophy, and Culture: Historical Perspective*. Columbia, MO: South Asia Books, 1995.

Chaudhuri, Haridas and Frederic Spiegelberg, eds. *The Integral Philosophy of Sri Aurobindo*. London: Allen & Unwin, 1960.

Coedes, Georges (Walter F. Vella, ed. and Susan Brown Cowing, trans.). *The Indianized States of Southeast Asia*. Honolulu, HI: East–West Center Press, 1968.

Coward, Harold G. *Modern Indian Responses to Religious Pluralism*. Albany, NY: State University of New York Press, 1987.

Coward, Harold G., ed. *Studies in Indian Thought: Collected Papers of Professer T.R.V. Murti*. Columbia, MO: South Asia Books, 1996.

Dasgupta, Ajit K. *Gandhi's Economic Thought*. New York: Routledge, 1996.

Dasgupta, Surendranath. *A History of Indian Philosophy*, 5 Vols. Cambridge, UK: CambridgeUniversity Press, Delhi: 1922–55 (Reprint) 1976.

Deussen, Paul. *Allgemeine Geschichte der Philosophie*. Leipzig, Germany: F.A. Brockhaus, 1920 (1922).

Deussen, Paul (Charles Johnston, trans.). *The System of the Vedanta*. Delhi: Karan Publ., 1987.

Dubey, S.P., ed. *Facets of Recent Indian Philosophy*. Columbia, MO: South Asia Books, 1996.

Farquhar, J.N. *Modern Religious Movements in India*. New York: Macmillan, 1915.

Gandhi, Mahatma. *Collected Works*, 90 Vols. Delhi: Publications Division, Ministry of Information and Broadcasting, Govt. of India, 1958–94.

Halbfass, Wilhelm. *India and Europe*. Albany, NY: State University of New York Press, 1988.

Heine, Steven and Charles S. Prebish, eds. *Buddhism in the Modern World: Adaptations of an Ancient Tradition.* New York: Oxford University Press, 2003.

Ibrahim, Ahmad, Sharon Siddique and Yasmin Hussain, comps. *Readings on Islam in Southeast Asia.* Singapore: Institute of Southeast Asian Studies, 1985.

Jadhav, Narendra. *Dr. Ambedkar's Economic Thought and Philosophy.* Columbia, OH: South Asia Books, 1993.

Jayatilleke, K.N. *Early Buddhist Theory of Knowledge.* London: George Allen & Unwin, 1963.

Jayatilleke, K.N. *The Message of the Buddha.* New York: Free Press, 1974.

Jones, Kenneth W. *Arya Dharm: Hindu Consciousness in 19th-century Punjab.* Berkeley, CA: University of California Press, 1976.

Jones, Kenneth W., ed. *Religious Controversy in British India: Dialogues in South Asian Languages.* Albany, NY: State University New York Press, 1992.

Jordens, J.T.F. *Dayananda Sarasvati, His Life and Ideas.* Delhi: Oxford University Press, 1978.

Juergensmeyer, Mark. *Fighting with Gandhi.* San Francisco, CA: Harper & Row, 1984.

Juergensmeyer, Mark. *The New Cold War? Religious Nationalism Confronts the Secular State.* Berkeley, CA: University of California Press, 1993.

Kalidas, Nag and Debajyoti Burman, eds. *The English Works of Raja Rammohan Roy.* Calcutta, India: Sadharan Brahmo Samaj, 1945–51.

Keown, Damien. *Contemporary Buddhist Ethics.* London: Curzon Press, 2000.

Kirkland, Frank M. and D.P. Chattopadhyaya, eds. *Phenomenology, East and West: Essays in Honor of J.N. Mohanty.* Dordrecht, Netherlands: Kluwer Academic Publ., 1993.

Kopf, David. *The Brahmo Samaj and the Shaping of the Modern Indian Mind.* Princeton, NJ: Princeton University Press, 1979.

Krishna, Daya. *Indian Philosophy: A Counter Perspective.* New York: Oxford University Press, 1996.

Krishna, Daya. *The Problematic and Conceptual Structure of Classical Indian Thought about Man, Society, and Polity.* New York: Oxford University Press, 1996.

Krishnamurti, J. *The Meditative Mind: A Selection of Passages from the Teachings of J. Krishnamurti.* Ojai, CA: Krishnamurti Foundation of America, revised edn, 1993 (1989).

Krishnamurti, J. *Total Freedom: The Essential Krishnamurti.* San Francisco, CA: HarperSan Francisco, 1996.

Krishnamurti, J. *Krishnamurti: Reflections on the Self.* Chicago, IL: Open Court, 1997.

Lester, Robert C. *Theravada Buddhism in Southeast Asia.* Ann Arbor, MI: University of Michigan Press, 1973.

Lutyens, Emily. *Candles in the Sun.* Philadelphia, PA: Lippincott, 1957.

Lutyens, Mary. *Krishnamurti: The Years of Fulfilment.* New York: Farrar, Straus & Giroux, 1983.

Lynch, Owen M., ed. *Divine Passions: The Social Construction of Emotion in India.* Berkeley, CA: University of California Press, 1990.

Malalasekera, G.P. and J.K. Jayatilleke, *Buddhism and the Race Question.* Paris: UNESCO, 1958.

Matilal, Bimal Krishna. *Epistemology, Logic, and Grammar in Indian Philosophical Analysis.* The Hague: Mouton, 1971.

Matilal, Bimal Krishna. *Logic, Language and Reality: An Introduction to Indian Philosophical Studies.* Delhi: Motilal Banarsidass, 1985.

Minor, Robert, ed. *Modern Indian Interpreters of the Bhagavadgita.* Albany, NY: State University of New York Press, 1986.

Moffat, A.L. *Mongkut, the King of Siam.* Ithaca, NY: Cornell University Press, 1961.

Mohanty, Jitendra Nath. *Reason and Tradition in Indian Thought: An Essay on the Nature of Indian Philosophical Thinking.* Oxford, UK: Clarendon Press, 1992.

Naeem, Ahmad. *Philosophy in Pakistan.* Washington, DC: Council for Research in Values and Philosophy, 1997.

Nhat-Hanh, Thich. *The Diamond that Cuts through Illusion: Commentaries on the Prajnaparamita Diamond Sutra.* Berkeley, CA: Parallax Press, 1992.

Nikhilananda, Swami, trans. *The Gospel of Sri Ramakrishna.* New York: Ramakrishna-Vivekananda Center, 1952 (1942).

O'Connor, June. *The Quest for Political and Spiritual Liberation: A Study in the Thought of Aurobindo Ghose.* Rutherford, NJ: Fairleigh Dickinson University Press, 1977.

Oommen, T.K. *Alien Concepts and South Asian Reality: Responses and Reformulations.* Thousand Oaks, CA: Sage Publications, 1995.

Panda, Rabinda K. *Anandabodhayati: Life and Philosophy.* Columbia, MO: South Asia Books, 1997.

Pappu, S.S., ed. *New Essays in the Philosophy of Sarvepalli Radhakrishnan.* Columbia, MO: South Asia Books, 1995.

Radhakrishnan, Sarvepalli. *Indian Philosophy,* 2 Vols. New York: Macmillan, 1923–27.

Radhakrishnan, Sarvepalli, trans. *The Principal Upaniṣads.* London: Allen & Unwin, 1953.

Radhakrishnan, Sarvepalli. *An Idealist View of Life.* London: Allen & Unwin, 2nd edn, 1957 (1932).

Radhakrishnan, Sarvepalli, trans. *The Bhagavadgita.* London: Allen & Unwin, 2nd edn, 1958 (1949).

Radhakrishnan, Sarvepalli, trans. *The Brahmasūtra.* London: Allen & Unwin, 1961.

Radhakrishnan, Sarvepalli. *The Hindu View of Life.* London: Allen & Unwin, 1961.

Radhakrishnan, Sarvepalli, trans. *The Dhammapada.* London: Oxford University Press, 1966.

Radhakrishnan, Sarvepalli. *Eastern Religions and Western Thought.* New York: Oxford University Press, 1990.

Radhakrishnan, Sarvepalli and J.H. Muirhead, eds. *Contemporary Indian Philosophy.* London: George Allen & Unwin, 2nd edn, 1952.

Rammohun Roy. *The Precepts of Jesus.* Boston, MA: Christian Register Office, 1828.

Rinehart, Robin. *Contemporary Hinduism: Ritual, Culture, and Practice.* Santa Barbara, CA: ABC-CLIO, 2004.

Sahoo, Shridhar C. *Subhas Chandra Bose: Political Philosophy.* Columbia, MO: South Asia Books, 1997.

Sarkar, Anil K. *Triadic Avenues of India's Cultural Prospects: Philosophy, Physics and Politics.* Columbia, MO: South Asia Books, 1995.

Schilpp, Paul A., ed. *The Philosophy of Sarvepalli Radhakrishnan.* New York: Tudor Publ. Co., 1952.

Searle-Chatterjee, Mary and Sharma, Ursula M., eds. *Contextualising Caste: Post-Dumontian Approaches.* Cambridge, MA: Blackwell, 1995.

Sen, Amartya. *The Argumentative Indian: Writings on Indian History, Culture, and Identity.* New York: Farrar, Straus and Giroux, 2005.

Sinha, Harendra P. *Religious Philosophy of Tagore and Radhakrishnan: A Comparative and Analytical Study.* Columbia, MO: South Asia Books, 1993.

Smart, Ninian. *Worldviews: Crosscultural Explorations of Human Beliefs.* New York: Scribner's, 1983.

Smart, Ninian. *The World's Religions: Old Traditions and Modern Transformations.* Cambridge, UK: Cambridge University Press, 1989.

Smith, Bardwell L., ed. *Hinduism: New Essays in the History of Religions*. Leiden, Netherlands: Brill, 1976.

Spiro, Melford E. *Buddhism and Society: A Great Tradition and Its Burmese Vicissitudes*. Berkeley, CA: University of California Press, 2nd edn, 1982.

Stcherbatsky, Theodore. *Buddhist Logic*, 2 Vols. New York: Dover, 1962.

Tagore, Rabindranath. *Gitanjali (Song Offerings)*. London: Macmillan, 1913.

Taher, Mohamed. *Muslims in India: Recent Contributions to Literature on Religion, Philosophy, History, and Social Aspects*. Columbia, MO: South Asia Books, 1993.

Vigne, Jacques. *Indian Wisdom, Christianity and Modern Psychology*. Columbia, MO: South AsiaBooks, (Reprint) 1997.

Vivekananda. *The Complete Works*, 8 Vols. Calcutta, India: Advaita Ashrama, 1948–55.

Von der Mehden, Fred. *Religion and Modernization in Southeast Asia*. Syracuse, NY: Syracuse University Press, 1986.

Walker, Benjamin. *The Hindu World: An Encyclopedic Survey of Hinduism*, 2 Vols. New York: Frederick A. Praeger, 1968.

White, David Gordon, ed. *Tantra in Practice*. Princeton, NJ: Princeton University Press, 2000.

Williams, George M. *The Quest for Meaning of Svāmī Vivekānanda*. Chico, CA: New Horizons Press, 1974.

Williams, Harold W. *The Swan's Wide Waters: Ramakrishna and Western Culture*. Port Washington, NY: Kennikat Press, 1974.

14. CHINA, KOREA AND JAPAN IN MODERN TIMES

Baroni, Helen J. *Ōbaku Zen: The Emergence of the Third Sect of Zen in Tokugawa Japan*. Honolulu, HI: University of Hawaii Press, 2000.

Brière, O. (Laurence G. Thompson, trans.). *Fifty Years of Chinese Philosophy: 1898–1950*. London: Allen & Unwin, 1956.

Burns, Susan L. *Before the Nation: Kokugaku and the Imagining of Community in Early Modern Japan*. Durham, NC: Duke University Press, 2003.

Carter, Robert E. *Becoming Bamboo*. Montreal, Canada: McGill-Queen's University Press, 1992.

Chan, Wing-tsit. *Religious Trends in Modern China*. New York: Columbia University Press, 1953.

Chan, Wing-tsit. *Chinese Philosophy, 1949–1963: An Annotated Bibliography of Mainland China Publications*. Honolulu, HI: East-West Center Press, 1967.

Ch'oe, Yôngho, Peter H. Lee and William Theodore de Bary, eds. *Sources of Korean Tradition, Vol. 2: From the Sixteenth to the Twentieth Centuries*. New York: Columbia University Press, 2000.

Chung, Chai-Sik. *A Korean Confucian Encounter with the Modern World: Yi Hang-No and the West*. Berkeley, CA: University of California, Institute of East Asian Studies, 1995.

De Bary, William Theodore (Tu Wei-Ming, ed.). *Confucianism and Human Rights*. New York: Columbia University Press, 1997.

De Bary, William Theodore, Wing-tsit Chan and Burton Watson. *Sources of Chinese Tradition*, 2 Vols. New York: Columbia University Press, 1960.

Dilworth, David and Valdo Viglielmo (eds.). *Sourcebook for Modern Japanese Philosophy: Selected Documents*. Westport, CT: Greenwood Press, 1998.

Elman, Benjamin A. *From Philosophy to Philology: Intellectual and Social Aspects of Change in Late Imperial China.* Cambridge, MA: Harvard University Press, 1990.

Fujita, Masakatsu (ed.). *Nihon kindai shisō o manabu hito no tame ni.* Kyoto, Japan: Sekai shisōsha, 1997.

Fujita, Masakatsu (ed.). *Kyōtō gakuha no tetsugaku.* Kyoto, Japan: Shōwadō, 2001.

Fung Yu-lan. (E.R. Hughes, trans.). *The Spirit of Chinese Philosophy.* London: K. Paul, Trench, Trubner, 1947.

Fung Yu-lan. (Derk Bodde, trans.). *A History of Chinese Philosophy,* 2 Vols. Princeton, NJ: Princeton University Press, 1952–53.

Goto-Jones, Christopher S. *Political Philosophy in Japan: Nishita, the Kyoto School, and Co-Prosperity.* New York: Routledge, 2005.

Han, Woo-Keun (Lee Kyung-shik, trans.). *The History of Korea.* Seoul: Eul-Yoo, 1970.

Hansen, Chad. *A Daoist Theory of Chinese Thought: A Philosophical Interpretation.* New York: Oxford University Press, 1992.

Heisig, James W. *Philosophers of Nothingness: An Essay on the Kyoto School.* Honolulu, HI: University of Hawaii Press, 2001.

Heisig, James W. and John C. Maraldo, eds. *Rude Awakenings: Zen, the Kyoto School, and the Questions of Nationalism.* Honolulu, HI: University of Hawaii Press, 1995.

Hirota, Dennis, ed. *Toward a Contemporary Understanding of Pure Land Buddhism: Creating a Shin Buddhist Theology in a Religiously Plural World.* Albany, NY: State University of New York Press, 2000.

Hsiao, Kung-chuan. *A Modern China and a New World: K'ang Yu-wei, Reformer and Utopian, 1858–1927.* Seattle, WA: University of Washington Press, 1978.

Hsiung, Shih-li. *Hsin wei shih lun.* T'ai-pei: Kuang wen shu chu, Min kuo 51, 1962.

Iwasaki, Chikatsugu. *Nihon kindai shisōshi josetsu ki zenpen,* 2 vols. Tokyo: Shin nihon shuppansha, 2002, 2004.

Johnston, Reginald F. *Confucianism and Modern China.* Westport, CT: Hyperion Press, 1986.

K'ang, Yu-wei (Laurence G. Thompson, trans.). *Ta T'ung Shu: The One-World Philosophy of K'angYu-wei.* London: Allen & Unwin, 1958.

K'ang, Yu-wei. *K'ang Yu-wei Ta t'ung shu shou kao (The Book of Great Concord),* 4 Vols. Nan-ching shih, China: Chiang-su ku chi ch'u pan she, 1985–.

Kiyota, Minoru, ed. *Japanese Buddhism: Its Tradition, New Religions and Interaction with Christianity.* Los Angeles, CA: Buddhist Books International, 1987.

Knight, Nick. *Li Da and Marxist Philosophy in China.* Boulder, CO: Westview Press, 1996.

Kosaka, Masaaki (David Abosch, trans.). *Japanese Thought in the Meiji Era.* Tokyo: Pan-Pacific Press, 1958.

Kosaka, Kunitsugu. *Nishida Kitarō o meguru tetsugakusha gunzō: kindai nihon tetsugaku to shūkyō.* Kyoto, Japan: Minerva Shobō, 1995.

Koschmann, J. Victor. *Revolution and Subjectivity in Postwar Japan.* Chicago, IL: University of Chicago Press, 1996.

Levenson, Joseph Richmond. *Liang Ch'i-ch'ao and the Mind of Modern China.* Taipei: Rainbow-Bridge, 2nd edn, 1959.

Levenson, Joseph. *Confucian China and its Modern Fate: A Trilogy,* 3 Vols. Berkeley, CA: University of California Press, 1968.

Li, Lincoln. *Student Nationalism in China, 1924–1949.* Albany, NY: State University of New York Press, 1994.

Li, Lincoln. *The China Factor in Modern Japanese Thought: The Case of Tachibana Shiraki, 1881–1945.* Albany, NY: SUNY Press, 1996.

Liang, Ch'i-ch'ao. *Ou yu hsin ying lu chieh lu (Recollections of a Trip to Europe)*. Shanghai, China: Chung-hua shu-chü, 1936.

Liang, Ch'i-ch'ao (I.C.Y. Hsü, trans.). *Intellectual Trends in the Ching Period (Ching-tai hsüeh-shu kai-lun)*. Cambridge, MA: Harvard University Press, 1959.

Liang, Ch'i-ch'ao (Li Yu-ning and William A. Wycoff, trans.). *Two Self-portraits: Liang Ch'i-ch'ao and Hu Shih*. Bronxville, NY: Outer Sky Press, 1992.

Louie, Kamm. *Critiques of Confucius in Contemporary China*. New York: Saint Martin's Press, 1980.

Mao, Tse-tung. *On Practice*. Peking: Foreign Languages Press, 1960.

Mao, Tse-tung. *On Contradiction*. Peking: Foreign Languages Press, 5th edn, 1965.

Mao, Tse-tung. *Mao Tse-tung's Quotations: The Red Guard's Handbook*. Peking: Foreign Languages Press, 1966 (1972).

Mao, Tse-tung (Jerome Ch'en, ed.). *Mao Papers, Anthology and Bibliography*. New York: Oxford University Press, 1970.

Mao, Tse-tung (Nick Knight, trans.). *Mao Zedong's On Contradiction: An Annotated Translation of the Pre-Liberation Text*. Nathan, Australia: Griffith University, 1981.

McNally, Mark. *Proving the Way: Conflict and Practice in the History of Japanese Nativism*. Cambridge, MA: Harvard University Asia Center, 2005.

Meissner, Werner. *Philosophy and Politics in China: The Controversy over Dialectical Materialism in the 1930s*. Stanford, CA: Stanford University Press, 1990.

Mou, Bo, ed. *Davidson's Philosophy and Chinese Philosophy: Constructive Engagement*. Leiden, Netherlands: E.J. Brill, 2006.

Neville, Robert Cummings. *Boston Confucianism: Portable Tradition in the Late-Modern World*. Albany, NY: State University of New York Press, 2000.

Nishida, Kitaro (Robert Schinzinger, trans.). *Intelligibility and the Philosophy of Nothingness*. Tokyo: Maruzen, 1958.

Nishida, Kitarō (David A. Dilworth, trans.). *Fundamental Problems of Philosophy: The World of Action and the Dialectical World*. Tokyo: Sophia University, 1970.

Nishida, Kitarō (David A. Dilworth and Valdo H. Viglielmo, trans.). *Art and Morality*. Honolulu, HI: University of Hawaii Press, 1973.

Nishida, Kitarō. (David A. Dilworth, trans.). *Last Writings: Nothingness and the Religious Worldview*. Honolulu, HI: University of Hawaii Press, 1987.

Nishida, Kitarō. (Valdo H. Viglielmo, with Takeuchi Yoshinori and Joseph S. O'Leary, trans.). *Intuition and Reflection in Self-Consciousness*. Albany, NY: State University of New York Press, 1987.

Nishida, Kitarō (V.H. Viglielmo, trans.). *A Study of Good (Zen no kenkyu)*. New York: Greenwood Press, 1988.

Nishida, Kitarō (Masao Abe and Christopher Ives, trans.). *An Inquiry into the Good (Zen no kenkyu)*. New Haven, CT: Yale University Press, 1990.

Nishitani, Keiji (Jan Van Bragt, trans.). *Religion and Nothingness*. Berkeley, CA: University of California Press, 1982.

Nishitani, Keiji (Graham Parkes and Aihara Setsuko, trans.). *The Self-Overcoming of Nihilism*. Albany, NY: State University of New York Press, 1990.

Odin, Steve. *The Social Self in Zen and American Pragmatism*. Albany, NY: State University of New York Press, 1996.

Palmer, Spencer J., ed. *The New Religions of Korea*. Seoul: Royal Asiatic Society, Korea Branch, 1967.

Piovesana, Gino K. *Recent Japanese Philosophical Thought, 1862–1996: A Survey: Including a Survey by Naoshi Yamawaki, the Philosophical Thought of Japan from 1963 to 1996.* Richmond, UK: Japan Library, 3rd edn, 1997.

Reischauer, E.O. *History of East Asian Civilizations,* 2 Vols. Boston, MA: Houghton Mifflin, 1960–65.

Roberts, J.M. *History of the World.* New York: Oxford University Press, 1993.

Sansom, G.B. *Japan: A Short Cultural History.* Revised edn. New York: D. Appleton-Century, 1943.

Scheiner, Irwin. *Japanese Thought in the Tokugawa Period, 1600–1868: Methods and Metaphors.* Chicago, IL: University of Chicago Press, 1988.

Schiffrin, H.Z. *Sun Yat-sen and the Origins of the Chinese Revolution.* Berkeley, CA: University of California Press, 1968.

Schram, Stuart. *Mao Tse-tung.* Harmondsworth, UK: Penguin, 1967 (1966).

Schwartz, Benjamin. *Chinese Communism and the Rise of Mao.* Cambridge, MA: Harvard University Press, 1951.

Sheng-yen (John Cook, ed.). *Illuminating Silence: The Practice of Chinese Zen.* London: Watkins, 2002.

Sheng-yen, Master, with Dan Stevenson. *Hoofprint of the Ox: Principles of the Chan Buddhist Path as Taught by a Modern Chinese Master.* Oxford, UK: Oxford University Press, 2001.

Smart, Ninian. *Mao.* Glasgow, UK: Collins, 1974.

Smart, Ninian. *The World's Religions.* Cambridge, UK: Cambridge University Press, 1989.

Smart, Ninian. *Buddhism and Christianity: Rivals and Allies.* Honolulu, HI: University of Hawaii Press, 1993.

Sun Yat-sen (Frank W. Price, trans.). *San Min Chu I, the Three Principles of the People.* Shanghai, China: China Committee, Institute of Pacific Relations, 1928.

Suzuki, D.T. *Mysticism, Christian and Buddhist.* London: Allen & Unwin, 1957.

Suzuki, D.T. *Zen and Japanese Culture.* Princeton, NJ: Princeton University Press, 1970 (1959).

T'ai hsü. *Lectures in Buddhism.* Paris: Imp. Union, 1928.

Tanabe, Hajime. *Suri tetsugaku kenkyu.* Tokyo: Iwanami Shoten, 1930.

Tanabe, Hajime. *Shu no ronri no benshoho.* Osaka, Japan: Akitaya, 1947.

Tanabe, Hajime (Takeuchi Yoshinori with Valdo Viglielmo and James W. Heisig, trans.). *Philosophy as Metanoetics (Zangedo to shite no tetsugaku).* Berkeley, CA: University of California Press, 1986.

Tang, Xiaobing. *Global Space and the Nationalist Discourse of Modernity: The Historical Thinking of Liang Qichao.* Stanford, CA: Stanford University Press, 1996.

Tu, Wei-ming. *Humanity and Self-Cultivation: Essays in Confucian Thought.* Berkeley, CA: Asian Humanities Press, 1979 (1978).

Tu, Wei-ming. *Confucian Thought: Selfhood as Creative Transformation.* Albany, NY: State University of New York Press, 1985.

Tu, Wei-ming (Alan M. Wachman, and Milan G. Heitmanek, eds.). *The Confucian World Observed: A Contemporary Discussion of Confucian Humanism in East Asia.* Honolulu, HI: University of Hawaii Press, 1992.

Tu, Wei-ming, ed. *China in Transformation.* Cambridge, MA: Harvard University Press, 1994.

Tu, Wei-ming, ed. *Confucian Traditions in East Asian Modernity: Moral Education and Economic Culture in Japan and the Four Mini-Dragons.* Cambridge, MA: Harvard University Press, 1996.

Twitchett, D. and J.K. Fairbank, eds. *The Cambridge History of China.* Cambridge, UK: Cambridge University Press, 1978–1991.

Wakeman, Frederic E. *History and Will: Philosophical Perspectives of Mao Tse-Tung's Thought.* Berkeley, CA: University of California Press, 1973.

Wargo, Robert J.J. *The Logic of Nothingness: A Study of Nishida Kitarō.* Honolulu, HI: University of Hawaii Press, 2005.

Watsuji, Tetsurō (Geoffrey Bownas, trans.). *A Climate: A Philosophical Study.* Tokyo: Printing Bureau, Japanese Government, 1961.

Watsuji, Tetsurō (Yamamoto Seisaku and Robert E. Carter, trans.). *Watsuji Tetsuro's Rinrigaku.* Albany, NY: State University of New York Press, 1996.

Welch, Holmes. *The Buddhist Revival in China.* Cambridge, MA: Harvard University Press, 1968.

Wilson, Dick, ed. *Mao Tse-tung in the Scales of History: A Preliminary Assessment.* Cambridge, UK: Cambridge University Press, 1977.

Wilson, Thomas A. *Genealogy of the Way: The Construction and Uses of the Confucian Tradition in Late Imperial China.* Stanford, CA: Stanford University Press, 1995.

Wood, Alan T. *Limits to Autocracy: From Sung Neo-Confucianism to a Doctrine of Political Rights.* Honolulu, HI: University of Hawaii Press, 1995.

Yusa, Michiko. *Zen and Philosophy: An Intellectual Biography of Nishida Kitarō.* Honolulu, HI: University of Hawaii Press, 2002.

Zavala, Agustin J. (David A. Dilworth and Valdo H. Viglielmo, eds.). *Sourcebook for Modern Japanese Philosophy: Selected Documents.* Westport, CT: Greenwood, 1998.

15. AFRICAN PHILOSOPHIES

Abraham, Willie E. *The Mind of Africa.* Chicago, IL: University of Chicago Press, 1962.

Appiah, Kwame A. *In My Father's House: Africa in the Philosophy of Culture.* New York: Oxford University Press, 1993.

Asch, Susan. *L'église du prophète Kimbangu: De ses origines a son rôle actuel au Zaire, 1921–1981.* Paris: Editions Karthala, 1983.

Beidelman, T.O. *Moral Imagination in Kaguru Modes of Thought.* Bloomington, IN: Indiana University Press, 1986.

Benson, Peter. *Black Orpheus, Transition, and Modern Cultural Awakening in Africa.* Berkeley, CA: University of California Press, 1986.

Betts, Raymond F., ed. *The Ideology of Blackness.* Lexington, MA: D.C. Heath, 1971.

Blyden, Edward Wilmot. *Liberia: Past, Present and Future.* Washington, DC: 1869.

Blyden, Edward Wilmot. *Christianity, Islam and the Negro Race.* London: W.B. Whittingham, 1888.

Chidester, David. *Religions in South Africa.* New York: Routledge, 1992.

Chukwudieze, Emmanuel, ed. *African Philosophy: An Anthology.* Malden, MA: Blackwell, 1997.

Deutsch, Eliot and Ron Bontekoe, eds. *A Companion to World Philosophies.* Malden, MA: Blackwell, 1997.

Douglas, Mary. *The Lele of the Kasai.* London: Oxford University Press, 1963.

Dupré, Wilhelm. *Religion in Primitive Cultures: A Study in Ethnophilosophy.* The Hague: Mouton, 1975.

Eboussi-Boulaga, F. *La crise de Muntu: authenticité africaine et philosophie.* Paris: Présence africaine, 1977.

Eboussi-Boulaga, F. *Christianisme sans fétiche: révélation et domination.* Paris: Présence africaine, 1981.

Eboussi Boulaga, F. (Robert R. Barr, trans.). *Christianity without Fetishes: An African Critique and Recapture of Christianity*. Maryknoll, NY: Orbis Books, 1984.

English, Parker and Kibujjo Kalumba, eds. *African Philosophy: A Classical Approach*. Paramus, NJ: Prentice Hall, 1995.

Evans-Pritchard, E.E. *Nuer Religion*. Oxford, UK: Clarendon Press, 1956.

Eze, Emmanuel C., ed. *Postcolonial African Philosophy: A Critical Reader*. Malden, MA: Blackwell, 1997.

Forde, Daryll, ed. *African Worlds: Studies in the Cosmological Ideas and Social Values of African Peoples*. Oxford, UK: Oxford University Press, 1954.

Garvey, Marcus (Amy J. Garvey, ed.). *The Philosophy and Opinions of Marcus Garvey: or Africa for the Africans*. Dover, UK: Majority Press, 1986.

Gbadegesin, Segun. *African Philosophy: Traditional Yoruba Philosophy and Contemporary African Realities*. New York: Peter Lang, 1992.

González-Wippler, Migene. *The Santería Experience*. Englewood Cliffs, NJ: Prentice-Hall, 1982.

González-Wippler, Migene. *Santería: The Religion: A Legacy of Faith, Rites, and Magic*. New York: Harmony Books, 1989.

Gyekye, Kwame. *An Essay on African Philosophical Thought: The Akan Conceptual Scheme*. Philadelphia, PA: Temple University Press, 1995.

Gyekye, Kwame and Kwasi Wiredu, eds. *Person and Community: Ghanaian Philosophical Studies I*. Washington, DC: Council for Research in Values and Philosophy, 1992.

Hallen, Barry. *A Short History of African Philosophy*. Bloomington, IN: Indiana University Press, 2002.

Hallen, B. and J.O. Sodipo, *Knowledge, Belief and Witchcraft: Analytic Experiments in African Philosophy*. Stanford, CA: Stanford University Press, 1997.

Henry, Paget. *Caliban's Reason: Introducing Afro-Caribbean Philosophy*. New York: Routledge, 2000.

Hexham, Irving. *The Irony of Apartheid: The Struggle for National Independence of Afrikaner Calvinism against British Imperialism*. New York: Edwin Mellen Press, 1981.

Hord, Frederick L. and Jonathan S. Lee, eds. *I Am Because We Are: Readings in Black Philosophy*. Amherst, MA: University of Massachusetts Press, 1995.

Hountondji, Paulin J. *African Philosophy: Myth and Reality*. Bloomington, IN: Indiana University Press, 1996.

Idowu, E. Bolaji. *Olodumare: God in Yoruba Belief*. London: Longmans, 1962.

Kagame, Alexis. *La Philosophie bantu-rwandaise de l'Être; extraits*. Brussels: Académie Royale des Sciences Coloniales, 1956.

Kagame, Alexis. *La Philosophie bantu comparée*. Paris: Présence africaine, 1976.

Kebede, Messay. *Africa's Quest for a Philosophy of Decolonization*. New York: Rodopi, 2004.

Kigunga, Raphael. *The Anthropology of Self-Person and Myth in Africa: A Philosophical Reflection on Man in South-East-Africa*. New York: Peter Lang, 1996.

Kiros, Tedros. *Moral Philosophy and Development: The Human Condition in Africa*. Athens, OH: Ohio University Press, 1992.

Kwame, Safro, ed. *Readings in African Philosophy: An Akan Collection*. Lanham, MD: University Press of America, 1995.

Lévi-Strauss, C. *The Savage Mind*. Chicago, IL: University of Chicago Press, 1966.

Leyburn, James G. *The Haitian People*. New Haven, CT: Yale University Press, 1966 edn.

MacGaffey, Wyatt. *Modern Kongo Prophets: Religion in a Plural Society*. Bloomington, IN: Indiana University Press, 1983.

Mack, Kibibi Voloria, ed. *The African American Encyclopedia. Supplement,* 2 Vols. New York: Marshall Cavendish, 1997.

Makinde, M. Akin. *African Philosophy, Culture and Traditional Medicine.* Athens, OH: Ohio University Press, 1988.

Martin, Marie-Louise. *Kimbangu: An African Prophet and his Church.* Oxford, UK: Blackwell, 1975.

Masolo, D.A. *African Philosophy in Search of Identity.* Bloomington, IN: Indiana University Press, 1994.

Mazrui, Ali A. *World Culture and the Black Experience.* Seattle, WA: University of Washington Press, 1974.

Mbiti, John S. *African Religions and Philosophy.* Garden City, NY: Doubleday, 2nd edn, 1970.

Mbiti, John S. *Concepts of God in Africa.* New York: Praeger, 1970.

Mosley, Albert G. *African Philosophy: Selected Readings.* Paramus, NJ: Prentice Hall, 1995.

Mudimbe, V.Y. *The Invention of Africa: Gnosis, Philosophy, and the Order of Knowledge.* Bloomington, IN: Indiana University Press, 1988.

Mudimbe, V.Y. *The Idea of Africa.* Bloomington, IN: Indiana University Press, 1994.

Mujynya, E.N.C. *L'homme dans l'univers des Bantu.* Lubumbashi, Zaire: Presse de l'université nationale du Zaire, 1972.

Mulago, Vincent. *La Religion traditionalle des Bantu et leur vision du monde.* Kinshasa, Congo: Presses universitaires du Zaire, 1973.

Murphy, Larry G., J. Gordon Melton and Gary L. Ward, eds. *Encyclopedia of African American Religions.* New York: Garland, 1993.

Nelson-Richards, Melsome. *Poverty of Philosophy in African Studies.* Lawrenceville, NJ: Brunswick, 1990.

Nkrumah, Kwame. *Consciencism: Philosophy and the Ideology for Decolonization.* New York: Monthly Review Press, 1970.

Nzegwu, Nkiru. "Feminism and Africa: impact and limits of the metaphysics of gender", *Companion to African Philosophy,* ed. K. Wiredu, Cambridge MA: Basil Blackwell, 2004, pp. 560–9. Obenga, Théophile. *A Lost Tradition: African Philosophy in World History.* Philadelphia, PA: Source Editions, 1995.

Okere, Theophilus. *African Philosophy: A Historico-Hermeneutical Investigation of the Conditions of Its Possibility.* Lanham, MD: University Press of America, 1983.

Okere, Theophilus, ed. *Identity and Change: Nigerian Philosophical Studies I.* Washington, DC: Council for Research in Values and Philosophy, 1995.

Oruka, H. Odera, ed. *Sage Philosophy: Indigenous Thinkers and Modern Debate on African Philosophy.* Kinderhook, NY: E.J. Brill, 1990.

Oruka, H. Odera and D.A. Masolo, *Philosophy and Cultures.* Nairobi: Bookwise, 1983.

Pakenham, Thomas. *The Scramble for Africa, 1876–1912.* New York: Random House, 1991.

Parrinder, E.G. *African Traditional Religion.* London: Sheldon Press, 3rd edn, 1974.

Pittman, John P., ed. *African-American Perspectives and Philosophical Traditions.* New York: Routledge, 1996.

Ray, Benjamin C. *African Religions: Symbol, Ritual, and Community.* Englewood Cliffs, NJ: Prentice Hall, 1976.

Salzman, Jack, David Lionel Smith and Cornel West, eds. *Encyclopedia of African-American Culture and History,* 5 Vols. New York: Macmillan Library Reference, 1996.

Sartre, Jean-Paul (W. Allen, trans.). *Black Orpheus.* Paris: Présence africaine, 1976.

Schmidt, Wilhelm. *Der Ursprung der Gottesidee, eine historisch-kritische und positive Studie.* Münster, Germany: Aschendorff, 1926.

Senghor, Leopold S. *Les fondements de l'africanité ou negritude et arabité*. Paris: Présence Africaine, 1967.

Senghor, Leopold S. *Anthologie de la Nouvelle Poésie Nègre et Malgache de Langue Française: Avec: Sartre, Jean-Paul. Orphée Noir*. New York: French & European Publ., 1985.

Serequeberhan, Tsenay, ed. *African Philosophy: The Essential Readings*. Saint Paul, MN: Paragon House, 1991.

Serequeberhan, Tsenay. *The Hermeneutics of African Philosophy: Horizon and Discourse*. New York: Routledge, 1994.

Shutte, Augustine. *Philosophy for Africa*. Milwaukee, WI: Marquette University Press, 1996.

Summer, Claude. *Source of African Philosophy: The Ethiopian Philosophy of Man*. Philadelphia, PA: Coronet Books, 1986.

Sundkler, Bengt. *Bantu Prophets in South Africa*. New York: Oxford University Press, 1961.

Sundkler, Bengt. *Zulu Zion*. New York: Oxford University Press, 1976.

Taylor, J.V. *Christians of the Copperbelt*. London: SCM Press, 1961.

Tempels, Placide. *La Philosophie bantoue*. Paris: Presence Africaine, 2nd edn, 1961.

Theron, Stephen. *Africa, Philosophy, and the Western Tradition: An Essay in Self-Understanding*. New York: Peter Lang, 1995.

Thompson, Robert F. *Black Gods and Kings: Yoruba Art at UCLA*. Bloomington, IN: Indiana University Press, 1976.

Thompson, Robert F. *Flash of the Spirit: African and Afro-American Art and Philosophy*. New York: Random House, 1984.

Turner, Harold W. *Religious Innovations in Africa*. Boston, MA: G.K. Hall, 1979.

Tutu, Desmond. *Hope and Suffering*. Grand Rapids, MI: W.B. Eerdmans, 1984 (1983).

Wagner, Roy. *The Invention of Culture*. Chicago, IL: University of Chicago Press, 1981.

Williams, Michael W., ed. *The African American Encyclopedia*, 6 Vols. New York: Marshall Cavendish, 1993.

Wiredu, K. *Philosophy and an African Culture*. New York: Cambridge University Press, 1980.

Wiredu, Kwasi. *Cultural Universals and Particulars: An African Perspective*. Bloomington, IN: Indiana University Press, 1996.

Wiredu, Kwasi, ed. *A Companion to African Philosophy*. Malden, MA: Blackwell, 2004.

Wright, Richard A., ed. *African Philosophy: An Introduction*. Lanham, MD: University Press of America, 1984.

Zahan, Dominique (Kate Ezra Martin and Lawrence M. Martin, trans.). *The Religion, Spirituality, and Thought of Traditional Africa*. Chicago, IL: University of Chicago Press, 1979.

Zuesse, Evan. *Ritual Cosmos: The Sanctification of Life in African Religions*. Athens, OH: Ohio University Press, 1979.

16. CONCLUDING REFLECTIONS

Althusser, Louis (Ben Brewster, trans.). *Politics and History: Montesquieu, Rousseau, Hegel, Marx*. London: NLB, 1972.

Appiah, Kwame A. *Cosmopolitanism: Ethics in a World of Strangers*. New York: W.W. Norton, 2006.

Baghramian, Maria and Attracta Ingram, eds. *Pluralism: The Philosophy and Politics of Diversity*. New York: Routledge, 2000.

Brock, Gillian and Harry Brighouse. *The Political Philosophy of Cosmopolitanism*. Cambridge, UK: Cambridge University Press, 2005.

Bullock, Alan and Stallybrass, Oliver, eds. *Fontana Dictionary of Modern Thought*. London: Collins, 1977.

Burridge, Kenelm. *New Heaven, New Earth: A Study of Millenarian Activities*. Oxford, UK: Basil Blackwell, 1969.

Cavarero, Adriana. (Serena Anderlini-D'Onofrio and Aine O'Healy, trans.). *In Spite of Plato: A Feminist Rewriting of Ancient Philosophy*. New York: Routledge, 1995.

Code, Lorraine, ed. *Encyclopedia of Feminist Theories*. New York: Routledge, 2000.

Copleston, Frederick C. *Philosophies and Cultures*. Oxford, UK: Oxford University Press, 1980.

Derrida, Jacques (C. Spivak, trans.). *Of Grammatology*. Baltimore, MD: Johns Hopkins University Press, 1976.

Derrida, Jacques (Alan Bass, trans.). *Writing and Difference*. Chicago, IL: University of Chicago Press, 1978.

Derrida, Jacques (A. Bass, trans.). *Positions*. Chicago, IL: University of Chicago Press, 1981.

Derrida, Jacques (A. Bass, trans.). *Margins of Philosophy*. Chicago, IL: University of Chicago Press, 1982.

Derrida, Jacques. *Acts of Literature*. London: Routledge, 1992.

Douglas, Ann. *The Feminization of American Culture*. New York: Alfred A. Knopf, 1977.

Dreyfus, Hubert L. and Paul Rabinow. *Michel Foucault: Beyond Structuralism and Hermeneutics*. Chicago, IL: University of Chicago Press, 1982.

Dummett, Michael. *Frege: Philosophy of Language*, London: Duckworth, 1973.

Dummet, Michael. *The Seas of Language*. Oxford, UK: Oxford University Press, 1993.

Dummet, Michael. *Truth and the Past*. Oxford, UK: Oxford University Press, 2005.

Dummet, Michael. *Thought and Reality*. Oxford, UK: Oxford University Press, 2006.

Edwards, James C. *The Authority of Language: Heidegger, Wittgenstein and the Threat of Philosophical Nihilism*. Tampa, FL: University of South Florida Press, 1990.

Fay, Brian. *Contemporary Philosophy of Social Science: A Multicultural Approach*. Cambridge, MA: Blackwell, 1996.

Fricker, Miranda and Jennifer Hornsby. *The Cambridge Companion to Feminism in Philosophy*. Cambridge, UK: Cambridge University Press, 2000.

Garry, Ann and Marilyn Pearsall, eds. *Women, Knowledge, and Reality: Explorations in Feminist Philosophy*. New York: Routledge, 2nd edn, 1996.

Glover, Jonathan. *Humanity: A Moral History of the Twentieth Century*. New Haven, CT: Yale University Press, 2000.

Habermas, Jürgen (F. Lawrence, trans.). *The Philosophical Discourse of Modernity*. Cambridge, UK: Polity, 1987.

Habermas, Jürgen (E. Medieta, ed.). *Religion and Rationality: Essays on Reason, God, and Modernity*. Cambridge, MA: MIT Press, 2002.

Harvey, David. *The Condition of Postmodernity: An Enquiry into the Origins of Cultural Change*. Oxford, UK: Blackwell, 1989.

Heidegger, Martin (J. Macquarrie and E. Robinson, trans.). *Being and Time*. Oxford, UK: Blackwell, 1980.

Hennessy, A, ed. *Intellectuals in the Twentieth-Century Caribbean,*. 2 Vols. London: Macmillan Caribbean, 1992.

Hutchinson, John A. *Living Options in World Philosophy*. Honolulu, HI: University of Hawaii Press, 1977.

Jackson, Kevin T. *Charting Global Responsibilities: Legal Philosophy and Human Rights*. Lanham, MD: University Press of America, 1994.

Jaggar, Alison M. and Iris M. Young, eds. *A Companion to Feminist Philosophy*. Malden, MA: Blackwell, 1998.

Kuhn, Thomas S. *The Structure of Scientific Revolutions*. Chicago, IL: University of Chicago Press, 1970.

Leaman, Oliver, ed. *The Future of Philosophy: Towards the Twenty-First Century*. New York: Routledge, 1998.

Lear, Jonathan. *Radical Hope: Ethics in the Face of Cultural Devastation*. Cambridge, MA: Harvard University Press, 2006.

Leiter, Brian, ed. *The Future for Philosophy*. New York: Oxford University Press, 2006.

Martin, David. *A General Theory of Secularization*. New York: Harper & Row, 1978.

McGrath, Alister E. *The Blackwell Encyclopedia of Modern Christian Thought*. Malden, MA: Blackwell, 1995.

Mortimer, Edward. *Faith and Power*. London: Faber and Faber, 1982.

Patterson, Dennis, ed. *A Companion to the Philosophy of Law and Legal Theory*. Malden, MA: Blackwell, 1996.

Plott, John C. *Global History of Philosophy*, 5 Vols. Delhi: Motilal Banarsidass, 1977–89.

Rawls, John. *A Theory of Justice*. Cambridge, MA: Harvard University Press, 1971.

Ricoeur, Paul (Emerson Buchanan, trans.). *The Symbolism of Evil*. New York: Harper & Row, 1967.

Ricoeur, Paul. (Charles E. Reagan and David Stewart, eds.). *The Philosophy of Paul Ricoeur: An Anthology of his Work*. Boston, MA: Beacon Press, 1978.

Ricoeur, Paul (George H. Taylor, ed.). *Lectures on Ideology and Utopia*. New York: Columbia University Press, 1986.

Ricoeur, Paul. *Fallible Man* (Charles A. Kelbley, trans.). New York: Fordham University Press, revised edn, 1986.

Ricoeur, Paul (Kathleen Blamey, trans.). *Oneself as Another*. Chicago, IL: University of Chicago Press, 1992.

Ricoeur, Paul (David Pellauer, trans. and Mark I. Wallace, ed.). *Figuring the Sacred: Religion, Narrative, and Imagination*. Minneapolis, MN: Fortress Press, 1995.

Rorty, Richard. *Philosophy and the Minor of Nature*. Princeton, NJ: Princeton University Press, 1979.

Rorty, Richard. *Contingency, Irony, and Solidarity*. Cambridge, UK: Cambridge University Press, 1989.

Rorty, Richard. *Essays on Heidegger and Others*. Cambridge, UK: Cambridge University Press, 1991.

Rorty, Richard. *Objectivity, Relativism, and Truth*. Cambridge, UK: Cambridge University Press, 1991.

Ryle, Gilbert. *The Concept of Mind*. London: Hutchinson, 1949.

Scharfstein, Ben-Ami, ed. *Philosophy East/Philosophy West: A Critical Comparison of Indian, Chinese, Islamic and European Philosophy*. Oxford, UK: Oxford University Press, 1978.

Singer, Peter. *One World: The Ethics of Globalization*. New Haven, CT: Yale University Press, 2002.

Smart, Ninian. *Beyond Ideology*. San Francisco, CA: Harper & Row, 1981.

Turner, Harold. *Bibliography of New Religious Movements in Primal Societies*. Boston, MA: G.K. Hall, 1977–92.

Wyschogrod, Edith. *Saints and Postmodernism: Revisioning Moral Philosophy*. Chicago, IL: University of Chicago Press, 1990.

INDEX

a priori propositions 291

'Abduh, Muhammad 374–6

Abhidharma 63

Abhinavagupta 61

Abravanel, Judah 233

Absolute 40, 41, 94, 213–14, 234, 236–7, 295, 300, 312

Absolute Idealists 294, 295–7

Abulafia, Avraham 235–6

ācāryas 4

Addams, Jane 350

Adorno, Theodor 328

Advaita Vedānta 42–6, 388

Aenesidimus 171

African philosophies 450–2; context 433–5; new movements 444–5; themes 435–6

African religions, theology 448–50

agape 189–90

agnosticism 30–1, 300

Agnostics 17

ahiṃsā 29, 392

Ahmad, Mirzā Ghulām 373

Ahmadiyahs 373

Ājīvikas 17

al-'Adawiyah, Rābi'ah 195

al-Afghani, Jamal al-Din 373–4

al-Ash'arī 193

al-Baṣri, Ḥasan 195–6

al-Bisṭāmi, Abū Yazīd 196

al-Fārābī 199–200

al-Ghazālī 203–8

al-Ḥallāj 197

al-Hudhayl 'Allāf, Abu 193

al-Kindī 197–8

al-Ma'mūn 192, 193

al-Nūn, Dhū 196

al-Quḍāt, Ayn 197

al-Rāzī 198–9

Albigensian movement 244

Alcinoubinus 165

'Ali Nuri, Mirza Husayn 372

Althusser, Louis 459

Ambedkar, B.R. 401–2

Ambrose 183

American pragmatism 338–42, 348–9

Amida 133

analytic philosophy 343–5; Anglo-American 346–8

anarchism 311

Anaxagoras 158–9

Anaximander 152–3

Anaximenes 153

ancestors 435
Ancient Learning School 146–7, 148
Anselm of Canterbury 245–6
anthropology 439–40, 456
apartheid 444
Aquinas, Thomas 2, 4
Arcesilaus 165
arhant 32
Arielism 356–7
Aristotle 2, 5, 167–70, 188–9
ascetics 16, 17
Ash'arism 193–5
Atatürk, Kemal 376
atheism 51
ātman 19, 23–4 *see also* self
atomic theory 158, 278
Atomism 5, 46–51, 158–9
Augustine 182–5
Aurobindo Ghose 393–5
Avataṃsaka 91–3
Averroes 208, 210–12
Averroism 231–2
Avicenna 200–2
Ayn Sof 234–5
Aztecs 355

Bacon, Francis 268–9
Baha'is 372–3
Baha'ullāh 372
Bakunin, Mikhail Aleksandrovich 311
Bantu people 438–9
Barth, Karl 305
Beccaria, Cesare 299
ben Gershom, Levi (Gersonides) 231
ben Maimon, Moshe (Moses Maimonides)
    229–30, 239–40
ben Nahman, Moshe (Nahmanides) 236
Bentham, Jeremy 299
Berdyaev, Nikolai 313
Bergson, Henri 308–9; influence on Islam
    378–80
Berkeley, George 285
Besant, Annie 395

Bādarāyaṇa 40–1
Bhagavadgītā 31, 38–41
bhakti 31, 39 *see also* devotion
Bhattacharya, K.C. 398
Blavatsky, H.P. 395
Blyden, E.W. 441
Bodhisattva 35
Bonaventure 246–7
Bondy, Augusto Salazar 368
Bosanquet, Bernard 298
Bradley, F.H. 297–8
Bradwardine, Thomas 256
Brahma Sūtras 40
Brahman 23–4, 40–1, 42, 43
Brahmins 14–15, 16–17
Bramo Samaj (Divine Society) 385–7
Britain, ethical theories 283–4
British empiricism 284–7
British idealists 297–8
Bruno, Giordano 267–8
Buber, Martin 335
Buddha 4, 6, 17–18
Buddaghoṣa 54
buddhis 25, 47
Buddhism 8, 32–3, 53–4; basic teachings
    17–22; development and trends 403–5;
    India 13–14; Japan 126–7, 148–9, 425–6;
    Korea 117–18; late developments 62–3;
    modernism 400; modernization in China
    408–10; persecution 97–8; spread of 3,
    13–14; success in China 88–9; syncretic
    128–9; Uttar Pradesh 16; Western impact
    on 399–403
Burgos, Abner of 240
Buridan, Jean 256
Byzantine philosophy 181–2

Caitanya 62
Calvin, John 267
Cambridge Platonists 278–9
Cardano, Girolamo 265
Carnap, Rudolf 343–4, 347
Carsun Chang 417

Casas, Bartolomé de las 355

caste system 31–2

Catechetical School of Alexandria 177

Cathari 244

causation 36, 66, 168; al-Ghazālī 206; ibn
    Rushd 211

Chaadaev, Peter 309–10

Chan Buddhism 93–7; *see also Zen Buddhism*

Ch'an (Chan) 78

Chang Tsai (Zhang Zai) 100–2

Chen Que 113

Ch'en Tu-hsiu (Chen Duxiu) 411

Cheng brothers 101–3

Cheng Chung-ying 421

Chinese philosophy 2–3; Enlightenment
    415; intellectual heritage 421; key
    divisions 70–1; after Mao Zedong
    414–16; pragmatism 415–16; themes
    115–16; Western challenges 406–7

Chinul 119

Ch'ont'ae (Tiantai) 119

Chou Tun-i (Zhou Dunyi) 99

Christian philosophies: development of
    175–7; medieval 261–3; up to and beyond
    Constantine 177–9

Christian scholasticism 240–1

Christian Science 336

Christianity, Africa 444–5

Chulalongkorn 400–1

chün-tzu (junzi) 74–5, 81

Church of Jesus Christ of Latter-day Saints
    336

cit 67–8

Clement 177

Cohen, Hermann 241

Collingwood, R.G. 325–6

Common Notions 277–8

compassion 33–4

Comte, Auguste 307–8

conceptual issues 463–4

Confucianism 70, 72–6, 148, 149; in Japan
    144; Mencius (Mengzi) 81–2; mythic
    and cosmic background 71–2; recent

developments 410; revival 98–9, 455;
    and Shinto 141; Shushi (Zhuxi) 144–5;
    Xunzi (Hsun-tzu) 83–4

Confucius 6, 9, 72–3, 75

consciousness 61, 67–8

contemplation 37

Copernicus, Nicolas 267

cosmology *see* cosmos

cosmos 27, 40, 52, 59, 153–4, 177–8, 235,
    260, 270, 282, 394

Council of Nicaea 180–1

Cratylus 5

creation 57, 202, 295–6; Aquinas 251;
    Gersonides 231

Crescas, Hasdai 232–3

critical realism 342–3

critical theory 328

criticism 8

Croce, Benedetto 322–3

Cruz, Sor Juana Inés de la 366

Cudworth, Ralph 278–9

Cynics 171–2

Daodejing 77–8

Dasgupta, Surendranath 396

de Valladolid, Alphonso 240

deism 277–8, 332

del Rio, Julian Sanz 357–8

Deloria, Vine, Jr 350

Democritus 158

Deng Xiaoping 414

dependency theory 361–2

dependent origination 20–1, 37, 38, 92

Descartes, René 270–1

determinism 233, 240

Deussen, Paul 316, 390–1

Deustea, Alejandro 358–9

devotion 31, 41 *see also bhakti*

Dewey, John 341–2, 349

dharma 33, 39, 92–3

Dharmakīrti 65

Dharmapāla, Anagārika 401

dialecticians 79–80

dialectics 4, 5, 149, 295
Diamond Vehicle 53, 63
Diderot, Denis 288
Dignāga 65–6
Dilthey, Wilhelm 324–5
Dinka people 437
Diogenes 171
discrimination 26
Divine Being 177; diversity 42; Islam 193; personal and impersonal 40
divine virtues 21
Doctrine of Emptiness 35
doctrines 9
Dōgen 136–7
Dogon people 438
Donatists 184–5
Dong Zhongshu 85
dualism 27
dualistic Vedantā 58–60
Dubois, W.E.B. 350
Duns Scotus, John 253–4
duty 39

East Asian philosophies, summary 148–50
Eckhart, Johannes (Meister) 257–60
Eddy, Mary Baker 336
education 10–11, 262, 456
Edwards, Jonathon 331, 350
Eisai 135–6
elements, theory of 157
emanationism 205, 212
Emerson, Ralph Waldo 333–4
Empedocles 157–8
empiricism 109, 279–81; British 284–7, 298–300; William of Ockham 254–5
Enchin 128–9
Encyclopédie 288–9
encyclopedists 182
Engels, Friedrich 301–2
Ennin 129
Epicurus 171
epistemology, Indian philosophy 64–6
Eriugena, John Scotus (Erigena) 244–5

eros 188–90
essences 35–7
ethical theories, Britain 283–4
ethnicity, identity and name 367
etiquette 73
Europe, new directions 458–61
European colonialism 456–7; Africa 434; Islamic world 370; South and South East Asia 384–5; South East Asia 399
Eusebius of Caesarea 179
evidential research 109–11
evil 251
evolution 26, 308–9, 377–8, 394, 440
experience 44

fa 80
Fa-tsang (Fa Zang) 92–3
falsafah 192, 197–9
fate 17
feminism 351–2, 365–6
Feng Kuei-fen (Feng Guifen) 407
Feuerbach, Ludwig 301
Fichte, Johann Gottlieb 293–4
Ficino, Marsilio 263–4
First Principle 205
Florentine Academy 263
Fon people 438
Forms 169 see also Theory of Forms
Four beginnings 122–3, 124
Four Noble Truths 18
Fourier, François-Marie Charles 307
France, nineteenth century 306–9
Franklin, Benjamin 332
free will 226, 233, 251, 255–6, 374–5
Frege, Gottlieb 346
Freud, Sigmund 336–7, 402
Frondizi, Risieri 368–9
Fujiwara Seika 144
fundamentalism: Islamic pre-modern 371–2; modern Islam 382
Fung Yu-lan 4, 417
Fuzukawa Yukichi 423

Galilei, Galileo 268
Gandhi, Mohendas (Mahatma) 391–3
Garvey, Marcus 443
Gauḍapāda 42
gender 365–6
Gentile, Giovanni 323–4
Gilligan, Carol 352
Gilson, Etienne 333
globalization 11, 456–7
'Glory of God' 372
gnosis 48; Sufism 196
Gnosticism 173–4
God: African religions 436; al-Ghazālī
    204–5; Anselm of Canterbury 245–6;
    Aquinas 247–51; Aristotelianism 168–9;
    bantu religion 439; Eckhart 257–8;
    Gersonides 231; ibn 'Arabi 213–14; ibn
    Sīnā 202; John Scotus Eriguena 245;
    Kabbalah 235; Liberation Theology
    362–3; Maimonides 230; Platonism 165;
    Sa'adyah ben Yosef 225; self-dependent
    59; as self within 39; Spinoza 273; Yoga
    47
goodness: acquired 83; innate 81
Gorgias of Leontini 161
Gramsci, Antonio 314–15
Great Empty 100–1
Great Ultimate 99–100, 104–5, 122
Great Vehicle Buddhism 34–8
Greek philosophy see also Hellenistic
    philosophy: context 151–2; Hellenistic
    period 170–2; love 188–90
Gregory of Nyssa 179
Gregory Palamas 190
Guide of the Perplexed 229
gunas 25

ha-Levi, Yehuda 227–8
Habermas, Jürgen 328
Hakuin 139–40
Han Dynasty 84–6
Han Fei (Hanfei) 80
Han Yu 98

Haraway, Donna 352
Harlem 350
Haṭha Yoga 48
Hayashi Razan 144–5
Hayek, Friedrich 415
Ḥayy bin Yaqẓān 208–10
He Lin 417–18
Heaven 74, 79, 97
Hegel, Georg 5, 9, 295–7, 301–2
Heidegger, Martin 5, 326–7
Hellenistic philosophy 186–7 see also Greek
    philosophy
Hempel, C.G. 344
Heraclides Ponticus 165
Heraclitus 155
Herbert, Lord Edward of Cherbury 277–8
Herzen, Alexander 310
Hesychasm 182–3
higher knowledge 24
Hinduism 3, 14–15; classical 31; Gītā and
    Brahma Sūtra 38–41; revival 455–6;
    schools 53
Hirata Atsutane 142–3
history 10, 465
Hobbes, Thomas 275–7
Holocaust 242
Hōnen 131–2
Horace 7
Hsiung Shih-li (Xiong Shili) 409
hsuan-hsüeh (xuanxue) see metaphysics
hsüan-hsüeh (xuanxue) 86
Huang Zongxi 114
Huayan 91–3
Hui Neng 95–6
Huishi 79–80
humaneness 73, 74
Hume, David 285–7
Hung Hsiu-ch'üan (Hong Xiuquan) 406
Husserl, Edmund 324
Hutcheson, Francis 284
Hwaom (Huayan) 118–19
hylomorphism 247–8

ibn 'Abd al-Wahhāb, Muhammad 372
ibn 'Arabi 212–14
ibn Bājjah 208
ibn Daud, Avraham 228–30
ibn Falaquera, Shem Tov 240
ibn Gabirol, Solomon 227
Ibn Khaldūn 215–16
ibn Rushd 208, 210–12, 231
ibn Sīnā 200–2
ibn Tufail 208–10
idealism 67; Japan 145–6
idealists, British 297–8
identities 11
identity: developing 456; ethnic 367; and
    liberation 365–7
ideology 10–11
ignorance 44
illuminationism 217–19
illusion 55–6
impermanence 18–19
Incas 354
Indian philosophy 3, 14, 27–8
individualism 331–4, 449
individuals: *Bhagavadgītā* 39; composition
    19
inference 65, 66
Ingenieros, José 359–60
innate goodness 81
Inoue Enryō 423–4
Inoue Tetsujirō 424
instrumentalism 341–2
intellectual changes 455–8
Ionian School 152–3
Iqbal, Sir Muhammad 378–80
ishraqi 217–18
Islam: five pillars 191; fundamentalism 382;
    influence on Hinduism 53; influence
    on Western thought 222; intellectual
    strands 191–2; postmodernism 381–3;
    pre-modern philosophy 217–22; revival
    455; secularism 376; South Asian reforms
    376–8
Islamic empires, decline 370–1

isolation 26
Itō Jinsai 147

Jains 16, 17; philosophy 28–30
James, William 339–41, 349
Japan, Western challenges 407
Japanese philosophies: overview 126–7;
    response to the West 422–5; summary of
    trends 148–50
Jaspers, Karl 328
Jayantha Vimukthi Peramuna (JVP) 403
Jefferson, Thomas 332
Jesus 6–7
Jesus, Mai Chaza 447
Jewish philosophy 223–4 *see also* Judaism;
    contemporary 242; context 223–4; end
    of medieval 233–4; modern 241; recent
    developments in study 238–42; Spain
    227–33; summary 237–8
jingshi 115
jīvanmukti 45
jñāna 39
John of Damascus 182
Jones, Sir William 390
Juche 422
Judaism 173, 334–5 *see also* Jewish
    philosophy
Jung. C.G. 337

Kabbalah 234–7, 240–1
Kagame, Alexis 439
Kaibara Ekken 145
Kalām 191–2
kami 140–1
Kaṇāda 49
Kang Youwei 407–8
Kant, Immanuel 290–3
Kaplan, Mordecai 335
Kardec, Allan 358
Kardecism 358
karma 20, 39, 56, 59
Khan, Sir Sayyid Ahmed 376–8
Kharijites 192

Khmer Rouge 403
Khomeini, Ayatollah Ruhollah 382
Ki Taisŭng 121
Kierkegaard, Søren 304–5
Kim Il-Sung 422
Kimbangu, Simon 445
Kimbanguism 445–6
Kireevsky, I.V. 310
knowledge 39, 45, 274, 280; acquisition 65;
    Yoga 48
Kogaku (Ancient Learning) 146–7
Kokugaku (National Learning School) 141–3
Kong, K'ung *see* Confucius
kongan (riddle) 96
Korea: premodern thought 125; Western
    challenges 407
Korean philosophy: historical context
    117–18; modern period 421–2
Korn, Alejandro 360
Krause, Karl Christian Friedrich 357–8
Krausism 357–8
Krishnamurti, Jiddu 395
Ku Yen-wu (Gu Yanwu) 109, 110
Kuhn, Thomas 347, 461
Kung-sun Lung (Gongsun Long) 79
Kuo Hsiang (Guo Xiang), 87
Kuomintang 410–11
Kusumānjali 50

language 19
Laozi 76–7
Latin American philosophies: context 353–4;
    existence of characteristic philosophy
    368–9; scholasticism 355–6
Lavrov, Peter 310–11
Learning of Mind 105–6
Learning of Principle 417
Legalists 80
Leibowitz, Yeshayahu 242
Lele people 436–7
Lembede, Anton 449
Lenin, Vladimir 302–3
Lesser Vehicle Buddhism 33–5

Lessing, Gotthold 289–90
Leucippus 158
Levinas, Emmanuel 242
li 73, 83–4, 99–103, 113, 120–1
Li Ao 98
Li Po 7
Li Yong 115
Liang Ch'i-ch'ao (Liang Qichao) 408
Liang Shu-ming 417
liberal theology 332
liberalism 279–81
liberation 23, 45, 47, 51
Liberation Theology 361–5; background
    361–2; and philosophy 365; themes
    362–5
Liebniz, Gottfried 281–3
light 219
Lin-chi (Linji) 96
linguistic philosophy 318–20
Liu Shu-hsien 420–1
living liberation 45
Locke, Alain 350
Locke, John 279–81
logic, Indian philosophy 64–6
logical positivism 318, 343–5
logicians 6, 79–80
Logos 173, 177
Lokayatas 17
Longino, Helen 352
Lonshina, Alice 446–7
Lossky, Nicholas 313–14
Lotus Sūtra 134–5
love 188–90
Lu Hsiang-shan (Lu Xiangshan) 105–6
Lukács, Georg 314
Lumpa 446–7
Luria, Isaac 236–7

Macchiavelli, Niccolò 265–6
machismo 366
MacKinnon, Catherine 351–2
Madhva 58–60
Mahābhārata 31

Mahabodhi Society 401

Mahavira 29

Mahāyāna 34–8

Maimonidean Controversies 239–40

Maine de Biran, François-Pierre 306–7

Malebranche, Nicolas 272

Mani 174

Manichaeanism 174–5

Mao Zedong 412–14

Marcus Aurelius 171

Marcuse, Herbert 328

Marías, Julián 322

ma'rifah 196

Maritain, Jacques 333

martial arts 137–9

Marx, Karl 301–2

Marxism 5, 411–12, 413; Liberation
    Theology 362, 364; Russia 314–15

materialism 30–1, 112–14, 462

mathematics 153–4, 267

Matilal, B.K. 398–9

Maximus the Confessor 190

medieval Christendom 243–4

Meditation Buddhism 135

Meiji 422–3

Melissus 156–7

Mencius (Mengzi) 81–2

Mendelssohn, Moses 241

Merleau-Ponty, Maurice 327

metaphysics 5; Duns Scotus 253–4

Miki Kyoshi 430, 431

Mill, John Stuart 298, 299–300

Mīmāṃsā-Vedānta 46

Mīmāṃsā 28, 46, 51–3

Ming-chia 79

ming-chiao (mingjiao) 87

Mirandola, Pico della 264

missionaries 444–5

Mo-tzu 79

modernism, Islamic 374–6

Mohanty, J.N. 399

Moism 79

mokṣa 51

Mongkut 400

monism 43

Moore, G.E. 298, 316–17, 346

moral responsibility 33–4

morality 292

Mormonism 335–6

Moses 229–30

Motoori Norinaga 141–3

Mou Zongsan 418, 419–20

Mudimbe, V.Y. 446

Mullā Ṣadrā 218–20

munis 5

Muslim Brotherhood 381

Mutai Risaku 428

Mu'tazilah 193, 194

mysterious learning 86

mysticism, and philosophy 257

myths 9–10

Nāgārjuna 35–7

Nagel, Ernest 343

Nakae Tōju 145

National Learning School 141–3

nationalism 328–9, 370–1, 399–400, 422,
    443–4, 449–50, 456

Negritude 441–2

Nehru, Jawaharlal 392–3

Neo-Advaita 390–1

neo-taoism 86–8

Neoconfucianism 99–102; Japan 145–6;
    Korea 119–21; rejection of metaphysics
    109–12

Neohinduism 11

neoplatonism 165–7

Neurath, Otto 347

New Confucianism 416–21

New Culture Movement 411–12

New England Transcendentalism 333

New Logic 66

Nichiren 134

Nichiren Buddhism 134–5

Nicholas of Autrecourt 256

Nicholas of Cusa (Nicholas Cusanus) 260–1

Nietzsche, Friedrich 5, 305–6
nirvana 20
Nishi Amane 423
Nishida Kitarō 426–8
Nishitani Keiji 429
Nkrumah, Kwame 449
nominalism 276
non-dualism 42–6
non-identity theory 48, 66
non-injury 29
North American philosophy: context 330–1;
    recent issues 461–3; reflections on
    345–52; social and political thought 351
nous 158–9, 166
Nozick, Robert 351
Nuer people 437
numbers, Kabbalah 235
Nung-chia (Nongjia) 81
Nyāya 28
Nyāya-Sūtras 49
Nyāya-Vaiśeṣika 46, 57–8

Olcott, Henry S. 395
Origen 177
original enlightenment 128–9
Orphism 154
Ortega y Gasset, José 321–2
Otto, Rudolf 39
Ōyōmei 145–6

Padmasambhava 63
Paine, Thomas 332
Pāli Buddhism 33
Pāli canon 17
Pāli Text Society 402
pan-Africanism 442–4
Parmenides 155–7
particularities 49
Patañjali 47
Pelagius 183
perception 55–6, 64–5, 66, 219
Perfection of Wisdom 34, 35
performance 73

Personalists 33–4
perspectives, Jainism 29
Phaedrus 188
phenomenology 324, 398, 399
Philo of Alexandria 173
philosophical method 9
philosophies 7–8
philosophy: as contested concept 2;
    developments up to World War I 315–16;
    functions 8; 'great three' 2–3; and human
    types 4–6; scope 6–9
Photius 182
pien-che (bianzhe) see dialectics
Pierce, Charles Sanders 338–42, 348–9
pilgrimage 32
Plato 2, 161, 162–4
Platonism, early and middle 164–5
Plekhanov, Georgi Valentinovich 314
Pletho 182
Plotinus 2, 4, 165–6
pluralism 282–3
politics, Confucianism 76
Popper, Karl 320, 461
Porphyry 166–7
postmodernism, Islam 381–3
prakṛti 26, 39
Presocratic philosophies, and eastern
    movements 159–60
Price, Richard 284
Prime Mover 188–9
principle 99–103, 120–1
Proclus 167
professional philosophers 6
projections 37–8, 44–5
prophecy 201
Protagoras 161
protestantism, American 331–4
protoscience 49, 63–4
Psellus, Michael 182
Pseudo-Dionysius 184–5, 189–90
psychoanalysis 336–7
pudgalavāda (puggalavāda) 33–4
Pure Land Buddhism 131–2, 133–4

purity 140
Putnam, Hilary 347
Pythagoras 4, 153–5

qi 101, 103, 122
questioners 5
questioning 8
Quine, Willard Van Orman 344–5, 347

racism 443
Radhakrishnan, Sarvepalli 396–7
Radical Reformation 266, 331
rajas 25, 26
Rāmānuja 40, 54–8
Rawls, John 351, 462
realism 56, 67
Realists 33
realities 27
reality 36, 55–6, 66, 68–9
rebirth 20, 68, 153–4, 157
reciprocity 74
Reform Judaism 334–5
Reformation 266–7
Reid, Thomas 287
reincarnation 23
relativism 17, 29
ren (jen) 73, 74, 408
Renaissance 261–3
representation 303
Representation-only school 37–8
revelation 50
Rg Veda see vedas
Rhys Davids, T.W. 402
Rinzai Zen 139–40
ritual 52
Rodó, Jose 356–7
Roman Catholicism, USA 333
Rorty, Richard 348, 462
Rosenzweig, Franz 241
Rousseau, Jean-Jacques 288–9
Rouvroy, Claude-Henri de 307
Roy, Ram Mohan 385–6
Royce, Josiah 337–8

Rramakrishna 388
Ruijiao 84
Russell, Bertrand 9, 317–18, 346
Russian Marxism 314–15
Russian philosophy 309–11
Ryle, Gilbert 319

Sa'adyah ben Yosef 224–7
sacrifice 23
sages 4, 6
Saichō 128
saint-hood (Buddhism) 32
Śaivism 60–1
salvation 56, 59
Sampan, Khieu 403
Saṅgha 18
Śaṅkara 41–6, 54, 390–1
Sāṅkhya 19, 24, 25–7, 39
Sāṅkhya-Yoga 27–8
Sanskrit 52
Santeria 447–8
Sarasvati, Dayananda 387–8
Sartre, Jean-Paul 327
Sarvāstivāda 33
sattva 25
Schechter, Solomon 335
Schelling, Friedrich Wilhelm Joseph von 294
Schleiermacher, Friedrich 294
Schmidt, Wilhelm 448
Schopenhauer, Arthur 303–4
science 267–9; and religion 377; rise of 261–2
secularism, Islam 376
sefirot 235
self 23–4, 43, 44–5, 50, 55–6, 67–8 *see also
ātman*
self-cultivation 431
Self-strengthening Movement 407
selfishness 34
Sen, Keshab Chandra 386–7
Seng-chao (Seng Zhao) 94
Senghor, Leopold 441–2
Seven feelings 122–3

Shao Yung (Shao Yong) 100
Shembe, Isaiah 446
sheng 103
Shingon 129–31
Shinran 133–4
Shinto 148, 422; and Confucianism 141;
    principal ideas 140–1
Shoah 242
shu 74
Shushi (Zhuxi) Confucianism 144–5
sincerity 123–4
Six Darśanas (Six Viewpoints) 27
skepticism 5, 30–1
Skeptics 17, 171
small societies, identities 453–5
Smith, Adam 284
Socrates 5, 161
Soloveitchik, Joseph 242
Solovyev, Vladimir Sergeyevich 312–13
Sophism 160–1
Sōtō Zen Buddhism 136–7
soul 19–20, 26, 55–6, 157, 163, 251–2, 388
South Asia: classical philosophy 31–4; Islam
    376–8; scope 13
Spanish philosophy: Islam 208–9; Judaism
    227–33
Spencer, Herbert 300
Speusippus 164–5
Spinoza, Baruch de 272–5
spiritual analysis 4–5
śramaṇas 15, 16, 24
sramanic movements 15
Sri Lanka 53–4
State 163–4, 296
Stewart, Dugald 287
Stoicism 170–1
subjectivisism 67
subjectivity 37–8, 44
Śuddhādvaita 61–2
Sufism 195–7; al-Ghazālī 207–8; ibn 'Arabi
    212–14; trends 214–15
Suhrawardī 218
Sun Yat-sen 410–11

Śūnyavāda 35
super-scientists 5
Suso, Heinrich 260–1
sūtras 27–8
Suziki, D.T. 425–6
Swami Vivekananda 42
Syādvāda 30
Symposium 188
synthesis 179

Tagore, Debendranath 386
Tai Chen (Dai Zhen) 109, 110, 113–14
T'ai Hsü (Tai Xu) 409
Taipings 406–7
Takahashi Satome 430
Takuan Sōhō 138–9
tamas 25
Tanabe Hajime 428
Tang Dynasty 97–8
Tang Junyi 418–19
Tantra 41, 60, 129–31
Tao-sheng (Dao Sheng) 94
Taoism 3, 70, 76–9, 82–3, 106–7, 149
Tauler, Johannes 259
Taylor, Charles 351
Tempels, Placide 438
Tendai 128–9
testimony 64
Texts, Old and New 111
texts, translation 385
Thales 152
The City of God 184
The Idea of the Holy 39
the Way 77–8
theism 47, 51
Theory of Forms 162–3
Theosophy 395, 401
Theravāda 33–4
Thiry, Paul-Henri 288
Thomas Aquinas 247–53
Thomé Fang 418
Tiantai 89–91
Tibet 53; Buddhism 63

tikkun 237
Tillers 81
Tokugawas 144–5
tolerance 280–1
Tolstoy, Leo 5, 311
Torah 230
Tosaka Jun 430–1
transcendental intuition 44
transformation theory 21, 48, 66
transnationalism 456
Trimśika (Thirty Verses) 38
Trinity, doctrine of 9, 180–1
truth 282; levels of 42, 45
truth pragmatism 339–41
Tsong-ka-pa 63
Tu Wei-ming 420
tzimtzum 236

Udayana 50
Ueda Shizuteru 429–30
Uich'on 119
Uisang 118
Unamuno, Miguel de 320–1
unity 55, 82
universalism 454
universals 201
universe 162
universities 243
Upanishads 16–17, 22–5, 40–1, 55, 58–9
Uttar Pradesh 16
Uttara-Mīmāṃsā 28

vaiśeṣas 49
Vaiśeṣika 28, 49
Vaiṣṇavatheism 61–2
Vallabha 61–2
Varona, Enrique José 359
Vasconcelos, José 360
Vasubandhu 37–8
Vedānta 23, 28, 54
Vedas 14, 16, 19, 22
verification principle 318
vidyā 45

Vienna Circle 318
Vijnānavāda 37–8
virtues 169, 171
Viśiṣṭādvaita 54–8
Visuddhimagga 54
viveka 26
Vivekananda 388–91
Voltaire, François-Maire Arquet de 288
voluntarism 413–14
Voodoo 447–8

Wahhābīs 371–2
Wang Fuzhi 112–13
Wang Pi (Wang Bi) 86–7
Wang Yangming 107–9
Watsuji Tetsurō 424
Western orientalism 371
Western philosophy 3
Whitehead, A.N. 342–3
William of Ockham 254–7
Winthrop, John 349
Wise, Isaac M. 334
Wittgenstein, Ludwig 2, 318–20, 346–7
Wŏnhyo 118–19
world order 464–6
worldviews 7–8; African religions 436–8, 444–5; Americas 447–8; Aquinas 252; Eckhart 258–9; Inca and Aztec 354–5; Kabbalah 234–7; Pierce 339
wu 87
Wu Chi-hui (Wu Zhihui) 411

Xiong Shili 418
Xu Fuguan 420
Xunzi (Hsun-tzu) 83–4

Yamaga Sokō 146–7
Yamazaki Ansai (Suika) 141
Yan Yuan 115
Yang chu (Yangzhu) 80
Yi Dynasty 119–21
Yi T'oegye 120–1, 123–4
Yi Yulgok 120, 121–4

Yin-Yang 78, 100
Yoga 27
yoga 394–5
Yoga, classical 46–51
Yoga-Sāṅkhya 46
Yoga-Sūtras 47
Yogācāra 37–8
Yoruba people 437–8
Yuasa Yasuo 431–3

Zea, Leopoldo 368

Zen Buddhism 135–6, 429; and martial arts
   137–9
Zeno 156, 170
Zhi Kai 89–91
Zhu Xi 103–6, 110
Zhuangzi (Chuang-tzu) 82–3
Zionism 335
Zohar 234
Zoroastrianism 172–4
Zulu Zionism 446
Zurvanism 172